Stepan Anastasovich Mikoyan

Stepan Anastasovich Mikoyan

An Autobiography

Translated by Aschen Mikoyan

Airlife
England

Translation into English © 1999 Aschen Mikoyan

First published in the UK in 1999
by Airlife Publishing Ltd

British Library Cataloguing-in-Publication Data
  A catalogue record for this book
  is available from the British Library

ISBN 1 85310 916 9

Typeset by Phoenix Typesetting, Ilkley, West Yorkshire
Printed and bound in Great Britain by
Biddles Ltd, Guildford and King's Lynn

Airlife Publishing Ltd

101 Longden Road, Shrewsbury, SY3 9EB, England

Foreword

The book you are holding in your hands was written not by a writer but by a former military test pilot. It is not a novel or a piece of fiction but the story of my life and of my professional career in the Soviet Air Force.

When I first set out to put my thoughts and memories into writing, the only possible readers I had in mind were my colleagues, both known and unknown to me. However, as I moved on, and as I wrote down more and more of my general recollections, many of which did not solely deal with aviation, I began to think of a more general reader. So, to avoid baffling this general reader with too much 'aviation talk' or too many technicalities, I shortened, and to some extent popularised, the technical passages in the book – although there was no way I could do without them altogether.

It is quite possible that some of the people remote from aviation might want to know a little more about aeroplanes and about a test pilot's work; and those readers who are not interested in either flying machines or people who fly them may perhaps be attracted by the 'civilian' parts of the book, which I hope reflect the way of life and the atmosphere of the former Soviet Union, and some of the painful or bizarre experiences that its people had to face. In short, I hope that there will be at least something of interest to every reader who opens the book; then my two years' work on it will not have been in vain.

Stepan Anastasovich Mikoyan

Acknowledgements

I would like to thank my lifelong friends and fellow test pilots, Alexander Shcherbakov, Alexander Bezhevets and Norik Kazarian, for the help they gave me by providing some details of the events in our professional careers which I wished to describe, thus ensuring a more vivid and accurate account. I would also like to express my gratitude to USAF Col Terry E. Tomeny for his support and his willingness to resolve some of the difficulties encountered in the translation of technical passages in the book.

I thank my daughter Aschen, a lecturer in English and translation at Moscow State University, who devoted nearly a year of intensive work to translating my memoirs into English. Due to her heartfelt involvement with the book, she also undertook the voluntary task of editing my original version even as she was translating it, thus making some parts of it livelier and more succinct. For all the help I gave her with aviation terms and highly technical passages, her work still remained a challenging feat for somebody as remote from the field of technology as she is.

In the final stages of working on my book and in preparing the typescript, I was willingly and patiently helped by my eldest grandson, Alexander. I would like to express my thanks to him, as well as to my wife Ella, who, as a professional editor and the first reader of the initial Russian version of my text, made valuable comments and useful criticisms, and to my entire family for their support and enthusiasm about my undertaking.

I would also like to thank all my fellow test pilots, aviation engineers and all those who, like myself, dedicated their lives to aviation – all those, with whom I have ever worked and with whom I shared the joys, the difficulties, the risks and the losses which the profession of a military test pilot involves.

Stepan Anastasovich Mikoyan

Contents

CHAPTER 1

Bolshevik Roots

My entire adult life has been devoted to aviation, and therefore in this book I will be writing about flights, aircraft and pilots, but not exclusively. I will also write about the family into which I was born and in which I grew up, about the things and events that I remember along the way and that I consider to be interesting or characteristic of the life I have lived and of the people I have come across.

Until the 1920s, my parents – Anastas Ivanovich Mikoyan and Ashkhen Lazarevna Tumanian – lived in the Caucasus. My father, a future Soviet politician, was born and grew up as a child in the ancient Armenian village of Sanahin, perched high in the mountains over the nearby valley town of Alaverdy. His father, a village carpenter, was called Hovannes, and his mother's name was Tamara. My own mother was born to Lazar Tumanian, a salesman in a shop in Tiflis, and his wife Virginia was Tamara's cousin. Far back in the eighteenth century, an ancestor of the Mikoyans, called Sarkisian, lived with his wife and family in Nagorny Karabakh. In 1813, during a massacre of Armenians, he and his wife were killed, but their two sons – twenty-year-old Alexander and thirteen-year-old Mikhail – escaped and found refuge in the village of Sanahin. Their parents had named them after the sons of Emperor Paul I of Russia, but everybody called them Alexan and Mikael. The priest of the monastery at Sanahin gave the brothers new surnames derived from their Christian names, as was the custom with refugees, and thus the future 'clans' of the Alexanians and the Mikoyans began. The Alexanians later moved to a different village, while the Mikoyans continued to live in Sanahin.

Apart from being a self-employed village carpenter, Hovannes Mikoyan also worked as a carpenter at a copper plant in Alaverdy. Both Hovannes and his wife Tamara were highly respected in their village. Hovannes had a reputation of being a sensible, decent and honest man, an honesty that sometimes verged on naivety. He would easily agree to build somebody a house on credit and then be left without payment for his work, and he would readily lend money to his fellow villagers, sometimes risking all he had at the time. As a young man he had spent several years as an apprentice in a carpenter's shop in Tiflis, and so in his appearance he was more like a member of an urban professional guild than a typical village master, always very neatly dressed and making a point of wearing town-bought, not makeshift, shoes. Though he was illiterate, he worked out his own way of keeping a record of his jobs and orders, and he pencilled them in a system of signs no one but he could operate in a special notebook, with which he never parted. Another thing he had with him at all times was a silver spoon; he never ate with a wooden one, which was what everybody else in the village would use at the time.

9

Hovannes and Tamara had three sons and two daughters. First came their daughter Voskeat, then a son, Ervand, who became a worker at a copper plant; next in line was my father Anastas, then another daughter, Astrik; finally, the youngest of all, Anushavan, or Anush for short, who eventually became the world-famous aircraft designer Artem Ivanovich Mikoyan. Hovannes died of pneumonia in 1918 at the age of sixty-two, but my grandmother Tamara lived to be ninety-three and died in my father's home in Moscow in 1960.

In the village of Sanahin there was an old and widely known monastery of the same name, and in that monastery there was a monk who enjoyed a particular reverence among a number of villagers. That monk and the priest were the only two literate people in the community, including the entire village. One day Anastas saw the monk engrossed in a book, and he asked him about it. The monk was pleased at the boy's interest and offered to teach him to read and write. Anastas made quick progress and soon became literate. About that time a new settler appeared in the village, an educated and cultivated man who was probably an Armenian 'narodnik'* hiding from the secret police. The newcomer opened a small school in a disused cottage in the monastery grounds where he offered to teach the village kids for a nominal fee – just enough for him to survive on. His offer was accepted, he received a class of twenty children and Anastas was among them. Their teacher taught them to write and read, instructed them in arithmetic and gave them classes in physical training. He also taught them to be neat and clean, to wash their hands before meals and rinse out their mouths after (there was a spring of pure mountain water nearby, which is still there today), and other basic rules of a cultivated way of life. But after a while the man left the village for good, and the school closed down.

Shortly afterwards the little cottage in the monastery received another temporary occupant – the Armenian bishop of the diocese of Tiflis, who came to spend the summer in the mountains. He hired my grandfather Hovannes to build an extension to the cottage. Anastas, who was ten-and-a-half years old, helped his father. One day the bishop asked him if he could read. Anastas replied that he could, but only a little, and would like to learn more. The bishop suggested to Hovannes that he take his son to Tiflis and promised to find the boy a place in the theological school there (known as 'the Seminary'). His mother's cousin Virginia and her husband Lazar took Anastas in, although there was hardly any spare room in their house. Hovannes did not want to approach the bishop directly, so he dictated to the bishop's cook, who was from the same village (and who could write), a petition requesting admission for his son. As a result, Anastas was enrolled in the second preparatory form of the Seminary.

He was a good student, and the Armenian Charity Society, which helped the poorest among the students, gave him free meals and paid for the room which he shared with three of his classmates. He also made some money giving private lessons. He was an avid reader and devoured a great number of Armenian books,

---

* A member of the populist and anti-monarchist movement initiated by Russian liberal intelligentsia in the second half of the nineteenth century, from the Russian word 'narod', meaning 'people'.

and later, when he became fluent in Russian, he took to reading Russian books as well, especially history and poetry. Later still he began reading works by the natural scientists K. Timiriazev, Charles Darwin and Dmitry Mendeleev, by the historians Theodore Mommsen (*The History of Rome*) and Jean Jaures (*The History of the French Revolution*), and by the Russian literary critics Vissarion Belinksy and Nikolai Dobroliubov. Another critic and historian of literature whose writings and views, according to my father, greatly influenced his outlook and his personality as a whole was Dmitry Pisarev. The next step was the discovery of Russian literature in the form of novels by Turgenev and Goncharov, Leo Tolstoy and Dostoyevsky, Veresayev and Garshin. As for Alexander Pushkin, at that time his prose appealed to Anastas more than his poetry. Among the foreign authors read in those years were Dickens and London, Hugo and Dumas, Ibsen and Schiller. The novel *What Is To Be Done?* by Nikolai Chernyshevsky led Anastas to the works of Thomas More and Charles Fourier, Claude Henri de Saint-Simon and Robert Owen.

Despite his being a student at a theological institution and the son of a deeply religious woman, Anastas's reading and subsequent reflection on the books he read gradually brought him to complete atheism. In his Scriptures class he was the one who was always ready to debate issues of divinity and the existence of God. Yet, since his formal knowledge of the subject was quite good, the teacher was obliged to pass him.

The wave of revolutionary movement had reached Tiflis from Russia by 1911. The walls of the theological school proved poor protection against the new ideas; a number of students from Anastas's class formed a secret political circle with a view to studying the available revolutionary literature together and deciding which political party to join. They started off with Kautsky's book on Marx's economic theories and then went on to Plekhanov's work entitled *On the Monistic View of History*. One day, when Anastas went to see his distant relation Danush Shaverdian, a Bolshevik and already aware of the students' circle at the Seminary, Danush lent him a book by Lenin entitled *The Development of Capitalism in Russia*. Thus, under the influence of Shaverdian and another confirmed Bolshevik called Borian, Marxist views found their way into the students' circle and took firm root in the students' minds. Many Seminary graduates took an active part in the revolution of 1917, some going on to become eminent Soviet politicians and party leaders.

At the outbreak of World War One many Armenians began to hope that Russian army operations against Turkey would lead to the liberation of the western Armenians (of whom there were about two million) from Turkish rule (as is well known, later, during the massacre of 1915, nearly a million and a half Armenians were killed in Ottoman Turkey). In November 1914 a group of the most 'belligerent' young men from the theological seminary, among whom was my father (just turned nineteen), volunteered for the front line and joined the army of the legendary Armenian commander Andranik, who had distinguished himself in the Armenian guerrilla war in Turkey and in the anti-Ottoman liberation movement in Bulgaria, for which he was decorated with the highest Bulgarian orders. Anastas was at the front line until April 1915, when he became

11

seriously ill. His illness was caused by a violent reaction of his system to meat, which was an essential part of the soldiers' rations and which he had never eaten before. Since early childhood he had lived on vegetables and dairy products, especially cheese, which he would eat with bread three times a day, often as his main and only course. It was only later, in Baku when he was twenty-two, that he gradually 'trained' himself to eat meat. Back in 1915, on top of the strong allergy to meat, he was attacked by a severe form of malaria and ended up in hospital.

His war was over, but his political self-education went on, and the piece of writing that finally determined his own political views was Lenin's brochure entitled *What Is To Be Done?* His choice was made, and in November 1915 he joined the Bolshevik party. On his return to the Seminary he was admitted to the sixth form, from which he had gone to war with a promise to do a two-year course within one year. So in December 1915 he successfully passed his exams and moved on to the seventh form, which was the Seminary's graduation class. As before, he earned a little pocket money by coaching weaker fellow students.

Unlike various secular schools where education cost money, the theological seminary was in fact a charity institution, accessible to the children of poor or even very poor parents. Therefore its general atmosphere and the contingent of its students were certainly more democratic than in other schools and more susceptible to revolutionary ideas. Most of the teachers had been educated at the universities in Germany, Switzerland and France, and many of them held liberal views. The only cleric among the teaching staff at the Seminary was the priest, who taught the Scriptures and another four religious subjects on the curriculum. All other subjects taught were in the scope of general education: mathematics, geography, literature, physics, chemistry, botany, zoology, psychology and physiology. Unlike senior lay schools (known as *gymnasia*) there was only one compulsory foreign language to be studied; however, apart from Russian and Armenian, the students did a compulsory course in Old Armenian. In addition they had classes in Armenian history and underwent a course in pedagogy, for the Seminary was in effect a teacher-training institution, preparing masters for Armenian primary schools.

The art teacher at the Seminary was a well-known Armenian painter, Amshishian. In my father's class there were two successful students of drawing, my father and a boy called Karo Alabian. Anastas was very proud of the teacher's high praise of his drawing from life of an ancient stone viaduct across the mountain river Debed near Alaverdy, the viaduct which carried the road to his native village of Sanahin. But, as my father later recalled, he could not match Karo's achievements, for the latter had a real artistic talent (which eventually led him to a celebrated career as an architect).

Anastas successfully passed his final exams and received a school leaver's certificate in which twenty out of twenty-nine were top marks ('excellent'). He had 'good' marks for Russian conversation classes, in three religious subjects and in another three subjects; the lowest pass marks ('satisfactory') were for singing and the Scriptures. (I remember how my father once read through a school essay of mine and found a couple of spelling mistakes which I had not noticed. I was

12

ashamed – he had never been to a Russian school and I was about to finish one, and besides I had a reputation of being a very good student.)

On graduating from the Seminary at twenty, Anastas decided to continue his education at the Armenian Religious Academy at Echmiadzin, an ancient town near Yerevan. The Tiflis Seminary graduates were admitted to the Academy without entrance exams. The tuition at the Academy was free; the students lived in a boarding-house and got three free meals a day. As Anastas and his parents were quite badly off, such terms were very appealing. Despite its official name, the Academy prepared advanced specialists in Armenian studies rather than dedicated priests. Except for the Rector (as its head was known) of the Academy and the Greek master, all staff were laymen. Great emphasis was laid on Armenian history, from ancient times though the Middle Ages and on to modern history. Historical geography of Armenia was also taught, as well as Armenian literature and language, from its early history onwards. Anastas developed a deep interest in languages and asked a fellow student who was fluent in Georgian to teach him to read and write in it, while another of his friends was giving him lessons in the Azerbaijani language (some people believe that these three languages are closely related, but in actual fact they have little in common except mutual borrowings, and all three belong to different linguistic families).

My father recalled how in 1958 he arrived in Yerevan to meet his constituency, and afterwards attended a state banquet, where among the guests was the Catholicos of All Armenians (the official head of the Armenian Church), Vazghen I. My father came up to him with a glass of wine in his hand, greeted him and then said, jokingly, that he had a guilt complex because he had failed the expectations of the Armenian Church and had rendered all its efforts at his clerical education totally wasted. 'I am a defective product of the Armenian Religious Academy', he said. The Catholicos smiled and said, 'You are mistaken. Far from lamenting the fact that a man like you has come out of our Academy, we take pride in it. The more of such defective product, the better!' My father naturally took these words as a polite compliment from an urbane and courteous person. They drank a toast to the prosperity of Soviet Armenia and parted with mutual respect.

Of what was going on in Russia as a consequence of the continuing world war, in Armenia they heard only rumours. Little was known about the social unrest caused by the deprivations and hardships suffered by the population, about the strikes of Petrograd workers, women's riots in bread queues, or about the clashes between workers and the police in February 1917. Therefore the telegraph message about the overthrow of the monarchy came as a surprise, but was enthusiastically received by the students. Having secured permission to put off his exams until the autumn, Anastas left for Tiflis where he attended the first legal meeting of local Bolsheviks, chaired by Misha Okudzhava (uncle of the well-known Russian poet Bulat Okudzhava).

At one of their further meetings at the end of March they read and discussed the letter that had been sent from Baku by a well-known revolutionary leader, Stepan Shaumian, who had just returned from political exile. The letter described the current situation in Baku, and in conclusion Shaumian asked for a 'reinforcement' in the shape of the experienced Bolshevik Mravian, who was called on to help with the political agitation among the Armenian expatriate workers in Baku. However, Mravian could not go for family reasons, so Anastas volunteered to go in his place. He took with him a note of introduction written by Danush Shaverdian, which he presented to Shaumian on his arrival in Baku in March 1917:

> Dear Stepan! The bearer of this note, Anastas Mikoyan, is a newly baptised Social Democrat who has had good training. I sent him to you to help in the struggle against the Dashnaks. He's a very able young fellow. I ask you to give him your special attention. He'll tell you about the current state of affairs.
> Yours, Danush.*

In March 1917 my father was twenty-one. Stepan Shaumian, whom he was meeting for the first time, made a very powerful impression upon him. As he would tell us later, he grew very fond of Shaumian and always felt enormous respect towards him. Shaumian was not a very tall man, but well built and handsome, with a pleasant and intelligent face and a kind smile. At that time he was just under forty. He was a sedate and even-tempered person, and whatever he said was always well grounded and persuasive. Shaumian was a thoroughly educated man. He had graduated from the faculty of philosophy at Berlin University and wrote a number of works on philosophy, art and literature, and also on the key issues of the revolutionary theory as formulated by Marx and then Lenin. He was an outstanding personality by any standards. He possessed many of the talents and qualities required of a major statesman and politician of the time: he was well versed in the Marxist theory, was a brilliant organiser, an eloquent public speaker, a man of firm principles, determination and great personal courage. And, above all, for all the steadfastness of his political views and sympathies, he was flexible and resourceful where tactical decisions were concerned. Some newspapers of the time dubbed him 'Caucasian Lenin' (in my opinion, he had at least one indisputable advantage over Lenin: he had none of the latter's ruthlessness or intolerance). Shaumian commanded respect even on the part of some of his political opponents, to say nothing of his allies and confederates, for whom he was an undisputed leader. It is easy to imagine what Shaumian's career would have been like had he lived until Stalin's 'ascension'. The higher respect and authority he inspired among his fellow party members would have made Stalin see him as a dangerous rival. Besides, Shaumian would probably have seen the danger of Stalin's usurpation of supreme power in the 1920s, which most of the earnest Bolsheviks, including my father, unfortunately failed to realise at the time.

In those days Baku was the largest industrial city in the whole of Transcaucasia, and its workers greeted the February revolution with enthusiasm,

---

* This note, written on the reverse of Shaverdian's card and kept by Shaumian's wife, was many years later returned to my father as a gift from Shaumian's son Sergei.

celebrating their own contribution with a general strike which involved all oil works, factories and workshops. On 7 March 1917 a Soviet of Workers' Deputies was convened, with the majority formed by the Socialist Revolutionaries, the Mensheviks and other non-Bolshevik factions. Nevertheless, at the very first meeting of the Soviet Stepan Shaumian was elected chairman – a Bolshevik, yet a man respected by all. Apart from the Soviet, there existed an elected municipal council known as the city Duma, where the majority belonged to the capitalists and right-wing socialists, with a sprinkling of Armenian and Azerbaijani nationalists, known as the Dashnaks and the Musavatists respectively. The largest political representation in the Duma was that of the Socialist Revolutionaries. After the fall of the provisional government the Duma claimed political power in the city, placing itself in opposition to the Soviet.

Anastas attended numerous rallies and meetings of Baku workers, where he spoke to the participants in Armenian, explaining the Bolshevik policy to them and answering their questions. To earn a living he took a job as a telephone operator, which Shaumian helped him to get. Soon, however, he was given a position as a propagandist on the staff of the Baku party committee. The salary he received for that job could not pay for any rented lodgings, so he slept on a table in one of the rooms occupied by the committee.

One day Shaumian invited Anastas to visit him at home. He was living with his wife Ekaterina, three sons and a daughter in three rented rooms on the first floor of a small house. Apparently the reference given to my father carried weight, for Shaumian was prepared to like and trust him from the very start. Later Shaumian asked him to join the board of the paper of which he himself was the editor, the weekly *Social-Democrat*. Shaumian was too busy to give enough time to it, so eventually Anastas became its *de facto* editor.

Towards the end of the summer Anastas returned to Tiflis and took up his former lodgings with the Tumanian family. My father's mother's cousin Virginia Tumanian (my maternal grandmother) had no formal education, although she could read and write. Knowing very little about politics, she was still an ardent supporter of the revolution and of the Bolsheviks. She was a very wilful woman and the real head of the family. Her husband Lazar, related to Armenia's great poet Hovannes Tumanian – either his cousin or his nephew, both men hailing from the Lori district in Armenia – was a conscientious worker and a very decent and honest man. Every day he read the conservative Armenian paper *Mshak*, from its first line to the last, and fully believed every word of it. He kept all the issues of that paper and occasionally had them bound. Later, when Anastas was already working in Moscow, Virginia and Lazar Tumanian, as well as my father's mother Tamara, often stayed for a long time at his dacha outside Moscow. After the war they moved in permanently. I still remember Lazar Tumanian as an old man in an armchair with the eternal newspaper in his hands. He would still read his paper from cover to cover, though it was no longer the *Mshak*, but *Pravda*. He died in 1946 at the age of eighty when my son – his great-grandson – was about three months old.

I remember Virginia, my grandmother, as an even-tempered, kind and sober-minded woman, old but still quite agile and as ready to manage her husband (and her docile cousin Tamara as well) as ever. Even we, her grandchildren, listened to her opinions with respect. Despite the mistakes she made and her heavy accent, she could still express herself in Russian quite well, whereas Grandmother Tamara could barely get by in Russian. She was then a tiny, quiet, gentle old woman whose principal emotion was her love for her sons, particularly her youngest, Anush, and her grandsons. In the last two years of her life she could hardly see at all, despite the very strong glasses she was wearing, and no longer knew one of us from another. We had to 'introduce' ourselves whenever we were with her. Virginia and Tamara grew as close as sisters, and they died within a week of each other, Virginia at the age of eighty-five and Tamara at the age of ninety-three. Both my grandmothers and my grandfather Lazar were buried in Novodevichy cemetery in Moscow, thus starting what has since become the family tomb. Tamara survived her husband, my paternal grandfather, by forty-two years.

Lazar and Virginia Tumanian had four children: a daughter Ashkhen, a son Haik, and another two daughters, Haikush and Mano (Maria). While Anastas was living with the Tumanians during his student years he fell in love with Ashkhen, but he did not dare to make it known for she was his second cousin. Armenian tradition forbade marriages between second cousins. For as long as four years he kept his feelings to himself, behaving towards her in a severely polite and aloof manner. Even while Ashkhen was staying with the Mikoyans in Sanahin, where Anastas was coaching her for her re-examination at school (she had been seriously ill through the scheduled examination period), he behaved in a no-nonsense way and never allowed himself to talk on any 'irrelevant' subject. For her own part, she was extremely diligent and conscientiously did all the tasks received from her austere tutor. Anastas's father grew very fond of her. One day, Anastas could bear it no longer and told her of his feelings. She said that she herself had been in love with him for a long time, but had been totally discouraged by his callous and distant manner which she had naturally taken to mean that he did not like her at all. They became man and wife in 1921, when already in Russia.

While in Tiflis in the summer of 1917, Anastas participated in the All-Caucasus Congress of the Bolsheviks as the delegate of the Alaverdy copper factory. Shaumian was the principal speaker at the congress, and in his speech he said, among other things, that as early as 1913 Lenin had suggested an amendment to the party programme as regards its national policy, in accordance with which the principle of regional autonomy was preferred to the previously favoured idea of local self-government with more limited authority. Shaumian himself was in favour of relations between the Caucasus and Russia being built on a federal basis. He pointed out in his speech that there was no reason to fear 'decentralisation', and quoted Lenin's slogan: 'Let Russia be a union of free republics!' Shaumian, appointed by Lenin 'extraordinary commissar for the Caucasus', invited my father to return to Baku to work for the Soviet there (where by that time the Bolsheviks and their left-wing supporters from the SR party had won a majority).

On 26 October 1917 the news of the fall of Russia's provisional government and the transfer of supreme power to the Petrograd Soviet reached Baku. Five days later, on 31 October, the Baku Soviet proclaimed itself the only legitimate power in the city. No armed opposition followed, until March 1918, when there was an insurrection against the Baku Soviet, whose main hostile force was the 'wild division' of the Azerbaijani national army. After three days of intense street fighting the insurrection was crushed, and the surviving soldiers of the 'wild division' fled to those parts of Azerbaijan where the Baku Soviet had not yet assumed power. My father took part in this fighting and was wounded in the leg. When he was discharged from hospital, Shaumian insisted that he move in with his family (he still had no home of his own). He lived with the Shaumians as a member of the family for a long time, during which he had an opportunity to see a lot of Shaumian himself and to meet the people who came to see him. That made him much more aware of party matters and affairs of state than he would have been under different circumstances.

In February 1918 Azerbaijani, Armenian and Georgian Mensheviks convened an All-Caucasus Assembly which soon began to collude with Germany and Turkey, and the government of Georgia gave its consent to a free passage of German troops through the republic *en route* to Baku. The newly formed bourgeois governments of Armenia and Azerbaijan followed suit, announcing their independence from Russia. Until that time Transcaucasian bourgeois parties had not pursued the aim of secession from Russia, giving preference to a federal structure. Shaumian, in accordance with Lenin's opinion, also insisted on establishing three Transcaucasian national autonomies whose relationship with Russia would be based on a federal principle. However, his view was not supported by the Caucasian Congress of the Bolsheviks, at which the old Bolshevik idea of regional self-government with limited authority won the day. My father, along with most of the others, failed to understand Shaumian's idea and did not give him his vote. It was not until 1919 that the Bolsheviks in Baku came round to the idea of an independent Soviet Azerbaijan in close relationship with Soviet Russia.*

In April 1918 the Baku Soviet of the People's Commissars (a local government) was formed. It mainly consisted of Bolsheviks and a few left-wing SRs. Stepan Shaumian was elected chairman, and among the commissars were Dzhaparidze, Narimanov, Korganov, Fioletov, Kolesnikova and others. Anastas did not become a commissar.

In June 1918 the Turkish army invaded the Caucasus and began a march towards Baku. My father left for the front line with the 3rd Red Army Brigade. Baku became a scene of mass rallies which debated the feasibility of inviting British troops from across the Caspian Sea to help deter the Turkish threat. The workers who voted at those rallies for inviting the British were swayed into this decision by the hardships and deprivations they were suffering and by their fear

---

* This formula, only without the word 'Soviet', basically reflects the present state of affairs between the two countries; therefore those who are blamed by our over-zealous 'patriots' for having destroyed the Soviet Union in 1991 can be said simply to have returned to the ideas of 1919.

of Turkish invasion. They believed that the 'cultivated' British troops would come to the aid of their allies against the Turks and save the city.

On 29 July 1918 the Turks broke through the front line, and almost at the same time there was a coup in Baku, as the result of which the power in the city went to the Mensheviks, Socialist Revolutionaries and the Dashnaks. They formed what they called the Central Caspian Dictatorship and invited the British Expeditionary Force deployed in Iran, sending a number of ships of the Caspian Naval Fleet to collect them at the Persian port of Ensile. On 4 August the ships with British troops on board started arriving at the Baku port. The Bolsheviks convened a Workers' Conference at which Shaumian suggested removing the revolutionary force from Baku to Russia, for there was no hope of them holding their ground fighting both the Turks and the British, and no chance of receiving help from Soviet Russia (because of an extremely serious military situation on the Volga). The majority of those present voted for his suggestion. My father was among those who voted against. He stayed behind in Baku to take part in the underground party work.

The Red Army soldiers commanded by Petrov, members of the Baku Soviet of People's Commissars (known since as 'the Commissars of Baku') and other party leaders and functionaries embarked on several steamboats and sailed towards Astrakhan. However, they had not gone far when they were surrounded by the naval ships sent by the Central Caspian Dictatorship and escorted back to the naval port of Baku. The soldiers were then disarmed and allowed to leave for Astrakhan on the same steamboats, but thirty-five people, among whom were Stepan Shaumian and all the other Commissars of Baku, as well as other party executives, were arrested. Those of the Bolsheviks and their left-wing allies from other parties who had escaped capture because they had not been on those boats put together an ultimatum in which they demanded the immediate release of their unlawfully arrested comrades. The demand was reinforced by the threat of physical elimination of every member of the Dictatorship if so much as a hair fell off any of their comrades' heads.

In the meantime the Mensheviks and their allies held an election of a new Baku Soviet, aiming to get rid of the Bolsheviks in the Soviet. Yet, despite all they could do to prevent it, twenty-eight Bolsheviks were elected, including nine of those under arrest, and also my father and Sturua. The newly elected Bolshevik members insisted on the release of their fellow deputies, but the Dictatorship refused to comply.

By 14 September the Turks had come very close to Baku. The Mensheviks and their allies began to leave the city, and there appeared a very real threat that the Bolshevik prisoners would suffer or die at the hands of the invaders. Anastas organised a deputation from the Baku Soviet to the leaders of the Central Caspian Dictatorship which demanded their release and transport to Astrakhan. As a contingency plan, a group of seven armed men headed by Suren Shaumian, Stepan's son, was instructed to make a surprise attack on the prison and free the Bolsheviks under arrest. An arrangement was made with the captain of the Soviet steamer *Sevan* which had just arrived from Astrakhan, to assist in their escape from Baku. Anastas went to the Central Caspian headquarters, where he found a member of the Dictatorship called Velunts. The latter, not wanting to be responsible for potential violence, gave his consent to releasing the prisoners and their evacuation. Having received a written authorisation, my father, accompanied by several soldiers of the guard, headed for the prison. The superintendent of the prison had been wondering what to do with the prisoners, with the Turks almost as good as there already, and so he was happy to wash his hands of them. They left the prison with Turkish bullets already whistling over their heads.

That was the end of the Baku Commune. The Turkish troops entered the city, and their commander, Nuri-Pasha, let his *askers* have their way with the citizens and their property for three days. These were the days of bloody massacres, rape, arson, plunder and other atrocities, the chief victims of which were the Armenians. About thirty thousand of them were slaughtered over a few weeks. The Turks didn't leave Baku until the beginning of November, when Germany and Turkey signed a truce with the Entente. Their place was then taken by the British.

When the released prisoners and the soldiers of the guard came to the naval dock, the *Sevan* was not there. It turned out that it had been seized by Central Caspian troops. Somebody suggested escaping on another boat, the *Turkmen*, which was already filled with refugees and armed soldiers. Shaumian's sons, Dzhaparidze's wife and the wives of other leaders were also on board that steamer. The *Turkmen* was supposed to be part of a convoy of vessels directed to the port of Petrovsk, to where the Central Caspian government had 'retreated' from Baku. My father suggested to Shaumian that he should persuade the captain to break away from the convoy and sail to Astrakhan, which was controlled by the Bolsheviks. And so, at night, the steamer began to change its course, slowly breaking away from the others. However, as soon as the change of course had become apparent to the crew committee, which consisted of Socialist Revolutionaries, it voted for sailing towards Krasnovodsk where the British were and where the situation with food supplies was much better than in Astrakhan. The committee members were supported by many of the refugees and soldiers on board. Later it turned out that the decision to head for Krasnovodsk was taken under heavy pressure from the Dashnak commanders and two British officers who were on board.

Towards the evening of 16 September the steamboat arrived at Krasnovodsk, but, contrary to usual practice, it was not allowed to dock and unload on arrival. The launch that came out to meet it received on board only the two British officers and an unknown Armenian with a Cross of St George on his chest. His excuse for disembarking ahead of everyone else was that he 'had some important information for the local authorities'. Next day the steamboat was ordered to weigh anchor and dock at another wharf, where it was met by a larger unit of armed men. In the group of British officers and local officials who had assembled on the landing were the two officers who had got off the *Turkmen* earlier and the Armenian with the Cross of St George. On going through the checkpoint all the Bolsheviks and those who were with them were identified with surprising and suspicious ease and escorted onto a small harbour ferry called the *Vyatka*. Altogether thirty-five people were arrested, on the orders of the Krasnovodsk

Strike Committee, as it was announced to them (that committee was at that time the only governing body in the city with any real power and it was controlled by the Socialist Revolutionaries). In the evening the *Vyatka* docked at the Krasnovodsk port. The prisoners were told that since the prison could not accommodate them all some of them would be kept under custody in a separate prison-house. On the list of the people to be taken to that place was Shaumian, another eleven men and five women. My father was not on that list, but he asked to be included, for he was hoping that Shaumian and he would be able to organise a jailbreak.

In the middle of the night of 20 September the prisoners were roused by the unexpected arrival of the Chief of Police, Alania, accompanied by a group of other people. It later turned out that among them were the chairman of the Socialist Revolutionary government in Ashkhabad, Funtikov, and several other members of that government. Alania announced that in accordance with the decision of the government certain prisoners were to be immediately transferred to the central regional prison in Ashkhabad, pending trial, and the rest would be released. He proceeded to read out the list of those to be moved to the Ashkhabad prison. My father's name was not on it. He asked to be put on that list – as he later told us, he was still dreaming his jailbreak plans. However, Alania replied that he was not authorised to make any alterations. Shaumian took Anastas aside and instructed him that if they were indeed released he should take his sons, Surik and Leva, try to reach Moscow to get an interview with Lenin and tell him about what had happened. Shaumian's plan was to ask Lenin to arrest several eminent right-wing Socialist Revolutionaries and Mensheviks and then negotiate an exchange of prisoners. The morale of the prisoners was quite high. They believed that some of them would be set free, while others would await trial, which in itself meant that not all was lost. It was only in Shaumian's eyes that my father saw some alarm on parting.

On what basis the Ashkhabad government and the representatives of the British military command had compiled their list of twenty-six people out of the thirty-five prisoners became clear from the written account given in June 1925 by Suren Shaumian, who was examined as a witness in the investigation of Funtikov's case. The account is cited by my father in his book of memoirs, and what follows is a slightly abridged reproduction of the same document:

> In the middle of August 1918 we were arrested in Baku by the British and Menshevik authorities. Among those arrested, besides the twenty-five comrades who were later shot, were Mudryi, Meskhi, Samson Kandelaki, Klevtsov and I, Suren Shaumian – thirty people altogether. Zevin (one of the twenty-six) was elected headman, and he had the list of all the prisoners, which he used to distribute the provisions brought to us by the comrades who came to visit us in prison.
> [. . .] Comrade Kandelaki got dysentry and was removed to the prison hospital. Therefore his name was crossed from the list. I was released on bail two days before the evacuation from Baku. My name was also crossed out from the list. Meskhi, Mudryi and Klevtsov did not get on our steamer with us [. . .]

When we were arrested in Krasnovodsk, the list that I mentioned earlier was found on our headman Zevin during the search. After that they began identifying and arresting people from the crowd of refugees (600 people) with the help of that list.

Apart from those whose names were on the list, several other people were arrested, namely: 1) Anastas Mikoyan, 2) Samson Kandelaki, 3) Varvara Dzhaparidze, 4) I, 5) my younger brother Leon, 6) Olga Fioletova, 7) Tatevos Amirov, 8) Maria Amirova, 9) Satenik Martikian, and 10) Maro Tumanian. The people here named were not known to the authorities in Krasnovodsk, and they were arrested because they were given away by the provocateurs among the refugees. Tatevos Amirov was the only one they had known as a famed guerrilla fighter, and that was why he was later added to the twenty-five, and that was how the number 'twenty-six' was accounted for.

This explains why such eminent Bolsheviks as Anastas Mikoyan and Samson Kandelaki stayed alive, while a number of lesser party members (Nikolaishvili, Metaxa, Bogdanov Jr) and even some people whose being there was an accident of fate (e.g. Mishne) found themselves among the twenty-six. Accidentally arrested in Baku, they had their names entered into the headman's list, which subsequently happened to become prescriptive. If Kandelaki had not got dysentery, he would have remained on the list, and so would I, had I not been released on bail just before the evacuation.

The Socialist Revolutionaries in Krasnovodsk decided that if the people on the list had been arrested in Baku, they were the very people they were after, and they had to be eliminated.

If Comrade Zevin's list had not been found, it might have happened that 1) all the arrested people would have been shot, or, 2) only the leading Bolshevik activists, whose names had been known to them, would have been executed . . .*

Suren forgot to mention another name, that of Emmanuel Ghigoyan, member of the Revolutionary Committee of the Caucasian Red Army, who was also removed from the list when he fell sick in the Baku prison and taken to the prison hospital (he died in the 1970s).

The Bolsheviks imprisoned in Baku were the ones who were arrested on board the steamboats *en route* to Astrakhan during their first attempt to leave Baku just before the arrival of the British troops. Mikoyan did not leave Baku then, for he, along with some others, had decided to stay on for underground work. That was why he was not arrested then and therefore his name never appeared on Zevin's list. Although Suren Shaumian refers to my father as one of the 'eminent Bolsheviks', he was perhaps only approaching that category at the time. He began to be well known later, during the struggle for the establishment of Soviet power in Baku and particularly after his return there from the Ashkhabad prison. Although he was very enterprising and energetic, he was

* Quoted by Anastas Mikoyan in *Dorogoi Borby*, Moscow, 1971, p. 225.

younger, less experienced and of a lower profile (especially to his political adversaries) than his senior fellow Bolsheviks such as Shaumian, Dzhaparidze, Azizbekov, Fioletov, Korganov, Ghigoyan, Kandelaki and Amirov.

It was a month after the tragedy that the remaining prisoners heard about it. A railway guard happened to be an eye-witness. In the small hours of 20 September, between the stations of Akhcha-Kuima and Pereval, the Commissars of Baku were ordered to leave the train and were led into the sands, where most of them were shot and the others killed with sabres. The execution was supervised by Feodor Funtikov, Sedykh and Semion Druzhkin in the presence of the head of the British mission in Ashkhabad, Reginald Tigg-Johns. Among the twenty-six were the four key Bolshevik leaders of Baku: Shaumian, Dzhaparidze and Azizbekov, who represented the three Transcaucasian nationalities as an Armenian, a Georgian and an Azerbaijani, and Ivan Fioletov, a Russian. About them and several others my father always spoke to us with great warmth and respect.

Despite the drastic 'reappraisal of values' in the past few years in Russia, there is no doubt that all those people and the majority of other revolutionary leaders of the time did what they did and sacrificed themselves for a genuine faith in socialist ideals, in their heartfelt conviction that their struggle was for the sake of a new system synonymous with justice and happiness.

The official inquiry into the murder of the Commissars of Baku began in the Soviet Union in 1925. Most of those involved in the carnage had fled abroad before Soviet power was established in Baku. However, one of the main instigators and an actual participant in the execution, Feodor Funtikov, was arrested and put on trial. In spring 1925 Funtikov's case was heard at a session of the Supreme Court of the USSR held in Baku. The court established that the one-time head of the Caspian government in Ashkhabad had instigated and organised an armed insurrection against the Soviet power and its deposition in Kyzyl-Arvat, Ashkhabad and Krasnovodsk, and had formed an alliance with the British military command (headed by General Malleson) encouraging the occupation of the areas east of the Caspian Sea by British troops. Funtikov was also pronounced guilty of the murder of nine Commissars of Ashkhabad, and later of Shaumian and twenty-five other Commissars of Baku. He was sentenced to death and shot. Lev Shaumian, in an interview with the magazine *The Soviet Union*, quoted part of Funtikov's written account dating back to the time when the British troops were still in Ashkhabad: 'The representative of the English mission in Ashkhabad, Tigg-Johns, spoke to me personally before the shooting of the Commissars about the necessity of shooting them, and afterwards expressed his satisfaction with the accomplished fact. Ashkhabad, March 2nd, 1919, 4.35 p.m.'*

While in the Krasnovodsk prison, my father began suffering from severe pain

---

* When, in the 1960s, my younger brother Sergo visited Delhi to research for his PhD, he looked for the papers referring to those events in the National Archives of India. He found reference to them in the catalogue, but the files themselves were missing – removed and probably destroyed altogether.

in his gums. The pain grew so bad that he could hardly eat the bread that was his ration. Finally, he was taken to the prison dentist, who turned out to be a young and good-looking woman. She examined his gums and declared, 'Your only cure is plenty of fresh fruit and fresh air.' Such a treatment prescribed to a prisoner could well be taken for a deliberate insult, but her tone was sincere and kind. My father thanked her and returned to his cell. Forty-one years later, in 1959, when my father was on a visit to the US, he attended a performance of a Soviet dance company called Beriozka. He was watching the performance from a box where he was seen by one Judith Shuiskaya, who turned out to be the very same dentist. In an interview she gave to an American paper she said that she had recognised her patient of old by his eyes. She also described their encounter in Krasnovodsk almost exactly the way my father remembered it.

After a month and a half the remaining prisoners were transferred from Krasnovodsk to a prison in Kyzyl-Arvat. Something happened during their time in that prison which my father could never forget and always spoke about with great regret. As I have already said, Shaumian's sons, especially the younger ones Lev and Sergei, were like family to us. They often came to see us, particularly at the dacha at weekends, and Sergei even lived with us for a long time with his mother Ekaterina Sergeevna, and later, when she died, on his own. What happened was that some time after Lev had joined the Red Guard he was accidentally shot in the leg by a former classmate. The wound seemed to heal well, but almost a year later, when Lev was in the Kyzyl-Arvat prison, it became inflamed and swollen. The paramedic who was brought in to have a look at Lev's bad leg (instead of a qualified doctor) prescribed massage, and Anastas, anxious to help the boy, zealously applied the treatment. The pain, however, grew worse, and the following day the prisoners insisted on a visit from a real doctor, who said, 'What have you done? The pus in the knee is now spread along the entire leg!' Lev was taken to a hospital in Ashkhabad. To save his life, his leg had to be removed from above the knee. For a long time afterwards he was on crutches, until some time in the 1930s when a good artificial leg was made for him in Germany. It could bend in the knee, and with it Lev could do without the crutches, although he always used a walking stick. My father always maintained that the whole thing was his fault, although in fact he only did what the paramedic had instructed him to do.

Stepan Shaumian's elder son, Suren, also came to see us, but in 1936 he died of a grave illness. Suren was only thirty-four when the disease developed. He was sent to Vienna with his wife, but the doctors who treated him there could do nothing to save him. I still remember the grief that pervaded the house when the sad news reached us from Austria. My own memory of Suren is not very distinct, but I knew him well enough through what my father and my uncles told us about him. My father always spoke of him with great fondness and warmth.

Suren was fifteen when he joined the organisers of the first union of students in Baku. At the time of the Baku Commune, Suren's father sent him with some important and confidential papers to Lenin in Moscow. Suren had to go via Astrakhan and Tsaritsyn (now Volgograd), and at the time, when transport communications were disrupted and danger was around every corner, such a journey certainly required great courage and presence of mind. After his release from the Ashkhabad prison, Suren disguised himself as a merchant and, with great difficulty and a number of dangerous adventures *en route*, found his way through Turkey to the Crimea and then to Kharkov (both controlled by the White Army at the time), changed his disguise for that of a White lieutenant, reached the front line and crossed it so as to get to Moscow. Once there, Suren entered a military academy, and upon graduation from it he was appointed Chief of Staff of the Azerbaijan Division. Later, as the head of an infantry school in Orel, he initiated its reorganisation into the first armoury college in the country. Suren's next appointment was Commander of Armoured Forces of the Belorussian and later Leningrad military district. Thus, Brigade Commander Shaumian became one of the leading figures in the newly created Red Army armoured force.

Lev Shaumian moved from being a party activist (in Tsaritsyn and Rostov-on-Don) to a newspaper reporter (from 1932) and then editor of several successive papers, among them *The Urals Worker*, where he was editor during the war years. From 1949 to the end of his life Lev was on the staff of the Soviet Encyclopaedia Publishers. In 1954 he became deputy editor-in-chief of that large publishing house, which, as the name suggests, published all successive editions of the multi-volume Soviet Encyclopaedia. Lev was a highly educated, erudite person, and, like his brother Suren, had an even and pleasant temper.

The third of the Shaumian brothers, Sergei, was not much older than I, and we were on friendly terms. He was an art-lover and a great theatre-goer. I still remember the great admiration and respect with which he spoke of the leading actors of the day, especially of Igor Ilyinsky. I believe it was due to his influence that I came to love the theatre, particularly drama (although later I became fond of ballet as well). For many years and until his death, Sergei was a lecturer (and then a professor) at the so-called Higher Party School. Unfortunately, at the time of Khrushchev's 'thaw' Sergei, unlike Lev, failed to understand the changes or to come to terms with the more relaxed ideology that brought them about. He remained a Stalinist to his last day. I remember how back in the 1930s he blotted out photographs of purged party leaders and political figures from the photo albums of the party congresses prior to their arrest. There is one such album in my father's personal archive, and it also lost some of the photographs due to Sergei's efforts to erase them, although some of them can still be discerned. I always felt there was something wrong about it and did not like him doing it, but I was too young to really understand the situation and thus be able to stop him.

Let me go back to the events in 1919. Some time after the Commissars' execution the remaining prisoners were transferred from Kyzyl-Arvat to the Ashkhabad prison. On 27 February 1919 they were released. They spent another day in Ashkhabad and then got on a train to Krasnovodsk as free men, although once in Krasnovodsk they were escorted to the pier and onto the steamboat, where they were guarded by British soldiers. When the steamboat docked in Baku it was met by a delegation which presented the captain with an official paper ordering the immediate release of the group. As it turned out, the

Presidium of the Workers' Conference (a permanent body of workers' representatives in Baku), supported by the entire workers' contingent, had succeeded in
extorting it from the British military command. Even the Mensheviks, Socialist
Revolutionaries and Dashnaks joined them in that demand.

Once back in Baku, my father returned to revolutionary activity. After a while,
during the re-election of the Presidium of the Workers' Conference, he was
chosen as its deputy chairman. Now that their senior comrades were no longer
with them, the young ones – Ivan Anashkin, Levan Gogoberidze, Anastas
Mikoyan, Levon Mirzoyan, Sarkis and others – had to devise the tactics and
make decisions themselves, even though the situation was no less involved than
before. Despite his youth and his fiery temper, my father showed himself to be –
and remained in the years to come – a clever tactician not inclined to act rashly
or impetuously. The following episode may serve as an illustration. One day he
discovered that the party committee of Baku had formed a paramilitary group
(in which, among other volunteers, was Gevorg Alikhanian, his former classmate
at the religious school). As he later wrote in his memoirs, my father was stunned
when he heard at a meeting that they claimed to be ready to start an armed insurrection, and when many of those present voiced their support of the idea.
When Anastas expressed his doubts, the committee moved that he get together
with the paramilitary group to assess the situation and prepare a report for the
next meeting. Having looked into the details, he reported to the committee – in
the presence of the three leaders of the group, Alikhanian, Ghigoyan and
Kovalev – that the group had no real power to carry out a successful insurrection
and expressed his doubts about the political aspect of the issue. He said that an
armed revolt at that moment in time would be nothing but an adventurous undertaking doomed to total failure and conducive to the ultimate defeat of the party
organisation in Baku. He succeeded in proving his point to the committee
members.

Whatever plans there were for an armed insurrection, they certainly had to be
tied in with the plans of the Red Army advance. Besides, there were certain issues
concerning party work on which the party leaders of Baku could not come up
with a unified point of view. It was over a year since any member of the Baku
committee had visited the Central Committee, so it was decided that a trip to
Moscow was a must, and Anastas was elected as the one to go.

The way to Moscow lay across the Caspian Sea, and the choice of vessel was
limited to a fishing boat by the same route along which petrol was smuggled into
Soviet Russia at the time. With great difficulties and utmost secrecy, my father,
accompanied by another party activist from Baku, Olga Shatunovskaya, and a
few others set out for Astrakhan in a fishing boat. The crossing was long and
fraught with danger; the sea was rough almost throughout the voyage and the
approaches to Astrakhan were patrolled by General Denikin's navy. It must have
been this experience, never forgotten by him in later life, that inspired my father,
born and bred in the mountains, to a love for the sea and its tempestuous nature.
I remember his recollections of his later encounters with the sea; how he, then
already the Food Industry Commissar, went out to sea with Murmansk fishermen during a storm, and how he sailed together with the Caspian Sea fishermen.

He told us proudly that he was a good sailor and felt as fit as a fiddle even when half the crew was sea-sick. He also had the experience of going out to sea on naval ships, and in 1945, again during a storm, he sailed to Kamchatka with a call at the Kuril Islands on the way on an American ship, one of those received through the lend-lease agreement. It was different, of course, during his holidays on the Black Sea, but there too he took every opportunity to go out on his own for an hour or longer in a small rowing boat.

Having met Kirov in Astrakhan, my father then got on a train and safely reached Moscow, where he was received by Lenin and attended several meetings: the Second Congress of the Communist Organisations of the Peoples of the East, the Eighth All-Russian Party Conference and the All-Russian Congress of Soviets. At that congress the twenty-four-year-old Anastas was elected an alternate member of the All-Russian Executive Committee (the prototype of the Supreme Council).

Father stayed in Moscow for about two months. Then, at the beginning of January 1920, he, Olga Shatunovskaya and two others left Moscow for Baku. This time they went via Tashkent and Krasnovodsk, for there was ice in the north part of the Caspian Sea and so the Astrakhan route was no good. A launch was sent from Baku to pick them up at Krasnovodsk. The plan was to land somewhere in Azerbaijan and then secretly find their way to Baku, but the compass on board the boat failed, they lost their way and ended up at Petrovsk (now Makhachkala), north of Azerbaijan. They were greeted there by Red Army soldiers of the 11th Army, whose headquarters were at the local railway station in an unfastened lounge-car. Taken to the headquarters, Anastas again saw Ordzhonikidze and Kirov and met the Army Commander M. Levandovksy. Anxious to reach Baku as soon as possible, my father asked Kirov and Levandovksy for help, and they sent him there on an armoured train as an official representative of the Army Council. And so he arrived in Baku on that first armoured train, in the vanguard of the 11th Army.

The next day, 28 April 1920, even before the main forces of the army approached the city, Soviet power was proclaimed in Baku with the new provisional government – the Military Revolutionary Committee – headed by Nariman Narimanov, its chairman. Soviet Russia, well aware of the interest in its oil resources from Britain and other countries, was always very unlikely to leave Azerbaijan outside its sphere of influence.

CHAPTER 2

A Kremlin Childhood

In September 1920 my father was informed of the Central Committee's decision to post him to Nizhny Novgorod to work for the district party committee (as became known later, it had been suggested by Lenin). At a party conference that took place shortly before my father's departure for Nizhny, he met Vyacheslav Molotov, who had worked there earlier. He told my father that it would be a difficult job for him because in the Nizhny Novgorod district committee everybody was hand in glove with each other, and outsiders were not welcome. As my father later heard, Molotov had been more or less kept in isolation and eventually had to leave Nizhny. He certainly did not have the flair for getting along well with people or for creating a relaxed and friendly atmosphere around him, something my father was naturally good at.

The initial welcome my father received was, indeed, somewhat cool and wary. He was assigned to work for the district executive committee. The experience received while working there, and later for the district party committee, proved of great value for his future work as a minister in charge of (at one time or another) trade, food industry, supplies, etc. It was in Nizhny that my father first became involved in something for which he had a liking and aptitude: economic and industrial management and organisation of trade and production (mainly of food and consumer goods). This activity was what he was mainly engaged in and truly dedicated to throughout his subsequent career up to 1964, when he was elected chairman of the Supreme Council of the Soviet Union.

Back in Nizhny, it was not long before the ice between Anastas and his new colleagues was broken and he succeeded in winning the trust and respect of those with whom he was working. Soon he was elected member of the district committee, and then its secretary – the real purpose of his posting there. After a while my father wrote to his second cousin Ashkhen Tumanian, asking her to come and join him in Nizhny. The two of them had had an 'understanding' for some time and had already secretly decided to get married, so she came accompanied by her younger brother Haik, who had just finished school.

In January 1922 my father received (through Stalin) Lenin's assignment to go to Novo-Nikolaevsk (now Novosibirsk) to warn the local party authorities against delegating a large number of former Trotskyists to the coming party congress (a characteristic example of Lenin's tactics in dealing with the opposition; he would never let things take their course when active interference was possible). That trip was the first in the series of many delicate missions my father was to be assigned to in the future, both under Stalin and Khrushchev.

The time was soon approaching when Anastas and Ashkhen expected their first child to be born. My mother required a good diet, and as the Nizhny Novgorod district almost verged on famine, there was not enough food at home.

My father wanted her to go home to her parents in Tiflis where she would be fed well and cared for by her mother. At first Ashkhen resisted, saying that she could not return to her mother; when they had become man and wife she had written to her in Tiflis and received a reply full of anger and indignation. Her mother as good as cursed her for doing such an unheard-of thing, violating the time-honoured Armenian custom that forbade marriages between second cousins. But Anastas knew his wife's mother; she was a woman of strict principles but she also had a keen sense of justice and was by no means unkind. He was confident she would never turn her pregnant daughter away. On consideration my mother agreed to go, and so, when my father had to go to Moscow to attend a party conference, he took her along, and from there sent her to Tiflis under the protection of a few fellow Caucasians returning home from the same conference. The welcome my mother received from her parents in Tiflis was as affectionate and warm as my father had supposed it would be.

In May 1922 my father was transferred to Rostov-on-Don and elected secretary of the South-East Bureau of the Central Committee. I was born in July. My mother and I were brought home from hospital by Sergo Ordzhonikidze in his car (he was working in Tiflis at the time). He suggested staying in Tiflis until September, when Voroshilov would be passing through Tiflis in his special train carriage, and then go with him to Rostov to join my father. My mother did as he suggested. Which I should now consider to be my 'native' town in the broader sense of the word, I do not really know – Tiflis, where I was born but where I remained only for about two months, or Rostov, where I spent the first four years of my life, the period which some believe to be crucial for the development of one's personality? Or Moscow, where I have lived ever since?

From his very first days in the North Caucasus my father had to face an issue which was very important and complicated, if not painful, at the time (it has recently recovered its importance and come to the fore of Russian politics): the Cossacks and the relationship between them and Bolshevik power, which mainly relied on the new settlers among peasants, the latter being at odds with the Cossacks. The party line at the time my father first encountered the problem was to obliterate the Cossacks' deep-rooted traditions, and indeed anything that marked them out as a distinct group of population (and formerly a very privileged group too): they were forbidden to wear their traditional clothes, to say nothing of their swords or daggers; they had no more of their famous horse shows at which they used to compete in fancy riding and target shooting; even their songs were banned. In short, the new power was taking it out on the Cossacks for the civil war, in which many Cossacks had been fighting with the White Army. My father opposed that line from the very start. He went round many Cossack villages and talked to people, listening to the catalogue of grievances and offences. He then did his best to persuade the local party leadership that the Cossacks, instead of being further alienated by such a severe and unreasonable policy, could be won over through tolerance of and regard for their traditions and their feeling of identity.

Later my father reported on the new tendencies in the work of the regional party committee at a plenary session of the Central Committee in Moscow. On the basis of the Rostov experience the session adopted a special resolution on party policy towards the Cossacks which for the first time emphasised the need to take their traditions and customs into consideration. I believe it was my father's initiative in this respect and his successful handling of the sensitive issues in the relationships between the many nationalities of the North Caucasus that won him the respect of the Central Committee members.

After the Central Committee plenary session of July 1926, my father was summoned by Stalin who told him that the Politburo had moved to appoint him the Commissar (Minister) of Foreign and Domestic Trade in Kamenev's place. My father refused on the grounds that he did not have the experience needed for the job, and also because he did not want to leave his post in the North Caucasus. Stalin insisted, but my father did not give his consent and left for Rostov, hoping the matter would end at that. However, totally undaunted by his refusal, the Politburo voted for dismissing Kamenev and appointing Anastas the Commissar of Foreign and Domestic Trade. An exchange of telegrams between Stalin and my father followed (my father still hoping that the Politburo decision would be reconsidered), until finally an official telegram from Moscow informed him that the decision was ratified by the entire Central Committee and was to be made public. Later, of course, Stalin would handle such matters in a markedly different manner. In 1939 he was looking for a suitable man to take charge of the newly formed Commissariat (Ministry) of Textile Industry. My father, who during a visit to Leningrad had met Alexei Kosyghin, recommended him to Stalin as a good candidate for the post and suggested that he should be invited to Moscow to talk it over. 'Why talk?' said Stalin. 'Put together a written resolution about his appointment and that's that.' As Kosyghin later remembered, he was summoned to the Kremlin without any explanation and learned about his new appointment from a morning paper he bought getting off the train in Moscow.

So in the end my father had to give in. The official resolution of the Central Executive Committee was signed on 14 August 1926, following which the Council of the People's Commissars (the equivalent of the Cabinet) made him a member of the Labour and Defence Council. To be honest, I do not understand why my father so stubbornly resisted that appointment; he had always been an excellent organiser and had a distinct flair for economic management. On the other hand, he was totally devoid of careerism or self-seeking ambition and never sought or solicited any high position for himself. This, I believe, was one of the reasons for his political longevity.

In my father's personal archives I came across the written record of his talks with Mr Dirksen, the German ambassador, in April 1929. Their main subject was trade between the two countries, and one of the ambassador's remarks reads as follows: 'In Germany we greatly appreciate the circumspection with which you draw up your foreign trade plans, and know that your payments are always guaranteed.' Somewhere in the course of these talks my father said: 'We must and shall be able to purchase the necessary foreign goods for cash, if the credit terms offered to us happen to be unfavourable from our point of view. We shall not accept unfavourable and unprofitable credit terms any more.' Another interesting document I came across in my father's archives was his memorandum to Vyacheslav Molotov written in September 1930 (when my father was still the Commissar of Trade) in connection with the Soviet trade experts abroad. A special commission under the auspices of the Central Committee which had the sinister function of purging the party membership was going to recall to Moscow those of the experts who 'had spent too much time abroad' (the assumption being that the longer they were staying abroad, the more susceptible to 'capitalist influence' they became). In his memo Anastas wrote: 'If their long stay abroad had affected their moral integrity, I would have agreed with you, but since there is no evidence of that, their long experience of working abroad is certainly an advantage rather than a drawback.' In a memo written in the same year by my father's deputy, Kissin, the main issue is the necessity of major construction work in the food industry with the help of foreign specialists and expertise. 'For the first time since putting all food industry under the auspices of the People's Commissariat of supplies,' Kissin wrote, 'the question of foreign technical aid has been raised. Comrade Mikoyan has approved the plan of inviting seventy-five foreign engineers – specialists in various fields.'

I must say that my father always respected and valued true professionals, people who knew what they were doing in their jobs. In fact he did a lot to promote professional and vocational training in the Soviet Union. Thus, before 1930, when the food industry became a prerogative of the new Commissariat of Supplies (there was no Commissariat of Food Industry then), at the head of which was my father, there had not been a single higher educational institution for training food industry specialists, but by 1933 there had appeared over a hundred and thirty such institutions, both secondary and tertiary ones.

Over the past few years there have been a number of publications in the Russian press concerning the sale of paintings and other artistic items abroad in the late 1920s and 1930s, and Anastas Mikoyan has been named as the person responsible. In actual fact the use of various *objets d'art*, paintings and antiquities as 'currency' for trading, urgently needed to save Soviet Russia from famine and economic collapse, according to the contemporary Russian historian Yuri Zhukov, had begun back in 1921. The scale on which the treasures were being sold abroad was growing steadily, and the peak fell in 1927 to 1930 as a response to the slogan of intensive industrialisation declared by the 15th Party Congress (1927) and the official adoption of the first Five-Year Plan. My father was the Commissar of Foreign and Domestic Trade from 1926 to December 1930, so it does look indeed as if he was directly responsible for that activity, but it is obvious that decisions of that calibre – i.e. aimed at the realisation of the 'grandiose plans of the party' – were made at the highest level of the party leadership, and the Commissar of Trade was expected to carry them out without question. Incidentally, that was the time when the construction of such giant industrial enterprises as the car plant in Nizhny Novgorod and the Stalingrad tractor plant began, and it was carried out with the active participation of foreign engineers and construction experts. Their work and expertise had to be paid for, and that was just one of the many urgent reasons why the country needed currency to survive and develop. It is interesting that after 1930 the export of Russia's artistic legacy began to decrease, and by 1940 it stopped altogether. From 1938 onwards the Commissar of Foreign Trade was again Anastas Mikoyan.

My younger brother Sergo, in response to a question about the sale of paintings in one of the interviews he gave, said that he was quite ready to suppose that Anastas, not being a connoisseur of art, might have not been sufficiently aware of the value of those paintings and of the damage suffered by our cultural legacy due to their loss. After the publication of that interview, Sergo received a phone call from Z. Sheinis, a former Foreign Office executive and the author of a book about Maxim Litvinov (Commissar of Foreign Affairs 1930–9, Soviet Ambassador to the US 1941–3), who said: 'How could you suppose such a thing? I was present at a meeting where both Anastas Ivanovich and Litvinov declared that they were against selling particularly valuable works, but their opinion was ignored and the decision taken anyway.' Together with Anatoly Lunacharsky, and possibly on his suggestion, Anastas compiled 'The List of Antiquities and Works of Art Not to be Taken out of the Country', but a few days later this document was supplied with an additional clause which considerably limited its 'protective' power. No doubt that clause was a directive 'from above' – most likely from Stalin himself, to whom the list had to be shown.

At my father's first official meeting (1926) with the executive personnel of his new Commissariat he said to them, with what must have been rather unusual candour, that he was a novice in the job and that he relied on their help and advice for gaining knowledge and experience. He made it clear that it was not like him to be embarrassed to ask when there was something he did not know, and that in such cases he would turn to them. He said he hoped it would not belittle him in their eyes, for 'if you don't know something it is better to ask someone who does than remain in ignorance pretending to be a know-all'. He stuck to this principle throughout his entire life.

The Trade Commissar's deputy for foreign trade in 1926 was Leonid Krasin. My father always remembered him with great warmth and described him as a man of high culture, erudition and great personal charm. But their association was to be very brief: in November that same year Krasin died during a business visit to London. About a year later a selection of his articles on foreign trade was published by the Commissariat as a tribute to his memory. My father did all he could to promote that publication and even supplied it with a foreword. Shortly after the volume had come out, Stalin surprised my father with a question about it: 'Why did you allow the publication of Krasin's book, and with your own laudatory foreword at that? Don't you know that Krasin had made some grave mistakes, both at the time of the Baku underground, where he and I had worked together, and more recently too? You must know that he grossly overrated the significance of foreign capital for our economy, and actually made his fallacious views public in a speech at the 12th Party Congress.' No doubt Krasin, had he not died in 1926, would have been declared an 'enemy of the people' in the 1930s, as many on the staff of the Commissariat were – later, when my father was no longer working there. Whenever he afterwards recalled his own time at the Commissariat he had nothing but words of praise to say about those people.

In those years my father used to see Stalin almost every day, and many of those meetings were quite casual and informal. The usual pattern was meeting up for a late dinner at Stalin's dacha. In those days Stalin was still capable of listening to all the information on the affairs of state and the opinions of his guests attentively and calmly, making quick and reasonable decisions there and then. According to my father, it was much later, during the last few years before his death, that Stalin was no longer able to control his irritation when told about problems and complications.

In 1926, shortly after his appointment as Commissar of Trade, my father was elected a candidate member of the Politburo. From then, and until 1964, he worked within the structure of the Soviet version of the Cabinet, starting off as Commissar, then Deputy Chairman of the Council of Ministers, and finally First Deputy Chairman (i.e. First Deputy Premier). Apart from his being a member of the Politburo (from 1935) and the Central Committee he had no position in the party and was mainly concerned with trade, production and supplies, and also international relations.

Some time after our arrival in Moscow the family was given an apartment in the Kremlin, in the building known before the revolution as the Horse Guards. Only a small part of that building survives today, adjoining the Palace of Congresses built between 1959 and 1961. The eight-room apartment stretched on either side of a long wide corridor. We, the children, lived in three small rooms with an adjoining bathroom, next to my father's study. My parents' bedroom and their bathroom were on the same side of the corridor. On its opposite side were the dining room, the sitting room, the kitchen, the loo and a small guest room, often occupied by one of my grandmothers when they came to town from the dacha, or my mother's sister Haikush.

At that time many Soviet leaders, members of the administrative staff and service personnel lived in the Kremlin with their families. There were many children. I remember the mock fights we sometimes had on a vacant plot of land (there is a park there now) not far from the Tsar Cannon. We built shelters of sand and sheets of plywood. It was anything but an idle precaution, for pebbles and even small stones were used in our 'battles'. A chance encounter with a top government or party official in the Kremlin was more or less a matter of course in those days. I vividly remember two such occasions from my early experience: once my brother and I 'ran into' Stalin and Voroshilov, and another time into Bukharin and Ordzhonikidze. Both 'pairs' stopped for a chat and a laugh with us. The nickname they all had for us was 'the little Mikoyans'. On the stairs of our house I once met Abel Enukidze, who lived in the same building. He invited me over to his flat, treated me to some sweets and made me an unexpected present of a foreign-made tool kit in a leather case, which was a great rarity then. I often met Kalinin and Andreev, Politburo members who lived one floor down from where we did. Next to us lived Tomsky, who later shot himself to escape imminent arrest, and Krestinksy, who also vanished before long.

Following the assassination of Sergei Kirov in 1934, all the families except those of the top-rank officials were moved out of the Kremlin, and after the purges of 1936–7 only Politburo members and their families were left to live within the Kremlin walls. At that time the Kremlin could not be entered without a special pass. I invited my classmates a number of times, for my birthday parties and also when we got together to prepare an issue of our school newspaper, but I always had to ask for a single pass for each guest. The same went for my parents' guests.

There were five sons in the family. My youngest three brothers and I were named after the men whom my father respected and was fond of: Stepan Shaumian, Alexei Dzhaparidze and Vano Fioletov (the leaders of the Commissars of Baku shot in 1918), and also Sergo Ordzhonikidze, who was my father's life-long friend. Their second son was born in the year of Lenin's death and was named Vladimir after him. Big portraits of all these people hung in dark wooden frames on the walls of my father's study, together with a picture of Stalin (from the years of the revolution) and a photograph of my father. At the time of my childhood, my father usually wore a kind of semi-military outfit, with a field shirt, riding breeches and high boots. With his slender waist accentuated by a leather belt, that outfit was very becoming. But after his first trip to the US in 1936 he took to wearing ordinary civilian clothes, with a jacket and tie. He always dressed very neatly and wore his clothes well, which was partly due to my mother's care.

There was only a seven-year difference between me and my youngest brother Sergo. One can imagine what a noisy and naughty lot we were. We must have given our mother a lot of trouble and been a constant source of anxiety to her. Although there was a housekeeper and, when in the country in the summer, a nanny, my mother gave a lot of her time and attention to her children and to the housekeeping. From my early childhood and adolescence I remember her best of all with a duster in her hand or with a pile of our things (which she always washed and mended herself) to be sorted out, darned and put away. Thanks to her untiring efforts, the flat was always spotlessly clean and in perfect order (in so far as it was possible with five boys 'at large' in the house).

Some time ago, as I was looking through a collection of memoirs entitled *The Bygone Days*,* I came across B. Babina's account of Jana Kozlovskaya's recollections of her life in the Kremlin. The Kozlovskys lived in the same building as we did. 'The Mikoyans had many children,' says Babina, 'while the Kozlovskys had only two – Jana and her brother . . . Mikoyan's wife, with her six [*sic*] children could not work, while in Kozlovsky's family both he and his wife worked. Mikoyan's wife used to come and borrow money from us almost every month, for they could hardly make ends meet.'

My mother was extremely kind, though quick-tempered at times, very conscientious and fastidious, both in the direct and in the figurative sense. She was remarkably modest, even shy, and invariably polite with people irrespective of their position or social status. As to her own 'elevated' position, she never showed off or put on airs because of it; if anything, she was almost self-conscious about it. She had an enormous sense of duty which revealed itself both in her domestic

---

* Progress Publishers, Moscow, 1990, vol. 2, p. 385.

life and in the voluntary work she did outside her home. These, I believe, were also the criteria on which she based her attitudes to other people and which she applied in bringing us up. After finishing school in Tiflis, my mother had spent some time working as a school mistress. Later, when we were at school, she was very active on the parents' board, and years later I heard many nice things about her participation, and none of these accounts failed to stress her amiability and modesty.

My father stuck to the same basic principles as my mother where we were concerned, but he was rather stern, exacting, at times even severe and certainly not always tolerant. At the same time he loved us very much and was in general very fond of children. He was happy with and proud of his large family and often complained in front of friends that his wife had not given him a sixth child, which had been on its way when 'those stupid doctors forbade her to have it'. My mother always got annoyed when she heard him say that. Being kissed or hugged by our parents was something we hardly ever experienced, and even though my mother would sometimes 'forget herself' and give one of us a hug or a kiss, my father never would. Years later, when he was already retired, he would sometimes say to his other relatives that he was proud of his sons, each of whom had grown up to be a deserving and worthy person. And once – just once – he said it in our presence, during a toast at a family celebration. My mother tried to keep our petty mischiefs from my father, and her most effective 'correction' gambit was the words 'Your father won't like it if he finds out'. We were in awe of his anger. Very nearly the greatest sin in the eyes of my parents was any manifestation of immodesty on our part or lack of respect towards other people. A well-known episode of family history (which I did not witness myself but heard about several times) was when my father, punishing one of my brothers for immodest behaviour, accompanied his smacks on the culprit's bottom with the words, 'It's not you who's a Mikoyan, it's me!'

My parents, when talking to each other or to their relatives, would often use Armenian. My father's mother, who lived with us most of the time, spoke very little Russian, and apart from my maternal grandmother and my mother's sister, both of whom often stayed with us, we had frequent visits from various relatives from Armenia. Two of my favourite uncles also used Armenian in those days, yet we, the children, did not pick up the language. Our native tongue was Russian. I could follow Armenian speech better than any of my brothers, but all I knew was the simplest everyday vocabulary, of which I now remember about a hundred different words and phrases. As a young boy I was more or less fluent in German, which I studied both at school and at home with a private teacher who was also teaching German to my father. Much later, after the war, I took lessons in English from a very competent teacher called Nelly Gershevich, an American expatriate who had come to the USSR with her father, an engineer. He had arrived in Russia to take part in the construction of a car plant in Nizhny Novgorod and stayed for good.

We had a very good library at home: complete works by Russian and foreign writers, a large series of books entitled 'Contemporary Foreign Novel', contemporary Russian literature, and volumes published by the Academia publishers. I would not say that my parents really supervised or guided our reading – for my own part I read avidly whatever came my way – but occasionally my father would say, 'Read such-and-such book (or article)', and it was unthinkable to ignore his advice. What would I say when he asked me what I thought of it? Telling my father a lie was utterly out of the question. The other avid reader in the family was my youngest brother Sergo, while my other three brothers were not so fond of reading. And only two of us, Volodya and I, went into sports on a serious scale.

We did not see our father very often: when we were leaving for school he was still asleep, and when we were going to bed at night he was still at work. In those days the government leaders worked from ten or eleven a.m. until the small hours of the morning. Only occasionally my father would come home for dinner, and then go back to work afterwards. But at weekends, throughout the year, the family usually got together at the dacha.

The dacha had fairly large grounds surrounded by a red-brick wall. There were three separate houses known, respectively, as the 'big house', the 'small house' and the 'service block'. The dacha was called Zubalovo after the former owner of the estate, an Armenian oil magnate from Baku. Tradition had it that Zubalov had feared assassination and therefore had built a stone house without balconies with a high wall around it (while we were living there a large balcony was built over the veranda on the ground floor). The 'small house' had been built for the manager of Zubalov's estates. About a mile from that estate lay the former property of Zubalov's son, known to us as Zubalovo-2. Both its main house and the grounds were somewhat smaller than at Zubalovo-1. It was Stalin's dacha. While his wife, Nadezhda Alliluyeva, was still alive he came there often, but after her death he hardly appeared at all. It was his children, Vasily and Svetlana, who lived there. Once or twice I saw his elder son, Yakov, there as well.

In the early 1930s our dacha was shared by several families. The 'big house', apart from us, was occupied by I. Unschlicht (an old Polish Bolshevik and a secretary of the Central Executive Committee), A. Varsky (another Polish émigré) and, for a while, the deputy Commissar of Defence, Ian Gamarnik. One of the rooms on the first floor, where we lived, was given by my father to Stepan Shaumian's widow, Ekaterina Sergeevna. The 'small house' was occupied by K. Voroshilov's family, but later, when a separate dacha was built for him, Ian Gamarnik moved in. The so-called 'service block' was the home of the Alliluyevs – Stalin's wife's brothers and sister, and her widowed sister-in-law. Their neighbours in that house were Dzerzhinsky's widow Sofia Sigismundovna, deputy Commissar of Foreign Affairs Karakhan, and Alesha Svanidze, Stalin's first wife's brother. What with all their offspring (only the Varsky couple had none), the place was swarming with children of all ages. It was there that I first met Timur Frunze, who eventually became one of my best friends. Upon the death of their parents – Commissar of the Armed Forces Mikhail Frunze and his wife – Timur, and his sister, Tanya, lived in the family of Voroshilov, one of their officially appointed guardians (the other two had been purged).

In the purges of 1937 several of the dacha's inmates were arrested – first Unschlicht and Varsky, then Karakhan and Svanidze. The number of families (and of the children) living at the dacha grew smaller. A new tenant appeared in the 'small house', the General Staff Commander B. Shaposhnikov. We also had frequent visits from Vasily Stalin, who joined us in playing ice-hockey in winter, cross-country skiing, skating and, in the summer, swimming in the nearby river. Sometimes I would visit Vasily in Zubalovo-2, where another friend would join us – Artem Sergeev, son of the late Bolshevik Artem. He lived with his mother at a dacha a few miles off and cycled to us or to Zubalovo-2.

My brothers and I initially went to the same school, until I transferred to a special military school. We were never taken to school in the car, except for Monday mornings, when we came straight from the country. Even so, we were loath to be seen getting out of the car by other kids, and we always asked the driver to drop us round the corner half a mile off.

It was school No. 32, known as a 'commune'. It had been founded by Panteleimon Lepeshinsky in Belorussia in 1918, the original pupils being orphans. In 1919 he had moved them all to Moscow where Lenin's wife, Krupskaya, helped to set the school going. In those days it was really a 'commune' as both the pupils and most of the teachers lived there. Everything was based on self-government and self-service; all issues, including admission and expulsion, were decided by vote at the pupils' and teachers' general meetings. They said that Trotsky's son Sergei had been expelled in this manner for some grave offence when his father was still in power and greatly popular. By 1930 the school had ceased being a commune, but its old spirit of comradeship and its democratic tradition were still there.

Among the pupils were people of different nationalities – children of Polish and Hungarian Communists, many Jewish children, etc. – but nobody ever minded about ethnic background; there was no trace of anything like anti-Semitism or any other nationalist prejudice. We had very good and competent teachers at that school, among them the authors of several well-known textbooks which were then and for decades to come used in all Russian secondary schools. Among our favourite teachers was the PE master, who is still vividly and warmly remembered by all his former pupils. An officer of the Russian army before 1917, a participant of the Russo–Japanese war of 1904–5 and later an instructor at a military cadet school, he was a smart-looking, reserved, no-nonsense man who had a way with children. I still remember our summer hiking tours and winter skiing trips under his leadership, particularly the expedition to the field of Borodino, scene of that great Napoleonic battle, with a campfire in the evening and the night spent in a hayloft.

The school was in the centre of Moscow, in a side street just off Ostozhenka. Most of the pupils were from that area and lived in and around Ostozhenka and Kropotkinskaya (now, as before 1917, called Prechistenka). The school gave an annual thirty per cent quota to the children of the workers of a nearby factory, but there were also many pupils from what is now known in Moscow as the 'House on the Embankment' (after the title of Yuri Trifonov's famous novel set in and centred around that building), a huge constructivist residence block on the other side of the river. It received its first tenants in 1931, and most of the children who lived there studied at the school which was closer to it, right next to the British embassy and across the river from the Kremlin. In those days the building was called the 'House of the Government', for many of its apartments were allotted to higher executives of various government offices, high-ranking Red Army commanders and other well-known figures (e.g. famous Arctic explorers and distinguished pilots, etc.).

Our school had a 'patron' in the shape of the nearby Vakhtangov drama theatre, and the children of the actors who lived in the neighbourhood were also among the pupils. For example, the son of Ruben Simonov, the company's art director, was in the same class as my younger brother Alyosha. Known to us as Zhenya (a familiar form of Yevgeny), he later became a famous theatre director himself. Another famous father among the school parents was the actor Boris Shchukin. Actors of the Vakhtangov company sometimes performed at our school, and some of them were active members of the parents' board.

During our early school years we were seen to and from school by our nanny, Dasha. We used to walk from the Kremlin to Ostozhenka past the Cathedral of the Saviour. Dasha had once promised to take me inside, but one day all we saw was a great length of hoarding around the place where the cathedral had been: it had been blown up over night. It happened in 1931, when I was in my second year at school. It now stands there again, rebuilt from scratch in 1996.

It was due to the elevated background of many of my schoolmates that the purges of 1937–8 were very strongly felt at our school. Not only the parents of many were arrested, but some of the pupils as well – the sons of Drobnis, for example, and of the Polish émigré Communist Ganetsky. Shura Drobnis, the sister of the boy who was arrested, was in my class, as was my good friend Serezha Metallikov, whose parents were both purged, and Nina Kuchinskaya, who lost her father.

Towards the end of the 1930s I was already at the age when children began to listen to their elders' talk with attention and interest. In their conversations (often joined by my two uncles, Anushavan Mikoyan and my mother's brother Haik Tumanian) my parents frequently mentioned the names of well-known people, many of whom at that time or later disappeared without a trace, and natural death was not the reason. My memory has kept many of those names, some of which began to appear in various publications at the start of the *perestroika*. When my parents did not want us to understand what they were saying they would use Armenian, but making out names was not difficult, and I learnt the word *nestats* that meant 'arrested'. Such conversations were always conducted in sombre tones, and my mother always spoke about those people's fate with great sadness, which naturally intrigued me even more. I do not recollect the faintest sign of malicious joy or gloating satisfaction. We, the young ones (just as, I believe, the majority of the country's population), did not understand what was really going on and believed the stories of the 'enemies of the people' in the newspapers, films, etc. Yet, the emotional tenor of those conversations at home was not lost on me and no doubt contributed to my somewhat uneasy and wary attitude to the events.

As were other members of the Politburo, my father was allowed to bring various state documents home to read, including the secret ones. He piled them up on the desk in his study, and I must confess I sometimes sneaked in to take a look at them. One day I chanced upon a paper which turned out to be a record of an interrogation of a prominent party leader (unfortunately I do not remember the name). Among other things he was asked about his clandestine meetings with foreigners, and whether or not he was performing subversive assignments. The man's answers confirmed all the accusations, and his full confession was there as well, leaving no room for doubt about his guilt. Many years later, thinking about those events, I imagined how difficult if not impossible it must have been to doubt or refute those well-documented accusations against various people. And it also must be remembered that Stalin's policy was generally and implicitly believed to be infallible as such. As for the tortures which forced confessions from those people, nobody, not even those in high places, could have imagined they were practised.

Once I heard from behind the shut door of my parents' bedroom my father's sharp exclamation, 'I don't believe it, I don't!' It was said with pain and distress in his voice, and I guessed it referred to Ordzhonikidze's suicide, the news of which he had just received. It became known shortly afterwards that Stalin had been about to declare him an 'enemy of the people' (later it was supposed that Ordzhonikidze's death had been staged to cover his assassination on Stalin's secret orders).

Years later I thought of the horrible psychological pressure under which my parents must have been living during those years, and also after the war until Stalin's death, seeing so many well-known and distinguished people, including their good friends and acquaintances, vanishing one by one. There had been no immunity for anyone, and my father must have been inwardly prepared for a sinister knock on his own door any day. I had met many of those people who later disappeared, and I remember some of them vividly to this day. In those days my parents still had plenty of visitors and guests, whereas after 1937 the only people who came to see them were relatives or those friends and acquaintances who held no positions of prominence. Party leaders and top government officials stopped socialising in each other's houses after 1937 for fear of being accused of plotting, and the tradition of mutual friendly visits became extinct. But until then, many prominent people had been coming to see us.

Sergo Ordzhonikidze was one of them. I remember him well, for he came several times and always played with us – it was clear he loved children a lot. Another celebrity I remember was the writer Maxim Gorky, to whose dacha we (the eldest three sons) once accompanied my father. The grown-ups went into the house and we stayed outside, and then Gorky came out to see my father off. I can still see him very clearly in my mind's eye, but at the time the three of us were much more impressed with a little pet monkey which lived in his garden and amused us with its deft way of peeling tangerines.

So in the first half of the 1930s my father used to see many of his friends and acquaintances. Among them were his former classmates from the Seminary. Two of them, the well-known architect Karo Alabian and Napoleon Andreasian, remained his life-long friends. Their class at the Seminary produced about a dozen well-known Bolshevik activists, but only two of them – my father and

Alabian – survived Stalin's purges. Andreasian was the only one of those arrested to be released in 1939. In the 1950s, at some official celebration, Khrushchev saw a familiar face in the audience and asked my father, who sat next to him in the presidium, 'Could it be Andreasian sitting over there?' My father said it was. During the interval Khrushchev went down into the audience, embraced Andreasian heartily and said to those around them, 'Of all the district party secretaries in Moscow of that time he and I are the only ones who have survived!'

My parents were on very friendly terms with the Uborevich family, known to them since their time in Rostov when Jeronim Uborevich was the Commander of the North Caucasian military district. In 1928 he was appointed Commander of the Moscow military district, and our two families grew even closer. They had even lived for some time in my parents' apartment on their arrival in Moscow until they got a place of their own. Uborevich's wife Nina and my mother became very close friends. After his posting to Moscow, Uborevich was appointed Commander of the Belorussian military district and left for Smolensk, where the district headquarters were. His wife and his daughter Mirra continued to live in Moscow, joining Uborevich every summer at the dacha near Smolensk that came with his new job. Nearly every time business called him to Moscow, Uborevich came to see us at our dacha. Nina came very often, and so did Mirra, who was my childhood friend and whom I always liked very much. When I saw her in Moscow some time ago she recalled how in those days we would call for her in the car at their house in Vorovksy street, going to the country for the weekend. I remember Mirra's parents very vividly, especially Nina, who was lively and attractive. In my adolescent view she was a real beauty, and I was secretly in love with her. Mother and father remembered later that we, the children, had been very fond of Nina Uborevich and would obey her eagerly when she gave us a mock order to line up and present our hands and ears for inspection.

In May 1937 Uborevich was arrested on a train which he had boarded to answer Voroshilov's summons to Moscow. On 12 June, after a one-day 'trial', he was shot, together with Mikhail Tukhachevsky, Jonah Yakir and other eminent commanders. My father later told me that he had been deeply shocked and distressed by the so-called 'case of the military', when many brilliant Red Army commanders were executed on trumped-up charges of espionage or sabotage. He named several of them – Uborevich, Yakir, Gamarnik and Yefremov – as his friends. (Yefremov had for some reason escaped execution and later, following my father's direct appeal to Stalin, was released.) The talent and experience of those people would have been invaluable during the war of 1941–5.

Among our closest friends whom we often saw both in the country and in town were the Gamarniks. Their daughter Veta (Victoria) was a pal of my brothers and me. Our fathers were good friends too, and I often saw them taking a stroll around the grounds together and talking on their return to the dacha at the end of the week. Two days after Tukhachevsky's arrest, Gamarnik shot himself. The wives of Uborevich and Gamarnik (as of the other arrested commanders) were first exiled, then arrested, and finally executed three years later. The children were put in an orphanage and then also arrested at the age of eighteen. After a term in a labour camp they spent several years in exile, and in 1949 were put under arrest again. At present both Mirra Uborevich and Veta Gamarnik are living in Moscow.

Not long ago Veta told me about the circumstances of her father's death as described to her by a medical nurse whom she had seen upon her return from exile. The nurse was on duty in Gamarnik's apartment in Moscow in those days on account of his acute diabetic condition (Veta was in the country at the time). He was in bed. On 29 May 1937 my father came to see him, and they had a long talk behind closed doors. Next morning, while the nurse was making his bed, she saw a gun under his pillow, which had not been there before. As Veta told me, my father must have warned Gamarnik of the clouds gathering over his head. A few days before that Gamarnik had been visited by Marshal Blukher. Apparently Blukher had been commissioned by Stalin and Voroshilov to persuade Gamarnik to join the military tribunal which was to condemn Tukhachevsky and other commanders, and thus save his own life. (It has since been revealed that Blukher himself had joined that tribunal and signed the verdict, but it did not save him, for he was soon eliminated too, shot by Yezhov, chief of the secret police and the architect of the first purges, as rumour had it.) On Monday 31 May, Gamarnik's apartment was visited by the deputy General Staff Commander, Smorodinov, who demanded the keys to Gamarnik's safe at work on the pretext that they had to look at some of the papers there. He barely had time to leave the flat before a shot was fired in Gamarnik's bedroom. Veta Gamarnik also told me that when she and her mother were leaving to go into exile, my mother came to see them off at the station and gave them money. It is obvious that, given the situation, she would never have done this without her husband's knowledge and approval. I knew at the time, and it was confirmed later, that my parents never ceased to keep a fond and bitter memory of those two families, as well as of other perished friends, even though it was something they did not advertise.

Veta Gamarnik also told me the story of her return from exile in 1954. She came secretly and found temporary shelter with her old friends. The next day she phoned Alexander Barabanov, my father's chief of staff. So as not to inflict the KGB's displeasure on her friends, she told Barabanov that she had spent the night on a park bench. At the same time she gave him her friends' phone number, saying that she had been in touch with them and they had agreed to take a message for her. Next day there was a phone call to instruct her to report at the official entrance to the Kremlin where she would receive a pass to go inside and into the main government building. Her friends tried to dissuade her from going, thinking that it was a snare for an arrest, but Veta was confident of Anastas Ivanovich's kind attitude to her. She received her pass, entered the Kremlin and walked into Mikoyan's reception room. In her own words, she cut a pathetic figure in a cheap calico dress with an old pair of canvas shoes on her bare feet. The receptionist on duty stared at her in bewilderment. Soon Barabanov came out of the main office, went straight to Veta, hugged her and said that she would shortly go in. When he approached the desk, the secretary asked him in a low voice who it was. Barabanov answered loudly, 'Comrade Gamarnik's daughter'.

Hearing her father's name in combination with the word 'comrade' after all that had happened was too much for Veta. She nearly fainted there and then. When she entered my father's office he embraced and kissed her warmly and then asked her about her situation and everything else. Afterwards he phoned the chairman of the City Council and instructed him to find a suitable flat for her. Finally he gave her money to see her through settling in her new home and took her to his Kremlin flat where they had lunch together (my mother was in the country at the time). On Sunday that week my father brought Veta to the dacha, where she and my mother, both in tears, sat together for a long time remembering the past, fluctuating between sadness and joy.

CHAPTER 3

Aviation – My Dream

In the summer of 1936 my parents decided to spend their holiday in the Crimea together with all five of their children. Until then they had only taken any of us with them once – in 1924, when I had just turned two years old and my brother Volodya was a four-month-old baby. We were looking forward to the trip with excitement, but when the great day came – my mother flustered and busy packing, her children bouncing around in anticipation of a long journey on a night train – my father returned home from work to announce that the family trip to the Crimea was off, and he and mother were shortly going to America instead. We, the children, were bitterly disappointed and excited at the same time – a trip abroad was a rare thing in those days, and as for Politburo members, nobody ever heard of them going abroad at all. My father had certainly not been out of the country before (except for a holiday spent in Latvia in 1922), though my mother had once been to Vienna, taking treatment for her impaired hearing (which had deteriorated after her fifth baby). The treatment helped to a degree, but her hearing never returned to normal. As it turned out, the Politburo had moved that my father go to the US with a group of experts to study the American food industry and to purchase equipment and technologies for our food factories. Stalin suggested that he should take his wife with him, for it was considered good form in the West for a state visitor to be accompanied by his spouse on a trip.

All in all, thirty-four years of my father's career were devoted to the food industry. In 1930, various food processing factories which had been 'scattered' among a number of commissariats were put in the charge of the Commissariat of Supplies, which he headed at the time. When, subsequently, a separate Commissariat of Food Industry was formed, he was put in charge of that. And afterwards, when he became Deputy Chairman of the Council of People's Commissars, and later First Deputy Chairman of the Council of Ministers, the food industry always remained his particular area of responsibility. In the 1930s my father dedicated himself with great zeal to the task of modernising and improving the Soviet food industry. He initiated the construction, with the help of foreign specialists, of advanced fish and meat processing factories for producing tinned food, modern slaughterhouses, automatic bakeries and other food production enterprises.

Some of the newly built food factories were named after him, but in 1957, under Khrushchev, the Central Committee voted against giving the names of living people to industrial enterprises (the motive behind that decision was to get rid of the names of Molotov, Kaganovich and other members of the 'anti-party' group). His name was removed from the official designation of those factories and was not restored to any of them after his death. Nevertheless, one of the

42

largest meat processing factories in Moscow is still commonly referred to by Muscovites as the 'Mikoyan factory'.

Another large area of my father's responsibilities was trade, both foreign and domestic (he was Minister of Trade for some years before and after the war). It was on his initiative and under his direct supervision that the famous Yeliseev food store (so-called after its pre-revolutionary owner) was restored to its former glamour, and it was on his insistence that the Politburo agreed to return retail trade to the old shopping arcade on Red Square, thus establishing the famous GUM in the building which since the revolution had been occupied by various offices and warehouses. Towards the end of the 1950s my father initiated another new development, the first self-service supermarkets, as well as specialised stores dealing in photo and radio appliances, sports goods, hunting gear, etc. Another of his ideas was to open in Moscow and the main cities of other republics in the Soviet Union shops and restaurants representing various area-specific goods and national cuisine.

Sending food industry experts abroad had been something he himself had suggested some time before 1936. Now, at last, the decision was made. The twelve-strong delegation headed by Anastas Mikoyan paid a two-month visit to the US, going round a large number of factories and firms and purchasing various kinds of machinery, industrial refrigerators and production samples. They were interested in such areas as fresh fruit and vegetable delivery systems, production of sparkling wine, beer and soft drinks, automatic baking systems, army rations, supermarket design, packaging, refrigeration, deep freezing, production of tinned food, ice-cream, mayonnaise, cornflakes, biscuits, etc. They visited small and large retail shops, as well as a stock exchange, Ford's car plant in Detroit and even an aircraft plant in Los Angeles (I found all this information in my father's archives). It was as a direct result of that tour that the Soviet Union began the mass production of cheese, ice-cream, frankfurters, various fruit juices, condensed milk, margarine, sweetcorn and green peas in tins, cornflakes and so on.

Our ambassador to the US at the time was Alexander Troyanovsky, the first Soviet ambassador since the establishment of diplomatic relations between the two countries. He did his best to help the delegation members in their work. My parents liked Troyanovsky and his wife very much, and they remained on good terms with them for years afterwards. Their son, Oleg Troyanovsky, and I are good friends to this day.

I remember my parents' departure for the States quite vividly, for I was allowed to accompany them on the train, which took them as far as the western frontier in Belorussia. Our party occupied a special saloon-car and consisted of my parents, my father's PA Barabanov, his security chief, Nina Vladimirovna Uborevich and me. Nearly half of the carriage was taken up by a large saloon where we spent the daytime hours and took our meals (the kitchen was at the tail of the same carriage). The experts were in the carriage next to ours. Some of them visited our saloon during the day. The last station before the frontier was called Negoreloye, and there Nina and I said goodbye to the others and went back in the same railway car.

In those days people mostly travelled to America by boat, so my father's party first went by train to Paris, where they stopped for two days, then on to Le Havre to board the *Normandy*, a new packet boat and one of the three largest and best known ocean liners of the time (the other two were the *Queen Mary* and the *Queen Elizabeth*). Their voyage to New York took a little over four days, much less time than an ordinary passenger boat would take. My mother told me afterwards about the comfort and luxury of the liner. I remember I was particularly impressed by the fact that there was a swimming-pool and a tennis court, and by her description of their de luxe cabin – a suite of two rooms with a private bathroom.

On the way back from Negoreloye, Nina and I stopped in Smolensk, where her husband was stationed as the Commander of the Belorussian military district. She invited me to stay at their dacha for a few days. Her husband joined us in the evening, after work. He, as before, impressed me with his 'dapper' looks – a slender, well-groomed man in a white jacket, with intelligent eyes behind a pair of pince-nez.

At the end of that same year I joined a riding school which was based in the centre of Moscow, just off Vorovsky Street. Since then (with the exception of the war years) I went in for riding. As a young man I took part, with some success, in jumping competitions (*concours hippiques*) and in later years, until fairly recently (until I turned sixty-nine), I took every opportunity to go for a ride in the woods and have never stopped loving horses. My brother Volodya soon joined that school too. We both went in for the same sports: cross-country skiing, skating, ice hockey, volleyball and shooting (Volodya also did gymnastics). When at the dacha, Volodya and I played tennis, although we never had any formal coaching. One of our favourite winter 'sports' was skiing on tow behind a car along a snow-covered country road. In the summer we spent a lot of time on the river swimming and rowing (all government dachas in the neighbourhood shared a bathing house and a moorage with a small 'fleet' of motor launches and rowing boats).

My father was fond of riding too. He used to ride as a young man before the revolution, and then when on holiday in the Caucasus. After the war and until the late 1950s we had three riding horses brought to the dacha for the summer months from the Defence Ministry riding-school stables (the same privilege was enjoyed by Voroshilov, Budenny and Kaganovich). The horses were looked after by a soldier who came with them, and every Sunday there arrived an officer who accompanied my father on his rides into the woods. I often joined them on the third horse, while my father's security officers followed our small cavalcade in a jeep. The officer often came on weekdays too, to exercise the horses. I sometimes went riding with him and the soldier, but more often I ventured out on my own.

At the riding school we mostly went in for the *concours hippique*, and once even took part in a hippodrome race. In that race I unwittingly let a few of my fellow horsemen down. Those of them who knew the horses in that race well placed a double bet on my brother's thoroughbred Galas, and on Sabur ridden by our friend, Kostya Gridnev. My Bird was not considered a serious rival at all. For half of the distance I was holding my filly back (she was very excited), but then

I let her go, still in a steady fourth place, as everyone had expected. And then, at the last bend they all ended up on the outside while I managed to keep to the inner side of the track. My horse was exhausted, and I had to use my whip to keep her going, but I overtook Kostya and another jockey. They nearly overtook me again on the run-in, but I still managed to come second, after my brother, who won. My trainer, Elizar Levin, was very pleased with me, but a groom in the stable gave me a gloomy look and said, 'D'you know what you've done?' It was only then that I realised that he and the others had put their money on a different result.

One of the jockeys in that race was Rimma Leuta, an attractive petite brunette. Her father was a well-known soccer player who was later arrested together with two other famous soccer players, the brothers Starostin. Some time ago she told me about her attempt to have her father released at the beginning of the war. After several evenings of 'patrolling' the street where Lavrenti Beria, the last chief of the secret police under Stalin, lived, she managed to waylay him on his way home, despite the bodyguard's attempt to prevent her. She told him about her father, insisting that he was an honest man who must have been arrested by mistake, and asked Beria for an intercession. He answered hypocritically that it was not his 'domain' and told her to address Mikhail Kalinin, who was the Chairman of the Supreme Soviet at the time. Rimma managed to get an audience with Kalinin, but he said something evasive and unconvincing to the effect that as soon as the war was over the 'misunderstanding' would be cleared up and her father released. Rimma could not have known that Kalinin's own wife was in a labour camp at the time.

Horse-back riding, particularly jumping and cross-country riding, develops many sporting qualities, to say nothing of sheer physical fitness (contrary to what many people think, riding is very demanding physically). It builds up courage, reaction, a sense of time and distance and the ability to control both yourself and the horse, to understand its temper and its habits. All these qualities (except controlling the horse, of course) are essential for a pilot. I am sure that my regular riding sessions, as well as my early passion for driving, to some extent contributed to my success in learning to fly. An aircraft, even though it is not a living being, also has to be controlled and it has its own 'temper', and quick reactions are even more essential for a pilot than for a horseman. It might not have been accidental that in the early years of aviation would-be military pilots were mostly recruited from cavalry troops.

Since my early childhood I had been interested in various technical gadgets and weaponry, though it was not weapons as such that I admired but the intricacies of their technical design. I took delight in handling my father's Mauser, admiring its beautiful grip with silver-gilt decoration and its wooden holster which could be converted as a butt – a battle award for his work in the civil war (I believe it is now in the collection of the Russian Army Museum). Many times at the dacha we had shooting sessions supervised by my father's security officers, when we shot at targets with pistols and rifles, learning, among other things, to handle weapons with care. When in town I sometimes visited the shooting gallery of the Red Commanders' School in the Kremlin, where I was allowed to shoot with a real carbine. I am interested in weaponry to this day, although I am by no means a bellicose man.

But what fascinated me most of all were cars and aircraft. In the Kremlin, opposite the building where we lived and almost next to the armoury, there was a large garage for government cars (Stalin's cars and those of his security men were kept in a small separate garage in the arsenal courtyard). In charge of both garages was Pavel Osipovich Udalov, one of Stalin's former drivers. My brothers and I spent a lot of time in the garage, where we found everything, especially the work of the car mechanics, extremely interesting. The Kremlin fleet of the time consisted only of foreign cars, and I became so familiar with them that I needed but one glance at a passing foreign car in the street to name the firm, the model and even the year when it was made. Up to the mid-1930s the garage had been stocked with Rolls-Royces and Lincolns, and later there appeared Packards, Cadillacs and Buicks. There were a few Fords too, but they were used only by security officers. The year 1937 saw the appearance of special vehicles for Politburo members, 1936 Packards with bullet-proof windows and bodies. The glass in those cars must have been no less than eight or nine centimetres thick. At the end of the 1940s, these cars were replaced by armoured ZIS-110 limos based on a later model of the Packard.

I learnt to drive at the age of twelve. Later, when I was in the eighth form and was already a decent driver, I joined a teenage motor club so as to study the design of the car and get a driving licence. I successfully passed the exams at the end of the course, including the driving test taken in a lorry, but as I was only sixteen I did not receive a licence until a year later. I announced the news proudly to my father, who said, 'You should have given more time to your German instead!'

In September 1937, when the new school year had already begun (I was in the eighth form then), I heard about a new type of secondary school to be opened: military cadet schools for boys from the eighth form to the tenth. I must say that the attitude of young people to the army and military service in those days was totally different from what we see now. We were growing up in the belief that the Soviet Union was surrounded by hostile countries whose principal goal was to destroy our political system, and we could not imagine life without that system, for we sincerely believed it to be better than any other. We knew that sooner or later we would have to fight a war, particularly since the Nazis had seized power in Germany. Most boys really wanted to go into the army, and there was a certain romantic aura associated with the idea of a military career. Even some girls were attracted to such sports as shooting, aeroplane flying and parachute jumping. It was not surprising, therefore, that many boys joined those military cadet schools, including quite a few of my own schoolmates and friends – Artem Sergeev, Vasily Stalin, Igor Boytsov and others. Five such schools were formed, and my friends and I chose special school No. 2.

At first there was no particular emphasis on any military profession, but later it was announced that all these schools would specialise in artillery. My best friend Timur and I were disappointed, yet we decided to stay. Soon we all received a specially designed uniform which we were proud to show off during the May Day parade on Red Square, the first time schoolchildren were included in the military parade programme. All the cadets in our school continued to live at home; there was nothing like army barracks or anything of that kind. In addition to the subjects on the secondary school curriculum we had special military training, for example ordnance and parade drill. In the summer we were sent to a military camp where we lived in tents and obeyed the army service regulations, went on marches and studied various types of guns and methods of aimed artillery fire.

Among my fellow cadets was a boy called Oleg Frinovsky, a tall, handsome smart-looking fellow whom I liked. I had visited him at home several times and at his parents' dacha, and then, in 1938, both his father and mother were arrested. We remained friends as before, and I could see how painful it was for him. Once we were all at a party at the house of Naum Friedman, a classmate of both Oleg Frinovsky and Vasily Stalin. There were a number of boys from our schools and their girlfriends. Suddenly somebody rang the doorbell and asked to see Vasily. He went out of the room, talked to the people at the front door, then returned and told Oleg that they were asking for him. Oleg left the room, and Vasily whispered into my ear that they had come to arrest him. We looked out of the window and saw him put into a black car and driven away. Later we were told that he was a member of a 'teenager anti-Soviet group'. I never saw him again and never heard anything about him except that he did not live to be released. It was only recently that I learnt that his father had been one of Yezhov's deputies, and Yezhov by the time of Oleg's arrest had already been executed.

Another close friend whose father was arrested was Igor Boytsov. Timur and I remained on friendly terms with him until he was drafted. Once I was at Timur's place (he lived in Voroshilov's flat in the Kremlin) when Igor phoned. On hearing who had been on the phone, Voroshilov's wife, Ekaterina Davidovna, a dedicated party member, became alarmed and asked Timur to break off his friendship with Igor. Timur was indignant at her request. The last I heard from Igor was a letter from the front in August 1941.

I was in the ninth form when I started going out with a girl. Her name was Kalya Kaziuk. We went to the cinema together and to dances, and several times I took her to parties at my friends' houses. Once I saw a paper on my father's desk with Kalya's name on it. It was a kind of 'character reference' from the NKVD – the secret police. I was stunned. I could not resist reading it of course, and I was enraged by their treacherous trick of sneaking in a slanderous lie disguised as truth. What they said in that paper was that she was 'an acquaintance of Oleg Frinovsky' (who had already been arrested by that time), the implication being that she came from the circle of an 'enemy of the people'. She had been, indeed, acquainted with Oleg, but it was I who had introduced them to each other! I was waiting for my father to say something to me about Kalya so as to refute the insinuation, but he never did.

For as long as I can remember I have been fascinated by aviation. I read all I could find about pilots, aircraft and the history of aviation, about the polar expeditions of Roald Amundsen and Umberto Nobile, about our then very famous polar pilot Chukhnovsky, and so on. One of the 'idol figures' of the time was the American pilot Charles Lindbergh, who had been the first to fly (in 1927) from the US over to Europe on a single-engine aircraft. Lindbergh had even visited the USSR, and later, while in Germany, he gave an unfavourable account of Soviet aviation in his talks with Hitler and his publications in the German press. Whether it was true or not, he became a *persona non grata* in Russia, and his name was no longer mentioned. Another well-known pilot was Willie Post, who performed the first round-the-world flight. With great interest I read a book by the American test pilot Jimmy Collins, and *Your Wings* by Assen Jordanov, which in effect was a popular manual of flying, with amusing drawings and aphoristic 'rules' (e.g. 'Changing decisions during a forced landing is tantamount to a crash'; 'If you run out of fuel in the air, there is no one to blame but yourself').

The story of the steamboat *Cheluskin*, iced up in the Arctic Ocean in 1934, and the spectacular rescue operations that followed stirred the entire country, and I, like all Russian boys at the time, knew the name of every single pilot involved in those operations. It was those pilots who became the first ever Heroes of the Soviet Union for what they did. I read all that was then written about the record flights by Shestakov, Gromov, Chkalov, Kokkinaki, Polina Osipenko and others. My imagination was excited by the extraordinary boldness of the flight over the North Pole to the US performed by Chkalov, Baidukov and Beliakov on a single-engine ANT-25 in 1937, and immediately afterwards by Gromov, Yumashev and Danilin. One day, on the way home from school, I saw (what an incredible piece of luck for a boy addicted to aviation!) Chkalov and Baidukov in person getting out of Chkalov's Packard. Everyone knew that he had received that car as a gift in the US after his famous flight, and it had 'V. P. Chkalov' engraved in small metallic letters on one of the doors.

It was the time of the civil war in Spain, and later of the fighting against the Japanese at Halkin-Gol. The front page of the *Pravda* often published photographs of those who distinguished themselves at the front and were awarded the titles of Heroes of the Soviet Union 'for performing a special government mission'. Pilots featured in that context more than anyone else. I made clippings of their photographs and kept them. The participation of our volunteers in the Spanish war was then a secret from the people at large, but my friend Timur Frunze and I knew what they were awarded for. We also heard about Mikhail Yakushin, a Soviet pilot fighting in Spain who was the first to shoot down an aircraft at night-time. He was rewarded by the Spanish Prime Minister with a Chrysler, together with the commander of the Soviet fighter pilots in Spain, Anatoly Serov. Later, during World War Two, I met Mikhail Yakushin and we became good friends.

All those events, both peaceful and wartime, contributed to the young people's interest in aviation. One of the most popular spectacles of the time, and one of my most exciting childhood memories, was the annual airshow that took place every eighteenth of August at the Tushino airfield in the north of Moscow. The date was chosen because we then had a 'six-day week', and every sixth day was a day off (like a Sunday), so in each month the days off always fell on the same dates: the 6th, the 12th, the 18th, the 24th and the 30th. Many older pilots still regard 18 August as their professional holiday, the Aviation Day, although nowadays it is officially celebrated (with airshows and all) on the third Sunday in August.

The Commissar of Defence, Kliment Voroshilov, took a close personal interest in many famous pilots, and his particular favourite was Stepan Suprun. His family, along with many other Ukrainian families, had emigrated to Canada before the events of 1917. In the late 1920s the Supruns returned with their four children to Russia. When the eldest, Stepan, already a qualified pilot by that time, decided to become a test pilot, he immediately encountered problems. His former life abroad was considered an obstacle. He turned to Voroshilov for help and was allowed to be a test pilot as a result. He had a very successful career and very soon became well known. Two of his younger brothers also went into aviation: Feodor, first as a pilot and then as a testing engineer, and Alexander, as a fighter pilot in the war and a test pilot afterwards. He and I served together for several years in the same fighter testing unit where his brother Stepan had served before the war.

Once, at Voroshilov's dacha, I met Pavel Rychagov, a pilot and a legendary hero of the Spanish war, who by that time had been appointed Deputy Commander of the Soviet Air Force. I could not take my eyes off him. Back in 1936 he had been a senior lieutenant, and just a year later he commanded the Soviet Air Force contingent engaged in China. Such impressive career 'leaps' were made by quite a number of the Spanish war participants in our armed forces. One of the reasons, apart from the occasional arbitrary decisions of those in charge who confused personal courage with the gift to command, was the acute shortage of high-ranking officers and commanders as a result of the purges of 1937–8.

Just a few days before the German invasion of June 1941, Pavel Rychagov was arrested, together with another volunteer of the Spanish war, twice Hero of the Soviet Union Yakov Smushkevich. On 28 October 1941 both were put in front of a firing squad, along with Generals Stern, Loktionov and other eminent high-ranking commanders. Their fate was shared by Pavel Rychagov's wife, Maria Nesterenko, a well-known pilot and a deputy commander of an air force regiment. It was only recently that I discovered the date of their execution, and I was really shocked. A great war was on, our army was suffering severe losses and defeat, and in the meantime experienced battle commanders, instead of being relied upon for saving the situation, were hurriedly put to death! I heard that they had first been packed off into the rear, and then Beria's telegram followed with the order of immediate execution. It is painful to imagine the feelings of people who, at a time of acute danger to their country, were awaiting death at the hands of their own compatriots.

My choice of vocation was certainly also affected by my uncle, my father's younger brother Artem Ivanovich Mikoyan. In those years he was a student of the engineering faculty of the Zhukovsky Air Force Academy.* Artem, like my

* So named after Nikolai Zhukovsky (1847–1921), the founder of modern aerodynamics.

other uncle Haik Tumanian, had no children of his own yet, and was extremely fond of and attentive to his nephews. Once he took me with him to the Tushino airfield to see a test flight of the small aeroplane that he had designed and built together with his two fellow students. It was equipped with a low-powered foreign engine. The aeroplane took off and flew westwards, turned back towards Moscow and then, suddenly, we saw its propeller stop. The engine had jammed. The pilot turned to the left, glided down to the edge of the airfield and landed safely. As far as I remember the aeroplane never flew again; they failed to find another suitable engine. While at the Academy, my uncle took flying lessons and did parachute jumping (both were 'extras', of course). He told me that Valery Chkalov had several times gone up with him as his instructor. At Artem's home I saw his drawings for an aircraft design – his graduation project.

All this decided my choice. I could not imagine myself taking up any other career but aviation. My priority was to become a pilot, but I was interested in engineering too. For my birthday after finishing secondary school I received a case of drawing instruments from Artem, with an engraving: 'A pilot, an engineer, a designer'. His 'prediction' came almost entirely true; I became both a pilot and an engineer, and, although I am not a designer, I am now working at a designer firm. Timur did not share my interest in engineering and teased me, 'What kind of fun is wearing out your trouser seat sitting at a desk?' He wanted to be a pilot – nothing else.

We both liked it at the artillery school, but our passion for aviation did not flag. While we were in the ninth form we thought of joining an aviation club and even passed a compulsory medical examination, but then Vasily Stalin, who had come on leave from his flying school (which he had joined in the autumn of 1938), told us there was no point going to an aviation club, for at the air force school they preferred to teach flying 'from scratch' rather than retrain 'amateur pilots' from civilian aviation clubs.

At the summer military camp after the eighth form I became very close with two of my classmates, Alexander Babeshko and Andrei Kertes, who have remained my best friends to this day. Having done yet another year at the artillery school, the three of us transferred to an ordinary school, planning to join an air force flying school after the final year. Timur did not follow suit so as not to upset Voroshilov by leaving the military cadet school. Andrei's father, Franz Kertes, was a Hungarian who ended up in Russia after he had been captured during World War One. During the civil war in Russia he joined the Bolshevik party and fought against the White Army as a partisan in Siberia. Later he became a railway engineer. Upon Hitler's invasion of the USSR Franz Kertes, along with many other immigrants, was transported to a labour camp beyond the Urals. After the war he was allowed to return to Moscow and continued his career as an engineer. At the time of Khrushchev's 'thaw', his Hungarian origin was remembered again, but this time in a different light: he was invited to work for the newly formed Soviet–Hungarian Friendship Society, which gave him an opportunity to meet Hungarian visitors and to make several trips to his home country.

Nearly all graduates of cadet schools continued their training at artillery colleges and then, as young artillery officers, found themselves at the front at the beginning of the war – a time which was hardest on our army. Many of them did not return. My friend Alexander Babeshko, although he left the cadet school when I did, still became an artillery officer and fought the war in a 'Katiusha' rocket battalion. After the war Alexander graduated from the Artillery Academy and continued to serve in the army as a senior officer until he finally retired at the rank of Lieutenant-General. Andrei Kertes served as a aircraft mechanic during the war, and afterwards graduated from the Institute of Roads and Transport. Since his graduation and to this day Andrei has worked at the Moscow Experimental Machinery Plant producing various special-function vehicles and machines for the maintenance of urban roads.

Shortly after the three of us had left the cadet school, it moved to new premises in Kropotkinskaya Street. There has been a school in that building ever since, an ordinary secondary school after the cadet school had ceased to exist. There is a small but carefully preserved museum of the artillery school in the building, and a stele in the school yard commemorates those of its pupils who did not return from the war.

My friendship with Timur Frunze continued as ever, despite our being at different schools. We still went riding together, both at a riding school in town and at Voroshilov's dacha where Timur lived during the summer. I was a frequent guest at that dacha throughout the year. I remember a small but pleasant party held at the dacha to celebrate the arrival of 1940: Piotr Voroshilov and Nayda, his wife, Timur and his sister Tanya, Voroshilov's nephew Nikolai, Nadya's sister Vera and I. None of us was a heavy drinker, but we had all had some wine before Voroshilov came home after midnight. He had been celebrating too and was in a party mood. Pleased to find young company at home, he generously treated us to his champagne. It was all very well until a few hours later when, in the small hours of the morning, I became severely sick and my hangover lasted all next day. I spent it in bed in their house, and when Voroshilov returned home after work he came to see how I was and blamed himself profusely for having caused all that trouble. Since then I have disliked champagne.

Despite all the disparaging things written about Voroshilov since the beginning of *glasnost*, I must say that in his lifetime he was certainly very popular and well liked by those who knew him personally. At least that was the impression I could not help having. My father also seemed quite fond of him. Whether he deserved it or not, Voroshilov was one of the most celebrated figures in the country and a great favourite with the people. However, at that time we knew nothing about his rather sinister role in the tragic fate of Marshal Tukhachevsky and other high-ranking Red Army commanders. At the same time it is a fact (known, among other sources, from Khrushchev's memoirs) that when Stalin, at a Kremlin meeting, chastised Voroshilov for the Red Army's defeats in the Finnish war, Voroshilov answered back, pointing out quite bluntly that it had been the result of the purges within the Red Army command, thus effectively suggesting Stalin's own responsibility. In private life Voroshilov was a pleasant, amiable and fun-loving man who was fond of music and painting and interested in literature. At the same time, even then it was obvious to us, the young ones, that politically and ideologically he was rather narrow-minded and inflexible, and he saw things in a light totally different from ours. We put it down to his elevated position which prevented him from knowing 'real' life as we knew it.

My teenage years fell in the late 1930s and the atmosphere of that time is very difficult to describe to those who were not living in the Soviet Union. On the one hand, it was the time of mass purges the full scale of which no one could imagine, not even those in the governing élite, to say nothing of young people like us. Many people were aware that something sinister was going on, and it could not but affect the general atmosphere. At the same time it must be admitted that most ordinary people genuinely believed in the existence of anti-Soviet conspiracies and of the spies and saboteurs who were behind them, and Stalin's authority was, of course, absolute and unquestioned. I do remember how Timur and I would sometimes doubt the validity of the charges against some particular people, yet I do not think we ever seriously questioned the general party line. Once, while the Finnish war was on, Timur and I were going somewhere together by tram and a common-looking drunken man got on it at one stop, muttered something under his nose and then suddenly raised his voice and said: 'Now it's Finland they're after!' Those who heard it hissed at him, but Timur looked at him with apparent compassion and said to me bitterly, 'There are still so many people at odds with our way of life!'

In 1939–40 the economic situation improved noticeably, especially in comparison with that of a few years before, and the first major wave of purges had subsided by that time, so life could really be said to have become 'better and merrier', as Stalin declared at the time. A combination, let alone a 'happy union', of two such contradictory factors is difficult to imagine or to take in, yet that is how it was and we all believed that the hardships suffered by ordinary people and all the difficulties the country had would soon be behind us. All the people and the country at large had to do was to build up real industrial power and advanced agriculture, and life would quickly and irrevocably improve. Had we only known then that no radical changes in the standard of living were in store, that our agriculture would be driven to shameful and disastrous decline and that our industry would mainly work for the defence and its own corporate interests!

In the construction boom that seized Moscow at that time there were two particularly memorable highlights: the newly built underground and the impressive premises of the All-Union Agricultural Exhibition Centre. The first underground station, Palace of Soviets (now Kropotkinskaya), and a length of the tunnel were being constructed right on our way to the school, and Timur and I watched their progress with great interest. We promised ourselves to take a ride on the opening day, and indeed we did. On 15 May 1935 we took our first ever underground journey along the entire stretch of the line. The agricultural exhibition opened in 1939. The architecture of the original pavilions was in much better style than the buildings which replaced them later (and which are still there), far less pompous and not as ornate. Soviet architecture of the 1920s and early 1930s favoured the austere constructivist style and its best examples were in the vanguard of world architecture of the time. My friends and I liked walking around the exhibition grounds. I remember the elation we all experienced during our first underground trips and our first visits to the exhibition; it was a glimpse of the happy future, as we believed our socialist future to be, and we were certain it was soon to come.

Another great breakthrough of the time was the advent of television. In 1939 or 1940 a television set was brought to our dacha. It had been assembled from American parts at a Soviet factory. It was a large upright wooden 'box' with the tube facing upwards and the picture reflected in a mirror which was attached to the lid. The latter, when opened, stood at an angle of forty-five degrees. The picture was pale and fuzzy but we still regarded it as a miracle. Some time before the television sets, at the dachas and in Moscow apartments of all highest officials there appeared large American RCA radio gramophones. They were also set inside large upright wooden cases, and had excellent all-wave receivers and gramophones that could be 'charged' with as many as eight records, automatically played one after another. It was also seen as a technological miracle because what we had before was a gramophone that had to be wound up by hand for every record.

Maybe the optimistic spirit I shared with my friends at that time was just a natural accompaniment of youth, of growing up, and a 'foretaste' of the joys of living? But it could not have been just that, for the same kind of elated optimism is remembered by people who were already quite mature at the time. This brings to mind a line by the poet David Samoilov: 'How it all was! How it all coincided – war, anguish, dreams, and youth!'

CHAPTER 4

The Flying School

The year 1940 was my final year at secondary school. My friend Timur Frunze was still a cadet at the artillery school, but we were both as keen as ever to become pilots. We sent our applications to the Air Force Training Command, and were soon summoned for an interview. We asked to be posted to the Kacha AF Flying School in the Crimea, the oldest Russian institution of its kind. It was there at Kacha on 9 September 1913 that the celebrated Russian pilot Nesterov, then an instructor at the school, performed the aerobatic figure which has since been known in Russia as the 'Nesterov loop'.

We arrived in Sevastopol by train on Aviation Day – 18 August. The Kacha school bus that was meeting the would-be cadets at the railway station brought us to our destination. The road from Sevastopol to Kacha ran along the Black Sea coast. It was the first time I saw the sea (not counting the time when I was two years old). The Kacha Flying School premises were also on the coast, by the mouth of a small river of the same name. The bus stopped outside the headquarters building and we reported to the officer on duty, handing in our letter orders to him. After a while he took us to meet the School Commander, AF General Major Alexander Turzhansky. With his military bearing and slender figure he reminded me of Uborevich; the resemblance seemed even stronger when I later saw General Turzhansky in a white uniform jacket and with an officer's dirk at his belt. His brother, as we knew, was the well-known test pilot and hero of the Spanish war, Boris Turzhansky. Shortly after the breakout of the war 'our' Turzhansky, the School Commander, was arrested, and I did not see him again until the 1960s.

Timur and I were posted to the 2nd Squadron. There were seven squadrons altogether, each consisting of two detachments, and each detachment of four flights. Each flight was subdivided into several groups of pilot trainees. Our instructor pilot was our flight commander, First Lieutenant Konstantin Korshunov. Soon a number of new arrivals joined our group – Volodya (short for Vladimir) Yaroslavsky, Volodya Saburov, Ruirik Pavlov and Yuri Tyomkin. Later appeared Oleg Barantsevich, my fellow cadet at the artillery school, and Alexander Shavrov. Thus our 'special' group was formed. It was considered special because it consisted of the sons of eminent people, but its distinction ended there. In all the rest – the daily routine, the living conditions, the rations, the fatigue detail, etc. – our group was exactly the same as any other. The only special favour we ever got was the permission to go on a short leave to Moscow over the New Year. None of us ever claimed any special treatment or attitude: in fact, *not* wishing to be singled out in any such way was a natural outcome of the upbringing each of us had received, and of the principles we all shared. Besides, had any of us ever showed any lack of modesty it would have caused great anger on the part of his parents. At least with my parents it certainly would – of this I was (and still am) quite sure. Even if other students had been initially somewhat wary of us, their wariness soon disappeared, and we became aware of having been 'accepted'. Most of us soon made friends among students from other groups.

The 2nd Squadron occupied a two-storey red-brick barracks where each flight had a large room to itself. In the room allotted to our flight there were about fifty iron beds, each with a small bedside table at its head and a stool at its foot. Sitting on the bed during the day was against the rules, so the stool was the only seat each of us could use in our spare time. On going to bed at night we were supposed to put our neatly folded uniforms on the stools, with the folds strictly flush with the edge of the stool. The master sergeant on duty during his rounds of the barracks at night would never deal with even the slightest untidiness he might notice himself; he would always wake the student and make him refold his things. I wouldn't say we liked that; we got so tired by the end of each day that we dropped off the instant we reached our beds. That master sergeant, a tall, good-looking Azerbaijani called Kasumov, has remained in my memory thanks to the thunderous voice with which he announced the hateful reveille each morning.

Our instructor pilot, Korshunov, was a pleasant young man of twenty-seven or thereabouts. To students of a flying school their instructor pilot is a very special figure. His authority is indisputable, and his word is law, not only in matters of flying but in nearly all others as well. Apart from helping his students to learn to fly – and that is why people join a flying school in the first place – a good instructor pilot also carries out pastoral duties and becomes a true friend and 'guardian' of the students. Korshunov was like that: he was a frequent guest in the barracks and he spent much time with the trainees in addition to the time needed for flight preparation and analysis. His influence on us was very power-ful, and we liked him, respected him and obeyed him without a word. I am sure that I owe a lot to my first instructor pilot and I remember him gratefully to this day.

We were told about an accident that had taken place at the school before our arrival. A flying instructor and a trainee on the UTI-4 fighter-trainer had lined up onto the runway for take-off when the runway detail student spotted a tractor that had appeared on the airfield. He raised the red flag to signal danger, and then pointed it at the tractor to explain the reason for the delay to the pilots in the fighter. The pointing gesture was identical to the clearance signal of the white flag, for which the much-faded red flag was easily mistaken against the sun. Failing to notice the tractor for the limited forward view, the UTI-4 began the take-off. Seconds later, already off the ground but still just above it, its wheels hit the tractor and the aircraft broke up into pieces after a few somersaults in the air. The pilots were injured but survived; the tractor driver was killed. As a result of the accident the instructor, Vladimir Lutsky, would have been discharged from the school but for the School Commander, V. Ivanov, who declared he could not afford to lose such excellent flying instructors. Both pilots later became my 'comrades in arms' during the war. Vladimir Lutsky and I were in the same squadron in the 32nd Regiment of the Guards, and the student, Konstantin

Kruikov, was my squadron commander and friend in the 12th Regiment of the Guards. Both were first-class pilots and both became Heroes of the Soviet Union during the war. Lutsky retired from the air force as a lieutenant-general, and Kruikov as a colonel.

Being a flight instructor is a very useful experience for a pilot. Instructor pilots as a rule control the aircraft with greater precision than combat pilots and pay closer attention to the instruments while monitoring the flight. This develops their ability to analyse the flight. Once in action, former instructors usually made very good combat pilots. Characteristically, instructor pilots have very often been the most successful candidates among the would-be experimental test pilots, primarily due to their skilful instrument flying and their ability to analyse aircraft handling qualities and flight.

Almost immediately on arrival we began studying the theory of flight and the training programme manual (TPM), where all flight regulations and air safety rules were explained in detail. There was a saying to the effect that the TPM had been 'written in blood', with the implication that many of the rules in it (as well as in the aircraft manuals) had been born of the fatal experiences of many an aircrew. Another much repeated adage was that 'an intelligent person learned from his mistakes, a more intelligent one from the mistakes of others'. Two unwritten rules of the fighter pilots I often used to hear later and repeated to younger colleagues myself were that the pilot must act 'fast yet without haste', and that the aircraft should be controlled 'briskly but smoothly'.

Soon we began flying Polikarpov's U-2, the 'classical' basic trainer of the time. My first ever flight was on 5 September 1940. What I remember most vividly are the tiny cows in a meadow below and the breakers on the sea that looked like the ripples on a small river. It felt a bit frightening flying over the sea. It's difficult to explain, but even much later I felt that the sea under the aircraft seemed to hold greater danger than the earth, maybe because when flying over the sea, without any reference points to set the scale, the real altitude was harder to establish.

The instructor suggested I take over the controls. I got hold of the control stick and the aircraft immediately started rocking and banking away. 'Let go of the stick. Look, I am not holding it. She's flying nice and straight – let her be!' That was the first lesson I learnt in the air, to make no superfluous movements at the controls. Rules of this kind I have since called 'philosophical' as they are applicable to life in general. Thus, it is a good rule for anyone in charge of other people; the more initiative and freedom of movement is left to subordinates the better. The same is true in bringing up children.

The routine of the initial training programme began, what was known as 'area' and 'circuit' flights respectively. The area flights were flights to the aerobatic practice area, allocated for free manoeuvres and for practising various turns, gliding, climbing and so on; the chief aim of circuit flights was practising take-offs and landings. The required flight parameters were to be very strictly observed; the set airspeed, especially when climbing or gliding before landing, had to be maintained with precision. The given flight attitude was maintained by the position of the nose as regards the horizon. We were required to draw diagrams in our workbooks showing different projections of the nose onto the horizon in various flying attitudes.

Although the flight route from take-off to landing within the airfield area was known as a 'closed circuit', it formed a rectangular figure with four turns (which still remains the standard training route pattern for all types of aircraft). The turns were numbered from one to four, and their position in relation to the runway always remained the same. The turn performed right after take-off or after flying over the runway was always number one, and the final turn taken to align with the runway centreline was always number four, even if it was the first turn you performed coming in for landing. For the students' training flights the runway was divided into two parallel 'strips', for take-off and landing respectively.

Each flying group had an aircraft attached to it. The students waiting for their turn to fly were in the 'square' – the area marked off by the flags between the two 'strips' of the divided runway. The flight supervisor with his binoculars (there was no radio communication then) and a student appointed to watch over the aircraft took their posts nearby. A cadet next in turn for a flight would meet the returning aircraft as it was taxiing off the landing runway, and run along with it, holding on to the wing. The pilot's forward view while taxiing a plane with a tailwheel (which sat low on the ground with the nose up) was in those days limited by the engine cowling at the head of the aircraft, so it was the accompanying student's duty to warn the crew of an obstacle on the way by tapping lightly on the aileron. Running (sometimes quite fast) side by side with a taxiing aircraft in clouds of dust and under the blazing southern sun did not rate high among our favourite pastimes, but, as the Russian saying goes, 'If you like sleighing down-hill, you should like pulling your sleigh uphill'. As the aircraft stopped by the 'square', the trainee climbed out onto the wing and listened to what the instructor had to say about his performance. Then the next cadet took the front seat. After that it was his predecessor's turn to see the taxiing plane to the take-off position. Having done that, the cadet would write down the instructor's criticisms and advice and the marks he scored into his workbook. I have kept all my school workbooks as mementoes of my first steps along the road that determined my entire life.

The first flight on a new type of aircraft is always an event in the career of every pilot; to a student who is about to do his first ever solo flight it is an event of great excitement and emotional strain. Before he is allowed to go for his first solo, his performance is checked by the squadron commander, who then allows the solo. Back in 1940 our group received a special 'distinction': apart from the detachment and the squadron commanders we were 'checked out' by the school's second-in-command and General Turzhansky himself (they were just being over-cautious about us). As a result we had flown more hours before our first solos than other students, up to fifteen hours each.

And then, at last, on 24 October, the rear seat of our U-2 received a new 'passenger' – a sackful of sand, fondly referred to by generations of cadets as 'Ivan Ivanovich' and used to compensate for the absent instructor's weight. I was the first in the group to do two solo circuit flights, and Timur was next. It is impossible to put what I felt into words, just as it is impossible to forget that feeling. I remember a lot of exciting moments associated with my many subsequent flights, but that first flight on my own has always remained a unique memory.

In our daily classroom sessions we studied flight theory, airframe structure and engine design, as well as navigation, meteorology, and so on. Each day was very full. For our early morning flights (which began at dawn) we were woken up at three or four a.m. After breakfast we would all march to the main airfield where we helped the technician to prepare the aircraft. Afterwards one of us (the lucky one!) would get into the pilot's seat, with the instructor at the back, and fly the machine over to the airfield of our squadron, from where they would begin the first training flights of the day, while the rest of us were taken there in army lorries. Towards midday the school van would arrive at the airfield with what was known as 'Voroshilov breakfast' – coffee with milk and a bun for each of us (that was an addition to the pilots' rations introduced on Voroshilov's command). Those who were flying at the time when the van appeared would always hurry with the landing on spotting it. A couple of hours later we would be driven back to the main airfield and taken to lunch. After lunch it was back to the airfield to wash and clean the aircraft. Then, after an hour's rest in the barracks, we had to go to the teaching block for classroom work, which lasted until dinner time. After dinner there was about an hour of private time, and then off to bed. On Sundays we were mostly free (no classes or flights), except for 'household chores' that we had to perform: mopping the floors, washing the lavatories, airing our straw mattresses and pillows, and cleaning the grounds. The school compound had its own club (called the Red Army House) with a decent library, which we usually went to on our days off.

At the end of 1940 the school was visited by the famous test pilot Stepan Suprun, who, as an elected member of the Supreme Council of the USSR, had come to meet his constituency at Kacha. He spoke at a meeting of the school commanders and instructors, telling them of his air combat experience in China (against the Japanese Air Force). Thanks to Timur, who had met Suprun before, he and I had the privilege of hearing him speak.

By the end of December 1940 we had completed the U-2 training course. Due to non-flying weather conditions in that month we were spending most of the time on classroom work, and then a joyful surprise came: 'for commendable work and excellent performance' we were rewarded with a leave to go to Moscow for New Year's Eve.

After that brief holiday at home, Timur and I returned to Kacha on the same train. I still remember the long heart-to-heart talk we had in the dining car in the evening. Timur reminded me that back at the flying school he had sometimes teased me so that a couple of times we had been at the point of fighting (not that I had ever liked fighting, not even as a boy). He now confessed that he had deliberately provoked me so as to 'harden' my nature, which in his opinion was much too soft. Although I had borne him no grudge at all, I remember that his confession eased my mind and brought us even closer together.

In February 1941 we began flying the UT-2, an advanced trainer designed by

Yakovlev. It was a faster aircraft than the U-2, and a more demanding one. When I first went up in the UT-2 with an instructor it seemed a difficult machine to handle, and its landing speed felt unusually high. In fact I doubted I would be able to adapt to it fast enough. However, I got rid of those doubts in my next flight, and after my seventh training flight I was ready to fly solo.

One day we heard about a fatal accident at one of our training airfields. A student and his instructor spun and crashed in their UT-2 after a simulated engine failure. A fairly simple aircraft on the whole, the UT-2 had a feature rather unpleasant in a trainer: if a yaw developed at low speed it tended to go into a spin, which could easily turn into a flat one. In a flat spin the aircraft is spinning almost horizontally, and not with its nose down as in a vertical spin. The recovery in this case is more difficult, and with some aircraft impossible. To avoid stalling and spinning one had to take care not to lose speed and to perform 'co-ordinated' turns, i.e. the deflection of the rudder should match the bank angle. Over-pushing the pedal made the aircraft yaw and slip, which easily led to spinning. The instrument to control this was called a 'slip indicator' and it consisted of a bow-shaped glass tube with a small 'ball' moving inside: when a turn was performed without a slip, the ball stayed in the centre of the tube (no lateral forces involved). This indicator remains an important cockpit panel feature in most modern aircraft.

A group of inspectors headed by Colonel Lakeev arrived from Moscow to examine the Kacha cadets. Ivan Lakeev was a well-known pilot who had fought in Spain and was also known as the leader of an aerobatics team, the 'Lakeev Five', which distinguished itself at the air shows at Tushino. The inspectors spot-checked the flight performance of a number of cadets. I was one of those selected for the check, and Colonel Nikolayev, who went up with me, gave me the top mark.

Finally the day came for the probation flights on the UT-2 with the detachment commander, prior to the first solo flights. One of the tasks to be tested was the ability to cope with simulated engine failure. I had hardly gained a dozen metres in height after take-off when the inspector suddenly closed the throttle. I pushed the stick to maintain the speed and went gliding to land straight ahead – the standard procedure in the case of a low-altitude engine failure. The inspector reopened the throttle, and we continued the flight. He closed and opened the throttle without warning several times during the circuit flight. Our airfield was very close to the sea, and I went somewhat too far over it on the down-wind leg. The commander apparently decided to demonstrate what the consequences could be, and unexpectedly closed the throttle again. I pushed the stick, made a turn and started gliding towards the coast. Very soon I realised that if I continued at the same gliding angle I would hit the rocky stretch of the coastline. To adjust the angle would mean losing speed and increasing the angle of attack (i.e. the angle between airflow and wing plane), which in its turn might easily lead to spinning. Taking care to maintain optimum speed, I continued at the same angle. By the time the aircraft had come level with the cliffs we were still about two hundred metres short of the coast. If the engine failure had been real, I would have tried landing on the narrow stretch of the beach; as it was, the instructor opened the throttle, enabling me to gain height. I had learnt my lesson. Incidentally, he still gave me the top mark, with one laconic criticism: 'went too far over the sea'.

Towards the end of winter 1941 my uncle, the designer Artem Mikoyan, and Stepan Suprun arrived at Kacha attended by a group of specialists whose task was to do the final tests of the MiG-3, an aircraft of the new generation, to which the latest fighters by Yakovlev and Lavochkin (the Yak-1 and LaGG-3 respectively) also belonged. The test flights were to be performed by the company pilot Arkady Yekatov. Timur and I visited them at their hotel, overjoyed at the chance to meet such celebrated pilots. Needless to say, I was also happy to see my uncle. He and Stepan Suprun soon left, and on 13 March, in his last scheduled flight, Yekatov was killed in a crash. His engine supercharger disintegrated, a fragment must have hit him in the cockpit, and the aeroplane went into a fatal dive.

Having completed our UT-2 training programme, we proceeded to prepare to fly a real fighter – the I-16. That fighter, designed by N. Polikarpov, remains one of the best-known aircraft in Russian aviation history. If I am not mistaken, it was the world's first mass-produced monoplane, and definitely the first monoplane with a retractable undercarriage. It had been tested by the famous test pilot Valery Chkalov. Some people later believed that Chkalov should not have recommended the I-16 for serial production; with its low-stability margin, it was an 'over-sensitive' machine that reacted to the minutest deflections of the control stick. The slightest over-pulling of the stick would send it into a spin. Moreover, the aerodynamic 'shaking' that normally warns the pilot of an imminent stall and spin in the I-16 came nearly at the same time as the stall itself.

I believe that to the pilot of today who has never flown piston-engined fighters of the I-16 and La-5 type, many of their features would seem odd or even dangerous. Upon landing, those aircraft required extreme precision of piloting. If, for example, the three-point landing attitude was assumed when the wheels were still twenty centimetres or more above the ground, the I-16 could stall and hit the ground with a wing. On the landing run, it was essential to stick to one's strict heading, with the cowl kept steady against a chosen reference point on the horizon. The slightest deviation from a straight line would lead to an accelerated turn and, if the speed was still high, to a nose-over. Another unpleasant feature of the I-16 was its limited forward view. But at the same time the I-16 was the kind of machine that developed a pilot's 'feel of the aircraft' and his precision when it came to control inputs. Experienced pilots used to say that those who were good at flying the I-16 could fly anything. For my part I believe that it was the training I received in the I-16 under the guidance of our instructor that formed the foundation for my qualifications as a pilot and ensured my future – I must say fairly successful – flying career.

To practise handling the I-16 on the runway, we were assigned a special 'ground' aircraft with the wing-skin removed to prevent it from taking off. Before going solo, we had to do a series of check-rides with the instructor in the two-seat version of the I-16, the fighter-trainer UTI-4. It required an even greater precision of piloting than the I-16, and had almost no stability margin.

Thanks to the retractable landing gear the I-16 had a speed of up to 460 kph, which was quite high by the standard of the time. The I-16 had served well as a combat fighter in Mongolia, against the Japanese Air Force in China, and in the Spanish war. It was also used at the beginning of the Great Patriotic War* but it had already become largely obsolete by 1941 and was no match for the German fighters in air combat.

In April 1941 our 2nd Squadron, together with another one, was transferred to a summer camp on the sea coast north of Kacha by the mouth of the river Alma. The move was used as an excuse for a training march. We marched with rifles, haversacks and overcoat rolls. The day was hot and we had to cover eighteen kilometres. After about two hours on the march there was a surprise gas-attack drill. We had to put on our gas masks, and then came another command, 'Double-time march to the line of defence!' and we ran towards a small gully a few hundred metres away from the road. By the time we reached the campsite we were dead tired, but before we could rest we had to obey yet another command: 'Set up the tents!'

Our group was in one tent. It was still very cold at night, and we covered ourselves with overcoats on top of the blankets. We invented a way of 'heating' the tent on chilly mornings: we lit a newspaper with a match (we had shingly beach for a floor) and received a few seconds of warmth, just enough to jump out of beds and pull on our trousers, T-shirts and boots, then out of the tent to do morning exercises. Our days at the camp were full, and it was only on Sundays that we were 'set loose' on the beach and could sunbathe, swim and wash our socks, the sea water being as good on them as the best detergent. In those brief spells of freedom we almost forgot we were in the army. While at Kacha we had hardly had any time on the beach at all. We took our meals in a fenced-in part of the campsite next to the kitchen. There were long tables with benches on either side, and an awning over them to protect against the rain. Each cadet had a tin cup and a spoon, and a mess tin used for the soup and the main course in turn. Timur and I saved time by using one of our respective tins for a double portion of soup, and the other for a double portion of the main course, eating out of one tin together.

On the occasion of May Day our group was rewarded with a real treat: we were put on a small bus (together with our instructor) and taken for a day trip to the south coast of the Crimea. Although in those past six months we had seen the sea many times, both from land and from up in the sky, the view that opened to us after a long serpentine climb to the crest of a mountain was stunning, and it is hard to put into words what I felt. I still remember the joy of suddenly, quite suddenly, seeing the dark blue sea, which began somewhere down below and seemed to end almost level with the mountain peaks. The mountain slopes and the coast were a solid mass of green, punctuated with the tall slender pyramids of cypresses. Such a striking contrast to the bare steppe of the western coast, where our school was.

We drove into Yalta and were allowed to wander around on our own. Timur and I chanced upon a dance pavilion, and we stayed there for a while. It was a

---

* This is the name by which World War Two – from Hitler's invasion of the USSR in 1941 to VE-Day in May 1945 – is known in Russia.

warm spring afternoon before the war, and May Day into the bargain; carefree merriment and joyfulness reigned supreme. I took a great fancy to one girl and danced with her several times. On parting I told her I would always remember her. Timur chuckled at my sentimentality, but I do indeed still remember her, if only as a symbol of that blissful day.

In the middle of June our group, together with our instructor, was reassigned to No.1 Squadron located at the main base. We returned to Kacha. It was ten days before war broke out.

CHAPTER 5

The War

Saturday 21 June 1941, was the final day of training prior to parachute jumping, and the instructor announced that on Monday we would perform our first jumps. After that the subject was never brought up again.

On Sunday night we woke up to Master Sergeant Kasymov's loud reveille and battle alarm command. We had been raised by practice alarms several times before, and so the only question we asked ourselves while dressing hastily was who could have thought of having a practice alarm on a Sunday. The word 'battle' that preceded the word 'alarm' did not register with us at first. We knew that we had the standard two minutes to leave the barracks, and that those who lingered would receive an extra fatigue, but this time there was no master sergeant with a stopwatch outside the door.

We lined up in the yard with our rifles, expecting to hear the usual command, 'All clear, dismissed!', after which we could go back to bed, but instead we heard, 'Double-time march! To the line of defence!' We ran, trying to keep a formation of sorts, out into the field outside the school compound, where we were ordered to lie down in a line in twosomes, each twosome about fifty metres from the next. I was with Timur. We fell asleep as soon as we 'landed' on the grass, and were woken up at dawn by a lorry that drove up to the line. It brought ammunition for our rifles. That was when we learnt a war was on. We continued lying in a line, no longer wondering what the point of it all was. We knew we were expected to deal with the enemy should the Germans attempt an airborne landing.

Sleep was forgotten. Everyone was talking excitedly, and our main concern was that the war would end (with our victory, of course) before we had time to graduate from the flying school and get into action. Later, back in the school compound, we heard Molotov's radio address which ended with the words, 'Our cause is right! The enemy will be destroyed, and victory will be ours!' It was then that we began to feel increasingly alarmed although we had not yet taken in the full extent of the danger the country was suddenly facing.

We no longer slept in the barracks. We were moved to one of the school airfields, where we continued flying and where we ate and slept on piles of hay under the wings of our aircraft. Every night we watched the German air raids on Sevastopol. We could discern the bright dots of bombers in the searchlight beams and could hear anti-aircraft guns and bomb explosions. Lastly another sound came: the unfamiliar drone of enemy aircraft making a left-hand turn over our heads on their way home. We could sometimes make out their dark shadows against the black southern sky. At daytime we could see Soviet bombers, the DB-3s, passing north of us *en route* to Ploesti in Romania. When they returned, we could see that their 'nines' were no longer complete. Ironically, the first war casualty at the flying school was an instructor pilot who ignored a sentry's command to halt and was shot.

Back in the early days of June our instructor had written in our workbooks: 'ready for a solo in the I-16 fighter'. The familiar procedure followed: two or three senior officers took check-rides with each of us and repeated the instructor's 'verdict' in our workbooks, but still would not let us fly the I-16 solo. The twenty-second of June changed everything. The next day, after two check-rides, we were sent up in the I-16s. From that moment on we were considered real pilots and, in accordance with the existing tradition, could let our hair grow by two centimetres and sew the much-cherished wings onto our sleeves (to be honest, we had already sewn them on for the few days spent in Moscow over the New Year – we just couldn't resist a bit of showing off).

In one of those solos I had the first of many experiences in my flying career when luck seemed to be all that saved me from very unpleasant, if not fatal, consequences. The I-16, unlike the U-2 and the UT-2, was equipped with wheel brakes. Once, upon landing, I was about to use the brakes, but at the last moment decided I had better not, for I had landed a bit short of the landing 'T'. Instead, at the end of the landing run, I added power and pressed the left toe-pedal to taxi off the runway. The machine suddenly turned round sharply of its own accord. I closed the throttle and the aircraft came to a halt. It turned out that one of the brake shoes had split and jammed the wheel. Had I used the brakes on the landing run when the speed was still high, the aeroplane would have nosed over and my flying career (and maybe my life as well) might have ended there and then.

Lady Luck had first helped me when I was just over a year old. According to my parents, I had caught a very bad strain of dysentery and was actually dying. In my father's words, I looked like death itself: a skeleton covered with skin. The old doctor who had been treating me suddenly stopped his daily visits and did not appear for two days. My mother phoned my father at work and tearfully told him about it. My father sent a car to the doctor to ask him to come to see him. The doctor was blunt. He said that with so many sick children on his hands he could not waste time on a hopeless case, even if it happened to be the son of a Central Committee member. My father accepted his argument but naturally said nothing to his wife. He was sure I would die, and, as he was leaving Rostov for Moscow that evening, he asked his secretary to find some other doctor just to reassure my mother, and to see to the funeral arrangements when the inevitable happened. On the way home from work he ran into a former schoolmate, Sarkisian, who said he knew a young doctor whom he trusted and he would bring him to have a look at me. Shortly afterwards my father caught his train to Moscow. The doctor, whose name was Osinovsky, came the next day and said he would try to save the child, as long as my mother did as she was told. While in Moscow, my father did not know how things were at home; there was no telephone connection with Rostov then and he did not want to send a cable asking whether his son was alive or dead. So it was only when he heard a child crying behind his front door on his return that he learned I was alive.

Early in July it was announced that the school was to be evacuated to Krasny Kut near Saratov on the Volga. We loaded the train at night. I was in the guard detail at the station and was soaked to the bone by the incessant drizzle. My over-coat remained wet throughout the journey. We spent nearly five days in covered goods wagons, sleeping on two-level plank beds, seven people to each bed. We were so crammed on those beds that unless three or four people were always on their sides there was not enough room for everyone. We ate once or twice a day when the train stopped at various stations on its way. Our last hot meal had been in a station canteen on the third day of our journey; all we had had since then was some rationed tinned food and bread. Whenever the train stopped we would run to the station master for some hot water, although we had no tea. Just before 22 June I had received a food parcel from home, but it did not take us long to get to the bottom of it. I still had a tin of condensed milk left, though, and I had it with me on the train. I rationed it out to everyone in our wagon, one spoonful to a cup of hot water, and it lasted long enough for each of us to have two cups of the drink.

Our destination, Krasny Kut, was part of the Autonomous Republic of the Germans of the Volga basin. In August that year it was abolished. We heard stories about the mass expulsion of German families, the recurrent motif of those stories was their alleged disloyalty to the USSR (in view of the German invasion, of course). In one of the tales we heard an old German woman said something like, 'Just you wait till Adolf comes! He'll show you!'

Dry, treeless and dusty, Krasny Kut possessed one true oasis of green grass and birch trees where a small river made a loop near the airfield. It was my favourite retreat in the rare spare minutes, and I still remember the feeling of peace I enjoyed lying on the soft grass and looking up at the blue sky through the leaves of the trees.

Once, on a Sunday at the end of July, one of my fellow students came running to my haven with the news that my brother Volodya had arrived. It was a total surprise. He had finished his ninth form at school and he had just turned seven-teen, still a year before conscription. He told me he had pressed our parents into letting him join a flying school. For a little over a month, before our group left the school in early September, we were there together.

At the beginning of August two air force inspector pilots arrived at Krasny Kut in brand new Yak-1s. One of them was Stalin's son Vasily. Already a captain, Vasily had graduated from flying school as a lieutenant – only about a year and a half earlier.* We were fascinated by the Yak-1; the latest Soviet fighter, it looked and felt so different and so advanced in comparison with our good old battered I-16s. I was impressed by its various technical innovations: the use of compressed air for starting the engine and for retracting and extending the landing gear. The wheel brakes were also activated by compressed air. The engine had an automated two-speed supercharger which meant that at take-off there was no need to control the boost by ear, as in the I-16 (so as not to over-stress the engine).

---

* In the Soviet armed forces the rank of lieutenant was subdivided into three 'ranks': junior lieutenant, lieutenant and senior lieutenant. Captain was a rank between major and senior lieutenant. The system remains in use.

Our graduation time came. Our head examiner was the school's Assistant Commanding Officer, Major Sidorov. All students except two received top marks, and Volodya Yaroslavsky and I passed with distinction. The rank each of us received on graduation was that of lieutenant. Timur, Volodya and I were asked to stay at the school as instructor pilots, an offer always made to those cadets in each group who had graduated with the best results. It was the standard method of recruiting school instructors. We thanked them for the offer and refused.

We were due to report at the Air Force Personnel Command in Moscow. While on the train from Kacha I saw a low-flying fighter through the window and cried, 'Look! There's a MiG, a MiG!' Timur gave me a censorious look, and I felt embarrassed at my impulsive show of 'family pride'. The three of us were assigned to the 16th Fighter Regiment stationed at Lubertsy near Moscow. It was a regiment known as a 'parade unit', for before the war it had always performed fly-pasts over Red Square during military parades on 7 November and 1 May. I will never forget what I felt on entering the pilots' mess for the first time in my leather raglan overcoat, sitting down next to 'real' fighter pilots. Could it be true that we too were real pilots at last?

The regiment flew MiG-3s and I-16s. The I-16 was of a different modification to the type we had flown at the school; known as 'type 24', it had a M-63 engine (instead of the M-25) and two 20 mm guns in addition to the two machine-guns. There were other distinctions as well, so we had to go through transition training for it, but Vasily Stalin, then the AF inspection commander, intervened with an offer to transition us for the Yak-1. He took us from the regiment to the Central Airfield in Moscow, where the air force inspection aircraft were based. On the same day he took each of us for two rides in the Yak-7V (a trainer modification of the Yak-1). I liked the aircraft very much. After the over-sensitive I-16 it felt particularly stable and easy to handle, at take-off and landing as well as in flight. The cockpit felt comfortable too, and there was less engine noise. The pilot's forward view was much better as well, for its liquid-cooled V-engine had a smaller cowling cross-section than that of the air-cooled radial engine of the I-16.

Next day Vasily asked me, 'Will you fly solo?' I was somewhat taken aback but did not show it. To me, a recent student, the idea of letting anyone fly solo after just two training flights (and without a check-ride on the day of the solo either!) seemed almost too bold. At the school every day began with a check-ride no matter now confident a student might have been, and we were now talking of a new type of aircraft! I naturally said that I would, although I was a little nervous. I performed two circuit flights and did rather well, and so did both Volodya and Timur.

Next morning, in the car on our way to the airfield, Vasily briefed me on an aerobatic flight and named the speed for the tight turns. I thought I heard 250 kph. In the I-16 it was 240 kph, and, although I knew the Yak-1 was a faster aircraft, I thought that, given its stability, 250 kph must be enough. I should have made sure, but I did not. While performing a steep turn I felt the fighter was rocking and on the verge of stalling – the speed was definitely too low. I brought it up to 300 kph and performed all the remaining manoeuvres without a hitch.

After I had landed, Vasily rudely told me off (he certainly knew how to do it!). Clearly I had misheard the figure; what he had said was 350, and not 250. They told me later that while I was in the air Vasily was swearing loudly on the airfield, as if he thought I could hear him in the sky (radio communication was not yet in use then)! As for me, I silently thanked my school instructor, who had taught me to recognize the point when the aircraft was about to stall.

However, I did not avoid a spin in one of the flights that followed. I decided to perform a loop and, having climbed to the vertical position, I glanced at the airspeed indicator. The speed seemed to be falling too fast, so I pushed the left pedal and moved the stick to the left to turn the aircraft to the horizon line. Instead of turning, it went into a spin. It was inevitable, of course. I had made a very bad mistake: even with the speed being too low, I should have continued the loop, taking care not to yaw or to increase the angle of attack. As it was, the rudder deflection caused the aeroplane to slip outwards, which in turn led to a spin. Luckily, the Yak-1 was easy to recover. Later I realised that the rate of deceleration had been quite normal, but how could I have known it if it had been my first loop ever!

Shortly before the war aerobatics had been restricted in the air force 'due to the high accident rate', so our school training programme did not include aerobatics, except for the spin, steep turns and wing-overs. Combat unit pilots did not engage in complicated aerobatic manoeuvres either (unless they did it 'on the sly'). I am sure that restricting aerobatics was a very unwise step and it affected the performance of our young pilots at the outbreak of the war. Aerobatic manoeuvres develop the pilot's competence and his feel of the aircraft, as well as his ability to handle any attitude of his machine. Ultimately, it certainly increases flight safety, to say nothing of giving an invaluable advantage in air combat. Unfortunately this was not the only example of a restrictive decision in our air force, prompted by the 'what-if-something-happens' attitude. Thus, in 1950, there were several fatal spin recovery failures caused by pilots' errors in the swept-winged MiG-15. A series of special research flights were then performed by military test pilots (my future colleagues) to investigate the reasons, and additional recommendations for the recovery techniques were worked out as a result. However, the Air Force Supreme Command forbade any intentional spins in combat units, even with an instructor. As a consequence, there were accidents, caused by the pilot's lack of confidence or even fear of an unintentional stalling. Incidentally, this restriction is still in force.

Later, aerobatic manoeuvres were also banned in the Su-24 attack bomber. For my own part, I am convinced that every pilot should at some stage be trained in aerobatics and in handling the spin or, at least, the departure – the phase that precedes spinning. The pilot will stop fearing the spin only if and when he learns to recognise the threat of departure, and when he knows from his own experience that spinning can be prevented and that recovery from a spin is quite possible. It also applies to pilots who fly various non-manoeuvrable aircraft (including passenger liners), for whom there should be an in-service training programme in light manoeuvrable aircraft involving intentional departure. Such experience is invaluable for developing flight attitude perception and the feel of the aircraft, which can help if the machine accidentally slips into an unusual attitude as regards the horizon. No attitude of the aircraft in the air should be frightening or incomprehensible to the pilot, and he must always be capable of recovering the normal position – as long as the altitude margin allows it.

A case in point is the 1985 crash of the passenger Tupolev-154 in Central Asia. Due to excessive altitude, the liner approached the critical AOA (angle of attack). The pilot took the high AOA vibration for a sign of the engine surging and pulled the throttle back. The aircraft departed and began to fall, rolling in a slack spin, while the pilot was still pulling at the wheel. Had he allowed the machine to lower its nose (thus lessening the angle of attack) it would have regained speed and returned to normal flight.

Back in 1941 Vasily Stalin unexpectedly announced that he could not go on training us himself and that we were to depart for the No. 8 Reserve and Training Regiment stationed north of Saratov. As he was himself going to Saratov for an inspection visit of the Saratov aviation works, he took us with him as passengers in his C-47 (the American prototype of our Li-2). It was two days before the 'panic day' of 16 October when a breakthrough of German tanks on the approaches to Moscow and the emergency measures taken by the State Defence Committee caused a panicked flight from the city. A few days earlier our Air Defence pilots had spotted large German tank formations about 160 km south-west of Moscow, with no Soviet troops between them and the capital. It was during that fretful month of October that we learned of the death of Konstantin Korshunov, our much-respected instructor pilot from 2nd Squadron. Vasily Stalin had helped him to get a posting to the front line, a cherished wish of instructor pilots at flying schools all over the country. He was shot down by a German anti-aircraft gun while escorting attack aircraft which were strafing an enemy airfield on the approaches to Moscow.

On the way to Saratov we landed in Kuibyshev (now Samara), the city on the Volga to which the government, all ministries, foreign embassies and other institutions were being evacuated. Our families were there too. When we entered the house where Stalin's family was lodging (Stalin himself had never been there, and its only occupants were his daughter Svetlana and Vasily's wife Galina), the guard on duty congratulated Vasily on the birth of a son, who had come into the world that very day, 14 October.

Finally we arrived in Saratov, and together with Vasily went straight to the plant that was producing the Yak-1 fighters. In the evening we accompanied Vasily to the home of his former schoolmate Nina Orlova, the wife of a well-known film cameraman, Roman Karmen. She had also been evacuated from Moscow. I still remember the depressing picture of an evacuee's life: a corner separated from the rest of the room with a sheet, a baby in a cot, the washing hanging on a line across the room. In those drab surroundings Nina herself did not impress me with her looks at all; it was only later, when I met her again in Moscow, that I saw her for what she was reputed to be – one of the first beauties in town.

The reserve regiment we came to join was converting pilots for the Yak-1 fighter for the replenishment of combat fighter regiments. It was also where the regiments received new aircraft. We asked to be assigned to No. 163 Regiment, which as we knew was soon to be sent back into action. The answer was that we would receive our appointment once back in Moscow. We lived in a long dugout, or rather a barracks that was sunk deep into the ground. There were about 200 inmates mostly sleeping on two-level plank beds. In one end of the barracks, however, were a few iron beds, and that was where we were put. One of my vivid memories from those days is how on 6 November 1941 we all stood in the barracks listening to Stalin's speech broadcast from the Mayakovskaya metro station in Moscow, where that year's official meeting to celebrate the 1917 Revolution anniversary was held. Timur, who knew and loved Russian history, was very pleased when Stalin mentioned the national war heroes of the past, Prince Alexander Nevsky and the famous commanders Kutuzov and Suvorov.

After we had done the conversion course we were ordered to report at the Air Force Personnel Command in Moscow. We decided to go through Kuibyshev so as to visit our families on the way. Besides, in Kuibyshev there was a better chance to get on a flight to Moscow than from Saratov. *En route* to Kuibyshev we 'got a lift' in a big old TB-3 bomber that was taking some passengers to Syzran, part of the way to Kuibyshev. From there we were to continue by train, but at the last moment I heard that a liaison U-2 was about to fly to Kuibyshev and, having made sure that my friends would not mind, asked the pilot to take me with him. It turned out that the rear cockpit of the two-seater was already occupied by a girl, also a pilot, so she and I, both in fur-lined flying suits, literally cuddled in the tiny cockpit, for there was no other way to fit into it together.

My family were living on the first floor of a small town mansion not far from the local drama theatre. The ground floor was taken by Mikhail Kalinin. The conditions were of course incomparably better than those in Nina Orlova's lodgings. I spent a whole day with my mother and my three younger brothers. Mother told me that my father had remained in Moscow all that time, except for a four- or five-day visit to Kuibyshev together with Molotov at the end of October, when they came to inspect the work of the evacuated Council of the People's Commissars.

The day after my arrival, on 15 December, Voroshilov was returning to Moscow in his special C-47. He took Timur, Volodya Yaroslavsky, Volodya Saburov and me with him. The next day we reported to the AF Personnel Command and received appointments to combat regiments. Timur Frunze was assigned to the Monino airfield thirty kilometres from Moscow, and I had to report to the No. 11 Fighter Regiment stationed at the Central Airfield in Moscow. It was ten days since our troops had begun a counter-attack, and we were forcing the Germans away from the capital.

CHAPTER 6

Timur, Volodya, Leonid

In the critical days of the Battle of Moscow in October 1941, when the Wehrmacht troops were as close as ten kilometres north-west of the city, No. 11 Fighter Regiment, which flew the Yak-1, was performing the unusual function of strafing the enemy's ground troops. The Yak-1 fighter had no armour plating except for the armoured seat-back and a small bullet-proof windscreen. Its original armament was not adequate for strafing tasks, but soon it was armed with under-wing unguided rockets. It will be easy to imagine just how close to Moscow the German troops were if I say that the strafing mission from the Central Airfield, which was well within the city itself, took about eighteen minutes from take-off to landing! The same function was assigned to another fighter regiment based at the same airfield (in which I later served for some time), No. 12 Fighter Regiment of the Guards, as it became known for its distinction in the Battle of Moscow.

As a result of its ground support action, 11 Regiment suffered heavy losses. On the very day of my arrival at the regiment I heard of two pilots who had not returned from their sorties the day before – V. Golovatyi and V. Mikkelman. Both, particularly Mikkelman, were remembered with great warmth, and everyone grieved their loss. Apparently Golovatyi had already been shot down twice before and had twice returned to the regiment, but now there seemed to be no hope. Then, three or four days after I had joined the regiment, Golovatyi returned again! Shortly before that the Germans shot down V. Kovalev, who took his last revenge by diving right into the midst of their large troop formation. Upon my arrival the regiment had only twelve pilots and eight aircraft left. New aircraft were not coming, so even the Yak-7V trainer, supplemented by an armoured pilot seat-back for the purpose, was used for combat sorties.

That winter the snow on the airfields was not rolled out flat, so the wheels of the fighters were replaced with skis which pressed to the wings when retracted. All aircraft were painted in white for camouflage. At that time, a new Yak-1 was transferred to the regiment from the air force headquarters squadron and assigned to me. The aircraft had not been repainted for winter camouflage and remained an ordinary green colour. This had a certain bearing on what happened to me later.

We were quartered in a red-brick building opposite the Peter Palace on Leningrad avenue. The building is still there. Daylight hours were usually spent in a dugout on the airfield or near it, where the regiment aircraft were parked. For meals we were assigned to the canteen at the Zhukovsky Air Force Academy in the Peter Palace, which was quite a distance on foot from the airfield, so we usually skipped lunch (for it was a busy time for sorties on short winter days), and when darkness came we went over to the Academy and ate both lunch and supper with a short interval in between. Over the meal, our squadron commander, Verbliudov, distributed coupons for the daily drinks rations, the well-known wartime 100 g of vodka.

My wartime and later association with combat fighter pilots, whom I always deeply respected and admired and who were not averse to liquor, did not teach me to enjoy drinking. I have never been fond of liquor and have never smoked; neither have my brothers. In fact, none of our family was a drinker or a smoker. My father gave up smoking when he realised that after his tuberculosis it was particularly bad for him, but I also think he did not want to give a bad example to his sons. He usually had dry or semi-dry wine with his weekend lunch or dinner, and as a young man he had not even tasted either vodka or brandy. Until he turned twenty-two, he had only had wine twice: for his twentieth birthday and then a year later. As he later told us, he sometimes had to drink spirits at Stalin's dinner parties, but he always drank as little as he could get away with. Stalin, who himself preferred semi-sweet wines and champagne, perversely insisted on his guests drinking vodka or brandy. My father remembered how, after a large glass of brandy which he had been forced to drink at Stalin's insistence, he slipped into a small room next to the dining-room where there was a wash basin and a sofa. He splashed some cold water on his face and then took a short nap on the sofa, after which he returned to the table refreshed. He managed to perform the same manoeuvre on two or three similar occasions, until he was found out by Beria, who gave him away to Stalin. Stalin came up to him and said, slowly and with venom, 'Want to be smarter than the rest, don't you? See that you don't regret it later.'

The remaining pilots of the war-ravaged regiment were real 'veterans'. They had participated in repelling the first air raid of Moscow on 22 July 1941. Many of them were decorated with various orders: my flight commander Vladimir Lapochkin had the Order of Lenin, and the squadron commander Verbliudov the Red Banner Order.

By mid-December the strafing sorties had stopped as the German troops had been driven beyond Volokolamsk. We now performed fighter cover tasks for General Dovator's cavalry which was fighting in the German rear. However, the weather was dull, with clouds hanging low, and, except for German anti-aircraft guns firing at us, nothing exciting was happening (I once saw several shells burst about 200 metres from my tail behind me). One day, after the take-off of our six, a sudden snow blizzard hid the airfield and the area around from view. The leader ordered a one-by-one approach. I could not see the ground until I was just about fifty metres over it and the visibility was no more than 300 to 400 metres – tough for any pilot, especially one as young and inexperienced as I then was. I realised I was flying over Begovaya Street, recognised the building of the Hippodrome and, navigating myself by familiar streets, found the way to the airfield. I could already see the landing 'T', but I was approaching it from the side, at an angle. I had a happy thought to extend the flaps and, after a 360-degree turn at about forty metres over the airfield, I saw the landing 'T' again, but this time I was able to land properly. It turned out that except for the leader and myself, everyone landed at various angles across the runway.

This landing brought me my first commendation in combat service.

Another incident. Once, when I was about to lower the undercarriage before landing, I saw that the system air pressure was low. I decided not to create counter-pressure by selecting the 'up' position of the lever before turning it down (as the standard procedure required), so I extended the landing gear straight away and then heard a much louder noise than usual. I knew that the under-carriage was down, but the green indicator light of the left strut for some reason did not appear. On touching down, the aircraft gently leaned on the left wing tip and made a ninety-degree turn. It transpired that despite the low pressure in the air-bottle the impact on the strut was too strong, and the brace of the strut split in two (there must have been some defect in the metal). No wonder the green light was not on – the strut was hanging loose and had folded up as I landed. Thanks to the snow the wing was not damaged; only the under-wing rocket rails were bent.

Throughout my flying career I always tried to analyse the flight situation and to take a decision dictated by the situation itself. I never liked the idea of acting 'blindly' by the book without thinking. In the above incident I would have done better if I had followed the instructions, but in some other cases my conscious, situation-bound deviations from them helped me to avoid serious accidents. I cannot resist adducing a brief quotation from the 1910 Circular of the Marine Technical Committee of Russia, which I came across when already a test pilot and which agreed with what I felt myself: 'No instruction can stipulate all duties of an official, or anticipate all possible situations with an exhaustive list of recom-mendations of how to act in each of them; therefore Messrs Engineers should use their initiative and, guided by their professional knowledge and considerations of the common good, should zealously endeavour to show themselves worthy of their positions.'

On 16 January 1942 my flight commander and I were sent on an interception sortie: a Junkers 88, possibly a scout, had been spotted near Istra, a small town west of Moscow. It was my eleventh sortie. When we got to the area there was already no sign of the enemy aircraft. The flight commander gestured to me to move ahead of him and lead on. I was euphoric, happy to be a real combat fighter, enjoying a kind of devil-may-care feeling. What happened next taught me a lesson I have never forgotten. Whenever I feel exceedingly elated, I mentally remind myself to be alert and not to get carried away. I think this habit has guarded me against self-assurance and helped to avoid some dangers and mishaps.

I suddenly saw three fighters heading towards us. When they were above me and slightly to the left, I performed a chandelle and got some 700 metres behind them. I recognised them as Yak fighters and began a turn away to the right, while not taking my eyes off them. Suddenly their left wingman made a sharp turn, heading for my tail. I entered a tight turn while the white Yak with red stars continued hanging on my tail at about fifty metres. Since I was performing a maximum-rate turn, I could not be hit by fire from an aircraft of the same type. Having made two or three 360-degree turns I decided to level off, for the Yak was definitely a friendly aircraft. As soon as I had levelled off I saw green jets of tracer bullets just about a metre away from my cabin. I shrank into my seat, hoping for the protection of the armoured seat-back, and rocked the wings to show that I was a friend. Then I performed a split-S and dived down. After I had levelled off again I saw that the plywood wing-skin close to the fuel tank was in splinters, and flames were coming out through the holes. As I understood later the aiming was not so accurate thanks to my levelling off with the ailerons alone (without the deflection of the rudder). It made my Yak side-slip to the right, and the other pilot, while aiming nearly point-blank at the fuselage, hit the wing instead. My luck was with me again – had he succeeded in hitting the fuse-lage he would have got me, for he was firing his cannon as well as his machine-gun, and the armoured seat-back was not much of a protection against cannon shells.

Unfortunately it did not occur to me to bail out, which would have been the only sensible decision. Instead I made a steep descent and approached for landing, with my undercarriage up, on a small snow-covered field. By that time the flames had reached inside the cockpit because of a leakage from the fuel tank into the fuselage. I was shielding my face with my left hand but the woollen gloves on both hands caught fire too. I had a one-piece fur-lined flying suit on, a leather helmet and goggles that saved my eyes, and, in a flash of memory, I remembered that I had nearly put on the large-cuffed uniform leather gloves but had then rejected them for the ordinary woollen ones. Now was the time to regret my choice! The leather gloves would have protected both my hands and my face. As I was levelling at landing, the fire in the cabin was so fierce that I, as I have vaguely remembered since, was screaming with pain. I do not quite remember the moment of touching down; the next thing I knew the plane was coming to a halt. I climbed over the port-side board and, tearing off the strap of my burning celluloid map case, tumbled down onto the wing. After that another memory gap. What I remember next is lying on the snow some ten metres away from the blazing aircraft. I thought, 'The cannon shells will start going off now', and made an effort, with a sharp pain in my knees, to crawl away from the plane. I believed the pain came from bullet wounds, but it turned out later that my right knee was broken (I must have hit it against the wing) and my left knee badly burnt (the trouser leg had completely burnt through).

A Yak-1 flew low over me – it was Lapochkin, my leader. I waved an arm to him to show that I was alive. It must have been a very colourful picture: a green aircraft in flames against the white snow. I used my elbows to crawl a little further away, and at that moment the shells started bursting. After a while three teenager boys from a nearby village appeared. They pushed several skis under my body and dragged me towards the road, which luckily was not too far. On the road they put me on a horse-drawn sleigh. It was very cold and my burnt face and hands were freezing. Someone covered my face with his cap and put mittens on my hands. I was brought to the nearest field hospital set up in an old mansion house in the suburbs of Istra. My burns turned out to be pretty bad – they were third-degree, and in places fourth degree. The pain was excruciating. The nurse soothed it by applying light manganese solution, but soon the pain returned and I started groaning again. The hospital was overcrowded. There were beds carrying the wounded in the hall and even on the landings. Groans came from every corner.

The next day an ambulance came from Moscow and with it my father's personal assistant Alexander Barabanov, who had known me as a child. I was transferred to the so-called 'Kremlin' hospital, where I spent about two months. For a long time my face below the eyes was covered with a thick black scab, with a hole between the lips through which they gave me drink and liquid food from a feeding cup. Professor Bakulev, who was my doctor, carefully removed tiny pieces of the scab with pincers, assuring my mother and me that there would be no traces left when my face healed. Later, when it became clear that he had been right (there were almost no visible traces left), he confessed that he had been saying it only to comfort my mother, while being sure all the time that there would be scars on my face, just as there were (and still are) on my hands and on my left knee.

As it turned out I had been shot down by a fighter pilot of the 562nd Regiment (my friend Volodya Yaroslavsky, who served in that regiment, later told me their side of the story), Junior Lieutenant Rodionov. On his return from that sortie he said, 'I'm afraid I've shot down a friend.' And then added, 'Well, he had no business getting onto my tail.' He must have got caught up with the excitement of a combat sortie and probably got confused by my Yak being green, not white. Yet it seems odd; I had already begun to turn away from their formation when he got on my tail. Besides, I had levelled the wings and stopped my defensive manoeuvres to show that I was a friend. As I was later told, the order issued in connection with that incident commanded Rodionov to be court-martialled, and 'the degree of Lieutenant Mikoyan's guilt to be established upon his recovery'. However, as far as I know there was neither a court-martial for Rodionov nor an investigation regarding myself, although recently, in 1994, General Yakushin (a well-known pilot who had fought in the Spanish war and World War Two) told me about the visit he had paid me in hospital. Apparently he had come with the task of clearing up some details of the incident. I have no memory of that visit at all, although later Mikhail Yakushin and I served together for some time and became friends.

On 3 June Junior Lieutenant Rodionov was killed. He had rammed a Junkers 88 in the wing, but the bomber had continued its flight so Rodionov rammed again into the fuselage. The Junkers fell out of the sky and Rodionov, while landing onto a field with his undercarriage up, crashed into anti-tank obstacles. He was made a Hero of the Soviet Union posthumously.

My mother came to the hospital for several hours every day, helping the nurses in their work and sitting by my side. My father visited me twice. In February Vasily Stalin and my brother Volodya came to see me together. Volodya had just come from his flying school. Vasily was already a colonel, although he had only been a captain in October and a major in November. He had 'skipped over' the rank of lieutenant-colonel, which was between major and colonel.

Five or six days after I had been brought to that hospital I was visited by Voroshilov. I asked him if Timur was writing home. 'Oh yes, he is, he's writing often', he replied, without meeting my eyes. I did not pay attention to it at the time, but remembered it later when I was told that Voroshilov had come to see me on his return from Timur's funeral near Novgorod. He had been shot down on 19 January, some two months before his nineteenth birthday.

Timur's regiment had been moved to the north-west front, but there had been a decision to transfer Timur to another regiment so he could remain near Moscow. He had asked Voroshilov to intervene and help him to stay in his regiment. Voroshilov had complied, and Timur was not moved to a different unit. He had sounded very happy when telling me the whole story over the telephone on New Year's Eve. It was the last time we talked. As I heard later, Timur Frunze and his flight commander Lieutenant Shutov had attacked and shot down a German aerial spotter, after which a group of Messerschmitt fighters appeared. They shot one down, but Shutov's Yak was shot down too, and Timur was left to confront the remaining 'Messers' alone. The then Chief of Staff of the 32nd Regiment, Major Prostoserdov, happened to witness the finale of that combat. According to his description he saw a Yak-1 flying low, listlessly rocking its wings, with two Me 109 fighters in close pursuit. After a burst of machine-gun fire from one of them the Yak-1 pitched down and crashed into the ground. Prostoserdov ran up to the wreckage, removed a Komsomol membership card from the dead pilot's breast pocket and read the name: Timur Frunze. Knowing Timur as I did, I have always been sure that he must have been seriously wounded some time before the Me 109s' final attack, otherwise he would never have behaved as passively as Prostoserdov described.

Timur had been buried in a small town near Novgorod, and after 1950 his remains were transferred to the Novodevichy Cemetery in Moscow. He was posthumously awarded the title of Hero of the Soviet Union. Not far from the cemetery where he is buried, on the street bearing his name, is a school where the pupils and teachers organised a small 'museum' in Timur's memory. For many years until 1994, on Timur's birthday, his classmates and some of his fellow fighter pilots got together for a meeting with the pupils and staff of this school. We talked to the children, sharing our memories of Timur and of the war. At those meetings, as well as at similar gatherings at the school where my brother Volodya had been a pupil, I used to say to the children that neither Timur nor my brother had performed any remarkable deeds of great heroism; they had simply not been given time, although in their hearts they had been ready for them. And so they were remembered, by those who had not been their relatives or friends, as 'symbols' of millions of very young boys who had given their unlived lives for their country.

Timur as a person was a combination of very different features: on the one hand he was 'an offspring of a good family', on the other just an ordinary boy, full of good-natured naughtiness. Tall and slender, Timur was very fit physically and went in for many sports: riding, gymnastics, wrestling and shooting. He was extremely sociable, great fun to be with and, above all, a very good friend. He hated deceit and malicious cunning, though he was a great one for mischief and harmless practical jokes. At school he was a favourite with classmates and teachers alike – a rare combination. He was very well read and hard working. He loved literature and painting, history and languages. He was easily carried away, high spirited and recklessly brave. One of the instructor pilots at our flying school once said to him that with his foolhardiness he would not fly for long. 'You'll get yourself killed one day', he remarked.

My treatment continued for a long time after I had been discharged from hospital. My fractured right knee still ached and I limped heavily, and the burns on my left knee were not healing properly. I went over to Kuibyshev to stay with my mother and brothers. One day, at the clinic where some wounded officers continued their treatment, I met two senior lieutenants: Ruben Ibarurri, son of the famous La Pasionaria, and Khrushchev's son Leonid. Both had already been decorated with the Red Banner Order. We became friends, though Ruben left for Moscow soon after we had first met. Later I heard that he had been assigned to an airborne division as a machine-gun company commander and had fought at Stalingrad where he was badly wounded in the stomach and had shot himself before anything could be done. Leonid Khrushchev, a fully-fledged pilot from before the war, had been in action from its very first day. He had done over thirty sorties in the Ap-2 bomber, until in late July 1941 his aircraft was hit by a German fighter. Leonid barely made it to the front line and crash-landed in no-man's land. One of the four crew members had been killed while still in the air, and Leonid broke a leg on landing; in his own words, 'the bone was sticking out through the boot'. They were picked up by our infantrymen. The field hospital surgeons were going to amputate Leonid's leg but he, brandishing his pistol, did not allow it. The leg was healing very badly and his treatment continued for over a year.

While in Kuibyshev, Leonid and I became friendly with two young ballet dancers of the Bolshoi theatre company. Earlier, back in Moscow, I had met another dancer, one of the two leading ballerinas of the Bolshoi, Olga Lepeshinskaya, who became a lifelong friend. These meetings inspired my interest in ballet, which has remained with me all my life. In the end Leonid left for the front without waiting for his leg to heal and got retrained to fly the Yak-7 fighter. He and I met briefly in Moscow when he was passing through on the way to the front. A pilot later transferred to my regiment, who had taken part in Leonid's last air combat, told me about his death. In a dog-fight on 11 March 1943 he saw as a Focke-Wulf 190 that was flying in a turn on Leonid's tail opened fire at him from the rear, and then Leonid's aircraft went into a dive. The air was full of smoke, so he could not see Leonid fall and crash. The fact that a Focke could get a more manoeuvrable Yak in a tight turn could probably be explained by Leonid's limited experience of manoeuvre pilotage in a fighter aircraft; he had been a bomber pilot and had had very little time for retraining. Such was the sad irony of fate: had he not prevented the surgeons from amputating his leg, he would not have died. The actual site of his final crash, although looked for after the war, has never been found. It was not surprising considering how fierce the fighting had been in the area.

As soon as my burns had healed (but not my fractured knee, for I was still limping heavily), I returned to Moscow. My brother Volodya, who had done an intensive course at the flying school, was then going through additional training at the air force inspection squadron. Vasily Stalin was very fond of my brother and was acting as a kind of self-appointed 'guardian' to him, but my brother disapproved of Vasily's drinking, his wilfulness and his frequent outbursts of rudeness towards his subordinates and friends. I remember he once returned from a party with Vasily very annoyed and said, 'What a cretin!', his favourite word of censure, several times before finally telling me that Vasily had again used obscene language in the presence of women.

When his training was completed Volodya was posted to 434 Fighter Regiment of the Supreme Command Reserve, and that was where I was posted on my return from Kuibyshev too. The regiment had been formed by Vasily Stalin, who took advantage of his virtually unlimited opportunity to choose and give appointments to whomever he wished. The flying officers were either former instructor pilots from the Kacha flying school or fighter pilots with front-line action experience. Three of the flying officers were Heroes of the Soviet Union, as well as the regiment commander, twenty-four-year-old Ivan Kleshchev, who by that time already had sixteen personal victories and shared many more with other pilots. The least experienced of all and the youngest were my brother and I.

The regiment was based at the Lubertsy airfield outside Moscow, where we started off by retraining for the Yak-1B, a new version of the Yak-1 which I had flown before. When off-duty we were still living our 'normal' lives and were even allowed to sleep at home instead of the barracks most nights. Once Volodya and I returned home late after a party and were surprised to see that our mother was still up and looking flustered and concerned. She told us off for partying at such a time and said that there had been a phone call to say that the regiment was leaving for the front line early next morning. Mother packed our things, we said goodbye to her and went off to Lubertsy straight away. That was the last time she saw Volodya, 3 September 1942.

I remember we were impressed that our CO Ivan Kleshchev was seen off by the famous film actress Zoya Feodorova, though we knew they were living together as husband and wife. As her daughter Victoria later said in an interview, her mother often remembered her dearly beloved pilot who had been killed in the war. She also told everyone that he was Victoria's father, although in fact it was an American officer on the staff of the US embassy in Moscow, and it was for her affair with him that Zoya Feodorova was arrested at the end of the war.

The 434 Regiment flying officers were transferred in two transport Li-2s to Bagai-Baranovka, to the base of the No. 8 Reserve and Training Regiment, where we were to receive our aircraft. A number of Yak-7Bs were brought for us straight from the Saratov plant. The Yak-7B was armed with two large-calibre machine-guns as distinct from the rifle-calibre machine-guns of the Yak-1. Its cannon was of the same calibre – 20 mm. We immediately flew our new fighters and tried out the cannon and the machine-guns. We found that the latter were not always reliable. Soon afterwards we took off for Stalingrad.

The regiment was based on an airfield which lay some sixty kilometres north of the city. We slept in peasant log huts in the nearby village. At night we would often hear the roaring of a lone German bomber, which would sometimes drop a few bombs on the airfield area. A number of bombs fell fairly close to us, and it made many pilots very nervous; ground explosions sounded more frightening to them than cannon fire in the air. One afternoon, as we were dozing off on a haystack by the aircraft, we woke up to the sound of a close explosion followed by several others; a number of bombs fell neatly one by one along the line of parked aircraft belonging to another regiment at the far end of the airfield. Sasha Yakimov, who had been lying next to me, tumbled down the haystack and into the nearest trench even before he had had time to wake up, causing a hearty burst of laughter from all of us.

On another occasion we saw a Junkers 88 heading right towards our airfield, with a few Yak fighters from a neighbouring regiment in pursuit. The fighters attempted a somewhat clumsy attack, firing from a distance which was clearly too far. The Junkers entered a large cloud and hid from sight. The fighters nosed around, waiting for him to show between the clouds. Eventually a bomber emerged out of a cloud over the edge of the airfield. One of the Yaks attacked him and shot him down. The bomber went into a spin and exploded on crashing. We cheered, but it later turned out that it was one of our own Pe-2s that was shot down, while the Junkers had reversed in the cloud and made off unscathed. Just to think that several fighters had been wasting ammunition failing to hit a Junkers, and it took just one burst of fire to shoot down a friendly aircraft!

A few days later a Messerschmitt 109 flew low over the airfield. We fired at the German with our pistols and rifles, but it was all useless of course, and he had appeared and disappeared so suddenly that even the pair on duty did not have time to take off. Once I saw a Messerschmitt pursuing a Yak and heard a distant burst of gun fire, after which the Yak suddenly went into a loop which ended in a steep dive and a crash. The wounded pilot must have continued pulling the stick without knowing what he was doing.

One day our regiment received a reinforcement – an all-women flight consisting of four pilots and twelve mechanics, sixteen girls altogether. Their commander was Lieutenant Klava Nechaeva. To test the new pilots' competence, Kleshchev challenged them to a series of simulation dog-fights. Klava Nechaeva was the first to accept the challenge. At first she almost managed to get on Kleshchev's tail, but he dodged her and went astern of her instead. Trying to make off from him, she overpulled the stick and went into a spin. Her altitude was dangerously low, and the pilots who were watching from the ground could not help crying out 'Recover!' – as if she could hear them. Fortunately she did manage to recover, but a few days later, when she was on a group patrol of the front-line area, she was shot down by a Messerschmitt which made a surprise attack at a ninety-degree angle. Kleshchev was attending a meeting at the front headquarters at the time, and so when an officer walked into the room and reported that Major Kleshchev had been killed in action, he immediately knew who had been killed and why it was thought to be him: he had lent Klava his map case, and it was found in the debris after the crash. It was the first casualty in our regiment at Stalingrad. Another pilot from that female flight, Klava Blinova (whom I regularly saw at the annual veterans' meetings long after the war), was later posted to another regiment, shot down and captured. When she and a number of other prisoners of war were being transported by the Germans in a sealed railway carriage, they contrived to make a hole in the side of the carriage and escaped. Out of the sixteen people who had made off, only five managed to reach the positions of our troops. Klava Blinova was among them.

On 16 September 1942 our regiment was visited by the Air Force Commander-in-Chief, Air Marshal Novikov. While addressing the pilots he said that our particular 'charge' was to be the enemy's Focke-Wulf 189s, the artillery fire-direction aircraft that were giving a lot of trouble to our ground troops. Next morning CO Kleshchev was summoned to a meeting at the front headquarters. On his return he told us that on the next day, 18 September, our troops were launching a major offensive in the direction of Kotluban (a railway junction fifteen kilometres west of Stalingrad). The purpose of the operation was to encircle and isolate the German units besieging the city. Our troops were expected to gain a thirty-kilometre advance in one day.

Next morning our regiment took off in three large formations, heading for the front line north of the Kotluban junction. I was flying in the first formation as the CO's wingman. When we reached the area I saw a FW 189 (we called them 'frames', after their frame-like profile) performing a turn right in front of me. Kleshchev must have deliberately got out of the way to let me have a go. I attacked him, aiming carefully and calmly (which later, when I remembered it, seemed surprising). So as not to miscalculate the lead angle, I opened fire when it was still too large, narrowing it as I went on firing. Unfortunately both my heavy-calibre machine-guns jammed, and my only weapon was the cannon, whose low rate of fire made my chances of hitting the Focke very small. The 'frame' was turning at a steep bank and, as the distance between us shortened, I noticed that one of the shells had hit his wing. However, he then dodged my fire by banking even more steeply and finally diving. I chased him for a while and then returned to my place beside my leader. I had been expressly instructed before take-off to stick to the leader at all times. Our second formation was flying below us, and the Focke was finished off. It was my first experience of firing at a flying target.

Later we saw several dozen Heinkel 111 bombers flying in sections of three. Kleshchev and I were the first to approach them. I aimed the cannon, doing everything by the book again and feeling as calm as the first time. As soon as we had opened fire, the Germans started dropping their bombs (which we could see quite clearly) and making off towards the Don. It meant we prevented them from doing precision bombing, and their bombs might have in fact fallen on their own positions. The other machines in our formation and in the other two were shooting too. My machine-guns were still jammed, though I had done the reloading the instructions prescribed. I did not see any shot-down aircraft in front of me, but later I learnt that we had nine victories in that fight.

Suddenly I heard a female voice on the radio shouting, 'Messers above you! Messers!' It was the ground observation post warning us. Not all our aircraft were equipped with radio stations, nor were all of them working, but it did not take the pilots long to see the approaching Messerschmitts above us. We went into a defensive turn and then made a series of 360-degree turns during which I was reassured to see red-nosed aircraft (the distinctive marking used in our regiment) behind me. And then, suddenly, a yellow-winged machine flashed past about a hundred metres below me. A Messerschmitt! It was only later that I realised he had been trying to attack me, but in any case I could not get him into my gunsight as he was inside our turn circle.

One of the Yaks suddenly soared up above us and started vigorously rocking the wings. It was the CO ordering us to flock around him. It was time to stop making defensive turns and to start fighting. The pilots finally got their bearings and embarked on vertical manoeuvres; I joined one of the fighters as his wingman. Petrol was running low by that time, and the Germans must have had the same problem for they began to turn home. Back on the airfield the pilots avoided one another's eyes; such seasoned flying officers ought to have known better than to waste their time circling around defensively. I told the armament mechanics of my machine-guns' malfunction, and they assured me it would not happen again. Yet it did, in the very next sortie. The failures of this type of airborne machine-guns became such a common thing that even the top army authorities eventually got to know about them.

Our next sortie had the same pattern: we were first engaged with a large number of bombers and then came face to face with a fighter formation. As before, we returned home in desultory pairs and foursomes, making our way through a haze of smoke. Even through that haze I could see the flashes and explosions below – severe ground fighting was going on. It was mainly to that fighting that the smoke was due, rising up to three kilometres into the sky. Now and then the silver ribbons of the Don and the Volga flashed through the haze, and I saw the fires raging where Stalingrad was. The sky was swarming with aircraft, most of which were German. This picture has been imprinted in my memory ever since.

My brother Volodya was the youngest in the regiment, both in terms of age and in terms of experience. He had turned eighteen in June that year, and it was only six months before Stalingrad that he had come out of a pilots' school. Everyone in the regiment was fond of him. He made several sorties with a covering mission in the area of the regiment's airfield. The day before the offensive operation was to begin his machine malfunctioned, so he did not participate in our first combat sorties to the front line.

The two sorties of very intense action told heavily on the morale of most pilots in the regiment. There were no more jokes to be heard, none of the usual friendly leg-pulling in the mess, even though there had been no casualties yet. We must have shared a premonition of future losses. I still remember the unusual bitter taste in my mouth; it must have been an effect of the extreme nervous strain I was under. Kleshchev ordered me to rest and sit the next sortie out so that my brother could go up in my machine. Kleshchev himself stayed behind too, putting Squadron Commander Izbinsky in charge of the formation. Volodya took off as Izbinsky's wingman. When the formation was making the landing approach on its return home, we saw that it was two aircraft short. One of the missing fighters turned out to be Nikolai Shulzhenko's (he had bailed out) and the other was mine. Maybe Volodya automatically taxied over to his squadron's parking area?

Kleshchev put me in his car and together we drove along the lines of parked aircraft. My machine was nowhere to be seen.

As I heard later, the section of eight to which Volodya belonged had engaged the enemy's bombers when a group of Messerschmitts appeared from above. The leader of our other formation, Sergei Dolgushin, was about five kilometres away. He hurried to his comrades' aid and saw a pair of fighters climb in a turn after an attack on a German bomber, and a Messerschmitt dive and open fire at one of the fighters in the pair that had slightly fallen behind the leader. The aeroplane rolled over slowly and dived, but then it seemed to level out. Moments later, however, it dipped again and dived plumb down into the ground. Volodya must have been wounded heavily, struggling to control the machine, but then he must have blacked out, and it was all over. One of our pilots told me that he had tried to cut the German off with machine-gun fire, but his machine-guns jammed. Sergei Dolgushin saw Volodya's aircraft go in, and back at the airfield he showed the CO the exact spot on the map – about twelve kilometres into the German positions by a ravine south of the Kotluban junction. They did not tell me about it then, but my father later talked to Dolgushin on the phone from Moscow, asking him about the circumstances of Volodya's death. Quite recently Sergei Dolgushin has repeated his account to me again.

On our return from the airfield Kleshchev took me to the mess where the other pilots had gathered already. I could not even think of eating and was feeling horrible. Other pilots had scarcely touched their food either. The tension was enormous. Kleshchev called the senior officer of the service battalion and ordered vodka to be brought to every table. They poured a glass for me too, but I couldn't drink – my teeth were clattering against the rim. Still, they made me drink some, and everyone else emptied their glasses too. Nobody showed any sign of tipsiness, and I realised that the idea was to relieve the tension. I was still hoping for a miracle. Suddenly the report came that a wounded pilot had been found. 'Volodya!' I thought, but it turned out to be Sergei Paushev who had bailed out in the next sortie.

Strange as it might seem, this abortive attempt to destroy the German troops around Stalingrad in September 1942 is hardly ever mentioned in the literature on the war. All I have managed to find in relation to it are a few lines in a single edition. Apparently it was an operation which, as it failed and thus brought no credit to our military command, was considered unworthy of forming an episode in official Soviet war history. I heard later that after the final destruction of the German force at Stalingrad Marshal Zhukov had given orders for the search of Volodya's aircraft, but nothing was found. The fighting in the area had been so fierce, the ground literally turned over with bombs, shells and crashed aircraft, that if anything had been identified it would have been a miracle.

CHAPTER 7

On the North-West Front

In October 1942 No. 434 Regiment returned to the Lubertsy base near Moscow for re-forming. In the heavy fighting at Stalingrad our regiment had eighty-six victories, including those achieved in battles against the famous German wing of 'Berlin Snipers'. But our own losses were heavy too: sixteen pilots and twenty-five machines (in comparison in the regiment's previous engagement on the river Don there had been one lost pilot and two aircraft against thirty-four victories). Some of the losses were particularly painful due to their tragic absurdity. Karnachonok and Abrosimov collided in the air just after they had together shot down a Messerschmitt, and both crashed almost on top of it; Captain Starodub, having destroyed one Junkers 87, collided with another; Nikolai Garam force-landed on a minefield; the same happened to Marikutsa; Captain Ivanov was strafed by a Messerschmitt together with his aircraft as he was having a cigarette sitting on the wing after a forced landing.

The day after my brother's death Major Kleshchev was leading his formation home after a battle and saw a number of Messerschmitts at some distance. He broke off from his group and attacked six enemy fighters single-handed. I believe his desperate action was his personal revenge for Volodya, for he had been extremely fond of him. He got two of the Messerschmitts, but his own aircraft was set on fire and he was wounded. He managed to bail out, losing his Hero's Golden Star in the process (throughout the war all pilots flew into action with all their decorations pinned on). Vasily Stalin sent an aircraft to take him to Moscow, where he was treated in the 'Kremlin' hospital. On his recovery Mikhail Kalinin summoned him to the Kremlin for a new Golden Star to replace the lost one. This, to my knowledge, was the only such occasion in the history of this award. On 19 September Sergei Dolgushin's machine was damaged too. Volodya Lutsky and Sasha Koshelev escorted him home, but his bad luck continued: two days later he had to bail out of a burning aircraft.

In October 1942 Vasily Stalin had several pilots – Dolgushin, Garanin, Kleshchev (back from hospital), Baklan and me – transferred from No. 434 Regiment to the Air Force Inspection, which he commanded. In November 1942 No. 434 Regiment was renamed No. 32 Fighter Regiment of the Guards. Nearly all the regiment flying officers were decorated with various orders, and Vasily Babkov and Andrei Baklan became Heroes of the Soviet Union. I received the Red Banner Order.

The Air Force Inspection had its own flying squadron based on the Central Airfield in Moscow. The squadron had just received a small fleet of the new Yak-9 fighters, the series production of which had just begun. They differed from the Yak-7B in that they had metal, not wooden, wing spars. We flew those fighters from time to time. In those days fighter pilots took off and landed with the canopy open, for it was believed that its Plexiglas distorted the pilot's view on landing and prevented him from determining his precise height when touching down. When in action, the canopy was also left open for fear of its jamming under fire (our aircraft did not have the emergency throwing-off device yet) and also for the sake of a better rear view. One day I defied common practice and shut the canopy as soon as I had started the engine. I did three circuit flights without opening it, keeping it shut even while taxiing on the ground. I liked it a lot better that way; I felt warm, there was no wind blowing into my face, and I had no problem determining my altitude at landing. However, my 'complacency' was punished with a reprimand from the chief inspector.

New Year's Eve saw a tragic accident involving one of our best pilots: Ivan Kleshchev was killed in a crash. At the end of December he was sent with some mission to an air force airfield near Tambov. The day before his scheduled return to Moscow a heavy snowfall began. It never stopped snowing for hours, and there was no question of flying in such weather. However, on 31 December Kleshchev got fed up with waiting and took off. After a while he must have realised he would not make it to Moscow through the blizzard and turned back. As he was landing in heavy snow at the same airfield, he misjudged his height above the ground at the most critical moment, when it was time to flare before touching down. His plane hit the ground and disintegrated. A renowned pilot with the country's highest award, Ivan Kleshchev was not even twenty-five when he died. Many pilots blamed his death on Zoya Feodorova, the famous actress he was living with, saying he had risked his life to be with her for the New Year. I never thought it was fair to blame her, for his wish to be home for the New Year seemed to me quite natural, no matter who was waiting for him there. It is a pity he was not awarded a second Golden Star, even though he had twenty-four personal and thirty-two shared victories to his credit after Stalingrad. I am sure that if he had not died so absurdly he would have outshone Pokryshkin and Kozhedub, the most celebrated of the Soviet wartime aces.

Kleshchev's fatal accident makes me think of another outstanding pilot and a promising commander, Captain Konstantin Titenkov, who was also killed while landing during a snow blizzard back in October 1941. As a Squadron Commander in No. 11 Regiment, he had participated in the air defence of Moscow from the day of the first German air raid, during which he shot down the leader of the entire formation and five other aircraft into the bargain. Titenkov was posthumously awarded the title of Hero of the Soviet Union.

During that time Vasily often invited me to Stalin's dacha in Zubalovo, where he and his sister Svetlana lived. His parties often lasted long into the night. The company usually consisted of several pilots and an assortment of civilian celebrities: the writer Konstantin Simonov with his wife Valentina Serova, a well-known actress, the poet Alexei Surkov, the documentary cameraman Roman Karmen and Nina, his wife, the scriptwriter Alexander Kapler, the actors Nikolai Kriuchkov and Ludmila Tselikovskaya, the film director Mikhail Slutsky, the Bolshoi ballet dancer Eugenia Farmaniants, and others. One of the favourite pastimes was watching films in a small private cinema hall at the dacha. Vasily would usually drink and smoke a lot and hardly ate anything (a combination of habits that might have become the reason for his early death).

As I understood later, Vasily had been giving these late-night drinking parties in (perhaps subconscious) imitation of his father. It was Stalin's practice to summon the 'select' Politburo members to his dacha in the suburbs of Moscow late in the evening and keep them at his table until four or five a.m. He would then stay there and sleep until midday, while the others had to be at work by ten in the morning. In the post-war years these parties took place nearly every day. If any of the 'regular' guests suddenly was no longer invited it meant he had got into Stalin's bad books. Thus, Voroshilov was almost never invited after the war, and a year before his death Stalin stopped inviting Molotov and my father, but that is a subject for later. It was not just small talk that Stalin and his guests were engaged in at those parties. Affairs of state and political matters were discussed there a lot. Many important decisions were made on those occasions, and the fates of some people were decided there too. Tradition has it that Defence Minister Nikolai Bulganin, on the way to Stalin's dacha once, said to another guest, who was in his car, 'One never knows which way one'll go from the dacha – home or to Lubyanka.'

As for Vasily and his parties, his self-indulging habits eventually led to a scandal. He began flirting with the beautiful Nina Karmen and once, in the absence of his own wife and Nina's husband, he induced her to stay with him at the dacha for a few days. As I later heard from Karmen himself, he had found this out and had written an indignant letter to Stalin. Stalin gave way to his anger (Vasily's addiction to drinking being the main cause of it) and ordered that his son be stripped of his position in charge of the Air Force Inspection Command, locked up in a guardhouse for ten days – something that was never done to officers, let alone colonels – and finally packed off to the front line. Contrary to what has been said in some publications, I must make it clear that until then Vasily had paid only flying visits to the front line in his capacity as the Inspection Commander and had never made a single combat sortie, yet now he was posted to No. 32 Regiment as its CO. He decided to take several of 'his' pilots with him. On 11 February 1943 a group of nine Yak-9s took off for the North-Western Front. Among the pilots in that group were a number of distinguished aces and several experienced pilot flying officers. Being the youngest, I belonged to neither category, but was taken along anyway.

We joined No. 32 Regiment at the time of the so-called Spas-Demensk operation, during which we were based at an airfield west of Ostashkovo. The purpose of this large-scale operation was to encircle a major German force, but it ended in failure, for the Germans managed to escape.

Before our arrival, on which Vasily Stalin assumed command, the regiment had been commanded by Vasily Babkov, who became Vasily's second-in-command (Babkov survived the war and had an usually long flying career, continuing to fly fighter jets until he was over sixty). Sergei Dolgushin became my Squadron Commander, and among my fellow pilots were Alexander Shishkin, Vladimir Orekhov and Vladimir Lutsky.

One day a formation of our fighters was returning home from the front line.

The last to land were Ivan Kholodov and Arkady Makarov. As they were approaching their final turn we saw from the ground two Messerschmitt 109s which, one after the other, dived at them. The leader must have been about to open fire when both our fighters turned sharply to face them, and the leading Messerschmitt shot past the Yaks at high speed, without time to aim or fire, and his wingman scrambled up to a safer altitude. Makarov turned back after the German leader and tried to open fire but he had no ammunition left. The 'Messers' climbed up and made off. As Kholodov and Makarov told us on landing, they had spotted the German fighters as soon as they had begun their dive at them, but were putting their evasive manoeuvre off until the last moment to leave the Germans no chance of getting them. Amazing self-possession!

Soon after that all flying officers were ordered to report to the regiment head-quarters. As soon as we had assembled outside the staff dugout we saw a Junkers 88 heading right towards us about 2,000 metres up. The German must have been unaware of the airfield below him until our AA machine-gun opened fire. The Junkers then entered a turn for a bombing course intending to drop his load on us. By that time our pair in readiness had taken off, but the German did not seem to mind; he knew he could quickly hide in the clouds above him. He levelled out and we clearly saw six bombs separating from the aircraft's body. Somebody shouted 'Take cover!' (better late than never!) and everyone scurried away. I made it to the dugout, while many others, including Vasily Stalin, dived head-first into snowdrifts. Luckily, apart from three slightly damaged aircraft, there was no harm done and the Junkers climbed up into the cloud and was gone. The episode ended in a general burst of somewhat nervous laughter, the pilots pointing at one another, covered in snow from the waist up.

On another occasion, when our two formations were away from home, we saw three Junkers 88s flying towards us, also apparently surprised to see a fighter base below. The sky was clear and there was nowhere they could hide. We always used to have two or three aircraft standing by, and mine was among them that day. I ran up to it but my mechanic said it was not ready. I made a dash for the neigh-bouring squadron, but none of their machines were home. No. 3 Squadron's aircraft were parked at the far end of the airfield, but I could not make it there on foot in time. There was nothing I could do but walk back in disappointment. It was only Volodya Orekhov who took off and he climbed up to attack one of the Junkers 88s, which dived to low-level flight. Volodya went after him and set him on fire. At that time one of our groups returned home from the front line and the fate of the other two bombers was decided even as we were watching. One of them was shot down by Vladimir Lutsky, one of the regiment's best pilots and a very good friend. He was always ready to rush to a fellow pilot's aid, even if it meant turning away from the German he was attacking.

At a veterans' get-together many years later, my former mechanic confessed that he had lied to me about my aircraft on Vasily's orders, which he dared not disobey. Thinking back on that episode, I remembered that I had seen Vasily near my machine as I was running to it – our squadron was parked close to the staff dugout – but I had never given it a thought at the time. Vasily did not allow me to take part in the raids to the front line. After the war he told me that he had

had his father's express orders about it, but I could not have known it at the time and was waiting and hoping to be allowed. Apparently Stalin had given Vasily a piece of his mind after Timur Frunze's death had been followed by my brother's. As a result I flew on patrol and cover missions around the airfield area.

One day, as I wandered in the direction of the parked bus where we used to spend time between sorties, I saw a fighter flying very low towards me. It looked like the La-5 except for its fin, which seemed too high, and then it dawned on me that it was a Focke-Wulf 190. The German was coming at a height of fifteen metres or so, heading for the aircraft of the flight in readiness. Their pilots were already starting their engines. The German banked and, on seeing our machines with spinning air-screws, added power and came even lower than before. He must have been a young pilot who had lost his leader and was desperate to get away, and get away he did for he was out of our fighters' reach before they could take off.

We had several losses: Aniskin and Alexandrov were shot down, and so was Kholzunov from our squadron – he went after a pair of Focke-Wulfs, failing to hear the Squadron Commander who was forbidding him to chase them because he had spotted another group of German fighters on the way to attack him. In one of the regiment's severest air battles two of our fighters rammed the enemy's aircraft. Ivan Kholodov, as he came to Makarov's rescue, had to ram the Messerschmitt that was attacking him; his own damaged aircraft entered a spin after the ram, and Kholodov barely had time to bail out. The other ramming was done by Nikolai Koval, who then half-landed, half-fell into a river in his uncontrollable aircraft (Koval was severely wounded but survived).

I also remember the occasion when Vasily Stalin took off for what I believe was his one and only combat sortie (although by some accounts he made two). He went with a large formation to the front-line area where they had a fight with German fighters. The group included the veteran pilots who had joined the regiment together with Vasily. On their way home they failed to find our base because of bad weather and landed in Staraya Toropa, from where they returned on the next day.

One day Lieutenant-Colonel Vlasov and I were ordered to intercept a German reconnaissance aircraft that was moving at high altitude. After we had climbed to seven thousand metres or so, Vlasov told me on the radio that he could not go any higher due to oxygen deficiency and ordered me to follow him home. The reason was that all our aircraft were stripped of their oxygen equipment to reduce the weight. The maximum altitude at which a pilot can function normally without oxygen is five thousand metres, or so the official standards have it. I still seemed to be feeling all right when Vlasov's order came, but I knew I would not last much longer either. After that episode, two of the regiment's fighters received their oxygen equipment back, to provide for an occasion of this kind.

A German captive pilot was brought to the regiment one day. He had been shot down in an air combat, and the Iron Cross with Oak Leaves he was wearing told us he was a distinguished ace. I could more or less speak German, so Deputy CO Babkov (Vasily was away at the time) made me interpret for him while he was questioning the German. His name was Major Hans Han, and he was a group commander. He appeared totally composed and self-assured. Only once, when Babkov raised his voice after one of his answers, did he seem to go tense for a moment. One of the questions he was asked concerned his view of the Germans' defeat at Stalingrad. He said that it had been a temporary failure and that soon his army would be on the offensive again. According to him he had shot down 108 aircraft, forty-three of which had been in western Europe and the rest on the Eastern Front. He obviously thought it beneath his dignity to have been defeated by another fighter pilot in air combat and insisted that he had been shot down by an anti-aircraft gun. Describing his last combat (which was against the fighters of another regiment, our close neighbour) he claimed to have personally shot down two aircraft. That, as we knew, was indeed the number of aircraft lost in that battle, but we also knew that there had been another five German fighters taking part. The German's words, therefore, indirectly supported the belief shared by many of our pilots that when a distinguished German ace was taking part in an air combat the rest of his formation were expected only to cover and support him rather than attack.

Many sources quote very large numbers of personal victories for some World War Two German aces. Thus, Erich Hartmann is supposed to have shot down 352 aircraft, Gerhard Barchorn 301, and Gunther Ralle 275. To compare, the two best-known wartime Soviet aces, Ivan Kozhedub and Alexander Pokryshkin, had sixty-two and fifty-nine respectively, and the best American pilot of the time, as far as I knew, had forty shot-down aircraft to his credit. The high numbers of victories attributed to German pilots can hardly be taken for granted. Hartmann's first victory refers to November 1942; just before the Battle of Kursk in July 1943 he had a record of eighteen victories; by August 1943 he had ninety. This means that the majority of his 352 victories fell on the last third of the entire war period, when the Soviet Air Force had already gained superiority over the Luftwaffe. Another piece of indirect evidence of the inaccuracy of these figures is the entry in the war diary of the German First Air Fleet made in March 1943. According to this entry, the number of German victories was several times larger than the actual number of aircraft lost during that time by the Soviet Thirteenth Air Army, which was opposing the Luftwaffe's First Fleet in that area: 357 quoted victories against forty-four actual losses!*

German pilots used camera guns for recording their victories in the air. A camera gun was activated by the same trigger as the machine-gun and it filmed the target in the sight reticle and the actual hit. However, not every aircraft that was hit by machine-gun fire went down. Many of our pilots safely returned home with shell- and bullet-holes in their machines, which were then 'patched up', and continued flying. The Germans must have counted them as shot-down aircraft. True, each aircraft shot down by a German pilot had to be entered by him on a special card with another pilot's confirmation of his victory. Confirmation from the ground was also required. Yet during the final period of the war, when the

---

* I take these statistics from D. Khazanov in *Sovershenno secretno*, No. 11, 1991.

German troops were on retreat, these requirements could hardly have been consistently observed. Our pilots, on the other hand, were invariably required to supply confirmation from the ground, and when an enemy's aircraft was destroyed in the enemy's rear such confirmation had to be provided by other pilots, particularly by the crews of the escorted bombers or attack aeroplanes. Nevertheless, the rate of the German aces' personal victories, even if it is lower than stated, is impressive. They were, indeed, highly competent, experienced and courageous pilots who were obviously greatly valued and cared for by the German military command.

The tactics of military action also played their role. Our pilots, under the pressure of high-ranking ground commanders, were required to stay above the troops they were covering for as long as possible. This could only be done at low fuel consumption rates, i.e. at low speed. It made our fighters an easy target for the German aces, who would attack, diving at them from the sun side at high speed and immediately climbing up again. Those 'hunters' usually avoided dog-fights when they could. Their tactics misled many of our pilots, especially at the beginning of the war, into believing that the German fighters were faster aircraft than their Russian counterparts. As AF General George Bayevsky recalled, when the pilots of the élite No. 5 Fighter Regiment of the Guards were allowed to cut down on the time spent over the river crossings and started flying at high speeds, the Germans immediately lost their advantage. The illusion of the Messerschmitts' superior speed was dispelled.

But not every pilot in the Luftwaffe was up to that very high mark. R. F. Toliver and T. W. Constable, describing the career of the most distinguished German aces in their book *Fighter Aces of the Luftwaffe*, point out that they started off among thousands of obscure Luftwaffe pilots who lost their lives without a single combat victory to their credit. In another of their books, *Holt Hartmann von Himmel*, Toliver and Constable express their high opinion of Soviet wartime pilots, especially those who belonged to the Fighter Regiments of the Guards. They say they were the best Russian pilots of the true fighter-pilot type – aggressive, fearless, and intelligent tacticians who flew the best available aircraft and who surpassed the fighter pilots of the Allied forces in the number of their victories.

Shortly after we took our first German prisoner another German fighter pilot, an Unteroffizier who had bailed out, was captured and delivered to our base. We let him sit in the cockpit of a Yak, curious about his opinion. I was standing in the group of our pilots on the wing and interpreting for them. Somebody joked, 'See that he doesn't start the engine and make off!' The German was surprised that there was no canopy over the cockpit, saying it must feel very cold flying without it (at that time our canopies were removed altogether). He was also amazed to see that the Yak's oil cooler flap and its trimming tab were mechani-cally controlled by a trim wheel. In the Messerschmitt both these devices were electrically operated. We asked him about his senior officer Hans Han, but he said he knew nothing about him, for the Unteroffizieren in the Luftwaffe did not mix with officers. It was our turn to be surprised – they were all doing the same job flying together, weren't they?

Apropos of that trim wheel, when flying patrols on air alert missions I took to increasing the screw pitch by a few turns, knowing that the reduction of engine speed helped to save on petrol. Other pilots did not do it, either because they did not care how much petrol they used or else for fear that they would not have time to turn the wheel back to the fine pitch when maximum power might be needed. In debriefing, the regiment engineer once said approvingly that there was more petrol left in my tanks after each flight than in anybody else's, but my 'innovation' nearly failed me again. One day I forgot to turn the wheel back after a landing at coarse pitch, and at the next take-off I could not gather the unstick speed and fell behind my leader. As it dawned on me what the matter was, I barely had time to turn the wheel back, after which the engine speed built up and I finally took off. In fact, even landing at low engine speed was a risky business, for it could cause problems if I had to go around.

At the regiment Vasily did not give up his Moscow habit of late-night drinking parties. They took place in the largest room of the log hut in which he, two other commanding officers and I were billeted, and often lasted until midnight. My way of trying to cut them short was to declare that it was late and I was going to bed, but it hardly ever helped; I would be trying to fall asleep in the next room to the hum of their endless half-drunken conversation. We pilots had to be up and ready at the crack of dawn, whereas Vasily could afford to sleep in.

One day we took off in a group to escort a transport aeroplane in which some big-wig military official was travelling. We landed at Kalinin, refuelled and then flew homewards. Suddenly my engine died and I started gliding, looking out for somewhere to land, but soon the engine came to life again. In a few minutes it happened again, and again, and each time I half-expected it would not restart. Finally, when it failed for the fourth time, I saw an airfield to the right and I turned in for a landing approach. The airport later turned out to belong to Baidukov's division.* I was nervous and my inexperience must have told too, for I did my finals too close in. Overshooting seemed inevitable, for as things were I could not touch down anywhere before the middle of the strip and thus risked finishing my landing-run in the thick forest at its end. All I could do was open the throttle on the off-chance that the engine would restart, which luckily it did. I made a circle over the forest, praying aloud that it would not fail again, and it did not – I performed a normal final turn and landed. Another evidence of my special luck: a head-on run into that forest would have been no joke.

When the Spas-Demensk operation was over, our regiment was transferred to a base near Ostashkov for a respite, after which we left our aircraft behind to be used by another regiment and took off for Moscow in a number of transport aeroplanes. Later I heard of a tragic accident in which Vasily was involved. He took a group of officers fishing to some place near the Ostashkov base. The way they chose to do it was stunning fish with aircraft rockets. The regiment armament engineer started throwing rockets into the river, with the fuses set for delay. Either due to his own error or for some other reason, one of the rockets exploded

* G. F. Baidukov was V. Chkalov's co-pilot in his flight to the US over the North Pole in 1937.

in his hand. The engineer was torn to pieces and Alexander Kotov (a young pilot and Hero of the Soviet Union) was heavily injured in the spine. His flying career was over, and he has used a walking stick ever since. Vasily Stalin was dismissed as Regiment Commander on his father's orders and remained without a position for some time.

I have earlier mentioned Nikolai Vlasov, and I would like here to tell his tragic story. An instructor pilot at Kacha before the war, Vlasov began his combat career in a MiG-3, in which he shot down about a dozen German aircraft. In the action against the Germans who were advancing towards the Don, a Soviet dive-bomber was shot down over the German lines. One of the three crew members managed to get back through the front line and said that his wounded commander was being hidden by some villagers in the German rear. Vlasov crossed the front line in a low-speed liaison U-2 aircraft, found the wounded officer and brought him home. For this, in combination with his personal victories, he was made a Hero of the Soviet Union. He was twenty-six or so at the time.

In the summer of 1943 Vlasov was sent on an AF inspection mission in a light UT-2 trainer to Leningrad. The next thing we heard about him, from Vasily Stalin, was that he had defected and was serving on the German side. It was hard to believe – everyone knew Vlasov as a thoroughly good, brave and trustworthy man – but sooner or later, for lack of evidence to the contrary, it was accepted as fact. It was only in the 1960s that an article in *Pravda* relayed Nikolai Vlasov's true story. He had lost his bearings on the way to Leningrad because of bad weather and by accident had landed on the enemy's airfield. The Germans packed him off to a concentration camp. At a veterans' get-together in 1995, fifty years after the end of the war, I met a retired dive-bomber pilot, V. Gorshkov, who had been Vlasov's fellow prisoner in that camp. It was a special camp for captive flying officers in Poland. As Gorshkov told me, confirming the news-paper article, Vlasov had escaped from the camp, hiding under the body of a van, but he was caught and two days later brought back and severely beaten. He was then transported to another camp, where he was shot in his second attempt to escape.

Nikolai Vlasov's story brings to mind a remark made by Vasily Stalin in connection with his half-brother Yakov (Stalin's son by his first wife). In 1941 Yakov, an artillery officer, was taken prisoner, and what Vasily said about him was: 'What a fool – couldn't shoot himself!' I was aware even then that Vasily was echoing his father's view, whose attitude to our prisoners-of-war was no secret to me. What I could not see was why every captured officer or soldier had to be regarded as a traitor, whatever the circumstances of his capture. Because of Stalin's attitude the Soviet Union did not sign the Hague convention, and as a result our prisoners-of-war were treated by the Nazis far more cruelly than PoWs from any other army in the anti-Hitler coalition, and so most of them did not survive the camps. Most of those who did ended up in camps in their own country.

Over the past few years I have repeatedly met up with a friend of my brother Alexei, the well-known pilot Grigory Dolnikov. He was also shot down in the war and taken prisoner. What happened to him suggested to Mikhail Sholokhov the plot of his *Story of a True Man*. Dolnikov managed to escape from the Germans and return to his regiment, after which he shot down about a dozen enemy aircraft. Nevertheless, when the war ended he was suspended as a pilot and thoroughly 'checked out'. It was only twenty years after the war that he was decorated with the long overdue Golden Star of a Hero. In the book *Holt Hartmann von Himmel*, Toliver and Constable tell the story of Eric Hartmann's capture and subsequent escape, after which he was decorated and promoted – something directly opposite to what happened to Soviet officers and men returning from German captivity.

CHAPTER 8

No.12 Fighter Regiment
of the Guards

After the North-West Front our regiment was resting at the Lubertsy base near Moscow. One day Vasily arrived (it was before his dismissal), called all pilots to attention and read out the new regiment's lists. I was not on them and could not understand what it meant. Later I was informed that I had been posted to No. 12 Fighter Regiment of the Guards, part of Moscow's air defence force.

This force, apart from the AAA, consisted of No. 6 Fighter Air Corps equipped with the MiGs and Yaks; No. 16 Regiment also had Spitfires, and 28 Regiment Aircobras. Nos. 1 and 3 Squadrons in No. 12 Regiment flew ordinary Yak-9s with a ceiling of just over 10,000 metres, while No. 2 Squadron was assigned MiG-3s and the high-altitude modification of the Yak-9, equipped with a supercharger. Both had a ceiling a little over 12,000 metres. Nos. 2 and 3 Squadrons' mission was to cover Moscow itself, while No. 1 was based on an advanced airfield and defended the front communication routes. No. 12 Regiment of the Corps was based on the Central Airfield in Moscow, but we also used the airfields at Klin, Kubinka, Podolsk and Vyazma, which in 1943 was in the rear of the Western Front. The Regiment CO, Lieutenant-Colonel Konstantin Marenkov, was an experienced pilot and Vasily Stalin's former flying instructor. One of his squadron commanders was Alexei Katrich, who was made Hero of the Soviet Union for the first ever high-altitude ram.

It was not always possible to distinguish an accidental collision from a deliberate ram, but Katrich in his MiG-3 had neatly chopped off the elevator of a German bomber with his air-screw and returned home with minimal damage to his own machine. In 1943, together with Konstantin Kriukov, he shot down the very last of the German aeroplanes that ventured close to Moscow. Alexei Katrich survived the war and retired after a long and distinguished career in the air force as a colonel-general. At a recent veterans' meeting Katrich told me the following episode. In 1943 he shot down a Junkers 88 near Smolensk and made a note of its landing place. He returned to it later in a liaison U-2 and landed by it. He saw three surviving crew members in the cockpit, all heavily wounded (one of them was calling for his mother between moans), and regretted having returned to the site. He could not see them as his enemies at that moment; they were what he was himself: just very young soldiers at war, and their fighting was over. He asked the peasant women who came to look at the fallen Junkers to take the Germans to their village and try to cure their wounds. The women agreed. What happened to those German pilots afterwards General Katrich does not know.

Distinct from flying officers in the air force, the pilots of the Moscow air defence force often had to fly in bad weather, and therefore had to be quite good at instrument flying. In our flights we would often break through the clouds and fly with only the gyro bank-and-turn indicator (apart from the performance instruments) to rely on for our attitude orientation. Later our aircraft were equipped with radio half-compasses and American artificial horizons, and flying in the clouds became a much easier business. We often had to take off with a very low ceiling and cut through the clouds in close formations of two. I have kept my logbook of the time, with my weather minima recorded in it: visibility one kilometre, the ceiling 100 metres in daylight and 2 × 200 metres at night-time (in supersonic jets such minima were achieved only towards the late 1970s, when instrument landing systems were used; but of course the wartime Yaks had a much lower approach speed). In clear weather at night we would also normally fly in pairs. Such was our pattern of flying over Smolensk, for example, which we covered from Luftwaffe bomber raids after its recovery from the Germans.

I was appointed senior flying officer of No. 3 Squadron, which was commanded by Captain Maxim Tsyganov. On my arrival I heard about a rather remarkable episode in his war career. He had been shot down in a dog-fight and taken prisoner by the Germans, who locked him up in a wooden shed. He managed to break a board in its side at night and made off through the front line. When he reached his regiment he was promptly deprived of his party membership card, just because of that single day spent as a German prisoner. But at least the Regiment Commander managed to insist that he be allowed to fly as before. After a while it was decided that Tsyganov had 'proved his loyalty', and he was reinstated as a party member.

It was in that squadron that I first began flying at night. The Klin airfield, which was our station, was very sparingly lit at landing: there was one projector that threw diffused light on the touch-down strip and one searchlight at the approach end of the runway, with its beam 'lying' along its length. Taking off was done in pitch darkness, except for an ordinary lamp at the departure end of the runway which served as a beacon for direction on the run. At night we would fly from the Klin airfield (some ninety kilometres north-west of Moscow) on patrol. The area around Moscow was divided into sectors, and our squadron was responsible for the western and north-western sectors. One night, when I was in a formation of two with Tsyganov, very low rain clouds overtook us as we reached our sector near Istra, west of Moscow. Tsyganov ordered me to follow him home, but I could no longer see him, so I turned and proceeded on my own. The ceiling was about 100 metres and it was raining. I had to come down almost to 'hedge-hopping' level and headed north-east, looking out for the Leningrad motorway, which would guide me home to Klin. There was a danger of missing the motorway and shooting past it, for the car headlights were covered with special screens which made their light almost invisible from above. But I was travelling so low that I managed to identify the motorway by the faint light of the headlights and followed it to Klin. On the approach to Klin the clouds were a bit higher and it was not raining. I had no trouble finding the airfield and landed. The CO had landed shortly before me. Soon after the end of the war, Tsyganov and I went out to dinner together. Remembering that sortie, he said, 'That was when I realised you were a pilot all right. I had been sure you would not make it home.' It felt great to be praised, even in that understated way, by the usually reticent Tsyganov.

In the winter of 1944 I was transferred to No. 1 Squadron and appointed Flight Commander. The Squadron Commander at that time was Konstantin Kriukov (his predecessor, Alexei Katrich, had been promoted to the regiment second-in-command), with whom I later became good friends. After I had reported for duty, Kriukov said, 'Come on, let's go up together. I'll see if you're any good in formation aerobatics.' I looked up at the sky. The clouds were hanging low, without a single blue patch in between, and I doubted we would go up. However, I said nothing and walked over to my machine. We took off in formation and climbed up to the ceiling, which was at about 200 metres. I was sure there would be no aerobatics and we would go home, yet Kriukov entered a series of steeply-banked turns, vigorously rolling from right to left and back again. Being as I was five or six metres away from his wing, I could not afford to take my eyes off his machine even for a second. Every time I happened to be between Kriukov and the ground in a turn, I would throw a quick look at the ground; it was so close I almost seemed to be touching it with my wing. Incidentally, the 'aerial show' was going on over Kuntsevo, where both Kriukov and his future wife lived. My impression afterwards was that I had 'passed the test'; later I always felt he had confidence in me.

The squadron was stationed at Dvoevka aerodrome, about 200 kilometres west of Moscow. It was near Vyazma, an unfortunate, devastated town which was a sad sight from above. Once Kriukov and I were returning to Dvoevka from the Central Airfield in Moscow, and on the approach to Vyazma (still at high altitude) I heard a radio message from the ground to the effect that a Junkers was on its way to a nearby railway station. I felt excited at the prospect of a chase. We dived down towards the station at the 'never-exceed speed' and immediately saw a two-engine aircraft ahead of us. We came down below it and started closing in a shallow climb. My forefinger on the trigger, I suddenly thought that my target did not look like a Junkers 88. I had barely thought so when Kriukov's voice in my headset said, 'Hold your fire! It's a friend.' We flew past it – it was a Douglas A-20 Boston, an American bomber received by the Soviet Union through the lend-lease agreement. Its crew must have been blissfully unaware that we had very nearly opened fire, and somebody else in our place might easily have done it without thinking.

At Dvoevka we pilots took turns at readiness, i.e., actually sitting strapped-in in the cockpits ready to take off, a pair of fighters on stand-by at all times. We would start the engines at a signal flare and receive our heading and altitude detail over the radio after the take-off. Getting off to chase away German reconnaissance planes was almost a routine. Chase them away was more or less all we could effectively do; it was only once that one of them got 'caught' and was shot down, by the squadron second-in-command Gavriil Fastovets, a seasoned pilot who had begun the war in the obsolete I-16. That Junkers 88 remained the only victory on our regiment record for the summer of 1944.

Fastovets, an easy-going and cheerful person, was also a parachutist with some six hundred jumps to his credit. For a long time after the war he continued as a pilot in the air defence force and eventually became chief of parachute training and a colonel, without ever ceasing to fly. Many years after my wartime service under him I began regular professional (and social) contact with his son, Aviard Fastovets, a test pilot of the MiG Design Company whom everyone called Alec. In the mid-1970s Alec got involved in a unique incident. While performing a structure-strength test flight in a MiG-23 from the AF testing centre at Akhtubinsk, he pulled the maximum 8G load at Mach number 0.85, which proved too much for the wings and they broke off. In the second or two it took his aircraft to disintegrate in the air, Alec managed to yank out the ejector D-ring. Once on firm ground again, he made himself comfortable on the canopy of his parachute and turned his emergency radio beacon on for the rescue helicopter. The AF Research and Flight Test Institute Commander, General Gaidayenko, who was in that helicopter, did not even put his radio direction-finder on, certain that the pilot could not possibly have survived such an accident. Nevertheless, Alec was found and was safely brought home to the base, where there was no end of amazement and joy at his miraculous deliverance. In the 1980s Alec Fastovets became a Hero of the Soviet Union. He died in 1991 of a stroke, surviving his father by just one year.

If I remember correctly, the Moscow air defence force was equipped with its first ground-based air surveillance radars as early as 1941. There were both Soviet and British radars. Initially the radars were used only to warn about approaching aircraft and not as guidance devices. Radars began to be widely used to guide fighters to the enemy aircraft in 1943. We had such a ground-based radar at Dvoevka. The officer on duty at the command post would watch the radar returns of the enemy aircraft and of our own fighters, passing the data (heading and altitude) on to the fighter pilot. Eventually it was noticed that German 'scouts' were changing their course to deviate from the parameters received by our interception fighters from the ground-based radar. Our conclusion was that the Germans had in-flight radio operators who could understand Russian. As a rule they came in cloudy weather and were very good at hiding in the clouds at the first sign of danger to themselves.

Once, as I was climbing up with my wingman behind me to the 10,000 metre height detailed from the ground, and some time after the altimeter needle had reached the 7,000 mark, I suddenly woke up from a kind of drowsiness that had stealthily come upon me to see that the altitude had for some reason dropped to about 4,000 metres. I climbed up again, and the same thing happened. I reported it to the radar control post. They realised there was something wrong with my oxygen equipment and ordered me home. My wingman chose not to stay behind on his own and followed me back. I was still feeling dizzy from the shortage of oxygen, and my brain was dull and lethargic; this continued until I came down to a lower height. Back at the aerodrome it was revealed that the oxygen hose had got jammed under my seat.

On another occasion, after I had taken off at a signal flare with Yuri Baranov as my wingman and had received my heading and altitude, the German, having obviously overheard those instructions, started making off. I was chasing him at top power, and Baranov began dropping behind (his machine had a pretty old engine). After a while I heard over the radio that the Junkers was about twenty kilometres ahead of me and that they would soon lose us out of 'sight', for we were approaching the radar range limit. I was still heading straight on, expecting to see the German any minute, but there was no one in front of me (or behind, for that matter, as Baranov had turned for home). The German must have heard the last transmission too and shifted off his heading (or else was hiding in the clouds below me).

After another ten minutes or so I realised there was no chance I would catch the Junkers. There was nothing for me to do except return home, especially since I knew I must have got far beyond the front line into the enemy rear. I turned back and flew for some time without descending, hiding above a thick layer of solid clouds until I decided it was safe to come down. I cut through the clouds, coming down to 300 metres and continued to travel east. Soon I saw a railway station and descended to contour flying to be able to read its name. I went there and back along the rails three times but could not make out the words. As the boys told me later, I should have approached the signpost head-on instead of flying past it, then I would have read it easily. Luckily I did not have to worry about petrol: my machine was a five-tank modification of the Yak with nearly three hours' flight's worth of petrol in them.

I was still too far from home for the radio half-compass or the radio set to be of any use. It suddenly occurred to me to tune to the main national radio station broadcasting from Moscow which, I hoped, would be powerful enough to be heard. Indeed it was; my radio compass needle swayed away from the zero mark. I adjusted the nose to the needle and determined the radio station to be in the east. This meant that I was west of Moscow, and if I headed to the south-east I would eventually hit upon the Minsk motorway (running out of Moscow to the south-west) – that is, if I managed not to overshoot it. I had not even reached the motorway when I heard my own radio station in the headset and soon saw familiar terrain. At that moment the radar screen on the ground showed the mark of a moving aircraft, a tiny twinkling speck of light, and I was asked to make a turn. As the speck turned aside as well, the ground post was assured it was me the radar showed, and I was given the heading home. By that time I had picked up my bearings completely and knew my own way.

This episode gave me confidence in my navigating abilities, and I never lost my bearings again in the future, even though there were some difficult situations to cope with. In fact one of them followed shortly after that flight. Alexei Katrich and I were flying in a pair from Dvoevka to Moscow. Because of very low clouds ahead we had to come down to contour flying, and soon got a radio command to land at Kubinka because of deteriorating weather conditions. I looked side-ways at my leader, who waved a hand by his ear; 'We did not hear anything!' was the meaning of the gesture. I followed him on and soon recognised a road junction near a village that I knew. I realised that Katrich was going the wrong way, so I overtook him and rocked my wings to invite him to follow me. We were flying over the area that had been familiar to me since childhood, and I followed the

Anastas Mikoyan, Stepan's father, with Chairman Mao Tse-tung in February 1949.

Marshal Tito and his wife, with Anastas Mikoyan on a Soviet cruiser at Sochi on the Black Sea in 1956

From left to right: Aircraft designer Artem Mikoyan, Anastas and Alexei Mikoyan
— then a major.

During Anastas Mikoyan's visit to the USA in 1959. Left to right: President
Eisenhower, Ambassador Menshikov, Anastas and John Dulles.

Father and Mother: Anastas and Ashkhen Mikoyan in 1960.

Anastas Mikoyan with his great-grandchildren, (left to right) Alexander, Alla and Vanya in 1978, shortly before his death.

Lieut. Stepan Mikoyan shortly after graduating from the pilots' school in 1941.

Stepan Mikoyan and his wife Eleonora, son Volodiya and daughter Aschen in 1950.

Anastas Mikoyan, Nikita Khrushchev and Stepan, photographed in 1963 at the Black Sea resort of Pitzunda.

Stepan and his wife Eleonora with their grandson Alexander in 1972.

Air Force Major-General Stepan Mikoyan in 1980.

Akhtubinsk Air Base — from left to right: Visiting test-pilot and cosmonaut Lieut-General George Beregovoi, third Major-General Stepan Mikoyan, Second-in-Command of the Test Institute and fourth, Colonel-General Ivan Gaidayenko, the Test Institute's Commander.

The author in 1989

Stepan with the Chief
Test Pilot of Sukhoi,
Vladimir Iliushin, in the
1980s.

Stepan Mikoyan receiving his certificate as an Honorary Fellow of the Society of Experimental Test Pilots at the Beverly Hilton Hotel in the USA in September 1997.

Aschen Mikoyan, Stepan's daughter and also translator of this autobiography, in the cockpit of a Lockheed F-16 Fighting Falcon at the USAF Edwards Air Base in 1997. Stepan discusses the fighter's attributes with its American pilot.

roads, which were winding close to where our dacha was, past Arkhangelskoye, then to Tushino (where the visibility was already better), and finally we landed safely on the Central Airfield in Moscow. Later I heard that Katrich was told off for not landing at Kubinka as ordered.

Another time, as I was descending on the way home from a sortie, I switched the supercharger from the second stage to the first at 6,000 metres, as it had to be done, and a few seconds later the engine suddenly died on me. Fuel pressure was zero, so I decided that the fuel pump had failed and began a dead-stick approach. While I was gliding down before the base turn I was trying to figure out at what altitude I should begin making it so as to touch down at the top of the landing strip. I started the turn at a thousand metres and came down to the final at 500 metres, dropped the wheels just before the flare and landed plumb on the landing 'T'. At the end of the landing run I turned right and the aircraft stopped. I reported to Major Katrich, who was with the regiment engineer at the time. Katrich praised me for the landing, while the engineer went to have a look at my machine and then called me to it. I looked into the cockpit and saw that the supercharger lever was at the second stage and the fuel tap was closed. I had cut off the fuel supply myself by getting hold of the wrong lever! The cockpit layout was partly responsible for it too; the levers of such seriously different functions should not be placed so close together or have such similar shapes. Later, I frequently had to deal with such issues as a test pilot; back in 1944 the incident was taken as a lesson: in all aircraft of our regiment the fuel cut-off taps were fastened with elastic bands to prevent their accidental activation.

In the meantime another of my brothers, Alexei (Alyosha), became a pilot too. He had just begun his tenth year at secondary school when he left to become a student at the flying school at Vyazniki. On finishing his course in the autumn of 1943 he was posted to my squadron in No. 12 Regiment, and eventually he began flying with us at Dvoevka. (He passed his exams for the secondary school certificate after the war.)

One day our Regiment Commissar, Lieutenant-Colonel Gvozdev, was returning to Dvoevka from the Central Airfield in Moscow. While moving the landing gear control lever to extend the wheels, he must have accidentally touched the magneto selector with his glove cuff and cut the engine off. Unaware of what was wrong, Gvozdev entered a turn so as to land on the runway, and overpulled the stick. The aircraft went into a spin and crashed. The boys, including my brother, hopped into the squadron lorry and hurried to the site, certain that it was I who had crashed, for just a few minutes earlier I had taken off on a ferrying mission to Moscow. Not knowing that Gvozdev had been on his way from Moscow, they thought I had turned back home because of some failure.

Towards the end of 1944 a group of our fighters escorted a transport aircraft with a high-ranking general on board to Shaulai near Riga. My brother, flying in my machine, was in that group. On landing, right after the touch-down, one of his wheels suddenly pivoted sideways and the aircraft jerked to the left. Alexei applied the right brake, trying to straighten the run, and the machine nosed over. As it turned out later the safety wire had come off, and a bolt fastening the traverse bracket (the device responsible for the position of the wheel) had unscrewed. Alyosha's spine was injured and also his face, which had struck the gunsight. After a while I found out that the regiment security officer (from the NKVD) was harassing Chudakov, my mechanic, trying to accuse him of 'malicious intent'. At the first opportunity I told my father about it, and the mechanic was left alone.

Back from hospital, Alyosha continued to fly despite some lingering effects of his injury. After the war he graduated from the Air Force Academy and began his service as a military pilot and commanding officer, first at Kubinka as a fighter regiment second-in-command and then as its CO, then in Belorussia, where he also commanded a fighter regiment. After his graduation from the General Staff Academy he commanded a division in the Far North and then in East Germany, where he was eventually promoted to Air Corps Commander. After East Germany he was second-in-command of an air army and was then appointed Commander of the Air Force of the Turkestan military district, a post he held for seven years. Throughout his career as an air force commander he continued to fly jet fighters, mostly MiG-19s and MiG-21s. During the last several years of his life he was Deputy Commander of the Air Force ATC Directorate. A month after he retired he died of a heart attack, a day before his sixty-first birthday. He has been gone a long time, but I still hear kind words about him from those who knew him as a first-class pilot, as a brave commander and as somebody who never neglected the needs of his garrison and the people who served and lived in it. He was extremely sociable and had a great many friends, and an even greater circle of acquaintances from many walks of life. He was often approached with various requests, and he invariably did all he could to help.

For the covering and patrol work in which No. 1 Squadron had been engaged in the summer of 1944, its entire flying personnel was decorated: the Squadron Commander received the Order of the Patriotic War of the 2nd Degree, and all others the Red Star Orders. I am mentioning this in connection with the arrival at the regiment of Lev (or Leva, as all his friends called him) Bulganin, son of the Deputy Defence Minister Nikolai Bulganin. Leva had time to do only two or three sorties when he was unexpectedly decorated with the prestigious Order of the Patriotic War of the 1st Degree. Everyone was surprised, including Leva himself, who was also awfully embarrassed and never wore the order in the regiment.

Unfortunately Leva was not averse to rather serious drinking, which affected my brother Alexei's career and in the end cut Leva's own life short (he died at the age of fifty). In 1954, Alexei and Leva accidentally ran into each other in Moscow and went to a restaurant to celebrate the birth of Alyosha's daughter. After a few drinks over a meal – all perfectly respectable at that stage – they parted company to go home. At least Alexei went home; Leva apparently went on to some place for more drinking. He then made his way home with some difficulty, hardly fit to be seen by any member of his family, let alone his father, by that time already the Defence Minister. As ill fate would have it it was his father who was there and still awake when Leva returned. Having ascertained who

Leva's drinking companion had been that night, Bulganin ordered a commission set up to closely inspect Alexei's regiment. Up to that time the regiment had been considered one of the exemplary units in the force, and Alexei himself had been repeatedly commended for his service. It had been Alexei's regiment that flew their MiG-15s over Red Square in military parades on state holidays, with Alexei himself flying as the leader of the formation. He had even received the Red Banner Order for his regiment's performance in these parades. Nevertheless, briefed by the Defence Minister the commission came up with conclusions directly opposite to the recent commendations. Alexei was dismissed from his commanding position and packed off to a regiment stationed in Belorussia as its second-in-command. However, he soon distinguished himself again and was appointed the regiment's CO. As for that incident with Leva, I admit that Alexei was not without fault, for Leva's weakness was well known to him, yet his punishment was harsh.

In 1943 our family had suffered another trauma which had begun as somebody else's tragedy. Volodya Shakhurin, the sixteen-year-old son of the Minister of Aviation Industry, killed his girlfriend, daughter of the newly appointed Soviet ambassador to Mexico, K. Umansky. Being passionately in love with the girl he could not bear her to leave, so he first shot her and then himself. All this happened within seconds as they were coming down the steps on the side of the Bolshoi Kamenny Bridge over the Moscow river. My sixteen-year-old brother Vanya, who was a friend of Volodya's, was walking ahead of the young couple when it happened. The pistol that Volodya used belonged to our family. That day he had asked Vanya to let him wear the gun for a while, and my brother, naively unsuspicious, agreed. The NKVD's investigation that followed – hardly through the investigators' own initiative – was promptly endowed with political implications: 'an anti-Soviet youth organisation had been discovered'. Vanya was arrested, and a week later plainclothed NKVD officers came to our dacha for my youngest brother, fourteen-year-old Sergo. The son of General Khmelnitsky (Voroshilov's ADC) was also arrested, as was Stalin's wife's nephew and a few other boys of about the same age. At first the 'conspiracy' case was conducted by the well-known investigator Lev Sheinin, who must have realised it was nothing but a fabrication, for he was not tough or menacing during interrogations and even seemed sympathetic. Sheinin was soon replaced by Vladzimersky (later executed with Beria), whose interrogations were different. Although he did not have the boys beaten up or physically abused in any way, he succeeded in concocting a case against them, all no doubt done with Stalin's knowledge and in accordance with his directives.

My brothers spent over six months each at Lubyanka, in separate cells and without any contact with each other. In fact until his release Vanya was not even aware that Sergo was there too. They first saw each other in the room where my mother was waiting to take them home on the day they were both released. They had both flatly denied participation in any conspiracy and refused to plead guilty; each of them had been pressed to sign a paper to this effect. On leaving prison they were asked again, in threatening terms ('Or else you'll stay here!'), to sign those papers, and they again refused. However, mother told them that our father had instructed them through her to sign what they would be demanded to sign on the way out, and they did. They were both exiled to Stalinabad in Tadzhikistan (now Dushanbe) for a year, where Vanya was allowed to enter an aviation college, while Sergo went to school. Not long before the end of the war their term of exile ended and they returned home.

Before leaving for Central Asia, my brothers had written a joint letter to Stalin in which they assured him of their innocence and of their loyalty to their country. With my father's consent I asked Stalin's daughter Svetlana to pass the letter on to her father. She took the letter from me, and that was the last we heard of it. There was no reaction of any kind on Stalin's part. Many years later my father told us of Stalin's unexpected and alarming reference to my brothers in the late 1940s, when he asked him, completely out of the blue, 'And where are your sons that were convicted?' My father replied that the elder was a student of the Zhukovsky Air Force Academy and the younger an undergraduate at the Foreign Relations Institute. To this Stalin asked, 'And do they deserve to be students of Soviet higher institutions?' My father kept his silence. For some time after that he was sure my brothers would be thrown out of their respective institutions and maybe even arrested again (it was the time of a new wave of purges). However, nothing happened. Perhaps Stalin was distracted by something and forgot about them, which would then be an almost unique instance of forgetfulness on his part. After his death my brothers' convictions were officially expunged, and they received certificates of 'the unjustly convicted', although of course what they had been through could not be compared with the tragic fate and sufferings of the millions of other victims of Stalin's purges.

CHAPTER 9

The Cost of Victory

At this point I would like to digress from my story and share some thoughts and some of my personal observations on that part of World War Two which began for the Soviet Union with Hitler's invasion in June 1941. Something I, and many other people, have been thinking about a lot recently is the role of Stalin in that war. In this chapter, as elsewhere in the book, I must stress that I have made a point of relaying my father's accounts of the episodes in which he had participated or which he had witnessed *the way I heard them from him*, as distinct from the form in which they appeared in his articles on the war published after his death in a historical journal, where many details were glossed over or omitted through 'ideological' editing.

It is well known that since the very early days of 1941 there had been numerous reports and indications coming to the USSR from different sources, yet all to the same effect – that Hitler was preparing to attack the country. These reports naturally differed in their reliability as isolated pieces of intelligence, but even a smaller number of such reports in combination and perfect agreement with one another should have sufficed to show that there was truth in them. Two former officers of the Soviet embassy in Berlin, A. Korotkov (an intelligence officer) and I. Chernyshev (a professional diplomat from the Foreign Office), told me back in the 1950s about the detailed report to the Moscow leadership they had personally written together a month or two before Hitler's invasion. In that report they told of a massive movement of troops in the direction of the Soviet border. Another member of our embassy staff, B. Zhuravlev, recalled in a newspaper article (*Pravda*, 13.4.91) that on 19 June 1941 a secret report had been sent from the embassy to Moscow with the actual date of the invasion – 22 June. Stalin read the telegram on the morning of 21 June.

My father told me that two days before the war he had received a phone call from the harbour master at Riga port (my father in his capacity as Deputy Chairman of the Council of the People's Commissars was in charge of the merchant fleet), who reported that some twenty-five German ships that had been loading and unloading in the harbour had suddenly stopped all work and were preparing to leave. That was something unheard of in any port. The harbour master was asking whether he should detain the ships in harbour or allow them to leave. My father asked him to hold the line and immediately went over to Stalin's office. He reported on the phone call, suggesting that the ships should be detained as their sudden intention to leave was an unambiguous sign of war. Stalin said that if the ships were detained it would give Hitler cause to declare war against us, and gave clear orders not to obstruct their departure in any way. As my father said to me in connection with this episode, every man should have realised, especially against the background of intelligence data to the same effect, that a hasty departure of a large number of German ships could mean only one thing: a war was about to break out in the next few days, or even hours.

Some time towards midnight on the 21st Stalin was informed, in the presence of my father and several other Politburo members, of a German defector, a Feldwebel who had swum across the Dnestr and informed them that the attack was scheduled for the early morning of that very night – four a.m. on 22 June. Still Stalin would not sign the order to call the troops to combat readiness. Both Marshal Timoshenko (Defence Minister) and General Zhukov (Chief of General Staff), who had arrived with urgent late-night reports, insisted on that order. According to my father, many of the Politburo members who were in the room supported the military men. However, instead of the combat readiness order Stalin issued a different one calling for general vigilance and asking Soviet citizens not to yield to provocations.

The list of circumstances, caused by the absence of the combat alert order, which played a tragic role in the war could be very long. Suffice it to say, for example, that many units of the Belorussian military district (on the USSR's western border) had transferred their artillery to training ranges for firing practice. Many officers were on holiday, while many others were allowed to take that 'black' Sunday off. The military aircraft were parked on the airfields in accordance with the peace-time pattern, lined up close together with their wings nearly touching – a perfect target for bombing and strafing! The disastrous result is well known: on the very first day of the Nazi invasion we lost over eight hundred aircraft on the aerodromes in the western parts of the country (to say nothing of the losses in the air). Among them there were many MiG-3s, the most advanced fighters of the day. It was only the Commander-in-Chief of the Navy, Kuznetsov, who defied Stalin's directives by sending a cipher to all five of the Soviet fleets that said 'Immediate combat readiness. Kuznetsov'. All fleets were brought to readiness, and as a result there were almost no losses on the day when war broke out: the very first raid of the German bombers on our naval ports was met with dense anti-aircraft fire.

None of the intelligence reports about Germany's preparations for an attack on the USSR, none of the warnings that came from such sources as Winston Churchill himself or the Soviet intelligence agent Richard Zorge (whose cable from Japan named the exact date of the German invasion) was taken into consideration by Stalin. He regarded them as deliberate dissemination of false information by the Germans, and according to him the order of the day was 'not to react to provocation'. He forbade all preparations for military action 'so as not to trigger off a war'. Stalin's attitude to intelligence data reflected his extreme mistrust of people. In his opinion everyone was capable of deceit or treason. Very shortly before the German attack he ordered a recall of resident agents from abroad, i.e., those who had been sending alarming reports, in his own words 'to grind them into dust in camps'.

At the same time it would be wrong to think that Stalin was neglecting the country's general war preparations; quite a lot was done along these lines in the late 1930s, and he was not only aware of what was being done but had actually initiated some of the improvements himself. Those years saw a boost in war industries, the appearance and development of advanced armaments, of new types of military aircraft, tanks and artillery, and finally the accumulation of strategic ammunition stocks, as well as of food supplies and so on. A very active part in carrying out these preparations, in accordance with government decisions, was played by my father. He kept a close eye on building up, among other things, adequate stocks of grain, sugar and other staples. By spring 1941 the strategic food stocks accumulated by the country were sufficient for feeding the entire armed forces for over six months. But that was not all. Being also in charge of foreign trade my father was concerned with building up the top-secret strategic resources of those raw materials of which the country did not have enough or none at all, for example rubber, lead, aluminium, nickel, diamonds and various alloys.

Yet, as Stalin had convinced himself that Hitler would not break his pact with the USSR, and in any case would not go to war against his country until he had 'sorted out' Britain, he obstructed all attempts and measures directed at increasing the army's immediate readiness for an enemy attack. For somebody in charge of a whole country it was truly criminal short-sightedness. Some of the top officials in the country, including several Politburo members, as my father has told me, found such a policy very worrying and alarming, but the majority believed in the 'great leader's wisdom'. They thought Stalin knew something they did not know, and was acting accordingly. Some of the top commanders even showed somewhat excessive zeal in obeying Stalin's order about 'pacifying the Germans'. One of these commanders in my opinion was General Pavlov, who was later executed on Stalin's orders along with other members of the Western Front Command, chosen as 'scapegoats' after the devastation of that front by the Germans in the early days of the war.

There were many blunders made in the course of the war, and this is quite natural for any country at war, but the errors made in this war by the Soviet leadership and military command were rather specific in that they were peculiar to the Soviet system and its authoritarian, dictatorial rule. Judging by the conversations which accompanied the unhurried weekend meals at our dacha after the war, conversations in which my two uncles – Haik Tumanian (who had fought in the war from its first day to the last) and Artem Mikoyan – often took part along with my father's friend Lev Shaumian, my own thoughts here expressed are very similar to what my father and his dinner guests believed.

When, in the late summer of 1941, the Germans surrounded Kiev and gained access to the River Dnepr both north and south of the city, there was a real threat that the entire Soviet group of troops in that area might be encircled. The General Staff was aware of that threat, and so was Zhukov himself, who twice reported the danger to Stalin, asking him to recall the troops from Kiev. But Stalin was dead against giving up either Kiev or the Dnepr to the Germans – the river seemed such a strong line of defence (especially on the map!) – and he refused to agree to a retreat. At the end of August the Germans forced their passage over the Dnepr north of the city, then in September they crossed it in force in the south, and on 15 September they surrounded four of our armies in a close circle. Nearly half a million people were lost on our side, and only a handful of officers and soldiers managed to break through the circle. The Front Commander Mikhail Kirponos was killed, and so was his entire staff. The way to the east was open, and just a little over a month later the Germans took Kharkov.

The second major mistake was made during the attempted counter-attack of our troops at Kharkov in 1942. In his memoirs Marshal Ivan Bagramian recalls that when the offensive operations (suggested by Marshal Timoshenko and approved by Stalin) had begun, the operational intelligence data at his disposal made him see a serious threat of a large German tank unit striking our attacking forces from their left flank. Bagramian reported to Timoshenko, who refused to ask Stalin to stop the advance of our troops. Then Bagramian addressed Khrushchev as the Political Commissar of the Ukrainian Front, asking him to telephone Stalin and try to persuade him that the attack operations had to be suspended. Khrushchev did – and failed.*

Even before I read Bagramian's book I had heard the story from the other end, as it were, from my father, who had been present when Khrushchev phoned Stalin. Stalin was at his dacha at the time and he and a number of Politburo members, including my father, were sitting around the table in the dining-room, at the far end of which there was a small side table with telephones. One of them, the top-secret government line apparatus, started ringing. Malenkov answered it. 'Who's calling?' Stalin asked across the room. 'Khrushchev.' 'Ask him what he wants.' Malenkov listened to Khrushchev at the end of the line and said, 'He says the advance on Kharkov should be called off – there's a serious threat of our troops being struck from a flank and encircled by a tank army.' Stalin's reply to it was, 'Put down the receiver. As if he knows what he's talking about! Military orders must be obeyed and not discussed.' Having described the episode, my father added, 'He did not even bother to come to the phone. The man was calling him from the front line, with a battle on and people dying around him, and *he* would not walk ten steps across the room to hear him out!' As a result, another disaster: a large contingent of our forces was encircled and destroyed.

Incidentally, in his famous Twentieth Congress speech, Khrushchev mentioned an episode that had taken place at a Politburo meeting after the war. He said that at that meeting Anastas had directly pointed out that the refusal to stop our attack on Kharkov as Khrushchev had suggested resulted in a serious defeat, thus stressing Stalin's negative role in the episode. Stalin was enraged. After the defeat at Kharkov there was nothing to stop the Germans from their advance further east towards the Volga and Stalingrad. In fact it might be assumed with a fair degree of certainty that if it had not been for these two disastrous defeats in which we lost so much in manpower and armaments, the Germans would have hardly reached Stalingrad: the resistance on the way would have been much stronger and more efficient.

Finally, as the third very grave failure that was caused by Stalin's dictatorial decisions and that also had heavy consequences, I would name the Kerch operation of 1942 in which our large landing force was annihilated by the

* Ivan Bagramian, *Thus We Moved Towards Victory*, Voenizdat, Moscow, 1977.

Germans. This operation was carried out under direct pressure from the Stavka's 'political representative' L. Mekhlis, who was encouraged by Stalin and whose incompetent interference in the decisions of the military command on the spot contributed to the tragic finale.

The humility and submissiveness of many military commanders at all levels and their fear of being arrested, inspired by Stalin's tyrannical rule, often led to totally unjustified losses in the army units. Thus, scores of thousands of infantrymen met their deaths defending (or attacking) some nameless and often useless elevations, just because their commanding officers did not dare to suggest a change of tactics imposed on them from the Stavka in view of the changed situation. The never-ending 'game' of appointments, dismissals and reshuffles within the higher military command did not help things either; there were no permanent winners in that game, for no one could be sure to have his position for long, let alone for ever, and the danger of Stalin's displeasure loomed over each and every one of them.

On 9 May 1985, along with many other war veterans, I was watching the fortieth anniversary military parade from the stands on Red Square, where I had a rather memorable chat with two generals standing next to me. One of them, General Briukhov, was remembering the Berlin campaign of the Soviet Army in which, as he told me, there were enormous and totally unjustified losses on our side which could have been avoided. This is, in paraphrase, what he said: 'Why on earth did we need that head-on attack on the Seelow elevation, where the Germans had a very powerful and deeply echeloned defence? We did not move a step forward in the first two days, and made just an 800-metre advance on the third day, and it was only at the very end of that day that we finally broke through their defence. Some 360,000 people were lost! Konev [Marshal Konev commanded the troops of the 1st Ukrainian Front S.M.] had approached from the south and was ready to move through to Berlin, yet Zhukov forbade him to budge for two days – with Stalin's approval of course – so that his own front would march into Berlin first.'

Another thing to be remembered in this connection is the sadly known purges in the Red Army before the war. Over forty thousand Red Army commanders were arrested in the last few years before Hitler's attack on the country. The majority of them were executed or died in the camps. Most members of the Red Army supreme command were eliminated, including such brilliant commanders as Mikhail Tukhachevsky, Alexander Yegorov, Jeronim Uborevich, Jonah Yakir, Vitaly Primakov, Vasily Bliukher, Yakov Alksnis, and many others. All deputies of the Defence Commissar were arrested, as well as nearly the entire staff of the central military administration, all commanders of military academies, all corps commanders, the majority of division commanders and half of all regiment commanders. About 700 people among the purged officers held the rank of generals. Nearly all of them perished, and only about nine per cent of all arrested commanders were released shortly before the war.* Among them

* V. Papoport, Y. Geller, *High Treason*, 1995.

were Konstantin Rokossovsky, Cyril Meretskov, Alexander Gorbatov and others. Thus almost the entire officers corps in our armed forces was devastated. That was Stalin's crime against the country, and it can be neither justified nor forgiven.

The vacancies in the senior and supreme command which were thus 'provided' were often filled with incompetent, inexperienced and immature people. The standard of quality within the military command inevitably deteriorated. The rare survivors who kept their posts alongside the newly appointed commanders, having been scared by the purges, were not ready to show initiative, courage or the ability of independent decision-making, i.e. the qualities that are so essential at war or at the time which immediately precedes it. I have repeatedly heard from my father that the loss of the experienced, well-educated and thinking commanders on the eve of the war, especially in its first days and weeks, produced the single most damaging effect on both the preparation for repelling Hitler's attack and the course of the war itself. One can only imagine how much more efficient both the strategic and the tactical management of the war would have been if those commanders had been 'allowed' to remain alive and in charge of our armed forces.

However, it would be wrong to completely deny Stalin's 'organising' role during the war. His unlimited power and authority guaranteed that once a decision was made, it was carried out; and when it happened to be a correct or a sensible decision, it was very useful to have such a guarantee. Besides, for many ordinary soldiers at the front his name was a kind of symbol which to them represented what they were fighting for (although this aspect was strongly overrated and exaggerated by the official propaganda). But all this taken together did not and could not make up for the damage done. All things considered, I believe – contrary to the opinion of some war veterans who still say that 'we won the war thanks to Stalin' – it would be correct to say that we won the war *despite* Stalin's dictatorship. In any case, if it had not been for him, there would have been far less loss of life. It is no longer a secret to us in the former Soviet Union that our joint losses in military action alone were four or five times larger than those suffered by the German army.

The overall loss of life in the Soviet Union during the war was enormous. Apart from the soldiers and officers killed in action, apart from the losses among the partisans in the enemy rear, apart from the civilians killed in air raids and as a result of military action or, in occupied territories, as victims of the Germans' punitive operations, apart from about a million who died of starvation and hypothermia in besieged Leningrad, apart from our prisoners-of-war and civilians who perished in the German concentration camps and those who died in our own camps after they had survived the German ones, there were also thousands of people who did not survive the deprivations of war, the grave shortage of food in some areas and other wartime hardships. Thousands of people were also dying of hunger, hard labour and diseases in the camps of the Gulag. Neither the twenty-million figure officially announced after the war nor the recently adjusted figure of twenty-eight million reflects the real number of people lost.

There is another well-known figure: there were only three per cent of survivors among men born between 1921 and 1923. I believe this to be as arbitrary as the twenty-million losses figure. I am certain that many more of them survived the war. They say 'an example is not a proof', nevertheless I will give an example from my own experience. Before the war, as I said earlier, I happened to study at three different schools in turn, so after the war I used to take part in three separate meetings of former classmates nearly every year. Incidentally, one of 'my' classes was from the artillery school, nearly all pupils of which continued their military training and went straight to war as officers when it started. Yet even in this class there were more survivors than losses. In the two ordinary civilian schools where I had studied about a third of the boys in each of my former classes were killed in the war. After all, it was not as though every single boy of that age joined active service or was sent to the front. If the three per cent figure was accurate, we, the survivors, would have very little chance to meet people of our own age, which has fortunately not been the case.

My father's account of the situation within the Soviet leadership in the first few days following the German invasion is a sobering one. It was the eighth day of the war when several Politburo members, concerned about the course of events, together with Stalin, who arrived in town from his dacha in the suburbs, drove over to the Commissariat of Defence based not far from the Kremlin to get a clear idea of what was going on at the front. On arrival they only got a clear idea of what was going on at the Commissariat: nobody knew anything, there was no communication with the front line troops, no reliable information as to how far the Germans had advanced into Soviet territory, and no way of knowing whether the troops of the Belorussian military district were still combat-efficient. It was only then, my father said to me, that Stalin became fully aware of the disastrous consequences of his refusal to believe in the danger of Hitler's attack. He ordered Defence Minister Timoshenko and Chief of Staff Zhukov to give him information they did not have. My father told me that the tension was so great that Zhukov suddenly ran out of the room in tears. Finally Molotov suggested letting the military do their job and returning to the Kremlin. On the way out Stalin murmured, 'Everything's lost, all that was left to us by Lenin – we've lost it all.' He went straight to his dacha and stayed there for some time in a state of nervous breakdown, refusing to answer telephone calls.

The next day the Politburo members discussed the idea of setting up a State Committee for Defence, with Stalin at its head, and a number of other urgent measures. Towards the end of the day they drove over to Stalin's dacha. When they entered the dining-room where Stalin was sitting, he seemed to shrink into his armchair. His voice was tense when he asked them curtly, 'What have you come for?' As my father told me, he must have thought they had come to arrest him. At that moment he must have been aware of the blame that lay upon him and realised that there were grounds for deposing him. When he heard why they had come, he gave them a somewhat surprised look and visibly relaxed. After that he agreed to their proposal. When the list of five Defence Council members was read out to him, he asked, 'Why isn't Mikoyan on the list?' Voznesensky pointed out that for some reason he had been omitted too. Stalin suggested that both of them should be added to the list, but Molotov objected to enlarging the council. Let them concentrate on the work in the Council of People's Commissars, he said. Then my father interposed to say he did not need to be a full member, but it would be useful if he were appointed the Defence Council's official representative in charge of the army supplies of food rations, clothing and fuel, i.e. in charge of the areas which were related to his sphere of activity in the CPC. It was agreed, but in February 1942, on Stalin's proposal, both my father and Voznesensky were included in the Defence Council as full members.

Shortly before the 'day of panic' – 16 October 1941 – some pilots of the Moscow air defence force happened to spot a large German tank unit near Gzhatsk, much closer to Moscow than the front line was supposed to have been. There were no Soviet troops in front of those German tanks (I have heard this from M. Yakushin, then second-in-command of the Moscow Air Defence Corps, who personally flew over to the area to check out the report of his pilots; that is to say, there were no troops between the advancing enemy army and the capital).

The situation threatened to cause chaos and disruption at the front. As Air Force Marshal Golovanov told my future father-in-law, Mark Ivanovich Shevelev (who was Golovanov's chief of staff in the war, and from whom I later heard this episode), when he entered Stalin's office early that day (he had been sent for by Stalin) he saw him in a very depressed mood. He sat there saying, 'What shall we do? What shall we do?' several times. According to my father, on the morning of 15 October Stalin summoned all Politburo members to inform them of the situation, and then he proposed an urgent evacuation of the government, of all the commissariats, including that of defence, of important offices and government institutions, foreign embassies, and, in addition, of eminent political figures and other important people. Moscow, he said, had to be prepared for the eventuality of a massive breakthrough by German troops. He ordered all Moscow machine-building factories and other strategic plants and works to be mined. On the same day all these proposals were made law by an official decision of the Defence Council.

Towards the night of that day, commanders of the voluntary Home Guard battalions were ordered to occupy defensive positions on the approaches to the city. There was no address to the citizens, no official information or explanation to the people of the threatened city, yet alarming rumours travelled fast, and uncontrollable panic came in their wake. Thousands of people were fleeing Moscow in whatever transport was available. It was not until the next day that the Moscow party chief, A. Shcherbakov, addressed the remaining citizens over the radio on the orders of the Defence Council, declaring that the city would not be surrendered to the enemy and urging its inhabitants to defend it 'to the last'. He also assured the people that the principal members of the government and the Politburo were staying in the city, with Stalin himself as their head. The panic gradually subsided.

It has been stated in some relatively recent publications that most of the top leadership left Moscow on that day; however, as a number of first-hand sources confirm, that was not the case. Thus, D. Pavlov, then the Defence Council representative in charge of the ration supplies to Leningrad and to the troops of the Leningrad front, in his book *Stoikost*, recalls his visit to Moscow from Leningrad on 16 October when he was received in the Kremlin by the Deputy Chairman of the CPC (Anastas Mikoyan), to whom he had to report.* For my own part, I remember my father telling me of how he asked his chauffeur to drive him around Moscow on that day so as to see what was going on in the streets, and then went over to a car factory where he had a spontaneous meeting with the workers. He made a habit of visiting plants and factories during bomb raids – those plants and factories which were still working, or course. By all accounts, he almost never or very rarely went down into bomb shelters. One of his two drivers even asked to be replaced, afraid of driving around the city during air-raids. Once, during a raid, father walked out onto the square in front of the building where his Kremlin office was, 'just in time' to see a German bomb hit the Kremlin AA machine-gun post.

While I am on the painful subject of our victory's cost and our losses, I must say a few words about something that prevented them both from being even greater, namely the aid the Soviet Union received from its allies, especially from the USA and from Britain. The aid was supplied under the terms of the US Lend-Lease Bill passed in June 1942. The first deliveries had in fact begun to come much earlier, in the summer of 1941. For a long time after the war, and until fairly recently, the significance and role of the lend-lease aid was deliberately understated if not completely ignored. This was a totally wrong attitude, for the deliveries from the Allies were certainly a great help and no doubt enabled us to avoid a longer and more devastating war.

Even in my own experience as a fighter pilot in the war the lend-lease aid was something tangible and of great practical value, even in its relatively insignificant manifestations. Thus, during my service in the No. 12 Air Defence Fighter Regiment, our aircraft were equipped with American radio sets providing a far better quality and a longer range of transmission than the ones we had used before. A very useful innovation in our cockpits from the same source was the artifical horizon. The foreign ground-based radars I have mentioned earlier were British, and the leather jackets and two-piece fur-lined winter flying suits handed out to the pilots of some AF and Air Defence regiments also came from America. There were large deliveries of British and American aircraft. To be honest, the Hurricanes, which had come to us first, were somewhat obsolete and in some respects inferior to our own latest models. The Spitfire, on the other hand, was an excellent machine, although unfortunately we received very few of them. The American Kittyhawk and Tomahawk fighters did not distinguish themselves in any particular way, while the Aircobras and the Kingcobras (which came in large numbers) did a very good job. The famous fighter division commanded by Alexander Pokryshkin was equipped with those aircraft, as was its No. 9 Regiment, whose performance at the front gained it the reputation of one of the best units in the force. As for the bombers, the US Douglas A-20 and North American B-25 were described by our pilots as highly efficient machines. Our Navy, too, had their share of lend-lease aid in the shape of various warships, and

---

* D. Pavlov, *Stoikost* ('Steadfastness'), Politizdat, Moscow, 1983, p. 72.

the marines received several dozen large-capacity cargo vessels of the famous Liberty type.

The food consignments delivered under the lend-lease agreement were very considerable. All front-line servicemen had their share of American tinned pork, egg and milk powder, none of which had been known in the Soviet Union before. Another important type of delivery which is hardly mentioned at all was the strategically important raw materials. Among the latter was aluminium, used, among other purposes, for covering the wings of the celebrated Il-2 (Ilyushin-2) attack aircraft. I have heard from V. Bugaisky, then Ilyushin's right-hand man, that when the Germans had destroyed one of the sea convoys sent by the Allies, the Kuibyshev aircraft plant was left without aluminium, and for a while the covering had to be made of plywood. The Allies also shipped tanks, anti-aircraft guns, anti-tank rifles, machine-guns, chemicals, explosives, and so on.

My father used to stress the unique role played in the war by the American six-wheel trucks with their high cross-country ability, the Studebakers and Fords. We received over 400,000 of those vehicles! Thanks to them, much of our infantry was motorised and the artillery could stop using horses as its main tractive power; both changes were essential for the increase in the manoeuvrability and attacking efficiency of our army (incidentally, the famous Katiushas from the end of 1942 were mounted on Studebakers). Another important line of supplies was medical equipment and medication, including the vitally important penicillin, which had been totally unknown in the country before.

I am far from suggesting that the supplies delivered by the Allies played a decisive role in our future victory, yet I am certain that without them our victory would have come to us at an even higher cost. My father believed that without the lend-lease arrangement the war on our territory would have lasted at least a year longer. At the same time, I cannot help thinking that if the Allied forces' landing in Normandy had taken place about a year earlier, World War Two would have ended sooner and at a lesser cost to us (even if it would have meant more losses to the Allied forces, the overall cost of life in Europe and for the world at large would have been far less).

In his capacity as a fully authorised Defence Council representative (and eventually a full member), father was responsible for the war-related activities in the rear. He was in charge of supplying the armed forces with rations and medication, with ammunition, various engineering equipment, fuel, clothing and other vitally important deliveries. Besides, as a deputy of the CPC chairman (a post held by Stalin at the time) he was also responsible for the work of the Commissariats of Trade, Supplies, Food, Fishing and Meat Industries, as well as Sea and River Merchant Fleets and Arctic Navigation. Finally, as the People's Commissar for Foreign Trade, he oversaw the deliveries which came under the Lend-Lease Bill.

My father's most frequent visitors in his Kremlin office were Chief of the Red Army Rear General Khrulev and the Artillery Directorate Chief, General Yakovlev. They came to discuss and to report on the various army supplies issues. I saw them a few times on my occasional flying (the pun is unintentional!)

visits home from the regiment; father used to bring them along for dinner after a working session in his office. According to two independent accounts – that of D. Pavlov (Deputy Trade Minister in the 1950s), whom I saw fairly often in the last few years of his life, and Aram Piruzian, a food industry veteran, – my father, while ensuring that the army units received their supplies in good time and in sufficient quantities, was at the same time dead against any form of squandering the resources. He would personally check the army order lists for each coming month, banning unjustified surplus demands. As Piruzian remembered, he would insist, for example, that felt boots, which the servicemen wore in winter, should not be chucked out just because of a hole or two in the sole if the rest of the boot was fine; the soles should be mended or replaced, and the boots would be as good as new again (it was not, of course, that he was obsessed with felt boots as such, it was just an expression of his impatience with any form of unnecessary waste). He initiated the setting up of repair shops for the army which mended over twenty million felt boots, seventeen million overcoats and sixty-one million pairs of leather footwear. Father was also in charge of production and supplies of food and other essentials to the civilian population, the crucial part of his activity in this area being his supervision of the delivery of food rations to besieged Leningrad.

In March 1943 Anastas Mikoyan was commissioned by the Defence Council with yet another task. He was put in charge of forming the so-called reserve front, a powerful reserve force intended for the future Battle of Kursk (which was already being planned at the time), where it proved an invaluable addition to our forces in that battle.

Partly in connection with the war, partly because there might not be a better occasion in this book, I want now to try to draw a portrait of somebody I was greatly fond of and have always remembered with special warmth – my mother's brother and my uncle, Haik Tumanian. This uncle and my father's younger brother, Artem, were the nearest and the dearest of all our family's numerous relations. They treated me and my brothers as if we were their own sons and gave us a lot of their time and attention. We always called them by their first names, without the prefix 'uncle'. Haik was a man with a very eventful and exciting life story. Tall, good-looking, with a great sense of humour and very kind, he was a master of amusing and witty conversation and was nearly always ready to smile or share a laugh. In fact, when he did not smile or was not being amusing, it meant he had weighty reasons to be serious – and then he was very serious indeed.

I have earlier written about the Tumanian family, in which both my mother and Haik were born and grew up, and with which my father (their second cousin) was living as a student of an Armenian theological school in Tiflis. The elder Tumanians sympathised with the revolutionary movement, and Haik got involved in it as a teenager. Later he would entertain us with humorous accounts of his subversive 'adventures'. In one of them, he was asked by Kamo, the leader of a secret Bolshevik paramilitary group, to take a large amount of money to Baku. Haik, a sixteen-year-old schoolboy looking respectable in his uniform, took a first-class ticket ('It was safer that way!') and spent the entire journey sitting next to an unsuspecting officer.

In the 1920s Haik was a student in Moscow; he then went to a cavalry school, and later served in the Red Army. In the 1930s Haik became a military intelligence officer and spent five years as our agent in Harbin under the cover of the Soviet consulate office. I remember the Japanese children's books with colourful pictures of Tokyo street life which he brought for us from Harbin, and I remember my genuine surprise: how could it be that in that 'backward' country the streets looked more modern than in Moscow? I was particularly taken by the trams and buses in those books – I had never seen anything of the kind before. Another surprising novelty that Haik brought over from Harbin was an electric shaver. I don't think anyone in Russia even knew they existed, let alone used them.

He took part in the Spanish Civil War and was decorated with the Red Banner Order for his service. I asked him when he returned, 'Did you fire your gun there?' He said he had not. 'What's your order for then?' I demanded. He got away with some joke. After a while he unexpectedly showed me a paper clipping which stated that a transport ship that had been *en route* to Spain from Italy with a cargo of armaments was blown up on the way and sank. 'That's what my order is for', said Haik, and explained that the operation had been thought out and prepared by him and carried out by his subordinate. Haik's closest associate and comrade-in-arms in Spain was his old friend and fellow intelligence officer Khadzhi Mamsurov. They remained friends to the day when Khadzhi died, as a colonel general and Deputy Chief of Soviet Military Intelligence. In the war of 1941–5 Khadzhi Mamsurov commanded a corps and was decorated with the Golden Star of a Hero of the Soviet Union. He was a truly fascinating person, extremely full of life and energy, very good-looking and with irresistible personal charm (the same was true of Haik). His activities in Spain involved organising reconnaissance operations and subversive activity against the Frankists. He was mentioned by Hemingway in *For Whom the Bell Tolls*. Together with my other uncle Artem, they formed a very colourful trio and were greatly devoted to one another.

After the outbreak of war Haik had been Voroshilov's aide in charge of organising partisan movement, and was later appointed Commissar of the Tank Corps commanded by General Liziukov. Haik told me after the war how Liziukov and he, their pistols in their hands, had stopped an infantry unit that had panicked and fled, and organised the men into a decent line of defence. One of the officers, who would not stop running, had to be shot. Shortly after that there was a large tank battle in that area. A 'political officer' on an inspection visit from Moscow accused Liziukov of cowardice because he (for tactical reasons) left one of his brigades, the one in whose dispositions they all were at the time, unengaged. Not bothering to reply, General Liziukov jumped into a tank and led the brigade into battle. The Germans repelled their attack and Liziukov's machine was put out of action by a direct hit. Haik and Liziukov's staff officers, unable to interfere, watched through their binoculars as the Germans pulled Liziukov's body out of the tank. Shortly afterwards Stalin summoned Haik to Moscow and asked him to describe the situation at the front line and the exact circumstances of General Liziukov's death.

In the summer of 1942 Haik Tumanian was appointed Political Commissar of the 6th Tank Army. With this army he participated in the Battle of Stalingrad and went through all the other battles in which it was engaged, up to its final advance to Prague at the end of the war. Not once during all that time did Haik visit his home in Moscow, or Moscow itself for that matter. With his personality, his temperament and experience, he would have been better suited to the post of combat commander, and I believe he had considered such a turn in his career, but resigning from political organs of the army was not so easy – unless of course they wanted one to resign.

Upon the final defeat of Germany the 6th Tank Army was directed to the Far East. After his participation in a series of combat operations against Japanese forces, and their eventual capitulation, Haik happened to be among the officers of the 6th Army who took the Emperor of Manchuria prisoner. He had met the emperor before in his official capacity as a Soviet consular officer in Harbin. In my father's official archives a letter has recently been discovered. The letter, dated 1945, is addressed to Haik Tumanian and signed by Lin Bayo and leaders of the Chin ese Red Army. It contains a request for a delivery of rifles, machine-guns and other arms. I remember what Haik himself told me in connection with this request. He reported it to Stalin, asking his consent to supply the Chinese Red Army with arms; Stalin suggested that they should be brought secretly to some mountain caves, and that the 'Chinese comrades' should be discreetly informed of their whereabouts so that the 'transaction' would not appear as if it were official aid from the USSR.

In the same file as Haik's Chinese letter, I have discovered a clipping from an American (or so I believe) magazine with a cartoon showing Red Square and a number of people lined up along the balcony on top of Lenin's tomb, all wearing identical coats and hats. A foreign tourist beside the tomb is asking the man next to him, 'Listen, Frank, who're those guys up there with Mikoyan?' Whatever the intended implication of that cartoon at the time it was published, I'll use it as an excuse to say that my father did have a memorable face as well as a powerful and charismatic personality, and what John Gunther in his book *Inside Russia Today* described as 'a famously barbed tongue'. These features, together with his sharp intelligence, his inherent diplomatic skills, his sense of irony and humour and many other remarkable qualities, ensured that once met, seen or talked to, he remained, as the cartoon suggested, easily recognised and well remembered.

Although at the time of Stalin's regime Haik had not discussed his views with anyone, much later, when I thought about him, I realised, on the basis of some small details I recalled, that he must have been fully conscious and resentful of Stalin's dictatorial rule. As a seasoned intelligence officer he would never have given his feelings away, and I remember how he saw to it that we would not make a blunder either. Once, when my brother and I were in the midst of a conversation which he thought was 'not safe', he led us both into the bathroom, opened the tap and said: 'Now, talk away!' I also remember the bitterness with which he told me the story of his fellow intelligence officer, also a Soviet agent in Manchuria. Haik and his companions managed to organise his escape from Chinese prison and helped him make his way home. He returned to the Soviet Union safely, only to be arrested and executed shortly afterwards. Haik was nearly also arrested on his return; I believe it was my father's intervention that saved him.

Once my brother asked Haik, 'Why are most of the political officers so narrow-minded?' 'And how can they not be, always thinking one thing and saying another as they are!' he replied. And one other remark I remember (made during the Brezhnev period): 'Did we devote our lives to come to all this?'

Haik died at the age of seventy as a result of an acute kidney condition. An operation could have helped him, but he put it off until it was too late. Whenever I meet someone who knew Haik Tumanian, I invariably hear his name mentioned with great warmth and respect. He is remembered by all those who worked with him or under him as a highly intelligent, kind and considerate person with a fine sense of humour, great courage and spirit.

CHAPTER 10

The Air Force Academy

I was happy to be in Moscow for Victory Day and, moreover, to be at home with my mother. At about five a.m. on 9 May we all went to the airport to see my father off to Berlin. Leaving the Kremlin through the Saviour's Gate, we drove across Red Square, still full of rejoicing people who had spontaneously gathered there during the night to celebrate the news of Germany's capitulation.

My father was going to Germany at the head of a group of experts with the mission of organising medical aid and food supplies for the civilian population of that country. He was commissioned with the task by the State Defence Committee of which he was a member. He was met in Berlin by Marshal Zhukov. On arrival Anastas Mikoyan held a meeting to which were invited representatives of various German industries, of the transport and municipal services, of the health service and so on. I heard from Ivan Serov (a future high-ranking KGB official), who had been in that delegation, how at that meeting he had read out to the German audience the list of items to be supplied to the country as humanitarian aid from the Soviet Union. When, among other groceries, he named coffee, there was no reaction in the audience. 'Tell them we mean *real* coffee,' my father whispered. Serov, not at all sure it made any difference, nevertheless said as my father had prompted. There was a moment's silence and then applause. The Germans, who had lived on substitutes for a long time, could not have even dreamed of being promised real coffee.

Shortly after the end of the war two important events took place in my life: I got married and became a student of the Zhukovsky Air Force Academy. I met my future wife Ella (Eleonora) in the summer of 1940, not long before my departure for the flying school, in the country near her stepfather's dacha, just a few kilometres away from my father's. We spent some time together before I left for Kacha, driving around the countryside, often in the company of my brother Volodya, having picnics or swimming in the river together. Then I left for the flying school and in the two years that followed I only saw her once, by chance. I came to Moscow on a short leave in late December 1940, and I was invited to a New Year's Eve party at a friend's school. It turned out to be Ella's school too, and she was attending the same party. In the late autumn of 1942, when Ella and her mother returned after their evacuation to Krasnoyarsk and when my regiment was recalled from the Stalingrad front, we started going out together, whenever I got leave for a brief visit to Moscow from the regiment. On 1 May 1943 I brought Ella to our dacha to meet my parents, and just about three weeks after VE-Day, on 3 June 1945, we got married.

My wife's father, Piotr Lozovsky, was born in Latvia and was a pilot in World War One and then in the Russian Civil War afterwards. His courage in the civil war (he was fighting for the Red Army) earned him a Red Banner Order. Later

115

he became a test pilot at a Moscow aircraft plant, and in 1932 he was killed in a crash while performing a low-altitude aerobatic manoeuvre. By the time I met Ella, her mother Alexandra had been the wife of Mark Ivanovich Shevelev for six years, and both she and her daughter were living in Shevelev's house. Shevelev began his remarkable career as a young yet very capable Arctic explorer and navigator pilot who had taken part in many expeditions to the Far North, including the well-known expedition to the Kara Sea. He was the initiator and chief organiser of an entirely new service within Soviet aviation, Polar Aviation (its appearance as a single, systematic and well-run service immediately reduced the accident rate in polar flights). Shevelev was twenty-eight years old when he was appointed the first Chief of the Polar Aviation Directorate, and became the right hand and official deputy of Otto Schmidt, the Chief of the Northern Navigation Route Directorate, a celebrated polar explorer himself and a full member of the Soviet Academy of Sciences. Shevelev was actively involved in the organisation of the 1937–8 drift-ice expedition by four polar explorers led by Ivan Papanin. Otto Schmidt, as the commander of the expedition, and Mark Shevelev, as assistant-commander, were on board one of the aircraft which delivered the expedition to the Arctic, landing on drift-ice (Shevelev was created a Hero of the Soviet Union for his role and performance in the expedition).

When war broke out he was appointed second-in-command of the long-range bomber division formed on the basis of Polar Aviation units. Later he became Chief of Staff of the Long-Range Aviation Command, and at the end of 1943 his experience as a polar explorer and an aviation specialist made him an ideal candidate for taking charge of the Alaska–Krasnoyarsk air route which was used for ferrying lend-lease aircraft from the US. After the war he returned to his post at the head of the Polar Aviation Directorate. Over the forty years during which he oversaw Soviet polar aviation, AF Lieutenant General Shevelev supervised a great number of expeditions to the North Pole, was in charge of the ice reconnaissance along the length of the Northern Navigation Route, and had many other responsibilities related to the exploration of the Arctic and the Antarctic. He was the commander of the first flight from Moscow to the Antarctic, and much later, as a seventy-three-year-old man in 1977, participated in the air escort of the nuclear-powered ice-breaker *Arctica* in her expedition to the North Pole. Having retired from commanding posts, he began working at the Marine Ministry, in charge of ice reconnaissance. He died in 1991 just two weeks before his eighty-seventh birthday, having to his last day retained his sharp intelligence, a remarkable memory and his contagious *joie de vivre*. A serene, wise and very kind man, a lover of poetry and classical music, he was a walking encyclopaedia of knowledge about the Arctic and of the entire history of its exploration.

At the time of our wedding Ella was a student at a technical institute, but she left it some time before our first son was born. She became an undergraduate again later, in the 1950s, after all our three children had been born, and in 1958 she graduated with honours from the faculty of journalism at Moscow State University (it was rather brave in those days for a mother of three children to become a university undergraduate; most of the students around her were still in their teens). Her first job after she graduated became her life-long vocation:

from 1958 and until her retirement in 1990 Ella worked as a book editor at the country's largest publishing house producing books for children. A born perfectionist and a champion of accuracy, Ella would check and double-check every single reference, quotation, fact or date in each book she edited. As a result, our home gradually filled up with all imaginable encyclopaedias, dictionaries and reference books. My wife's other passion in life has always been classical music, and so she has gradually built an impressive collection of records too, representing all the world's classical composers and greatest performers.

I could say that we have always had three 'cults' in our family: classical music, Pushkin and books in general. The cult of music was introduced and has been nurtured by my wife, but all other members of the family supported it. As for Pushkin, he has always been our favourite poet, and both Ella and I believe him to have been one of Russia's greatest men. Our home library has never stopped growing, and it now amounts to about five thousand volumes or so. There are all kinds of books, and apart from classical and contemporary literature, poetry, biographies and so on, there are specialised 'sections' within the collection: reference books, books on music, art, history of literature, works on Pushkin, works on the history of Russia and Moscow, and, of course, on aviation.

My collection of aviation books was rather smaller when I made up my mind to become a student of the Zhukovsky Air Force Academy. I was the proud owner of a golden-edged secondary education certificate (the golden edge indicating graduation with honours), and I was entitled to be admitted to the Academy without any entrance exams. When I applied I was offered a place on a preparatory course designed for candidates who were fresh from active service. I refused, but they still suggested that I take exams in physics and maths. That was fair enough, for I certainly had forgotten a lot in the five years that had passed after school. After a month of intensive studies, I passed my exams with flying colours and became a first-year undergraduate. I must say I did rather well as a student, and managed to graduate with a record of seven 'fours' (in the five-point system used in most Russian education institutions) out of the total of fifty marks, the rest of which were all 'fives' (each mark was given for a separate course in the overall curriculum). At the end of 1946 I was promoted to major (after the standard four years at the rank of captain), and in 1950 I became a lieutenant-colonel.

My year within the engineering faculty (it specialised in aircraft and aircraft engines) represented the first full-capacity intake of undergraduates after the war. We were also the first lot of newly admitted undergraduates to be taught in accordance with a comprehensive state-of-the-art curriculum. Thus, the course on jet engine theory delivered to us by its original author, Academician Stechkin himself, had not been heard by any undergraduates before us, nor by any of the lecturers, and the entire staff of the jet engine department was attending his lectures together with the students. Other brand-new or freshly revised courses we heard were theoretical mechanics (with a section on variable-mass flight mechanics, particularly important in the subsequent development of spacecraft design), aerodynamics, thermodynamics, engine design and others. Most lecture courses were delivered by distinguished academics and well-known aviation specialists. The entire course lasted almost six years, with the last year chiefly devoted to the work on our respective graduation design projects. For our practical training we were assigned for three or four weeks at a time to an aircraft plant, an engine factory and an aircraft repair plant, as well as to an air force regiment. Most of the students in my year were combat unit officers, and many had fought in the war. The majority did a preparatory course before becoming students. About one third of the first-year students were secondary school-leavers who had also been required to do the preparatory course first, so as to get used to the military routine and order.

No. 1 Faculty produced aircraft engineers of wide professional qualifications; therefore as undergraduates we were involved in both the aircraft and the engine design projects. Thus, when I was in my fourth year, we were first required to design a piston engine, and then some structural part of an aircraft. Four of my fellow students and I decided to design an aircraft together and to enter it for a competition which was going on at the time. We distributed the tasks, and I got the fuselage. Our aeroplane resembled the An-2 (which had just appeared), but it was less than half its size and had a nosewheel instead of a tailwheel for its landing gear. Although we missed the competition deadline, we were still allowed to present our project to the jurors, and I was elected as our spokesman. The project was very well received, both by the competition jury and our lecturers at the Academy, and we were all given top marks for it.

The quality of teaching at the Academy was exceptionally high. Throughout my subsequent career in the air force and aviation industry I encountered many of my former fellow students, and most of them were highly competent specialists. I would say that the Academy background proved to be of particular benefit to those of us who became test pilots.

We began working on our graduation projects towards the end of 1950, by which time the swept-wing jet fighter MiG-15 and the jet bomber Ilyushin-28 had already appeared on the scene. Supersonic jets did not yet exist, but two of the graduation assignments received by the graduate students in that year concerned supersonic jet interceptors. One of them was assigned to our top student Vitaly Altukhov (a former instructor pilot), the other to me.

The qualities most valued in interceptors at that time were high rate of climb and high maximum flying speed (later it was the onboard radar and then also guided missiles that became the primary distinctions of an interceptor). The opinion that persisted within Academy walls was that only the interceptor would become a supersonic jet, while regular fighters designed for air combat manoeuvres would remain on this side of the sound barrier. But further afield, as it were, there existed other opinions, and I already knew at the time that at the aircraft design company headed by my uncle Artem Mikoyan they were working on a supersonic combat fighter project. No wonder it was this type of aircraft that I wished to attempt as my graduation project. The department chief and a celebrated aircraft designer in his own right, Victor Bolkhovitinov, gave his permission for the change of assignment and became my supervisor. Naturally, my project could only be a success if I used advanced specific data. My choice of wing type was based on the results of aerodynamic experiments with delta wings held at the Academy by Professor Burago. Professor Tigran Melkumov, who combined his position at the Academy with a post as head of the Air-Engine Construction Institute, let me have his data on thrust-specific fuel consumption and weight of the new jet engines.

Thanks to the latest parameters I was using, my supersonic jet was a success – on paper only, of course, where it remained. Incidentally, at that time nobody could imagine that a supersonic jet could have any externally mounted loads, which would create additional drag. What a surprise it would cause us all then to see a modern supersonic fighter virtually 'hung' with rockets, missiles and external fuel tanks! There were naturally no external loads on my jet, but I 'equipped' it with a built-in launcher with rockets, designed by a student of the armament faculty. My project earned special commendation from the graduation commission, and shortly after that I graduated with honours as an engineer-mechanic in the air force.

The graduation project of my friend Sergei Dedukh was supervised by the famous aircraft designer Sergei Ilyushin. On one of his visits to our project-design class he came up to my drawing board, made several criticisms and then spoke to me of the MiG-15, praising its design and saying that it would cut itself a place in history as a 'classical' machine of its kind. And that is exactly what happened.

This seems an appropriate place to digress and say some words about Artem Mikoyan. Like my father, he was born in the village of Sanahin and went to school in Tiflis. My father then invited him to come and live with him in Rostov, where Anush* finished at a technical school for young factory workers and gained employment at a plant. In the 1920s he moved over to Moscow. After some time, during which he worked at a large machine-building plant, Anush was conscripted. When his army service was over he became a student of the Zhukovsky Air Force Academy, and on his graduation was appointed military representative at Polikarpov's design company. Eventually he began his own designing work within the company, and was soon made Polikarpov's deputy in charge of the fighter I-153.

That was the time of the technical rearmament of the Soviet Air Force. As a result of a large meeting of aviation specialists convened by the government at the beginning of 1939, a number of design companies were commissioned with the task of creating aircraft of a new generation. A group of young enterprising engineers at the Polikarpov company developed technical propositions for a high-altitude fighter with Alexander Mikulin's liquid-cooled engine. Some members of that group eventually became well-known designers – N. Matiuk, N. Andrianov, V. Romodin and Yakov Seletsky. Mikhail Gurevich also contributed to their work. The project appealed to the management of the No. 1 Plant, a large aircraft production plant in Moscow to which Polikarpov's design company was assigned. It was decided to set up a special department at the plant

---

* Artem was addressed by family and close friends with the original Armenian version of his name, pronounced 'Anoosh'.

for the technical elaboration of the project. The group invited Artem Mikoyan to join the new department as its chief, to which he agreed on condition that Mikhail Gurevich would be a member too.

Eventually the department was transformed into an independent design company, with Mikoyan at its head and Gurevich as his deputy. So as not to miss the opportunity of its being chosen for serial production, the aircraft had to be built as soon as possible (both Yakovlev's and Lavochkin's new fighters were at the time approaching the flight testing stage). Anush suggested a new scheme for the designing process and it was supported by the plant management; in accordance with that scheme the production technologists were from the very start working together with the designers. Thanks to their co-operation, every assembly unit and every detail of the future aircraft was designed with due consideration of the possibilities of the existing machine-tools and technologies, and the plant started preparations for the production of the new aircraft well in advance. As a result, the company set a kind of record: the initial designing work had begun in late November 1939, and the prototype, known at that stage as the I-200, performed its maiden flight on 5 April 1940.

Upon the completion of the military certification tests, the new aircraft was given the name of MiG-1 – the acronym of the names Mikoyan and Gurevich. It was done in accordance with the recent decision of the government to designate new aircraft by the initial letters of their designers' surnames, and new engines by the designers' initials. Besides, the fighters were to be given odd numbers, and bombers and other types of aircraft even numbers. All subsequent generations of the MiGs, including the very latest, have retained this name, despite the fact that neither of their original designers is living.

It was the improved version of the first MiG, named MiG-3, that was launched at No. 1 Plant to be produced on a mass scale. The improvement mainly consisted in the addition of an auxiliary internal fuel tank for extending the range of flight. The range-of-flight issue became in indirect cause of a tragic episode associated with the MiG-3. In the tests performed by the Air Force Research and Flight Test Institute (RFTI), the aircraft failed to reach the range of 1,000 kilometres required by the military specifications, despite the additional (internal) fuel tank. The failure was even reported to Stalin as an obstacle to mass production of the aircraft. It had been intended to reduce fuel consumption at high altitudes with the help of a fuel-air ratio corrector, but Mikulin had forbidden use of the corrector until some imperfections of his engine were removed. To prove that the MiG-3 was capable of covering the 1,000-kilometre range, the MiG company persuaded Mikulin to allow one single demonstration flight with the corrector 'in action', and the 1,000-kilometre range was confirmed. The result was reported to the Aviation Industry Minister, who in turn reported it to Stalin.

After a successful demonstration of the new MiG's possibilities, who could have foreseen a disaster? Stalin appeared to have his own view of events, assuming, under Beria's sinister influence, that the military had deliberately 'played down' the performance of the aircraft so as to sabotage its mass production (even though the military had also insisted on the use of the fuel-air ratio corrector from the very start). The Commander of the Flight Test Institute, General Filin, was arrested along with some of his very experienced staff members. Filin was a man respected by all who knew him, including Anush. He was a highly qualified engineer and an excellent test pilot. In fact Stalin knew him personally too, and had always trusted his professional opinion. Nevertheless, Filin was arrested, and in November 1942 he was shot.

The MiG-3 had from the very start been intended as an air defence aircraft, and accordingly it was primarily its high-altitude performance that distinguished it from other fighters of the time. Alexander Mikulin's engine, AM-35, with which it was fitted, was a high-altitude modification of his AM-34 engine designed for bombers (incidentally, it was the only fighter of the time equipped with an engine of an original 'domestic' design' – the Yaks had the M-105 engine based on the Hispano-Suiza motor, and the La-5s were equipped with a development of the American Wright-Cyclone engines). To adapt the engine to high altitudes it was supplied with a supercharger which increased its power by increasing the pressure of the fuel–air mixture. As a result the rated altitude of the engine (i.e. the altitude up to which maximum engine power could be maintained) was 7,200 metres as against the usual 4,000 metres or so. Therefore the MiG-3 could perform at 12,000 metres plus, higher than any serial fighter of the day, while reaching at lower altitudes a speed of 650 kph. To compare, the Yak had a ceiling of 10,200 metres and a speed of 600 kph. However, there were several airframes of the modified Yak, dubbed 'Yak-9D', with a ceiling of 12,000 metres. Their weight was reduced by removing two of the three guns and some equipment, and they were provided with a turbo-supercharger.

I have never flown the MiG-3 myself, but I have heard other pilots' opinions of it: despite being somewhat 'heavy-going' in low flight, it was a wonderful machine to fly at high altitudes. My wartime fellow fighter pilot Sergei Dolgushin, who had flown the MiG-3 at the beginning of the war, told me that whenever a MiG-3 formation encountered Messerschmitts at 5,000 metres or higher, the latter would always try to escape without putting up a fight; at that altitude the MiG-3 was superior to all other aircraft. Although they had been purpose-designed for air defence, the MiG-3 fighters were actively used as combat fighters at the beginning of the war to make up for the shortage of aircraft (the total output of MiGs just before the war had been larger than that of the Yaks or LaGGs). A very common tactic of the Germans was to lure a MiG to a lower altitude – under 4,000 metres – where the Messerschmitts had an advantage. Incidentally, by the time there were virtually no MiG fighters left in the front-line units, the Germans had finally produced a high-altitude modification of the Messerschmitt, which enabled them to reverse their combat tactics: they would now tug our aircraft up instead of luring them down as before.

At the end of December 1941, three months after the No. 1 Plant had been evacuated to Kuibyshev, serial production of MiG-3s stopped. One important, if not the most important, reason was that the engine they had (AM-35) was practically the same type (and produced at the same factories) as the one in the Ilyushin-2 – the AM-38, also designed by Mikulin. The AM-38 was a low-altitude modification of the AM-35; there was a great demand for attack aircraft then, and there were not enough engines to cover both types of aircraft (it is well known that Stalin personally directed the plant management to increase the output of the Il-2 and stop the production of the MiG-3). The same reason affected another aircraft, the long-range bomber Pe-8 (which participated in the raids of Berlin). It had been equipped with engines produced by the same factory, but then its original engine was replaced with a different and less suitable one. However, the MiG-3s did a very good job in the Battle of Moscow at the end of 1941, to say nothing of their efficient service in the Moscow and Leningrad air defence.

The Mikoyan Design Company was evacuated to Kuibyshev too, and it continued its work on new models of aircraft in new conditions. One of their projects at that time (1944) was realised as a prototype high-altitude aircraft, derived from the MiG-3 and equipped with an AM-39 motor with two turbo-superchargers and a four-blade propeller. Its factory designation was the I-222 ('I' is the first letter of the Russian word for a fighter), or the MiG-7. As a combat fighter it had an unprecedented ceiling of 14,500 metres and a record high-altitude speed of almost 700 kph.

This reminds me of a characteristic episode which is well known to those involved in the air defence of Moscow. In 1942, pilots were continuously plagued by a high-altitude German reconnaissance plane, the Junkers 88, which would cruise high over Moscow with perfect impunity, its white condensation trail visible from the ground. I saw it myself one day, from the city centre. The German would travel complacently above the city at about 13,000 metres where neither our fighters nor our AA guns could get at him. It went on like this until two pilots from No. 12 Regiment (in which I later served) managed to catch up with the Junkers, only about 500 metres short of the altitude it was at – Eduard Nalivaiko in a high-altitude Yak-9D and Leonid Samokhvalov in a MiG-3D. They still could not shoot the German down, for a fighter cannot manoeuvre or raise the nose to aim at its maximum altitude. Nevertheless they chased him off, and he never returned again.

Two other projects of the Mikoyan company during that period were a modification of the MiG-3 with an air-cooled engine (similar to the La-5 fighter) and a twin-engined fighter with the same kind of engine. Both aircraft were in some of their characteristics superior to all existing fighters, but neither of them (nor the I-222) was launched into mass production, for at that time there was no question of stopping an aircraft production line for reorganisation, inevitable if totally new types of aircraft were to be produced. The only exception made was for Tupolev's new bomber, the Tu-2, which was put on the lines in 1943 to satisfy the need for an advanced competitive bomber.

Equally unfortunate were the new models by N. Polikarpov, one of the best-known aircraft designers of the time. Back in 1938 he had created the I-180, an advanced high-speed fighter based on his I-16. The aircraft was designed with an air-cooled engine in mind, which was a breakthrough in itself; the general opinion then was in favour of liquid-cooled engines due to the lower drag they created. This aircraft was involved in a series of tragic accidents. Its prototypes were tested first by Valery Chkalov, then Colonel Thomas Susi, both of whom crashed, as later, during the war, did another well-known test pilot, Colonel Vasily Stepanchonok. All three accidents were caused by the engine.

I would like to share my idea of the causes of Valery Chkalov's fatal crash-landing. He was no doubt an outstanding pilot – with God's gift, as we say in Russian – and a remarkable person as well, but he was also too much of a dare-devil type. It was the very first flight of the I-180 which proved to be Chkalov's last. That December day in 1938 was exceptionally cold, and the cowling of the I-180 had no jalousie, which meant that at low rotation speed the engine would inevitably overcool. It is known that the engine test team specialist refused to sign the aircraft clearance. In that situation the test pilot had to cancel his flight; Chkalov did not, and I must say I find it easy to understand: I know from my own experience and from that of other pilots how hard it is to deny oneself a flight, even in the most unfavourable conditions. The risk has almost an irre-sistible appeal, and one's pride seems at stake as well. They say Chkalov insisted on performing that flight, but having taken off in such weather he should have kept the possibility of engine stalling in mind. The most dangerous stage under such conditions would be the landing approach, when the engine, unprotected by jalousie, would be working at low speed for a long time and thus getting over-cooled. And that was exactly what happened: his engine stalled when he was still too far from the airfield. With the aircraft already flying very low, it was impos-sible to reach the runway gliding down. He crash-landed in a yard and was thrown out of the cockpit by the impact force, hitting his head on a large cable reel as he went down. Chkalov should have allowed for the danger of overcooling and should have started his approach from afar on a gently sloping glidepath, enabling the engine to work at increased rpm and thus preventing the over-cooling; or he could have approached on a steep and short glidepath, in a kind of descending spiral, so as to be able to make it to the runway even if the engine went dead. As it was, Chkalov chose an ordinary approach pattern, and it was a fatal mistake.

So very often in life, to say nothing of aviation, we say 'If only'. If only he had not hit his head on a hard cable reel; if only he had been wearing a helmet (which did not become standard until twenty years later), he would probably have survived.

Many people's lives and careers were affected by Chkalov's accident. Several people were arrested, including Polikarpov's own deputy, the well-known aircraft designer D. Tomashevich. I remember seeing on my father's desk at home a report to the government on the causes of Chkalov's crash. It said that over two hundred defects were detected in that I-180 by the test team on its leaving the factory. In itself that did not signify anything out of the ordinary: it is quite a usual thing for a post-production inspection to reveal a large number of small deficiencies, which might include traces of rust, surface scratches, uneven paint, etc. Some more serious faults are not out of the question either. Most of these defects would usually be removed before the aircraft's maiden flight, but the absence of louvres in Chkalov's machine was a very serious deficiency, which was not made up for in any way, and in that cold weather it cost him his life.

As for the test pilot Stepanchonok, his engine also stalled, although for a different reason. He did not make it to the airfield either and crashed into the roof of the aircraft factory building. In the I-180 flown by Colonel Thomas Susi, test pilot on the staff of the Research and Flight Test Institute, an oil tube burst in the air and hot oil spurted out of it straight into his face, forcing him to lose control.

Polikarpov continued his work on this type of aircraft with an air-cooled engine, and in the early months of the war produced his I-185. It was tested by the pilots of the Flight Test Institute and officially pronounced to be superior to all existing fighters in the world (at that time the Institute was testing all types of aircraft that were coming from the Allies via lend-lease, as well as all captured German aircraft). And yet the I-185 was not launched for mass production. Those in authority could not bring themselves to stop the manufacture of any other aircraft to convert the production lines to the new machine.

In the meantime Lavochkin also fitted his LaGG-3 (Lavochkin, Gudkov, Gorbunov) with an air-cooled engine. The initial result was a rather heavy-going machine. While our No. 32 Regiment was getting ready to go to Stalingrad, it was supposed to be equipped with these aeroplanes, dubbed the La-5s. A number of the regiment pilots tried the aircraft out and pronounced a very negative verdict. I remember Sasha Koshelev's words upon landing in the La-5: 'It's like flying a log! The MiG-3 is miles better.' (He meant at medium-altitude flying.) In the end Vasily Stalin made sure we got the Yak-7Bs. However, the La-5 was soon fitted with a new, more powerful direct-injection engine, and it became an aircraft immensely popular with most combat pilots. Moreover, its further modification, the La-7, came to be regarded as our best fighter in that war, along with the Yak-3. From the summer of 1943 onwards our regiment was also equipped with the modified La-5s and then with the La-7s.

In the end Polikarpov proved to be right: the air-cooled engine, even if it slowed down the aircraft's maximum speed, made it more 'survivable' than any aircraft with a liquid-cooled engine. I remember how a damaged La-5 from a neighbouring regiment belly-landed on our aerodrome at the North-West Front. It was riddled with bullets and its hydraulic tubes were shot through, as well as two or three of its engine cylinders, yet the aircraft made it to the airfield. A liquid-cooled engine would not have survived a single direct hit, for it would have lost its liquid, overheated and jammed.

Among my fellow students at the Academy there were quite a number of pilots, mainly those who had been in action during the war. There were two Heroes of the Soviet Union in our midst. Many of the pilots, including myself, although they had joined an engineering academy, were intent on continuing with their flying careers after graduation. In fact we never stopped looking for (and finding) opportunities to fly during our course of studies. The Academy had an air force regiment assigned to it for experimental flights (it was based in Monino, thirty kilometres east of Moscow), and we insisted on being allowed to fly with it. In 1946 the Academy was visited by the Air Force Commander-in-Chief Marshal Vershinin. I was delegated by the other students as their spokesman to address the marshal with a justification of our 'flying practice'. Vershinin accepted our arguments and 'legalised' our partisan flights, saying that there was a great need for test pilots with engineering education; the few such people that there were, were known to him personally and were held in great esteem by everyone in the profession.

The 'team' of those who wanted to fly numbered seven or eight people. Among them were George Bayevsky, Sergei Dedukh, Alexander (Sasha) Shcherbakov, Igor Yemelianov, George Zhitomirsky, and me. Two more people, one of them twice Hero of the Soviet Union, joined our group from a junior year. We were allowed to fly only those types of aircraft which we had known from prior experience, so I could fly the Yak-3 and the Yak-9. We received formal permission to fly every summer, and to have more time to fly we would usually take our end-of-term exams before the scheduled time and also use part of our official leave. By that time the regiment had moved to a different airfield eighty-five kilometres south of Moscow, close to the Academy's summer campsite on the Oka river. In 1948 all third-year students were supposed to fly during their 'term' in the summer camp, but while all others took familiarisation rides in the rear cockpit of the U-2 trainers with regiment pilots, our little group flew real combat machines – unchaperoned.

My flying skills must have inspired the Regiment Commander with confidence, for I was soon allowed to have a go at Lavochkin's fighters, which I had not flown before. During one week in the summer of 1948 I flew the La-5 and the La-7 (and later the La-9 as well). About the same time George Bayevsky and Yuri Nosenko suggested that I go to Vasily Stalin (who commanded the Moscow air force district then) and ask him to give us an opportunity to convert to jet fighters. Although I had been out of touch with Vasily for a few years, the idea was so tempting that I agreed. Vasily was quite easy about it and appointed Colonel Artemiev as our instructor for the Yak-17 jet trainer. The transition training was to take place at the air force training centre commanded by Colonel Akulenko, a celebrated pilot who had led the first ever formation of jet fighters, the MiG-9s, over Red Square during an air parade.

The MiG-9 and the Yak-15 were the earliest Soviet aircraft with turbo-jet engines. They made their maiden flights on one and the same day, 24 April 1946 (the MiG-9 going up three hours earlier). The Yak-15 was in fact a modification of the Yak-3 with its nose-mounted piston engine replaced by a German UMO-004 jet engine, whose exhaust jet ran under the fuselage. The MiG-9, on the other hand, was the first Soviet aircraft originally designed as a jet to be fitted with two BMW-003 jet engines behind and below the cockpit. Both these types of German turbo-jet engine began to be produced by our factories on the basis of the original samples from captured enemy aeroplanes.

The training centre was equipped with combat MiG-9 fighters and the Yak-17U trainer aircraft. As distinct from the Yak-15, the Yak-17U had two cockpits and a nosewheel landing gear instead of a tailwheel one. After a few check-rides with each of us in the Yak-17U, our instructor let us go solo. However, it was the MiG-9 that we were really tempted by – a far more 'serious' aircraft of an entirely novel type, and a faster one at that (the Yak-17U was hardly different in handling from the familiar Yak-3). The training centre CO, having checked us out in the two-seater, declared he was ready to let us have a go at the MiG-9, provided the Moscow District Commander gave his permission. I talked Colonel Artemiev into accompanying me to Moscow to see Vasily Stalin about that permission.

On arrival we went straight to Vasily's house on Gogol Boulevard. He was at dinner when we came, with a large group of officers as his guests. Many of them I knew well. Having heard what we came to say he instructed his second-in-command, Colonel Redkin (who was among the guests), to fly back to the training centre with us in the morning and to oversee our initial solos in the MiG-9. Some two hours after our return to the centre each of us made two solo flights in that fighter and returned to Moscow the same day. Thus, I flew four different types of aircraft in two weeks, two of them completely new jet fighter models. We were proud of those flights. It was not even two years since jet fighters had first been adopted by the Soviet Air Force, and in the entire Academy we were the only people who had a 'flying' acquaintance with them; all other students had only seen them in the training hangar, where first a MiG-9 and then a MiG-15 were displayed for the study of their airframe structure.

My first flights in a jet fighter gave me some familiar and unusual experiences. I was pleasantly surprised by the absence of vibration so common to piston-engine aircraft with air-screws. The jet seemed to fly as smoothly as a glider, and only the engine noise betrayed the difference, but even this noise was different from the noise made by a piston engine: it was even and without the characteristic exhaust 'explosions'. Another thing I liked was the landing gear with a nosewheel (although I had encountered it before in the experimental MiG-8 'Canard'). The nosewheel gave the aircraft stability on the landing run, unlike a tailwheel, with which it would always tend to swerve. Besides, an aircraft with a nosewheel was positioned on the ground almost horizontally, thus giving the pilot a fair forward view. Both the landing and take-off in such an aircraft are easier than in an aeroplane with a tailwheel which would require a three-point touchdown. The cockpit in those jets was nearer the nose, which gave a better forward view but at the same time left the wings too far back to be within vision. At first it made me wonder how the pilot was supposed to monitor banking; the habitual way, especially in aerobatics, was to be guided by the leading edge of the wing. It turned out, however, that the cockpit canopy frame could serve as an equally convenient reference point, and eventually it became so common that the question was never raised again.

To start the engine of those early jets, the mechanic would first pull the cord (like in an ordinary motorboat) of the small auxiliary engine which acted as a starter for the main power plant. The service life of those jet engines did not exceed twenty-five hours before overhaul. Their fuel consumption was much larger than that of the piston engines, while the fuel tank capacity of the jets, particularly of the Yaks, was not so large. To prolong the engine's service life and to save on fuel we would glide down the final with the engine out (something that is hard to believe today) – we would cut it off on the final when sure that the aircraft would touch down at, or close to the landing 'T'. After that there was no way back; another circle was out of the question. In the MiGs, which had two

126

engines, one of them was shut even earlier, on the base leg. At the end of the landing run we would turn off the runway to where a towing truck was waiting to take the aircraft back to the departure end of the strip, where the engine was restarted for the flight.

Another peculiarity of the MiG-9 was its tendency to 'rear' if you abruptly released the brakes at maximum power at take-off (because of the jetwash that ran under the fuselage and rarefied the air under the tail). To avoid its sinking on its tail, the brakes had to be released gradually.

In both of my first flights in the MiG-9, I touched down right at the landing 'T'. Colonel Redkin was pleased, and after a while he sent a formal commendation to the Academy administration, praising George Bayevsky and me 'for excellent solo flights'. And before that, on the flight back to Moscow together later that day, he said, 'I thought I'd have to kill a week looking after you there, and you've got it over and done with in half a day!'

Next summer I addressed Vasily again, and he allowed Bayevsky and me to do our training in the Yak-17B (a combat version of the Yak-17U trainer) in the regiment based at the airfield at Teply Stan, now a residential suburb in the south-west of Moscow. The CO, Nikolai Shulzhenko, had been my fellow flying officer in the No. 32 Fighter Regiment of the Guards. It was just a year since our initial flights in jet fighters, yet the manner of flying them had changed: the practice of cutting off the engine on the approach had been dropped, as well as the towing after landing (the service life of the engines had doubled).

Once, as I had extended the undercarriage at landing, a compressed-air tube suddenly burst, rendering the wheelbrakes utterly useless. The aeroplane ran along the somewhat humpbacked runway up to and over its 'crest' and then rolled downhill. While it could still be controlled with the rudder, I turned off the runway onto rough ground, where it would slow down more easily. Soon it came to a stop – five metres short of a ditch.

Shortly afterwards a real accident happened. As George Bayevsky was taking off on an aerobatic flight, one of his wheel rims suddenly disintegrated. The pilots on stand-by at the far end of the airfield noticed that an aircraft just airborne was one wheel short. They telephoned the CO, who decided that there was no point alerting Bayevsky on the radio or telling him to rush his landing, for the less fuel left in the tank the safer it would be to land with one wheel missing. That proved to be a dangerous error of judgement. I took off shortly after Bayevsky, and after a few aerobatic manoeuvres I saw George performing a loop at some distance from me with a trail of smoke coming out of his machine. I pressed the radio button and said, '121, you've got smoke behind your tail.' The CO heard me in the tower, realised what was happening and ordered an immediate landing.

As Bayevsky was coming in to the base leg, it was dead clear to all that his aircraft was on fire. As it turned out later his fuel tank had been punctured by the fragments of the broken wheel rim; the kerosene had leaked into the engine section and ignited. Bayevsky landed with his lame undercarriage down, on the ground near the runway. By that time I had approached the airfield too and saw him land and then climb out of the cockpit in one piece. Dozens of people were hurrying across the runway to where he stopped. I had not much fuel left by that time, but the people on the runway prevented me from landing. I did a couple of circuits and then had to fly low over their heads to make them clear the runway. In the meantime the mechanics who had reached the burning aircraft were trying to put out the fire, despite the CO's urgent commands to stay away from it. The aircraft was loaded with ammunition, and sure enough the shells started going off soon. One of the mechanics was badly wounded and died on the way to hospital. Had I not noticed George's aircraft in the air with smoke coming out of it, he would have been too far from the airfield by the time the fire got really bad, and bailing out would have been his only chance (though the mechanic would have then stayed alive). After that accident Bayevsky and I were summoned to the second-in-command of the Academy and told off in none too gentle terms. Worst of all, we were forbidden to fly with that regiment, although what had happened was none of our fault.

A few days before 7 November 1949 I went to see a horseback riding competition, where I ran into Vasily Stalin. He offered me to join him in his aeroplane for a fly-past over Red Square during the November parade – he would be flying the leading aircraft as the air parade commander. We took off in a brand-new, recently tested Tu-4 piloted by A. Perelet, a test pilot of the Tupolev Design Company (he was killed in a Tu-95 prototype crash in 1952). Vasily was in the co-pilot's seat and in radio contact with the ground control centre and the formation leaders. I perched on the flight engineer's small hinged seat between the seats of the pilots.

The Tu-4 was produced by Andrei Tupolev as a replica of the American B-29 bomber ('Superfortress'). The B-29 was both technologically and in its design a very advanced aeroplane of its time. Stalin, who commanded that a replica be made, forbade changing anything in the design or introducing any new features; the only alteration was to be the replacement of the machine-guns with Russian-made guns. I would say that the decision to produce an exact replica was very sensible, otherwise, under the pretext of 'improving' the design, many of the B-29's really good features might have been dropped due to the absence of relevant technologies in our aircraft industry. As it was, although the task gave an enormous headache to both the designers and the contractors, the net result was a real technological breakthrough in the Soviet aviation industry, both in terms of the materials used and in the novelty of the avionics installed. Later these new materials and this new equipment were used to produce other types of aircraft. Among those novel types of avionics and other airborne equipment were the systems of remote gun-turret control, the automatic direction finder, bombing and navigation radars, flexible fuel tanks and so on.

Back at the aerodrome I took the opportunity to ask Vasily to be given a chance to fly the then latest fighter, the MiG-15. In November 1949, after a briefing and a training ride in the two-seat MiG-15UTI with my old acquaintance Colonel Artemiev, I performed my initial solo flight in the MiG-15. Among other novelties that distinguished it, it was the first aircraft to be fitted with a Machmeter, and with a speed indicator that showed not only indicated speed but the true air speed as well. I still remember the thrill with which I watched the needle cross the 1,000-kph mark.

In the summer of 1950, when we were all to be assigned for combat practice to various air force regiments as engineers, I asked to be posted to Kubinka, where by that time my younger brother Alexei, a new graduate of the Air Force Command Academy in Monino, had become a deputy regimental commander. As I had hoped, I was allowed to go on flying the MiG-15. My friend and fellow student Sasha Shcherbakov, assigned to the same regiment for his summer practice, was converted for that fighter too. Colonel Artemiev also put us on the night-flight training programme in the Yak-11 trainer, which involved the use of a brand new 'blind-landing system' (OSP-48). Strictly speaking it was not a landing system, but a set of devices that facilitated non-precision landing approach through the clouds with the help of an ADF (automatic direction finder) pre-tuned to two ground homing radio beacons. The ADF indicator needle showed the direction to those beacons. One of the beacons was set up at 4,000 metres and the other at 1,000 metres from the top of the landing strip. At 200 metres above ground and within two kilometres from home, the pilot was already supposed to see the runway. Generally speaking, the weather minima, i.e., the ceiling and horizontal visibility, depend on the precision of the landing system and on the type of aircraft, or, to be more specific, on its approach speed. In the case of a low-performance aircraft both the visibility and the ceiling can be lower than in the case of a fighter. Naturally, if the pilot's qualification is not sufficient, his 'personal' weather minima will be higher than that secured by the landing system. The ADF was used very extensively in all types of aircraft (and is still used today as a back-up for the modern navigation and landing systems), not only on the landing approach but in flight as well.

At Kubinka I had more proof of my luck. As I was taking off in a MiG-15 one day, I released the brakes and increased the rpm, beginning the take-off run. Suddenly I heard a change in the roar of the engine and noticed that the indicator showed that rpms were falling. I reported this to the tower, but the controller's reply was, 'Go on, take off – you must be dreaming it up.' Nevertheless I repeated my report, aborted the take-off run and turned off the runway. When my mechanic took a look, he discovered that the fuel hose was broken at the inlet, so most of the fuel had been gushing out through the hole and all over the engine. Considering that the normal fuel pressure in the hose was 90 atm, it is not hard to imagine what would have happened a few seconds later, when the take-off could no longer have been aborted: apart from unintentional stalling, there was a clear threat of fire. This incident helped to detect a fault in the design of the fuel hose inlet connection, and as a result all the deficient fuel pipes were soon replaced with those of an improved design.

Shortly before our graduation, the Academy was visited by the head of the personnel section of the Flight Test Institute, who arrived to select candidates for future employment. During the meeting he held with the graduates several of us, including me, expressed our wish to become test pilots. He confirmed that the Institute administration was very much in favour of test pilots with an engineering background. He also said that the best specialists among their project engineers were those who had been pilots in the past. In short, a combination of flight experience with engineering education was an advantage all round.

After graduation, five of us were posted to the FTI as test pilots and another few graduates as test engineers. I was assigned to the 1st Section, responsible for the flight testing of fighters and other similar aircraft (interceptors, fighter bombers and reconnaissance aeroplanes based on a fighter airframe). My friend Sergei Dedukh became a test pilot of the 2nd (Bomber) Section, while Igor Yemelianov and Alexander Shcherbakov were posted to Section No. 3 to test helicopters and trainer aeroplanes. All three sections belonged to the Institute Department No. 1, which was in charge of testing all types of aircraft. George Bayevsky was assigned to Department No 2, which tested engines.

Among my fellow graduates from the Academy was Vladimir (Volodya) Ilyushin, son of the famous aircraft designer. A well-known test pilot in the future, at that time he had almost no flying experience at all. He was first taught to fly in an initial trainer, the UT-2, by Vladimir Kokkinaki, the chief test pilot of Vladimir's father's design company, who did it in his own time and as a personal gesture. On graduation from the Academy, Volodya passed final exams in a primary-training flying course at a flying school (as an external student) and then joined the test pilot school of the Aviation Industry Ministry. Later he became, and for many years remained, the chief test pilot at the Sukhoi Design Company, eventually earning a reputation as one of the best aviation industry test pilots.

Alexander Shcherbakov, although the end of the war had seen him as a flying officer, was still a relatively inexperienced pilot by the time we all met. After the Academy he spent a year at the FTI, and then left it to take a course at the same test pilot school. Eventually he became a highly qualified test pilot, particularly well-known for his achievements in spin testing. Both Vladimir Ilyushin and Alexander Shcherbakov were later made Heroes of the Soviet Union. As for Sergei Dedukh, at the beginning of the war he was flying the obsolete R-5s, which, like the U-2s of the Women's Bomber Regiment, were only used for night-time bombings. In that aircraft Sergei was shot down, just as I was too, by a friend, only in his case it was not another aircraft but an anti-aircraft gun.

My other friend George Bayevsky deserves a special place in my story. An instructor pilot at the outbreak of the war, he was posted temporarily to a front-line regiment where he distinguished himself as a daring fighter pilot, achieving two personal victories within a short time and winning over his fellow officers with his unfailingly good nature. He returned to the school with a petition signed by the Regiment Commander to support his own request to be sent back to that regiment for permanent service. His request was denied, so he left the school without leave – 'deserting to the front line'. By the time the demand to send him packing reached the regiment, George had distinguished himself in action again and they let him be.

Once he and his wingman Peter Kalsin were on a free hunting mission far behind the lines in their La-5s. As they came near a German airfield George spotted a Focke-Wulf 189, which he attacked and shot down. However, at the last moment the German gunner fired at George's La-5 and set it on fire. George belly-landed on a snow-covered field and tumbled out of the burning aeroplane in time to see his wingman land nearby with his undercarriage down. The risk

130

was tremendous: a small ditch or a snowdrift in the field would have made his aeroplane dip its nose down and break the propellor, or even turn over. Kalsin taxied over to George, who opened the hatch of the fuselage and squeezed inside it, his feet sticking out for lack of room. Kalsin opened the throttle, but one of the wheels got stuck in a hole in the ground. George climbed out, stood under the wing and struggled to lift it with his shoulders. The wheel got out of the hole, and George climbed back into the fuselage. They took off under the machine-gun fire of the Germans, who were running across the field towards them. As Kalsin approached home, the other pilots' spirits sank at the sight of only one aircraft returning instead of two, but to their great joy they soon saw George Bayevsky, badly burned yet in one piece and alive, climb out of the fuselage.

The CO immediately gave orders to write to the Air Force Command putting Kalsin forward for the title of Hero of the Soviet Union, as a pilot who saved his formation leader at risk to his own life. Unfortunately, a few days later Kalsin failed to return from an air combat. He was never awarded the title, not even posthumously, since there was no confirmation of his aircraft going in; he was reported missing in action, and the 'political commissars' in the Armed Forces Command tended to think of such people with suspicion. There were so many such victims of the war whose families were even denied a pension on the grounds that their fate was unknown.

His final two victories (out of a total of nineteen) George achieved over Berlin, the city which he had known well. His father had been head of the Soviet trade mission in Berlin and the family had spent several years living in Germany before he was posted to Sweden. In both countries George went to local schools, thanks to which he was (and still is) fluent in German and could speak Swedish. George Bayevksy is a very good and loyal friend and an exceptionally modest person. Far from showing off his awards and distinctions he has always been almost shy (particularly among fellow students at the Academy) of being a Hero of the Soviet Union and later a general.

CHAPTER 11

Politburo Members and 'Big Politics'

Shortly after my wedding and the entrance exams at the Academy, my wife and I went together to the Crimea for our honeymoon. We were given a suite of rooms in the service wing of Vorontsov Palace near Alupka, so called because before 1917 it had belonged to the rich and influential Russian nobleman Count Vorontsov. During the Yalta Conference of 1945 the palace had been given to Winston Churchill as his residence, and for a number of years after that it was used as one of the so-called 'government dachas' – holiday residences in the 'care' of the special No. 9 Department of the KGB (the department responsible for the personal safety of the Politburo members) – and occupied in turn by various Politburo members and their families. Occasionally these dachas on the Black Sea coast were also used to accommodate the visiting leaders of the 'socialist camp' countries. Vorontsov Palace was eventually returned to its pre-war status of a public museum, and certainly when my wife and I were living there in the summer of 1945 we would enter the main part of the building with all the respect and admiration due to a fine museum. I remember vividly the grandeur of the great dining-room with its impressive array of pictures on the walls, the glass-walled 'winter garden' with tropical plants, the library with hundreds of old books, the marble lions outside the front entrance and the beautiful park that descended steeply to the sea level and the beach.

Although some of these dachas were known individually as 'Stalin's dacha', 'Molotov's dacha' and so on, officially none of them was assigned to any particular dignitary. When a Politburo member was about to go on holiday on the Black Sea he would choose one of the dachas that happened to be vacant at the time. At the same time there were, of course, some personal preferences involved. Thus, Stalin would usually go to the Sochi area, to the dacha near Matsesta or to the one near Gagra. With Stalin's favourite dachas the situation was different: it was only at his invitation that anybody else occupied any of them. Molotov preferred the dacha at Miusseri, Voroshilov the one at Oreanda in the Crimea, or near Sochi. My father liked the dacha at Miusseri too, and the one at Mukhalatka in the Crimea. Stalin's favourite dachas were usually quite far from the sea and high above it; according to my father he was not fond of sea bathing and would hardly ever go to the beach at all (however, in a letter to his wife in September 1931 he wrote that he had swum in the sea). What he liked most was walking in the park and sitting on a park bench or on the terrace of his house.

At the end of the 1950s three new government dachas were built at Pitsunda in Abkhazia. The vast grounds encompassed a fine wood of ancient pine trees of a rare kind. (Many people were indignant when the wood was made inaccessible to the public, yet in the opinion of others the enclosure actually saved the trees from the sad fate of many other much-frequented natural havens; our holiday-makers in Russia are notorious for their careless treatment of the environment.) A brand-new sports complex with a sea-water swimming-pool added to the attraction of the place. It became a favourite holiday place of Khrushchev, Kosyghin and my father.

While on holiday, Politburo members would never detach themselves from work and affairs of state completely. Every day a special military aeroplane arrived from Moscow with a state messenger on board who brought various government papers for perusal (at some stage the messengers stopped coming on special aircraft and began using regular airline flights, accompanied by body-guards). Besides, each dacha had a telephone on a special secret high-frequency line linked to the Kremlin and the highest of the state officials.

When my father went on his annual holiday to the Black Sea he always took his grandchildren with him, usually seven or eight of them, or even the whole lot (by the mid-1950s there were ten altogether). Those of his sons and daughters-in-law who happened to be on leave from work at the time would also join them there for some time. Altogether we, the four brothers, had sixteen children among us (two of my brothers were married more than once). The first ten of my father's grandchildren more or less grew up together at his dacha, where they spent all their pre-school years and all their holidays and weekends while they were at school. It was like a family 'kindergarten', and it is probably due to their child-hood spent together that most of them have remained very close to one another to this day, hardly making any distinction between a brother or a sister and a cousin. The eldest of them all are my son Volodya (Vladimir in full, named after my brother who was killed during the war), born in 1946, and my daughter Ashkhen (Aschen, named after my mother), born in July 1949. In February 1952 our third child was born, a boy whom we named Alexander after Ella's mother, Alexandra. Volodya was educated as a biologist, and he is now working at an International Science Foundation in Moscow. Aschen is a lecturer in English as a foreign language at Moscow State University (of which both she and her elder brother are graduates, as well as her son, Alexander junior) and a translator. Their younger brother, Alexander, has always divided his life between his two main passions – music and car racing. Ella and I now have five grandchildren. Our eldest grandchild, Alexander, is twenty-seven, our youngest, Anton, just over two years old. In 1992 we were 'promoted' to great-grandparents when our granddaughter Julia gave birth to her little Sasha. Alexander's eldest son Dima is a student, and his youngest is just a toddler. As for my brothers, they have another thirteen grandchildren among them.

Father would usually spend most of the morning on the beach, where he would sit under a canvas awning for at least an hour and a half working on state docu-ments. While he was on the beach the government telephone line was transferred to the telephone in the beach-house. My father was a poor swimmer, in fact he could hardly swim at all, yet he loved being in water and would spend half an hour at a time keeping afloat with the help of an inflatable lifebelt, at a considerable distance from the shore. He also loved rowing and would regularly go far into the sea in a rowing boat, mostly on his own but sometimes with one or two of his grandchildren to keep him company. Whether he was swimming or rowing, he was invariably accompanied, at a discreet distance, by a rowing boat with two of his bodyguards in it (appropriately dressed in 'beach gear'). Sometimes one of them would go swimming with him. In the afternoon my father would usually devote another two hours or so to his papers, sitting on the open terrace of the house, and then spend some time there reading. One of his favourite pastimes was walking in the park, in any kind of weather. He was perfectly content to walk on his own (very likely grateful for some peace and silence, for his grandchildren were a noisy lot!), but he was equally pleased whenever any of his sons, daughters-in-law or elder grandchildren volunteered to join him. Some time before dinner a game or two of volleyball would be played on the pitch in the grounds, with some of the security guards or drivers forming up the teams besides my father and myself. After dinner the whole family would get together to watch a film, while those who were not interested would play billiards, go swimming in the sea or read. Every government dacha was equipped with a film projector and a wall screen in the largest room, and a full-size billiard table. During his holiday my father usually visited some collective farm or farms in the neighbourhood. Although I hardly ever stayed with him for the entire three or four weeks of his holiday, I remember accompanying him on at least four such visits, one of which was to a trout farm near Gagra.

One morning during a fortnight I was spending with my father and the children at Mukhalatka in the Crimea, I went to Yalta where I heard about a girl who was taken to a police station for walking around the town in shorts. Such a 'frivolous' manner of dressing was frowned upon at that time, even at a seaside resort. When I returned to the dacha I told my father about the unfortunate girl. Later that afternoon, after lunch, he was going to visit some construction site. I was waiting for him by the car, and soon he emerged from the house wearing shorts! Knowing that the local dignitaries would be 'in attendance' at the building site, he deliberately dressed like that to curb the zeal with which they were trying to oppose the 'subversive influence of the West'.

In the summer of 1946 I went to a sanatorium in the North Caucasus for a course of mud-baths for my knee (broken in my crash-landing during the war). The spa shared its spacious grounds with a government dacha. It was the house where my parents had stayed with my brother Volodya and me during my father's brief holiday in 1924. This time the dacha was occupied by Panteleimon Ponomarenko, First Secretary of the Belorussian Communist Party, who had been the partisan movement leader at the time of the German occupation of Belorussia during the war. An easy-going and sociable man, he spent a lot of time mixing with the inmates of the main building and would often take part in our daily volleyball games. During one particularly tense game one of the supporters loudly made a few good-natured jokes aimed at Ponomarenko's team. It was Zosim Shashkov, Minister of Inland Water Transport. Ponomarenko's team was in a bad shape, and Ponomarenko suddenly lost his temper at Shashkov's teasing. An exchange of sharp words followed, and Shashkov left the pitch. The same evening, when the large common room of the spa building was full of people who had gathered to listen to music and to dance, Ponomarenko entered and walked straight to where Shashkov was talking with a few other men. He joined their conversation as though nothing had happened. He had obviously been uneasy about his public outburst on the pitch, so he made the first step to reconciliation, which was as good as a public apology to Shashkov.

I have since respected Ponomarenko, and whenever I heard anything about him from anybody who knew him well, it was always nothing but sincere praise. I saw him once or twice after that, one of those encounters being in Poland where he was ambassador at the time when I was sent there to help Polish pilots convert to our fighters. The last time I saw him was shortly before his death, at a clinic in Moscow where we were waiting to be called in by our respective dentists. I naturally asked him how he was, and we talked of this and that, and eventually he mentioned Brezhnev (who was still 'at the top'), in none too flattering terms. He said that it was Brezhnev who had caused his premature retirement. He also told me how in the early 1950s Khrushchev had sent him and Brezhnev together to Kazakhstan as his chosen candidates to be elected secretaries of the local Central Committee of the party. Ponomarenko was expected to be elected First Secretary, Brezhnev his deputy. Khrushchev, whose authority had not yet become as complete as it was later, was somewhat apprehensive about the vote. Ponomarenko, by his own account, had played on the mutual rivalry of the two main factions within the Central Committee of Kazakhstan, managing to convince them both of his neutrality, giving them to understand that he was an equally acceptable choice from every point of view. As a result, both he and Brezhnev were elected. Ponomarenko got through to Khrushchev on the government line, and Khrushchev immediately asked 'Did they blackball you?', and was pleased to hear of their election. Later Brezhnev replaced Ponomarenko as the First Secretary. 'And now he has given me the boot!' he concluded with resentment.

On Stalin's death he was appointed Minister of Culture. One day a newly made Soviet film was shown to him for his approval, and he okayed its release. The chairman of the State Committee for Cinematography voiced his surprise: 'Should it not be shown at the top first?' he said, for before Stalin's death no feature film could be released without his personal approval. 'D'you mean that my wife should see it too?' Ponomarenko asked. (Incidentally, in the late 1940s Stalin issued an order according to which only eight films could be made each year, and each of them had to be 'very good'. I still remember the irony with which my father told us about it.)

In January 1949 we heard that father was to take a trip to the Far East. We assumed it would be the same kind of trip as he had made in the autumn of 1945, when he had spent over a month in the Far East with a group of industrial experts. They flew from Moscow to Russia's easternmost coastline, stopping on the way in Krasnoyarsk, Irkutsk, Khabarovsk and so on and visiting various industrial enterprises. Then they spent some time on a warship (received from the USA on lend-lease), which took them to the islands Sakhalin and the

Kurils, and to Kamchatka. Wherever they went they visited various plants and food- and fish-processing factories. (My brother Vanya accompanied father on that trip.) Now it was again officially announced that Anastas Mikoyan was going to the Kuril Islands on some food industry business. Actually he was going to China on a secret mission from the Politburo that involved negotiations with Mao Tse-tung. It was still eight months before the Communists took full power in China, so the trip was to be made in total secrecy.

Not long ago I received an opportunity to read archive material related to that trip. Apparently, Mao had received an invitation to come to Moscow back in 1947, and he was ready to come in the summer of 1948. According to a message from Dr Terebin, Mao's personal physician (a Russian doctor sent to Mao by the Soviet government), 'the suitcases were packed, leather shoes purchased (as everyone else in China, Mao would normally have worn canvas shoes) and an overcoat made'. Mao himself would often say in private conversations that he was willing to go. A series of coded telegrams was exchanged to discuss the best plan. The final decision was made in favour of going by air from a former Japanese airfield. Mao, accompanied by a retinue of twenty people, would make his way to the airfield, to which two aircraft would be sent from across the Russian border. Stalin agreed to that plan, promising that two aeroplanes would be there on the day named by the Chinese side. The whole operation was to be prepared and carried out in utmost secrecy.

Then suddenly Stalin informed Mao that from August to November most Soviet leaders would be 'scattered' around the country overseeing the harvesting, so if he wanted to meet them all he would have to postpone his visit. Mao replied with ill-concealed surprise at the fact that harvesting should demand such close attention on the part of the country's top leadership. In September 1948 Mao retaliated with a telegram informing Stalin of his illness, putting off his visit until December. On 30 December another telegram arrived from China with a detailed account of military operations against the Kuomintang army and a promise that Mao Tse-tung would visit Moscow as soon as the fighting was over. He seemed fully ready to start out at the beginning of January 1949, yet a telegram from Stalin dated 10 January advised that the visit be postponed due to the situation at hand. One of the considerations against the visit was that if it became known, the Communist Party of China would be discredited and openly accused of dancing to Moscow's tune. Dr Terebin replied that if Mao did not go to Moscow before the end of January he would probably not be able to go at all. On 14 January another telegram from Stalin insisted that the visit be put off, and suggested sending a Politburo member to China to talk it all over with Mao. A reply from Mao confirmed his agreement to that plan. On 18 January Stalin cabled the following secret message: '[To] Terebin. Inform Mao our representative arrived Dairen today. Surname Mikoyan conspiratorial name Andreev. Surname to be kept secret. 28.01.49. Stalin.'

I do not think that 'Andreev' was a very happy choice for a conspiratorial name since there was a Politburo member at the time whose real name was Andreev – Andrei A. Andreev. All telegrams to Stalin were to be addressed to the name of Filippov. All radio communication went through Dr Terebin, who also did the coding and decoding of messages together with Dr Melnikov, another Russian physician in Mao's 'retinue'. (Dr Terebin was later killed in an air crash near Sochi where he had been on holiday.) This exchange of telegrams was followed by another in which they discussed the tactics of the Chinese Communist Party in view of its imminent victory over the Kuomintang and its supporters. Thus, in connection with the CCP's intention to ban all other parties upon coming to power, Stalin informed Mao of Moscow's disapproval of this plan and recommended him to let some of the parties be, namely the ones that were in opposition to the Kuomintang regime. He even went as far as to suggest that they should be represented in the new government, which should be called a 'coalition government'.

Toward the end of 1948 the Americans began to probe the ground, intending to suggest negotiations between the Kuomintang and the CCP with the mediation of the US, France, Britain and the USSR. Stalin suggested that Mao should agree on the condition that Chiang Kai-shek and other generals were excluded from the talks. This condition was calculated to ensure the Kuomintang leaders' refusal to negotiate. 'It will look as if the CCP is willing to start peace talks,' Stalin wrote, 'therefore it will not be possible to accuse it of wishing to prolong the civil war. It will be the Kuomintang which will be responsible for the breakdown of peace talks. Thus, the peace-aimed manoeuvre devised by the Kuomintang and the USA will be disrupted, and you will be able to continue your victorious war of liberation.' This was Stalin's characteristic way, to talk of peace while thinking of war. Mao Tse-tung did not accept Stalin's scheme and suggested that the USSR should make a declaration to the effect that, in accordance with the principle of non-interference, it refused to act as a mediator. Stalin replied that by refusing an offer of peace talks Mao was laying his cards on the table and allowing the Kuomintang to use such a powerful trump card as an offer of peace. Later Mao Tse-tung changed his mind and published the 'eight conditions for peace talks', which were clearly unacceptable to the other party.

In my father's archive there is a paper dictated by him to his secretary in 1958 and devoted to his trip to China in 1949. In this paper he recalls that while preparing for the trip he put together a list of questions that were likely to be asked by the Chinese side and mapped out his own answers to those questions. So as not to ask for Moscow's approval at every turn of the future talks, my father went over to Stalin with his list of questions and they spent two hours discussing the answers. The list with those seventeen questions is still in the file.

Father was accompanied on that trip by an interpreter and I. Kovalev, Minister of Transport. Stalin sent him to 'look around', for he intended to appoint him as USSR's official representative in China once the CCP came to power. They took off for the Far East in an American-made transport aeroplane, a Douglas C-47 from the Soviet Air Force Special Transport Wing. Their first pilot was Wing Commander General Victor Grachev, a well-known pilot who had distinguished himself in the Spanish war. 'Grachev was an experienced and talented pilot,' my father wrote, 'and he gave us an easy flight to Khabarovsk.' (I can add that he was also a very good and pleasant man. Until 1991, when he died, he had been working as a lecturer at the Zhukovsky Academy.) To the local officials who met them in Khabarovsk my father said that he was 'going to the Kuril Islands about some fishing industry business. A formal excuse. Said this to Malinovsky [the future Defence Minister] and the others. But although I did not say anything, they guessed about my trip.'

Their next stop was Port Arthur, where only the Air Corps Commander knew that their aeroplane would next go to China. They took off at night-time and reached China at dawn. They were escorted by a formation of Soviet fighters as far as the frontier, and once over China they flew at the lowest possible height, hiding from the radars at the American air force and naval base, which at some point on their route was just a hundred kilometres away. Part of the route lay over the mountains, and visibility was low. Many years later Grachev himself told me how difficult and risky that flight had been. They landed on a formerly Japanese airfield about 300 kilometres south-west of Peking (which, as I established on a map, would make it about 600 kilometres as the crow flies from Port Arthur – a two-and-a-half-hour flight in the C-47). They found the airfield by a campfire lit by the Chinese in lieu of a landing light. The airfield had been out of use for some time, but the runway was still in decent condition. They were met by two members of the Chinese Politburo. The aircraft was sent on a return flight there and then, lest it be detected and destroyed from the air.

The journey was continued in a captured army Dodge another 170 kilometres or so (about six hours) along dusty country roads, past numerous villages and finally into a mountain gorge where the Central Committee of the CCP had its secret headquarters in a small village. Mao was lodging in a small wattle-and-daub peasant hut with two rooms and a courtyard. There was oil-paper in the windows instead of glass and a kind of quilted door-curtain instead of a front door. The house was not heated, and Mao was sitting there in a thick padded jacket while my father kept his heavy winter coat on his shoulders. The house to which he and Kovalev were taken after their initial interview with Mao Tse-tung was very small, but thanks to a little iron stove it was warm.

My father takes up the narrative: 'In Moscow we suffered from Stalin's habits. He would go to bed at four or five in the morning and get up at six or seven in the afternoon, or between noon and two p.m. in the summer. Every night he would invite us to dinner [that would often last until the small hours]. And we had to be at work by eleven a.m. . . . . It is not hard to imagine how tough this routine was. We suffered badly, for we could not neglect our work. On the other hand, one could not ignore Stalin's invitation or leave early. We were in a hard and hopeless position.' Father must have remembered Stalin's habits in connection with his account of his Chinese trip, because Mao turned out to have the same daily routine as Stalin. Like him, he did not go to bed before four or five in the morning or get up until two or three in the afternoon. My father's daily discussions with Mao did not finish before midnight or later, yet he made a point of organising his own time in a way as close to normal as he could, something he could never afford to do in Moscow. He would get up between eight and nine in the morning and take a long walk in the mountains. The consultations with Mao, which were also attended by Chou En-lai and other Chinese Communist leaders, began in the late afternoon. Earlier during the day my father would sometimes talk with these people without Mao. The interpreter who had come from Moscow with him did not know the dialect Mao was using, so the talks were interpreted by a Chinese who knew Russian, for he had lived in the USSR for sixteen years and had a Russian wife.

In the group of people who accompanied my father and Kovalev to China were two experts on disarming mines and neutralising listening-in devices. They went with Mao's son to Peking (which had just been captured by the Communist troops) to check out the buildings intended for the Central Committee and the government. Next in that paper I read: 'Stalin had always been paranoid about spies, he thought they were all over the place and could infiltrate the whole country and do anything; he feared that the Chinese leadership was surrounded by American and English spies, and so he specifically instructed me to find out if there were any Americans or English people anywhere near the Chinese [Communist Leaders]. He insisted that I find out and report to him.' Mao's Russian physicians told my father of two Americans that were around. My father had to report what he heard to Moscow. Stalin then directed him to recommend to Mao to have those two people arrested. 'I did as I was told.' Mao Tse-tung, however, was not convinced. My father had to report the outcome of their exchange on the subject to Stalin, who urged him to insist further. 'The Chinese were annoyed,' my father writes, 'they could not understand why we should interfere with their affairs. It produced a bad impression. Yet I had Stalin's strict instructions [to insist on the Americans' arrest]. It brought a touch of coldness into our talks, otherwise quite friendly and amiable. I admitted, of course, that I was speaking on instructions from Moscow, but rather than blaming Stalin I tried to present my own arguments in their favour. All this clearly displeased Mao Tse-tung. I was actually far from certain that I was right, yet I had to do what the Central Committee had instructed me to do.' There is a telegram from Stalin in the file that directly refers to the matter. It reads:

> [To] Mikoyan. To be reported to Mao Tse-tung. We have no doubt that Rittenberg, the American on the board of the CCP Central Committee's news-paper, is a US spy. We advise that he be immediately arrested and the network of American agents exposed through him. We have indisputable evidence that the American writer Ann-Louise Strong is a US spy. Over the past few years she has asked to be admitted to the USSR as a member of the left-wing faction in the workers' movement and as a Marxist with pro-Communist sympathies, but we declined her entry each time. In actual fact she has long served as an American spy. Our advice is not to allow her anywhere near your people or the areas controlled by the CCP. Stalin. 4.2.1949.

There was another telegram from Stalin along the same lines, this time about an American professor. According to the report of the then Deputy Foreign Secretary F.Kuznetsov, the professor 'had contacts' with the US ambassador in China, Stuart (which was perfectly natural, considering that Stuart was the former chancellor of the university in Peking at which that professor was teaching). In short, Stalin was behaving in his usual way, seeing spies round every corner and having people arrested on the basis of made-up or imagined 'indisputable evidence'. In the end the Americans were arrested. On Stalin's death, my father insisted that the Chinese be officially informed that there was no evidence against those people and therefore there was no need to keep them in custody. Shortly afterwards they were released.

Throughout father's stay in China he and Stalin exchanged daily telegrams. He had to keep Stalin informed of all the talks, while the latter responded with his directives and suggestions. The cipher clerks at both ends (in China they were the two doctors) must have had a hard time coding and decoding them. Another typical piece of advice given by Stalin to Mao via my father concerned the CCP's national policy. The Soviet Central Committee, he informed my father in his telegram, 'did not recommend the CCP to be too liberal on the national score by giving independence to national minorities and thus curtailing the territory of Communist China. They should be allowed to have autonomy but not independence.' My father writes that Mao was obviously pleased with that advice; it was written on his face that he had had no intention of giving independence to anyone.

When the talks were over the group was driven back to the same airfield where they were taken on board Grachev's C-47, which had been called in to collect them. When they landed in Vladivostok my father received a phone call from the chief of Stalin's secretariat, Poskrebyshev, who informed him that the Politburo was highly pleased with his mission in China. It turned out that Stalin had been reading my father's daily telegrams out to all Politburo members, and their content had been discussed at their meetings. According to Poskrebyshev, Stalin was impatient for him to return to Moscow and give him a detailed account of his trip.

Some time after my father's return to Moscow, he said that he wanted to have a word with me in private (it was at the dacha). It was a rare thing for him to say and something we had always feared, for it promised a serious dressing-down. In a very stern voice he demanded to know how I had found out about his trip to China and whom I had told about it. Stalin and the Politburo, he said, had always believed him to be a reliable person who would not blurt things out, and now I had let him down! I was mortified. I protested that I had not known about his secret mission to China, so there was no way I could have told anyone about it. I was genuinely at a loss and could not remember talking to anyone about it. And then I mentioned Svetlana Stalina, who had been at my place a short while before. My father, who had been urging me to remember, was immediately alerted and demanded, 'Well, what about Svetlana?' At first I could not tell, and then I had it all back in a flash: as I had been telling her of my father's urgent departure for the Far East, I had had a sudden idea as to what his destination might be, and I had shared it with her. 'And what if he calls on Mao Tse-tung?' I had said (in those days the victories of the Chinese Red Army were on everyones's lips). I realised that my father had been aware of the source from which my indiscretion had become known, but he waited for me to name it. He told me off severely, finishing with the words, 'Don't blab!' As for Svetlana, I do not know why she relayed my guess to anyone. I decided not to ask her about it.

Towards the end of 1948 or thereabouts, my youngest brother Sergo met Alla, daughter of Alexei Alexandrovich Kuznetsov, a member of the Central Committee of the party who had distinguished himself in the battle of Leningrad. They fell in love and decided to marry, though Sergo was not even twenty yet. It was at that time that Kuznetsov fell into disfavour with Stalin; he was dismissed from his position in the Central Committee and instructed to sign up for some military course. For a party official of his rank to be sent on a training course was a sure sign that something much worse than that was in store for him. Sergo and Alla got married on 15 February 1949, the very day when Alla's father lost his job. Shortly before it my father was accosted by Kaganovich, who said, 'You must be mad to allow your son to marry Kuznetsov's daughter – he might be arrested any day now!' My father replied that it was not Kuznetsov his son was marrying but his daughter, and that he was not going to interfere with his son's life. It was not until some years later that Sergo heard about this conversation from our father.

The wedding was to be celebrated at our dacha, and Sergo naturally expected his father-in-law to attend. Under some pretext or another Kuznetsov asked to be excused. Obviously he did not wish to put our father into an awkward position (if not at direct personal risk) by his presence at his dacha. Sergo told father of Kuznetsov's refusal to come and he (father) phoned him himself, repeating the invitation. Kuznetsov tried to excuse himself again on the grounds that he had no car available for a trip out of town. My father dismissed that excuse by declaring that he would send his car to bring him over. And he did. Kuznetsov did come, but he took care not to stay long – after about an hour he slipped away and left.

In August the same year, Sergo, with his young wife, our brother Vanya and me, was staying with my father at a government dacha in Sochi. A few weeks earlier my wife Ella had given birth to our daughter, so she stayed in Moscow with the baby. None of us had visited the Caucasus before, and my father decided we should see the 'land of our ancestors'. He allowed us to take his car, and his chauffeur drove us first to Sukhumi, then through Kutaisi and Gori to Tbilisi (where I was born). From there we went to Armenia, driving along a winding road high in the mountains. While in Armenia we stayed at the house of Grigory Arutiunov, Armenia's First Party Secretary. I remember him as a pleasant, well-spoken and cultivated man. Later I heard that he had been generally respected in Armenia, and most people were upset and disappointed at his eventual dismissal: after the 20th Congress of the CPSU there was a campaign to 'automatically' remove party leaders who had begun their career under Stalin. Arutiunov had a niece, Nami, who was then living at his house and whom he had adopted after her father had become a victim of Stalin's purges in 1937. Nami soon became the wife of Alexei, another of my brothers (they had met some time before), and in 1951 they had their first child, a boy, whom they named Anastas. One of our trips around Armenia was to the Sevan lake and from there, over a chain of mountains, to Alaverdy and finally to Sanahin, my father's native village, perching high on a plateau over a deep gorge.

At the end of August, when Sergo and Alla were still staying with the

Arutiunovs in Yerevan (Vanya and I had left for Moscow earlier, while the driver with the car had been sent back to Sochi by train a few days after our arrival in Yerevan), it became known that Alla's father had been arrested. Alla, unsuspecting, was trying to call home to her parents from Yerevan but their telephone was not answered. Later she learnt that every room in their flat except for two ('generously' left for Kuznetsov's wife and her younger children to live in) had been locked and sealed by NKVD officers who had come to arrest her father. The telephone happened to be plugged in in one of the sealed rooms, and there it remained, inaccessible to its owners. My brother Vanya (a wizard with his hands and a born engineer) arrived with a telephone apparatus and connected it to the cables that ran through the corridor.

Some time after his arrest Alexei Kuznetsov was executed, along with N. Voznesensky, P. Popkov and a number of other party leaders (all of whom at one time or another had worked in Leningrad). Then Kuznetsov's widow, Zinaida Dmitrievna (Alexei Kosyghin's wife's sister), was arrested and convicted (for the 'crime' of being an 'enemy of the people's' wife) to eight years in a labour camp. The children were left on their own: Alla, the eldest and now a married woman, her sisters Galya and Lida, and her eight-year-old brother Valery. They were evicted from their parents' spacious apartment and given a poky little flat instead, where they moved in and lived with their paralysed grandmother (my brothers Alexei and Vanya brought her to her new home and actually carried her upstairs, for she could not walk). My father had always respected Kuznetsov and never believed in the absurd charges against him, but there was nothing he could do to save him. It was part of Stalin's deliberate scheme to destroy all members of the Leningrad party leadership, and he was determined to carry it through, which he did.

The only help my father could effectively offer was to Kuznetsov's youngest children (to say nothing of supporting his new daughter-in-law, their sister) and he did all that was in his power. My parents took them into their care, and they began to be practically seen as members of our family. Father used to send his car to bring them to the dacha, where they would often stay for several weeks at a time. This must have saved them from the lot of so many other children in their position, from being exiled and forced to live in an orphanage. This kind of open support and sympathetic attitude on the part of my father (and the Kuznetsov children were not the only children of his purged friends whom he helped in some way or other) required courage and was rather a dangerous thing to do in those dark days, for it could easily be interpreted as a deliberate act of defiance. In fact it might have been one of the causes of my father's eventual fall into disfavour after 1951. Immediately after Stalin's death my father invited Kuznetsov's children to come to the dacha and said, 'Your father was no enemy of the people, or whatever. I wanted you to know this!' Their mother, Zinaida Dmitrievna, was released in February 1954.

In 1957 our family was struck by another tragedy: Sergo's wife Alla died. When earlier that year she had been examined at a clinic because she had not been feeling well for some time, an eminent blood specialist on the commission, Professor Kassirsky, phoned my father and asked to see him, and when they met he told him that Alla had leukaemia and her days were numbered. Sergo was told of it too. In the summer Alla began to feel better, and my father called Professor Kassirsky and said, 'Fortunately you seem to have been mistaken.' 'Alas, Anastas Ivanovich, I am not', replied Kassirsky, and explained that it was only a temporary and superficial improvement which would be soon followed by a relapse, with the process developing faster than before. He was right. Towards the autumn, Alla's condition grew seriously worse and she was taken to Barvikha, a government sanatorium in the country not far from our dacha. We, Sergo's brothers and our wives, were somewhat surprised when Sergo moved in with her into her ward; we did not yet know that Alla was fatally ill, whereas he was painfully aware that those were their last days together. My wife Ella and I visited them there. Alla seemed to be in high spirits and laughed a lot, but we could not help noticing a strange puffiness in her face.

A few weeks later, when I returned to Moscow from an outside duty trip, Ella told me that Alla was dying. I was stunned and could not believe what I heard. It seemed totally incredible. She had always been so full of life. We were all dearly fond of her. She was so charming, so lovable, so young. A slim and gracious girl, she was easy-going, friendly and cheerful. I remember how I once came to the dacha and saw my father walking along a path with Alla, who was wearing a smart new dress and looking awfully elegant. I gave way to my admiration: 'A true Parisian lady if there was one!' My father retorted almost angrily: 'Why Parisian? A Russian beauty!' The ease with which Alla could win people over had always amazed me; a total stranger after chatting with her for a few minutes would perceive her as a good old friend (my wife has the same gift with the people she likes). She must not have enjoyed her studies very much, and she quit the Institute as soon as she started having children. She was made for family life and for the love of and for the people around her. Alla and Sergo had lived together for nine years and had had three children before she died at twenty-nine, her youngest daughter just under the age of four.

Ella and I went over to the hospital. Alla was unbearable to look at; she breathed with difficulty and was unable to speak. She died the next day. Sergo, Alla's brother Valery and my wife were with her to the last. Literally a minute before she died the nurse led Sergo out of the ward. My father was informed and he came over straight away, his eyes, as Ella told me, full of tears. I saw my father crying too – for the first time in my life – at the funeral, over Alla's coffin. He had loved her dearly. He always treated my wife and his other sons' wives as his daughters and he loved them all (when asked, before any of us got married, if he regretted not having daughters of his own, he would always say, 'My sons will bring wives into the family, and so I'll have daughters'), but he was especially caring and protective towards Alla, maybe because her father's tragic fate was forever a painful memory.

Sergo is the only of my father's sons never to have had anything to do with aviation. He graduated from the Institute of International Relations (as, later, did his eldest son, Volodya) and his fields are modern history and politics. For nearly twenty years he headed the editorial board of the journal *Latin America*, then joined the senior research staff of the Institute of World Economy and

143

Foreign Relations within the Russian Academy of Sciences. For the past few years he has been lecturing on Russia's Soviet and post-Soviet history, politics and international relations at Georgetown University in Washington and several other universities. Since our father's death Sergo has been responsible for the publication of some of his writings, and he prepared the US edition of the first volume of our father's memoirs. He is the 'curator' of the unpublished part of Anastas Mikoyan's memoirs and of other family archives. Sergo has five children: two sons, Volodya and Sergei, and three daughters, Svetlana, Karina and Anastasia.

My other brother Vanya got married in 1950 when he was still a student of the Air Force Engineering Academy. When our parents heard of his plans to marry Zina – a professional dancer – they were somewhat taken aback but raised no objection to their marriage, and Zina became Vanya's wife. At first my father wanted her to quit dancing (she belonged to the world-famous Moiseev dance company), but Vanya was against it, and so was Zina, of course, and they won; my father gave in and soon he no longer minded. Zina performed under her maiden name. Lithe and good-looking, cheerful and bubbly, she was a dedicated and gifted dancer who enjoyed a long and successful career with Moiseev's company (since her retirement she has been teaching young dancers). Since his graduation from the Academy in 1953 Vanya has been working at the Mikoyan Design Company as project engineer and project designer for several generations of the MiG and as deputy chief designer of the company (which he is to this day). Vanya's eldest daughter, Olga, was born in 1952, a few hours before my youngest son; their son Anastas came about two years later.

My wife Ella was on friendly terms with all her brothers- and sisters-in-law, as, indeed, most members of our ever-growing family were with one another. But each of us naturally had friends outside our family circle as well. Some of those friends were life-long, some acquired through marriage, work or social life. One of our mutual friends at the time was somebody I had known since childhood and whom Ella met through me some time before our marriage. It was Svetlana Stalina, and I feel compelled to give her some space in my story. After her 'defection' abroad Svetlana for some time became 'the talk of the world', but I had known her well long before it and I would like to write of what I knew and what I witnessed myself. As I have written earlier, our respective dachas were very near each other, with only about a kilometre between them, and at our dacha there lived Svetlana's aunts and cousins on her mother's side. She came to see them once in a while. In the 1930s I often visited Svetlana's brother Vasily at their dacha and naturally saw a lot of her too.

Until the mid-1930s the Uspenskoye road (through Barvikha and Usovo) had been unpaved, and to get to either of these two dachas everyone used the road via Odintsovo. The road turned right towards and past the gate of our dacha and then went steeply downhill along the red-brick wall on the west side of our grounds. At the bottom of that downhill road was a little river, and the road continued across it and uphill again towards the collective farm called *Gorki-2*, near which Stalin's dacha was. I remember one winter evening when Svetlana unexpectedly turned up at our house, for the driver who had brought her all the way from Moscow refused to attempt the narrow, ice-covered, cobbled road leading past our gate to the bottom of the hill. Svetlana had to spend the night with us. (After the war the road was extended forward and down the hill from where it had turned towards our gate. A T-junction appeared, and those who were not coming to us went down the main road, no longer having to drive all the way up to our gate and negotiating the cobbles downhill.)

I have earlier mentioned that during the war, after our return from Stalingrad at the end of 1942 and at the beginning of 1943, I was visiting Vasily at his dacha again. He had more or less spontaneous parties almost every night, and Svetlana often sat at the table among his guests. Whenever I saw her there I was always impressed with how modestly and how quietly she behaved. It was at one such party that she first met Alexei Kapler, with whom she had an innocent, girlish flirtation that annoyed Stalin so much that he had Kapler arrested and exiled. A scriptwriter and a film critic, Kapler was an erudite, amusing and amiable young man – no wonder she had a crush on him. He must have also enjoyed talking with a bright and intelligent girl who loved books and music and who was happy to accompany him to museums and theatre performances. As far as I know there was nothing more to it; maybe a few kisses were exchanged, and that's all.

In 1944 Svetlana married Grigory (Grisha) Morozov. Ella (still my fiancée at the time) and I saw them a lot, and Ella and Svetlana soon became close friends. After the war, when we also got married, Svetlana, either on her own or with Grisha, often came to see us at our Moscow home or at my father's dacha. Everyone seemed to like and respect Svetlana as she was then. People noted her intelligence, modesty, tact and her pleasant and sociable manners. She would often be contrasted to Vasily, whose volatile temper and frequent outbursts of rudeness and aggressiveness were well known to most people who had met him. However, on looking back now, I remember that Svetlana as I knew her at the time was already developing, little by little, some of the rather unpleasant features that distinguished her later in life: selfishness, wilfulness, her inability to question her own opinion and her occasionally somewhat despotic treatment of people around her. I can see it now, but back in the post-war years, when we were all young, none of these features was pronounced enough to be really noticed. Svetlana's and Grisha's divorce came to us as a complete surprise. I have long suspected that it was brought about by Stalin himself, for he was a militant anti-Semite, and having a Jew for a son-in-law was probably more than he could put up with for long. There might have existed other reasons, of course. In any case Stalin had never once invited Svetlana to his house with her husband, and as for their son Joseph, he seems to have only seen him two or three times altogether.

In 1949 Svetlana remarried. Her second husband had Stalin's full approval: it was Yuri Zhdanov, son of Politburo member Andrei Zhdanov. Ella and I attended their wedding at Zhdavov's dacha. (My father later told me that after Svetlana's divorce with Grisha, Stalin had named Sergo Beria, the head of the secret police's son, and me as possible 'candidates'. But I was already married and Sergo Beria was either married to or about to marry Svetlana's friend Marfa Peshkova, Maxim Gorky's granddaughter.) I do not think there was any great love involved in that marriage. Svetlana and Yuri divorced before Stalin's death, shortly after the birth of their daughter Katya. I must say Yuri Zhdanov was a very nice and universally liked man, intelligent, sociable and extremely well educated, with two complete university courses (in chemistry and in philosophy) to his credit. He was a good amateur pianist, and would always willingly oblige friends at a party by accompanying their dancing.

A few days after the 20th Party Congress my father let me and Ella read a copy of Khrushchev's 'secret report' on 'Stalin's personality cult'. We decided to let Svetlana read it too. She asked Ella to sit with her as she was reading it. When she had finished, she said, 'The saddest thing about it is that it's all true!' Svetlana's personality flaws, which I have already mentioned, as well as her increasingly unstable temper, might have played a part in her later, at times somewhat bizarre behaviour. The things she did in her mature life were sometimes so odd that it was hard to believe they came from the sensible and unassuming person we had earlier known her to be. Her tumultuous love life, with a succession of several husbands after Yuri, is not a case in point; I am sure she was genuinely in love, or believed herself to be in love, with each of them. Every time she got carried away with someone she would say that 'this time it's real', and then be disappointed a few months later. When it happened, she would come to our place nearly every day (we lived in different sections of the same large block of flats – the 'House on the Embankment') and cry it all out on Ella's shoulder.

Some time in the early 1960s, Svetlana met and soon decided to marry Bradzhesh Singkh, an Indian Communist who was working in Moscow at the time. Getting married to a foreign citizen was a very difficult task at that time (especially for Stalin's daughter!), and Svetlana wished to introduce the man to my father, hoping that he would help her to get the relevant permission. (Several months prior to that Ella had managed to help Svetlana through my father, who made it possible for Singkh's contract in Moscow to be renewed for another term.) Ella passed Svetlana's request for an interview to my father, and he suggested meeting at his dacha on a certain day. It then turned out that on the day named some really outstanding concert by a visiting pianist was to take place at the Great Hall of Moscow Conservatory, to which my wife (a great lover and connoisseur of classical music) was going and which my father, once he heard of it, very much wanted to attend too. He asked Ella to ask Svetlana to put their meeting off until the day after. Ella phoned Svetlana and passed on the message. She knew she was talking to an old friend (and she also knew that one day did not decide anything in Svetlana's situation), and so, without beating about the bush or inventing false excuses, she told her the true reason, that both she and her father-in-law were very keen on attending that concert and so could she (Svetlana) please come and see him just one day later. There was a pause of a few seconds, after which Svetlana attacked Ella with an avalanche of accusations and insults. The gist of what she said, in a raised voice, was that Ella, allegedly, had plotted against her and deliberately enticed her father-in-law with the idea of attending that concert to prevent Svetlana's meeting with him. Having said all this and more to the same effect, Svetlana slammed down the receiver.

Late in the evening of the next day I returned home from Akhtubinsk and found Ella in tears. She had come home from the concert and found a letter, delivered by hand and put into our mail-box, from Svetlana. Without a word, Ella gave it to me to read. I could not believe what I read; it was flagrantly unjust and cruelly insulting. Needless to say that letter put a stop to Ella's friendship with Svetlana; they did not meet during the time before Svetlana's departure, and she left without apologising or saying goodbye. After some time Ella showed the letter to my father, who read it in amazement and said, 'Her own father all over – can't do without enemies!' Nevertheless, Svetlana saw my father the day after the concert and introduced her fiancé to him. She asked him to help her obtain official permission to become his wife, but my father, possibly because of her record of broken marriages, or maybe because he did not think Svetlana's marriage to a foreigner desirable, recommended that she should live with Singkh without marrying, just as he himself had lived with his wife, our mother, for forty years.

On 31 October 1966 Bradzhesh Singkh died. Svetlana asked to be received by Alexei Kosyghin (my father was no longer a member of the Politburo), hoping to be allowed to go to India to scatter her husband's ashes over the river near his native home, as the custom of his land required. Kosyghin suggested writing a petition to Brezhnev, which she did there and then. The next day a decision was made (through a telephone vote of the Politburo members) and the relevant paper was signed by Chernenko. The paper allowed Svetlana a seven-day visit to India with an escort of two people, and instructed the Soviet ambassador to India, I. Benedictov, to give her all the assistance she might require. In her letter to Brezhnev Svetlana assured him that nothing 'politically reprehensible' would occur as a consequence of the trip, but this is exactly what did occur.

While in India, Svetlana managed to persuade the ambassador to prolong her stay beyond the seven days that were originally allowed (she was staying with the family of her late husband). After she had obtained several such extensions one after another and her visit had extended to nearly three months, she again arrived at the Soviet Embassy to ask Benedictov to be allowed to stay on. This time he refused to co-operate, implying that enough was enough, and he presented Svetlana with a return ticket for a flight to Moscow due to leave the same night. One may assume that she came to the embassy with a plan ready in her head, but I believe that what she did next was dictated by one of her spontaneous, impulsive decisions provoked by what she had always hated: an opposition to her wishes. With perfect composure she said to the ambassador that she would go and do her packing and would shortly return. Instead, she went straight to the US Embassy. They organised her passage to Switzerland and from there to America (Svetlana had never been abroad and she might have some time earlier regretted that in her position she could hardly be allowed to travel outside the USSR).

It might now be difficult to imagine the uproar that followed. Stalin's daughter had secretly defected to the West! The Soviet leadership took it very badly. Even my father was bewildered. As soon as my wife and I heard what had happened, Ella went over to Svetlana's children, Joseph and Katya. For a long time afterwards she continued to look after them, trying to support them emotionally (and

147

materially as well) until they recovered from the shock. Joseph was twenty at the time and Katya just sixteen. Joseph referred to her defection as 'another of my mother's escapades', but Katya was too young for a show of bravado and her reaction was more overtly painful. In fact she could never forgive her mother that she had abandoned them. After a while each of Svetlana's children was granted a pension, to be received until their education was completed.

Rather than dwell on Svetlana's life abroad, I shall tell of her return eighteen years later. One day Joseph phoned my wife and told her the stunning news of his mother's unexpected arrival in Moscow. Ella immediately gave her a call at the Hotel Sovetskaya, where Joseph said she was staying, and they talked as old friends again, neither of them reminding the other of the breach. After that initial telephone reunion, Svetlana three or four times came to see Ella at home, and one of those visits took place when I was at home. Svetlana told us the story of her return. Apparently, when she had realised that she wanted to come back, she moved from the USA to England so as to get nearer home, as she put it. There she settled in some small town (to my question 'Why?' she replied that life was cheaper there than in London). She then went over to London with the intention of visiting the Soviet Embassy, but she was not admitted. Instead, she was recommended to present her request in writing. When she came again, her 'petition' in hand, she was let in and given a warm welcome. They must have consulted Moscow about the line they should take with her. So as to avoid possible complications which an open departure for Moscow could cause, it was suggested that she and her daughter Olga should first go to Greece, as if on holiday, and report to the Soviet Embassy in Athens (where Yuri Andropov's son was then ambassador). Svetlana did as she was advised, and arrived in Moscow from Athens. Having finished her story, Svetlana said, 'The wisest thing I have done in these eighteen years is coming back.'

Katya Zhdanova, Svetlana's daughter, a geologist, was working in Kamchatka at the time. She refused to come to Moscow to see her prodigal mother. As for her son (a doctor of medicine), Svetlana's selfishness and her despotic streak soon destroyed what had begun as a good and warm family reunion. Svetlana was offered by the authorities all she could need for a comfortable life in Moscow – an apartment, a free car, language tuition for her daughter and other things – but she declined. She made up her mind to settle in Tbilisi; one of the reasons, as she put it to us, was her wish to avoid a 'flow of reporters'. She also said that her daughter was not used to living in a large city.

Soon after Svetlana had moved to Tbilisi I was visiting that city on business. I came to see her in her nice and comfortable two-bedroom flat which she shared with her daughter. The girl enjoyed living in Tbilisi, she had already made friends, and she went riding at a nearby riding school. She was also taking lessons in Russian and Georgian and, according to her, enjoying Georgian better, with the result that she could already communicate in it quite well. She seemed to like Georgia very much, and when Svetlana pointed out that Olga would have to go back to England to finish boarding-school, the girl declared that she would afterwards return to Tbilisi to stay. Despite apparent well-being and comfort, I felt a touch of disappointment in Svetlana's tone. She suddenly said that they were living in a very dull part of town. 'The town centre, that's where life is!' The town centre was only a couple of bus-stops away. Maybe she was just conscious of a certain estrangement and isolation; quite a lot of people were feeling hostility towards her. The Stalinists hated her for having 'betrayed' her father, and the anti-Stalinists disliked her for being his daughter.

After some time Svetlana paid a short visit to Moscow, hoping to be received by Gorbachev. What she wanted to talk about we did not know, but in any case Ella advised her to wait until after the party congress for which they were preparing. However, Svetlana, once she had put something into her head, could not be dissuaded. She tried to press for a meeting and, as we expected, Gorbachev did not receive her.

Although while living in Tbilisi Svetlana had been sending Ella occasional postcards and had rung her a number of times, her sudden departure abroad came as a total surprise for both of us. She had never said a word about it, and she did not even ring to say goodbye. And we have heard nothing from her since she left. Maybe her departure in 1986 was a good thing. With all that has been said and written about Stalin since then (even though nearly all of it is true), it would not have been easy for her to be here. I once heard an opinion that she had been prompted to leave in anticipation of the coming *glasnost*.

CHAPTER 12

I am a Test Pilot

T he graduation day and my subsequent 'legitimate' leave behind me, I was driving in my own car into Chkalovskaya, the then base of the Research and Flight Test Institute situated about thirty kilometres east of Moscow. It was the day after our professional holiday – Aviation Day, celebrated on 18 August. On that same day eleven years earlier I had arrived at the Kacha Flying School.

The Institute's history began back in 1920 when the military 'Experimental Airfield' was set up at Khodynsky airfield in Moscow (later renamed the Central Airfield). The official order underlying this development was signed by the Commissar for Defence Leon Trotsky on 21 September 1920. However, it has recently become known that as early as 1914 a military unit stationed at Gatchina outside St Petersburg had been engaged in testing foreign and Russian-built aircraft, and a number of specialists from Gatchina, including their CO, A. Weghener, later joined the personnel of the newly established Experimental Airfield in Moscow, with Weghener in charge. So, having celebrated the Institute's seventy-fifth anniversary in 1995, we shall probably mark a different anniversary in the future.

Initially the Experimental Airfield had had about a hundred staff, including four test pilots. Most of the aircraft tested at that time were of foreign origin, but soon home-designed aeroplanes began to appear as well. The testing centre in Moscow – the only one authorised to conduct military certification tests – was growing along with the steadily developing Russian aviation industry and combat aviation. Eventually the centre became known as the Research and Flight Test Airfield, and then as the Research and Flight Test Institute.

In the 1930s, when our aviation industry was growing rapidly, the Institute was expanding at a matching rate. Among its staff were many outstanding aviation specialists – pilots, engineers and scientists. In those days the existing aircraft design companies did not have well-established flight testing facilities of their own, nor sufficiently qualified test pilots and engineers. Neither was the Aviation Industry Flight Research Institute (now known as the Gromov Institute) in existence then. The factory tests were confined to the very basic, preliminary level, and so it was the Flight Test Institute which was responsible for most of the flight testing. Often the well-known and highly experienced military test pilots were involved in testing a new aircraft from the initial stage onwards. Among them were such renowned pilots as Mikhail Gromov, Valery Chkalov, Konstantin Kokkinaki, Stepan Suprun and others (many of them later left the Institute to join individual testing teams assigned to design companies). Until the late 1960s the FTI was responsible for the testing of all passenger aircraft as well.

On arrival I was received by the Institute Commander General Redkin, the very same Redkin who had overseen my first flights in the MiG-9 three years earlier. As I realised later, flight testing was not his real vocation at all; he had been put in charge of the Institute through the influence of Vasily Stalin. In that first interview in his office he gave me a piece of advice which I did not like at all: he said I should look at test pilots with a critical eye, for they, in his opinion, were a spoilt and self-complacent lot. I had long been reading whatever I could find about test pilots, and had a great respect for those people and the profession itself. Until then I had met very few 'real' test pilots, and those I did meet I admired. Later, when I came to know many of them better, I was happy to see that my initial respect was perfectly justified. I have retained this attitude to the people of this profession throughout my life. Naturally there are undisciplined people in whatever walk of life you take, but the majority of the test pilots I have known were and are honourable and open-hearted people with a strong sense of duty and loyalty, truly devoted to their work, very alert and as a rule possessing a fine sense of humour, to say nothing of personal courage.

The reasons, as I see them, are simple. On the one hand the profession itself, being as challenging and dangerous as it is, naturally attracts and 'selects' people of this kind; on the other it encourages the development of these features, as well as of personal dignity and independence. The latter is especially evident in fighter test pilots, who mostly fly one-seat aircraft and often have to make crucial decisions on their own. Another very important professional quality is a constant psychological readiness for unexpected situations and for taking adequate and prompt action. I feel rather awkward writing this, having been a test pilot myself, but the last thing in my mind is to boast or to paint a flattering self-portrait. It is just that I simply wanted to say what I have always felt about my colleagues, as well as other test pilots whom I knew indirectly, through my pilot friends or through what I read or heard about them.

In due course I discovered the source of General Redkin's prejudice against test pilots. His appointment as the Flight Test Institute Commander followed a major 'dressing-down' given to its former administration by an outside investigation commission. Redkin must been influenced by the commission's unjust conclusions. Thus, one of the things the commission could not 'forgive' the Institute was the relatively high salaries received by its testing personnel, not only pilots and other members of each testing team, but also the specialists of various other test-related services, who in those days received a bonus estimated as a small percentage of the total received by all project test pilots of all teams; the team members' bonus was a percentage of their project pilot's reward. As for the inspection itself and the prejudiced attitude of the commission, it must have been caused by one particular incident.

During the war the pilots of the fighter corps commanded by General Savitsky complained that the Yak-9 did not reach the speed stipulated in its performance specifications. General Savitsky wrote a report to Stalin alleging that test pilots had deliberately overrated the capabilities of the aircraft. The Air Force Command then sent an FTI test pilot, Afanasy Proshakov, and the Yak-9 project engineer Mikhail Pronin to one of the best regiments of Savitsky's corps. They discovered that the aircraft were operated in the wrong way: the cockpit canopies had been removed, which increased the air drag, and anti-dust filters had been installed inside air inlets, which decreased the engine's power. Besides, it turned out that the pilots were in the habit of opening the oil radiator flap to the full so as to prevent the engine from overheating, with the result that the drag increased even more. Upon their discovery Proshakov and Pronin asked for one regimental aircraft to be returned to its initial condition (with all the amateur 'innovations' removed), and first Proshakov and then the CO took a ride in it, both of them reaching the specified speed without any problem. All this had to be reported to 'the very top'. General Savitsky found himself in a very awkward position, with a bitter grudge against the FTI.

Rumour had it that it was none other than General Savitsky who initiated an inspection of the Institute soon after the war; at any rate he was at the head of the inspecting commission. The commission's final report was devastating, and as a result several highly experienced pilots and engineers were fired – including Afanasy Proshakov, an outstanding test pilot to this day remembered by veterans with great respect. Another well-known test pilot to leave the Institute was General Stefanofsky. That was when and how Vasily Stalin's former second-in-command General Redkin became the FTI Commander. One of the charges of the commission against the Institute's most experienced pilots was that they flew too much for the sake of more money, 'snatching' the most highly paid tasks. It might have been true to some extent, for the way flight missions were sched-uled in those days was anything but formalised (which it became later), and it was said that many experienced pilots would not leave the airfield for hours, climbing from one aeroplane into another without time to take their parachutes off. Yes, they must have made a fair amount of money, but it was still *flying* they were doing, not selling things in the market or something! And God knows, there was a lot to fly and test in those days, for new aircraft and new modifications were appearing all the time.

The commission's report and the dressing-down received by the Institute was followed by the appearance of new regulations concerning payments to the testing personnel. For thirty years after that (until new regulations were issued in the 1980s), the military test pilot's remuneration for flight test missions remained from five to ten times lower than the analogous payment received by his civilian colleagues in the aviation industry, who did the same kind of work, and often their missions were simpler than those carried out by the Institute test pilots. The percentage bonuses formerly received by the ground flight-support services were cancelled altogether, the natural outcome being that those services were deprived of any material stimulus for maximum efficiency in their work.

What I would like to stress here is that members of the testing teams proper – the pilots, engineers and mechanics – always possessed (and still do, by all accounts) an unquenchable thirst for work. The same applied to most of their commanders. It was particularly evident in those days when there was in-comparably more freedom and flexibility in the way flight missions were assigned, and whatever money had to do with the pilots' enthusiasm for flying, that enthusiasm certainly never faded when they were assigned missions for which the payment was very low or, as the case sometimes was, non-existent.

Considerations of flight safety could be the only possible deterrent in checking the pilot's excessive craving for flying. I have never since known a team of people so passionately devoted to their cause and their work as the FTI Department No. 1, and especially its fighter flight test section to which I was assigned. To be fair, the character of the work itself had something to do with this devotion. It did not take me long to become convinced, on the basis of my own and other pilots' experience, that to those who chose aviation as their life's cause no work could be more exciting or more gratifying than flight testing. Maybe it is because in flight testing one constantly encounters new challenges; there is no room for stereotypes but plenty of room for imagination and creativity.

It is often believed that it is only new types of aircraft, so-called prototypes, that are tested by test pilots. This is not so at all. The reality is such that a greater amount of testing falls in fact on the aircraft already coming off the production lines (their quality and performance has to be constantly tested against their technical specifications and those of their prototypes; the previously discovered deficiencies in the design have to be removed; and at the same time new capabilities have to be developed and researched), as well as their new modifications and different versions with various improvements and changes aimed at achieving higher combat efficiency. Various parts and systems of the aircraft have to be tested as well, from the engine to a great variety of equipment types: avionics, radars (both airborne and ground-based), optical sights, missiles and rockets, guns and bombs, navigation aids and systems, instrument-landing systems, altitude equipment, rescue equipment, etc. Scientific research is of great importance too, carried out both in flight and in various stand tests. Nearly all kinds of testing and research work involve some new technological development, albeit sometimes just a very small one. This accounts for the element of creativity in the work and, by the same token, for the immense satisfaction it brings. Another aspect of a test pilot's work worth mentioning here is his participation in considering and discussing new projects and mock-ups of new types of aircraft, as well as in the analysis of various technical issues arising in the course of creating or testing a new aircraft. Finally, test pilots take part in the writing of instructions and manuals guiding the use and operation of the tested aircraft.

On my first day at the Institute the Commander's secretary explained how to find the building of the First Flight Test Department. That was a unique woman. She first came to work as the FTI Commander's personal secretary as a seventeen-year-old girl back in 1929; and she worked up to 1997 in the same position, having outlasted nearly twenty successive bosses. Highly sensible, amiable and composed, she was respected by one and all. Once in that building, I was shown to the pilots' briefing room. I entered, greeted those in the room and asked where I could find the section commander. 'There he is, at the chessboard', was the answer. I saw a stocky young colonel with a Hero's Golden Star on his chest. I knew the name already: Ivan Dziuba. I asked his permission to address him and reported my arrival as the military form required. He stood up from his chair, shook my hand, asked me to wait a little and returned to the chessboard. When the game was over he stood and invited me to follow him to his office. Within my first few minutes in the briefing room I became aware of the relaxing lack of formality in the relationship among the pilots, and I liked it very much.

While I was in Dziuba's office he was joined by Lieutenant-Colonel Vasily Gavrilovich Ivanov, the deputy in charge of flight testing. Their questions concerned my flight experience. I felt that they were pleased to hear that I had already flown jets, particularly the MiG-15; it was barely three years since the first aircraft of this type had appeared in some operational units, and I came to them straight from the student's desk, as it were. They also seemed to like that I had had some experience of night-time flying and had done a course of 'blind' non-precision ADF approach, which was still a relative novelty at the time. My immediate CO was to be Colonel Kuvshinov, a pleasant, friendly man, a teacher by profession and a test pilot since before the war. After Hitler's attack on Russia he had joined a combat regiment formed at the Flight Test Institute in the first days of the war.

The idea of forming such regiments from the personnel of the Institute had come from Lieutenant-Colonel Stepan Suprun (he had served in the same section as I was now posted to), who wrote to Stalin with his proposal on the second or third day of the war. Five days later, on 30 June 1941, they took off for the front line – two fighter regiments, two bomber regiments and an attack regiment. Their regiments were also joined by pilots and engineers of the Air Force Command, aviation academies, aircraft factories and other non-combat aviation bodies. One of the fighter regiments was commanded by Stepan Suprun himself, who had gained his combat experience fighting against the Japanese Air Force in China. Kuvshinov participated in the sortie in which Suprun was shot down. Nobody, however, saw the fatal shot. Nevertheless Stepan Suprun was post-humously awarded a second Golden Star of the Hero of the Soviet Union. Years later his crashed aircraft was discovered, half buried in the ground with his remains inside. Stepan's brother Feodor confirmed his identity by his teeth, and his remains were interred at the Novodevichy cemetery in Moscow. Several months after these regiments had arrived at the front line most of the test pilots and test engineers were recalled; the need for flight testing at wartime did not decrease, in fact if anything it became greater. On top of the Institute's 'routine' tasks, it had to address the deficiencies and imperfections which were discovered by combat pilots in action. Besides, the captured German aircraft had to be tested to determine the most effective ways of resisting and defeating them. Foreign aircraft offered to the USSR under the Lend-Lease Bill were also tested at the Institute. The FTI test pilots and engineers visited air force regiments at the front line to assess the combat efficiency of our aircraft in action.

Lieutenant-Colonel Ivanov had a ride with me in the trainer version of the MiG-15. He made a couple of criticisms, but on the whole he seemed pleased with my piloting performance. My instrument-flying skills were checked out by D. Pikulenko, who did not say a word to me after the flight, thus leaving me in some bewilderment, for I was certain that I had given him no cause for dis-appointment. Back in the briefing room he was still silent. Finally, when Ivanov asked him a direct question about my flight, he snapped, 'He flies all right, and stop nagging me!' Later I heard that 'all right' from Pikulenko was very high praise indeed. A top-class pilot, on the ground he was somewhat irritable and hot tempered.

At that time there was no military test pilot school, and each pilot newly posted to the FTI was 'attached' to one of the test pilots with experience, who helped him to master the flight testing techniques and methods. Test engineers in their turn gave young pilots classes and consultations. The fighter test section consisted of pilots, engineers and maintenance technicians. For each individual test programme one of the engineers within the section was appointed project engineer in charge of the programme. He was given another engineer as an assistant, and other members of the team were the project test pilot (there could be more than one pilot involved), a technician and a mechanic. The rest of the team was supplied by other sections and departments of the Institute, engineers responsible for specific aspects of the testing programme, e.g. flight performance, stability and controllability of the aircraft, the engine, the avionics and so on. These were known as speciality project engineers. There could also be speciality technicians. Last, but not least, the teams always included the 'evaluation' pilots, who in theory were supposed to fly out the tested aircraft at the completion of the testing programme to ensure the objectivity of conclusions. In practice, however, they usually did more than that, often being called for to take over from the project pilot when for some reason or another he could not fly or was not around.

The engineers in our section, in contrast to the speciality engineers from other sections of the Institute, were referred to by us as 'the aircraft men' to imply their broad qualification which encompassed the aircraft as a whole (something in the nature of a GP as against narrower medical specialists). As project engineers at the head of a testing programme they were responsible for the planning, the carrying out and the completion of the programme, for preparing test flight missions (on the basis of established regulations and methods of flight testing), for the test planning and test safety, for the interaction of speciality engineers on the team, and, ultimately, for writing the final statement at the completion of the programme. The test programme statement comprised the data collected by all the various specialists on the team. An important section of this document was 'Conclusions', and it had to contain definitive remarks on each of the testing parameters included in the test programme in question. Any malfunction, defect or peculiarity, even the very minor ones or the ones that were successfully removed, had to be listed in the statement. Usually three separate lists of faults were compiled: one contained the safety-related faults to be removed before the operational pilots took over the aircraft; the second listed those deficiencies that could be dealt with in the course of serial production; and the third list presented the recommendations of the test force as to how the aircraft or any of its systems could be improved. Another essentially important part of the statement was the assessment of the aircraft flight performance and handling written by the project test pilots in consultation with the evaluation pilots and signed by them all. No commander and no official could demand that the test pilots change their written assessment, although attempts to put pressure on them have been known.

Finally, the team leaders prepared an official 'verdict' concerning the feasibility or possibility of adopting the tested aircraft for the air force. This paper, as part of the test statement as a whole, was then 'sealed' with the signatures of the department commanders and the Institute Commander (and later approved and signed by the Air Force Commander-in-Chief). Sometimes, by the time it was finalised the aircraft in question had already been put on the lines. None the less, without this fully authorised official document no aircraft could be adopted by any of the operational units or flown by anyone but a test pilot.

A very good education for us young test pilots was our participation in the briefings with which every working day at our section began. They were attended by all pilots and engineers, sometimes also by those engineers from other departments of the Institute who were current members of the test teams. The benefit of those briefings was enormous. Each of the test pilots who had no higher education became 'a little bit of an engineer', and every engineer became 'a little bit of a test pilot', learning to understand the specific character of the test pilots' work. Later, in the 1970s, the structure of the Institute departments was changed. The test pilots were structurally separated from the test engineers, and the daily briefings unfortunately were no longer conducted for both together.

I received my identification card, which said: 'Test pilot of the fighter testing section of the No. 1 Department of the Air Force Research and Flight Test Institute' (later that designation became classified). It was so gratifying to read that! From that moment and until 1978, I was on the staff of the Institute. In August and September 1951 I performed several training flights, in one of which I was faced with the necessity to 'use my brain', as they say; to look for a way out from an unexpected predicament. I was to fly along a particular route in the north-eastern sector of the Moscow region (our allotted area of flight testing), going over a number of towns which were to mark my turning points on that route. I had planned my flight with the 5,000-metre altitude in mind. On the day of the flight the cloud ceiling turned out to be under a thousand metres, and I was allowed to fly at 500 metres at the highest. In those days a test pilot was in many respects a free agent. He was supposed to prepare and map out his flight himself. His flying commanders would monitor his preparations of course, but only in the most general terms. I liked that, but at the same time, unaccustomed as I was at that time to the absence of 'surveillance', I took off without readjusting my original plan to the changed conditions. It should certainly have been done, for in jet aircraft fuel consumption per kilometre (and consequently the range of flight) directly depends on the altitude: the lower the flight, the shorter the range. I knew it of course, yet I was sure I had enough fuel.

The discrepancy between what the fuel gauge showed at every turning point and the pre-estimated amounts of fuel grew faster than I had expected. About halfway along the route there was already less then half left. By the original plan I was supposed to continue heading south until I reached Pokrov, and only then turn westwards in the direction of home; as it was, I had to deviate from the plan and turn homewards there and then. Even so, I soon realised that at the rate fuel was running out I would be short of it before I reached the base. I decided to cut through the clouds and climb up to 5,000 metres so as to slow down fuel consumption (although I had no instrument-flight rating in that type of aircraft yet).

As I was approaching home over a thick blanket of clouds, guiding myself by the ADF, the red low-fuel light indicating that only the emergency fuel reserve was left came on. After a while I throttled down and began gliding down without knowing how far or how close the airfield was (it was before the introduction of on-board distance measuring equipment or constant radar monitoring of airborne aircraft from the ground). But my luck was with me again: I emerged from the clouds to see the airfield right in front of me and, having obtained the tower's clearance, landed straight in. If it had not been for the two emergency decisions I had taken while in the air, I would have had to belly-land on some field or bail out. It would not have been a very glamorous start to a test pilot's career!

One of the fighter section test pilots was Stepan Suprun's young brother Alexander (Sasha). I had first met him during the war, when he arrived at our regiment for a few days in a flight of Spitfires to participate in the night-time fighter cover of Smolensk. On my arrival at the Institute I heard that Sasha had performed rather unusual tests. There had been a series of accidents in operational units with the MiG-15s: on touchdown the aircraft would start bouncing. It was established through special tests performed by Sasha that bouncing could have occurred because of certain errors made by pilots. If the speed at touching down was too high and the nose accordingly too low, the nosewheel prematurely hit the ground and bounced up. The speed being too high, the machine lost touch with the ground, while the pilot, in order to arrest the bounce, pushed the stick forward too much, causing the nosewheel to hit the concrete even harder and to bounce even higher (it was described as 'progressive bouncing'). The speed in the meantime would diminish, and so the final touch down was more of a 'fall' than a landing, often resulting in serious damage to the undercarriage or even the fuselage.

To demonstrate that 'progressive bouncing' was really caused by pilots' erroneous actions, the section command decided to re-enact this type of landing. The No. 1 Department Commander, General Blagoveshchensky, signed his consent to the experiment, confirming that the test pilot would not be held responsible for any damage this intentionally dangerous landing might cause. Sasha Suprun performed the landing, deliberately repeating all the characteristic mistakes of operational pilots, and the aircraft obliged by bouncing, with serious damage as a result. The landing was filmed, and the episode included in the film later made about the Institute. It has never since failed to produce a strong impression on various audiences, particularly the point when one of the undercarriage struts hits through the wing on impact with the concrete and zooms away from the aircraft, wheel and all. The recommendations to operational pilots as a result of the tests were as follows: the touchdown should only be allowed at normal landing speed, and in the case of a bounce the stick should by no means be pushed forward. It was also recommended to lower the air pressure in the nosewheel shock-strut to prevent it from 'springing' too much.

The Department Command put Sasha forward for an award, for courage shown in deliberately performing a dangerous crash-landing, but the Institute CO, General Redkin, had a different view of the event. Across the recommendation paper he wrote 'A damaged aircraft is a damaged aircraft', and he threatened Suprun with a penalty even though everything had been done in accordance with a written order, and Sasha's damaged aircraft had very likely helped to prevent many similar accidents in operational units.

In September, after I had passed all the standard tests in flight testing techniques and methods, I was formally rated as a test pilot and put forward for the Grade 3 qualification. I performed my first test flight on 13 September. My task was to assess the icing of the canopy at high altitudes. My second mission was to check on the MiG-15's service ceiling. The missions I received at the beginning were relatively simple and complementary to other pilots' flight tests. In October I was testing the Yak-17 fitted with drop-tanks and also made three flights in the MiG-17, a new modification of the MiG-15 fresh from the military certification tests. Later I got an opportunity to fly the La-15, a fighter of the same type as the MiG-15. These two earliest fighters with sweptback wings had been going through military certification tests almost simultaneously, and the choice was made in favour of the MiG-15, some of whose characteristics (including the maintenance ones) were superior to those of the La-15. Therefore the La-15 was produced in a small series and adopted by only two regiments (one of which was based at Kubinka).

My flight in the La-15, although my first, still involved a test mission, albeit a simple one: I had to assess the range of the friend-or-foe identification system. As I was on the landing approach after my mission was accomplished, I moved the undercarriage control handle down before the final turn, but the red lights indicating that the landing gear was still up did not go out; there was no pressure in the hydraulic system due to some failure on the line. I did not fancy going around with the fuel nearly out, so I continued gliding down, and while I did, I just about had the time to turn the wheel, opening the auxiliary compressed-air bottle. The undercarriage came out at the eleventh hour, so to speak. Such was the end of my only flight in that aircraft.

In March 1952 I made several flights in what we called 'inspection' tests of the MiG-15 in a randomly selected specimen from the factory lines. In April and May I flew as Nikolai Korovin's co-pilot in the inspection test programme of a new two-seat version of the MiG-15. I learned a useful lesson in that assignment. I was to perform a flight to test the aircraft's strength at maximum G-load. Most of the flights in that aeroplane Nikolai and I performed together, but a G-load test had to be conducted by one pilot only, and I was chosen for the task. I had to pull the maximum load of 8Gs. I dived and then pulled the stick. The accelerometer needle reached 6.7 and froze. I thought that I had not pulled the stick hard enough and decided to do it again, even though I knew that only one attempt of maximum acceleration was allowed by the book (I had been reminded of it just before take-off). The rule was to go home and study the flight instrument readings before repeating the attempt, but I decided that since I had obviously been too far from the limit G-load there was no harm in having another go. I dived again, pulling the stick harder than before, yet the indicator needle stopped dead at the same 6.7 mark. That amazing coincidence should have served as a danger signal, but I failed to see it as such and made two more attempts!

Back home the project engineer, having taken the readings, immediately reported an extraordinary occurrence to the section commander. In four attempts one after another I had achieved G-loads of 8, 8.5, 9 and 8.7 respectively, exceeding the limit load three times running. It turned out that each time the indicator needle had simply jammed at the 6.7 mark. Fortunately the wings were not damaged; they just about got away with a slight permanent-wavelike set in the skin which did not affect the aircraft's further performance. Both Dziuba and Ivanov gave me a thorough dressing-down, and they were quite right too. That incident confirmed that the ban on repeated attempts (one of the rules 'written in pilots' blood', as the saying goes) was perfectly justified. It was another step forward in my 'schooling' as a test pilot.

It reminds me now of another, equally instructive episode which took place later the same year during the qualification tests of the MiG-17. I was performing night flights to assess the adequacy of cockpit lighting and landing lights. Once, having dropped my landing gear, I saw that the green light of the nosewheel strut did not come on, while the red light went off, showing that the strut was no longer locked in the 'up' position. I remembered then that during two flights the day before the green nosewheel light had not come on either – not until I actually touched down. The technicians had tracked it down to the malfunction of the downlock switch and had fixed it; I decided that the same defect had returned. On feeling two characteristic thuds instead of the three which normally accompany the undercarriage locking, I thought that two of the thuds had somehow merged into one.

However, on the landing run, as the speed began to slow down and the nose lowered, it suddenly dawned on me – I believe even before it actually ducked down – that I was one wheel short. The nose strut was not out. The first thought that flashed through my mind was to open the throttle and take off, and the second that I would not gain enough speed to stop the nose from hitting the ground and would simply make the impact harder instead. I let it be, and the nose dipped down, screeching against the concrete and issuing a trail of sparks longer than my MiG's tail – as an eyewitness told me later. The Mig-17's guns, including a 37mm one, were fitted under its nose. It was that big gun's barrel that my aircraft leaned on, running along the landing strip on two wheels and a gun barrel. I knew there had earlier been a fatal accident in an operational unit when a similar landing had been made on a runway paved with perforated sheets of metal. The gun barrels ploughed the surface, the aircraft burrowed underneath the metal sheets and blew up, pilot and all. This could not have happened on a concrete runway, yet the barrel might have stumbled against an uneven seam between plates.

After a few hundred metres of the run the screeching stopped to my surprise and the nose slowly came up. I felt the thump of the nose strut as it locked in the landing position. I taxied off the landing strip and, seeing a car that had driven up to me, I stopped and opened the canopy. The flying commander Colonel

Antipov came up to the aeroplane and asked, 'Who's just landed with a fireworks display?' I said it was me. 'But you've got all your wheels down!' 'Look at the guns.' I replied. The barrel of the large gun was 'trimmed' some five centimetres shorter. My much-tested luck had been with me again. What had actually happened was that the wheel had jammed between the hatch flaps, but when the gun barrel shortened, the flaps touched the ground, the contact making them shift and release the jammed wheel.

The debriefing was conducted by General Blagoveshchensky himself – a rare occasion. He told me off without letting me say a word (perhaps because he was afraid I would somehow manage to justify myself) and punished me with a week's suspension from flying. As it was, I was not going to try to justify myself. On the contrary, I wanted to say that what had happened had been an error of professional judgement on my part. Rather than taking a non-standard situation (in my case the failure of the green light to appear) as a consequence or repetition of something already familiar, one should always consider a possibility of its being a sign of a new, unexpected malfunction.

Some time prior to that episode, about a month after my first test flight, I decided to have a go in the Yak-23. We still had one of those aircraft in our park on some test programme or other, and although as such it was no longer the latest word, it was still a new aeroplane to me. I asked Lieutenant-Colonel Ivanov to allow me a flight in it, and he did. The Yak-23 was not very different from the Yak-17, which I had flown three years earlier, yet regulations still required that I be briefed on its distinctive features and its instrument panel (according to regulations it was only another pilot who could do the briefing, not an engineer). Ivanov, whom I asked to appoint someone for the purpose, seemed at a loss for a candidate, when the door of his office opened and a woman, in the same rank as he was, stepped into the room. Ivanov brightened up and said, 'Give him a pre-flight in the Yak-23, will you, Olga?' It was Olga Nikolayevna Yamshchikova, and I was surprised at Ivanov's request. I knew she had been a pilot, but it had been quite a while ago. I swallowed my surprise though, and we went along to the aircraft. It turned out that she had been among those who had tested the Yak-23 a few years back. She gave me a very thorough and clear briefing, after which I performed quite a decent flight.

Olga Yamshchikova was one of the most remarkable people I came to know after I had become a test pilot. She was in a way a legendary character. She had been the first Soviet woman parachute-jumping instructor and the first woman instructor pilot (back in the 1930s). Later, in 1942, she graduated from the faculty of engineering of the Zhukovsky Air Force Academy and, as the war was on at the time, she went into action and became the commander of an all-woman fighter squadron in an air force regiment. After the war she joined the Flight Test Institute as a test pilot and became the first woman in the USSR to fly jet fighters. I heard that two years prior to my arrival at the Institute she was still flying, concealing her pregnancy until she was in her fifth month. After she had a baby, however, the doctors banned her from flying, and she began working as a project engineer in test programmes. As a project engineer and test team leader, Olga was generally admired and respected. She was thorough, hard-working,

The initial trainer of the 30th — the Polikarpov U-2.

The Yakovlev UT-2, the pre-war trainer.

The Yak-18 trainer.

Students of the Air Force Flying School at Kacha, 1941. From left to right: Oleg Barantsevich (killed in action 1943), Timur Frunze (killed in action 1942), Vladimir Yaroslavsky; back row: Stepan Mikoyan, Riurik Pavlov (killed in action 1942).

The Lavochkin La-5 went into production in 1942 and was operated, with the Yak-9, as a low-altitude fighter.

The Yakovlev Yak-3. Over 37,000 Yak fighters, mostly Yak-9s, were built during the war.

Squadron Commander, Hero of the Soviet Union, Konstantin Kriukov and Flight Commander Stepan Mikoyan at an airfield west of Moscow in 1943.

The author at No.1 readiness in a Yak-9, 1943.

Stepan with his Yak-9 at the North-western Front in 1943.

Taken in 1944 in front of a Yak-9, pilots of the 12th Fighter Regiment of the Guards take a respite in the sun. From right to left: Stepan's brother, Lieut. Alexei Mikoyan, Second-in-Command of the Regiment, Major Alexei Katrich and Lieuts. Alexander Shcherbakov (Sasha), Vadim Ivanov and Lev Bulganin.

conscientious and demanding, as well as an expert in what she was doing. Although she could have seemed a bit 'simple' at first acquaintance, she was well-educated, sharp-witted and had a fine sense of humour, camouflaged by her slow, deliberate manner of speech. Even after she had stopped flying herself she remained our pilots' great friend and colleague, and was invariably invited to all meetings, parties and so on. And when we lost a fellow pilot, there was no one like her to comfort his family and friends. She ended her career in the air force as a colonel and head of a flight test sub-section at the FTI. I am pleased to remember that she and I had a mutual liking and respect for each other. She died in 1982.

There was another remarkable woman at the Institute, Nina Ivanovna Rusakova. At the time of my joining the FTI, she was testing only transport aircraft, but back in the 1930s she had been a fighter pilot in an ordinary regiment. She came to work at the FTI before the war, thus becoming one of the world's first female test pilots. She tested many types of aircraft, both fighters and bombers. In 1959 she was awarded the title of 'Honoured Test Pilot of the USSR' and was promoted to colonel. She was a demanding and no-nonsense crew commander in the air, and a quiet and unassuming woman on the ground. Even when she was eighty, it was still evident that she had been a beauty in her earlier years.

Finally the day came when I was appointed both project engineer and second test pilot on a test programme. We were testing fuel drop-tanks designed for the MiG-15. The new tanks were for the first time supplied with stabilisers to steady them at their separation from the aircraft. The project test pilot was Vasily Kotlov, a short, ordinary-looking man with no formal education beyond seven years at school, yet an extremely alert and shrewd person and an excellent pilot. He was a whirlpool of energy and a miracle of resourcefulness, and his passions besides aviation were fishing and shooting. He was also modest, reserved and a devoted and loyal friend. He once told me how during his service on the Kamchatka peninsula he had made a forced landing in his UT-2, not very far from the airfield but separated from it by a dead volcano. They were looking for him from the sky but failed to spot him. After a week on a diet of berries, he found his way to the airfield through the woods. In 1957, alongside several other test pilots, he was awarded the title of a Hero of the Soviet Union for achievements in flight testing.

Despite being only the second pilot on the project, I did half of all the flights on it. In one of them my mission was to drop the tanks at low speed – just 350 kph. I pushed the button when it was time, but the tanks refused to separate. I pressed it again and again, but still nothing happened. Then, as I began turning for a go-around, the tanks suddenly separated of their own accord. The prescribed area of tank dumping was the airfield itself, just off the side of the runway. While I had been waiting for them to come off, the dumping area had been left behind me, and the tanks landed in a grove next to the airfield, right onto the bomb dump, luckily without any explosive consequences. I had to accompany the technicians who went to collect the tanks, and I made my excuses to the man in charge of the bomb dump. He must have been mollified by the fact that a pilot actually took the trouble of coming to him with apologies, and so scandal was evaded.

On analysis it turned out that at low speed, when the angle of attack was high, the lift created by the body of the tanks and their stabilisers pressed the tanks to the wings, but when the aircraft banked at turning the balance was upset and the tanks separated.

The tank dumping was supposed to be filmed from a chase aircraft, but one of the team engineers devised a way of fastening the cameras onto the gun barrels under the nose of my machine. Therefore the tanks, one under my right wing and the other under the left, were filmed by two cameras at one and the same time. The film provided a very clear view of the separation of the tanks and what happened to them after it. It was much better footage than the kind of filming that could be done from a chase aircraft, which thus saved over a dozen flights. However, this nearly led to a major cut-down (nearly by half) on the bonuses due for the tests to the project pilot (and consequently to the others on the team). The fact was that the accountants calculated the money due for testing on the basis of the total number of flights performed; fewer flights on a programme meant less money to be paid out. Luckily, the man in charge of the Institute finances was a sensible person, and I succeeded in making him see that if the project mission was fulfilled through fewer flights than envisaged, it was a good thing and by no means something to punish the team for (especially since the overall number of flights in the tested aircraft itself remained as planned).

One day the 'novice' test pilots were ordered to take a high-altitude endurance test. Each of us had to spend thirty minutes in the altitude chamber at the equivalent of 5,000 metres without an oxygen mask, regarded as the maximum altitude to be tolerated without oxygen feed. It was to be my first experience in the altitude chamber and I was a bit apprehensive as to whether I would pass the test. Thinking that the less energy I burned off the better, I tried to breathe as shallowly as I could. Soon I began to feel dizzy and felt cold sweat on my forehead. The doctor, who was watching me through a porthole, must have noticed it because he reduced the simulated altitude. After the test he announced he could not allow me to fly and sent me to the Central Aviation Hospital for a medical inspection. I was thoroughly upset and worried that perhaps I really was unfit for tolerating a rarefied atmosphere. In hospital they dispelled my fear and explained that at high altitude one should breathe deeply, so as to inhale more oxygen. They 'checked me out' at the simulated altitude of 10,000 metres with an oxygen mask on and allowed me to fly without restriction. Our Institute doctor had obviously been overcautious; he could have explained to me about the right way of breathing himself.

At the end of 1951 an American fighter, an F-86 'Sabre', was brought to the Institute from Korea. It was a rule of American combat pilots, when an aircraft was damaged yet remained controllable, to head for the sea and eject over it after reporting on the radio. Their survival kits contained inflatable dinghies, and they could safely wait to be picked up. Their rescue service worked so well that within minutes of his ejection a pilot would be found and lifted up on board a helicopter. At some stage we managed to get hold of one of these survival kits, and had a good chance to study it. It contained many items that could come in useful to a pilot, both on land and on water. In addition to the dinghy there was a radio beacon, a flare gun and even a small mirror to attract the rescue helicopter's attention with reflected sunbeams, and special powder to colour the water around the dinghy. All these devices made finding the pilot a much easier and faster job. The kit also contained assorted medication, a water-purifying preparation, three days' supply of fruit jelly and water, a knife, some fishing tackle and even a small folding rifle for shooting game. A few years later a similar kit (minus the rifle and a couple of other items) was adopted by our air force as well. Recently I have learned that a special service for rescuing air crews in distress had existed in the Allied forces as early as World War Two. As for the Soviet Air Force, we certainly had no such rescue service during the war, and it was not until after the Korean war that it finally appeared.

Due to the practice of abandoning damaged aircraft over water, we could hardly ever capture an American aircraft in one piece. It was mostly the debris of crashed aircraft that was found. The Sabre we received at the Flight Test Institute in 1951 had a damaged ejector seat. It meant that the pilot could not have ejected and had been forced to belly-land on the coast in the rear of the North Korean army, so the aircraft was indeed in one piece – yet, unfortunately, no longer airworthy.

Rumour had it that it was none other than Stalin who gave orders to examine this F-86 and draw up a detailed report within a week. The team involved was headed by a highly qualified test engineer, Semyon Fradkov. It was known at our section that I was studying English, so, despite my being a relative newcomer, I was included in the team as well. It was a useful experience, both in terms of specialised English vocabulary and as an encounter with a piece of foreign technology. It was also a lesson in the analysis of an unfamiliar aircraft and in the craft of writing a description of it. I remember how Fradkov went through my draft of the report with a red pencil, crossing out the redundant or the superficial and correcting the essential. At the time of the notorious 'Doctors' Plot', when in 1953 a number of eminent physicians, most of them Jewish, were arrested and charged with attempting to poison party leaders, Fradkov, a Jew himself, told me how he was summoned to the Institute's so-called 'political section' and spoken to in the following words: 'You are a Communist – you must realise that you should be removed from the Institute!' And remove him they did.

The Sabre was then handed over to the newly re-opened Sukhoi Design Company to be reproduced (in fact it might have been re-opened for the purpose). Although for some reason a full replica of the F-86 was never made, some of its features were adopted for our aircraft, such as its small-sized accelerometer which was installed in the MiG-19s (formerly accelerometers of a much larger size had only been installed in the tested models). Other adopted features were the built-in red light in the cockpit instrument panel and the four-position control-stick switch for the elevator and ailerons trimming. The Sabre also had an excellent optical sight with a radio range-finder of the kind we did not possess at the time. Both the sight and the range-finder were installed in the MiG-17 for testing. I performed a bombing mission in that aircraft, dropping two bombs in a diving manoeuvre. Both bombs hit the circle. The sight and the range-finder were rated very highly by the test team, but it was only the range-finder that was subsequently put on the production lines. The F-86's optical sight was not copied because a similar device was being designed in Russia at that time. Unfortunately it did not appear on a mass scale until a few years later, and turned out to be somewhat inferior to its American counterpart. A number of other features of the Sabre were later used in the new Sukhoi fighters.

Our air force units engaged in the Korean war were equipped with the MiG-15s, which were also flown by Chinese pilots. The aircraft has gone down in aviation history as a classical example of a subsonic jet fighter with sweptback wings (as Sergei Ilyushin had predicted to me on his visit to the Academy). I once came across a very favourable description of the MiG-15 in an American aviation magazine. It was written after the defection of a Chinese pilot who had flown a MiG-15 to Japan. The aircraft was tested by US pilots and one of them, a pilot with combat experience, when asked in which aircraft he would have chosen to go into action was quoted as saying he would opt for the MiG-15 with the Sabre's optical sight. The MiG-15 was produced on a very large scale and was adopted by the air forces of many countries. It had a number of modifications and remained active up to the mid-1970s.

Because of the MiG-15's engagement in Korea, we had to conduct a number of special tests. At the end of December 1951 a directive came to test the possibility of landing the MiG-15 when controlled in pitch by nothing except the elevator trim tab. Apparently there were many instances when, with the elevator control rod destroyed by enemy fire, the pilot had to eject even though the aircraft was still airworthy, except for the loss of pitch control. The elevator trim tab is a small part of the elevator control surface which deflects independently, creating a force that affects the elevator's position and, as a consequence, the stick-force to be applied by the pilot. The stick-force can be made very small or even non-existent, in which case the aircraft will be balanced in a certain attitude. In the MiG-15 the elevator trimmer tab was controlled with a levered switch on the port-side panel of the cockpit (in later models the trim switch was transferred to the control stick).

On 30 December several pilots, including me, performed six or seven landings each, using nothing but the trim switch to control the aircraft in pitch (we kept the spread fingers of the right hand close to and around the control stick without touching it; should the trim tab prove too slow or ineffective, the safety of the landing would be decided within fractions of a second). To our surprise everything went well. We completed all the tests in just under two days and worked out recommendations for combat pilots. The final statement was ready the next day, a few hours before the arrival of the New Year. We all got into my car – Leonid Kuvshinov, my new friends Igor Sokolov and Leonid Fadeev as my passengers – and drove to Moscow, taking the precious paper straight to the Air Force Command. Having handed it in to the officer on duty we went together to a café to celebrate.

With the appearance of jet aircraft, with speeds considerably higher than that of piston-engine aeroplanes, a new notion was introduced into aviation vocabulary.

It was the notion of the Mach number, or M-number for short. The M-number is the ratio of the speed of an aircraft to the speed of sound. The point is that an aircraft's approach to sonic speed rather noticeably affects its flight. Even before it reaches Mach 1.0 (i.e. sonic speed), the local flow velocity over some concave surfaces of the aircraft, including the wing itself, can exceed sonic speed. When this happens the sound waves that always appear as the aircraft is flying through the air can no longer spread forward, and start overlapping and clashing with one another, forming what is known as the 'shock wave', with a great difference in pressure before and after it. This is accompanied by a sharp increase in drag and a change in the pressure distribution around the wing surface. Finally, it affects the balance of the aircraft. With an ordinary wing (i.e. not a sweptback one) the shock waves are stronger, and the aircraft might end up in an unintentional dive (due to the pitch-down moment that develops in such conditions) from which it will not be possible to recover. All this is characteristic only of the aircraft approaching Mach 1.0 (the transonic speed), while at larger Mach numbers (supersonic speed) the shock wave precedes the aircraft so the latter remains unaffected by it.

Before this phenomenon was discovered and described, a number of fatal accidents had happened both in the USSR and elsewhere in the world. Among the pilots who crashed because of it were the test pilot Geoffrey de Havilland in Britain and Victor Rastorguyev in Russia in 1945 (he was flying a Yakovlev fighter with a rocket booster). The crash of Captain Bakhchivandzhi in 1943 in the first Soviet rocket-engine aircraft, the BI-1, might have had the same cause. Their aircraft were much faster than those with piston engines, but their aerodynamic characteristics were not suited to such speeds. It is not the only instance of science falling behind practical achievements in aviation. The pattern is well known: first pilots encounter some dangerous or unpleasant phenomenon (and often with tragic consequences at that) and then a scientific explanation of this phenomenon is evolved, after which it is easy to say that 'everything happened the way it should have happened'.

The MiG-15 fighter had sweptback wings but the sweep was only thirty-five degrees and the wings were relatively thick, therefore its speed limit was M 0.92 (for an aircraft with a non-sweptback wing M 0.8 was the maximum). In the Korean war the pilots who were trying to escape the enemy or were chasing him in a dive at full throttle sometimes exceeded that speed. Whenever it happened they were supposed to throttle down or deploy the airbrakes, but in combat nobody really did it. So we, the test pilots of the fighter section, were instructed to test the MiG-15 in steep dives to assess the risk of that manoeuvre and to devise some practical recommendations for combat pilots. I was among those engaged in those tests. Thanks to the MiG-15's sweptback wings, its longitudinal control was not affected by high-speed diving, whereas its lateral control effectiveness decreased and the aircraft would roll to the left due to the engine rotation moment. It took us several flights to realise it, but once we did we evolved a certain pattern of diving in which a steep dive was entered with the aircraft already banking to the right. It turned out that even in a vertical dive at full power the MiG-15 was unable to reach M 1.0 – with its aerodynamic layout the air drag was simply far too great. Therefore we could report that there was no danger exceeding the limit speed in that manoeuvre.

I have said earlier that American fighters were equipped with a radio range-finder. The range-finder, like a radar, emitted electromagnetic impulses. One of the FTI test engineers, Vadim Matskevich, on his own initiative conceived and assembled a small device that reacted to such impulses. Igor Sokolov and I were commissioned to test that device in flight. It was fitted to the tail of our fighter, and the radiator (to imitate the work of the enemy range-finder) was set up on top of a tall building on the Institute premises. Igor and I took turns to fly low over that building. Every time we flew over it we heard a low-pitched 'howling' in the earphones. As the distance from it grew, the noise became high in pitch and lower in volume. Even so, it remained perfectly distinct within the distance of seven or eight kilometres. Such a clever 'tail-protecting' device, which warned of the danger of enemy attack far out of the range of his guns, could be of great help to our pilots in action, and sure enough it was very quickly installed in all MiG-15s engaged in Korea. (The device was based, of course, on the same basic principle as the modern 'anti-radar' used by speed-loving car drivers.)

Strange as it might seem, the device was at first received by combat pilots with mistrust. Many of them would even turn it off. But soon we heard of its first successful application. A regiment commander in a sortie with his wingman, on hearing a faint sound made by the warning device, craned his neck to look back-wards but saw nothing. The noise in the earphones persisted and seemed to grow louder. He looked back and around him, and again all was clear. He decided the gadget was playing up and turned it off. A minute later, as though something pushed him from within, he turned it on again. This time his ears were attacked by loud howling. He looked back just in time to see a pair of Sabres behind his tail about to open fire. He rolled his aeroplane into a steep turn, his wingman followed suit, and the two Sabres shot past them at high speed, unable to take aim or fire. This incident convinced all combat pilots that they were better off trusting 'that gadget', and many a life was saved thanks to it. Its inventor, Vadim Matskevich, was decorated with the Red Star Order, and his tail-protecting device, named 'Syren', became an attribute of all Soviet military and military transport aircraft.

In May 1952 my friend Igor Sokolov and I were summoned by the Section CO, Colonel Dziuba, who commissioned us to conduct inspection tests of the pre-production MiG-17.

The manufacture of military aircraft (and all other military products) as well as the necessary quality control were monitored by the Defence Ministry. One of the Defence Ministry's primary concerns was the correspondence of the air-craft coming off the lines to the stipulated military specifications. Every factory producing anything that concerned the Defence Ministry always had to host so-called 'military representatives' whose main responsibility was to see that these specifications were consistently met by the manufacturer. Every aircraft coming off the lines was first tested by one of the civilian test pilots assigned to the factory and then presented for the inspection and approval of the military representatives. If some faults were discovered, which was often the case, additional flight tests were called for after their removal. Once an aircraft was approved by the military representatives, it was handed over to an operational unit. In addition, once a year the production of each factory manufacturing a particular type of aircraft was spot-checked by the Flight Test Institute. One aircraft from each of these factories was sent to the FTI to be tested for its correspondence to military specifications, and this is what Dziuba wanted us to do with the MiG-17.

The list of defects revealed in the course of qualification tests was included in the test statement, accompanied by a list of rectifying measures to be taken. In the case of serious faults that could affect flight safety or the operational performance of the aircraft, the approval of this type of aircraft produced by the factory in question was suspended and another aircraft off the factory ramp was picked at random to be tested to find out whether the fault or faults were recurrent or accidental. The same pattern always applied to the testing of other similar products, for example aircraft rockets.

Of particular importance to the aircraft industry were qualification tests of pre-production specimens, conducted on the basis of a broader and more extensive programme than ordinary qualification tests. The purpose of pre-production aircraft tests was, and is, to ascertain the identicality between the first aircraft coming off the lines and the prototype. The prototype will by this time have been thoroughly tested and supplied with a formal statement of the test team, confirming the feasibility of its production and its adoption by the air force. Besides, pre-production aircraft tests were supposed to establish whether the manufacturer had followed the specific recommendations contained in the prototype test statement.

The large-scale production of aircraft was sometimes launched even before the completion of the military certification tests of the prototype. In such cases the very first machines to be manufactured were likely to possess the faults or shortcomings of the prototype, either already revealed in the course of tests or yet to be exposed before they were finished. In addition, the first mass-produced aircraft of a given type may sometime have had production defects which were absent from the prototype. Experience showed that in the course of several years in the life of a certain type of aircraft occasional new flaws continued to appear, although most of them were naturally exposed in the course of the tests, those conducted at the FTI and those carried out in combat units with the FTI's participation.

So, Colonel Dziuba, having outlined our task with the MiG-17, said, 'Each of you is both an engineer and a pilot, so it is up to you which of you is going to be project engineer and team leader, and which project pilot.' We decided to draw lots. It fell to me to be project engineer, but I wanted to fly too, so in the draft order on the composition of my test team, which in my capacity as project engineer I had to prepare for the Institute Commander's approval, I named Igor as assistant engineer and myself as the second test pilot. Of course my list of team members included other people besides us – specialists in flight performance, in engines, in stability and controllability, in airborne equipment. Igor and I conducted the tests together on an equal footing. Together we planned the test programme, set up flight missions and took turns to fly. When the tests were completed we prepared and wrote the final statement together as well.

Igor Sokolov was a wonderful and understanding friend to have; he was kind, intelligent, reliable and possessed a remarkable sense of humour. Often, during a perfectly serious conversation, he would say something ostensibly innocent, and at first nobody would notice; then suddenly we would all become aware of the comic touch to the situation, which his words had subtly revealed. He was a good pilot, although not in the top-class category. At the same time he was an extremely capable engineer and possessed a very sharp mind and technical aptitude.

In the course of that test programme we had to perform a flight with the 8 G-load factor to test the aeroplane's structural endurance. I believe that many people who have heard the term 'G-load' might be rather uncertain as to what it really means. G-load is the result of acceleration (or inertia), and to some extent it can be felt in a car when it is speeding up or, on the contrary, slowing down. The same kind of load factor appears in an aircraft which is gaining speed on a take-off run. This is the longitudinal G-load, directed along the so-called air-path or body axis. It can be easily neglected, except when a fast-moving car or aircraft collides with an obstacle. What gives real trouble is the vertical G-load (the Z-axis load factor). It is known as 'positive' acceleration (G-load) when it acts down-ward, from head to pelvis, pressing the pilot into the seat, and as 'negative' acceleration when it acts upward, from pelvis to head, trying to tear the pilot's body from the seat. The negative acceleration appears, for example, when the aircraft is pitched down sharply from a steep climb into a dive. If this manoeuvre is performed at a rate when the centrifugal force equals the force of gravity (i.e. counterbalances it), the state of weightlessness (known as the 'zero-gravity condi-tion') is created. This is exactly how the weightless state is achieved in the aircraft used for training cosmonauts.

In a straight and level flight, however fast, the vertical G-load, above the normal gravity force, is not applied, but as soon as you start turning or pulling out after a dive the centrifugal force begins to press you into the seat. The force of inertia applies to all parts of your body and all parts of the aircraft. Their weight seems to increase several times, so the 8 G-load, for example, would mean that the plane and everything in it, including the pilot, have become eight times heavier. This increased weight has to be borne by the aeroplane's wings, and their strength is tested in special flight tests. Naturally the future aircraft is always designed with a certain safety margin in its airframe, and the ground structural endurance tests are conducted in a special test airframe beforehand, so normally there is no danger of the wings disintegrating during a test flight (although I know of at least one such case which I described earlier, in Chapter 8). The proof of sufficient strength of the wings is the absence of any residual strain (deformation) in the airframe after the flight.

The impact of vertical G-load on a man's body depends on the length of its application. The load factor of as much as 10 or 11 G can be tolerated if it is applied for just one or two seconds, but even the relatively low load factor of 6 or 7 G becomes too much if it is applied for over ten seconds. It first affects the pilot's eyesight (even before it happens the eyelids grow so heavy that it becomes hard to keep your eyes open) and then causes a blackout. When the pilot is in a reclining, semi-horizontal position, the acceleration acts from chest to back and is much more easily tolerated, therefore the limit G-load in this position is higher. At ejection, however, the acceleration is extremely high, up to 16 or 18 G, but it does not last longer than a few fractions of a second. To increase the maximum tolerable G-load a special flying suit was designed in the US. Compressed air that at high acceleration regimes filled the built-in bladders of the suit and squeezed the legs, preventing the blood from accumulating in the lower part of the body. During the Korean war we got hold of one of these suits; it was copied by our designers and several newly made samples were sent to the FTI to be tested by the pilots of our section. We wore them in various flight missions, including simulation dog-fights. The anti-G suit was approved by all test pilots, and it soon became part of our operational fighter pilots' flying gear.

In connection with the MiG-15 and MiG-17 fighters, I would like to tell the story of the engines with which they were fitted. I have said earlier that the first Soviet jets were equipped with German engines, or with engines copied from the German ones. They were rather heavy and had a large specific fuel consumption (the amount of fuel burnt per hour for every kilo of thrust developed). The new types of aircraft being designed in the USSR at that time needed more advanced engines. In 1946 a group of Russian experts went to Britain to purchase engine specimens. Britain had a very advanced engine-building industry then, and their engines are highly rated still. The delegation was led by Artem Mikoyan and our chief engine designer Vladimir Klimov. The war was only recently over and both our countries still treated each other as allies. So first everything went very smoothly, and it was agreed that several samples of the state-of-the-art British engines would be sold to us. However, the wind soon seemed to change; the representative of one of the big engine companies sensed the mood that prevailed in the government and wavered. My uncle told us all later, in his characteristic humorous manner, how as a guest in that man's house he was playing billiards against his host and half in jest offered him a game with the yet unsigned contract as their stake. If he won the game, his British host would have to sign the contract. The stake was accepted, but Artem knew what he was doing; he was a first-class amateur player and as soon as he started playing in earnest he had not too much difficulty winning. A bet was a bet, and it had to be honoured. The contract was signed.

The samples purchased were those of the Nene and Derwent engines with a centrifugal compressor. Their specific fuel consumption and their thrust-to-weight ratio were lower than in the captured German engines, and they were also more reliable. They were copied and launched to be produced on a mass scale. The hardest task of all was the creation of a metal alloy suitable for the turbine blades (they have to endure heavy loads and high temperatures, about 1,000 degrees Celsius). The material for the turbine blades proved such an important issue that it was discussed at a Politburo meeting, and Stalin instructed I. Tevosian, Metallurgy Minister and a well-known expert in the field, to take personal charge of the research and experiments aimed at receiving a suitable alloy. They said Tevosian literally did not leave the metal works for about a month, until the desired alloy was achieved. It is worth mentioning that before the war Tevosian spent a few years in Germany working as an engineer at one of Krupp's factories, the idea being to gain experience in dealing with the most advanced technologies. Experience he did gain all right, but he nearly lost his freedom, or life, later. Some time after his return home to Russia he was very nearly accused of being a foreign spy and declared an enemy of the people.

Once I dropped in on Artem at work and met Vladimir Klimov, who was sitting with my uncle in his office. We talked, and I asked him whether our RD-45 (the abbreviation stands for the Russian equivalent of 'jet engine') was in any way different from the Nene. 'Of course it is', said Klimov. 'You know, there is a tiny metal plate attached to the front part of the engine. On the English engine it says "Nene", and on ours "RD-45".'

Soon, however, the RD-45 engine was modernised. The high-quality alloy used in the turbine blades made it possible to increase the exhaust temperatures and, consequently, the thrust. The latter reached 2,270 kg (as against the 2,070 kg of the British Nene), yet the pre-overhaul life expectancy of our engine was lower than that of its British prototype. Later there appeared Klimov's new engine, known as the VK-1 (its designer's initials), which could develop a thrust of 2,700 kg. The new engine was fitted on the MiG-15, the MiG-17 and the Il-28 bomber. The engine based on the British Derwent became known as the RD-500, where '500' was again the name of the plant that produced it. It was used by Yakovlev for his fighters.

I have already mentioned the Chinese pilot who defected to Japan in a MiG-15 during the Korean war. Because of his defection it was discovered that the Soviet jet fighter was equipped with a Nene-based engine. There was quite a row in the British Parliament as a result about the source of the prototypes and the un-licensed manufacture of copies.

CHAPTER 13

Gaining Experience

On 1 May 1952, as usual, there was to be a military parade in Red Square. Aviation was also supposed to participate. In those days military parades were held twice a year on 7 November and 1 May, and whenever the weather permitted the air force would participate with formations of military aircraft flying over Red Square. The organisation of such air parades was the responsibility of the Moscow District Air Force Commander, Vasily Stalin. That year the weather was bad; it was overcast with the ceiling at about 200 metres and occasional 'loose' clouds even lower. The visibility was very poor. Naturally the reasonable thing to do on a day like this would be to call the air parade off; however, Vasily took a rather irresponsible decision to go along with it, thus causing serious trouble.

The fly-past was opened by a group of Tu-4 heavy bombers. They did all right except for a time delay due to the weather. A formation of a wing of Il-28 medium bombers that followed caught up with the rear Tu-4, its front aircraft getting on their tail. With the pilots barely able to see the other aircraft the formation broke up and there was serious danger of an accident. The Il-28s were commanded to turn off the fly-past route and return home, but two of them did not make it to the airfield: one crashed as it was making its way home through the clouds, and the other on the landing approach. The wing was commanded by my fellow pilot in the war, Colonel Dolgushin. The flight he was leading himself was the only one that kept the formation, the others broke up and returned separately.

The formation of the MiG-15 fighter division from Kubinka was led by my brother Alexei, who was already one of the regiment commanders. As his formation was *en route* to Red Square he saw that they were about to overlap with a group of the Il-28s that were close ahead. Alexei led his formation into a right S-turn to build up the distance between his fighters and the Il-28s, but when they got back on their route he saw several scattered bombers on their return flight. Alexei had to repeat his manoeuvre to evade overlapping, but since Moscow was already close, as a result of their second S-turn he and the other MiG-15s ended up off their original path. It was almost too late to get back on it, yet Alexei decided to give it a try. I was in Red Square at the time, watching the parade from the stands (the weather in Moscow was slightly better), wondering why on earth there was such a long pause after the heavy bombers. And then I saw the first fighter pilot appear, not from over the History Museum as was usual but to the left of it. They were coming in a right bank, about to recover their assigned path. Alexei levelled the wings right over the museum building, and each flight in his formation followed suit. After the parade Alexei received a commendation, while the leaders of the bomber formations and some ground commanders were

171

punished. Vasily Stalin, on his father's orders, was dismissed from his position and put on a course at the Air Force Academy.

The autumn of 1952 saw a fatal accident at the Test Institute, the first since I had begun working there. One day we were all alerted by the rumour that radio contact with Zuskevich, who was in the air, was lost. After a while Colonel Antipov entered the pilots' crew-room and said that the crashed aircraft had been found on the ground with the pilot inside. Zuskevich had failed to eject.

Lieutenant-Colonel Arkady Rogatnev (who had just been transferred with promotion from our section to Section No. 3) and Evgeny Zuskevich, in their two MiG-15s, had been climbing up through a thick layer of clouds after take-off, and as Rogatnev got on top of the clouds he could neither see Zuskevich nor hear him on the radio. Zuskevich must have lost his attitude orientation in the clouds and rolled over. Whether the artificial horizon had failed or the pilot had not coped with the instrument flight control, it was hard to say. Rogatnev was Zuskevich's CO; he had signed the flight mission sheet and he had taken off as the leader of their pair, so he was blamed for the accident. The official conclusion was that Zuskevich had been out of practice with instrument flying, and that Rogatnev should not have allowed him to fly. As a result Rogatnev lost his recent promotion and returned to our No. 1 section as an ordinary pilot. True, Zuskevich, as an engineer-pilot, had not flown regularly, and it could have played its role, but it is also true that even a well-trained pilot may sometimes lose attitude orientation in the clouds, especially if the artificial horizon fails. I shall try to describe what flying in the clouds, or 'blind flying' as we call it, is like.

People establish their position in space by various visual clues, and in their absence by the direction of gravity. In the early days of aviation it was believed that in a blind flight – through the clouds or at night, when neither the ground nor the horizon is visible – the pilot would be able to navigate with the help of his perception of gravity, without any visual clues. It soon became clear that it was not so. An aircraft hardly ever flies perfectly steadily; even in a straight and level flight it is affected by various forces which can be generated by air gusts, minor accidental disturbances of the flight path, yawing or the pilot's control inputs. The inertia forces which are then produced merge with gravity to form a single resultant force which is no longer acting towards the earth's centre. The pilot's brain, however, continues to receive 'normal gravity' signals, thus providing him with a wrong orientation. In addition, the angular movement factor affects the pilot's perception of the true vertical. When either the horizon or the ground (or both) is in view, visual guidance prevails over the gravity perception factor and the pilot has no orientation problem. When the visibility is nil, there are only the instruments to rely on for guidance, and the difficulty faced here by the pilot is that he must take in the readings of several instruments 'at a glance', as it were, or scan them while keeping the needles within certain limits and at the same time trying to ignore his distorted physical perceptions. Needless to say, the less sophisticated or readable the instruments, the more difficult the pilot's task of orientation.

In the early days of instrument flying, the instruments relied on in a blind flight were the turn-and-slip indicator (known in the Soviet AF as the 'pioneer', after

Pioneer, the company that produced the model adopted and copied in the USSR), the climb-and-dive indicator, the air speed and altitude indicators, and the tachometer. These instruments were also used to determine and maintain the attitude in banking and pitching, as well as the path of the aircraft in the vertical plane. The turn indicator is in fact a gyroscope which 'tries' to maintain its space orientation whatever the position of the aircraft. Its needle shows the rate and the direction of a turn. The indicator also includes a side-slip indicator, which looks like a level gauge with a ball inside. The 1930s saw the invention (in the West) of the artificial horizon, also based on the gyroscope principle. It actually showed a pictogram of the horizon line and the aircraft, thus providing a clear visual image of the attitude of the aircraft with respect to the true horizon. All these instruments are still in current use, but the turn-and-slip indicator has become an auxiliary instrument which confirms the readings of the artificial horizon.

I believe that every pilot who has ever flown in the clouds, at night or under the instrument hood (installed under the canopy for the simulation of nil visibility) has experienced false perceptions in defiance of the instrument readings. Even in an ordinary horizontal flight it sometimes seems that you are flying on your side or wheels-up, and you feel like levelling the aircraft, which in actual fact would mean rolling it over. A pilot qualified to fly in the clouds is not only capable of spatial orientation through instrument reading; it is essential that he does *not* trust anything *but* instrument readings and trains himself to disregard his own perceptions as to the attitude of the aircraft. There are times when it is fairly difficult. Occasionally even a highly experienced pilot might, for example, bank dangerously, misled by false sensations, especially if he is tired or suddenly feels unwell or something. It takes a powerful conscious effort to suppress what your body tells you and to operate flight controls, returning the instrument readings (those of bank and rate of climb or descent) to within the safe limits. Naturally, where there are two pilots in the cockpit (for example in a passenger aircraft) the danger of spatial disorientation is much less. The autopilot has made instrument flying much easier and safer. It usually has a mode for automatic levelling of the aircraft which can be activated even when the autopilot as such is not engaged, but the unfortunate Zuskevich had no such facility available to him.

At the end of May 1953 Moscow hosted the world basketball tournament. One of my former fellow students and now a fellow test pilot at the Institute, Igor Yemelianov, was a keen sportsman, and he and I together went to see the games every day after work. On 29 May Igor looked into our briefing room and said, 'Wait till I do another flight, and then we'll go.' He made that flight, but was immediately asked to make another, as the co-pilot in the prototype Mi-4 helicopter which was going through military certification tests. In the left seat was Igor's CO and a very experienced pilot, Kokotchikov. Just then Colonel Ivanov gathered all pilots of our section for a briefing. George Beregovoi was sitting by the window that faced the airfield. 'So tomorrow we will begin to fly helicopters', began Ivanov, but he was interrupted by Beregovoi crying out, 'A crash!' George had seen a helicopter colliding with an aeroplane over the runway, both of them crashing in.

As it turned out, the helicopter, having received clearance, took off from the ramp on the side of the runway and hovered low to check on the engine performance. At that time an Il-12 asked for take-off clearance, and the tower controller, failing to see the helicopter over the runway against the setting sun, decided that it had already gone and cleared the Il-12 for take-off. Just as the aeroplane got airborne the helicopter began climbing up and across the runway. The Il-12's first pilot saw the threat and entered a left climbing turn to avoid it, but the helicopter, also on the climb, hit his wing with its rotor blades and chopped it off. All five crew members of the Il-12 (there were no passengers) and the three helicopter crew members, including Igor, were killed. Throughout our entire flying career, Igor Yemelianov was the only accident victim among those of my fellow Academy graduates who became test pilots.

In September 1953 we received three serial MiG-17s produced by three different factories for inspection tests. It was decided to test all three together, in one test team. It was headed by Illarion Kriukov (project engineer) and had three pilots: Igor Sokolov, Nikolai Korovin and me.

One of our tasks involved carrying out gun firing and bombing tests. The Flight Test Institute had its own firing range near Moscow, but its limited size allowed only for medium-height bombing. As the MiG-17 tests required high-altitude firing, we had to ferry the fighters to a larger firing range (known as the Rocket Test Range, or RTR-4) over a thousand kilometres south-east of Moscow. We took off in a formation of four MiG-17s with Colonel Kuvshinov as the leader. His test mission was separate from ours but it also involved gun firing. It was the first experience of such a long formation flight (over 1,200 kilometres) in the MiG-17 for us all, and at the end of it we had to land on an unfamiliar aerodrome. As each of us began his landing approach, our fuel warning lights were all on.

RTR-4 was 140 kilometres south-east of Volgograd on the eastern bank of the Volga. Five years later my life and work would become firmly linked with that place for nearly twenty years, but on that first visit everything was still new and unfamiliar. We landed on the newly built concrete runway of the air base, whose entire working premises then consisted of six prefabricated bungalows. The living compound was situated off the base grounds between two villages, Vladimirovka and Akhtuba, and for the most part consisted of similar bungalows. There were just two or three two-storey brick houses, a single shop, and a water tower. The road between the compound and the air base was still only partially paved, and on a rainy day became almost impassable. Every other evening Igor and I went to the village post office to call home to Moscow. A large part of the way to the village lay through an empty field. When I returned to the air base three years later the compound had already reached the edge of the village, and by the 1960s it had expanded in every direction and grown into a sizeable town.

In the eleven days that we spent at the base we performed all our scheduled firings and bombings. In one of the test flights my fire warning light suddenly came on. I looked through the 'periscope' (a special device with a mirror on top of the canopy) and saw no flames or smoke behind the tail. There was no smell of burning either. Still, I decided to land and began the approach. The tower controller confirmed on the radio that there was no smoke behind me. The warning light turned out to be a false alarm, but to bring the fire detector to its senses it would be necessary to remove the aircraft afterbody, which would create a lot of hassle for our hosts and disrupt the test schedule. It had to be my decision only, for the project engineer had no right even to suggest I should fly with the fire-alarm light permanently on. He was obviously pleased, however, when I said I would overlook the defect until we returned home. Needless to say, it was a serious breach of safety rules.

There have been cases when pilots who put too much trust in the fire-warning light took hasty decisions, while the alarm turned out to be false. Usually if the aircraft is on fire there are other warning clues as well, such as a system failure or a smell of burning – and then there should be no doubt left. This reminds me of a tragic accident that occurred many years later. A passenger Il-62 was taking off from Sheremetyevo airport near Moscow. Within seconds of take-off, fire-warning lights flashed for first one and then the other port-side engines. The flight engineer did what the manual prescribed, immediately cutting both engines off. The heavy aircraft, with its tanks full and with many passengers on board, had not yet had time to gain the speed needed for a stable horizontal flight on the two remaining engines. It began to lose height and crashed. The investigation that followed did not confirm there had been a fire before the actual crash, so in fact the indicators might have given a false alarm. Flight regulations allowed the engineer to kill the engine on fire without the pilot's command, but in this case it was a fatal mistake to do so. Even if an engine is definitely on fire it should never be cut off at take-off – not until the aircraft has built up the speed sufficient for horizontal flight. A pilot would not have made such a mistake. Thus, a small item in the regulations and the engineer's 'blind' obedience to it caused the death of over a hundred people. After that accident the regulations were changed so as to allow the flight engineer to cut off the engines only on the captain's explicit command.

In 1954 Piotr Belyasnik (a war veteran and a Hero of the Soviet Union for his part in the Battle of Stalingrad) and I began testing the SR-2, a high-altitude reconnaissance aircraft. Nikolai Borisov was our project engineer. The SR-2 was a modification of the MiG-17 fitted with a new and more powerful engine and an aerial camera, and oxygen feed for a full-pressure suit. I had to ferry the machine from the aviation industry flight test base at Zhukovsky, and it was handed over to me there by a Mikoyan Design Company test pilot, Vladimir Nefedov. On taking off from Zhukovsky aerodrome I pulled the stick nearly all the way, as I would normally do in a MiG-17 for rotation (i.e. to unstick the front wheel), but the SR-2 reacted unexpectedly: it began to nose up too fast. My quick reaction helped: I pushed the stick forward, and after that handled it more gently. It turned out that because of the shift of the centre of gravity further to the back (in comparison with the MiG-17), the SR-2 required a much smaller stick

175

deflection for rotation at take-off. I said a few 'unkind' words about Nefedov under my breath for his failure to warn me of that feature, but then I thought that perhaps he was so used to it himself that he simply forgot about it.

It does sometimes happen that a test pilot, having got used to this or that feature of the tested aircraft, might unintentionally veil its shortcomings. So, according to a very important rule adopted at the Research and Flight Test Institute, every machine was at some stage flown out by a test pilot outside the given test team. It provided for a fresh, unbiased view of the aircraft and its performance. Paradoxically, the pilot's high qualifications might sometimes affect his judgement: he might fail to pay attention to certain minor shortcomings of the tested aircraft which a less experienced test pilot might 'stumble on'. Therefore, another golden rule adopted at the FTI was to assess the aircraft from the 'average pilot's' reference point.

In the flight tests of the SR-2, Piotr Belyasnik was mainly concerned with the engine, while I tested its overall flight performance. Besides, both of us made several photo-reconnaissance flights. In one such flight I did aerial photography at the SR-2's ceiling and reached an altitude of 17,600 metres. It was higher than the national record of the time (though we did not register my achievement as a new record). Besides, as far as I know it was the first jet test mission in the USSR performed in the newly tested first Soviet full-pressure suit (the prototype of the suit later used in our space flights).

Another innovation associated with the SR-2 was the dictaphone for recording reconnaissance observations, which we decided to use for registering instrument readings in test flights. It seemed much more convenient than the usual writing on the knee-board – the control stick no longer had to change hands (literally!) with the pencil. Yet it unexpectedly required more time. Talking into the dictaphone, I had to say several words for each instrument: for example, 'altitude fifteen two hundred; speed four hundred ten'. It took longer than jotting a few figures in the corresponding column of the chart. On the other hand the dictaphone allowed me to record various features of the aeroplane's performance. However, dictaphones were not adopted in test flying, and pilots still write everything down on the knee-board.

I did find myself in one somewhat embarrassing situation while testing the SR-2. By that time I had already become quite experienced in what is known as 'simulated dead-stick landing' – in other words, a landing with the engine at idle, performed as a training exercise in case of a real emergency. Dead-stick landing in a jet fighter with sweptback wings is one of the most challenging tasks. The aircraft glides down at a very steep angle – up to fifteen degrees instead of the usual three with the engine on – and pretty fast too; the rate of descent is up to thirty-five metres per second (as distinct from the normal four to five). If, with a real engine failure, you undershoot, i.e. end up some distance short of the runway, there is nothing you can do about it. But even when the aeroplane is close enough to the airfield the only course of action dictated by operational pilots' manuals in this emergency is ejection. Not so with test pilots: whenever it looks marginally possible to glide up to the runway, they usually try to land.

The first difficulty of the power-off landing is planning the approach in such a way as to touch down at the beginning of the runway. This involves a manoeuvre which enables the pilot to begin the final glide at the needed height: if the height is insufficient, the aircraft will undershoot; if it is excessive, it might overshoot the runway. Another difficulty is levelling-off on landing: if done too early the aircraft will lose speed and 'sink' or stall as a result, and if done too late it will hit the ground hard. Therefore gliding has to be done at excessive speed, thus causing an even steeper glidepath. First the aircraft is pulled out to the normal glide angle, i.e., the glide angle typical of the power-on landing (the preliminary pull-out), at which point the speed begins to drop. Then an ordinary flare-out is performed just before touching down. Like many other test pilots, I performed idle-engine landings as often as I could, for practice. Whenever the weather was all right and the air traffic not too heavy, all you had to do was request the tower for clearance. Unfortunately later, when the test pilots' work became 'constricted' by too much formalism, we could no longer ask for such a clearance on the spur of the moment. The intention to land with the engine at idle had to be entered in the flight schedule in advance, with the natural result that pilots began to have less actual practice.

At the end of the SR-2 test programme I had to try out its cannon. I ferried the aircraft to the air base 150 kilometres north-west of Moscow, near which there was a firing range, where I was soon joined by the engineers and mechanics of our team. My co-pilot on the project stayed behind at home, for one pilot was enough for the task (and he had some other mission to perform). I made ten flights with cannon-firing a number of different manoeuvres, including some high G-load ones. Every time, as I was returning to the aerodrome, I would move the power level to idle at an altitude of seven or eight thousand metres, and not touch it again until the end of the landing run. The first nine landings were successful; the SR-2 was a lighter aircraft than the MiG-17 and very responsive, and I would glide at a speed which was just 10 kph higher than at a normal landing. Whenever there seemed to be a danger of overshooting, I pulled the stick to bring the speed down by 20 kph. This caused my machine to 'parachute', i.e. to glide a little more 'flatly' and therefore more steeply until my glidepath was corrected. Then I pushed the stick again to return to the reference gliding speed of 260 kph. Had I been older and more mature, I would not have indulged in such stunts; the risk was too high. At power-off gliding there has to be a sufficient speed margin on top of the normal gliding speed, and my method of correcting the glidepath by reducing speed could very easily have brought me to disaster.

Anyway, during my final (tenth) flight, after which I was to return home, I was in high spirits and I must have forgotten my own rule to remind myself to be on guard every time I felt unreasonably elated or over-confident. I began the landing approach as before, at minimum power, having first extended the flaps to the take-off position. As I was about to extend them all the way I realised that my approach was a little short of the runway and decided to keep the flaps up a little longer. And then I forgot about them altogether. With the flaps at take-off position the air drag is lower and the aircraft takes a shallower glidepath. I soon realised that I was about to overshoot. Failing to guess the real reason, I reduced the speed at a height of some 1,000 metres. The aircraft started to sink. It was still 'parachuting', but much faster than I would have preferred because of the flaps not being fully down. The descent was so steep that the tower controller shouted in my earphones 'You're falling!', which did not rate high as a piece of news for I was already fully aware of it myself. I pushed the stick forward; the speed built up but I was already too low. It took some very energetic levelling off to avoid hitting the runway. Even so my touchdown was pretty rough, though both my machine and I seemed unscathed. On the landing run I took a look at the flap lever and realised what had happened.

As I climbed out of the cockpit I was confronted by the Institute Wing Commander Colonel Antipov, who, as bad luck would have it, happened to be at that aerodrome on that day. 'Now what's this supposed to mean?' he demanded, pointing at the tail. It turned out that I had performed not a two-point, but a three-point landing, the third point being the tail. The latter came out of this adventure slightly squashed (it later gave rise to the joke that I had tried to convert my SR-2 into a MiG-19, which had an oval-shaped tail). To level off my machine with the flaps not fully down, and the descent rate too high, I had had to create a higher angle of attack than was normal, and the tail hit the ground. Antipov punished me with a ten-day suspension from flying, and the fact was entered in my personal logbook, the only censorious entry in my entire career as a pilot. To add insult to injury, Piotr Belyasnik was summoned from Moscow to ferry the machine back home.

Afterwards I had ample opportunity to perform this frankly rather difficult task during the special tests of the MiG-19 in power-off landings. My friend Sergei Petrov was the project pilot, while I acted as an outside 'evaluation pilot'. The final flight of the MiG-19 test programme was performed by Petrov with the engine actually cut off on the final glide. He and I later published a joint article in an aviation magazine on the techniques of a power-off landing.* Later, in the 1960s, such tests were carried out in two types of fighter: the MiG-21PF (project pilot Victor Yatsun) and the Su-7B (project pilot Yuri Rogachev). I acted as an 'evaluation pilot' in both cases. Most of the landings were performed as simulated dead-stick landings with the engine at idle, but both the project pilots and I performed our respective final flights with the engine actually cut off at 7,000 metres over the runway. To be honest, although I knew I was doing everything correctly, the nervous tension was high, and as far as I remember my knees were shaking. The slightest slip on my part might have led to undershooting or overshooting the runway, and to go round again would have been impossible. When I landed in the Su-7B, Yuri Rogachev said approvingly, 'You must be the first and only general to have deliberately killed the only engine before landing!'

An important development in the design of the jet fighter was the appearance of engines with afterburners, which soon led to the conquest of the sonic barrier.

---

* S. A. Mikoyan and S. V. Petrov, 'Landing a supersonic aircraft with the engine out', *Vestnik Vozdushnogo Flota*, No. 2, February 1960.

My first acquaintance – on paper – with a jet with an afterburner had taken place in my final year at the Academy, when I got an opportunity to read the final test statement of the Yak-23. It was a jet fighter fitted with an engine with an afterburner chamber. It had been tested at the FTI back in 1948 or thereabouts. The tests had confirmed the speed increase, yet fuel consumption had grown too, and it could not be afforded in the Yak-23 with its initially small tank capacity. The endurance of the aircraft with an active afterburner had proved insufficient, and the military had rejected it. Thus a really advanced idea ended up dead and buried (at least for the existing subsonic jets) due to a formalist attitude to technological innovations. It was resurrected only when it was discovered that the new F-86D that had appeared in the American force in Korea was equipped not only with a radar but also with an afterburner, which gave it obvious superiority despite increasing its weight. Unfortunately, it was not the only case in the history of Soviet technology when a breakthrough project was for some reason rejected or held back until it became known that a similar innovation had been introduced in the West. 'A prophet is not without honour, save in his own country.'

So what is an afterburner, and how does it increase the thrust? In a jet engine the thrust is created by the exhaust jet stream gushing out of the nozzle. The larger the speed and mass of the exhaust gases, the more powerful the thrust. The exhaust jet of a turbo-jet engine still contains some oxygen, and it was discovered that if additional fuel was injected in the exhaust pipe and burnt there both the temperature and the volume of the exhaust jet increased. The jet stream velocity increased as well and produced additional thrust as a result. This is why the device was termed 'afterburner': it burns additional fuel aft of the engine gas turbine, increasing the thrust by 25 per cent and more. Shortly after the capabilities of the F-86D became known, there appeared the MiG-17F with the same engine as the MiG-17 but fitted with an afterburner (it was also provided with powered elevator control).

But first about the original MiG-17. By the time I joined the Flight Test Institute my commanding officer, Colonel Kuvshinov, had just completed the tests of the first MiG-17 (an advanced version of the MiG-15). I then got an opportunity to fly it twice, though later I used to fly the MiG-17 and its various modifications a lot. It differed from the MiG-15 in its longer fuselage (which gave it more stability) and a larger sweep of the wings (forty-five degrees as opposed to the thirty-five of the MiG-15), which increased its speed. Although the new version, the MiG-17F (tested by Alexei Solodovnikov), had a greater engine thrust thanks to the afterburner, and consequently a much higher rate of climb, it still came short of the speed of sound in horizontal flight. It could only go supersonic in a dive. Some published sources say that the Mikoyan company test pilot Ivashchenko achieved and even slightly exceeded the sonic speed in the prototype MiG-17 in level flight in February 1950, but in the MiG-17Fs tested at the FTI such a speed was never reached. Ivashchenko might have flown at very low air temperatures, when the speed of sound is lower and the engine thrust higher. In this case (or, perhaps, due to an inaccuracy of measurements) the needle of his Mach indicator could have gone beyond '1', but the rules of test flying dictate that all data be reduced to standard atmospheric conditions.

179

The MiG-17F was given dive tests identical to the ones performed in the MiG-15. We would perform a split-S manoeuvre at about 15,000 metres and then dive on full afterburner vertically down to about 3,000 metres. The speed would not go too far above the sonic speed; the actual Mach number stopped at 1.07 to 1.08, although the indicator might at times show up to Mach 1.15 (the discrepancy due to the delay of static air-pressure transfer to the speed indicator caused by a fast descent). Characteristically, on diving the speed would build up, down to about 7,000 or 8,000 metres, and then slow down because of the greater air density near the earth.

As a matter of fact, the first aircraft to have broken the sound barrier was an aircraft equipped with a rocket engine. Back in 1947, on 14 October, sonic speed was exceeded for the first time in history in a Bell X-1 by the American test pilot Charles 'Chuck' Yeager, whom I happened to meet later. But the X-1 was not the earliest rocket-engined aircraft. As early as 15 May 1942, the Soviet Air Force test pilot Grigory Bakhchvandzhi of the FTI performed a flight in a BI-1 with a rocket engine. The aircraft was designed by A. Berezniak and A. Isayev (under the supervision of V. Bolkhovitinov). In the same year there appeared the German Me 163, a fighter with a rocket engine which the Germans brought into action towards the end of the war (without much success, however). After the war, an experimental aircraft with a rocket engine was created by the Mikoyan company, while at the Yakovlev company they fitted an ordinary fighter with a rocket booster.

A rocket engine differs from a turbo-jet engine in that its oxidiser is in liquid form and is contained in a tank (as its fuel). This type of engine does not need atmospheric air for burning fuel. It is also known as the liquid-propellant rocket engine, as distinct from the solid-propellant rocket engine which also exists. The advantages of the rocket engine are confined to very high altitudes where the air pressure is very low or nil, whereas at higher air density the air-breathing engine (using atmospheric oxygen for burning) performs better. However, rocket engines, either liquid or solid, are widely used in many types of aircraft as take-off boosters and in all rockets where it is important to get high thrust for a short time. Even before the beginning of the 'supersonic age', in the late 1940s, both scientists and designers had already been working on the concept of a supersonic aircraft with a turbo-jet engine. They were aware that such an aircraft had to possess a different aerodynamic layout (with the wings swept back even more or made thinner, as was done by the Americans in the X-1) which would reduce the air drag at transonic speed. The second major development would have to result in a higher engine thrust without a noticeable increase in the engine size or weight. This could only be achieved with the help of an afterburner.

The first Soviet axial-flow turbo-jet engine with an afterburner was designed, developed and subsequently upgraded at Alexander Mikulin's design company (Sergei Tumansky later succeeded Mikulin as its head). Artem Mikoyan decided to install two such engines in his new fighter, initially designated SM-2. Finally, at the beginning of 1953, the FTI received from the Mikoyan company the first Soviet supersonic aircraft for military certification tests. Its high-altitude air speed was 1,430 kph, which corresponded to Mach 1.34. (The speed of sound near the earth in 'standard' atmospheric conditions is 1,228 kph, but it depends on the air temperature, so in the stratosphere, where it is much colder, the speed is 1,065 kph.) The SM-2 had the wings swept back at sixty degrees.

The test team was headed by the project engineer Vladimir Melnikov, and the project test pilots were Vasily Ivanov and Nikolai Korovin. Both Ivanov and Melnikov were first-rate professionals, and Korovin too, though perhaps lacking in technical knowledge, was a born pilot. Vasily Ivanov was our best and best-known test pilot of the post-war era. A fighter pilot in the first years of the war with a number of personal victories and a Red Banner Order to his credit, he became a test pilot in 1943 and was involved in the tests of the first Soviet jets. His formal education had not gone beyond secondary school, yet he was a man of remarkable natural talent and intelligence. Ivanov was the first among the test pilots of the Flight Test Institute to break the sound barrier. Besides being an excellent pilot (which is essential but not sufficient in flight testing), he had a great flair for practical technology and keen professional intuition. All this, combined with huge experience, made him a first-class test pilot. When it came to some technical problems in testing he would often be as good as our engineers in grasping them, and occasionally would come up with a solution before they did. Appointed Flying Commander of the FTI fighter test pilots in 1950, Ivanov remained in that position until his death from cancer in 1969. Many of our best pilots gained their experience and professional skills under Ivanov's guidance. I too regarded him as my teacher, and I continued to regard him as such when, due to my position within the Institute hierarchy, I became his CO.

Vasily Gavrilovich Ivanov (known to the entire Institute staff as 'VG') was an exceptionally honest and forthright man, and his work was his life. Whatever happened at work or with any of his colleagues he always took very much to heart. He was far from 'soft', and would often tell us pilots off (and sometimes engineers too), yet none of us would ever feel insulted or bear a grudge against him, for he always respected our dignity. An energetic, wilful and demanding commander and a handsome man (with a never fading sun-tan and an impressive 'Red Indian' profile), 'VG' enjoyed unlimited authority and respect among pilots and engineers alike. In fact he was respected by the entire Institute, and as for the pilots, they were genuinely fond of him and his word was law. Yet, for all his authority and prestige, he always remained 'one of us', never failing to take part in the pilots' social get-togethers and various celebrations, and he was all the more respected and loved for it. As a test pilot, Colonel Ivanov was of the same standard as Sergei Anokhin, the legendary test pilot on the staff of the Aviation Industry Flight Research Institute (the Gromov Institute), but I do not think that the kind and gentle Anokhin could compete with our 'VG' as a commander and teacher of pilots.

Most of the people I have so far named while describing my work were fellow pilots and engineers, but it is not a complete list. Naming all would be impossible, but I simply cannot go without paying tribute to such remarkable men as Alexander Rozanov and Victor Veselovsky. Rozanov was an engineer who trained to become a pilot, and while he was first a sub-section head and then the

No. 1 section commander he never stopped flying. He was a very intelligent, cheerful, easy-going and amiable person. Veselovsky was the section second-in-command in charge of test engineering work. Both he and Rozanov were highly experienced in testing and possessed remarkable professional knowledge and an independent way of thinking. The same applies to Vladimir Melnikov, whom I mentioned earlier. Quite a number of our engineers could well be described as unique specialists in their field, and their opinion was listened to and respected even by the famous aircraft designers. As distinct from design company engineers, who might have had a deeper knowledge of the particular types of aircraft they were immediately involved with, our test engineers had a very broad and extensive knowledge of a large variety of aircraft, as well as of the needs of operational units. The same can be said about the FTI test pilots.

I cannot help also paying tribute to the technical personnel, who not only ensured the maintenance of the aircraft but contributed to the assessment of the tested machines and of their maintenance characteristics. The man in charge of the technical staff was Piotr Onoprienko, later succeeded by Ivan Zhulev. The safety of our flights largely depended on the work of our mechanics and technicians. In those days they were mainly people of the war generation; they had no education beyond secondary school (which not all of them had completed), apart from technical training, so most of them to some extent were self-made men. Their practical experience and wits, their natural aptitude for their work and their uniquely conscientious attitude to it were the best guarantee we pilots needed that the aircraft we flew were always in perfect condition. As each of us climbed into the cockpit, he relied on his mechanics one hundred per cent, knowing that they would never allow any negligence. And we knew how concerned they were for each of us while we were flying 'their machines', and how anxiously they waited for our safe return.

CHAPTER 14

The Liberation

The official report of Stalin's death came on 6 March 1953, the day after he died. That day I was at work and had performed two test flights as scheduled. I remember feeling awfully depressed, and even while flying I could not get rid of the heavy thoughts that had been on my mind since I heard the news. Driving past the Kremlin gates on my way home after work I saw a long procession of government cars filing through at an unusually slow speed. It seemed to be a sign of universal grief. How would we go on without Stalin?

I must be frank and admit that, although shortly afterwards I became (and have remained) a confirmed anti-Stalinist, until the disclosures came I had trusted him and thought very much of him as leader. I believe it was an attitude shared by the majority of our people, and some of them have retained this blind trust in him and his policy to this day, despite all that has since become known of his inhuman and cruel rule. They say a work of art should be assessed only within the genre to which it belongs. I think the same principle should go for people, whose life and views should be assessed only within the historical framework in which they lived. Besides, nearly everything in life is relative, and even people who disapproved of the regime and were more or less democratically inclined at the time of Stalin's rule would still seem rather far from understanding genuine democratic values as they are seen today.

All I can say about myself is that I was never totally blind to what was going on in those days, and there were many things I disliked. One of these was the official attitude to the intelligentsia, which was never at that time regarded as a social category to be reckoned with, and which was labelled as a 'social stratum', a term that implied a very low 'rating' in the official hierarchy of society. For my own part, I had always respected the intelligentsia, and people in the literary and artistic world had always had a strong fascination for me. Another thing that secretly troubled me was the anathema declared on people whose professed views in some way deviated from the official party line. I believed that anyone should be allowed to have a private opinion, and even if this opinion was downright wrong it should not justify this person's persecution. I could not understand why Stalin described Social Democrats as the worst enemies of the workers' class; were they not opposed to capitalism just as the Communists were? I did not like it that at party meetings everyone voted the same as everyone else, i.e., in accordance with the guidelines received from 'above', and sometimes even without having seen the documents which we were supposed to approve or the articles we were supposed to condemn.

I had been a Young Communist League member, and then a party member, and in those days I sincerely believed in socialist ideals and in the fact that on the whole we were going the right way. It is hard to take in today – I can hardly believe it myself – yet it was so, and the majority of people before the war did honestly believe that the general line maintained by Stalin was correct. As for the negative sides to our lives and the flagrant abuse of the law that people would occasionally notice, none of it was associated with Stalin, let alone blamed on him. The general view was that all the bad things in our life happened due to the subversive activity of those who opposed Stalin and his good cause. The trust in him was implicit and blind; any thought of him being capable of erring was blasphemy.

During the war and after our victory many people began to change; their personal dignity and their self-respect had to some extent returned to them. It seemed that the beginning of a new life was at hand, and indeed, in the first few years after the war there seemed to be a little more freedom and life was not as constrained as before. But soon the respite was over, and things began to develop in a way I found impossible to accept unquestioningly. The persecution of genetics and geneticists, the Politburo's decisions concerning literature and art (and the people involved in them), the crusade against the 'servility to the West', as it was described – all this was hard to go along with, especially in view of the related ruthless activity of the ideological apparatus, secret police and party functionaries of all levels. I have since believed that attacks on literature, science and art are signs of what in idiomatic Russian is described as 'the screwing of loose nuts', i.e., a crackdown on freedom, however relative the latter might be. It happened again later, when Khrushchev gave his notorious dressing-down to artists and writers. This in fact was unwittingly strong evidence of the intelligentsia's important social role. Today the same could be said about the relationship between those in power and the mass media, but in the Soviet Union of the late 1940s and early 1950s there was no question of the journalists' independent position at all.

Things continued to get worse. There were persistent rumours of a new wave of mass arrests, and some of them happened very near home, both literally and metaphorically. Admiral Afanasiev, who had been working under my father during the war, was arrested just a few steps from where we lived (his apartment was on a different floor of the same section of the building); the so-called 'Leningrad case' and the arrest of Alexei Alexandrovich Kuznetsov touched our family to the quick; and as for the so-called 'Doctors' Plot', I had known two of its victims personally – Professors Preobrazhensky and Vinogradov, both of them first-class specialists and highly respected people. I cannot help agreeing with the opinion expressed by A. Afanasiev, a journalist who published an article about Kuznetsov in the *Komsomolskaya Pravda*: 'There appeared an urgent need to put an entire generation "in their place" – the generation that had emerged from the war victorious and enlightened.'

And yet I cannot remember having serious doubts concerning Stalin himself at that time. When he died, his body was laid out in state for three days in the Column Hall of the House of Unions, which Ella and I could enter through the door reserved for government members and their families (which helped to avoid the long queue of mourners outside the main door). I went there every day and sat there for about an hour or longer on one of the family's guest seats along the side of the coffin. Ella stayed there even longer, sitting supportively by Svetlana's side. On one of those days, as I was dining with my father at the dacha, I told him about my daily visits to the Column Hall. He said it was a daft thing to do, and I was dumbfounded. It was the first unambiguous clue I had ever received suggesting that Stalin could be thought of in critical terms, and that it was the way my father was thinking of him. Looking back today, knowing what I have learnt about my father's attitude to Stalin since then, I can recall other clues of the same nature, but until that day in March 1953 I had not even suspected it could be so. It was a turning point in my perception and understanding of what had been going on while Stalin was in power. My brother Sergo told me that he, feeling distressed by Stalin's death (as was his wife Alla, whose father had been shot at Stalin's orders and whose mother was in a labour camp), asked father, 'What will happen now? Will there be a war?' Our father replied, 'If there wasn't a war while he was around, there'll certainly be no war without him.'

Much later we learnt that in the last year of Stalin's life my father and Vyacheslav Molotov had fallen into disfavour with him. On 16 October at a plenary session of the newly elected Central Committee (the day after the closing of the Nineteenth Party Congress), Stalin astonished all those present (including the Politburo members) with a sharp and totally unexpected castigation of Molotov and Mikoyan. He was going on about the 'struggle against capitalism' and the need for stalwart and unflinching opposition to its 'pernicious influence' (as the Soviet cliché described it), and then suddenly lashed out against the two men, accusing them of a lack of decisiveness in that struggle, of insufficient steadfastness in their anti-capitalist position, of being too ready to yield to the 'enemy's demands' (in my father's case the particular charge was his insistence on the USSR paying its lend-lease debts), and finally of having a 'pro-Western bias' in their views. I have read a vivid account of that episode in the memoirs of Konstantin Simonov, a well-known Russian writer and the only one of those present at that session whose detailed recollection of it has been published so far.* Simonov states that all the Politburo members were sitting there as if transfixed, their faces turned into stone – tense, pale and frozen, not knowing who might be chastised next. Molotov and Mikoyan were both deathly white. Stalin was speaking in such tones that the least everyone could expect was that the two of them would be struck out of the Central Committee membership lists there and then. My father once spoke of this episode to me too, years before Simonov's recollections were published, but his account was reticent and without the touches that could only be observed by a relatively disinterested member of the audience like Simonov, who was a writer into the bargain. Father did not tell me just how severe Stalin's unexpected censure had been, but he mentioned one particular insinuation omitted in Simonov's memoirs: Stalin had pointed out that Molotov and my father had

---

* Konstantin Simonov, *Through the Eyes of a Man of My Generation*, Novosti, Moscow, 1989, pp. 241–4.

been the only Politburo members to have been to the West, and so their views could have been 'affected' by that experience.

As usual, Stalin's next move was equally unpredictable: he suggested electing a twenty-five-strong Presidium of the Central Committee instead of the old Politburo (which had consisted of some ten to eleven members), and to the surprise of those present neither Mikoyan nor Molotov was struck out. But Stalin was more subtle than this; his scheme was to exclude Molotov and my father from the top echelon of power. When the Presidium was elected, a small 'bureau' of eight was formed out of its members, and neither Molotov nor my father was included. They say the Presidium hardly ever convened at full strength and everything was decided by the bureau, or rather by Stalin himself with the bureau members' limited participation.

As for my father's and Molotov's position, their removal from the top of the party pyramid was certainly only the beginning. It was quite evident to us in retrospect (and my father must have known it all along) that if Stalin had lived a little longer Molotov and my father would have suffered the fate of Kuznetsov, Voznesensky and other Central Committee members arrested and executed three years earlier. It was Stalin's method of keeping everyone 'in order', by organising an occasional 'blood-letting' in the party leadership so as to maintain fear and tension in his immediate circle. It is not hard to imagine what would have happened had they been purged, for the grim pattern is unfortunately too well-known; it meant not only physical destruction of the people in question, but the imprisonment (and maybe annihilation) of their families, of their close friends and acquaintances and the people who were working under them, together with those people's families. That would mean death, prison or labour camps for dozens of perfectly innocent men and women (and orphanages for their children), all branded 'enemies of the people' of the country to which they had unreservedly given their lives.

After Stalin's death Lavrenty Beria displayed some vigorous administrative activity, which, as the other Presidium members knew only too well, promised nothing but a most sinister turn of events: he was obviously plotting for top power. In a move to gain popularity he even made some liberal steps. Thus, he publicly condemned the fabrication of the 'Doctors' Plot' and freed those who had been arrested in connection with it. The only way to prevent his ascension to power was to get rid of him. Beria and his closest associates were arrested and put on trial.

I had an opportunity to read the indictment against Beria and the others. Naturally I did not believe that he was 'an imperialist spy', but the rest of the charges were very convincing. As far as I remember, there were not many explicit references to the purges, but it was quite clear that they were implied. Great stress was laid on Beria's 'moral degradation'. The precise number of women, over a hundred and fifty of them (with some actual names), whom he had forced into a sexual relationship was given, and one of his ways of finding 'concubines' described. Apparently, Beria would have his chauffeur drive him slowly along the streets while he watched out for good-looking women among the passers-by. His security chief, who sat at the back of the car, would then be responsible for tracking down and delivering the women Beria had picked out. While reading this, I remembered my wife telling me once how as she was walking somewhere along a street Beria's car came driving slowly past her, and Beria nodded to her in recognition. So he indeed possessed the habit of watching people closely from his car.

Ella and I had visited Beria's dacha once or twice as guests of his son Sergo and Sergo's wife Marfa. At least on one of these occasions we all had lunch in his company. Although he ostensibly took part in our conversation, he said precious little himself. What was hard to forget was his seemingly friendly yet cold and piercing stare through his pince-nez. I remember feeling rather uncomfortable in his presence, although I had never felt intimidated or uneasy with any of the 'high and mighty'.

I can easily picture Beria's joy at Stalin's death – they say he did not even bother to conceal it. No wonder; not only did he evade retribution (in 1952 Beria had lost favour with Stalin and was dismissed as Minister of the Interior, so he must have been aware of what was bound to follow), but he was now a step away from the position of supreme power! He certainly did not expect the Presidium members to have the nerve to oppose him. Much of the credit for what they did goes to Khrushchev, although I find it hard to believe what Nikita Sergeevich later wrote in his book about my father's alleged hesitation in connection with Beria's arrest. I know very well what my father's attitude to Beria was. One of the indications I had was a brief conversation between my parents I had once overheard at the dacha. My mother said, with unmistakable pain in her voice, 'How can you all work with him? He is such a vile man!' My father did not contradict her but said, 'Be silent.'

A. V. Snegov, a one-time Central Committee member who was arrested under Stalin and then released and rehabilitated after Stalin's death, remembered a meeting back in 1931 at which various party leaders from the Caucasus were reporting. Snegov asked my father, who was sitting next to him, why Sergo Ordzhonikidze (a Politburo member and my father's old friend) was not there at the meeting. 'Why on earth should Sergo participate in Beria's coronation?' my father whispered in reply. 'He knows him well enough.' My father had already known then that Stalin was about to suggest promoting Beria (with whom he had just shared a holiday on the Black Sea) to Second Secretary of the Transcaucasian Party Committee. The proposal was indeed made and met with general opposition. The First Secretary of that committee declared, 'I shall not work with this charlatan!' Another man from Georgia asked Stalin, 'What was it you said, Koba? [Stalin's old conspiratorial name] Did I hear you correctly?' Failing to get support for his plan, Stalin angrily cut the discussion short with the words, 'Very well then. We'll settle it all without you.' Khrushchev recalled in his book how, within minutes of Stalin's death, Beria hurried to Moscow, and my father remarked, 'Dashed off to grab power, no doubt.' In other words, father was well aware of the Beria threat. I also remember my father's account of how Beria was arrested. Marshals Zhukov, Batitsky and Moskalenko, who had been entrusted with the task, could not enter the Kremlin armed because security rules forbade it. So as not to alert anyone to the plan, it was decided that three Presidium members would each 'smuggle' one marshal (or rather, his gun) in his car. As far as I remember, my father's 'passenger' was Marshal Batitsky.

I must say that in his book Khrushchev was rather unfair towards my father. It is well known that he was Khrushchev's staunch supporter and closest associate in the new state and party policy. He was a great enthusiast of reform, and directly assisted Khrushchev in much of what he was doing, especially in foreign affairs. Yet Khrushchev hardly mentions him in his book. Perhaps it is not an uncommon thing for the author of memoirs to avoid stressing his associates' role so as not to dilute his own. On the other hand, there could be a different reason altogether: shortly after his resignation my father became aware of indirect attempts to influence his attitude to Khrushchev. His secretary, Nina Kadolo (undoubtedly in the 'pay' of the KGB), passed on to him, supposedly from Khrushchev's chauffeur, some disparaging comments which Khrushchev had allegedly been making about him. The same kind of slanderous activity was aimed in the opposite direction as well, and Khrushchev was hearing unpleasant remarks that were falsely ascribed to my father.

I would like here to cite a few passages relating to my father and his relationship with Khrushchev from *Inside Russia Today* by the American journalist John Gunther. In Chapter 7 Gunther described a number of top Soviet officials, starting off with my father, whom he had apparently met at some public functions or receptions:

> Almost everything about Mikoyan seems excessive – the sharpness and glitter of his dark eyes, the flash of his clenched teeth, and the arch of his nose, which looks like a small twisted club. He has an emphatic character, with a famously barbed tongue, independence of mind (within limits), and a disputatious manner. [. . .]
>
> Mikoyan's chief quality is his glistening shrewdness. He is an Armenian, and all Armenians are notoriously expert traders. He was, in fact, in charge of the foreign trade of the USSR for many years, and had the reputation of being the best negotiator in the country. Nobody has ever doubted his alertness, tenacity and acute intelligence. [. . .] Mikoyan is fascinating to watch at a reception – controlled, almost sinister, but vibrant at the same time, with suppressed flashes of energy rippling across his face. Before Khrushchev became well known for candour, Mikoyan was supposed to be the only top-flight man who would answer questions frankly. He knows all the double-talk, but sometimes cuts through it. [. . .]
>
> He certainly has courage. Khrushchev told a little anecdote about him in the Twentieth Congress speech. Khrushchev had telephoned Stalin from the Kharkov front during a critical battle in the Second World War, appealing for a change of tactics and giving advice which Stalin rejected. The result was a very serious Soviet defeat. After the war, at a meeting of the Politburo, Mikoyan directly taxed Stalin with this, mentioning how unfortunate it was that Khrushchev's suggestion had not been adopted, and thus underlining Stalin's blunder. Stalin was furious. As a matter of fact, Mikoyan delivered at the Twentieth Congress a speech that paved the way for Khrushchev's, in which he was bold enough to say that there had been no vestige of socialist legality in

the Soviet Union for twenty years. No such attack on the Stalin record had ever been voiced before.

Earlier in the book, in Chapter 5, describing the Politburo work pattern, John Gunther wrote:

> Sometimes lively – even sharp – interchanges take place between members of the Presidium in public. During this same speech [Khrushchev was making a speech at the Polish Embassy, where John Gunther was present] Mikoyan, with his dark Armenian face, kept interrupting Khrushchev, who did not seem pleased. Khrushchev said that the Western Powers had done something 'idiotic'. Mikoyan muttered aloud, 'Too strong, too strong!' Khrushchev quoted Lenin to the effect that, if a man was utterly convinced that he was right, not wrong, he should proceed to the limit in executing his views. Mikoyan interrupted, 'But how do you know that you are not wrong?' On another occasion when I was present Khrushchev began his remarks with the phrase, 'Comrades, friends, gentlemen'. Mikoyan shot out, 'Sometimes friends are also gentlemen!'

Our former trade representative in Greece, A. Piruzian, in his book of memoirs quoted a passage from a 1961 issue of the Greek paper *Arax*. Translated by Piruzian into Russian and from his version into English, the passage reads:

> When asked by a Brazilian reporter about his impressions of the Soviet government, Chancellor Adenauer said, 'I have to admit that of all Soviet leaders whom I have met I have so far been most favourably impressed by the First Deputy Chairman of the Council of Ministers, Anastas Mikoyan. He is both a great diplomat and a highly capable economics expert, with whom one can sit across a table and exchange opinions. He is also very witty and often accompanies his words with jokes. If we have trade relations with the Soviet Union today, we owe them to Mikoyan's efforts and his clever diplomacy. However, one should be on one's guard near him for he is also a great trader.'*

Piruzian continued with his own recollections of his professional association with my father. According to him, my father worked fast and in a well-organised and efficient manner. He was rather quick-tempered and had no patience with any attempts at cheating or deception. He could be very sharp and severe in his dressing-downs, but his criticism was always to the point and never made at the expense of someone's personal dignity, no matter how angry he was. Many people who worked with him or under him knew that if he stopped criticising someone completely, it meant he had lost interest in that person.

In my earlier life I had opportunities to meet many people among the top leadership of the country. As a child I was talked to in the Kremlin by Stalin,

---

* Aram Piruzian, *The Life of the Country – My Destiny*, Nauka, Moscow, 1995, pp. 110–11.

Voroshilov and Bukharin, but I have very blurred memories of these occasions. Every now and then I ran into our nearest neighbours in the Kremlin: Kalinin, Molotov and Andreev. Ordzhonikidze was a more or less frequent guest at the dacha. My mother told me that in the 1920s Stalin used to 'drop in' at the Kremlin flat and play with us, but in my adult life I only saw him at a distance, during the annual air show at Tushino from a stand next to the government one, and during the celebration of his seventieth birthday while he was honoured by a large gathering in the Bolshoi Theatre, and at the banquet in the Kremlin afterwards.

The ceremony held in the Bolshoi Theatre involved a long series of greetings and eulogies 'recited' by various exalted guests, including the leaders of foreign Communist parties. The first of the foreign speakers delivered their speeches in Russian, and then we noticed that Stalin gestured to his security chief Vlasik to approach; as we found out later, Stalin was displeased that the speakers were not using their own languages. The next person to speak after that was Palmiro Togliatti, the leader of the Italian Communist party and a man very highly thought of in the USSR. He must have been told of Stalin's words to Vlasik, for he began in Italian. Togliatti was a born orator, and even though nobody could understand the words, everyone seemed affected by the vehemence of his speech. When he finished, he smiled and said in Russian, 'Since there is no interpreter, I will translate my speech myself.' And he repeated it all in Russian.

Another memorable episode of that evening was the speech of Mao Tse-tung. When he was announced, there was an ovation. Nearly everyone in the audience was seeing him for the first time; it was like a miracle, like a sudden appearance of a hero from a legend. In those early days of the 'People's China', as it had recently become known, Mao enjoyed tremendous popularity in the USSR (I thought afterwards that Stalin must have been rather piqued by the ovation received by Mao). However, when Mao began his speech the spell was almost broken: he turned out to have a high-pitched, almost squeaky voice which sounded totally dissonant with the heroic aura that surrounded his name.

In the post-war years I occasionally saw Molotov, Andreev, Shvernik and Malenkov when I visited their respective dachas as a guest of their sons or daughters. I met both Brezhnev and Kosyghin at one of the government dachas on the Black Sea coast when they came to see my father during his (and their) holiday. Khrushchev's dacha outside Moscow was very near my father's, and I saw Nikita Sergeevich when I accompanied my father on a visit (he also occasionally came to us). At Pitsunda on the Black Sea we saw him even more often, for when he and my father were on holiday at the same time they and their families lived next to each other in the neighbouring dachas and met casually during the day or in the evening.

Perhaps of all leaders of that time it was Voroshilov whose house I visited most frequently because of my close friendship with his adopted son Timur Frunze (until he got killed in the war). After the war I continued to come to his dacha, for I was on very good terms with his son Piotr, Piotr's wife Nadya, and Timur's sister Tanya and her husband Anatoly Pavlov, who used to spend almost every weekend at Voroshilov's dacha. Almost every time Voroshilov saw me he would repeat, for the umpteenth time, how he had rocked me to sleep in his arms while accompanying my mother on the train from Tiflis to Rostov-on-Don. The other episode he would invariably remember was his wartime visit to the hospital where I was treated for the injuries received on landing in my burning machine. He would repeat how shocked he had been at the sight of my burnt face and reproach me for not having sought out, upon my discharge from the hospital, the village boys who had found me in the field. This is something I have never stopped blaming myself for.

One summer in the early 1960s, when both my father and Khrushchev were spending their holiday at Pitsunda, they were visited by Voroshilov, who was resting near Sochi. The three of them, accompanied by assorted family members, went on a short sea voyage to Novy Afon in a large yacht. The yacht was a real luxury boat with all imaginable comforts and amenities on board, and it was said to have formerly belonged to Gering. The yacht was based at Sevastopol and was used mainly as a pleasure boat for Politburo members and high-ranking foreign guests. Having docked at Novy Afon, we disembarked onto the pier of a government dacha which was next to a public beach. There was quite a crowd of people on that beach attracted by the sight of the large and beautiful yacht. As we were walking along the pier people recognised the three dignitaries and I heard several people exclaim, 'Look, Voroshilov!' They must have been surprised and clearly pleased to see Voroshilov, a popular man yet officially no longer important, in the company of Khrushchev. (I do not know if Voroshilov heard those exclamations – he was hard of hearing then – but Khrushchev surely did.)

The place we came to used to be one of Stalin's favourite dachas on the Black Sea. It had a large park stretching from the sea to the foot of a mountain. The park had formerly belonged to a monastery (hence the name of the place: 'Novy Afon' means 'New Athos'). We entered a dark-green one-storey building in the upper part of the park furthest from the sea. The three veteran Politburo members stood in the large room which had served as a sitting/dining room and remembered their visits to Stalin and what had happened during each of them. How I wished I had a tape recorder with me! They remembered how Khrushchev had once arrived on Stalin's summons from his dacha and had to wait several hours until Stalin finally emerged from his bedroom. Khrushchev had been languishing in the garden all that time, not daring to leave.

Another occasional visitor to the Pitsunda dacha (while Khrushchev was still in power) was Brezhnev. I remember him coming twice in my presence. At that time his position was lower than that of my father and Kosyghin, both of whom were First Deputies of the Chairman of the Council of Ministers, namely Khrushchev. In later years, under Brezhnev, the post of First Deputy lost much of its importance. In fact the Council of Ministers itself under Brezhnev was deprived of its status and of its vital role in the country's life. Most decisions concerning the economy of the country were made by the Central Committee. In Khrushchev's time and even under Stalin, the Council of Ministers had enjoyed an important status at least for the simple reason that both of them combined their posts of the party's General Secretary with that of the Chairman of the Council of Ministers. Therefore all issues concerning economy, industry, trade and so on had been the prerogative of the Council of Ministers. In Khrushchev's absence my father often took over his duties as chairman.

When Brezhnev came to the top he gave great authority to various departments of the Central Committee in charge of various areas within the economy, industry and the army. They had great power without any real responsibility. They prepared the material on various issues to be discussed by the Politburo or considered by the General Secretary, and the 'angle' at which a particular issue was presented could very often predetermine the decision taken about it. I remember one conversation with my father somewhere in the late 1960s. I had expressed an opinion which he rejected, criticising me for a fallacy as he often did, and then I pointed out that it was wrong for the Central Committee to be directing the economy and defence. To this father said, 'Now you are talking sense!' I felt that I had touched a sore point. As a statesman with forty years' experience of running various areas of the country's economy (and to some extent its foreign relations), he must have deeply resented the newly assumed role of the party functionaries. Later in the conversation, in reply to something I had said about Soviet power, he unexpectedly declared, 'And we do not have any Soviet power!' It might sound quite commonplace today, but at that time I was quite unprepared to hear it. 'Soviet power', he continued, 'is the political power of the Soviets [elected councils], and our Soviets have no power of any kind, let alone political!' Back in my room I wrote it down in a notebook and hid it out of sight.

It could not, of course, be denied that my father was one of those who backed up Stalin at the time when he was building his power, although he (my father) did not have the same influence as, for example, Kamenev, Bukharin, Kirov or Ordzhonikidze. At the same time, in the 1930s when Stalin's terror began and later, my father was not among those party leaders who were actively supporting the purges and who signed the lists of condemned people to authorise the fatal verdict. I believe that somewhere along the way he must have become fully aware of what Stalin's regime was really like, and for a long time afterwards, maybe to the end of his life, he repented his association with it and did all he could to redeem himself (in the words of Yevgeny Yevtushenko, one of Russia's best contemporary poets, 'delusions redeemed by confession are not the same as delusions shielded by cowardice').

His repentance had little to do with words: it was as active as it could be. He was the first to raise the issue of the rehabilitation of Stalin's victims immediately after his death. He arranged for an interview between two recently released veteran Bolsheviks, A. Snegov and Olga Shatunovskaya, with Khrushchev, to whom they described the gruesome reality of Stalin's labour camps. He became chairman of the Central Rehabilitation Commission and insisted on setting up separate rehabilitation commissions in each camp so that they could prepare the relevant documents on site, providing for summary rehabilitation of all the people in each camp who had been convicted on certain charges (which had been applied to the alleged 'enemies of the people'). These commissions were opposed and even sabotaged by some of the 'old guard' Presidium members, but they still did their job, and thanks to them the liberation and rehabilitation of large numbers of people was done faster and more efficiently (they became popularly known as 'the Mikoyan commissions').

My father strongly supported Khrushchev's decision to expose the cult of Stalin's person, and the two of them were preparing 'to give battle' during the Twentieth Party Congress. As my father later told us, the issue was discussed at a plenary meeting of the Central Committee, which voted against any mention of Stalin's 'cult' in Khrushchev's official speech at the Congress. Then he and my father decided that Khrushchev would make a separate speech at the very end of the Congress, yet before Khrushchev made this famous speech my father spoke at one of the open sessions during the Congress, making the first ever public criticism of Stalin's regime. It was a revelation for most of the delegates. Ilya Erenburg in *People, Years, Life* wrote that when he had returned to Moscow from a foreign trip in February 1956, 'everyone was talking of Mikoyan's speech at the Congress: he mentioned Stalin's fallacy, spoke derisively of falsification of history and named Antonov-Ovseenko and Kossior, the Bolsheviks who had been destroyed in the days of the cult of the person.* That speech to a certain extent paved the way for Khrushchev. Shortly after the closing of the Congress my father delivered a four-hour speech exposing the atrocities of Stalin's regime to the representatives of Moscow intelligentsia invited to a special meeting under the auspices of the Central Committee. His audience had not heard Khrushchev's secret speech yet and were thoroughly shocked by his words.

'Everyone was responsible for what was going on!' has become a kind of catchphrase used in relation to the time of Stalin's rule, especially by those who are still defending him. It does sound plausible, but only superficially so. True, it took many people to carry out the purges: people who gleefully wrote anonymous denunciations of their neighbours, colleagues and so on; people who arrested, interrogated, tortured and executed; and, among the top leadership of the country, people (and I know for sure that my father was not among them) who showed particular zeal in exposing and condemning the 'enemies of the people'. But no matter how numerous the supporting cast, there was only one man who could stop that inhuman practice, who could put an end to the purges and restore legality. It was Stalin alone who could do it, no one else. Yet Stalin, far from attempting to stop it, was actually encouraging the party functionaries and the secret police to go on with it. Therefore it is he who was personally responsible for it all.

One particular episode from the 1930s which is, I believe, a case in point, is the assassination of Kirov. I have long been convinced that it was engineered by Stalin himself (through the then chief of the NKVD, Yagoda). My father was of the same opinion, particularly after the disclosures made by the special commission on the case, formed after the Twentieth Congress. It is a well-known fact that shortly before the Seventeenth Party Congress in 1934, a group of old Bolsheviks got together to discuss Stalin's race for power. Their conclusion was that he was well on his way to becoming a dictator and he had to be replaced.

---

* Previously unpublished chapters from Ilya Erenburg's book of memoirs *People, Years, Life*, the Ogonyok, No. 23, 1987.

The man they all agreed to nominate at the coming Congress was Sergei Kirov. One of them subsequently talked it over with Kirov, who refused to get involved and told Stalin about it, without giving any names (if he had not told him, Stalin would have found out through a different source and thought that Kirov was secretly plotting to usurp his power). Stalin thanked Kirov for the information and must have made a note of it. When the vote was taken at the Congress there were 292 votes against Stalin out of 1,059. Molotov and Kaganovich received over a hundred ballots against each of them. The head of the counting commission and Kaganovich together reported the results to Stalin. 'And how many [against] did Kirov get?' he asked. Four, they said. 'Leave me three against and destroy the rest,' he ordered (it was not for nothing that of all of his rivals in the election he asked only about Kirov).

I heard of this episode together with my father years later, in the 1950s, from his old friend Napoleon Andreasian during one of his visits to our dacha. Out of sixty-three members of the counting commission at that Congress sixty were arrested and shot, and the remaining three, including Andreasian, were also arrested but survived. A. Sevostianov, Sergei Kirov's trusted friend, cited Kirov's words said to him in the summer of 1934 at a hearing of the special commission: 'Now Stalin will not allow me to stay alive.'

Kirov's assassination is something that by association reminds me of the fire at the Berlin Reichstag in 1933. The arson was organised by the Nazis to be used as a pretext for the persecution of Communists and Social Democrats. It was a very tempting example for Stalin (Stalin and Hitler certainly appear to have occasionally borrowed each other's 'useful' tactics). The physical removal of Kirov meant getting rid of a potential future rival, but it was certainly not the only or even the principal goal. The principal goal, as with the fire at the Reichstag, was to manufacture an excuse for unleashing a campaign of total and unrestrained terror, first against his possible critics and opponents in the narrower party circles (the old Bolsheviks), and then, further afield, against society at large.

On the very day of the assassination, 1 December 1934, immediately after the telephone report from Leningrad, when nothing was yet known as to who could have murdered Kirov and why, Stalin hastened to write, in his own hand, a decree (ostensibly coming from the Central Executive Committee) commanding that the cases of all suspects be developed at 'emergency rate' and heard without the participation of the parties. Moreover, he demanded that there be no appeal allowed and, finally, that the capital punishment verdicts be executed without delay. There was no question of any legal procedure being observed. Before leaving for Leningrad later the same day, Stalin declared that the assassination had been organised by Zinoviev's circle, thus indicating to his investigators what sort of 'confessions' they were expected to extort from the accused. The next step was to invent the mythical 'Leningrad centre of Zinoviev's terrorists' and to get a good excuse to arrest Zinoviev himself. Exit Zinoviev on 16 December.

Fourteen people, including Nikolaev, the assassin, were shot as a result of the assassination case. Kirov's bodyguard, Borisov, was arrested too. He happened to have fallen a few steps behind Kirov seconds before the fatal shots were fired, because somebody on the way had asked him for a light – a simple yet effective delaying ploy. As the bodyguard was driven in a lorry after his arrest, an 'accident' happened: the guard sitting next to the driver suddenly grabbed the wheel and jerked it to the right so that the body of the lorry hit the wall of a house. Borisov ended up conveniently dead with a broken skull while two other guards in the car escaped unscathed (though later both were shot). The chief of the NKVD, Yagoda, did not survive the Zinoviev case either – he was arrested, tried and executed with the rest.

Stalin's implication in Kirov's murder is often deemed unlikely on the grounds that the two of them were very close friends. Even Svetlana Stalina emphasised their friendship in her book; she had often seen the amiable, lively and easy-going Kirov as a guest at her father's house. However, Stalin's friendship did not give immunity to anyone. He had for a long time been on very friendly terms with Nikolai Bukharin; until the early 1930s he used to stay at Stalin's dacha in Zubalovo with his wife and daughter almost every summer. It looked as though Stalin, like most people, was very fond of 'our dear Bukharin'. It did not, however, prevent him from plotting against Bukharin and eventually finding a 'good reason' to have him arrested, tried and shot, and he was not the only friend Stalin doomed to death without so much as batting an eyelid. According to the writer Lev Kassil, who was with Nikolia Bukharin when Stalin phoned to tell him of Kirov's murder, Bukharin put down the receiver and said, 'Now Koba will do what he likes with us.'

It seems that the authors of many recent publications about Stalin are unable to understand Stalin's psychology in relation to the people who were close to him. No measure of friendship or loyalty on their part mattered once he made up his mind to remove or destroy somebody for whatever reason. It could be somebody who happened to know what Stalin wanted to keep secret, or somebody whose sincerity he suddenly doubted, or somebody who said something he did not like. Or else, it could simply be done to teach others a lesson. So when some authors insist that Stalin could not have been implicated in Kirov's death because the two of them were 'good friends' and trusted each other, they quite simply fail to realise that neither friendship nor trust meant anything to Stalin once someone got in the way of his schemes.

Some time before the assassination Kirov had become a target for occasional indirect attacks. My father once told me about a certain satirical article published in *Pravda* in the summer of 1934. It portrayed a party leader of high rank, transferred from Baku to a post in Leningrad, who asked for a large apartment in Leningrad on the grounds that he had a large dog. There was no name given, but according to my father it was not hard for people in the party circuit or government officials of all ranks to guess that the satire was targeted at Kirov. There was no way a satire aimed at a Politburo member could appear in a paper without Stalin's direct command. On another occasion about the same time, somebody unearthed a pre-revolutionary paper with Kirov's article (signed by his real name, Kostrikov) on the 300th anniversary of the Romanovs. The issue was discussed at a Politburo meeting, and at the end of the discussion Stalin said something to the effect that they should let 'bygones be bygones' and forget about the matter. As he was describing this episode, father remarked that such tactics were typical of Stalin, who would first bring up a matter and then pretend that he did not think it important (until further notice, as it were).

What followed Kirov's assassination is well known: first the notorious political trials, then the summary death verdicts and convictions. Lists of a hundred or more names of the people condemned by fearsome *troikas* (three-member tribunals) of the NKVD would be presented to Stalin to sign, and he would write 'To be shot' on them without so much as enquiring into the charges, let alone the evidence. A fair trial was a totally forgotten notion. It might be remembered here how Stalin, then on holiday on the Black Sea, had a telegram sent to the heads of administration of certain regions reprimanding them for having exposed fewer enemies than in other parts of the country, as if it were a question of failing to keep up with a plan of industrial output or something!

A large part of the nation was under the hideously deforming influence of what was going on, of the powerful official propaganda (and the growing tension in Europe), believing the accusations and treason charges. Some were zealously denouncing the 'spies' and 'enemies of the people'. For several decades the country was living an unnatural and tragic life, and the vestiges of that poison, with which almost the whole country was permeated, are to some extent discernible to this day.

Sometimes people barely had the time to express their indignation at the treason of newly exposed 'enemies' when they were arrested themselves – as was the case with Maria Svanidze, the wife of Stalin's brother-in-law. Her recently published diary of 1937 shows that she did not doubt the charges against many well-known people: 'Pen in hand, I am at a loss how to begin. Hard to describe all that has been happening in these past months. [. . .] Continual removal of people with names, those who for years were standing side by side with the country's best people, who were trusted and rewarded for their work – and who turned out to be hostile to our system and its traitors in the pay of our enemies [. . .] How could we have overlooked them, how could it have happened that this hostile element blossomed so freely? [. . .] And now, twenty years since the revolution, these chameleons have finally betrayed their devilish nature. They have no honesty, no patriotism, not even the most primitive attachment to their country. To harm, to betray, to hiss, to hate and to deceive – anything but allow the well-being of the best ever social system.'* Fewer than five months after that entry in her diary Maria Svanidze and her husband Alexander Svanidze were arrested. Alyosha (as he was known since his early revolutionary days) was executed on 20 August 1941, his wife in March the following year, charged with 'the concealment of her husband's anti-Soviet activity, criticism of the punitive policy of the Party, and terrorist plans concerning one of the Party and Government leaders'.

I remember both Maria and Alyosha Svanidze well: they and their son had been our neighbours at the dacha. After their arrest their son was put into an

---

* Yuri Murin (ed.), *Joseph Stalin in the Family Embrace*, Rodina, Moscow, 1993.

orphanage and later exiled. Maria Svanidze had been a singer, and she was a woman to be noticed: she dressed more flamboyantly and used more make-up than most other women I knew, particularly my mother, who always dressed very modestly and never wore make-up. Did Maria Svanidze understand, in the four years she spent languishing in jail before she was executed, the true worth of the charges cooked up against the so-called 'enemies of the people'? Did she understand that the architect of her own 'case' and that of thousands of similar cases had been none other than her relative and, as her diary shows, the man she had been quite friendly with?

Among other frequent causes of arrests were various industrial accidents, mishaps or serious malfunctions in any technical sphere. Any such occurrence at work could (and did) lead to charges of sabotage and the arrests of those involved as saboteurs and 'enemies of the people'. And many people were becoming obsessed with suspicion, and there were also those who satisfied their vindictiveness by reporting on their personal enemies. And so I will repeat: Stalin was the only person who could have put a stop to all that and he did not, and therefore I believe him to be solely responsible for the terror and purges during his rule. I am also convinced (although many people will probably disagree) that no one in the leadership, apart from the successive chiefs of the NKVD/KGB and their most trusted subordinates, could at the time imagine the real scope of the genocidal activity that was going on in the country. At the same time I am aware that to have held a position of authority in the government, even if that authority mainly covered the country's economy, and to have remained totally uninvolved was impossible. Yet I know that my father was much less involved than many other Politburo members at the time.

There was one episode in his career which I have never liked to remember: his speech at a meeting on the occasion of the NKVD's anniversary (the documentary footage of that meeting was shown on Russian television some time ago) – by no means anything to be proud of. Yet how could he have refused to speak at the meeting when the Politburo (i.e. Stalin) had appointed him their spokesman for the occasion? It is a fact that shortly before this Stalin had invited my father to become chief of the NKVD, which he had flatly refused. It is very likely that Stalin's motive in naming Anastas Mikoyan to the Politburo as their spokesman at the NKVD celebrations was to deliberately compromise him as a punishment for his refusal to have anything to do with the secret police. The Politburo took their vote in my father's absence; he was away from Moscow at the time and there was nothing he could do about it when he returned. He asked the NKVD headquarters for a text and read it out verbatim at the meeting so as to detach himself from the content of that 'eulogy' as much as he could (it was perhaps the only speech which he ever *read*, for he was in fact well known for his spontaneous manner of speaking in public). The heaviest burden on us all as a family is the recently exposed massacre by the NKVD of several thousand captive Polish officers. The decision of the Politburo was signed by six people: Stalin, Molotov, Voroshilov, Kaganovich, Kalinin and – Mikoyan. But not to sign, if he was present at the meeting in question, was impossible. This has to be understood.

I would like to quote what my brother Sergo has said in an interview about our father, for this is what we all knew about him and how we remember him:

> Father was a highly intelligent person. He was a good judge of the situation and a master of self-control. He was a very clever politician too. Stalin valued him first and foremost for his remarkable talent as an organiser of the economy – somebody no regime can ever do without. Father was downright fanatical in his devotion to work and his energy seemed inexhaustible. He seemed to be working all the time. He would read his documents over breakfast and in the car on the way to work, while resting on the riverside or sitting in the garden. He had an excellent memory and always dealt with various working issues fast, never trying to delegate the responsibility to somebody else. In serious matters that concerned his work he was very demanding and could sometimes be rather harsh; he had no patience with idle talk or guesswork. His mind worked like a computer; he would grasp the essence of things, even the ones he had been unfamiliar with, very quickly, and would sometimes come up with more precise words than used by the person who was explaining the matter to him. [. . .] One could not help admiring his powerful intellect, feeling slightly oppressed by it at the same time.

We, his sons, often argued with him. We would tell him about the many things we learned outside our home that we disliked. Our conversation would often grow into very heated discussions. According to my younger brothers I was the most argumentative of all, always trying to prove my point. After one rather sharp dispute, Sergo told me that father asked him to tell me not to argue with him so much in the evenings: 'I can't sleep after that,' he said. We must try to understand his position, my brother said, and imagine what he thinks and feels being helpless to remedy this system, the faults of which we are so ready to attack. Later I realised that Sergo was right, and I felt ashamed for myself and sorry for my father. This is something I still remember with pain. I have since understood that his counter-arguments, rather than reflecting his disagreement with our charges, were forced by his position, in which he simply could not afford to admit certain things in so many words. It could sometimes be felt during those discussions, particularly in his later years, that he was painfully aware of how far reality was from the ideals of old. I know my father had been taking the atrocities of Stalin's regime close to heart, and he was happy when that regime was over. I remember well how he changed. For the first time in years he was coming home from work in high spirits and he recovered the pleasure of talking to people and having guests.

I remember with a particularly warm feeling our Sunday afternoon talks around the big dining-table at the dacha in the company of my uncles Artem Mikoyan and Haik Tumanian, as well as Lev Shaumian, my mother's brother-in-law Anush Arzumanian and some other family members and guests. Father would tell us a lot about Stalin, Molotov and others, talking about certain past events and about the way some government decisions had been taken. Others contributed their memories and their opinions of the past regime (which they had never expressed before). These conversations were like the opening of a secret door; we had heard nothing of the kind at home in Stalin's time. Unfortunately I don't have a consistent and full memory of what was said during those family get-togethers, but much of what I have relayed in this book is based on what I heard at my father's dacha in the years of the 'thaw'.

In those years it was apparent that for my father his life had an aim and a meaning again, that he was confident he had a role to play in 'humanising' his country. For instance, one of the first decisions of the new post-Stalin government concerned the working hours of government officials and civil servants of all levels, all of whom had been forced, directly or indirectly, to keep very erratic working hours by Stalin's habit of engaging Politburo members in his late-night parties at his dacha. The new regulations stipulated a fixed working day ending at six p.m., with the implication that those who could not have their day's work done by that time lacked efficiency. The document actually stressed that every civil servant or member of the government was entitled to a private life. It gave birth to a joke, with the punchline to the effect that the new regulations gave a private life to the husbands but one deprived of their wives.

Another instance of my father's determination to humanise the new government was his attitude to armour-plated cars. Until after Stalin's death, Politburo members were driven around in such vehicles. At least once, the plating came in useful and possibly saved my father's life. It happened during the war when he was driving out of the Saviour's Gate of the Kremlin. Several rifle shots were suddenly fired at his car from the direction of St Basil's Cathedral. One of the bullets hit the right side of the car opposite the front passenger seat where my father was, but did not get through the armour plating. The official version we heard afterwards was that the shots had been fired by a 'clinically depressed' soldier from the front line. Apparently he recognised Kalinin in the car that had preceded my father's, let him go by unharmed and fired at the next car. What happened to the soldier afterwards I do not know.

Despite that incident my father believed it was wrong to drive around in armour-plated cars, especially when the war had ended. Yet he could not change anything on his own, for Stalin would have been annoyed and would have suspected him of opposing himself to the others. Literally the day after Stalin's death my father asked for a regular Zis-110 limo in place of the armour-plated one. At one of the Presidium meetings that followed he suggested getting rid of the escort cars (with security guards in them) which had always followed their limos. His suggestion was not accepted at first, but he repeated it later, after Beria's arrest, and then it was agreed to. The escort ('tail') cars were cancelled, and only one security guard was retained for each Presidium member 'on the road'. He was to travel in the same car as his 'charge' and accompany him wherever he went. The security at the dachas remained, although the number of guards on duty was somewhat reduced. Under Brezhnev, escort cars for the three top men in the country were introduced again.

After 1960, when Khrushchev began to lose perspective in his judgement of himself and his role, my father's elation began to evaporate. He was against the military crackdown on the Hungarian revolution in October and November

1956. As soon as the events had begun he and Mikhail Suslov were delegated by the Politburo to Budapest. In a few days my father returned to report on the situation, but before he could do so he learnt that the decision about Soviet military interference had already been made. This is what Khrushchev wrote in his memoirs: 'When I told him [Anastas] of that decision, he objected very energetically, insisting that an armed interference would be a mistake and would ruin the reputation of our government and of the party. I said, "The decision has been made, and I approve it." Anastas Ivanovich was greatly agitated. He even threatened to do something with himself – in protest.'*

Among the foreign policy matters to which my father made his contribution were our relations with the United States. Everyone knows (or at least used to know) about Khrushchev's official visit to the States in 1959. Much was written about it in the press, there was a documentary film made and even a book written. At the same time very few people seem to remember (or indeed to know) that his visit was preceded and largely made possible by my father's unofficial trip to America in January 1959. It all started with Khrushchev delivering a thoroughly anti-American speech in connection with Berlin, in which he threatened to drive the Allies out of it. The Americans were naturally offended. After that my father persuaded Khrushchev that there was nothing to gain by breaking the Potsdam Treaty, and Khrushchev sent him to America to heal the breach.

It was to be the first post-war visit to the US of a high-ranking Soviet official, not counting Molotov's attendance at the UN-forming conference in 1945. Stalin had been officially invited by the US government to come on a visit in 1946 at a time when the chances of a positive political outcome were still high, but he declined the invitation (my father said he had not been sure of his safety; in other words he was simply afraid to go, although there was hardly any danger at all). Although father ostensibly went as the Soviet ambassador's 'private guest', the US administration was excited at the prospect of a visit that promised an improvement in their relations with the USSR and honoured the visitor with a reception commensurate with his rank as Khrushchev's First Deputy. My father's visa was issued within hours of the application to the US Consulate in Moscow.

The visit was full of interesting and useful meetings, some of which might not have taken place on an official state visit. These meetings – with industrial and financial magnates, with the press and university students – took place all over the country, in Washington and New York, in Detroit, Chicago, San Francisco, Los Angeles and Cleveland. Among the people my father met was David Rockefeller, which was the first Wall Street meeting between a Soviet official and a US financial tycoon. In Cleveland he had lunch with Cyrus Eaton, an industrialist and an eminent public figure, and in Chicago he dined with Adlai Stevenson who had been the Democrats' candidate in the 1956 presidential election and became the US ambassador to the United Nations two years later. He was invited to the leading business club in New York and the Press Club in

* Quoted, in translation, *Izvestia*, 25 September 1990.

Washington. According to Oleg Troyanovsky (Khrushchev's adviser and our future ambassador to the UN, and then to Japan and China), who accompanied him as his interpreter, my father made a very good impression on the journalists at the Press Club, and he made them laugh with his spontaneous jokes and witty repartees. That was obviously something the independent-minded members of the Washington Press Club appreciated very much (and among the questions he had to answer were some very 'delicate' ones about the events in Hungary, about Beria, the 'anti-party group' and so on). Most important of all, the Soviet ambassador's 'private guest' had two meetings with President Eisenhower and five with John Foster Dulles, the then Secretary of State.

The two trickiest issues that were discussed were, of course, the status of Berlin and the unification of Germany. My father said that the current situation provided for a rapprochement between eastern and western Germany. Eisenhower made a point of reminding him that 'the US government and the US people do not know of any way of resolving national issues other than by democratic vote – the traditional American method'. In some cities visited on that trip there were demonstrations of Hungarian immigrants who linked my father's name with the crackdown on the Hungarian revolution (they could not have known that he, for one, had strongly objected against the Soviet armed intervention). At first the police did nothing about the demonstrators, but then Eisenhower interfered and they began driving them away. Once my brother Sergo, who was accompanying my father on that trip, had fallen behind the delegation and as he was trying to catch up with it a policeman took him for a demonstrator and hit him with his baton on the back. At first my father had not intended to take any members of his family with him on that trip, but in the end he took Sergo on Khrushchev's explicit advice. When they returned, I asked him why he had not wanted any of us to accompany him, and he said that he had seriously supposed that something might happen and he would not return. Not that he was suspicious of the American authorities' intentions, but he was inwardly prepared for a terrorist act from some 'unofficial' organisation.

In fact something did nearly happen that would have had tragic consequences. When my father was returning home in a four-engine SAS airliner, first one engine caught fire and then another. The crew were already preparing to crash-land on the water, but luckily the fire was put out and they turned back towards the American coast. The engines that had been on fire were now dead, and the two remaining ones did not have enough power between them to keep the aircraft in horizontal flight, so it was steadily descending. The air hostesses, trying to hold back their tears, explained to the passengers how to use their life-saving devices, while my father was smiling, making jokes and doing his best to cheer them up – although later he told us that deep down he was sure it had been an act of terrorism against him and that they would not survive. Both Oleg Troyanovsky, my good old friend, and my brother, from whom I heard all I have just described, said that the aircraft had already been flying very low over the ocean, when they made it to Argenten, a US Air Force base on the Atlantic coast. The commander of the base invited my father to look around and to see whatever he wanted to see. My father replied that he was not interested in military objects, but would be happy to take the opportunity to meet and talk with the personnel of the base. He was taken to see the compound where married officers were living in separate bungalows and the single ones in a ten-storey hostel with a sports complex, a club, a mess and a bar. He was quite impressed with the facilities and also with what he was told about a special aircraft, 'loaned' weekly by the commander to the wives to take them to the nearest big city to do their shopping.

Life is stranger than fiction, and my father and everyone else in that aircraft might well have been saved by my brother's failure to arrive at the airport in time. He had gone off to do some last-minute shopping in a large department store, and, confused by its numerous exits, could not find the waiting car for a long time. As a result he was late for the airport, and the aircraft had been waiting for twenty minutes with the engines running. Father was very angry; Sergo says it was enough to see his face, even if he did not say a word. However, if they had taken off on schedule, by the time the fire began they would have been too far over the Atlantic to make it back to the coast.

The American government authorities offered to send a replacement aircraft from New York, but the airline management, obviously suspecting that the whole thing was not accidental, ordered another machine from Europe. The investigation, as we heard later, revealed nothing, so either it had really been a pure accident or it was decided to hush up the results of the investigation. Once back in Moscow my father organised for souvenirs to be sent to each crew member to thank them for the flight that ended well due to their professionalism.

CHAPTER 15

The Sweptback Wing, Nuclear Tests and Radar

A curious incident once took place with the new fighter SM-2 during its test programme. It happened on the very day Stalin's death was announced, 6 March 1953. After I had finished my flight schedule for the day I asked Colonel Ivanov's leave to go home. VG said I could go, and went over to the airfield to his SM-2. He had to do a stability test flight in it. I got my things together, spoke to a few people, and eventually got into my car and drove up to the security gate of the base. Then, for God knows what reason, I stopped to make a call to our briefing room. What prompted me to I do not know, but I asked, 'How's VG? Has he landed?' 'Yes, it's all right now, he has', I heard. There was something peculiar in that answer, but what mattered was that Ivanov had landed, so I rang off and drove home.

The next day I heard it all. VG had gone into an unintentional spin from which he nearly did not recover. It was after he had pulled the 2.7 G-load at 10,000 metres, as his flight mission required. His SM-2 pitched up and Ivanov in no time realised that it was pitching up too sharply, so he eased on the stick. Still the G-load was increasing. He pushed the stick fully forward but the aircraft continued to pitch until it exceeded the critical angle of attack and entered a spin. Ivanov applied the controls for recovery twice over but the aircraft refused to obey. He then sent word to the tower that he was about to eject, but he gave the controls one last try. The altitude was already less than 5,000 metres by that time, the air density had increased, and the controls had become more effective. At the eleventh hour the spinning stopped and VG pulled out to level flight.

The test programme was suspended. For several months a large team of specialists from the Mikoyan Design Company and the Central Institute of Aerodynamics were trying to determine the cause of the instability of the SM-2. Its factory flight tests had been conducted by Grigory Sedov, a remarkable person in every respect as well as a first-class pilot and engineer (he later became a Hero of the Soviet Union and AF General, and was eventually appointed deputy head of the Mikoyan company). He had not encountered the instability problem then, for the factory tests had not involved such G-load factors or such altitudes. Their wind tunnel tests, it seems, had not revealed it either.

I have since regarded Colonel Ivanov's flight as historic, in the sense that it revealed a certain feature of the sweptback wing of which aerodynamic experts might have known in theory for a long time but which they had not expected to manifest itself so forcibly in practice. The 'natural element' of the sweptback wing is speed – the sonic or high subsonic speed. At low speed, however, it behaves worse than the ordinary wing. The distinctive character of the airflow over a sweptback wing, into which I shall not go, accounts for the fact that at high angles of attack typical of low-speed or large G-load flying, the centre of the lift force moves forward and there develops an aerodynamic moment that pitches the aircraft to an even higher AOA. This phenomenon is known as G-load instability, or AOA instability, and pilots call it 'overshooting'. A stable aircraft resists overshooting under G-load by creating what is known as the 'pitch-down moment'. In an aircraft that pitches up, the pitching moment can eventually exceed the control authority: in other words, the machine will go out of control. This is exactly what happened in Ivanov's case.

After several months of research, experiments and wind tunnel tests, a solution was found which involved a number of alterations to the aerodynamic layout of the aircraft. One such alteration was made in the position of the horizontal stabiliser from the tip of the fin down onto the fuselage to avoid the downwash from the wings. Eventually the stabiliser, fitted with an elevator, was replaced with the so-called stabilon – an all-moving stabiliser. In addition, the height of the wing boundary layer fences was increased to about thirty centimetres. As a result of these and other alterations, the AOA instability 'disease' of the SM-2 was cured. The improved version of the SM-2 had the factory designation SM-9, and as it started coming off the lines it was dubbed MiG-19, with the letter 'S' added as it was equipped with a stabilon.

Unfortunately, other types of aircraft occasionally suffered from the same 'disease'. In the late 1950s there were three fatal accidents involving the earliest Soviet passenger jets, the Tu-104s. The aircraft got out of control and crashed. Another incident of the same nature involved a Tu-104 belonging to a Czechoslovak airline: the aeroplane entered a spin but the crew managed to recover it close to the ground. Their account made it clear that they had been through the same kind of trouble as Colonel Ivanov in his SM-2 a few years earlier. Until then nobody had thought that the Tu-104 (or its military twin, the Tu-16 bomber) could encounter the same emergency as the SM-2, even though the aerodynamic layout of the two aircraft was nearly identical; or if they had thought of it, they must have decided that an airliner was not likely to encounter the large angles of attack that could cause instability.

This is a real-life illustration of Murphy's law: what can go wrong, will go wrong. Whether it was originally perceived as a joke or not, this 'law' has been confirmed and vindicated by experience far too often. In the above-mentioned accidents of the Tu-104 airliners, they had encountered so-called 'thunder heads' (large thunder clouds with tall 'peaks'), which the flight safety manual forbade (and still does) aircraft to enter because of the strong up-going air streams and the dangerously violent turbulence inside them. They had to fly above the clouds, at altitudes which were close to the ceiling of the aircraft. The higher the altitude, the lower the air density and the engine thrust. To maintain horizontal flight the aircraft has to be kept at a larger pitch angle, with the nose up. This means a higher angle of attack at a lower indicated air speed. The smallest gust of air or a tiny backward movement of the wheel would have been enough to cause the aircraft to become unstable and get out of control.

Another factor that must have contributed to the fatal outcome in the case of the Tu-104 (as distinct from that of the SM-2) was the torsion deformation (or twisting) of the wing. It would have further decreased the lift at the wing tips, raising an additional pitch-up moment. It might have been possible to recover from the spin at a lower altitude (where air density is higher), which was what the Czech pilots did. The fact that our pilots could not do it confirmed what I have always believed (and have earlier said in this book), that airline pilots, as all others, should be trained in some suitable aircraft to cope with and recover from unusual flight situations, including the spin. The Tupolev pilots might not even have been aware they had entered a spin. To cure the Tu-104 of that dangerous 'disorder', their structure rigidity was increased and they were banned from flying at low air speed and at altitudes beyond 12,000 metres on scheduled commercial flights.

Earlier, in 1956, this unpleasant feature of sweptback aircraft had revealed itself in another type of aircraft: the interceptor Yak-25. It possessed an onboard fire-control radar (FCR) with a large antenna and a weapon-aiming control calculator which made it possible for the first time to fire cannon at targets at night or in the clouds. The system called for a second crew member, an FCR operator. The Yak-25 had sweptback wings, but their rigidity was not sufficient, which made them prone to torsion deformation under load. In one of the tests of the Yak-25, as our test pilot Piotr Kabrelev pulled the G-load specified in his flight mission (well within tolerated limits), he suddenly felt the aircraft overshooting. He pushed the stick forward, yet the G continued growing and finally exceeded the limit level. He landed all right, but his wings showed residual strain. Special tests revealed G-load instability, and the test pilots entered a somewhat drastic verdict into the test programme statement: 'to be removed from operational service'. The Institute Command was less radical, however, and in their conclusions they recommended that the Yak-25 not be used for aerobatics.

The Yak-25 episode had unexpected consequences that immediately concerned me. Once, in the summer of 1958, my wife and I accompanied my father to a ballet at the Bolshoi Theatre. As we walked out of the theatre after the performance my father took me aside on the way to the car, as though taking a little walk for a breath of fresh air. Then he asked me how I was getting on at work. I said all was well; I was on good terms with my fellow pilots and my COs, and as I was assigned to serious test programmes I was probably regarded well too, both as a pilot and engineer. I also told him that six months earlier I had been appointed second-in-command of the fighter test section. He listened to it all and then suddenly said, 'You'll have to leave this job.' I was stunned and could not understand what it was about. I demanded to know what he meant, and this is what he told me.

Apparently the Designer General Alexander Yakovlev, during a meeting with Khrushchev, had pointed out to him that 'one Mikoyan is designing aircraft, and another testing them', with the implication that it was not right (he could also have added, 'and yet another is flying them in an operational unit'). When I heard it I felt deeply hurt. He had obviously been hinting at my possible (or so he must have thought) partiality towards MiGs. That was thoroughly unfair, for I had always been totally unbiased as regards various designer firms, and if anything, I was more demanding and particular about the MiGs. It also hurt because I had met Alexander Yakovlev socially a number of times and I had always believed that he thought well of me.

The next day at work I was informed of the Institute Commander's order to report to the Air Force Commander-in-Chief, Marshal Vershinin. When I entered Marshal Vershinin's office, I saw that the AF Personnel Commander, Colonel General Gudkov, was also there. Vershinin said, 'I have made enquiries about you at the Institute, and I have heard nothing but praise. I haven't anything whatever to criticise you for, but I'm afraid I'll have to offer you another job. I think you know why.' General Gudkov began to name various postings, none of which was related to flight testing. I declined them all, inventing a different reason every time, and then Marshal Vershinin said, 'All right, go on where you are for the time being, we'll think of something.' I'm not sure whose idea it was, but I rather think it was the Institute Commander who saved me from being transferred. He invented a new post within the Institute, that of assistant commander in charge of interception complexes (a new direction in fighter aviation). *De jure* I was no longer on the staff of the fighter testing section, but actually I continued to be active as a test pilot, though no longer as the pilots' CO. I did not remain in that position for long, for about a year later I was appointed to a higher post: commander of the newly formed fighter flight testing department (Yakovlev's complaint was ostensibly 'forgotten').

In 1972, when my fiftieth birthday was celebrated at the Institute, I received many formal and informal birthday greetings from all imaginable institutions and operational units that had anything to do with new aircraft and aviation equipment. Most of the aircraft designer firms and aviation factories sent their representatives to the party I gave at the Institute, with flowers and cards signed by their colleagues or just warm words and wishes, but not a word came from the Yakovlev company. A week later, Yakovlev's deputy arrived with a formal birthday greeting from his company, where the only signature missing was that of Yakovlev himself. I was totally nonplussed and unable to see the reason for his dislike of me. It was only a few years later that I discovered that reason. I was then working on a dissertation devoted to high-angle-of-attack manoeuvres and the related G-load instability. Among other test programme statements which I used as data sources in my research, I looked through the test statement on the Yak-25. The section reserved for the pilot's comment contained several names and signatures of the evaluation pilots, with G. Beregovoi's name among them. However, instead of Beregovoi's signature opposite his name, there was mine! And it suddenly came back to me in a flash, as they say: George had been away that day, so I had made the flight instead, afterwards signing the severe verdict on the Yak-25 along with the other pilots. The mystery was solved. It was that signature Yakovlev had held against me all that time, even though I had been neither the project test pilot on his fighter nor the compiler of the text of the statement.

About ten years prior to this discovery I might have unwittingly given Alexander Yakovlev an additional grudge against me. It was at the formal reception in honour of our first cosmonauts in the Kremlin in the early 1960s. I was standing beside my uncle, Artem Mikoyan, while he was talking to Yakovlev and someone else. Yakovlev suddenly turned to me and asked, 'Isn't the Yak-25 a good aircraft?' I was not aware of any hidden motive behind the question, so I said what I honestly thought. 'It's fine in a cross-country flight or in instrument flying, or for attacking a non-manoeuvring target. But for air combat manoeuvres or aerobatics it's no good.' Yakovlev did not say a word in reply.

In 1954 the Institute received for testing another modification of the MiG-17, designated SN. It was a fairly unusual version, fitted with movable cannon. The fact is that in all fighters up to the present day the cannon have always been fixed along the body axis of the aircraft so that the aiming is done by manoeuvring the aircraft as a whole. The SN was armed with 23 mm guns that could move up and down the vertical slots on either side of the nose of the fighter. They were operated by turning the throttle handle, together with the movable gunsight. The SN was tested by Colonel Molotkov (the then commander of the fighter testing section) and Major Solodovnikov. I was appointed one of the evaluation pilots and performed one flight, 'firing' a camera gun at a ground target and at a flying Il-28.

Thanks to the vertical mobility of the cannon an air target could be approached at very close range without any risk of a collision, for the flight path of my fighter did not coincide with my line of sight. Even in a head-on attack I was able to hold the target in the gunsight down to no more than 200 metres' range. With the cannon mounted along the fuselage axis it would have been impossible: I would have had to turn off much earlier to avoid collision. In firing at the ground target I could remain in horizontal flight while lowering the cannon at the required angle and tracking the target for a longer time than in diving without the risk of going in. In short, the advantages were as clear as daylight, and we reported them to the decision-making air force authorities. However, the new device was bulkier than conventional armament and increased the weight of the aircraft. In the end it was decided to produce a small series to be tested in some operational regiments, but it was never done. The SN remained a fact of history, nothing else. Twenty-odd years later a similar system was conceived for the Su-17 fighter-bomber, but only as supplementary armament. The cockpit-controlled movable cannon were mounted in underwing pods.

Also in 1954 I was sent to my first long-term posting away from Moscow, where I encountered a totally unfamiliar area of technology. In September I was unexpectedly recalled from leave and informed that I would be going away. The destination was not named. Together with a number of engineers from various divisions of the Institute I was summoned to a meeting of the Air Force Command attended by specialists from other military aviation institutions. We were still in the dark as to where we would go and what we would be expected to do. Being the only pilot in the group, I asked if the mission would involve flying and whether I had to take my flying gear on that trip. The answer was no.

The secrecy was complete. We were not even given our train tickets before-hand, and they warned us that no one should come to see us off at the station; our families were not even supposed to know the general direction in which we were going. We met at the station and the person in charge of the group handed out our tickets. They said Novosibirsk, but our final destination turned out to be even further. It took us four or five days to reach Novosibirsk, where we got on a train for Semipalatinsk, from where an army bus drove us along the bank of the River Irtysh for another few kilometres until it entered a fairly large and tidy-looking living compound surrounded by a fence and barbed wire. We soon learnt both its official coded designation, 'M', and what it was called by the locals: 'M-stadt'. As to what this place was and why we had come to it, we did not know until the first joint meeting of our group with 'local' specialists: it was the now famous but at that time completely secret nuclear weapons testing site.

Several days later we were driven into the steppe to a cluster of army barracks that stood together as a small village in the middle of nowhere. One of the barracks became our 'home' for the period of each successive bomb test, between which we returned to the compound. The actual range was further into the steppe, about twenty-five kilometres from the barracks village. The range was furnished with various combat materiel, including different types of aircraft which we, the aviation experts group, were superintending. That is to say, we moved them around the range, placing them at varied angles and distances from the supposed epicentre of the explosion. Other experts would then place cages with mice into the cockpits and tie sheep near the aeroplanes. The idea was to establish the character and the extent of a nuclear explosion impact on living organisms and combat materiel. We heard from the locals that for some of the previous nuclear tests several fragments of life-size houses had been built, and a stretch of an underground tunnel dug out.

The bombs were dropped from a Tu-16 that would travel each time all the way from the Crimea, where the airborne nuclear armament testing base was situated. After each explosion special aircraft would take specimens of the air from the area around the bombsite so as to establish the degree of contamination and the direction in which the cloud moved. For a few days prior to each test we were forbidden to write home, and if anyone did, his letter would be held back at the local post office until the 'work' was done. They said a magazine reproduction of a nuclear 'mushroom' had been discovered in a soldier's letter home; he was immediately suspected of an attempt to reveal the nature of his military service.

The bombs that were being tested at that time were of low trityl equivalent, from three to ten kilotons I believe (the low-power bomb turned out to be more difficult to create than the high-power one). Only one of the bombs was really big, at twenty kilotons. At the time of the bombing we would be near the barracks, watching the explosion through dark glasses. Despite the relatively low power the flash was very bright and the 'mushroom' rather formidable. I remember I was particularly impressed by the sound wave, which was not heard but *seen* in the leaning of the grass. It seemed to approach us rather slowly, and as it reached us there was a powerful thunder-like clap. Right after the blast we would get into a lorry and drive to the aircraft positioned around the range.

We were accompanied by an army officer with a dosimeter, who read its readings aloud as we were approaching. If radiation was not above the safety level we examined the aircraft, jotting down the data in special notepads (an 'express report' had to be handed in as soon as possible, and a more detailed one followed later). Usually on the first day we would only work a short time. Once the radiation was so strong that we were not even allowed to stop or to get out of the vehicle. Instead, we took turns to make a number of short dashes towards the aircraft in a jeep (with several drivers replacing one another in turn) to collect data for the express report. None of us could understand why it had to be so urgent. A detailed examination of the exhibits was only possible two days later. Some of the aeroplanes would catch fire at the blast, others were shifted from their position or even overturned. The ones nearer the epicentre were seriously damaged. It was painful to see the sheep, with their coats and skin charred and burnt on the side where the blast had hit them.

Each of us was handed a personal dosimeter, which was to be carried in our breast pockets at work. On return to the barracks we had to hand them back so that everyone's daily dose could be added up for a total estimate. By the end of my stay there I had received twenty-five roentgen, which was slightly below the limit dose. We were shown the field where the first hydrogen bomb had been tested a year earlier. Although termed a 'field', it could hardly be called that; it was a vast surface entirely covered with lava where no kind of life could be imagined. The radiation was still at one roentgen per hour.

We made our way back from Novosibirsk to Moscow in a military transport plane. It was during that flight that we heard of a tactical exercise at Totsk in which a nuclear weapon was used. It is a sadly known episode now, but at that time it was top secret, just as what we had witnessed near Semipalatinsk, and for years we were not allowed to breathe a word about it to anyone.

A few months after my return from Semipalatinsk I had an interesting flight testing experience. In all our aircraft of the time the pitch (the up-and-down movement of the nose) was controlled with the help of elevators hinged to the fixed or adjustable stabiliser. At the same time the US Sabre possessed a novel pitch-control device which consisted of a mechanically interconnected elevator and stabiliser, allowing for much more effective pitch control. The Mikoyan company produced a modification of the MiG-17 with such a combined stabiliser and elevator, and in 1955 the machine arrived at the Institute to be tested (under the designation of SI-10). I was appointed both project engineer and project test pilot of the test programme. The team naturally included other specialists as well, for example an engineer who was an expert on aircraft stability and controllability, the most important parameters to be tested on that programme.

Although the new pitch-control system had some minor shortcomings, we approved it on the whole, but it was not adopted for production because the MiG-17 was becoming obsolete. A second version of the MiG-19, which was soon to be produced instead, had a more advanced and more effective all-moving stabiliser – the stabilon – which alone could ensure adequate control authority in supersonic flight. The point is that supersonic speed causes a change in pressure distribution on the wing surface, which in its turn shifts the aerodynamic centre of the aircraft towards its rear, creating the need for more powerful controls when a change of the flight path is in order. But the more powerful the controls are, the harder they are to operate by the pilot's muscle force alone (which is sufficient for controlling a subsonic aircraft). The dilemma is solved with the help of hydraulic boosters, thanks to which the pilot's physical effort is confined to sliding a valve, while the oil pressure in the booster cylinder creates the force needed for the controls. For the pilot to be aware of his control inputs, artificial feel-of-control devices are installed.

Testing the SI-10, I had an 'adventure'. I was performing a flight to test the stick-free longitudinal oscillation damping. I pulled about 3G and released the stick. The aircraft pitched down so sharply that I was tossed up from my seat and bumped my head against the canopy. Then it pitched up, and I was pressed down into the seat. After a series of such violent and hardly bearable jolts I finally decided to get hold of the stick, and the aircraft steadied down. My head was booming like a church bell and ached – I was only wearing an ordinary leather helmet. When the instrument readings were studied afterwards it turned out that there had been nine up-and-down jolts in eight seconds, with the positive load (pressing me into the seat) up to 10G and the negative up to 3.5. In other words, I had been jerked off the seat and rammed into the canopy with a force three and a half times larger than my own weight (although the harness – the seat belts – had eased the impact somewhat).

To make sure it was not caused by the heavy force-measuring control stick, it was decided to replace it with an ordinary one and to repeat the flight with a crash-helmet on. By that time it had not yet become part of our standard flying gear, but some pilots had taken to flying in steel infantry helmets for canopy-jettison tests (I had been somewhat surprised to see those helmets in the briefing room on my first day at the Institute). However, we knew that the flight gear and survival equipment design company headed by Semyon Alexeev possessed two or three American crash-helmets from Korea. 'VG' Ivanov sent me to Alexeev to ask for one of them. In my second flight with the same mission the whole thing happened again, the only difference being that my head did not ache quite as much.

I liked that helmet with its built-in earphones very much, and subsequently I always wore it, until its Soviet replica appeared a few years later in a limited series. My friend Sasha Shcherbakov flew in another of those captured American helmets (the third was used as a model for reproduction), so he and I became the first Soviet pilots – and for a long time remained the only ones – who would always wear a crash-helmet while flying. Eventually crash-helmets became compulsory for military pilots, but the type adopted in our air force was modelled on the British helmet and worn on top of an ordinary leather one. I preferred the American type that could be worn over a canvas helmet liner; or even without it. Later this type of helmet was adopted for all operational units.

In August 1955 we received a somewhat unusual task. We had to ferry a number of Yak-25s from the factory in Saratov to an airfield near Shauliai in Lithuania. According to its performance data, the Yak-25's range allowed us to cover that distance in a non-stop flight but without much reserve fuel. Combat commanders were reluctant to risk their pilots, so the FTI Commander General Blagoveshchensky did what he had done several times before and undertook to perform a combat pilot's task with the help of his test pilots. A group of twelve pilots was formed and each got a navigator from the bomber testing section attached to him. I was also included in that group, although I had never flown a Yak-25 before. After I had made three familiarisation rides in our own Yak-25, the group took off for Saratov in a military transport plane.

The factory airfield at Saratov had a rare feature: it was laid out on a hill, so the difference in height between the middle of the runway and its ends was over eight metres (almost the height of an average three-storey building). Past the bottom of the runway the slope went down even steeper and ended in a deep ravine that separated the airfield from the city. I must say it was no routine business taking off on this runway with maximum take-off weight (with external fuel tanks) when you could not see ahead until halfway through the strip, after which the aircraft ran downhill, still short of the take-off speed, with the city hovering in front of you somewhere above the ground level. All airborne, we headed for Shauliai, our navigators seeing to it that there was not the slightest deviation from the scheduled track. Even so, we began our landing approach to the Shauliai aerodrome with the fuel-low warning lights on, but everything went smoothly enough.

The mid-1950s saw another breakthrough in fighter aviation (apart from the breaking of the sound barrier): the appearance of airborne radar. The design work on such radar had begun in the USSR back in the late 1940s. In 1951 the FTI received several two-seat twin-engine aircraft with airborne radars from the companies of Mikoyan and Lavochkin, but their tests were aborted at an early stage. The first airborne combat radar for fighters to be fully tested (together with the MiG-17P, in which it was installed) and launched into production was RP-1, 'Izumrud' ('Emerald'). It was designed for cannon fire (there were no rockets then) at air targets at night and in the clouds. The radar had two modes: search and aiming. In the search mode the target would appear on the display at 7 km or 8 km, the pilot would update his flight path towards it, and at 2 km the radar would automatically switch to the aiming mode, when the antenna stopped scanning and 'locked' on the target.

I did not take part in the initial tests of the MiG-17P, but I had ample opportunity to fly it later, especially its modification with an afterburner, the MiG-17PF. I really enjoyed testing this kind of equipment; in fact such flight tests were among my favourite. However, stability and controllability tests remained at the top of my personal hierarchy. They were a real challenge in terms of piloting qualifications and required some understanding of physics. On the other hand, testing radars and navigation systems was extremely interesting from the technical point of view. The overall experience of testing and promoting advanced types of aircraft equipment shows that no matter how thorough the tests may have been, how detailed and conscientiously written the manual, it will still be some time before operational units learn to use it properly and appreciate its merits. The lack of smoothness at the beginning of serial production and the sometimes insufficient experience of the maintenance personnel in regiments cause minor reliability problems, and production factories almost invariably have to form technical support teams and send them to where their equipment is being used. Operational pilots cannot always immediately feel at home with new equipment either, and they sometimes get prejudiced against them. Airborne radar was a case in point, as the following episode shows.

One night in 1953 an American military aircraft crossed the USSR border over Transcaucasia. The air defence pilots failed to intercept him and the American returned home unscathed. After that incident the FTI sent two of our test pilots, Yuri Antipov and George Beregovoi, radar engineer Major Dubenko and radar guidance officer Lieutenant-Colonel Krivtsov to Baku to demonstrate the merits of airborne radar. Dubenko checked out the onboard radars in two MiG-17Ps, after which both pilots in turn took off in them (one some time after the other) for a demonstration. Neither of them had any difficulty searching, tracking and locking on their target (an Il-28 medium bomber) with the help of their radars. The radar guidance officer in the tower was guiding each fighter by means of the ground surveillance radar, on whose display the target and the fighter images were changing their respective positions every six seconds (one full turn of the antenna). The aircraft camera guns recorded the final stage of the interception, and it could later be seen in the film how the target had been 'sitting' in the cross-wires of the sight at the right distance for aimed cannon fire.

Ground radar guidance straight from the screen (of which Krivtsov had become quite an expert) was another major novelty then. Aircraft target guidance in AF units was still performed by means of the plotting board at the tower. An operator received into his earphones from the radar operator an update on the respective azimuth and distance of the interceptor and the target and entered them onto the plotting board. The guidance officer would then de-termine the right heading for the interceptor and transmit it to the pilot on the radio. The overall lag in the transmission of commands and their carrying-out could reach up to ten seconds or more. Needless to say, it affected the success of interception missions.

In order to teach the use of advanced aiming and guidance systems to more air defence units, the FTI Commander Blagoveshchensky suggested organising a demonstration for air defence commanders at our home base. It took place on a very dark night, and a target, an Il-28 bomber, took off from a neighbouring airfield. It was flying with its navigation flights off. My close friend Leonid Fadeev took off from our airfield in his MiG-17P. The two aircraft were commu-nicating with the tower at two different radio frequencies so that the target pilot would not hear the commands transmitted to the interceptor. The guests who had arrived for the demonstration stood watching the ground surveillance radar display while the guidance officer was guiding the interceptor to the target. Directing Fadeev's heading and altitude, he guided him onto the target range at which Fadeev's own onboard radar showed the target blip on its display. All Leonid had to do after this was to close in on the target and, as his radar locked on, to adjust the aiming and 'fire' his camera gun.

As it had been done earlier in Baku, the film from the camera gun was shown to all the guests and everyone could see how neatly the target was placed in the sight reticle when the camera gun was shooting. The demonstration was then repeated, with an equally convincing result, by another pilot, Nikolai Zakharov. After that a number of teams were formed of the test pilots and engineers who had done the original testing of the onboard radar; they 'toured' operational units and gave demonstration and training sessions to their flying officers and maintenance personnel. (Such on-site demonstrations in combat units were in fact standard practice at the FTI, both before and after the radar episode.) Later, even a special in-service training course was organised at Chkalovskaya air base for air defence squadron commanders.

By the early 1950s the FTI test pilots had become quite experienced in bad-weather flights with the help of the recently adopted landing approach system, which consisted of the automatic direction finder (ADF) and the ground-based non-directional radio beacon (NRB). We felt perfectly confident flying at the weather minimum or even below it. I liked those flights and was so much at ease in them that whenever good weather broke, it made me happy in anticipation of another 'blind' flight. The landing weather minima of both the MiG-15 and the MiG-17 had been two kilometres' visibility and 200 metres' ceiling (2×200). To start with, we had the same weather minima for the MiG-19. However, many operational pilots (my own brother among them) considered them too 'tough' for an aircraft with such a high approach speed as the MiG-19. They suggested that its weather minima should be temporarily raised to 3×300, and, to most test pilots' regret, it remained at that level for ever. It was only for specific flights that some test pilots were individually allowed to reduce the minima to the original 2×200 level, as I was on several occasions while testing the MiG-19P.

Another innovation we were testing at that time, apart from the ADF/NRB, was the ground-controlled approach system (GCA). Its operator, the landing control officer, watched the aircraft image on the displays of the localiser and glidepath radars and gave guidance clues to the pilot. I was once performing a training flight in an Il-28 bomber trainer with Igor Sokolov in the front cockpit as a passenger. As we were roaming the sky high above the clouds we decided we wanted some music and tuned in on the ADF to an ordinary broadcast station. I hoped, as we did so, that our radioman Anatoly Yablonsky was listening to the air base; I did not know that he in fact was talking to someone else. At some point, as though I felt something was wrong, I switched to the command radio frequency and immediately heard my radio call. The voice sounded anxious: clearly they had been calling me for some time. I replied and was commanded to land at once. They also said it had started snowing heavily over the base and visibility was very low. I was sure there was no need to rush the landing; it was the time of year when a snowfall could not last long, and the visibility being already quite low, it could hardly get any worse. Nevertheless the command had to be obeyed and I made a fast, half-circle, 'fighter-like' approach which turned out to be precise, which the landing control officer confirmed on the radio ('On course, on the glide slope!'). His update on the distance to the runway was a great help (we had no distance-measuring equipment on board then). I saw the ground at about eighty metres height, a lot lower than my weather minima, but no correction was needed as the runway was right in front of me.

In high spirits because of a good job done in adverse conditions, I walked from my Il-28 to our building. I saw three of my commanding officers standing together by the airfield gates – Molotkov, Ivanov and Antipov. I walked on towards them, anticipating a word of praise for a neat landing. Instead, Antipov started telling me off for having got out of radio touch with the tower. Later I understood that I had given them cause to be worried, but at the time I was hurt and deflated. It even seemed to me that my immediate commanders disagreed with Antipov, but they were silent. I sulked and said nothing either. Antipov finished off by suspending me from flying for two days.

The next day, gloomy and resentful of my unjust punishment, I was sitting in the corner of the pilots' briefing room and jealously watching them study their flight missions. Suddenly an order came on the phone: all pilots had to assemble on the airfield. It turned out that six of our aircraft – two MiG-19s, three MiG-17s and a Tu-16 bomber – had just been caught in a heavy snowstorm. The five fighters landed safely with the help of the GCA, but the pilot of the Tu-16, who had plenty of fuel, did not risk the landing and went off to an alternative base. The only critical point occurred when Volodya Sereghin, the pilot who later crashed in the same aeroplane as Yuri Gagarin, descended to a dangerously low height rather too far from the airfield, but levelled off on a command from the GCA. Colonel Antipov told the assembled officers about the landings and announced a formal commendation to the pilots. I could not help remembering how my landing had been 'commended' by him – it seemed even more unjust now. But suddenly Antipov added, 'And yesterday Lieutenant-Colonel Mikoyan also got into exceptionally difficult landing conditions in an unfamiliar aircraft and did very well. I commend him too.'

Yuri Alexandrovich Antipov was among our best-known test pilots after World War Two. He held the titles of both a Hero of the Soviet Union and an Honoured Test Pilot of the USSR. He had been in action from the very first days of the war with No. 402 Fighter Regiment, until, like most other test pilots and test engineers, he was recalled from the front to resume testing aircraft. Antipov had tested the earliest Soviet jets and was the air force project test pilot for our first sweptback jet fighter, the MiG-15. In the ten years that Antipov was the No. 1 Department Wing Commander deputy in charge of test flying, he flew every aircraft, including helicopters, that came to the Institute to be tested. After his retirement from active service Antipov worked for many years as a guide at the Monino Aviation Museum near Moscow.

I would like to end this chapter with a brief description of an interesting, even unusual project that was at that time designed by the Mikoyan company together with a ground equipment firm – a system of catapult take-off without an airfield. It consisted of a heavy truck with 'runway' rails about ten metres long. A MiG-19S with an external solid propellant booster that could deliver forty tons of thrust was mounted on it. The pilot gave maximum rpm, engaged the after-burner and then pressed the booster button. The booster thrust cut the retainer pins holding the aircraft on the rails. As the aircraft left the rails, the speed would not yet be sufficient to let it fly on its own wings, but the booster would push it up and forward. By the time the booster ran out of fuel, the speed would have reached about 320 kph, at which point the MiG-19 could fly independently. The booster was then automatically dumped.

In the factory tests the catapult was tested by the famous test pilots George Shiyanov and Sergei Anokhin. When it arrived at the FTI, the system was tried out by Mikhail Tvelenev, George Beregovoi, Leonid Kuvshinov and Vasily Kotlov. Even the Institute Commander, General Blagoveshchensky, could not resist having a go at it (I must say he, like Antipov, flew every new aircraft that came to us to be tested). The last pilot to test the catapult was 'VG' Ivanov. I had only just reported back from leave and was in time to see his take-off. The catapult was set up on the edge of the airfield quite near the forest. The take-off was filmed, with the trees in the background, as it had to be shown that the system could be used to take off from a clearing in the woods. As the MiG started gliding along the rails, with the roar of the booster added to its own considerable engine noise, my heart sank; it seemed that it would get to the end of the rails and topple down. But the rocket booster was thrusting it on and upwards, then the booster noise abruptly stopped and the booster itself came off and went tumbling down while the aircraft soared up into the air, gaining speed. I was now tempted to have a go at it myself, but, alas, 'VG' had used the last booster.

The system was not adopted in the air force for it only tackled one side of the problem: the landing still had to be made at an airfield. It was written in the test programme statement that the issue of the short, carrier-type landing had to be developed, but the recommendation remained on paper. Nevertheless, the performance of catapult take-off was a remarkable achievement of the day.

CHAPTER 16

Wider Horizons
and Narrow Escapes

In January 1955 I was fortunate enough to get a two-week posting to Leningrad. Until then I had only been to Leningrad once, as a schoolboy. My destination was an equipment design company which had some time before designed the first Soviet airborne range radar. Its initial specimen had already been tested by us at Chkalovskaya and sent back to Leningrad for improvement. I had flight tested it then, and now the company invited me to assess the modification results on site before sending the device back to Chkalovskaya to be tested again.

The weather in Leningrad was foul – thick low clouds and continuous rain. No question of flying. For two days I hung idly around the airfield at Pushkino (just outside the city) without so much as climbing into the cockpit, and finally got fed up. In the week that followed I did not go to the airfield at all but phoned the commander of the AF regiment at Pushkino (in whose machine I was supposed to fly with the range radar) to ask if there was any flying weather on the way. There was not, and I stayed in town. I had friends living in Leningrad then: Voroshilov's son Piotr and his wife Nadya. Piotr was already a general and commanded a tank-proving ground near Leningrad. I saw them both every day. While Piotr was at work Nadya took me out (despite the foul weather) to walk around their beautiful city and to visit museums, and in the evening the three of us either went to the theatre or had dinner in their house. Nadya's father and mine had worked together in Rostov in the 1920s. Later, in the 1930s, when Piotr Voroshilov and Nadya were already married, her father was arrested and shot and her mother sent off to a labour camp. Nadya and her sister Vera were left 'in peace' (probably thanks to Voroshilov's protection). Nadya's mother, Maria Fokeevna, and mine had been friends before it all happened. They began seeing each other again as soon as she returned from the camp, and remained good friends until my mother's early death in 1962. Maria Fokeevna herself lived until 1991, and whenever I saw her in Moscow she would always talk about my mother with great warmth.

At long last the weather improved; it became crisply cold and beautifully sunny. I went straight to the airfield without wasting time on phone calls. Alas, although the sky was clear, the runway was now covered with ice. The Regiment Commander, Alexei Mashenkin, whom I had met in a reserve fighter regiment back in 1941 and had not seen since, said, 'I would not allow anyone else to take off on this ice, but you and I will do it together.' So he flew with me as my target.

Such a take-off was not altogether new to me. In March 1954 I had been testing our first anti-skid automatic brakes. They made it possible to increase the pressure in the brakes almost to the point of skidding, thus providing for more effectual braking. Once, when our runway at Chkalovskaya was totally iced and all flights suspended, my headstrong project engineer, Vasily Popov, went from one commander to another until he reached the very top and managed to persuade the Institute Commander himself that it was essential to test the anti-skid brakes on ice, so I was allowed to perform two flights. What an unusual experience it was! In those two take-offs at Chkalovskaya, as well as at Pushkino later, the main difficulty was the runway alignment. I had made a couple of 360-degree 'pirouettes' each time before I finally succeeded in aligning the machine with the runway. Upon landing it was even 'curiouser': just as it touched down and I started braking, the aircraft turned against the wind like a weathercock and skidded sideways along the runway at a fifteen- or twenty-degree angle to its axis. Taxiing to the parking apron became quite a feat. Clearly the iced runway proved too much even for the anti-skid brakes, but then it had been known all along. Popov's idea was to test them in extreme conditions just to see how they would behave. It was not until the MiG-19 that anti-skid automatic brakes were adopted for production, and since then they have been installed in almost every type of aircraft. Strangely, the car industry, even in the West, has only recently adopted this useful device, and as for Russia the notion of introducing it has apparently not occurred to anyone yet, which is a shame, for in our climate and on our roads anti-skid car brakes could be especially useful.

The next day over Pushkino it was overcast again, and Mashenkin and I made two flights over the clouds. In those days pilots were still paid extra for flying in adverse weather conditions and above the clouds – two roubles per minute in the pre-reform money (about twenty pence at the rate of the time). I had almost run out of cash by that time and could do with an extra two hundred roubles or so.

In May 1956 I was promoted to colonel, five and a half years after my last promotion. Later the rank of colonel would be conferred only on Grade 1 pilots, but at the time I got mine that rule had not been adopted yet. I got my Grade 1 rating about a year later, in March 1957.

During that same year of 1956 I received several postings abroad, although the first of them was cancelled. In April that year Khrushchev and Bulganin were to go on a state visit to Britain, and initially it was supposed that they would fly in the first Soviet airliner jet Tu-104, recently tested at the FTI. Colonel Starikov and Major Yakovlev, who had been its project tests pilots, were appointed to fly it to London. As I could speak English it was suggested that I precede them to England and translate the Heathrow tower commands to them on their approach and at landing. I spent a few days in preparation, making up a list of relevant aviation terms, phrases and commands and watching our own ground-controlled approach operators in action, at work with radar equipment similar to that used in the West. However, the government delegation in the end went to Britain by sea on a naval cruiser, and although the Tu-104 was still sent over there as back-up transport, the responsibility was no longer quite as serious and my 'mission' was called off.

The 'trip that never was' came to mind unexpectedly in rather uncommon circumstances the following year. In the summer of 1957 Moscow became the scene of a rather remarkable event: the International Youth Festival. It took place a year or so after the Twentieth Party Congress and celebrated the 'thaw' on a really grandiose scale. Some of the bans and restrictions that had constrained people's lives in Moscow had already been removed by the time of the festival. To give just a couple of examples, the Kremlin had finally been opened to the public, and the ridiculous ban on taking pictures in Moscow had been lifted. Not many people would remember or in fact know today that until 1956 ordinary citizens were not allowed inside the Kremlin except on an organised visit to the Armoury Museum (which was not easy to arrange either), and that no one but formally accredited correspondents, and with a special licence at that, could take outside photographs anywhere in the city.

The very idea of Moscow's hosting such an event as the festival was, of course, a sign of the Soviet Union's new (if still very relative) openness. Just over a year before no one would have imagined that Moscow could be suddenly 'invaded' by thousands of foreigners, and very young people at that – hardly to be expected to be very sedate or 'prim and proper' in their ways. I remember one evening at the beginning of the festival when a large crowd of young people, foreign and Russian together, filled the entire space around the Tsar Cannon and the road outside the Great Kremlin Palace. Live bands were playing at a number of spots all over the Kremlin, and many people were dancing. But of course not all of them were there for enjoyment; some were 'on duty'. I happened to be near a young foreign couple who were dancing rock-and-roll and their movements were growing more and more energetic and became rather 'bold' (the kind of dancing that was not encouraged in Russia in those days). Finally, as the boy deftly hurled his partner over his shoulder, two plainclothes fellows emerged from the circle of fascinated onlookers and broke the couple apart.

I sought to practise my English with 'real' English people or Americans. Finally I met a group of young people from Britain. In the few days that followed I met up with them three times; I drove them around Moscow in my car, had dinner with them at Moscow's only Chinese restaurant one night, and once even brought them all home (my family were in the country then). One girl in the group, Dorothy, was a real beauty, but I spent more time talking to Jacqueline, an attractive dark-haired girl. I even took her alone for a drive once. The day before my new friends were to leave (the festival was over), I went over to their hotel for a brief farewell meeting, and the whole group and I met up outside the building. We stood there for a while chatting, and then we all said goodbye and I left.

Two or three weeks later I got a phone call to say that the State Security Minister Serov wanted to see me. For the first, and I hope the last time in my life I got an unsought-for opportunity to visit the well-known KGB building on Dzerzhinsky Square, known to most Muscovites as Lubyanka. General Serov knew me well; we had met several times while on holiday and had even played tennis together once or twice. On such occasions he had always been very sociable and easy-going. In his office he greeted me in a simple and outwardly friendly manner. He asked me casually of my meetings with that group from Britain and showed three photographs. They had obviously been taken on the last day outside the hotel, although naturally I had not seen anyone there taking pictures. They must have used some kind of secret camera, although the photographs were large and of good quality. They showed me and another Muscovite talking with the group, while the third picture was just of Jacqueline and me standing together in the same setting. I realised he had no other evidence besides these three photographs, so I told him of two meetings only. Then Serov asked me, completely out of the blue, whether it had been in England that I had met that girl (he must have supposed her to be a British agent instructed to seek me out in Moscow). I told him I had never been to England. 'How do you mean "never been"? But you have been granted a British visa!' I explained about my cancelled business trip to London. Serov crossed something out on the paper on his desk. I thought, 'Didn't they *know* who went to England in that group and who didn't?'

That was the end of the story. It had no consequences for me whatsoever. As I gathered from Serov's words, he was going to report the matter at the next Politburo meeting. Since my father did not say a word about it to me afterwards, I understood that he (and possibly other Politburo members as well) saw nothing wrong in my 'international' experience; otherwise, knowing him, he would have given me a piece of his mind. Perhaps it was rather careless for somebody in my position – an air force colonel and a test pilot – to mix with total strangers from the West, but I, like many other Soviet people, had been carried away with the euphoria of the 'thaw', which misled us into wishful thinking. But I, of all people, with my life-long awareness of our security service (my father's bodyguards and all that), should have known that the KGB were as vigilant as ever. In the not-so-distant past any unauthorised encounters with foreigners, especially by the military, were treated as a grave offence. Even in 1957, had any of my colleagues done what I did he would not have got away with it so easily and might have been forced to say goodbye to flight testing.

Back in 1956, after my promotion, I was posted to Poland, where an aircraft factory had obtained from us a licence for the production of the MiG-17. My mission was to convert a number of Polish test pilots for testing that machine. On arrival in Warsaw I reported to the Polish Air Force Commander, General Turkel. He was, in fact, a Soviet general, and there were three or four other high-ranking Soviet officers in the Polish AF High Command at that time. The next day I was accompanied by a Polish officer to the aircraft factory in Mielec. We went there by car, and I suddenly saw Soviet tanks on the road. My companion, who had bought a morning paper on the way, told me there was a revolt in Poznan. The subject was never mentioned again while I was there.

I had to convert seven test pilots. Three of them belonged to the Mielec factory and two were from an aircraft repair depot. The remaining two were the ones I have particularly remembered since: Tadeusz Olendzski and Andzej Ablamowic.

219

Andzej and I became good friends and many times met in Moscow afterwards. None of my charges really spoke Russian, but at least they had no difficulty understanding me. Very soon I began to understand them too, especially when we talked about flying, although the difficulty was that a few years before my visit Polish aviation had replaced the internationally accepted English and French aviation terms with their Polish equivalents. After preparatory ground work, the Polish pilots made several flights each in a single-seat MiG-17 following the flight missions I had written for them. Then Andzej asked me to give him a spin-training ride in the two-seat MiG-15UTI. I had made about a dozen such flights in that two-seater and in the MiG-17 before, but I did not possess an instructor's licence. But how could I, a Soviet pilot, lose face before my foreign colleagues? I agreed, and three other pilots besides Andzej volunteered to try. As a result of these rides I got such a feel for the spin that I almost became an instructor in earnest. I learned to apply the stick (the ailerons) against or with the spin in such a way as to change the character of spinning at will, from an unstable, 'oscillating' spin to the 'classical' stable one.

There was a somewhat anxious moment during one of these flights. As one of the Polish pilots was recovering from our first spin he was a bit indecisive with the controls, and the aircraft continued to spin. After four or five turns I had to take over and, since we had lost quite a bit of altitude, I made a point of applying the controls strictly by the book: I pressed the rudder fully against the spin, then pushed the stick fully forward aiming neatly at the centre (marked by the white line on the instrument panel). If that method had failed I would have had another chance by pushing the stick forward and to the side with the spin, which was known as the number four recovery method. However, the spinning stopped and all that remained was to pull out the aircraft to level flight. Although I had been rather uneasy for a few seconds I did not show it to my trainee and suggested trying another spin. While he was climbing up I calmly explained his mistake to him, and after that everything went well. In the meantime word reached Warsaw that we were making spin-training flights, and three engineers arrived at Mielec from the Aviation Institute. They were experts on the theory of the spin phenomenon but had never actually seen a sweptback jet fighter spin. So I had to oblige and do another spin by myself, and not at 7,000 metres as stipulated by the book but at 5,000 to give them a better view, although it was certainly a breach of safety rules.

We completed our flight schedule in two weeks and I was ready to return to Warsaw. The machines we had been flying had to be ferried there, and Andzej asked me to let him fly the MiG-17 while I was left with the MiG-15 trainer. As I approached the airfield outside Warsaw I asked for landing clearance in Polish. The answer came in near-perfect Russian – my accent had betrayed me. We arrived in Warsaw on 12 July, my birthday. Andzej took me to his house for a party that Zocia, his wife, organised in my honour. Tadeusz and his wife Theresa also came, and we spent a very nice and warm evening together.

In Warsaw I unexpectedly received an opportunity to fly as well; there was a problem with two MiG-17PFs that belonged to a fighter division stationed near the city. Apparently they failed to climb up to their assigned ceiling and I was asked to 'sort them out'. While I was there I paid a visit to the Military Testing Institute and was surprised to discover that its commander was my old acquaintance, formerly an engineer at Chkalovskaya (some time after that all Soviet officers and generals were recalled to the USSR). I went to our embassy to see the ambassador, who was also an old acquaintance – Panteleimon Ponomarenko, whom I have mentioned earlier. He invited me to join him and his family for an outing in the country the following Sunday – at a 'dacha' for the diplomats from socialist countries.

My new friend Andzej Ablamowic was a delightful man, calm, sociable and witty. He was a qualified engineer and an excellent pilot, and later became head of the Flight Research Department of the Aviation Institute in Warsaw. Thanks to Andzej, who took me on a visit to his Institute, I got an opportunity to fly three aircraft that were new to me: the Polish trainer TS-8, a Czech aerobatic aeroplane and the American twin-engine Cessna-78. Then Andzej and I flew over to the airfield of a sports club on the other bank of the Visla, where we made two flights in a glider (it was towed up by an aeroplane and then 'let off the hook' in the air). Andzej then suggested that I did another flight with a Polish girl, a glider pilot, whom he chatted with for a minute or two when we arrived. This time the glider was hooked onto the cable attached to a tractor engine on the ground. 'Will you take off or shall I?' asked the girl. I had not a clue as to how such a take-off should be performed, so I 'generously' let her do it, saying that I would take over once we were unhooked. The cable tugged us up to about 800 metres and I assumed control and eventually landed quite decently. On the way back Andzej confessed that he had presented me to the girl as a Soviet glider instructor. It was my first and last experience of flying a glider.

It was time to return home, and I dropped in on Andzej and Zocia on my way to buy an Aeroflot ticket for the next day. Zocia, a stewardess with LOT, the Polish airline, said, 'I am off duty tomorrow anyway, so you may fly Aeroflot if you like.' But the Aeroflot flight was sold out, so I bought a ticket for a Polish flight. In the evening, when I came to say goodbye, Zocia told me that an air hostess for my flight had fallen ill, and she was to fly instead. Whenever she got a few minutes free on that flight Zocia came and sat next to me, and we chatted amiably away, though she could hardly speak Russian at all. We went from the airport to the city together and I collected my car and showed her a bit of Moscow, after which I drove her back to the airport.

I have kept very warm memories of the time I spent in Poland and of my new friends. Andzej and I saw each other again fairly soon; he came to Moscow to take part in contrastive tests of three different trainer jets: our own Yak-30, the Czech L-29 and the Polish 'Iskra'. Later he came again, to evaluate the passenger Yak-40 that was to be purchased by the Poles. Once he and Zocia came together; they had spent their holiday at one of our Black Sea resorts and were stopping in Moscow for a day or two on the way back. Two or three times my daughter stayed with them as their guest in Warsaw.

In September the same year my father was to go to China as the head of a Soviet delegation invited to attend their Communist Party Congress. It was decided to take them there in a Tu-104. It would have been the Tu-104's first real passenger flight, and a VIP passenger flight at that. The rule is that in such cases neither of the pilot seats can be vacated during the flight, not even for a few minutes. The flight was to be a long one and a third pilot was obviously needed, so I asked to be selected.

Although I had of course always been a fighter pilot – both by my professional choice and due to my long experience – and I had always enjoyed flying fighters more than anything else, I was interested in occasionally trying heavy aircraft as well. It was interesting to fly something that was so different from a fighter, not only in size, performance and handling but also in that it had to be controlled by a crew, each member of which had his own function. Back in May 1954 I had flown solo the Il-28 tactical bomber (since then I have made over thirty flights in it); in June 1956 I flew as the co-pilot (and later from the left seat) in the Tu-16 bomber. The Tu-104 which was to go to China in September 1956, in accordance with the regulations, had to be checked in flight before taking off with passengers on board. I took this opportunity to practise and flew it from the captain's seat.

We made two landings on the way to Peking – in Omsk and Novosibirsk. The flight took just over eight hours – quite remarkable for those days. Although I had come as crew, I was regarded by our hosts as a member of the delegation, and so was my brother Alexei, who came along as well. They knew that we were both sons of the head of the delegation. My father, since my mother's health made it impossible for her to accompany him, often invited my wife to go on a foreign visit with him, either on her own or with me. On other occasions he was accompanied by Sergo, or Vanya with his wife or, as it was on this trip to China, by Alexei.

In Peking we lived at the villa which was reserved for my father and another VIP on the delegation, Boris Ponomarev. One morning over breakfast, Ponomarev was talking about the events back home and made an angry comment about some members of our Academy of Sciences who had declared that the Supreme Council election should be conducted on an alternative basis. I said I was of the same opinion. My father did not pull me up on what I said, which he would certainly have done if he had thought me wrong. Yet he did not get into an argument with Ponomarev, obviously letting me go on with it if I wanted.

One day my brother and I attended a session of the Congress. What was going on did not make much sense for we did not understand a word (there were no earphones where we sat), but one visual impression stuck: each of the participants had a tall china tea mug with a lid on it. They were taken away by the attending girls, who made fresh tea in them and brought them back in accordance with the numbers written on the mugs. However, Alexei and I spent most of the time sightseeing in the company of a young Russian-speaking guide who showed us many interesting places and things. We even got a chance to see Shanghai, where we were taken in a military transport aircraft, the Li-2. We were as yet unaware of the tension which was then developing between our two countries and there was nothing in that trip to make either of us suspect it. Wherever my brother and I went we got a very warm welcome. But there had been a different mood brewing at the top, and so the true goal of my father's visit must have been his talks with the Chinese leadership. It is well known that they did not like it that Stalin's personality cult had been exposed or that the truth of his regime had been revealed so bluntly.

The closing of the Congress was celebrated with a reception at the Peking, a large hotel in Tianenmen Square. My father had gone off to North Korea to have talks with Kim Il-Sung, yet my brother and I were nevertheless invited. The vast dining-hall of the hotel was furnished with many round tables with twelve seats around each. Wherever there were any foreign guests sitting there were two or three Chinese leaders representing the hosts. My brother and I were ushered to the same table as Ponomarev, and we found ourselves to be in the company of Liu Shao-ch'i and Mao Tse-tung. Mao was cordiality itself. Alexei, a great one for practical jokes, announced through the interpreter that I had particularly enjoyed one dish on the menu, some extremely spicy meat which I could barely finish. Mao got off his seat, came round to mine and spooned some more of that meat onto my plate from the large dish held by a waiter.

On the way home to Moscow we also landed twice, this time in Irkutsk and Krasnoyarsk. Wherever we arrived, my father would meet the local admini-stration, who would take him to see the city and some factories or other enterprises. My brother and I usually went too, and thus we saw Lake Baikal, to which we were taken on a drive from Irkutsk. All in all, that trip to China was a unique and memorable experience.

Towards the end of the same year Nikolai Zakharov and I began the testing of the second prototype MiG-19P with the RP-5 radar. The first prototype had been tested by George Beregovoi, who had had difficulty target-tracking due to the hyper-sensitivity of the pitch control. Beregovoi played an essential part in removing that defect. I remember these tests, among other reasons, for a number of difficult situations which in all truth were narrowly escaped accidents.

I liked the MiG-19 a lot. A beautifully shaped aeroplane, it always seemed to be reaching upwards, even when on the ground. It was also a powerful and a fairly manoeuvrable aircraft. Yet for all its obvious merits there were a number of technical failures in the first machines adopted by operational units, and many combat pilots considered it to be hard to handle.

Nikolai Zakharov, an engineer-pilot like myself, had participated in testing the earliest Soviet radars and so was regarded as an expert in radar equipment. That was why he was invited to take part, as a co-pilot to Andrei Kochetkov, in the factory tests of the new interceptor designed by Lavochkin, the La-250. In the very first flight they encountered a lateral control problem; the control was so sensitive that the aircraft began rocking at take-off, and the pilot's attempts to stabilise it only made the rocking more violent. Kochetkov aborted the take-off, but the aircraft was seriously damaged. Fortunately the pilots got away with nothing worse than bruises.

As early as its mock-up stage, the FTI pilots had pointed out that its low-placed cockpit and long nose (to which it owed its nickname, 'Anaconda') would create visibility problems for the pilot. The mock-up commission demanded that the layout be changed to raise the cockpit higher, but Lavochkin persuaded Marshal Savitsky (who chaired the commission) to leave the first three machines unaltered. In one of his flights in the first machine, Kochetkov had to approach for landing in very bad weather. His forward view was poor and the weather made it worse. Kochetkov, unable to see the ground, made a dangerously low approach without realising it. He hit some piping and crash-landed short of the runway. His landing gear legs broke, the aircraft went forward dragging on its belly and caught fire. Kochetkov tried to get out of the cockpit, but the canopy jammed. With truly amazing presence of mind, Kochetkov had time to think that if he pulled the D-ring slowly, just a short way, the canopy would come off, but the ejector-seat 'gun' would not fire (it was before the appearance of the ground-level ejector seats). The risk was great, but there was no other way out. He did that, and the canopy opened a crack. Kochetkov hit it hard with his fists, and it came off. He had barely run some distance from the machine when it exploded.

This is one of those incidents which show that the opinion of pilots should be seriously taken into account, as any other professional's opinion about a piece of technology he uses in his work. The accident was a serious setback in the work on the La-250, which slowed down as a result, and, as bad luck would have it, Khrushchev's sadly known decision of reducing the air force came at just about that time. Thus, the last manned aircraft designed by Lavochkin never made it as far as the factory tests.

The MiG-19P, besides two hydraulic systems that drove the controls, the undercarriage and wing flaps respectively, had an electrical emergency system for actuating the stabilon. If the pressure in both hydraulic systems fell below a certain value, they were cut off and the electric pitch control system switched on. However, it could only turn the stabilon by four degrees per second, instead of the twenty-five to twenty-seven-degree deflection per second provided by the hydraulic system. In normal flight a four-degree turn of the stabilon was as a rule sufficient, but take-off and landing sometimes require fast and large deflections of the stabiliser.

Once, as I was taking off in the MiG-19P, I pulled the stick all the way and waited for the nose to go up. When the rotation began, and I was about to push the stick a little forward to hold the nose at the take-off attitude, I felt I could not move it at all. The pitch angle kept growing, and to let it go on would mean to lose speed completely and crash. I was pushing the stick forward as hard as I could and eventually felt that it was yielding, but very slowly, far more slowly than I needed. I realised that the electrical emergency system had come on, and so no matter how hard I pushed the stick would move no faster than the system allowed. Meanwhile the pitch angle slowly began to decrease, and I eased on the stick, but now the nose was pitching down and the aircraft was heading towards the ground, though I was already pulling the stick hard. The reason was simple: while fighting its steep climb upwards I deflected the stabilon too much, and all I needed now was to undo what I had done. Yet despite all my frantic pulling the aircraft continued heading down. I can still, to this day, see that grey concrete surface into which I was about to crash. And then, literally within inches of the ground, the machine pulled out and became more obedient. The speed was now higher and the stabilon grew more effective, so smaller deflections were needed. The aircraft gained height and the control returned back to normal, or nearly so.

I performed my flight mission – tracking a target aircraft with my radar – and turned home, trying to figure out what was wrong with my machine. The pressure in the hydraulic system was normal at 160 atm, but the aircraft was evidently controlled electrically. The emergency system switch was, as it should be, in the 'hydraulics' position. I tried switching it to the reverse position, but nothing changed. I switched it back to 'hydraulics', and immediately felt the hydraulic system finally come on. The controls were now perfectly normal.

My 'spectacular' take-off happened to be seen by the Section Commander, Anatoly Molotkov. A capable engineer-pilot well familiar with many types of aircraft, he grasped the situation in no time and immediately, not even waiting for my return, informed the MiG Design Company. The fact is that my own troublesome take-off had been preceded by five or six take-off accidents ending up in serious damage or even disintegration of the aircraft. One of the pilots involved in them had been the chief test pilot of the company, Grigory Sedov himself. I had barely had time to change after the flight when Sedov arrived at the base and bombarded me with questions about my experience. A brain-storming session followed, and as a result the reason, which for a long time had remained obscure, was now established. It was considered before then that switching to the electrical system was 'legitimate' due to a fall in hydraulic pressure, but why the pressure should fall in the first place nobody could under-stand. My flight provided the explanation: pressure had nothing to do with the problem, and it was the emergency system valve that was the culprit. It had a piston whose function was to cut off the hydraulics and turn the electrical system on as soon as hydraulic pressure fell below the limit. At one of the factories which assembled the MiGs the valve was installed in such a way that its 'electric' position corresponded to the downward position of the piston. In the upper posi-tion it was normally kept by friction alone – but not at take-off, when the aircraft could jolt. Whenever the friction was less and the jolting a little more vigorous, the piston slid down and cut the hydraulics off. In none of the accidents that had preceded my experience had the reason been discovered, and now everything was finally clear. All factories were instructed to install the valve in such a way as to reverse the cutting movement of the piston. Since then there have been no more accidents of this kind.

I cannot forget what Sedov said to me at parting: 'There's no judging the winner, as they say – I damaged my aircraft, and you did not. Yet, you should have aborted the take-off as I did. It's a miracle you didn't crash while going on with it.' So, my luck had saved me once again, but subsequently I changed my take-off method: I would not pull the stick until the proper rotation speed was gained.

The designers' failure to foresee the possibility of spontaneous self-activation of the valve was a fairly typical case. The designer's mind is usually 'tuned' into the way his system or device *should* work, and he is not always capable of thinking out or imagining its possible or likely failures and defects. That is what test pilots and test engineers concentrate on, always asking themselves questions beginning with 'What if . . . ?' But they are also human and cannot foresee everything either.

Four years after that revealing experience with the MiG-19, a fatal accident resulting from a failure of design occurred at the Akhtubinsk air base. Anatoly Koznov, a test pilot of the Sukhoi Design Company, was taking off in a Su-7B with the help of the solid-fuel rocket boosters attached to either side of the fuselage. Such boosters had a manufacturer's access hole in the side next to the fuselage, permanently plugged with a metal stopper. This stopper in hundreds or thousands of cases before that day securely remained in place, but Murphy's law was not taken into consideration. During Koznov's flight in that Su-7B one of the booster stoppers was blown out. A jet of gas from the burning powder gushed out of the hole, like a welding torch, into the fuselage right opposite the stabiliser control rod. The latter burned out in no time, the aircraft got out of control, pitched up and then lost speed and crashed down with an explosion. Why the designers could not have planned the access hole in the opposite side of the booster is impossible to say, but their mistake cost us dear.

The electrical emergency control system was also once responsible for a fatal accident. As Vladimir Nefedov, a MiG Design Company test pilot, had reached supersonic speed in the prototype of the MiG-21, his engine stalled and surged, and the restart system failed too. Nefedov began a power-off landing approach, having aimed carefully at the approach end of the runway, but he must have overlooked that with the engine 'windmilling' the hydraulic pump would barely be able to keep up the necessary pressure. He had been gliding down steeply at first and then started pulling out vigorously near the ground. This immediately boosted the hydraulic fluid consumption and the pressure plummeted as a result. The electrical emergency control system came on automatically at the most critical moment, when the aircraft was heading towards the ground and the final flare had to be done. The stabilon control rate fell down at once and its deflections were no longer sufficient for levelling off. The machine hit the ground roughly, bounced and turned over. Volodya Nefedov died in hospital in the evening of the same day. In his brief conscious moments he kept repeating, 'It was my fault'. I knew what he meant: had he foreseen the fall in hydraulic pressure he would have levelled off the machine more smoothly, taking care not to pull the stick too far back. In fact, at a gradual pull-out, even if the electrical system came on it would still be possible to cope. But no one had yet attempted a power-off landing in a supersonic jet before. After this accident the electrical back-up control system was replaced in the MiG-21 with an emergency electric-hydraulic pump.

The test programme for the MiG-19P also involved cannon fire at an air target with radar aiming. In November 1957 I took off in my MiG-19P for an air defence firing range at Krasnovodsk. I was following my navigation leader, a Yak-25 piloted by Kabrelev and navigated by Bogachev. We were followed by a transport aeroplane with our team of test engineers and mechanics on board. The flight was to be in two legs, with a landing at the already familiar Akhtubinsk air base. On the approach to Akhtubinsk I discovered that the pressure in my main hydraulic system was nil, but as the other system was working I had no problem landing. The fluid pipe turned out to have broken, and while a replacement pipe was being obtained and installed the good weather broke and we got stranded at Akhtubinsk for five days.

The first thing we heard when it became clear that we would have to stay was that all their guest-houses were full. Somebody suggested addressing the newly appointed Air Base Commander General Finoghenov (I would later work side by side with him for many years). He sent me to General Ghiller, the air base chief of administration and technical services. (As I later heard, he had been Chief of the Rear of General Gromov's Air Force Army in the war, and in 1952, during Stalin's anti-Jewish campaign, he was posted off to Sakhalin like my wife's step-father, the celebrated polar explorer Mark Shevelev. They both remained on Sakhalin until Stalin's death.) Under General Ghiller the living compound of the Akhtubinsk base was very well supplied. Apart from his efficiency and organ-isational genius, Ghiller was assisted by the useful connections he had in many vital places, as well as by the high status of an air force rocket range. Unfortunately he died young, at fifty, failing to survive a heart attack. He was often fondly remembered by those who had worked and lived at Akhtubinsk under his care.

Ghiller confirmed that all the guest-houses were full, but there was just one room that was ready and furnished in the brand-new VIP-quarters building (the 'generals' hotel', as it was eventually dubbed; it was later to become my 'home from home' for five years). He said he was ready to put me in that room, while the others (the Yak-25 crew) would have to go and sleep in the barracks. I refused to accept the room on that condition, and General Ghiller grudgingly agreed to let all three of us occupy his precious VIP room. So we spent five days there biding our time, which was in fact not completely wasted, for Bogachev taught Kabrelev and me to play Preference, a moderately sophisticated card game that gave us some enjoyment.

We flew from Akhtubinsk to Krasnovodsk over Baku, travelling at high alti-tude. The tower controller of an airfield near Baku asked us on the radio if we had any special survival equipment on board. We did – inflatable dinghies, added to the parachute kit in view of the Caspian Sea crossing. Krasnovodsk was a fairly small city then, built on the coast of the bay next to the port. Most houses around the city centre were traditional one-storey wattle-and-daub buildings. I had personal interest in Krasnovodsk for my father had been here long ago. I went to see the building which had acted as the jail where he had spent some time and from where the twenty-six Commissars of Baku were taken to be shot in the sands. When I told my father on my return that I had been to see the building, he was pleased. My account gave rise to a flow of memories, and he told me much of what he had been through in those days.

The air defence division stationed at Krasnovodsk was equipped with MiG-17s. The MiG-19, in which I arrived, was a novelty which none of their pilots had seen. It caused such great interest on their part that I was asked to give a detailed talk, not only on the MiG-19 but on the recent innovations in aviation I had encountered or tested. And then I went from words to deeds and showed them what the MiG-19 was capable of. I took off on the afterburner and zoomed up at 360 kph at a very large climb angle. When I had climbed up to 2,000 metres,

I looked down and saw the departure end of the runway beneath me, which meant I had climbed at forty-five degrees. An impressive show no doubt, but rather pointless in practical terms. Then I speeded her up near the ground and performed a double Immelmann.

While I was at Krasnovodsk, I added (strictly unintentionally!) a couple of potentially very dangerous episodes to the eventful history of my relationship with the MiG-19. One of them took place in the flight where my mission was to climb all the way to the aircraft's ceiling on full afterburner, firing the cannon at top speed and top height until the ammunition was used up. I did not turn the afterburner off until I had finished firing, and then I descended and landed. Having taxied up to the ramp I noticed that the usual 'meeting committee' – the project engineer Vasily Popov and my mechanic Vadim Karepin – were not even looking at me but staring at the tail of my machine. I climbed out and saw that its aluminium skin had turned yellow. It became clear on inspection that the engine exhaust pipe had burst along the welding seam and the hot gas from the afterburner had leaked into the fuselage. It must have happened shortly before I turned the afterburner off, otherwise the stabilon link could have burned through (the way it happened in Anatoly Koznov's Su-7B), and then my only way out would have been to eject.

In one of my next missions in the MiG-19P I was to fire unguided 57 mm rockets to determine their dispersion trajectory. I was launching them two at a time, one from each of the rocket pods under either wing (each pod contained sixteen rockets). I had two special cameras suspended under each wing as well for a stereo footage of the rocket firing. As I was launching my next pair, instead of the usual 'farewell-to-the-barrels' whistle of the rockets I heard a loud clap and then a whistle of a different sort, that of engines flaming out. Both of them died at once. My altitude was too high for a restart so I turned homewards and began gliding. The commander of the host division happened to be at the tower at the time and he overheard my radio report. As I heard afterwards, he anxiously asked Popov, my project engineer, who was there as well, 'What shall we tell him? What is he to do?' Popov apparently replied, 'He knows what he's got to do. Just give him the in-bound heading and a distance update.' The commander, in whose experience a combat pilot in an emergency would always be given step-by-step instructions from the tower, gave up and walked out, washing his hands of us.

I glided from 15,000 metres down to under 9,000 metres, where I could restart the engines. There was a thick blanket of clouds from 10,000 metres down to about 300, so I restarted the engines in the clouds and arrived safely home. Again, my engineer did not come to the cockpit as I finished taxiing but went to look at the nose instead. My mechanic put the ladder up, and as I climbed out and looked where Popov was looking, I felt a chill down my spine. The nose was riddled with holes. One of the launched rockets had gone off prematurely, the splinters hitting the nose. My cameras had recorded that the explosion had been about three metres from the tip of the nose, and that was why the engines had flamed out. If the rocket had burst a fraction of a second earlier the splinters would have gone right into the cockpit.

There have been perhaps only four or five cases in the post-war history of

Soviet aviation of rockets exploding close to the aircraft they were launched from, and two of them were mine! My second experience of this kind was at a later date, in the mid-1960s. I was firing the same type of rockets at a towed air target from a MiG-21. I was launching one rocket in each attack, and as I fired my third rocket there was an unusual noise and the rocket seemed to be somersaulting in the air. I began my next attack, but the uneasy feeling that something was wrong would not leave me. My finger already on the trigger, I decided to abort the mission and return home. I reported to the tower that there was trouble on board and began the landing approach. As I landed and climbed out I saw that the skin of the left rocket pod was badly torn, and the aircraft had large splinter holes in it. One splinter must have hit the wing fuel tank, for kerosene was flowing out of it onto the rocket pod. What happened was that the rocket engine had exploded in the pod. If I had launched another one, its exhaust jet would have inevitably ignited the kerosene and set the aircraft on fire. Grigory Sedov, who happened to be visiting the air base at the time, walked up to my machine and observed the damage, silently shaking his head. At this moment the project engineer of the Su-11 team came running up and said, 'Such luck you have landed early, General! We're waiting for you to do an air target mission for us.' Afterwards Sedov told me that he was amazed I did not even seem to think twice before going off for another rocket-launching flight, minutes after my narrow escape. But in fact it did not even occur to me to be nervous at the prospect of another similar mission. Besides, as the saying goes, one shell-hole does not get hit twice, or something to that effect.

In Krasnovodsk I had yet another unpleasant experience in the MiG-19P, which was perhaps one too many for the same type of aircraft. However, this time it was not caused by malfunction. I was performing cannon firing at a towed air target (the MiG-19 had two 30 mm cannons). The firing range bordered on the south coast of Kara Bogaz Gol Bay, from where it stretched further east. Firing was allowed only in the easterly direction, so the tow aircraft and I would fly eastwards over the entire length of the range, about 100 km, then return idly to the starting point and back to the east again. My fighter was again fitted with two underwing cameras for filming the flight of the shells and registering the hits.

I was aiming by the target mark, which the radar projected onto the sight reflector in front of me. Between the reflector and the canopy glass, there was a screen that prevented me from seeing the actual target in the sky. However, every time the radar locked on the target I craned my neck to see over the screen and to make sure it was the target it found and not the Il-28 that was towing it. That is exactly what happened several times, so each time I had to repeat the attack. As a result I had used up nearly twice the amount of fuel planned and had little left in the tanks, yet there was the last, fifteenth attack to perform, otherwise the data would be incomplete. Having made it I saw that I had just about 600 litres of kerosene left – slightly above the emergency reserve level. I was travelling at 4,000 metres (and fuel consumption at such altitudes is high) and was over 150 kilometres away from home. I knew that if I continued flying at that altitude I might run out of kerosene on the way. I decided to opt for the maximum fuel economy regime, doing everything by the book. I turned to the in-bound course and rammed on full throttle to 'military power', or maximum power without the afterburner, although I was not happy doing it, for the engines immediately began to eat more fuel. However, I knew I would make up for it once I was at high altitude.

I speeded up in level flight to optimum climbing speed, 930 kph, and the fuel warning light came on at once: only the emergency fuel reserve was left. As soon as I had climbed up to maximum range altitude, 11,000 metres, I cut off one engine (it was no longer 'by the book'): I knew that fuel consumption would be lower since the remaining engine would be working at higher rpm, which usually pays more in range. As I approached the airfield area there were solid clouds over it with the ceiling some 300 metres above ground – just the weather minima at this airfield, to which the final approach was achieved through a gap between two mountains. I broke the clouds and saw the runway in front of me. I lowered the undercarriage and landed. There was just enough fuel left to taxi to the ramp nearest the runway, and when my mechanic climbed up the ladder to the cockpit I pointed to the fuel gauge. 'Look!' The needle was at the zero mark. If I had omitted one of the fuel-saving measures I had taken I would not have made it to the airfield, and would have either had to eject or crash-land in the middle of nowhere on the way home.

There was a case at Akhtubinsk later when one of our new pilots was left without fuel on the way home because the fuel from his drop tanks was not fed due to some failure. When he finally noticed it he did not think of dumping the useless tanks to reduce the weight and the drag of the aircraft; nor did he think of climbing to an economical altitude. As a result he did not make it home and had to eject. Admittedly my own case was rather a close shave, and strictly speaking I should not have allowed it to come to the last drop of fuel. Yet I have always believed it normal for the fuel warning light to appear on the final approach. Moreover, if the fuel light did not come on at landing after I had completed the mission, I used to feel that the mission was not adequate in 'size' and should have been made larger. That is what, after all, the warning light is for, to warn the pilot that fuel is running out and it's time to come in. Otherwise, why do we need it at all? Normally, from the moment the red light comes on there is enough fuel left for a fifteen-minute low-altitude flight, perfectly adequate for landing if the aircraft is near home. Yet in operational units they (and some of our test flight commanders as well) consider it a breach of the norm, an occurrence verging on a flight incident, if the fuel warning light comes on during a flight. This attitude effectively limits the capabilities of the aircraft.

Later in 1957, in May and June, I had an opportunity to fly at the Krasnovodsk base again. By that time the MiG-19 had been adopted in combat units and we had been receiving reports on certain recurring faults that many of its serial specimens seemed to share. One of them was that the engines would flame out as the afterburner was turned on. There were also complaints about cannon failures and poor performance of the radar. The AF Flight Test Institute co-operated with the manufacturer, Gorky Aircraft Factory, in an unprecedented venture: jointly performed tests of a batch of serial aircraft. They were three

MiG-19Ss (a version with the stabilon) and three MiG-19Ps, and the task was to establish whether the defects had been successfully eliminated. The test flight team consisted of a number of factory pilots and those from the FTI: George Beregovoi, Nikolai Zakharov, Piotr Kabrelev and me.

It was during those tests that we became particularly aware of the difference in remuneration for flight tests that we, air force test pilots, and civilian test pilots received respectively. Once, one of the factory pilots, Leonid Minenko, and I were simultaneously performing our respective flights with identical missions, in which we first took turns attacking each other to test our radars and then went our separate ways to test our afterburners. After we had both landed Leonid asked me how much I would be paid for that flight. For military test pilots these tests were in the category of inspection tests, which had its fixed 'monetary value' independent of the number of flights performed. A typical inspection test project would involve twenty-seven flights. On the current project I knew there would be just over a hundred flights altogether, so each flight was accordingly worth much less. I made the division in my mind and gave Leonid a quote, and then he told me what his rate was. It was nearly twenty times as much as mine! 'How come?' I asked him, and he said, 'Because I have first acted as your target, then I used you as mine to test my radar, and then I tested my engine. Each of the three tasks with us is rated separately, and each of these rates is higher than you military pilots would get for several full flights.'

Incredible and unfair as it was, it was unfortunately true. The discrepancy in the official remuneration rates for civilian test teams and military ones was enormous. For most categories of tests the civilian rates were about ten times higher than ours. The only category where payment was the same was testing missiles and rockets. It led to a paradoxical situation where we, military test pilots, would be paid much more for, say, launching a rocket (which did not take particularly high qualifications) than for an extremely complicated and demanding mission of testing the stability and controllability of the aircraft. I am perfectly certain that with most test pilots it is not the reward for the flights which is their priority, but the flights themselves. They have a drive to fly, to perform challenging tasks, returning home with valuable data, to defy danger and cope with complicated situations in the air, asserting (first and foremost to themselves) their competence and professionalism. This gives enormous gratification and raises the pilot's self-esteem. A reward for a flight which is adequate to its complexity plays a similar role – it is a recognition of the value and usefulness of the mission performed by the pilot and of the worthiness and status of his work. I never used to think before a flight whether I would be paid for it or how much, but afterwards, the more challenging and sophisticated the flight mission had been the more satisfaction I got from the reward received. Yet most of the time the military pilots' reward did not match the complexity of our flight missions, and besides, in some tests we did not get paid extra for flight testing at all.

In the 1970s I was personally involved in preparing and 'pushing' a new statute regulating the remuneration of flight testing and the rates for particular categories of flights, and at long last it was approved and became law. However, I had resigned from test flying by that time so the new statute did not affect me personally in any way.

Towards the end of our programme in Krasnovodsk three pilots from an air defence unit arrived at the base to participate in the tests. Their task was to ascertain that the faults they had encountered earlier were removed. One morning, after I had made a flight in a MiG-19S with cannon firing at high-G manoeuvres, one of the air defence pilots, Petrov, took off in the same machine and for the same flight mission which, among other things, involved cannon firing at negative G-load. The G-load 'pressed' the oil out of the engines (cannon recoil might also have been responsible) and the bearings got overheated and jammed. The engines went dead. Petrov belly-landed on a shell-covered sloping coast of the bay, and the friction set the aircraft on fire. The pilot, from force of habit, started climbing out over the port side of the cockpit, which happened to be in the direction the wind was blowing. Petrov got caught in the flames and received rather severe burns. He was picked up and rescued from the site by a liaison Yak-12.

The next day a group of engineers and technicians set out to reach his landing site in a lorry to have a look at the machine and decide what needed to be done. My friend Sergei Petrov (the unfortunate pilot's namesake), who happened to be at the Krasnovodsk base at the time, and I decided to go with them. When would we get another chance to see a real desert? And real it certainly was – just sand and salt marshes for as far as the eye could see. For a while we were driving along a more or less visible track which brought us to an air defence post, a radar station in the middle of nowhere, a water well, a bungalow for three officers and a barracks for about thirty soldiers or so. It was over fifty kilometres to the nearest habitation. To call it cheerless would be a massive understatement!

We drove on along a narrowish, seemingly endless stretch of salt marshes. We had to get on the other side of them, so when its darkest part had passed us and what followed looked like firm ground, the driver turned onto it, hoping for a short cut. 'Short' it was all right, for we had not driven fifty metres when the wheels started sinking in and slimy black slush seeped out through the ground. The driver tried to back out but it was no good: our four-wheel-drive lorry, for all its supposed cross-country ability, was sinking like a ship, up to the wheel axles in black mud. That was when the desolate radar station began to seem an oasis, but it was over fifty kilometres behind us and not a living soul within any imaginable distance around us. The air temperature was over forty degrees Celsius, and a cask of water in the lorry was all we had in the way of vital supplies. But we did not have engineers among us for nothing! One of them had a brain-wave and suggested dismantling the bolted sides of the lorry's body to use as planks. We did it in no time, then put one plank crosswise, setting up the jack on it, and jacked up the back wheels. Then we placed the other planks lengthways under them and repeated the whole operation with the front wheels. The rest was easy. We got her out all right, laughing and shouting with childlike joy, and celebrated our salvation by writing on the ground with a stick a humorous warning (in not too decent terms) to other 'adventurous' travellers who might find themselves in that place.

232

We drove on around the marsh and through the now roadless desert, among the sandhills to where our aeroplane was to be. Suddenly we saw some weird structures ahead and wondered what they could be. As we came closer we realised that it had been a mirage, caused by the half-burnt aircraft lying on the empty, shell-covered beach. The engineers and technicians gathered all the data they needed, and before long we embarked on a thoroughly uneventful return journey.

CHAPTER 17

Guided Missiles

In November 1957 I had my first encounter with guided missiles, which subsequently became a significant part of my work. At the rocket test range at Akhtubinsk they were testing air-to-ground underwing missiles, ground-to-surface missiles and guided air-to-air missiles. Due to the characteristic secrecy that was maintained even within one and the same force, we at the FTI knew virtually nothing about their work.

Eventually the missile testing base received their first jet fighter in which guided missiles replaced cannon as its standard armament. It was the MiG-19PM, a version fitted with four beam-riding K-5Ms. When the radar antenna locked on the target, such a missile, as the name suggests, when launched would 'ride' on its beam until it reached the target. The air base's own pilots had tested those missiles with radio-controlled unmanned aircraft as their targets, but for the aeroplane to receive military certification it had to be tested for performance, stability and controllability up to extreme regimes in full gear, as it were, i.e., with the missiles in place under the wings. The missile air base pilots had neither experience of, nor the qualifications for, this kind of work, so the Air Force Command instructed the FTI to direct a test team to Akhtubinsk for the task. Vasily Popov was appointed project engineer and I was the project pilot. Thus I found myself at Akhtubinsk again.

As soon as we had completed the necessary preparatory work, the flying weather broke. For nearly a week we were doing nothing until at last I could perform my first two, relatively simple, flights of the twelve planned in the test programme. There were another three flights scheduled for the next day, for the extreme regimes and stability tests. The morning dawned fine and clear, it was time to go to the airfield, but I had been feeling quite ill since late the previous night. As I was getting dressed I was wondering what I should do. If I did not fly until I got better, the whole team would be loitering around the base again. I went to the airfield with the decision that I would somehow manage one flight, which would keep the team busy processing the data for a while, and I would get better in the meantime. I did not say anything to Popov, but was worried that I would fail the compulsory medical check before the flight. The air base doctor took my pulse and blood pressure, and since both were within the norm he did not bother to take my temperature. He could not have known, of course, that both my pulse and my blood pressure were normally a lot lower than the values he registered, and the way I was feeling I knew I was running a fever. I told him nothing about it though, and left.

I had barely returned from the first flight when Popov came up to me with the mission sheet for the second. I still said nothing, though I was feeling even more feverish than before. So I made the second flight, and then the third. The flights were quite stressful: from take-off zooming right up to the ceiling with the after-burner on, then speeding up in a shallow descent to the limit Mach number of 1.34 (the air speed about 1,430 kph), finally reaching the maximum indicated air speed at a lower altitude – a flight condition in which the aircraft is subjected to the design limit of dynamic pressure. In addition, every stage of each flight involved control inputs to test the stability and controllability of the aircraft.

This might be a suitable point to explain the notion of indicated air speed. The speed at which the aircraft is flying is measured with a barometric instrument that responds to the full pressure of the head-on airstream entering the so-called pitot tube. It also registers the ambient pressure. The difference between these two kinds of pressure is the dynamic pressure, which moves the speed gauge needle, indicating the air speed. Yet as the altitude grows the air density lessens, and with the same actual speed the dynamic air pressure is lower, and so are the readings of the instrument. At high altitudes the discrepancy between the true air speed (relative to the air mass) and the instrument readings can be quite large. Thus, at a true air speed of 1,000 kph and an altitude of 5,000 metres the air speed indicator shows 775 kph, while the same true air speed at the 10,000-metre altitude will be indicated as only 580 kph.

For navigation purposes it is of course the true air speed that matters first of all. It serves as a reference point (with the necessary adjustments for the force and direction of the wind) in establishing ground speed, i.e. the distance covered over the ground within an hour's flight. However, in terms of actual flying and controlling the aircraft it is the indicated air speed which is a priority parameter. The point is that the behaviour of the aeroplane, the lift and the air drag also depend on the air density. At an indicated speed of, say, 400 kph at low altitude the aircraft's handling qualities will hardly differ from those it displays at the same indicated speed at 12,000 metres, though the true air speed will have grown to nearly 800 kph! The air drag in both cases is the same, therefore the engine thrust required for the flight also remains at the same level, producing a speed twice as high. That is why in a high-altitude flight a jet aircraft consumes much less fuel than at a low altitude. (All this is true, however, only for subsonic speed.) The air speed indicator shows both kinds of speed: indicated air speed is shown with its main, broad needle, and true air speed with an additional narrow needle.

After my third flight that day the project engineer, pleased that the day's schedule had been so promptly fulfilled, said, 'Well, Stepan Anastasovich, what do you say to just another quick flight?' I could barely stand on my feet at that point, and so I confessed that I was not well. He immediately got very anxious and dragged me to the medical unit where they took my temperature. It was quite high: 38.6 degrees Celsius. Popov took me to my hotel, put me to bed and for a few days looked after me like a nurse, and certainly not just because I was the only pilot on the project. I knew he was sincerely fond of me. The three flights I had made gave plenty of material to our two technician girls, who had to process all the recorder tapes, pick up the data and draw graphs to be analysed later by the engineers. The work took them two days, and then Sunday came. By Monday I was ready to fly again, so the team had hardly any idle time at all on my account.

Towards the end of our test programme I had a session with the regiment pilots, telling them of the test results and of the MiG-19's characteristic behaviour at extreme regimes.

That year, 1957, turned out to be a tragic year for No. 1 Section of the Institute. Since 1950 there had been no fatal accidents with the pilots of our section, just one non-fatal accident (a future cosmonaut, Vasily Lazarev, had belly-landed on a field), even though we were then testing aircraft of a new, more sophisticated generation and also went beyond the sound barrier. But on 8 August 1957 Nikolai Korovin was forced to eject from his E-50 after flying it out from the Zhukovsky air base. The aircraft, a prototype MiG-21 with a liquid-propellant rocket booster engine fitted into the root of the fin, was undergoing production acceptance tests. The booster exploded in the air and damaged the empennage and control surfaces. Korovin transmitted to the tower that he was spinning, then, after a pause, that he was recovering, then spinning again, and finally ejecting. His aircraft was fitted with a new-type ejector system: the seat was fired out of the cockpit together with the canopy, which was to shield the pilot from the airflow at high speed. The system must not have been fully developed yet, for after the ejection the canopy did not separate from the seat and Nikolai was prevented from leaving it and opening the parachute. He crashed into the ground in his seat.

On 23 November one of my closest friends, Igor Sokolov, was killed too. That morning he, another two of our colleagues and I were driving to work from Moscow in my car. After a few overcast days the weather was fine again, and we were anticipating new flights. Igor was then testing a new-generation aircraft, the Su-7, the first Mach 2.0 fighter. That day he was to perform his third flight in this machine. I had a mission in a MiG-19P, and as I was already in the cockpit, 'VG' Ivanov came up and instructed me to fly as Sokolov's target, for the machine assigned for the task was out of order (the Su-7 was a top-priority aircraft then). Igor attacked me several times to check out his ranging radar and then said he was going to land. I asked him to go ahead of me so that I could test my air combat radar. 'No time', replied Igor in a tense voice and switched to the landing radio channel. A few minutes later I did the same and heard Igor's words, 'The engine's out, I'm going for an approach.' He was quite close to the airfield, so he turned outbound and immediately extended his undercarriage, which was a mistake. When he turned inbound again he was too low to make it to the runway. I was in the air about two kilometres away from him, and I saw him gliding over the nearby town. Igor could have ejected, but his machine would have crashed into the town. To make it over the town and the railway station on its edge, Igor gradually reduced the glidepath angle, but it led to a loss of speed. By the time he left the town behind him his speed was so low that he did not touch down but hit the ground with a large vertical speed. As I saw him land roughly, I still hoped against hope that he would pull out alive, but, alas, he suffered severe internal injuries and broke his skull against the gunsight.

Maybe one really feels when his end is near. I remembered that after Korovin's death Igor seemed to have changed; it was apparent that he was nervous. A few days before the tragedy I had flown as his co-pilot in a trainer Il-28. Sometime during the flight our pump for transferring fuel from the front to the rear tanks failed, causing a forward shift of the centre of gravity. Igor began to worry that the elevator pitch-up authority would be insufficient for landing. I tried to calm him, saying that if the worst came to the worst we would do a high-speed landing. I suggested putting the port-side engine to idle and speeding up the other, which was fed from the front fuel tanks. The centre of gravity moved backward and we landed without a mishap. His worry had seemed excessive to me, but I did not attach any significance to it. If I had only known what was about to happen. And what if I had? Could I have told our CO Ivanov that Sokolov was getting nervous, and that he had better be replaced in the Su-7 tests? Would they have understood me? And would Igor have understood me himself?

What was particularly painful to know was that the real cause of the tragedy was the deficient layout of the cockpit, which led to Igor's fatal mistake. After he had completed his attacks Igor wanted to turn off the range radar switch, which was one in a long row of similar switches on the starboard panel of the cockpit next to a vital engine switch, the one that turned off the engine automatics for compressor-flow stability at low rpm. When his machine was examined afterwards it was discovered that the engine automatics switch was in the 'off' position, while the radar switch was still on. So Igor turned off the wrong switch. At first it did not affect the engine, but as he throttled down the engine surged and flamed out. A surge is a violation of the normal airflow in the engine or in the engine air inlet when the incoming mass of air is larger than the engine can 'swallow'. It can happen when the engine is throttled down at high speed, and the air stream begins pulsing, causing the turbine blades to overheat or the engine to flame out. To let the excess air out the engine was provided with an air outlet valve, and it was this valve control that Igor turned off by mistake. Unfortunately, deficiencies in the cockpit layout are a fairly common thing. I have earlier described an incident from my own experience, when I got hold of the wrong lever (of the two nearly identical ones next to each other) and cut the engine fuel supply.

Not long after Igor's accident I was summoned by the No. 1 Flight Test Department Commander, General Rychkov, who told me of the decision to introduce the position of another No. 1 Section Deputy Commander in charge of flight missions and to appoint me to it. I was a little surprised to hear that, for I had never had any thoughts of promotion at all. I did not consider myself experienced enough for one thing, and besides, I had never coveted any commanding positions.

Although the word 'section' as such can hardly seem impressive, in those days our flight testing section was a very important unit within the Institute. I have earlier said that it comprised pilots, engineers and aircraft technicians, and its overall staff consisted of nearly two hundred people. Our park normally housed up to twenty-five aeroplanes – our own machines plus the ones we received for testing. Moreover, the flight test section was the principal structural unit of the Institute for determining the technical policy for each given category of aircraft. The final decisions were naturally made by the department, the Institute and the

Air Force Command, but they were prepared and vindicated by the section, which was thus answerable to the State for the quality and safety of flight testing and for the accuracy in the assessment of tested aircraft. Besides, the section participated in evolving the relevant military specifications.

By that time Molotkov had been appointed Deputy Institute Commander and Ivanov was the Section Commander, with two deputies: Melnikov (in charge of test projects) and Beregovoi (in charge of flight missions). One of the most highly respected pilots, Kuvshinov, had become the Institute inspector pilot, and another three veterans had for various reasons resigned. Next in line, both in terms of experience and in terms of his authority with the pilots, was Vasily Kotlov. I pointed it out to General Rychkov. 'No, we wouldn't appoint Kotlov; he has no higher education.' I said I would think it over and went straight to Kotlov to tell him of the conversation. He was visibly upset, yet said, 'True, they'd not appoint me anyway, so go ahead and accept.' Almost immediately after my appointment Ivanov got seriously ill, and I was put in charge of the section for nearly two months.

Never ever in my life, before or after, did I feel so unnerved and embarrassed on account of a promotion. Just to think that I was to enter our briefing room as a commander, the room where I used to sit together with all the other pilots, and not in the front row either; the room where I used to rise with them all at the commander's entry. And now my fellow pilots and friends (several of whom I considered to be more experienced than I was) were getting up to their feet at the 'Attention!' command called out when I came in for a briefing. It took me a long time to get used to it, and I suspect that my embarrassment was no secret to anyone. I never had a commander's ambition possessed by some of my colleagues, who would be perfectly at ease in their new position as soon as they had been elevated to it. I have never been like that, and I may claim without false modesty that whatever positions I was appointed to in my career, I never changed my behaviour towards other people, and I could not help feeling that they repaid me with their respect. I would hardly ever use a 'commander's tone' and certainly never raised my voice to give an order to reprimand a subordinate – for 'lack of character', as some thought. Maybe my character did have something to do with it, but the main reason was that yelling at people has always been very far from my idea of a commander's true authority.

In 1958 we received a new aircraft to be tested, the SM-12, a modification of the MiG-19P and basically similar to it, but a much faster one. Its nose air intake had sharp edges (not rounded ones as in the MiG-19), which served to reduce pressure loss at supersonic speed. Its central air intake cone, which also covered the ranging radar antenna, was designed to extend in the forward position at a certain Mach number, reducing the intake cross-section and, accordingly, the air flow intake, thus protecting the engine from surging. Besides, the SM-12 had an afterburner with a greater thrust, and a number of other improvements.

The project engineer for the SM-12 was Konstantin Osipov, and Kuvshinov, Kotlov and I were appointed project pilots (there were several other evaluation pilots too). It fell to me to test the SM-12's maximum speed and ceiling. Thanks to the innovations I have described, both its maximum speed and its ceiling turned out to be higher than that of the MiG-19, by 500 kph and over 500 metres respectively. In two flights I reached the speed of 1,930 kph. It was the first such result in the experience of the Institute; only two of Sukhoi's prototypes had achieved higher speeds at the time (they were flight tested at Zhukovsky air base by two pilots 'borrowed' from our section, Vladimir Makhalin and Nikolai Korovushkin). In testing its static ceiling I went up to 18,000 metres, and then over 20,000 metres by the dynamic method, i.e., in a zoom from a maximum speed. A more powerful afterburner naturally increased the fuel consumption, whereas the tanks were no bigger than before. So there was just about enough fuel to achieve the top speed or the ceiling, after which only the so-called 'bingo' (emergency) fuel was left. That was when my experience of dead-stick landings came in handy.

My maximum speed flight would proceed like this. I would first climb outward up to 10,000 metres and then turn back towards the airfield, speeding up to top speed in level flight with full afterburner on. At the end of the run the acceleration got slower while fuel was running out faster, and soon the fuel warning light came on: 550 litres left. My eyes would race from the speed indicator to the fuel gauge, from the fuel gauge to the airfield (the weather was clear), and again and again. Finally, the speed indicator needle would freeze: I had reached the limit speed. There would be no more than 220 litres of fuel left by that time. I would throttle the engine to idle and start gliding, without touching the throttle lever, up to the end of the landing run after touchdown. By this time I would have only about 100 litres left in the tanks, barely enough for three minutes' work of the engines. All my flights at maximum speed or maximum ceiling in the SM-12 ended in this manner.

In the draft of the test statement (and in the pilots' comments attached to it) we wrote that the aircraft could be recommended for serial production with the removal of certain faults. One of them was the deficient cooling of the exhaust tube, and the other the insufficient fuel quantity. The Institute Commander, who signed the final version of the statement, changed '*with* the removal' for '*after* the removal'. It would seem the same thing, yet there was a difference: in the former case the removal of the defects would have gone parallel with its production on the factory lines, and in the latter the production could not begin until the faults were removed and the aircraft retested. Artem Mikoyan, on reading the statement, gave up on the machine altogether. Nobody could be sure it would be approved for production after the additional work, and besides, he had a new aircraft about to be ready, the prototype MiG-21, designated E-6.

It was a pity that this machine was not adopted in the force. It represented a unique case where a major improvement in flight performance could have been achieved through a very minor alteration of the design, which would not even require a change in the manufacturing process. Nor would transition training of either the pilots or maintenance personnel be needed. One could say the upgrading would have been accomplished at no cost at all. Even if its maximum speed was not practicable without the addition of new external tanks, it was still better than the MiG-19 in that it achieved the MiG-19's top speed and ceiling faster and with lower fuel consumption. Incidentally, in China they used the SM-12 improvements in the machine they were manufacturing under a Soviet licence and successfully produced it for several years.

Later that year I was again sent to Akhtubinsk. They received four Yak-27K prototypes to be tested for a new armament system which consisted of an airborne radar and the K-8 guided missiles (designed by M. Bisnovat) with infra-red homing heads. The Rocket Test Centre Air Regiment Commander Khitrov and the industry test pilot Zavadsky (as his instructor) were taking off for what would have been Khitrov's first flight in one of the new machines, when the aircraft pitched up sharply after they began the rotation, unstuck prematurely, went steeply up and, having lost speed, crashed, killing both pilots. It was established that the reason was the Yak-27K's angle-of-attack instability, similar to what we had experienced in the SM-2 and Yak-25, of which I have told earlier. After that accident operational pilots were forbidden to fly this machine, and FTI pilots were called in: George Beregovoi, Piotr Kabrelev and me.

In these tests my radar operator Burlakov and I shot down a radio-controlled target aeroplane Il-28 with a K-8 missile for the first time. It was my first guided missile launch at an air target. The ground-based radar guided us towards the target and the operator in the rear cockpit detected the target on the radar screen and locked on it, after which the target blip appeared on my radar indicator. I performed fuselage aiming at the target blip, and at a range of about 3,000 metres the 'missile-head-lock-on' light came on, followed by the 'launch permitted' light. I pressed the firing button but the missile didn't budge from the rails. I asked the operator if there was something he forgot to do; he replied no, he had checked it all. In the meantime our target for some reason gained height while losing speed, and we caught up with it. I had to reduce speed to the minimum, so my machine started rocking, but the distance still kept shrinking until we were about 1,000 metres from the target (to launch a rocket at a closer range would be dangerous because we could be hit by the splinters). I kept the firing button pressed all the while, but nothing happened. And then, as I was about to abort the attack, the missile came off the rails and headed for the target. Almost immediately there was a powerful explosion and a cloud of splinters. To dodge them I had to turn off rather sharply, which at our low speed meant doing it on the verge of stalling.

In one of the subsequent flights, performed by Piotr Kabrelev, another potential hazard developed. The missile only partially came off the rails and jammed nose-down under the wing. Kabrelev and his operator Inkov had every reason to eject, for at touchdown the rocket could hit the ground and explode. However, they opted for a risky landing and Kabrelev managed it well. The chief designer showed his appreciation of their courage (which saved the machine) with valuable gifts.

One day, when George Beregovoi and I were in the briefing room together, our project engineer came in to say that the infra-red homing heads had to be tested in night flights. He asked us how long we would require for practising (we had neither flown these machines nor used that airfield at night). George and I exchanged glances, and George said, 'You may plan test flights for tomorrow night.' To the engineers' great satisfaction we did all the required night-time testing in two aircraft in two nights. However, it was not all that easy; it turned out that night flying was more difficult from this airfield than from our Moscow base. In Moscow, when you flew under the clouds you saw many lights which helped your attitude orientation; in Akhtubinsk, when I emerged from under the clouds after my mission was done, all I saw underneath was solid blackness, as if I were flying over the sea. Although my altimeter was showing 800 metres, it seemed that I was about to hit the ground, and I could not make myself descend any further. It was only during the final, when I actually saw the landing lights, that I began to descend. This experience brought back memories of my night flights during the war.

These tests, together with the parallel programme of launching missiles from the MiG-19, became the starting point of a new stage of my work, which for many years linked me with the air base and the living compound at Akhtubinsk (at that time called Vladimirovka, after the nearest village).

In the mid-1950s, during one of the recurrent peaks of the Cold War, there were several incidents when US reconnaissance aeroplanes flying over Soviet territory proved to be out of reach of our fighters. Besides, the Americans launched a great number of high-altitude balloons with fairly sophisticated photo-reconnaissance equipment. The balloons reached up to twenty kilometres and more, and, carried by the regular eastbound air currents, flew over the Soviet Union as far as South-East Asia, where they were picked up (the container attached to the balloon had a pictorial instruction showing that if such a balloon were found it had to be reported to the nearest US mission). The US Air Force also had high-altitude bombers and high-altitude cruise missiles. In view of all this, our aircraft design companies were instructed to create a machine that could intercept an enemy aircraft at twenty kilometres and higher.

The Mikoyan company created a version of the MiG-19, the MiG-19SV, with an upgraded afterburner which increased both its vertical speed and its ceiling. Yet it could only reach the required height by the dynamic method – in a climb, trading speed for altitude as it were, and therefore only for a short while. At the same time Mikoyan was developing another version of the MiG-19 with a pod-mounted rocket engine supplied with additional fuel and oxidant tanks. This aircraft had a ceiling of twenty-four kilometres. Its factory tests were conducted by aviation industry test pilots (among them my friends V. Vasin and A. Shcherbakov) and the military certification tests by our engineer-pilots, Piotr Kabrelev and Sergei Petrov, both recent graduates of the Zhukovsky Air Force Academy. Two air defence pilots also took part in the tests. Their project engineer was Vasily Belodedenko. As a result of that test project Kabrelev and Petrov became the first Soviet Air Force pilots to negotiate altitudes considerably higher than twenty kilometres.

However, the tests showed that a high-altitude fighter with cannon armament and visual estimation guidance by ground-based radar screen could not ensure high-altitude interception. At very high altitudes the pilot normally had far more trouble detecting another aircraft visually than at lower heights, especially if the guidance received from the ground lacked precision and the onboard radar had insufficient range and scanning angle. Even if you caught sight of the target, the very high true air speed at which your fighter flew at extreme altitudes made it very difficult to approach it close enough for aimed cannon fire. So it was decided that a more precise automated guidance from the ground was essential for interception, and that the aircraft should be armed with guided missiles.

First Sukhoi and Lavochkin, then Mikoyan, and finally Yakovlev and Tupolev joined forces with missile designers and the radio industry for the development of what became known as 'interception complexes'. They consisted of a fighter, armed with guided or homing missiles, and a ground-based automated guidance system, designed to suit all types of aircraft. The first such complex to be tested was the Su-9-51, which proved to be an important development in our aviation technology and played a large part in my flying career. The complex was based on Pavel Sukhoi's delta-wing Su-9 fighter fitted with the AL-7 engines. Its air combat radar was designed by the company unofficially known as the 'Beria Design Company', for one of its former (until mid-1953) heads had been Lavrenty Beria's son Sergo. The fighter was armed with four K-5 beam-riding guided missiles (already familiar to me from the MiG-19PM). There was no other armament on board.

The new element of the system was the guidance system 'Air-1' (the digits in the names of the complex components formed its production designation, the Su-9-51). The Air-1 guidance system consisted of a number of ground radar stations linked to one another through an automatic data communication network (dubbed the 'web'). All data were accumulated by the command guidance centre and converted to its co-ordinates. The computer installed at the centre figured out the interception track on the basis of the data received (the azimuth, distance and altitude of the target aircraft) and evolved the steering commands to the interceptor: the heading and the speed (initially it had been an analogue computer, later replaced with a digital one). These commands, complemented by the interception altitude and the discrete range-to-range information, were automatically transmitted through the data radio channel to the pilot's indicators. The pilot approached the target astern by adjusting the instrument needles with the command marks that were controlled from the ground until the target was detected by his own onboard radar. Having come within seven or eight kilometres of the target, he selected the radar lock-on mode, adjusted the aiming at the target symbol on the gunsight reflector and, once the missile-effective range was reached, he could launch his missiles. The minimum and the maximum limit ranges were indicated on the target symbol.

The Su-9-51 tests were conducted by Beregovoi, Korovushkin and Fadeev, while the design company was at first represented by Ilyushin, Kobeshchan and Koznov. The team was led by Vasily Belodedenko of the FTI. The test programme was superintended by a state commission headed by Colonel General Agaltsev, with the First Deputy of the Aviation Industry Minister, Boris Kuprianov, as his second-in-command. By that time I had been appointed Assistant Institute Commander, and I was sent to the Akhtubinsk air base to supervise the test flights and to represent the Institute in the state commission. Besides, I was named as the evaluation pilot on the project. These must have been the first military certification tests conducted on such a scale and with such active participation of the aviation industry (they were officially named 'Joint Military Certification Tests'). They began in November 1958.

I made my first flight after the three project pilots on 27 December. (In my personal logbooks there are the dates of my first flights in the other new-generation Mach-2-plus aircraft: the Su-7 on 29 November 1958; the MiG-21 on 17 December 1959; and the Su-7B on 6 February 1960. In March 1960 I was the first pilot to fly the MiG-21 at night.) I liked the Su-9 very much – its handling was benign and its controls light and sensitive. Elated at its responsiveness, I got carried away and performed an aileron roll right over the runway threshold at a thousand metres, rather hoping that no one would spot me doing it. There was no comment upon landing, but Boris Kuprianov later told me that he had seen my 'stunt', adding that no one had done any aerobatics in that machine before. The Su-9 sped up very easily and climbed up fast. As a matter of fact for a long time it remained the absolute leader among our aircraft in flight performance in terms of ceiling, rate of climb and acceleration. The MiG-23 exceeded the Su-9 in speed alone. It was only the MiG-25, which appeared in the late 1960s, that had a higher speed and a higher ceiling than the Su-9, but it was an aircraft of a new generation.

The point is that the development of fighter aviation was at that time more or less confined to fitting the aircraft with more and more powerful radars, missiles and automated control systems. As a result the aircraft gained in weight and lost in the thrust-to-weight ratio. The aeroplanes themselves, seen simply as flying vehicles, were deteriorating in their flight performance parameters even though their interception and battle performance were improving due to greater target acquisition and missile firing ranges. The prevalent view of the day was that the appearance of missiles had rendered close-distance manoeuvrable air combat unimportant. The fallacy was not realised by the high command until later, during the war in the Middle East, when it became clear that there was a great need for high-performance and manoeuvrable aircraft as well as for cannon on board. I must say that our Institute had always maintained this view.

Some time afterwards I made the Su-9's maiden interception mission, with a Tu-16 bomber as my target. I was guided to the target by the Air-1 ground system, and the flight was performed at subsonic speed and medium altitude. Later, the Su-9 project pilots performed interceptions of the Yak-25RV at altitudes of about twenty kilometres. The Yak-25RV had been created as a kind of counterpart to the US U-2 reconnaissance aeroplane but without its reconnaissance equipment. It was a derivative of the Yak-25 interceptor, whose sweptback wings were replaced with straight ones with a high aspect ratio. Thanks to this alteration the aeroplane could climb up to about twenty kilometres at subsonic speed.

In the subsonic Yak-25RV, as in the American U-2 and later in Myasishchev's M-17, strange though it might seem, the ceiling was limited to the minimum indicated air speed at which it could maintain level flight. The minimum air speed, which is measured according to the dynamic air-flow pressure, is roughly the same at all altitudes, but the higher the altitude the lower the air density, and the aircraft has to fly at a much greater true air speed in order to maintain the given indicated speed. At twenty kilometres the indicated air speed of 200 kph corresponds to the true air speed of nearly 800 kph, which is quite close to the speed of sound (Mach 0.78). If the aircraft climbs any higher, its true air speed (at the same indicated speed) and the Mach number will grow, which in an aircraft with a straight wing is simply out of the question. Therefore, the ceiling could only be increased (provided the engines had adequate thrust) by reducing the minimum indicated speed for a level flight. This was not a trivial task and it involved the lengthening of the wing, which of course affected the weight of the aeroplane. Another method, later used by Myasischev in his M-17, was to increase the lift power of the wing by adding various kinds of flap. As a result, the M-17's minimum indicated speed dropped down to almost 160 kph, with its design maximum altitude rising to twenty-four kilometres.

We used the Yak-25RV as a target aircraft 'personifying' an enemy reconnaissance plane in our interception flights in the Su-9. It was then piloted by my friend Alexander Shcherbakov. (Later the Yak-25RV was modified to be used as an unmanned target.) The Yak-25RV would fly at about 19,000 metres at the true air speed of 800 kph or so. The interception of such relatively 'slow' aircraft is a harder task. The interceptor's high-altitude speed was at least 1,800 kph, so its closure speed with the target was over 1,000 kph. The pilot had just about forty seconds after the appearance of the target blip on the radar screen to adjust his course, to lock on the target, to perform fuselage aiming and finally to simulate the missile launch at a safe range. In attacking a high-speed target, the time available was much longer.

The Su-9-51 tests could be described as 'pioneering' in many respects, first of all in terms of speed. Speeds of over 2,000 kph at high altitudes were conquered for the first time, with the first ever missile launches performed in such regimes. These flights did not always go smoothly, and solving the problems which accompanied them proved essential for aviation development as a whole. As targets for such launches we used balloons. A balloon was to rise up to about twenty kilometres and arrive at the firing area, which was fairly limited in size, but the balloon obeyed the air currents and they were different at different heights. We would first launch a pilot balloon to determine the speed and direction of the wind, and then calculate the optimum starting point for the target balloon so that it would drift into the firing area by the time it had climbed up to the necessary height. The calculated starting point often turned out to be somewhere far into the roadless steppe. It is easy to imagine what difficulties the target launch team had to go through, especially in winter or in periods of rain and slush. Sometimes, even as they were making their way to the starting point, the wind would change and they had to move to a different place, or else the wind would change just after the launch and the balloon would go astray, frustrating all work.

The missile launch flights were mainly performed by George Beregovoi. Several of his flights developed according to the same unfortunate pattern. When, after all mishaps and misadventures, the balloon was at last about to appear in the firing area, George took off, got up to 10,000 metres, accelerated to Mach 1.9 and climbed up to 20,000 metres and then his engine surged! He had only six or seven seconds to close the throttle so as to cut off the fuel or else the turbine blades would have overheated and burned. Beregovoi acted confidently and neatly: he shut down the engine and descended for a restart, but the missile launching was disrupted. A number of balloons were wasted in this manner. In one flight George noticed that the exhaust gas temperature needle shifted from its position, and he immediately cut off the engine without waiting for the actual surge, for a series of previous flights had taught him to expect it.

At the briefing afterwards the industry representatives expressed doubt that a surge had been about to start and blamed him for disrupting a missile launch. Unfortunately it is only too common for a test pilot's report of a malfunction or the aircraft's misdemeanour to be mistrusted or questioned by the designers or manufacturers. As a result, Beregovoi began thinking that he had imagined the shifting of the temperature needle. However, when the instrument readings were taken it turned out that the temperature really had begun to rise, and George had spotted the growth of just about twenty degrees on a 1,000-degree scale! So, instead of being blamed he had to be commended for his high professionalism, keen observation and prompt reaction.

I (as many other test pilots, I am sure) also occasionally found myself in situations when I began to doubt my own in-flight experiences and perceptions under the pressure of probing questions and objections. Unfortunately, many aircraft designers and manufacturers share the tendency to blame failures and malfunctions on the pilots' mistakes rather than on a deficiency of design or a defect in the machine as such. (In combat units an opposite tendency exists: the commanders often blame almost everything on the materiel so as not to be charged with the inadequate training of their flying personnel.) I have always resented this approach. The pilot's account should be trusted without reservation (bearing in mind that it was *he* who had been in a difficult situation which might have directly threatened his life). Only if objective information (e.g. instrument readings) contradicts what the pilot is describing may his words be questioned.

Complete truthfulness when it comes to reports is one of the test pilot's essential professional qualities. Any mistake honestly admitted can be forgiven, but never a deception. Here is an episode to illustrate my point. One of our new pilots was performing a test flight for somebody else. His mission was to depressurise the cockpit at high altitude. He had his furlough papers in his pocket, as it were (and there is a belief among pilots that one should not fly the day before going on holiday: there have been several fatal accidents involving pilots who were about to go on leave), although in his case there was no particular risk involved. The pilot was wearing a high-altitude suit and everything would have gone well, but he lost his nerve and did not depressurise the cockpit. Had he confessed his momentary panic he would have got away with a reproach, but he lied that he had performed the mission, not knowing that there had been a barograph installed in the cockpit. When its readings were taken it became clear that the pilot had told a deliberate lie. Nobody could trust him after that, and he was dismissed from the Institute.

After a number of Beregovoi's flights after target balloons it became clear that the two-position air intake cone in the nose of the Su-9 did not ensure the steady work of the engine. Since that test programme was top priority, Deputy Minister Kuprianov ordered a new electronic air intake control system to be delivered. Officially it was still at the finishing stage, but its installation in the Su-9 immediately put an end to surging by automatically adjusting the intake cross-section in accordance with the flight speed, the outside air temperature and the engine rotation speed.

One day, as he was flying the Su-9, Beregovoi felt that the control stick had partially jammed: it would not move backward. The jamming of controls is one of the three most hazardous flight situations (the other two are the dis-integration of the airframe and an in-flight fire), in which ejection is usually the only option left to the pilot. After a series of useless attempts to move the stick, George jerked with all his might and it yielded. It later turned out that the stick had been jammed by a stray bolt that had somehow got into the control rod crank. George's powerful jerk on the stick flattened the bolt and it slipped out. As a token of his gratitude and his appreciation of George's self-control and presence of mind, thanks to which the machine was saved, Sukhoi presented him with a film camera and a projector.

The initial flights for the night test programme were made by Leonid Fadeev. At that time the Su-9 had an attitude indicator in which the artificial horizon line in a steep climb disappeared beyond the scale frame. On a very dark night, as Fadeev was climbing, he pitched up too steeply without knowing it and he could not see it in the attitude indicator. Soon he noticed that the speed was coming down and eased the stick a bit, yet the speed was still falling, so he pushed the stick again and again. Finally the speed came down to the stalling level, but Fadeev managed to avoid stalling by pushing the stick forward even further. He landed safely, and Boris Kuprianov immediately telephoned Moscow for a brand-new, only just tested attitude indicator without its predecessor's fault. This new instrument was then promptly installed in all our aircraft and unanimously approved by all pilots. It has remained in use to this day.

In interception test flights with the Air-1 ground guidance system there were a number of cases when the pilots failed to detect a high-altitude target by radar. It was then discovered that when the Su-9 was speeding up from subsonic speed to high Mach numbers at about 10,000 metres a deviation built up in its gyro-compass, making it pass the target by. The problem was solved through the installation of a new, precise compass system in which gyroscopic deviation was automatically corrected.

Another innovation used in the test programme was the pressure helmet, which complemented our usual partial-pressure suit. To put the helmet on, the pilot had to pull on a rubber stocking with an airtight collar round the neck. At low altitude you could fly with the visor off, but at high altitude the visor had to be tightly shut, with compressed oxygen fed underneath it. I later had to use this pressure helmet a lot, and I cannot say it was a pleasant experience. If your nose started itching, for example, there was nothing you could do about it, and if a mosquito happened to find its way under the helmet before you shut the visor it had a field day with your face. Even breathing normally in that helmet was not easy – it took getting used to. I remember how once, as I took the helmet off after a flight and bent my head down, nearly a cup of sweat came out from under my chin where it had been collected by the airtight collar. Later a better helmet replaced this first model. It fastened onto a ring connected to the collar and could be taken off on the ground while waiting for the flight.

The pressure helmet is needed in case the cockpit gets decompressed at high altitude. In the hermetic cockpit of a fighter, thanks to the pressure feed from the engine, the air pressure is maintained at the level corresponding to the altitude which is less than half of the actual flight altitude. Thus, at 20,000 metres the 'altitude' in the cockpit is between 8,000 and 9,000 metres. At such altitudes an ordinary oxygen mask is perfectly adequate. However, if what is known as 'explosive decompression' of the cockpit (for example, the canopy glass breaks) occurs, the pilot is abruptly 'tossed' up to a much higher altitude, which cannot be survived without a pressure suit and a pressure helmet. Even at fourteen kilometres normal breathing is impossible without additional oxygen fed under pressure, and with the outside air pressure very low the lungs will expand and there will not be enough muscle force to exhale. At higher altitudes it is even more dangerous. As is well known, the boiling point of liquid falls with a fall in pressure. At an altitude of 19,200 metres the outside air pressure comes down to a point where the boiling point of blood coincides with the body temperature: 36.6 degrees Celsius. What is scientifically known as 'cavitation' takes place and the blood flow stops.

In most high-altitude flights it is the so-called partial-pressure suit (with a crash helmet or a pressure helmet) that is mainly used in fighter aviation. It is covered with a system of air hoses which stretch the suit fabric to create pressure on the entire body, except hands and feet, thus making up for deficient atmospheric pressure. A hermetic full-pressure suit is occasionally used too (I had first worn one as early as 1954 to fly the SP-2), with a mixture of oxygen and air pumped up underneath it. In our air force this suit is only worn by long-range bomber pilots, for they might face a long high-altitude flight in a decompressed cockpit (a partial-pressure suit does not give protection for long in a depressurised cockpit at high altitudes).

In view of the large-scale and complicated tasks faced in the testing of air defence interception complexes, as well as in testing fighter aircraft and their various modifications, the Air Force Command made a decision to form a separate Fighter Aircraft Flight Test Department. Its official birthday was in May 1959. The new department was based on the fighter test section of the No. 1 Flight Test Department of the FTI. The newly formed department comprised test units specialising both in the aircraft as such and in all its components, so it united specialists on radar and optical aiming systems, avionics, engines, guided and unguided missiles, cannon, bomb armament, ground-based guidance systems and target aircraft. Many of them came from other departments of the Institute, and the missile and target sections were transferred from the Akhtubinsk base, together with a number of pilots of the regiment stationed there. The department received its own radar guidance control centre consisting of the Air-1 system and a remote radar station 230 kilometres into the steppe from the Akhtubinsk airfield.

I was appointed commander of the new department, and I invited Andrei Arsenovich Manucharov, our former deputy section commander, to become my deputy in charge of test projects. I was also happy to succeed in appointing my other deputy, in charge of flight missions, 'VG' Ivanov (the fact that he had no formal higher education was a serious obstacle in the eyes of my commanders). It was the best choice I could have made: an outstanding test pilot and flight commander, Ivanov was respected and loved by all.

For about a year and a half all the specialised sub-divisions which now formed the new department continued on their original premises. At Chkalovskaya we were allotted a hangar with various annexes in which there were a number of services and offices, including mine. Most of the testing was by that time conducted at Akhtubinsk, and the pilots and engineers who were involved in them were posted there for the period of the tests. My deputy Manucharov and I alternately superintended the work at Akhtubinsk and at Chkalovskaya. The next year, however, the entire department moved to Akhtubinsk.

CHAPTER 18

Charles Yeager

In 1959 Moscow hosted a conference of the International Association of Aviation (FAI). Among other guests who arrived in Moscow for the occasion were two celebrated American pilots: the record-holder Jacqueline Cochran and the famous Charles 'Chuck' Yeager, the first pilot in the world to break the sound barrier.

One day my fellow test pilot Sergei Petrov and I were summoned to the Institute Commander, who told us that Yeager, who had been a military test pilot himself, had asked to meet some Soviet Air Force test pilots. Sergei and I were picked out for that meeting. We were called into the No. 10 Department of the Defence Ministry for a briefing. One of the decisions made at that briefing was that I would not introduce myself to Yeager by my own name; my father being a Politburo member, they wanted to avoid 'irrelevant' questions (I chose my mother's maiden name, Tumanian). I asked whether I could talk to Yeager in English, and an official replied that I had better not. Luckily the briefing was attended by Anatoly Pavlov, a long-time acquaintance. He was there as a representative of the Chief Intelligence Department of the Defence Ministry. He countermanded that official's directive by saying, quite sensibly, that it would be much better if I could talk with Yeager without an interpreter – the conversation would be much more natural and easy.

At eleven o'clock next morning, in accordance with the plan, Sergei and I took a table at the Bega restaurant at the Moscow Hippodrome. Within a few minutes we saw Charles Yeager walk in with an Aeroflot representative, or so he introduced himself, though neither Sergei nor I was fooled for a minute. Yeager seemed at first somewhat strained, but as he became aware that we were real pilots and not somebody made to pose for them, he visibly relaxed and the conversation grew very friendly and animated. He addressed me directly in English, and the 'Aeroflot representative' helped Petrov to take part in the conversation.

From the restaurant we all drove to Charles Yeager's hotel in my car. There we met several other American pilots, and a group photograph was taken and immediately presented to us (we had never seen a Polaroid camera before). Among the guests was a well-known US military doctor, General William Lovelace. He made me a present of a book on the history of aviation medicine in the USA called *Doctors in the Sky*. It was from this book that I later learned of William Lovelace's contribution: in the 1930s General Lovelace, together with two other colleagues, had designed the first oxygen mask for pilots to be adopted throughout the world. In 1943 he tested his mask with an emergency oxygen bottle in a parachute jump from over 12,000 metres. It seems incredible, but it was his first ever jump! Shortly afterwards Lovelace was elected president of the US Aero-Medical Association, and remained in that post for three years. In the 1970s I was extremely sorry to read in an American aviation magazine that General Lovelace and his two daughters had crashed in his private aeroplane.

From the hotel the four of us (Yeager, his 'minder', Petrov and I) drove to Sokolniki park where an American exhibition was being prepared for the opening. On the way back the 'Aeroflot representative' surprised us by asking me to drop him off: apparently we were driving past his house. The three of us were left alone – three test pilots who, despite their belonging to different worlds, still had a lot in common and, at least when it came to their profession, understood one another perfectly well. We found a table in an open-air café in the Garden Ring and sat there chatting away for a long time. Although questions concerning the aircraft and equipment did of course 'pop up' every now and then, we did not insist on answers if they were evaded, and avoided asking about classified technology.

I vividly remember Chuck Yeager's story about his flight from USA to Okinawa at the head of a formation of twelve F-104s. They had to cover about 7,000 kilometres and they spent eight hours in the air, with two in-flight refuellings. He told us how nervous he was feeling when, with about fifteen minutes' worth of fuel left, he (and the others) met up with the air refueller in the appointed area and began coupling with the drogue, uncertain whether he would make it. And what would he do if he failed? There was, of course, a dinghy in the survival kit apart from the parachute, and there was supposed to be a warship standing by in the area of refuelling, but whether it would find any of them or not if he ejected was a big question.

At the time of our meeting Charles Yeager was only thirty-six, like Sergei Petrov, and I was a year older. However, Yeager had accumulated nearly three times more flying time than either of us. We knew that US pilots flew more hours than those in the Soviet Air Force, but Yeager told us that even by American standards he had flown a lot. With us it is only instructor pilots who have so many flying hours. Later my colleagues and I tried to find an explanation of such differences in flying time. One reason was that American pilots spent less time than we did on excessive ground preparation, a large part of which in many cases was nothing but a formality. They would also make more flights each week; with us Monday was, as a rule, a 'no flying' day, and in our combat units they alternated a day of flying with a day of ground preparation. The duration of an American pilot's individual flight could also be longer than that of his Soviet counterpart, for their aircraft had a larger fuel reserve on board than ours. Another factor reducing our flying hours was the rigidity of the flight schedule: sometimes a flight registered for a particular day would be cancelled due to unsuitable weather for the mission at hand, some malfunction or because of the previous test flight results, and to replace it with another in the schedule chart was a very difficult task. It could rarely be accomplished without a time-consuming and nerve-twisting struggle with bureaucracy, although in the 1950s the system was in fact more flexible and decisions were often made very promptly. Besides, we heard that the Americans in those days used to calculate their flying time, not from the brake release at take-off to the end of the landing run, as we did, but from the start of the engines to the moment they were shut off after taxiing to the parking ramp. This would give a noticeable addition to the total flying time, particularly on busy airfields and bases where there would be a long queue for the runway at take-off. (However, I have been recently told that today US pilots calculate their flying time the same way as we do, but with an addition of five minutes' taxiing time for each flight.)

As for us engineer-pilots, we had 'lost' six years of our total flying time while studying at the Air Force Academy, when we had very meagre opportunities to fly. Besides, flight testing did not consist of flying alone: quite a lot of time would go on the preliminary study of the new machines, on participation in various technical meetings and commissions (often involving visits to various cities), and on the investigation of accidents that took place in operational units. Yeager and other US test pilots must have had at least some of these commitments too, but maybe to a lesser extent than us; besides, whenever sent somewhere on business they would mostly fly there in their fighters, and the time involved would naturally be added to the sum total of their flying hours, whereas our pilots were not allowed to do that (I occasionally managed to do it later, but not in fighters – in transport aeroplanes).

At the time of his visit to Moscow Yeager was no longer a test pilot but a squadron commander in a combat unit. He said he had been a test pilot for about ten years – over three 'rounds' as he put it – and added that it was a lot. We were surprised, for with us none of the test pilots would ever go back to being an operational pilot. Instead, everyone would fly as a test pilot, unless they got killed or were prematurely grounded for health reasons, for about fifteen to twenty years or more, up to their retirement.

Both Petrov and I had a very warm and pleasant impression of that meeting with Charles Yeager, with whom we parted with a feeling of mutual friendliness. I am stressing this here because in 1991, when I attended a conference in England and was afterwards briefly staying with my daughters' friends Marina and John Firth in Nottingham, John showed me a book written by Yeager. In that book I came across his description of our Moscow meeting. Not only was the tone of that description totally different from the impression I had had and still remembered so well, but even the circumstances of the meeting itself were presented rather inaccurately. To start with, he wrote that it was me, not him, who had sought the meeting (naturally, 'with reconnaissance purposes'), and that I had introduced myself to him at a reception in the Kremlin (at which, incidentally, I had not been). Sergei Petrov was absent from his account altogether. I was mentioned in his book under my own name, but presented to the readers as the chief test pilot of the Mikoyan Design Company, which was something I had never been. Despite what I read I have not changed my friendly feelings towards Charles Yeager, and I prefer to think that it was something he did not really choose to write himself; it must have been done by someone else who deliberately endowed that account with the spirit 'appropriate' to the Cold War times.

Incidentally, my first meeting with John Firth took place long before my 1991 trip to the United Kingdom (where I was invited to give a paper at a conference on World War Two history held at Leeds University on the occasion of the fiftieth anniversary of the German attack on the Soviet Union). We first met in the 1970s during an international aerobatic competition in Kiev. I was there as vice-chairman of the FAS (the USSR branch of the FAI), and John, who was active in the FAI Aero-Medical Commission, accompanied the British aerobatic team (Marina was the team's interpreter, assigned to them by the Soviet hosts). In 1990 my daughter was on a three-month exchange course at Nottingham University, where Marina was a part-time teacher of Russian. On hearing my daughter's last name, Marina introduced herself and invited her home to meet her husband. They both remembered our meeting in Kiev, although there had been no contact between us whatsoever in all those years.

A few years prior to my acquaintance with Charles Yeager I had another interesting meeting with foreign colleagues. A group of Indian aviation specialists, including three pilots, paid an extended visit to the Kubinka air base to get acquainted with the MiG-17F. They had an interpreter assigned to them, of course, but he was at a loss with aviation terminology or aviation technology as such. Our Institute was applied to for help, and the Institute Commander posted me to Kubinka. To my knowledge I was the only aviation specialist in the country at the time who was not only fairly fluent in English but a test pilot into the bargain; in other words, I had both a practical 'inside' knowledge of the subject and could talk about it in English. Besides, I knew the MiG-17F quite well. My task was to describe its distinctive features, its performance and its cockpit equipment to the Indians and to brief them for their first flights in our fighters. While any of them was flying, I stood next to the tower controller and translated his commands to one of the Indian pilots who transmitted them to his colleague on board in the terms they were accustomed to. They started off by having rides in the two-seat MiG-15 with a Russian instructor pilot, and I had to translate even the onboard cockpit-to-cockpit talk. The Moscow Air Force District Commander, General Rubanov, who was superintending the joint project, said that if they had known of my knowledge of English they would have made things simpler by appointing me the Indians' instructor pilot. As it was, the order covering all aspects of the work and signed in higher quarters could not be deviated from in any way.

One of the Indian pilots, Wing Commander Suri, was a test pilot, the other two, AVM Singh and AVM Dutt, were operational unit commanders. Singh always wore a turban, which he never took off in public. Before a flight he would shelter behind some car and change his turban for a leather flying helmet. Colonel Suri had finished at a test pilots' school in Britain. He was very fluent in English, which the other two pilots spoke quite well too. I remember that as I was explaining the instrument panel layout, the Indian pilot in the cockpit seat seemed to shake his head every now and then; he would turn it to the side, only slightly inclining it down. At first I thought he did not understand what I was saying, and then I heard that he was saying 'yes' as he did it. I realised that the turning of the head was a sign of agreement or understanding, the same way as with the Bulgarians.

The Indians liked the MiG-17. They had never flown at such speeds before and wanted to know how close they came to the sonic barrier, but that type of aircraft was not equipped with a Mach number indicator; it had not been installed since it had been established that the MiG-17 would not misbehave at any Mach number it could reach, not even in vertical diving. So we had to calculate the Mach number on the basis of the true air speed they achieved. Colonel Suri was allowed to fire cannon in a dive at the target which was specially outlined on the airfield at a distance from the runway. When their flying was over for the day everyone lunched together (at the Air Force District Command's expense) in the air base mess. The last day of the project ended with a large farewell dinner in honour of our guests.

Several years later I got involved in such a project again. It was when two Indian test pilots, accompanied by aviation experts, came to Kubinka to get acquainted with the MiG-21, for which the Indian government was going to buy a production licence. This time I was directly responsible for the entire course of the pilots' ground briefing and their flights, while our engineers were engaged with the rest of the Indian delegation. The Kubinka Division Commander, Colonel Dubinsky, was for the most part only looking on and seeing to the work of the tower.

At Kubinka they did not possess a two-seat MiG-21 in their park yet, so the Indians had to fly a real combat machine from the very start. On the first day they had an official interpreter with them, but the very next morning, after he had brought them to the air base in his car, he asked me if I could bring them back to town after work and left. The pattern repeated itself the following day and on all other days of their visit. I would brief them before each flight and they would describe their flight experiences and impressions to me afterwards. Later we would have lunch with Dubinsky and then I would drive them to Moscow in my car.

One day I took them back along a different route, along the Uspenskoye road instead of the Minsk motorway. This road wound through the most beautiful parts of the Moscow countryside, in the neighbourhood of our dacha. They expressed their admiration with the words, 'It's like the countryside near London!' (both of them were graduates of a British test pilots' school). I had already been to England once by that time, so I could confirm that it had very beautiful scenery too. One of them said to me in the car one day, 'You must come to India', and then added in a low voice after a pause, 'You can't imagine what a poor country it is.'

After two or three days of the joint project I was called, with the engineers, to a meeting at the Chief Engineering Department, responsible for the selling of our military equipment and matériel abroad. We were shown the list of criticisms handed over to them by the Indians. The list was extensive, but most criticisms coincided with the ones that had earlier been entered by the FTI test pilots and engineers into the MiG-21F test programme final statement. The MiG-21F was no longer our latest machine at the time; we had already tested the more advanced MiG-21PF, from which many of the earlier faults, including those noticed by the Indian pilots, had been removed. However, we had no right even to mention this aircraft to them. Their major criticism of the MiG-21F was that it had no radar. It was frustrating to hear, not being able to say that our latest machine had it all right! The last we heard at that meeting was that the Indian side were not particularly keen on purchasing the aircraft we had been demonstrating to them.

The following Sunday, over lunch at the dacha, I told my father of the work with the Indian group (at that time he was still superintending the country's foreign trade). I said that every advanced fighter in the world except fighter bombers was already equipped with onboard radar, our MiG-21F being a notable exception, due to which the deal with India was not likely to go through. My father asked me if we possessed a more advanced machine than the MiG-21PF (there was a ban on selling the very latest specimens of military technology at that time). I replied that we were currently testing a MiG-21S with a more sophisticated onboard radar, known as 'Sapfir' ('Sapphire'). It had a larger search range than the 'Emerald' installed in the MiG-21PF. Two days later we were summoned to the Chief Engineering Department again and instructed to demonstrate the MiG-21PF to the Indian party with a full briefing on it. As a result, the production licence was bought and India manufactured the MiG-21PF for many years to come.

This incident reminds me of some other similar cases when I inadvertently happened to assist my father's work with some information I gave him. Thus, back in the early 1950s, my wife and I were on holiday in Czechoslovakia and from there made a fleeting visit to Vienna. On our return we handed over to my father some prospectuses on motor-scooters which we had picked up in a shop in Vienna, as well as some paper carrier bags with handles and company logos (which had contained the souvenirs we had bought). After that the USSR purchased a production licence for scooters and also began producing paper carrier bags, of which our people had no notion before. On another occasion I called in at a hardware and instrument shop on Kirov street and heard from a salesman there that the shop was about to be closed down (it was the only, and extremely popular, shop of its kind in Moscow). I told this to my father, and the shop remained as it was. In 1953 Ella and I were in Czechoslovakia again, and on our return Ella showed my father the cotton tights she had bought for our children. At that time tights, whether for women or for children, were totally unknown in Russia. Father 'requisitioned' two pairs and handed them over to the 'hosiery people' as samples. Soon children's tights appeared on the shelves of Russian shops and were an immediate success.

In the summer of 1960 a demonstration of combat aircraft to government members was organised at the Akhtubinsk air base. The group of guests was headed by Khrushchev himself, and included Politburo members Brezhnev, Kozlov and a number of bigwigs from the Central Committee. All chief aircraft designers came too, as well as the ministers of defence, aviation, radio industry and defence industry, the commanders-in-chief of all branches of the army and other high-ranking officials. The demonstration began on the ground, where the guests were shown various aeroplanes, missiles and other pieces of aviation technology.

I was delegated to tell them about the Su-9-51 interception complex. The guests were seated on the chairs placed in an open space outside the building of the guidance centre, with a display of relevant posters arranged in front of them.

After my talk (with which everyone seemed to be satisfied) they were shown an actual high-altitude interception of a Yak-25RV by a Su-9 interceptor. The guidance station room was too small to accommodate all the guests, so it was only Khrushchev, Defence Minister Malinovsky and another official who were there during the interception. The Su-9 was piloted by George Beregovoi. Khrushchev was seated in front of the radarscope and I was standing by his side and giving explanations. He was watching and listening with apparent fascination. As the target was detected by the remote ground radar station, the relevant data were transmitted from that station to the computer of the guidance centre, which evolved the commands for the interceptor: the heading and air speed, the ultimate altitude, and the target distance data. Suddenly the mission engineer, Captain Rumiantsev, came up to me and whispered into my ear that the automatic command relay system had failed. I decided to let the guests know the truth and repeated his report aloud, explaining that the computer commands would be transmitted to the pilot over the radio. Later I regretted not having taken that opportunity to point out the advantages of a piloted aircraft over guided missiles to Khrushchev. As for the demonstration itself, Beregovoi did an excellent job and the interception with a simulated missile launch was successful.

After that there was a series of demonstrations on the firing range: bombing, actual missile launching and real cannon fire, with disused aircraft and tanks as targets placed in the field two or three kilometres from the guest stands (erected on the firing range for such occasions). A number of unmanned radio-controlled target aeroplanes were guided over the range and shot down with missiles from fighters right in front of the stands.

A characteristic episode took place during one of the ground aircraft demonstrations. All the distinguished guests, with Khrushchev at their head, were seated under an awning set up in front of a MiG-21PF, and its test project engineer, Colonel Bako, was reporting on this machine. Its designer, my uncle Artem Mikoyan, was in the audience too. I, as the new Flight Test Department Commander, was standing next to the principal guests. At the end of his report, having pointed out all the merits of the aircraft, Colonel Bako said, 'However, the MiG-21PF has one serious shortcoming.' 'What is it?' asked Khrushchev promptly. 'It has no gun.' Khrushchev waved a dismissive hand. 'Why does it need a cannon if it has missiles?' It was, in fact, a matter of great importance. Our engineers and pilots, as well as the Institute Command, were convinced that guns were an essential part of fighter armament. We knew that there could occur wartime situations when fighter aircraft, failing to destroy all hostile aeroplanes in the first attack, would confront the enemy at close range and get engaged in a dog-fight. In such a situation the cannon was the only practicable weapon, for neither the K-5 missile nor its successors could hit a highly agile target at close quarters (later there appeared a new type of missile, the K-60 agile missiles, but they did not remove the necessity of cannon either).

However, Khrushchev's obsession with missiles, as was the custom of the time, was taken up by the whole government and all high-ranking commanders. As a result, the fighters armed with missiles were no longer fitted with cannon. It even suited the designers, for they were spared the layout problems: it was not an easy task to fit a cannon into the nose of an aeroplane packed with radar antennae and other equipment. The original MiG-21 had been armed with two 30 mm cannon in the front part of the fuselage; the MiG-21F, which had two K-13 missiles, was left with one cannon on the right side. Even that was done away with in the MiG-21PF, which was equipped with a radar. Several years later, however, the experience of the Middle East and the Vietnam wars showed that we had been right all the time. Cannon reappeared on fighters (usually fitted under the belly), and the manoeuvrability of aircraft became the order of the day again.

Many years later, in 1972, there was a similar demonstration of military aviation to the leadership of the country. Brezhnev, Kosyghin and Podgorny, accompanied by a great many military and civilian officials, arrived at the Akhtubinsk air base after a visit to the ballistic missile range in Kapustin Yar. My position at that time was already that of the First Deputy Commander of the Flight Test Institute, so together with other members of the Institute Command and several generals from Moscow I met the distinguished guests on their arrival. As they got out of the cars and walked past our reception line, shaking everyone's hands, Brezhnev saw me and said, 'Ah, Stepan, I saw you here last time, didn't I?' I confirmed that he was right. As before, the visitors were first shown the aircraft and their armaments on the ground. Alexei Kosyghin called me to his side and asked me to give him some additional explanations. I still keep the photographs taken on that day. Like the first time, it culminated in an actual warfare demonstration on our firing range.

Back in 1960, the pilots and the Institute commanding officers who demonstrated the aircraft and armaments to Khrushchev and other guests were rewarded by the Defence Minister with 'valuable gifts'. The pilots and I received sporting guns. My friend Mikhail Tvelenev, a war veteran and a dedicated fisherman and hunter, said, 'Stepan, you don't hunt, and you've got a more powerful gun. Let's swap – mine is of a smaller calibre.' I agreed, and we changed the name plates on the guns.

The MiG-21PF, which we had shown to Khrushchev and the others, was then being tested as part of our second interception complex. The ground-based guidance system was the same as with the Su-9, but the aircraft missiles were different. They were the new K-13 missiles, which I have already mentioned and of which I shall now say a few words. It was an exact replica of the US Sidewinder, which we received from China (with whom the Soviet Union was still on friendly terms then), on whose territory a few unexploded Sidewinders had fallen. They had been launched during some air clashes with Taiwan. Both Chinese and Soviet designers (for us it was I. Toropov, later succeeded by A. Lyapin) set out to copy them.

An ordinary guided or homing missile is in fact a kind of small unmanned aircraft. It has an engine, which accelerates it to a great speed within seconds, after which it is pushed forward by its own momentum. Like an aircraft it has aerodynamic control surfaces, and the pilot's role is performed by its homing head and by an autopilot which controls and stabilises its flight. There are two standard types of homing heads: the infra-red (IR) and the radar homing heads.

The infra-red detects and locks on the heat radiation of the target engine, while the radar homing head locks on the target with the help of the radar beam emitted from the launching aircraft and reflected from the illuminated target. Such missiles are supplied with two types of fuse: the proximity fuse and the impact fuse. The former will detect a target if the missile is passing close to it, and detonate the charge.

The Sidewinder was quite a breakthrough in missile technology. It is still in service in the majority of countries that possess fighter aviation. Its smart design allowed it to do without an autopilot (its infra-red head and homing head commands are directly transmitted to the controls) and therefore made it a much simpler and cheaper product. The pilot aimed at the target with the help of his gunsight, with a level sound signal of the homing head in his headphones. As soon as the missile head spotted the source of heat radiation, the tone of the signal changed. The change indicated to the pilot that the target was detected and locked on, and a missile could be launched. In contrast with other missiles, the Sidewinder reacted even to very low heat radiation, and had an unusual optical impact fuse. They say that the inventors of the Sidewinder had received an honorary award for the originality and simplicity of its design.

I happened to participate in the very first tests of the K-13 missiles, fitted on two of our SM-12 machines. The tests began at the end of 1959. For a start, we launched the K-13s at illuminating bombs, and then at unmanned radio-controlled MiG-15s and Il-28s. I was the first pilot to hit the Il-28 target at a wide aspect ratio. I began the attack almost at a right angle to the target flight path, but the rocket was launched at the fifty-degree aspect ratio. It performed a tight turn, caught up with the target and exploded at its tail. The Il-28 was destroyed and fell down in fragments.

The next stage in the missile tests was the high-altitude target mission. By that time an unmanned radio-controlled version of the MiG-19 had been made available, and we used it as our high-altitude supersonic target. It flew at 16,000 metres and was attacked by three aircraft one after another. Vasily Kotlov and I were in MiG-21s, and Eduard Knyazev in a SM-12. Unfortunately none of us succeeded in hitting it; the fuse time delay was too short in relation to the speed of the target and the missiles exploded a few metres short of its tail. I was the last of the three. My launch having ended the same way as the previous two, I came up rather close to the MiG-19 and for a while flew on its wing. It was a striking yet bizarre sight: a beautiful aeroplane against the deep-blue sky with a blazing afterburner stream behind it and no one in the cockpit! It was time to return, and I forced myself to break off and turn for home. In the meantime the tower sent a 'liquidation' command to the target, cutting off the engines and applying full ailerons for roll. I could no longer see it, yet I felt strangely sorry for it, as though it were a living creature about to die.

The missile fuses were later improved, and a high-altitude MiG-19 target was successfully destroyed. I must explain that the first two of the attacking aircraft usually carry missiles with their warheads removed. The idea is to use one and the same target for a number of launches, thus receiving more data. The missile does not necessarily have to hit the target; it is sufficient if the fuse action occurs within the so-called warhead radius of effects. The fuse action moment is filmed by ground-based cinetheodolite stations. In addition, telemetry proximity data can often be received from the target itself. The last of the attacking aircraft launches missiles with warheads, or so-called 'live' missiles. In this way one and the same target is normally used for up to five or six missile launches before it gets destroyed. However, there have been cases when the target received a direct hit from the very first rocket, and the others, to the test pilots' and engineers' disappointment, were left without a target. In such cases there were less data received as a result of the tests.

In one such 'combat work', as we called these missions, Eduard Knyazev found himself in a difficult situation. In preparation for a flight, two live missiles were hung onto his SM-12, and nobody remembered that his fuel reserve was smaller than that of the other attacking aircraft, the MiG-21. The mission took a little longer than usual, and the target flew off rather far from the airfield. Knyazev was the last to attack and hit the target. On the way home after the attack he realised he was short of fuel and might not make it to the airfield. His actions were level-headed and very sensible: he climbed up to 11,000 metres and travelled at that altitude until he was sufficiently near home to glide down to the runway with the engines off. The fuel was almost up, and to use it for the glide-down meant he could be left without a drop, and it might be needed for the final approach. Knyazev made a bold decision and cut both engines off. Some of our test pilots, including me, had had to cut one engine off to save fuel on the glide-down, but to kill *both*? He restarted the engines on the landing circuit and touched down safely.

In 1960–1 Leonid Peterin, Arkady Bersenev and I were project pilots in the tests of the interception complex with the prototype MiG-21PF. In one of the flights I made rather a silly mistake. I happened to be the first (as before, in the Su-9) to perform an interception mission with guidance from the ground-based Air-1 system in radio silence, i.e., with no voiced commands on the radio. I was flying by the commands radio-transmitted from the ground straight to my flight and navigation indicators. After a while the tower asked me what my heading was. On hearing my reply, they commanded, 'Mission cancelled, return to base.' I was surprised and asked what the matter was. 'Your heading is incorrect', came the answer. I realised what had happened. In accordance with my mission I had to press the heading co-ordination button (to co-ordinate my gyro-compass to the magnetic one) only after lining up for the take-off. So I had not done it on leaving the ramp, as I habitually did, and by the time I reached the runway for take-off I forgot about it. As a result my machine was guided not towards the target but far away from it. The mission was frustrated and the flight had to be repeated. I was terribly upset, especially so because I had failed to live up to my reputation as an interception expert, and also because in that test project the aviation industry was represented by none other than my younger brother Vanya, the MiG-21PF project designer.

It is common knowledge that military aircraft are fitted with ejector seats, which in the case of an accident are ejected from the aeroplane with the help of a gunpowder charge or a rocket engine. The first ejector seat was designed in Germany towards the end of World War Two. In our aircraft the mechanism operating the seat was interlocked with the cockpit canopy so that it would not be activated until the canopy came off. But if the canopy jammed (and in a real combat situation it might be damaged by cannon fire) then the pilot's only escape route would be blocked. That was why I always believed that pilots should have another life-saving possibility – perhaps not a very reliable one, yet still a chance – ejecting through the canopy if it failed to come off. We knew of an incident during the Korean war when the pilot of a damaged MiG-15 did just that: his canopy failing to separate, he unlocked the ejector mechanism (there was a device allowing him to do so) and ejected through the glass. The MiG-15 canopy was divided lengthways in halves with a steel beam to which the glass semi-spheres were fastened. The seat broke through the beam and the pilot got away with slight facial injuries, even though he was wearing only an ordinary leather helmet.

The MiG-19 was equipped with an ejector seat of a new design. It was activated by pulling a special screen from out of the headrest. The main function of the screen was to protect the pilot's face from the airstream at high-speed ejection. However, that seat did not have an unlocking device. When this ejection system was discussed at a mock-up board session at the Mikoyan Design Company, I (then an ordinary and relatively young test pilot) put up a demand for an unlocking device. The company resisted that demand for a long time, but eventually gave in, and the device was added. It was activated by a hook on the side of the headrest and was rather hard to reach, yet it was better than nothing.

My insistence on the installation of an unlocking mechanism was later justified by two tragic episodes. In one of them a pilot was trying to eject from a MiG-19 which had got out of control, but the canopy jammed and the pilot crashed with the aircraft. From the position of his body in the seat it seemed probable that he was trying to reach the unlocking hook. He must have remembered about it at the last moment and stretched his arm to it but failed to get hold of it before his aircraft went down. Some time afterwards an air defence pilot in Kazakhstan failed to eject from a burning Su-9 for the same reason: his cockpit hood jammed and the ejector seat could not be activated. There was no unlocking device in the Su-9 at all. The pilot had time to say goodbye on the radio and ask that his family be taken care of.

It so happened in my career that I never had to eject – my luck must have protected me. There were a number of situations verging on the point when ejection would be the only course, but God was obviously on my side. The entire flying personnel was required to practise parachute jumps (at least three jumps each), but I managed to get away without a single jump in my life. While at flying school my parachute jumping course was pre-empted by the war, and then I was for many years forbidden to jump because of my wartime knee injury. I knew of only one other colleague who had never made a single parachute jump, the distinguished test navigator Nikolai Zatsepa. At the same time a large number of excellent pilots and navigators completed their flying careers without emergency ejections.

Once, while I was the Fighter Test Flight Department CO, I had to give the order from the tower to a pilot in the air to abandon the aircraft. One of our new test pilots, Stepanov, was flying a Su-7B and as he was preparing to land, his right wheel strut jammed and refused to come out. Stepanov tried to lower it with the help of the stand-by compressed-air system, but he forgot to release its detent before pressing the lever, and broke it. I had just landed myself, and had barely climbed out of the cockpit when I was urgently called to the tower to make a decision. I talked to Stepanov on the radio and made sure it was no longer possible either to extend the jammed strut or to retract the other one. A landing with only one wheel out was a very risky business, so I commanded Stepanov to climb up to 3,000 metres and eject. As a helicopter was flying us to his landing site, I could not stop worrying that the ejection had not gone well, but soon we saw Stepanov safe and sound, sitting on his parachute below. The accident, as the regulations required, was reported in written form to the Air Force Commander-in-Chief. Marshal Vershinin wrote in the margin, opposite the words about my order to leave the aircraft, 'Correct decision'. If this kind of failure had occurred in my own flight, I believe I would have attempted to land with one wheel down; but it is one thing risking one's own life and another – somebody else's. I simply had no moral right to order another to do the same.

On 1 May 1960 there happened an event which immediately became known all over the world. A US reconnaissance aeroplane, the U-2, was shot down with a surface-to-air missile as it was flying over Soviet territory. The pilot, Francis Powers, did not have the time to eject; he was tossed out of his seat as his aircraft disintegrated and his parachute opened. Paradoxically it saved his life, for without his knowledge his seat had been fitted with an explosive unit which would have gone off at ejection (the idea was, of course, to prevent Powers from falling into our hands alive). The fragments of his U-2 were delivered to us at the Institute and placed in an empty hangar at the Chkalovskaya air base. Immediately afterwards a large group of aviation experts, including all the eminent aircraft designers, arrived to examine them. Our Institute engineers studied the fragments in great detail and prepared them for a secret display which was arranged in closed premises in Moscow. They also gave explanations to the visitors of that unusual 'exhibition', answering their questions about each 'exhibit'.

The incident came in the wake of a considerable warming of our relations with the USA – the first post-war *détente*, resulting from Khrushchev's visit to America (which was preceded, as I have written earlier, by my father's 'paving-the-way' trip of January 1959). Most people would have been pleased to see the end of the Cold War and were looking forward to the coming visit of President Eisenhower, who was to be received with honours then highly unusual for a state visitor from a capitalist country (he was to be the first foreign visitor of his rank to be taken on a trip to Siberia and Lake Baikal, where a guest house was urgently built to accommodate the distinguished guests). After the U-2 incident everyone was holding their breath, afraid that Eisenhower's visit would be called off and the tension would return. And this is exactly what happened.

The day after the exhibition of the U-2 fragments had opened I was driving from Chkalovskaya after work with my two pilot friends in the car with me. We decided to go and see the display. Thanks to our colleagues who were there as 'guides', we had no difficulty being admitted. We were looking at one of the stands near the entrance when we suddenly heard some bustle outside, followed by the appearance of a group of people with Khrushchev leading the way and a cluster of reporters in the rearguard. A spontaneous press conference took place. My friends and I were about a dozen metres from Khrushchev (he knew me well, but naturally did not notice me in the crowd). Almost at the very start a foreign correspondent asked bluntly whether Eisenhower's visit was still on. Everyone froze. Khrushchev hesitated, and I had a feeling that we were present at the moment when the decision was taken. Finally he said, 'How could I receive, with honours, the head of a state who sends spying aircraft to us? How could I present him to the Soviet people?' My heart sank, and it seemed that everyone in the room was crestfallen. Such a great store had been set on the US President's visit; so many hopes depended on the improvement of our relations with America, and now it was all over.

Khrushchev played his trump card well. The Americans were confident that the pilot was dead and would not be able to confess his mission, so they explained that the U-2 had crossed the Soviet border by accident due to a mistake by the pilot, who had been performing a meteorological flight outside Soviet territory. Only when this 'explanation' had come did Khrushchev reveal, for all the world to hear, that Francis Powers was alive and captured and had confessed his true mission. The Americans found themselves in a very awkward position. I believe that after that President Eisenhower made a mistake. He admitted that he had been aware of the US reconnaissance missions over our territory. Thus he pre-determined Khrushchev's reaction. All states engage in espionage activities against one another, but their heads of state should not admit to having anything to do with it. Eisenhower ought to have maintained that all those missions were organised by the military 'behind his back'. Khrushchev would have very probably pretended to believe him, and the movement towards *détente* could have continued.

When Powers was flying over Soviet territory at an altitude of more than 20,000 metres, several attempts to intercept him with our fighters, including the newly adopted Su-9, were made, but none of them was successful. The combat pilots on those missions failed to climb up to the height at which the U-2 was travelling, even though it was within the capability limits of the Su-9. I was instructed to send a test pilot from the Institute to the combat regiment in question to establish why the altitude had not been reached and to give recommendations for the future. When Leonid Fadeev arrived at the regiment's airfield in Kazakhstan he discovered that the regimental pilots had not quite mastered the Su-9 yet and did not know how to climb up in it correctly. The point is that the ceiling of a supersonic jet is achieved in a certain pattern. First the aircraft must break the sound barrier at 10,000 to 11,000 metres, then speed up to Mach 1.8 or so, and only after that start climbing up to the ceiling at this speed. Trying to reach the ceiling as fast as possible, the pilots had started to climb at an insufficient Mach number, unaware that at that speed the ceiling of the aircraft was much lower. In my opinion there was another, though less important, reason for the pilots' failure to intercept the U-2. They took off for that mission, wearing, for the very first time, partial-pressure suits with pressure helmets. These suits take some time to get used to, and until you have, your movements are somewhat encumbered and you feel tense and out of sorts.

The U-2 incident was accompanied by a tragic circumstance on our side. Within seconds after Powers had been shot down one of our interceptor fighters was shot down too. When the U-2 mark had disappeared from the ground radar display, the officers in charge thought it was due to some technical fault and did not report its disappearance. In the meantime a new target mark appeared on the radar screen of an anti-aircraft artillery post, and the crew launched a missile at it, sure it was the U-2. Alas, it was Captain Safronov's interceptor, and that mission became his last.

Later in the year we began testing the Su-11, a new modification of the Su-9. It was meant to be part of the same interception complex, with the difference that its radar range was much larger and its K-98 missiles were much more powerful than the K-5s (they were a modification of the K-8 missile with which I, in a Yak-27K, had hit an air target for the first time). Unlike the K-5, which was guided by radar, the new missiles came with infra-red or radar homing heads.

One day, before the flight testing began, they changed the engine in the Su-11 that had been ferried to the Akhtubinsk air base to be tested, and the factory test pilot Anatoly Koznov had to fly it out. The day was overcast with solid clouds hanging low over the airfield. Although Koznov's flight was the factory management's business and had nothing to do with us, I was still in charge of all flight testing activity on that programme. I put my foot down, declaring that the flight should be put off until better weather arrived, which was essential for a first flight with a newly installed engine. Koznov kept his silence and I realised that his opinion was the same, although he did not dare to contradict his bosses. Boris Kuprianov (Deputy Aviation Minister) was annoyed with my 'slowing down the work', as he put it, and threatened to report my interference to the Air Force Commander-in-Chief. I was sure he would cool down and forget it, but he did not, and shortly afterwards I received a phone call from the Institute Commander General Blagoveshchensky. 'What happened?' he asked, and when I explained he said, 'And right you were!'

The next day the weather cleared up and Koznov took off to fly the engine out. It surged, several turbine blades were scorched, and Anatoly barely made it home. Had it happened the day before, over a thick blanket of solid clouds, he would have had to eject and the test specimen of the Su-11 would have been lost: landing with the engines half dead in bad weather is next to impossible. Boris Kuprianov made no comment to me, but I was sure he no longer thought my interference inopportune.

The most active of our test pilots in the Su-11 tests was Eduard Knyazev, but I made several flights as an evaluation pilot. The day when I flew it for the first time the chief designer of the aircraft, Pavel Sukhoi, happened to be at Akhtubinsk. I saw him strolling along the edge of the airfield as I was lining up for take-off. When I saw him after my return from that flight, he said, 'I was very worried for you, but when I saw your landing I realised I needn't have been.' Spoken by the usually very reticent and uncommunicative Pavel Sukhoi, it was great praise.

Also in 1960 my department at Chkalovskaya was visited by the First Deputy Air Force Commander, Marshal Rudenko. A visit by such a distinguished guest was very unusual and, moreover, totally unexpected. Marshal Rudenko first came to my tiny office, and then asked me to take him round the premises. While we were visiting the rooms where our engineers and technician girls were working on their charts and diagrams, as well as the equipment testing laboratories, the marshal kept muttering something about our 'office stuff' or 'record-keeping'. I did not have any idea what he could possibly mean, but it was soon made only too clear. It turned out that he had come to ascertain that we had no equipment or facilities that were too bulky or too complicated to be moved to a different location. In short, he had come to make sure that the entire department, with all its sections and sub-divisions, could be transferred to Akhtubinsk.

The Air Force Command was thinking of us as if we were some ordinary operational unit which could be ordered to move – lock, stock and barrel – to another base. But with us things were different. Among the test experts of all profiles we had a large number of excellent and unique specialists with many years' experience. They would have had no difficulty finding employment elsewhere. Many of them were no longer very young, and they did not cherish the prospect of giving up their homes near Moscow and moving their families to a small military compound in the steppe several thousand kilometres from where they used to live.

Akhtubinsk lay between the villages of Vladimirovka and Petropavlovka. Petropavlovka is a large village (or a small town) with a landing pier and a wharf on the Volga, to which Russia's second railway for carrying salt from Lake Baskunchak had been laid long ago. By the 1960s the separate settlements had merged into the town of Akhtubinsk (which owes its name to the river Akhtuba, a tributary of the Volga).

In Akhtubinsk we were assigned three barely finished three-storey blocks of flats on the living compound. They could not accommodate all our personnel and we were forced to put three young families into each three-room apartment (a room to a family), where they had to share the kitchen and all other amenities. Even so, many of the young officers who moved with us or were posted to Akhtubinsk later had to rent rooms and even sheds from the local villagers. For many years to come we experienced enormous difficulties assigning the scarce additional accommodation the department would receive every now and then to those who had no homes of their own and those who had been forced to share the initially allotted flats. I will never forget the painful interviews I had with the dozens of people who came to me in my reception hours to talk about their desperate housing situations. If I had yielded to the AF Command's pressure and insisted on the move, not only of young officers, but of our senior specialists as well, the people who had well-established homes at Chkalovskaya, our housing problems at Akhtubinsk would have been even more hopeless, not to mention the fact that we would simply have lost many valuable specialists who would have left the Institute rather than move. I have always felt proud that I managed to resist the pressure from my superiors and thus keep many highly experienced people and first-class specialists at the Institute. Their contribution to our work, including the work of my department, was enormous.

Yet, thanks to the professional enthusiasm of our test force and their devotion to their work, only very few people left the Institute for good to avoid moving. Most of our experienced specialists agreed to be posted to Akhtubinsk without moving their wives and children. For years they continued to work there, despite all the difficulties their situation involved. They were not receiving any travel allowance, for officially they were still in the disposition of their unit; neither did they receive it when they were sent on business to Moscow, because their families lived nearby. They did not receive any accommodation allowance either and had to pay for their hostel and guest-house rooms in Akhtubinsk out of their salaries. The younger officers and specialists, particularly those who did not yet possess homes of their own, agreed to move to Akhtubinsk with their families, only to face the housing problems I have already described. I have always believed that all those people deserved great respect for their steadfast loyalty to their work and their profession, which they loved in spite of all the difficulties their new situation threw at them. As for me, I lived and worked at Akhtubinsk for nearly nineteen years, between 1959 and 1978, under the conditions I have just described for those who left their families behind in Moscow.

Maybe because most of us at Akhtubinsk were working there as if on a temporary posting (with our wives and children far away), we were on especially warm and friendly terms with each other and spent much time together during off-work hours. We would often meet in somebody's hotel room or in the flats of those who had moved their permanent home to Akhtubinsk. But the best meetings we had, which I have always remembered with particular warmth, were our regular weekend outings. In the long spell of warm weather that lasted from April to October most people would spend their weekends near the water on the banks of the numerous rivers and tributaries which formed the huge delta of the Volga river. Usually several families and their closest friends among the real or 'forced' bachelors formed steady groups which would habitually go out together to a particular spot they favoured. In the summer many of the officers were joined by their wives and children, and our outings grew livelier, noisier and more crowded. At first we used to go out in special buses, but gradually there appeared more and more private cars and motorboats, so people would go out in cavalcades or arrange to meet at a favourite spot by the river.

My children (Volodya, the eldest, leading the way) and occasionally my wife also visited me in the summer (with a very demanding full-time job in Moscow, Ella could not get away often or for long). The most regular visitor however was my daughter, who loved coming to Akhtubinsk and enjoyed 'keeping house' for me while she was there, especially in August when the worst of the heat was over and all the fruit and the watermelons ripened. From the age of fourteen or so she would spend about a month every year in Akhtubinsk until her boy was born in 1972. After that she could only occasionally come for a few days (usually for my birthday in July), although when her son was a little over two she brought him with her and they stayed several weeks. My small single-room 'bachelor' flat was not very well suited for putting up visitors, so when Aschen was there with her son the two of them had to 'camp out' in a neighbour's flat at night, using mine as their day-time base.

One summer, before Alex junior was born, my own son Alex was staying with me in Akhtubinsk and we were expecting his sister to join us. She arrived with a surprise package in tow, her cousin Olga (Vanya's daughter), whom she had spontaneously talked into flying with her only the day before. There were four of us to one bed-sitting-room now, but nobody seemed to mind, least of all me, for I enjoyed having the family visit me. A couple of camp beds had to be borrowed from the neighbours in addition to the one I had, and the girls improvised a makeshift partition to divide the room into the 'boys' and girls' quarters' for the night. It was an occasion to test the truth of the saying 'the more the merrier', and it certainly worked for us well.

I believe that the closest and friendliest group among my colleagues, both at work and at leisure, were the fighter test pilots. Most of them came from Chkalovskaya where they had worked together, and in Akhtubinsk they lived together at the hostel (it was known as a 'hotel', but was more like a hostel for single officers). They usually got together for riverside picnics and fishing at the weekends, often joined by those of the flying officers who were renting rooms in the local village. Many of our dedicated fishermen would set up a tent and spend the whole weekend on the river, joined by the others during the day. I always enjoyed the sight of a sunlit river bank with occasional clusters of tents under the trees. Fishing was the principal hobby of most of my fellow pilots. Their main method was spinning, although several other ways, including not very legal ones, were also favoured. That area was a fisherman's haven, and much of the fish caught was fried on the camp fire or used to make soup, eaten there and then as the highlight of the picnic menu.

One day the fighter pilots decided that it was time to acquire a communal motorboat large enough to accommodate a couple of dozen people plus assorted wives and children. We all clubbed together to purchase a boat and bought a large wooden vessel with a long pointed nose. We fitted it with a car engine, and both the boat and the engine were so old and took so much time to fix before they could be used, that somebody (I believe it was 'VG', though I am not sure), on seeing it, exclaimed, 'You call it a boat? It's a nightmare!' Then somebody else suggested naming it *Nightmare*. The idea appealed to the pilots' sense of humour, and our boat was officially registered as *Nightmare*. Every Friday morning the pilots' immediate commander, Piotr Kabrelev, would write the following words on the blackboard in the briefing room: *Sign up here for a nightmarish boat trip this weekend.* I was one of the *Nightmare*'s constant passengers. It was a very spacious boat, and I once counted twenty-eight people on board (although that included several children). Occasionally we would go to the lakes, and then crawfish would be our main picnic fare (apart from the supplies of fresh fruit, vegetables, bread and the magnificent local watermelons brought from home). Sometimes volunteers were sent to a nearby lake for crawfish even when our camp of the day was on the river. I am not much of a fisherman myself, but I often tried my hand at spinning for the sake of exercise. All in all my achievements were very modest, though I managed to catch a number of decent fish.

A few years later the *Nightmare* was sold, but we pilots continued our collective weekend outings, often joined by various people from other departments. Such more or less steady groups of friends existed in many other sub-divisions of the Institute. Those many carefree leisure hours spent together by the river, our wonderful picnics among friends, with whom each of us shared a dangerous and difficult job, have remained as my fondest memories of the years spent at Akhtubinsk. The tradition of spending the weekends together by the riverside continued through the time when most of those working at Akhtubinsk were living there permanently. However, when I visited Akhtubinsk in 1994 I was sorry to hear that the old tradition had almost died, because from the 1980s onwards officers were receiving allotments of land around the compound. Many built summer cottages and planted gardens and kitchen gardens, and fishing gave way to gardening as the leading hobby. The climate is ideal for growing fruit and vegetables, with the supply of water the only problem. Although there was nothing I could say against the pilots and engineers having their own gardens (which no doubt produced a welcome addition to their family diet), I have since felt sorry that the unique camaraderie of collective weekend outings was no longer known to them. It is only on special occasions that such riverside expeditions and picnics are now organised on a large scale – to celebrate Aviation Day, for example, or to entertain some important guests from Moscow.

Today, on the edge of the compound on a high bank of the Akhtuba stands a monument to test pilots, made of stainless steel and shaped as a stylised wing of a giant bird. The monument is inscribed with the words, 'To test crews who did not return from their flights'. Next to the monument there are several granite blocks with the names of the pilots, navigators, radiomen and one cameraman who were killed since the time when the Institute in its present form had been established and moved to Akhtubinsk from Moscow. The first name to appear was that of Victor Andreev, who crashed in 1962, and there are more than forty of them altogether to date. Shortly before the idea to erect such a monument appeared and a sculptor was found, I had been at the Bourges Salon and had seen their pilots' monument, shaped as an upright aircraft wing like a fragment of a crashed plane sticking out of the ground. It had a laconic inscription which I liked: 'To a test pilot and his crew'. I suggested something similar for our own monument, but the other idea prevailed. The area around the monument gradually developed into a small park stretching along the bank, with footpaths and flowerbeds and specially planted trees. It became a favourite meeting place of the people living in the compound, a promenade and a popular site for holiday festivities and fireworks. The paved square in front of the monument is also the site for ceremonial assemblies, military oath-taking and VE parades.

CHAPTER 19

Flying over the Steppe

Towards the end of the summer of 1960, after the Su-9 military certification tests had been completed, the pilot Vladimir Pliushkin performed some special air intake stability tests for this aircraft. These tests were meant to establish the surge boundaries at different positions of the air intake cone. The pilot's task was to turn off the automatic cone control at various planned speeds, beginning with the limit Mach number, retracting the cone manually little by little (with the help of a switch) until surging began, which he would immediately feel by the shaking of the aircraft and a rapid succession of loud claps.

After Vladimir, I had to perform the same mission as an evaluation pilot. I knew it was a particularly demanding kind of test flight, but I happened to encounter unexpected danger even before I properly took off. According to the latest recommendations, the exhaust nozzle of the Su-9 was to be opened with a special switch when taxiing towards the runway so as not to overheat the engine. Just before the take-off the nozzle had to be reduced to its normal size again, otherwise the engine thrust would be insufficient. Usually the nozzle is at its minimum diameter; it opens up automatically only when the afterburner is on and the volume of exhaust gas increases. Having opened the nozzle during taxiing, I forgot all about it at take-off. The nozzle warning light, which had already appeared on the instrumental panels of many Su-9s, had not yet been installed in the machine I was in. Since there were no missiles under the wings, I decided to take off without the afterburner. Very soon I realised that my acceleration was not fast enough; by the time I had covered half the runway I had only gained 270 kph (and to become unstuck I needed 320 to 330 kph). I thought the hot weather was responsible for poor engine thrust and lowered the nose again to reduce the air drag. The speed came up a bit, but not enough. The concrete runway was almost over and it was too late to abort the take-off, for the unpaved safety run in front of me was not long enough for me to stop before I hit the radio-beacon building at its bottom.

I opted for selecting the afterburner, but reluctantly, for I knew it would reduce the thrust even further before boosting it up (for the exhaust nozzle opened before the fuel began to burn). However, to my surprise the thrust did not go down, and only then did I realise that the nozzle had been wide open all that time. I pitched up the nose as high as I could and unstuck, almost at a snail's pace, at the very end of the runway, if not at the beginning of the unpaved safety run. Keeping an eye on the antenna on the roof of the beacon building before me, I began a smooth turn away from it, just as my afterburner came on and my speed went nicely up. As often happened, it was only when the danger was past that I felt cold sweat running down my face. I could not even wipe it off, for I had a pressure helmet on. The pressure helmet required even breathing, but maybe

267

because I had just been through a very stressful spell I could not manage to breathe evenly; instead, my breath was coming in frequent ragged gusts, and I had difficulty breathing out. It took a special effort to concentrate on the instruments to maintain the appropriate climbing air speed. Gradually my breathing came back to normal and I relaxed.

Interestingly, the very next day the same mistake was repeated by another pilot. Valery Baranov lined up for take-off in a different Su-9, having forgotten to close the nozzle. His machine was equipped with a warning light, but when it came on Valery could not figure out what it was telling him, so he closed the throttle and opened it again, only to see the warning light reappear. This time he remembered what it signalled and closed the nozzle. If there had been no warning light on his instrument panel he would have attempted to take off at low thrust, as I did the day before.

I climbed up to 13,000 metres and began the test. I sped up to the limit Mach number, 2.1 (2,240 kph), and pressed the air intake cone retraction switch to pull in the cone. As soon as I heard the first surge claps I extended the cone, and they stopped. I jotted down the cone position at which the surging began into the prepared chart on my knee-board, and repeated the whole pattern at Mach 2.0, and then at three other Mach numbers. Pleased to have fully performed a difficult mission, I reached for the auxiliary instrument panel to switch the instrumentation recorder off – and to my horror I discovered that it had never been on! I must have forgotten to turn it on because of my unnerving experience at take-off.

At landing, besides my mechanic, I was met by the powerplant project engineer Victor Pashkov. 'Victor, I've done it all, but can you imagine, I forgot to turn the recorder on!' I said. 'To hell with the recorder!' the engineer exclaimed. It turned out that as I was taking off just beyond the paved runway my jet stream had raised such thick clouds of dust from the ground that the aircraft was entirely lost from view, and poor Victor thought I had crashed. They told me he had actually dropped on the ground, half-conscious from shock. No wonder he did not care about the recorder after that, and he was perfectly content with what I had written on my knee-board.

The next day was a Sunday, and our usual company of pilots was picnicking by the river. We talked, as we often did, of our work, and Vladimir Pliushkin reproached me for not having checked on the position of the nozzle switch before my take-off the day before. He added that I had been lucky, for the whole thing might easily have ended badly. It might sound strange, but I, a colonel and the Department Commander, was pleased to hear a criticism from an ordinary pilot, a captain. It was something I really treasured, this attitude of the pilots which meant that they saw me as one of them, and respected me as such, knowing that I would always understand and accept a just word.

At the beginning of 1961 a major reorganisation of military testing institutions took place. Our Institute received a 'reinforcement' in the shape of three previously independent organisations: the anti-submarine aviation armament testing centre based at Feodosia in the Crimea, the missile testing centre that had always been based at Akhtubinsk, and the airship testing centre at Volsk. After the reorganisation the FTI specialists continued to play an essential part in the elaboration of service requirements, and especially of general military specification requirements. The latter are the requirements compulsory for all types of aircraft, and they mainly concern flight safety, ease of employment and maintenance worthiness. The Akhtubinsk air base was named as the principal location of the enlarged FTI. Apart from my Fighter Flight Test Department (which by that time had fully settled in Akhtubinsk), the air base received from Chkalovskaya the newly formed Missile-carrier and Bomber Flight Test Department, with all the sections in charge of the relevant equipment and armament. The Department Commander was General Rychkov. Later, when a new building appeared at the air base, yet another unit was transferred to Akhtubinsk from Chkalovskaya: the so-called Special Equipment Department. It was responsible for testing a very wide range of equipment, from airborne radios and navigation aids to instrument landing systems. It was commanded by Colonel Polsky.

Of all the independent units initially located at Akhtubinsk two remained unchanged: the Flight Path Measuring Department, comprising several remote measuring posts with cinetheodolites and radars for recording flight trajectory data, and the Maintenance Equipment Test Department, which became responsible for testing and launching radio-controlled target aircraft. What was left at Chkalovskaya officially became a branch of the Institute, consisting of three departments. The first was responsible for testing transport aircraft, helicopters and paraborne equipment, the second for testing aircraft engines, and the third for testing safety and survival equipment for both pilots and cosmonauts.

Many FTI veterans, including me, did not approve of the idea of moving the Institute headquarters and all its principal flight test departments so far away from Moscow. We were all for the merging of various test-related structures, but we believed that the Akhtubinsk base should function as their main testing ground, whereas the 'brain centre' should remain at Chkalovskaya. The Institute had very busy professional contacts with all aircraft and equipment design companies, with certain departments within the defence and aviation industry ministries, Air Force Command and other organisations, the majority of which were based in Moscow. In the new circumstances these contacts became noticeably encumbered.

There was another essential factor which had hardly ever been taken into consideration in the USSR – human resources. The FTI was a mine of first-class expertise and knowledge in the field of state-of-the-art aviation technology. The exceptionally high professional level of its testing and research personnel was accounted for by the very character of their work and by the unique role assigned to the Institute in the testing of new aircraft and equipment. It was the kind of work that left no room (or time) for stereotyped methods or routine approach; it was a constant challenge, demanding imagination, creativity and boldness in terms of professional thinking and decision-making. Our best test pilots and engineers were valued by all the various aviation industry organisations and enterprises with which our Institute had professional contacts. Their authority on professional matters was almost never questioned. They sometimes revealed a deeper insight into the new models of aircraft than the people who designed them, for their overall experience was broader and included many different types and categories of aeroplanes and equipment. All this ensured the exceptionally high reputation of the Institute as a whole. There was hardly a serious test project or a challenging flight mission carried out in the country without a pilot or an engineer from the FTI. We believed that a transfer of the entire Institute to Akhtubinsk would be followed by a decline of the overall standards of its personnel and the role of the Institute in the development of new aircraft and equipment. Unfortunately we were eventually proved to be right, although our pessimistic prediction did not come true at once, and not quite to the extent we had imagined.

In the summer of 1959 a tragic event had occurred that might have played a certain role in the decision to remove most of the flight testing from Chkalovskaya. A Tu-16 bomber lost height on its final approach in heavy rain and crashed, hitting several houses in a nearby village. It was a naval aviation aircraft temporarily attached to the Institute for a particular test project. I arrived on the scene of the tragedy an hour after it had happened. What I saw was a truly harrowing sight. It had grown dark, and the aircraft and three houses were still ablaze, the darkness around them full of terrified people, all of whom seemed to be crying, moaning or screaming with horror and pain. I was bitterly reminded of the scenes during the war.

The fatal accident was used as a pretext for dismissing General Blagoveshchensky from the post of Institute Commander. A veteran of two wars, Hero of the Soviet Union and an energetic and demanding commander, he was not even fifty then. He was a great loss to the Institute. There must have been other reasons for his dismissal apart from the accident. On very good terms with the previous Air Force Commander, Marshal Zhigarev, General Blagoveshchensky might not have been getting on too well with his successor, Marshal Vershinin; certainly Vershinin's deputy and our immediate commander at the Air Force Command, General Ponomarev, was not among Blagoveshchensky's admirers. I once heard him say that Blagoveshchensky was 'uncontrollable'. The autocratic Ponomarev did not particularly favour subordinates, whether they were generals or lieutenants, who dared to assert an opinion that differed from his own.

General Blagoveshchensky was invited by Andrei Nikolayevich Tupolev to take charge of his flight test base, and his position at the head of the Flight Test Institute at Chkalovskaya was given to General Pushko, transferred from an operational unit. General Pushko was not sufficiently educated for his new job and produced an impression of a rather narrow-minded yet cunning person. He knew little about flight testing on his arrival, nor did he begin to understand it in the years that remained until his retirement. He was the last person to be expected to defend the position of the Institute in relation to its transfer (to be fair, at that stage probably no one could). After the reorganisation, the enlarged Institute was put under the command of General Finoghenov (former CO of the Akhtubinsk missile centre), General Molotkov became his second-in-command, and Pushko remained in charge of the Chkalovskaya branch.

A few months after the reorganisation, in May 1961, together with three other department commanders, I was promoted from colonel to major-general. Although I had had a notion that I might sooner or later be promoted to the next rank to match my position in the Institute hierarchy, I still found it hard to believe that it had really happened. For some time afterwards I felt rather self-conscious about naming my new rank when I had to introduce myself according to form. Later I heard that the list of promotions (which had to be handed over to Khrushchev for official approval) contained my brother's name as well. At some stage somebody must have decided that the two brothers Mikoyan promoted together was one too many, and Alexei was crossed off the list – as the younger of the two, I suppose. He became a major-general the following year.

The position of a major-general in the Soviet armed forces was worlds apart from the position of all other officers, including colonels. Becoming a major-general in effect meant entering a qualitatively different category in terms of salary and various privileges. I always believed it to be wrong, and I heard that in Western armies the gap between major-generals and other officers was not quite so large. To be promoted major-general one has to have occupied a position corresponding to that rank for at least two years (with my previous position of Institute Assistant Commander I had had nearly three years in a major-general's position). However, it sometimes happens that promotion never comes. A case in point was Valery Migunov, the Fighter Flight Test Department Commander in the 1980s. He was nominated for promotion several times but every time some accident happened (through no fault of his) and his name was struck off the list. And so, after several years in charge of the largest and most important of the Institute divisions, he retired as a colonel, although he had been made a Hero of the Soviet Union for courage shown in flight testing.

A department like No. 1 Flight Test Department, at my time, would have about 1,000 personnel, most of whom would be officers, with several dozen colonels and about a hundred flying officers among them (including navigators and radio operators). The department was (and still is) responsible to the government and the country at large for the testing and assessment of new aircraft and for the recommendations concerning their adoption or rejection for service. The role and responsibility of the person in charge would be at least as important and high as those of an air force combat division commander, which had always been a major-general's position. The same applied to some other departments within the Institute, for example the Anti-Submarine Armament Test Department at Feodosia, which had its own base and testing facilities, as well as a large living compound the size of a small town.

Yet, in terms of the major-general's rank, the Institute was sometimes treated rather meanly. In the 1970s the Department Commander category, if the department in question had no test flight units in its structure, was brought one rank down and became a colonel's position. By the 1990s this 'downgrading' had gone even further, and only the Institute Commander's position and that of the Chief of Staff were left in the generals category, which was unfair towards the department commanders. Moreover, in 1990 the Institute was restructured and the word 'Research' from the Flight Test Institute's official name was lost on the way, despite the fact that up to one sixth of all working time at the Institute at large had always been given to scientific research.

In 1961 I was included in the Soviet delegation to the Farnborough air show in England. The delegation was rather representative: apart from the well-known designers Ilyushin and Antonov, Deputy Civilian Aviation Minister Kulik and other officials, there were a number of important people from the Air Force Command. I represented the Flight Test Institute, and the official leader of the delegation was Deputy Aviation Industry Minister Leshchenko, with the 'power behind the throne' in the shape of Igor Milovidov, ostensibly a representative of the State Committee for Science and Technology but in actual fact a colonel of the KGB (who later became a notorious figure in the West).

Once in London we checked into a cheap hotel near Queensway St, Ilyushin and Antonov sharing one twin room and General Belyunov from the Air Force Command and I another. It would have made an amusing (though not to us!) story in some English tabloid if any reporters had happened to discover us: two eminent aircraft designers (heads of large design companies) and two Soviet Air Force generals forced to share rooms in a cheap London hotel! Alas, our meagre travel allowance would not cover the cost of a single room each.*

Our programme started with a briefing at the embassy conducted by Anatoly Pavlov (Tanya Frunze's husband, whom I have already mentioned). His official position at the time was the USSR Embassy Secretary for Science and Technology, but his real profession was military intelligence. We spent three days visiting the air show at Farnborough, the usual venue of annual demonstrations of British aviation technology. If I am not mistaken, it was after 1961 that Farnborough acquired international status and became a biennial event, alternating with the Salon at Bourges (which I got the opportunity to attend four years later). Every day we were guests of some aviation company and watched aerial demonstrations from their 'chalets'. After the demonstration they invited us to lunch – an arrangement that, with our limited means, suited us perfectly.

One of the innovations shown that year was the 'zero-zero' ejector seat, designed to save the pilot at zero altitude and zero speed by means of a rocket engine ejecting the seat very high up. (The seats we had back home, for example the one in the MiG-21, could also save the pilot at zero altitude, but they needed a minimum of 130 kph forward speed.) The ground mount for the demonstration of the zero-zero seat in action was set up at the far side of the airfield opposite the stands for the public. As I was talking to a British test pilot (whose name I have unfortunately forgotten) in the AVRO chalet, I said I wished their ejector seat mount was closer to the stands so that I could film it with my 8 mm camera. To my surprise he offered to take me to it. The two of us drove up to the gate in his car, he showed his ID to the guard, and we were waved in. He stopped by a

---

* In those days Soviet tourists were allowed to have only a ridiculously small amount of money, about $30 altogether. People who went on business trips and as members of delegations, etc. were not permitted to have any money on top of the official 'travel allowance' (which 'fluctuated' from the rate of $10 to about $20 per diem) and a very modest 'hotel allowance'.

large marquee and we went inside it. My 'guide' introduced me to the officers who were there, the pilots who took part in the aerial demonstration. Then he showed me where I could stand to film the ejector seat mount. In those days it seemed absolutely incredible: a Soviet test pilot filming a state-of-the-art ejector seat on a British flight test airfield!

In the next three days our delegation split into several groups of four or five, and each group visited a number of different companies. I was most impressed by our visits to Ridiphone, a company specialising in aircraft simulators, and to Marconi, the famous radio equipment company. In our little group I was appointed interpreter, which was not an easy task, for I was far less familiar with English radio vocabulary than with their aviation terms. At Ridiphone we were led into a training room where they showed us the Boeing 707 simulator. I was allowed to make a circuit 'flight' in it. I had no experience with four-engine aircraft then, to say nothing of the fact that the Boeing was a totally unfamiliar machine, yet my 'flight' seemed to go well enough. They had not warned me that it was a moving-base simulator, and when I pulled the steering wheel for rotation on the take-off run I felt that the nose was rising! I turned to look at the English specialists who were standing in the cockpit behind me, and they all smiled, guessing that I liked their surprise.

We were also shown, from a distance though, a fighter simulator with a cockpit mounted onto the rod of a giant hydraulic cylinder. It was a six-degrees-of-freedom (or 'full-motion') simulator. The Boeing which I had 'flown' a few minutes earlier provided only for the pitch movement: at 'take-off' the cockpit inclined backwards and I was pressed into the back of my seat. It created a very plausible illusion of acceleration. After 'touching down' the cockpit inclined forward, and I was pressed into the safety belts, the illusion being that I was really using the brakes. The same effects accompanied vertical acceleration and slowing down during the 'flight'. The effect of vertical acceleration, or G-load, created by a full-motion simulator is more realistic, and thus the flight simulation itself is more true to life. The point is that the very first feedback the pilot receives in response to his control inputs, especially in instrument ('blind') flying, is a change of the G-load, especially of the vertical G-load. In a fixed-base simulator the response received by the pilot is confined to the second 'stage', i.e. the indicator readings alone, therefore the feedback is delayed and incomplete. That is why many pilots complain that such a simulator does not give an accurate imitation of actual flying.

In 1961 a flight simulator as such was no longer news to us Russian test pilots. We had already tested and were tentatively using our first full-flight, fixed-base MiG-19 simulator. At first I had treated the very notion of such a simulator with scepticism, refusing to believe that it could be of great use, for nothing could really replace actual flight experience. Once, on my first day back from leave, I ran into Wing Commander Antipov in a corridor of our building. 'Fresh from leave, are you? We'll go up in the MiG-15 trainer after lunch – a pilotage check-ride for you.' Such pilotage checks, testing the pilots' instrument flying skills, were given to each of us once every two or three months, during which we were doing our routine flying work, but I had not been inside a cockpit for two months. Every pilot knows that it is his instrument flying skills that a break in flying affects first of all. I shared my concern with some of the pilots, and somebody suggested I should practise in our new simulator first. I did, giving myself a half-hour 'flight' in it, and to Antipov's surprise my check-ride with him went well. I passed the pilotage check with flying colours and was converted in favour of flight simulators.

Later I even participated in testing simulators, and became thoroughly convinced that a full-flight, full-motion simulator with a plausible imitation of a normal flight and of various malfunctions or emergencies (many of which would be impossible or too dangerous to create deliberately in a real test flight) was a useful device for training and maintaining piloting skills at a high level. Naturally, a flight simulator cannot fully replace training flights, mainly because there is at least one important thing it cannot simulate: the pilot's awareness of real danger and of the possibly fatal consequences of a mistake. But it allows for a reduction in the number of training flights and enables pilots to keep in good form when for some reason (bad weather, for example) flying is suspended. Although today a really sophisticated in-flight simulator costs more than an aircraft, at the end of the day it is undoubtedly cost-effective. Even a simulator representing a 'wrong' type of aircraft is a useful means of instrument-flying practice. It teaches the pilot to distribute his attention over the instrument panel, to scan the main instrument displays, and to react to instrument readings (altogether it is known as the 'instrument survey').

Some pilots would disagree with the latter statement, for there is a belief that a pilot should practise his reactions and control inputs in a particular type of cockpit until they become automatic. For my part, I have always been against 'automatic' piloting skills. The pilot should always think and always be aware of what he is doing; he should pilot the aircraft in a constant dialogue with it, applying the controls when the situation requires. Of course his hand should be trained to find the necessary switch easily and promptly, but this sort of mechanical memory is very quickly achieved in actual flying. I must say that test pilots, who have an experience of flying different machines – sometimes two or three different kinds of aircraft in one day – very rarely make mistakes in the use of cockpit instruments or controls. As soon as you settle in your seat in a particular cockpit its layout comes back to you in a flash. All your acquired conscious and subconscious links with this particular type of aircraft quickly return from the back of your mind to the surface.

Eventually we got moving-base in-flight simulators too. Although a full-motion simulator creates a G-load effect lasting for a few seconds only (the cylinder rod full travel time), in terms of piloting practice the duration of G-load effect does not really matter. The point is that the pilot mainly reacts to a change in the G-load rather than to its certain fixed level. And a change in the G-load is what a full-motion simulator provides quite easily by rocking the cockpit backwards and forwards, and by pitching it up and down to imitate acceleration and slowing down.

Perhaps the most interesting meeting I had during that visit to England was with the well-known British pilot Colonel Paul Richey, to whom I was introduced at Farnborough. Richey had fought as a fighter pilot with No. 1 Squadron of the Royal Air Force, which from the very first days of World War Two had been based in France. Richey invited me to his London house. For a member of a Soviet delegation abroad to visit a private home on an Englishman's invitation without telling anyone was at that time impossible, especially since Richey invited me in the presence of some members of our group. I went to see the ambassador and asked his advice. He had nothing against my going, but suggested that I take Igor Milovidov along.

We took the underground, following the directions I had received from Paul Richey. They brought us to a prosperous-looking neighbourhood, and we stopped in front of a three-storey detached house with a Rolls-Royce parked outside the front door. We rang the bell and were admitted into the house by a liveried butler. From the looks of the house we were expecting to be received in some beautifully decorated drawing-room, yet the butler took us down to a den in the basement. There were other guests in the room already, some eight people or so, with an RAF air marshal among them. I remember the conversation I had with his wife. She said something that made me ask, 'You don't like the Russians, do you?' 'And why should I like them?' she replied. I was rather taken aback at first, but then I thought, 'And why should she indeed?'

Paul Richey presented me with his book *Fighter Pilot* (with the words 'To Stepan Mikoyan from a brother pilot, Paul Richey, London, 7.9.1961' written on the flyleaf in his hand), about his squadron and its operations in France until her surrender. The book had been written in 1941, and I had great pleasure reading it. Much of it reminded me of my own experiences as a fighter pilot in the war, and I could not help comparing my memories with what Paul Richey was describing. There was a lot in common of course, but naturally there were also a number of differences, not only in the general circumstances but also in some small things as well. One such difference that comes to mind is that as early as 1940 British pilots were already using onboard radios, which with us Russian fighter pilots did not come into broad use until the beginning of 1943.

On 29 October 1962 I received a phone call in my Akhtubinsk office from the Air Force Command in Moscow. They told me that Victor Andreev of our Fighter Flight Test Department had crashed in Novosibirsk. It was five years since the last two tragic accidents with our fighter pilots, in which we had lost Nikolai Korovin and Igor Sokolov. Unfortunately, in the years to come fighter pilots began to get killed more often.

Victor Andreev had come to us from Kubinka, where he had served in the regiment commanded by my brother Alexei. It might have been the reason why I was always aware of Victor's particular friendliness towards me. He was a fun-loving man, fond of friends, parties and women (not uncommon characteristics among our fighter pilots, I must say). He had a good tenor singing voice, and at our get-togethers he would often entertain us with popular opera arias. The last time I heard him sing was at my fortieth birthday party, three months before his fatal flight. We would often remember Victor and talk about him for a long time afterwards, and it would be his indomitable good humour and his ingenious practical jokes that would invariably be recalled by his friends. One of the many amusing situations he had a knack of getting into went as follows. He was returning early one morning to the pilots' hostel from some party that had kept him awake all night and came face to face with his commanding officer, who had just come into the yard for his morning exercises. Victor was not confused; he immediately began stretching his arms and breathing deeply, as if he was finishing his own work-out.

After the phone call from Moscow I went straight into the pilots' hostel on the way from work, and we all drank together to Victor's memory as the Russian custom was. Victor had been flying out the first production Su-11 to come off the lines of the Novosibirsk aircraft factory (it was common practice to invite one of the test pilots who had performed the military certification tests to participate in the production aircraft tests). He was travelling over the city when the engine rpm 'hung up' – the thrust 'froze' at a level insufficient for horizontal flight, and the aircraft began losing height. As soon as Andreev became aware that he would not make it to the factory airfield, he said on the radio that he was about to eject. At that time he was flying over a large chemical plant, and he must have realised that if his Su-11 crashed into that plant the consequences might be disastrous. He did not eject and tried to land on a light-aircraft airfield nearby. The runway was far too short, and Victor landed with his undercarriage up so as not to overshoot the airfield on the landing run. The possibility of belly-landing in a modern fighter with sweptback or delta wings was something we pilots had discussed more than once. Most of us had agreed it was a very risky business, for this type of aircraft touched down at a large pitch angle with its nose pointing high. As its tail touched the ground the nose would go smashing down against the ground, and the pilot would be exposed to a very heavy G-load. I remembered that Victor had not seemed to take that argument seriously, yet it was exactly what happened in his case: the impact of the fuselage against the ground was so strong that Victor received severe internal injuries and died within half an hour of landing. To be honest, it could hardly have ended differently if he had landed with his undercarriage down: the airfield was small, and it edged onto a forest.

The very next day there was another death: the parachute tester Piotr Dolgov was killed while testing high-altitude pilot gear in a record-altitude (over twenty-five kilometres) parachute jump from the gondola of a stratosphere balloon. His companion, Evgeny Andreev, who was wearing a partial-pressure suit, landed safely having opened his parachute at a little over 1,000 metres above ground level after a free fall of twenty-four kilometres. Dolgov was testing a full-pressure suit and was supposed to open his parachute at once. As he was leaving the gondola he caught his suit on some projecting detail and tore it. The inside air leaked and the pressure in the suit was lost. At a height where the air pressure is over thirty times lower than on the ground his blood immediately boiled and his circulation stopped. Piotr's parachute opened automatically, but he landed a dead man. Victor Andreev and Piotr Dolgov were buried at the same time and at the same place: the pilots' cemetery on the premises of the Chkalovskaya air base. Both were awarded the title of Hero of the Soviet Union, as was Evgeny

Andreev. Victor's name was given to one of the streets in our living compound in Akhtubinsk.

Piotr Dolgov and his CO, the well-known parachutist Nikolai Nikitin, had been parachute testers on the staff of our Institute and had trained the first Soviet cosmonauts of the so-called 'Gagarin group'. The entire group attended Piotr's funeral. Apart from Gagarin, Titov, Nikolayev and Popovich we knew no one in the group, but I remembered a tall, thin, lively-faced lieutenant. Later I learnt it was Alexei Leonov, the first man in the world to step into open space. It was a bitter irony of fate that Victor Andreev and Piotr Dolgov had been close neighbours in Chkalovskaya, with their front doors literally facing each other on the landing. After the double funeral everyone came from the cemetery to join the families for the traditional funeral repast that was offered simultaneously in both flats. Many people wandered from one flat to the other, for most of us had known both Victor and Piotr equally well. Yuri Gagarin and I did the same, and after a while we went two floors down to the flat of another pilot, my friend Sergei Petrov, and sat there in a narrower circle of old friends and fellow pilots, remembering Victor and Piotr and drinking to their memory. Then we all walked with Gagarin to his house and he 'dragged' us upstairs to his flat. There we sat talking and listening to his stories, not about his space flight but about his experiences as a combat pilot flying the MiG-17 in a regiment based beyond the polar circle.

The next day, 3 November 1962, almost as soon as I had returned to Akhtubinsk from the Chkalovskaya funerals, I received a phone call from Moscow through the high-frequency 'government line'. 'A call for you from Comrade Mikoyan's secretariat', a voice said, and a moment later I heard Feodor Lobochkin, my father's former security guard and now one of his secretaries. 'Stepan Anastasovich,' he began (he usually addressed me by my first name), 'such tragedy! Ashkhen Lazarevna has died.' It was my mother. The same day I flew back to Moscow.

My father was away in Cuba in connection with the missile crisis. He was accompanied, apart from officials, by my youngest brother Sergo, who had once been with our father to Cuba before, in 1960. On that visit he helped father, acting as another secretary. The funeral was set for 10 November (after the two-day official holiday), and we hoped father would be able to come. The next day Sergo returned alone, for father had to stay behind in Cuba.

A day or two before the funeral Khrushchev's son Sergei phoned Sergo (they were good friends) and said that his father was inviting Sergo and me to have lunch with him at his dacha. We had to accept, and when we arrived we saw that there would be no one for lunch but the four of us. Khrushchev was telling us about the dramatic events and the tension of the past few days, of how the Americans had discovered our missiles in Cuba and how the danger of a military conflict with disastrous consequences had surfaced. He also told us of his telephone talks with Kennedy and of Fidel Castro's 'getting hysterical'. 'Can you imagine, he insists that we deliver a missile attack on the USA! As if he doesn't understand it would mean a global catastrophe! So we had to send Anastas Ivanovich. He alone, with his inborn diplomatic tact, can make Fidel see reason.'

From what Khrushchev was telling us, I realised that he had hoped the deployment of our missiles in Cuba would remain a secret. It was incredibly naive, yet it was not the first instance of it on the part of state leaders I had come across. Thus during the Korean war, I understood, from something my father has said to me, that in the Politburo they seriously thought our pilots' engagement in Korea would not be discovered. I explained to him then that all the Americans had to do to discover it, was to take an ordinary radio set and tune it in to the frequencies used by our airborne radios.

Nikita Sergeevich said that as soon as he heard of our mother's death he had sent a coded cable to Anastas in Cuba with permission to interrupt his mission and return to Moscow for the funeral. But, he continued, Anastas had sent a reply in which he said that the situation was extremely grave, Castro was on edge, their talks were only just beginning and he could not possibly leave Cuba at such a moment. He asked for the funeral to take place without him. None of us at home could reach our father on the phone in Cuba.

My mother's funeral was on 10 November. The hall at the Defence Ministry club in Kuibyshev street where her body was laid out for a few hours was visited by a great number of people, friends and strangers alike. After the very warm words Khrushchev had said to us about our mother at his dacha only two days earlier, it hurt to see that he chose not to come. However, Nina Petrovna, his wife, and Rada, his daughter, were both there.

In the meantime my father was doing his duty in Cuba, having extremely difficult talks with Fidel Castro. Fidel, though he had met him at the airport on arrival, for two or three days afterwards did not invite him into his presence. According to the then Soviet ambassador in Cuba, A. Alexeev, father received the news of his wife's death a few minutes after the beginning of his very first talk with Castro in the latter's office. Before the paper with the official telephone message was handed to father, the attendant who brought it warned Castro of its contents. Alexeev remembers that my father, having read the message, went over to the window and stood there alone in silence for some time. After a while Castro broke the silence to suggest putting off the talks, but my father refused and they soon continued. In the end his goal was achieved. Fidel Castro relented and the agreement about the withdrawal of our missiles and the Il-28 bombers was achieved. On the way back to Moscow father stopped over in Washington and had a meeting with John Kennedy. Subsequently Castro and my father treated each other with mutual respect and friendliness. When later Castro arrived in Moscow on a visit, he came to see my father in his Moscow home and spent a few very relaxed hours in his company and the company of my father's ten grandchildren. My wife and I were there too.

My father flew back to Moscow two weeks after my mother's funeral, and from the airport he went straight to the cemetery to see the grave of his wife, whom he had known since childhood and with whom he had lived happily for over forty years. Some time after his return he collected and sorted out all mother's photographs, beginning with her few childhood pictures – over fifty pictures altogether. He had them copied and enlarged at the government photo studio and pasted into several large identical photo albums which he had ordered for the purpose. He kept one of them for himself and gave one to each of his sons, together with a number of beautifully enlarged and framed photographic portraits of mother.

The more time elapsed since my mother died, the more acutely conscious I became of the great loss her death was to me, to my father and brothers and to our family at large. She had been our family's soul and conscience. An extremely kind person, though quick-tempered at times, mother was remarkably honest, scrupulous and modest to the point of self-consciousness and shyness. She was utterly incapable of doing anything for her family, let alone herself, at the expense of others. Her sense of duty was overwhelming. For all her love and devotion to her sons she had not made the slightest attempt to protest against my joining a flying school, nor did she later, with the war already on, try to stop my next brother, still a schoolboy, from also becoming a fighter pilot. And with me already shot down and badly burnt and Volodya killed in action a few months later, she did not prevent her third son, a teenager and a schoolboy, from joining a flying school too (nor me from becoming a test pilot later), although for all I know she must have been sick with worry for Alexei and me and consumed by her unfading grief for Volodya.

Volodya's death in air combat at Stalingrad was a shattering blow to all of us, but of course most of all to my mother, though despite everything she could not accept that Volodya was dead and for some years after the war she still hoped against all reason that one day he would come back alive. The loss of her son, and the eventual loss of hope for his return, the nerve-racking anxiety for our father in the last year of Stalin's life and constant worry for her two sons who never stopped flying – all that and a lot more proved too much for her rather fragile health, and in the end led to her death when she was not even sixty-six. The last days of her life were full of concern for my father and her youngest son, in the epicentre of a crisis verging on another world war. Who knows how much longer she would have lived without that last new worry added to all she had already suffered?

At that time my father was already living on Lenin Hills in one of the residences purpose-built in the 1950s for Politburo members. The idea was said to have been conceived by Malenkov's daughter Volya, an architect by profession. The plan as such was probably not so bad for the time – personal residences for the top leaders of the country, many of whom had formerly lived in the Kremlin. The trouble was that the plan was realised, as was so often the case in Russia, without any notion of moderation in mind. As a result there appeared five identical, excessively large and fairly luxurious mansions, each surrounded by large walled-in grounds (later another row of smaller houses was added on the opposite side of the road). At the bottom of the road at the end of the row of houses they built a sports complex with an indoor swimming-pool, a tennis court and a gym, and a conference and reception venue adjoining it. All the neighbouring gardens had communicating gates in the side walls, providing for a private footpath along the length of the road.

My father was allotted the second house from the top of the road (nearer the Moscow University main building), and Khrushchev occupied the one next to the sports complex. My father moved in with all three of my brothers and their families, i.e., with seven of his grandchildren out of ten. For all its size (it had six or seven bedrooms apart from the master suite), the house was pretty full. My wife, my three children and I always lived separately. I remember that Voroshilov, who had also moved into one of the mansions with his wife, found it too big and too depressing just for the two of them. They both missed their old flat in the Kremlin so badly that soon they could not bear it any longer and moved out of the residence to go back (later they moved to a flat on Granovskaya street). My father, who loved being in the country and who used to take every opportunity to escape to the dacha after work, could now pretend he *was* in the country while he was walking around the spacious grounds every evening, with nothing but trees between the back of the house and the public promenade running along the river at the bottom of the hill.

After Khrushchev's deposition it was decided that everyone should move out of the residences, especially since Brezhnev and Kosyghin had never lived there. My father and Sergo with his three children moved together into a flat in a new apartment block on Alexei Tolstoy street.

CHAPTER 20

The Evil Genius of Aviation: The Spin

In April 1961 at the Zhukovsky air base near Moscow, I happened to be the first of the military test pilots to fly a new version of the MiG-21, fitted with a totally new system: the blowdown, or boundary layer control device (where 'boundary layer' is the layer of air closest to the surface of the wing). The function of this device was to increase the lift of the wing at landing, thus reducing the touchdown speed. It operated by means of blowing compressed air from the engine into the airflow over the upper wing surface through special outlets. It accelerated the airflow over the wing which ensured its steadiness and increased the lift.

I was briefed for that flight by the Mikoyan company test pilot George Mosolov. He and a company engineer explained the functioning of the new system to me and described its effect on the behaviour of the aircraft. Very soon I experienced it all 'in action'. As I was gliding with the switch of the boundary layer control device on, the blowdown was automatically activated as soon as I extended the flaps by forty degrees, and the behaviour of the aircraft changed at once. It seemed to have settled on a 'cushion'; I could feel how much more steadily it was supported in the air.

While holding off in my first landing immediately before touchdown, I had a feeling that the aircraft was behaving somewhat unusually. It seemed to require different control movements. After my second and third landings I became fully aware of what the difference was: instead of pulling the stick back gradually into the flare, I had to push it forward. It betrayed an evident speed instability of the machine. A stable aircraft would always react to the reduction of speed by 'ducking' the nose down, as though trying to make the speed faster. Therefore at landing the pilot would normally have to gradually pull the stick back. Mosolov had not warned me about the instability after the flare. When I mentioned that feature at the debriefing afterwards, Mosolov and the others smiled. I realised they had not warned me for a purpose; they wanted to test the reaction of a pilot who would encounter this feature for the first time. I must say I did not think it very ethical on their part to have kept that feature from me. What if the aircraft's unexpected behaviour had caused me to make a mistake?

Soon afterwards the MiG-21 with the blowdown device was passed on to the FTI to be tested by the pilots of our department. After a series of test flights there were several days of general discussion during which opinions were divided. On the one hand the aircraft's instability before touchdown was unacceptable in

281

terms of military specifications, so our engineers and some of the pilots spoke against approving the boundary layer control system which caused it. Most of the pilots, and I was among them, insisted that the blowdown device should be adopted for its obvious advantages in terms of the reduced landing speed and the required length of the runway. Our arguments were that it would not be too difficult for pilots to get used to the stability problem. Besides, they would not have to turn they system on if they did not want to. This last argument decided the outcome of the discussion. The system was soon adopted and, as far as I know, became widely used in the operational force.

In that discussion I also pointed out that an aircraft's very steady flight (when it seemed to be 'sitting on a cushion', as I put it) on the landing glide before the flare had its negative side. When the speed is reduced to a very low level an ordinary aircraft reacts by becoming somewhat unstable, or limp on the controls, as the expression goes. Now, the MiG-21 with the blowdown device was uncommonly steady throughout the loss-of-speed stage, thus failing to signal a very low speed to the pilot. At the same time it had a stronger loss-of-speed tendency than an ordinary aeroplane because of the greater drag. So one had to keep a close eye on the speed and take care to restore it in good time by increasing the engine thrust. We entered a warning to this effect into the MiG-21 manual.

Despite the warning there was one unpleasant incident caused by this feature of the new machine. An air force instructor pilot was performing a night-time training flight in a MiG-21 with a blowdown device and failed to notice the loss of speed on the landing glide. By the time he came down to several dozen metres above ground the speed had become too low. Although the blowdown device prevented the aeroplane from dropping off on a wing, it sank and landed heavily. Luckily there was nothing worse than minor aircraft damage as a result.

Next year there appeared a new interception complex – the Tu-128-80. It was to be tested jointly by the FTI and the Tupolev company. The complex consisted of the Tu-128 interceptor and the ground-based guidance system Air-1. The Tu-128 was a product of the current tendency of improving combat performance of interceptors by developing their armament at the expense of the flight capabilities of the aircraft. It was a heavy machine, and its performance was worse than that of other interceptors. Its maximum Mach number was only 1.6, and its ceiling was just above 13,000 metres. At the same time it was equipped with a radar which had a larger search and lock-on range, and four powerful long-range missiles of the K-80 type. The only way such aircraft could hit a high-speed air target from behind was by firing a missile while lagging behind it, for it would be unable to catch up with it. So its main function was supposed to be frontal attack on a head-on target. In fact, for air defence purposes a frontal attack is preferable since it saves the time taken to get behind the target and therefore allows for attacking the target at a larger distance from the line of defence.

The frontal-attack method became possible due to the increased range of the onboard radar and the installation of a radar operator on board. Later the frontal attack became possible for one-seat fighters as well, but not until both the aircraft and armament control processes became automated. The speed at which an interceptor approaches the target in a head-on attack is very high; it can exceed 3,000 kph. The attack itself takes only seconds, so the pilot is very hard pressed to perform all the necessary operations with the radar and the missiles while controlling the aircraft at the same time. As for the Tu-128, the broad searching zone of its radar and the presence of the radar operator on board provided for greater independence from the ground-based guidance system. The latter guided the Tu-128 into the area where an enemy aircraft was expected to appear, but the actual search of the target was performed by the crew on their own. It was important for the air defence of the areas where a network of ground radar stations could not be created, for example over an ocean or in polar regions. In fact it was in those areas that the Tu-128 interceptors were mainly employed in the future.

A similar aircraft had been built at the Lavochkin Design Company a couple of years earlier: the La-250. I have already mentioned the two accidents with the La-250 due to which this aeroplane was abandoned; then the task was handed over to Tupolev. We were surprised when we heard of it, as the Tupolev company had had no experience with fighters or smaller aircraft in general. That was why their interceptor turned out to be heavier than it might have been. In my opinion, as an aircraft the Tu-128 was inferior to the La-250, though to be fair we did not have the time to assess it in test flights.

Our famous aircraft designer Andrei Tupolev, for all his great talent, was not devoid of weakness. Thus he had a prejudice against hydraulically boosted flight control systems, and rejected the idea of installing such a system in the elevator controls in his Tu-16 bomber (which appeared in the 1950s). As a result this very good aeroplane had somewhat 'heavy' controls. But the Tu-128 was a supersonic aircraft and it could not possibly do without an all-moving horizontal tail. Tupolev had to agree to the installation of a hydraulic actuator, but his prejudice was clear from the fact that the manual controls remained as well. The idea was that in the case of hydraulic failure the pilot would release the elevator (until then rigidly fixed to the stabiliser) with the help of special levers and control it manually. No wonder the Tu-128 came out heavier and showed a more complicated control system design, and I do not know of a single instance when the back-up manual controls were used. To allow for the possibility of manual control, the Tu-128, like all Tupolev's machines, was equipped with a wheel instead of a control stick.

In November 1962, for the first time in our aviation history, an air target (the Il-28) was shot down with a missile launched from a Tu-128 in a head-on attack. The military test pilots who conducted these tests were Igor Lesnikov, Eduard Knyazev and Yuri Rogachev, with George Beregovoi taking part at the beginning. The joint test team was headed by V. Melnikov, and N. Borisov was the project engineer. In those tests the Tu-128 revealed the same kind of pitch instability we had earlier discovered in the MiG-19 and the Tu-104, and which was characteristic of most aircraft with sweptback wings. When Yuri Rogachev was performing a stability test at about 10,000 metres, the aircraft pitched up (as had earlier happened with 'VG' Ivanov in the MiG-19) and, despite the wheel being pushed fully forward, it exceeded the critical angle of attack and went into a spin. Yuri's navigator Mozgovoi was about to eject but Yuri commanded him to stay put in his seat, in none too polite terms, and recovered from spinning less than 5,000 metres above the ground level. As the Department Commander I recommended the crew for a decoration for having rescued the test specimen of the new aircraft. Tupolev supported my recommendation and Yuri was decorated with the Red Banner Order, Mozgovoi receiving the Order of the Red Star.

While I am on the subject of the Tu-128 I shall recall a number of episodes, including a tragic one, related to this aircraft. The Tu-128 had a feature which had revealed itself in other aircraft with hydraulically powered controls as well, a delay in the response of the actuator to the control stick (or wheel, as in the Tu-128) inputs. In the event of pitch oscillations, attempts to stop the aircraft from pitching up and down were counter-productive and led to an increase in the amplitude of pitching. Thus, when the pilot pushed the stick forward to prevent pitching up, the response did not come at once and so the pilot pushed further forward, which was already too far. On noticing that the aircraft was 'over-reacting', the pilot pulled the stick back, and the pattern repeated itself in the opposite direction. So due to the delayed action of the hydraulic system the pilot was swinging the machine himself even as he was trying to steady it. The phenomenon became known as 'pilot-induced oscillations', though it was the faults in the aircraft control system which were responsible for it.

We at the Institute had first encountered this phenomenon in the MiG-19, and we established that as soon as the control stick was fixed in the near neutral position the oscillations immediately stopped. At the same time we found that even a pilot prepared to expect these oscillations and knowing what to do, started off by making a few instinctive attempts at the stick in order to counter them, thus increasing the pitching further before remembering to neutralise the stick. In fighter aircraft, with the airframe designed to carry a much larger G-load, excessive pitching normally would not be of any consequence, whereas with heavy aircraft, designed for a lower G-load factor, excessive pitch oscillation could threaten the airframe integrity. The two ways of getting rid of oscillation are reducing the delay in the hydraulic system and fitting the aircraft with pitch dampers.

Before the Tu-128 was equipped with a pitch damper, excessive pitch oscillation was encountered by one of our test pilots, Igor Dovbysh. After three 'swings' up and down, Dovbysh remembered that the wheel should be fixed. It all ended well, for the Tu-128 sustained the load of nearly 5G without any damage to itself. However, similar circumstances encountered by a Tu-22 missile carrier, an aircraft with a smaller margin of strength, once led to a tragic outcome. This aircraft was designed with negative subsonic stability so that at supersonic speed, where stability is always higher, it would not affect the controllability of the machine. At subsonic speed stability was ensured by two pitch dampers. The crew, which consisted of the test pilot Chernoivanov, the navigator Tsaregorodtsev and the radioman Luzanov (all of them Institute men), were to perform a stability test with one of the dampers on. They switched one damper off as their mission required, and the other one turned out to be out of order. The aircraft began pitching up and down, and at the third deep 'swing' it started disintegrating. The pitching began so sharply and unexpectedly that the pilot had no time to switch the first damper back on. The navigator ejected at the last moment and landed safely, but the pilot was a fraction late and his parachute did not have time to open. The radioman remained in the aeroplane and crashed with it. After that accident pitch dampers in the Tu-22 were complemented with another safety device: a control column deflection rate limiter which prevented the pilot from making dangerously sharp control movements in pitch.

The Tu-128 had another shortcoming typical of aircraft with sweptback, relatively high-aspect-ratio wings. Such wings possess less torsional stiffness than short or delta wings. At high indicated air speed the torsional strain of such wings usually affects the aileron authority, causing the aircraft's disobedience, and if the strain is very high it can lead to what is known as aileron control reversal, where the aircraft banks in the direction opposite to that intended by the pilot.

This structural defect of the Tu-128 caused a fatal accident in 1971. The pilot Vyacheslav Mayorov, and his navigator, Gennady Mitrofanov, were testing aileron authority for rolling out from the bank which developed after launching two missiles from the same wing (with two missiles left under the other). Their prescribed altitude was 10,000 metres with a Mach number of 1.6. The indicated air speed was not supposed to exceed 1,010 kph, the level at which the aircraft still obeyed the lateral control inputs. It was the indicated air speed that was of primary importance here, for it reflected the dynamic air pressure. Mayorov accelerated, coming down from a higher altitude to 200 metres below the prescribed height, with the Mach number at launching slightly above the pre-set level. Neither of the deviations was large, yet both of them increased the indicated air speed to over 1,020 kph, which was the aileron authority limit. After launching the two missiles, Mayorov waited the prescribed four seconds before resuming control of the aircraft (the idea being to imitate a combat pilot's possible mistake). The delay proved fatal. The aeroplane rolled to the left with its nose down, and when Mayorov finally applied the wheel to counter the roll, the bank had already reached forty-five degrees and was still growing. The aircraft turned wings over and went into a dive at increasing speed. The Tu-128 had not been designed for high-speed diving, and so ejection was the crew's only way out. The pilot did eject, but his lapbelt was broken by the strong airstream and the lower part of the seat came off, hitting him hard as it did so. His parachute opened automatically, but Mayorov was dead when he reached the ground. As for Mitrofanov, for some reason he did not eject at all.

Mayorov must have been too preoccupied with watching the Mach number and the height, and so failed to notice that his indicated air speed had gone above 1,020 kph. Perhaps the engineers omitted to stress at the briefing that the indicated speed was the chief parameter of aileron authority, that he should on no account exceed 1,010 kph. There was also a chance that Mayorov might have recovered from banking if it had occurred to him to apply the rudder, but in any case all he had were fractions of a second. I arrived at the site of his landing in a helicopter right after the rescue helicopter had found him. Mayorov was lying on the ground covered by the parachute, and his aircraft was nothing but a pile of debris.

Towards the end of 1963 a group of pilots was individually awarded the title of Honoured Test Pilot of the Soviet Union, and I was one of them. The titles of Honoured Test Pilot and Honoured Navigator for those engaged in flight testing were introduced in 1959, and the first people to receive them were the pilots and navigators of the aviation industry testing centres and my colleagues from the Flight Test Institute. Honoured Test Pilot's badge No. 1 was received by the Aviation Industry Flight Research Institute (Gromov Institute) pilot Sergei Anokhin, and the Honoured Navigator's badge No. 1 was awarded to Nikolai Zatsepa from the FTI. The investiture of our group took place in February 1964 in the Kremlin. I was presented with a badge together with General Molotkov, Colonel Kabrelev and several other immediate colleagues. The ceremony was supposed to be conducted by Leonid Brezhnev, the then chairman of the Supreme Council of the USSR, but he was away and one of his deputies was acting on his behalf. If I had been awarded that title about six months later I would probably have received the badge from the hands of my father, who succeeded Brezhnev as chairman of the Supreme Council Presidium.

In 1963 the FTI was testing a new gunsight installed in the Su-7B for pull-up and over-the-shoulder bombing. It was a totally new method of bombing for fighter-bombers, mainly designed for nuclear bombs. The aircraft approached the target in a low-level flight and then either performed a pull-up (if it came short of the target) or an Immelmann (if it had overshot it). The bombs were supposed to be dropped from a steep-climb attitude so that they would fall on the target in a ballistic trajectory. This method allowed for a stealthy approach to the target and helped to dodge anti-aircraft fire. After bombing the aircraft descended at top speed and went home hedge-hopping again, evading the sonic shock wave.

The tests were performed by Vadim Petrov and Vladimir Grotsky. One unfortunate morning Grotsky took off in the Su-7B and did not return. The aircraft crashed and he went in with it. It was the second loss of life in our new department. The analysis of the causes led to an unexpected discovery. The aircraft was approaching the target at 1,050 kph at a height of just under 100 metres. Suddenly its landing flaps extended (there might have been an electric circuit closing or the pilot might have accidentally pushed the flap control knob). The air speed was nearly double the flaps-down limit speed, and a large portion of a flap broke off, hitting one of the horizontal stabilons and chopping it off (the flap portion was the first to fall on the ground, with the stabiliser fragment following). What happened next was hard to believe: the aeroplane went down almost at once, although with the speed it was flying at it should have carried on under its own momentum for some time. The Su-7B had taken off with three 100 kg bombs, but after the crash the bombs were not found among the debris, and the lugs that had held them on the wings were torn. The lugs were designed to hold up to 3,000 kg, so the load before the crash must have been about 30 G! Nobody had expected that an aircraft could experience such an immense G-load (the structural load limit was only 12 G).

The Evil Genius of Aviation: The Spin

The reason was the breakage of the horizontal stabiliser. The point is that a low-altitude flight at a high indicated air speed creates a strong pitch-up moment, and to keep the aircraft level the pilot has to push the stick almost fully forward. Aerodynamic calculations showed that with half the stabilon gone there was no question of its remaining half keeping the aeroplane in level flight. The machine was simply bound to pitch the nose up and go up in a curve, with a load factor of no less than 25 G. It was as though the Su-7B had suddenly gone upwards in a direction perpendicular to its flight path and then lost speed abruptly. Its powerful steel longerons had broken like matches even before the ground impact. Its wheel struts, as big as howitzer barrels, were plucked out of the gear wells and twisted off by force of inertia of the wheels. As for the bombs, they came off the lugs and flew forward. The pilot could not have survived such an enormous G-load and must have been dead even before the crash.

Vadim Petrov had an emergency experience himself around that time. He was testing a Su-9 for engine restart and he shut off and restarted the engine several times, until suddenly it refused to restart (it later turned out that the ignition coil had failed). Vadim began a power-off landing approach, but he had no relevant experience yet and was understandably nervous. Although he approached correctly, his landing speed was too high and he overshot at touchdown. Vadim deployed the brake parachute, but it was torn off by his high speed, and if that was not enough the unpaved emergency strip he landed on was covered with ice. Vadim could see the air base closure fence getting near, but the aircraft was still running. To avoid crashing into it, all he had time to do was steer the machine into a gap between two concrete posts supporting lines of barbed wire. The aircraft ran through undamaged, except for the wing edges. In accordance with the safety manual the engine's failure to restart was a legitimate reason for ejecting. I recommended Petrov for a decoration for saving the aircraft, but General Ponomarev from the Air Force Command, whose decision it was, presented him with a camera instead.

One day I was to fly in a two-seat Su-7 as an instructor with Colonel Vasily Kotlov for a routine check of his piloting performance. Kotlov taxied up to the strip and requested clearance to take the runway. The tower said yes, and he taxied on. Out of long-standing habit I took a look left in the direction of the final approach and saw a Su-9 gliding towards the runway. That was very odd, for we had heard no one asking for clearance to land – that's why the tower had cleared us for taking the runway. I ordered Kotlov to stop, and the Su-9 flashed past us and landed. It turned out to be Sasha Kuznetsov, whose engine had cut off in a surge evaluation test flight. Due to vibration his entire electrical system had failed, as well as his radio. He was going to land on the long runway, but miscalculated and was approaching too short of it. All he could do was turn towards the shorter strip which was closer, and to which we were taxiing.

My closest friend among my colleagues in the fighter section at this time was Leonid Fadeev. When Igor Sokolov was alive, he, Leonid and I often spent time together after work. Fadeev, like Igor, was a lively and sociable man with a great sense of humour. He was one of those people who are described as the life and soul of every party. No gathering of our fighter pilots, whatever the occasion, could be conceived or could do without Lyosha (as everyone called Leonid). He was certainly a fun-loving man and a bit of a playboy, but he adored his wife Katya and their daughter and was devoted to his mother-in-law, who truly doted on him.

The news of his wife giving birth to a pair of twin boys was celebrated by the entire fighter pilot section. Lyosha proudly called them 'my guardsmen', and they were still known under this nickname when they both became fighter pilots. For a while both of Lyosha's 'guardsmen' commanded Soviet fighter squadrons in East Germany, and on their return home they became graduate students of the Air Force Academy.

Although Leonid Fadeev had no higher education, he was an excellent test pilot. I have earlier mentioned his participation in testing the first radars and the Su-9-51 interception complex. Soon after those tests he was sent to the Gromov Institute in Zhukovsky to take part in the initial spin tests of the Su-9. After a few revolutions in a spin Leonid applied anti-spin controls to recover, and after a slight delay the machine stopped spinning and dived. Fadeev advanced the throttle to pull up, but the engine speed hardly went up at all and the exhaust gas temperature needle was moving menacingly towards the danger mark. The engine 'hang-up' was due to the intake airflow distortion caused by spinning. Lyosha pulled up and began his landing glide without touching the throttle. He could probably have turned the engine off and tried to restart it, but he believed he would make it to the runway, for there was some engine thrust left. At about 1,000 metres Leonid realised that he was coming a little short of the landing strip and instinctively moved the throttle forward. The temperature jumped and the engine cut off. The descent immediately became steeper, and Fadeev landed on rough ground, short of the 'undershoot strip'. The aeroplane made several somersaults and literally fell into pieces.

I later saw photographs of the wreckage: the cockpit part of the fuselage had separated from the rest and had turned over on its own. The photograph showed it lying on the side. It was hard to believe that the pilot could have emerged from that crash alive, yet he did! But his spine was injured, and the medical board grounded him for good. After that Lyosha Fadeev, an Honoured Test Pilot of the USSR, worked for many years at the Sukhoi company as a member of their pilot manual-writing team. He died after two heart attacks at the end of the 1980s.

I have used the words 'spin' and 'spinning' so many times, that it might be appropriate to explain this phenomenon in some detail. No doubt most people have heard the word 'spin' in connection with aviation, but I don't think many people outside the profession understand what it really is. Ever since the earliest days of aviation, the spin has been one of the main hazards threatening the pilot. It was in those days that people first encountered the unexpected, spontaneous and uncontrollable downward spiral movement of an aeroplane. In Russia the phenomenon became known as a 'corkscrew'. An aeroplane can go into a spin when the angle of attack becomes greater than the critical angle of attack. This can happen due to loss of speed or as a result of an excessively agile manoeuvre. The airflow over the upper wing surface stalls and swirls, dramati-

The first Russian jet aircraft, the MiG-9.

The Yak-17 fighter.

Two **MiG-15s** (NATO code 'Fagot'). Number 417 was flown by the author for inspection tests.

The MiG-17 (NATO code 'Fresco') was a development of the MiG-15, but with redesigned wings and an afterburner.

The photo-reconnaissance version was known as the **MiG-17R**.

The interceptor version of the **MiG-19** (NATO code 'Farmer').

The MiG-19-SM-12 fighter.

ABOVE AND BOTTOM LEFT: The first version of the MiG-21 (NATO code 'Fishbed'). This tactical fighter was powered by a single Tumanskii R-25-300 turbojet rated at 15,650 lb st with afterburner.

Test pilots of the Test Institute in front of a MiG-21PF. The author is ninth from the left.

The MiG-21F-13 ('Fishbed-C') was armed with one NR-30 cannon and two AA-2 'Atoll' air-to-air missiles.

A Sukhoi Su-15 with X-98 missiles.

The MiG-23S (NATO code 'Flogger') first flew in 1967. This particular aircraft was flown by the author and was the first prototype of the design.

The **MiG-23M** ('Flogger-B') carried pulse-Doppler radar and AA-7 'Apex' missiles.

Three **MiG-27** ground attack/tactical strike fighter-bombers. They are optimised for low-level attack.

cally losing velocity. The lift on one wing goes sharply down, the aircraft banks – or, as pilots put it, departs – and spontaneous rotation or 'auto-rotation' begins. The reason, quite simply, is the large discrepancy between the respective lift of the two wings. This is what a spin is: the aeroplane is falling down while rotating around all three axes.

An aircraft with a straight, non-sweptback wing usually reacts to the stalling of the wing airflow by abruptly going into a spin. A sweptback aeroplane as a rule tends to 'linger' at the departure stage and can occasionally even roll back into the opposite direction. However, if the stalling occurs in a high-G manoeuvre – which is known as 'dynamic departure' – the aircraft falls into a spin at once, in a violent rotating movement. To recover from the departure stage or from the spin which is just beginning, all the pilot normally has to do is push the stick slightly forward to reduce the angle of attack. Sometimes just neutralising the controls is sufficient. To recover from a fully developed spin is far more difficult. First of all you have to slow down the rotation rate by pressing the rudder pedal full opposite, and two or three seconds later you have to vigorously push the stick forward to reduce the angle of attack. To increase the sweep of the elevator you should first draw the stick fully back before pushing. As soon as the rotation stops, the rudder pedals have to be neutralised at once to prevent spinning in reverse. As the rotation stops and the angle of attack decreases the spin as such is over, but the aircraft is still diving and it has to be pulled up to level flight when it builds up sufficient speed. This can be regarded as the second phase of spin recovery.

When the sweptback MiG-15 had just begun to be widely used in operational units there occurred a number of ejections and fatal accidents caused by the pilots' failure to recover from a spin. In 1950 the FTI was commissioned to carry out flight research of the MiG-15 spin. The test pilots who had taken part in that programme were later sent to various combat units to perform demonstration flights and to train commanding officers as instructors for their flying officers. The test programme and the subsequent demonstration and instruction tasks were performed by the best FTI pilots: 'VG' Ivanov, L. Kuvshinov, A. Rogatnev, G. Beregovoi (who earned the nickname of the 'king of the spin'), V. Makhalin and D. Pikulenko. By the time I joined the Institute the programme was nearly completed.

The features that were then for the first time discovered in the MiG-15 eventually turned out to be to some extent characteristic of all aircraft with sweptback or with delta wings. The point is that in terms of its behaviour in a spin and its recovery from it, an aeroplane with sweptback wings is far more affected by the slipping factor than a non-sweptback aeroplane. In a spin the aircraft usually slips in the direction opposite to that of rotation, thus in a right spin the plane slips to the left. In such a slip the lift of the left wing builds up due to the change in the angle between the wing and the airflow, while that of the right wing, where the airflow is stalled, is low. This increases the banking to the right and enhances the spinning. If at recovery, while pushing the stick forward, you do what seems the natural thing and deflect it sideways against rotation – in our case it would be to the left – the right aileron will be lowered.

Normally it would increase the lift on the right wing and make the aeroplane roll to the left, but in a spin the lowering of an aileron is counter-productive; it enhances both the spinning *and* the slip. That is why the deflection of the stick against rotation makes recovery from a spin impossible.

A case in point was an incident involving our well-known test pilot Colonel Antipov. He was an evaluation pilot in the spin tests of the MiG-19 (an aircraft with the wings swept even further back than those of the MiG-15), in which Vasily Kotlov was the project test pilot. He was accompanied by a chase aeroplane with a film cameraman on board. As he was recovering from the spin and pushed the stick forward, Antipov accidentally moved it sideways against rotation (he was a big and bulky man for whom the fighter cockpit was somewhat too small). The machine went on spinning. As Antipov told us later, after another unsuccessful recovery attempt he went into a kind of stupor, and was just holding the stick and the pedals in the same position and waiting. The altimeter needle was revolving fast, but it was as if he did not realise there was no altitude left for recovery. 'I know I would have sat like this until I hit the ground, if it hadn't been for Nikolai Divuyev!' The chase aircraft pilot Divuyev said to him on the radio, 'Height low, make a decision!', which in pilots' language means that it is time to eject. It was only then that Antipov came to and pulled the ejector drive. After that his canopy ought to have separated but it didn't. When there was hardly an altitude margin left for ejection, Antipov rammed the canopy upwards with both fists and it came off. The ejection gun fired almost too late, for Antipov's parachute deployed just over the ground. He landed safely in the end, but it was a very narrow escape. Such 'stupors' are rare, yet even a very experienced pilot of Antipov's class can occasionally experience them. Who knows how many of the unexplained fatal accidents were caused by them?

In 1951, after the completion of the major test research programme devoted to the spin (I was already working at the Institute then), there occurred an incident related to that work. A coded telegram arrived at the FTI from the commander of an air fighter division based at Petrozavodsk which said that while our pilot Vladimir Makhalin had been performing a demonstration flight with one of the division commanding officers, the aircraft had gone into an inverted spin. The telegram was signed by Makhalin as well. There followed quite a row. The Institute Commander got Makhalin on the phone and promised to fire him. The problem was that it had been registered in the final statement based on the military certification tests that the MiG-15 two-seat trainer did not enter the inverted spin, so it looked as though Makhalin had 'let the Institute down' by admitting that it could happen.

As soon as Makhalin returned a new series of tests was conducted with his participation. He showed in what circumstances it had happened. It turned out that in the normal intentional entry into an inverted spin, from the wheels-up attitude, the aeroplane would not go into it. At the same time, in an ordinary level flight at low air speed, if the stick was pushed fully forward and sideways while the opposite full rudder pedal was pushed the aircraft tumbled violently over the nose to one side and entered an inverted spin, with a few seconds of tail-first flight on the way to it. This was a totally unexpected and bizarre manoeuvre which Makhalin christened with an equally bizarre name, 'coordy-coordy'. A somewhat similar manoeuvre was later adopted in aerial sports, where it became known as an 'abracadabra'. So Makhalin justified himself, though he still got a thorough dressing-down from the boss for signing that telegram without first reporting to the Institute Commander.

Institute policy was that departure and recovery should be demonstrated to combat pilots in action, in two-seater aeroplanes. Gaining some first-hand experience of the characteristic cues of the near-stalling condition and of the control inputs required to avoid stalling would boost their confidence when it came to flying in the near-maximum-angle-of-attack regimes (the latter are essential for getting the most out of the aircraft's manoeuvrability in air combat). However, the spin-related accident induced the Air Force Command to forbid intentional spinning to all except test pilots, and the ban has remained to this day, so operational pilots get acquainted with the spin recovery techniques only in theory. The ban on spinning leads to a kind of phobia among combat pilots and effectively limits the use of the manoeuvring capabilities of fighter aircraft. Worse still, if a combat pilot *does* accidentally encounter a near-stalling condition he sometimes fails to recognise and oppose it, and once the spin is entered he is often totally lost and all he can think of is ejection (or not even that – there have been cases of totally unnecessary deaths too). In addition, a pilot who will try to recover is likely to make the mistake of inclining the stick against rotation. It is something that might have killed a number of operational pilots with no practical experience of spin recovery techniques.

A spin-related incident happened to my brother Vanya. Soon after I had become a fully-fledged test pilot I visited the flying club at Klyazma where Vanya, then a student of the Air Force Engineering Academy, was doing his initial flying training course. I had a ride with him in a light Yak-18 trainer and he performed a series of aerobatic manoeuvres, one of which was a spin. As he was pushing the stick forward to recover he moved it against the spin as if to level the wings. The Yak-18 obeyed, for it was one of the few aeroplanes that would forgive such a mistake. However, I told Vanya off for it, explaining that another aircraft in this situation would not have recovered.

That flight nearly ended in misadventure too. When Vanya pushed the landing gear handle down before landing, only one leg extended, while the other jammed. He tried again with the same result. Vanya decided to belly-land, but I told him not to hurry with it. The point is that my ride with him was not quite 'legitimate' and was only thanks to the lenience of his official instructor. So the last thing I wanted was a row in connection with the Mikoyan brothers landing with their undercarriage up. We did a number of high-G pull-outs (pulling out of dives made to create G-load) but it did not help. Then I suggested, 'Let's fly around a bit until the air-bottle pressure gets pumped up.' About fifteen minutes later the pressure in the air-bottle went up and I suspended the aeroplane at minimum speed so as to diminish the airstream counteraction against the movement of the legs, and both of them obediently came out. It turned out on inspection that one of the struts had got slightly rusted.

CHAPTER 21

The International Aviation Federation

In 1963 I was invited to take part in the work of the USSR Federation of Air Sports (FAS), which was then chaired by the celebrated test pilot and twice Hero of the Soviet Union General Vladimir Kokkinaki. From that time until 1994 I was involved with that federation. Officially it was an independent body, which was as such a member of the Paris-based International Aviation Federation (FAI). In actual fact, however, our federation was created 'under the wing' of a state organisation called DOSAAF (the acronym stands for the Russian words meaning 'Voluntary Society for Co-operation with the Army, Air Force and Navy'). Our association executive secretary was a DOSAAF official. The FAS representatives regularly (on the money issued by the government and the money received as annual membership fees) attended meetings of the FAI council and its commissions in Paris, as well as its annual general conference held in various capital cities of the world.

In 1964 Vladimir Kokkinaki, as one of the FAI vice-presidents, and I, as a board member, visited Paris together in connection with the FAI council meeting. One morning I received a phone call at my hotel from FAI Honorary President M. Allez. He said he wanted to have a talk with General Kokkinaki and asked me to interpret for him (into English). The three of us met in the lobby, and Allez almost immediately surprised us by asking what Kokkinaki would say if he was nominated at the next general conference for election as FAI First Vice-President. This meant that at the conference after next he would inevitably be elected president. For all I know it might have been a unique occasion when a USSR representative was put forward for election as the president of an inter-national association without an initial proposal from the Soviet Union itself. Vladimir Kokkinaki was no doubt held in great esteem by the FAI leadership. Kokkinaki was certainly flattered but he could not say yes without the approval of a corresponding department of the Central Committee of the Party. He thanked Allez and said that he had to consult his own federation board. Later we mailed Kokkinaki's formal consent from Moscow. He was elected First Vice-President at the general conference in the autumn of 1964, and two years later he became FAI President.

Unfortunately he had to lose that post before his full term was over. Two years after his election as FAI President a new election was to be held. In accordance with a FAI tradition, each president was usually re-elected for a second two-year term. The general conference of 1967 had voted for holding the next annual general meeting (when Kokkinaki was to be re-elected) in Athens, but by the time

292

it was to be held, Greece had fallen under the power of the 'black colonels'. The Central Committee department that was in charge of sanctioning official visits abroad (no Soviet delegation could leave the country without their approval) decided that Kokkinaki's trip to Greece under its new political regime was 'inadvisable'. It was obviously beyond them to understand that he was expected to attend the FAI conference, not as a Soviet representative, but as a figure of international status. Imagine a general conference of an international organisation whose president fails to attend! No wonder that a new president was immediately elected in Kokkinaki's place, while he, by another FAI tradition, became an honorary president. The irony of it was that the next year a Soviet football team was allowed to go to Greece without any fuss.

Several years later Vladimir Kokkinaki was succeeded as the Soviet FAS President by another remarkable person, the renowned wartime fighter pilot and Hero of the Soviet Union three times over General Kozhedub. I was elected his deputy. A few years after that, in 1979 or 1980, General Kozhedub had to leave his post due to a grave illness. I received an offer of nomination as president, but I could not accept until I received official clearance for all visits abroad. After my initial three FAI trips in 1964 and 1965, General Kulikov, Chief of General Staff, had forbidden another air force general on the FAS board and me to go abroad. As a senior commanding officer of the Flight Test Institute I had access to top secret materials and data, and as all other people in similar positions I had only been allowed abroad on official missions (and the representation of the Air Sports Federation was not regarded as such) assigned by my command, or else on a course of treatment to a health spa in a socialist country. I had been abroad before that several times: on official postings, on holiday at the Karlovy Vary health spa in Czechoslovakia, and when I accompanied my father on his state visits. Yet a foreign trip on behalf of a public organisation would not be allowed (to say nothing of a private visit on a friend's invitation).

However, at the time I was invited to become FAS President I was already working for the aviation industry, not for the air force, and had far less to do with classified materials. The DOSAAF wrote to the Aviation Ministry for clearance for my attendance at the FAI meetings, and the answer was that it was 'undesirable'. Our second cosmonaut German Titov was elected FAS chairman instead of me. Ironically, he was not allowed to go abroad either, for he was then holding an important position in the Ministry of Defence. I remained vice-president for several years, and in 1991 I was elected president. In 1994 I was succeeded by Svetlana Savitskaya and was elected an honorary chairman, following the pattern of the FAI.

The FAI General Assembly in 1964 took place in Tel Aviv. At that time, before the 1967 Six-Day War between Israel and Egypt, the USSR still had diplomatic relations with Israel. Our delegation was headed by General Kokkinaki, and the rest of it consisted of a DOSAAF representative, Tatyanchenko, and me. At midday on 14 October we landed in our Ilyushin-18 airliner at Nicosia airport in Cyprus. The Soviet airliner was *en route* to Baghdad, from where it would have been a shorter way to Tel Aviv, but it was considered dangerous to fly to

Israel over an Arabic country and therefore we had been advised to change at Nicosia for a direct British flight to Tel Aviv. On the way in through customs in Nicosia a customs officer beamed on seeing Kokkinaki's name in his passport: 'A Greek, aren't you?' We had a few hours to see the city before our flight to Israel, and a Soviet embassy officer took us around in his car. We drove up to the demarcation lines between the Greek and the Turkish parts of Nicosia and saw rather a bleak picture: a barricade made of sacks of sand, with more sacks blocking the windows of many houses, soldiers wandering around and armed sentries at certain points.

The same night we got on a British Comet 4 airliner, and some time after midnight we arrived in Tel Aviv. We were surprised to see reporters who had obviously been waiting for us and who bombarded us with questions about Khrushchev's deposition. We were stunned and totally at a loss; though apparently the sensational news had been announced on the day we were travelling, we had heard nothing at all. We tried to hide our shock as best we could, and Kokkinaki dismissed further questions by announcing that we were a sports delegation and had no interest in politics; rather an ill-chosen reply by any standard, but the papers next day confined themselves to saying that we knew nothing. Was it possible that our ambassador in Nicosia, on whom we had called to say goodbye before leaving for Tel Aviv, did not know anything either? Or maybe he simply chose to say nothing to us to avoid discussion? Another surprise was awaiting us outside the arrival terminal: a large crowd with flags and welcoming posters. People shouted (in Russian) 'Hurrah!', 'Welcome to Tel Aviv!' and 'Peace and friendship!', and we even heard some of them call out our names. We shook a lot of hands on the way to the car, and there were camera flashes going off left, right and centre.

All conference participants had been booked into the Sheraton (some of them came with their wives and children), where the conference itself took place. The hotel stood right on the sea coast and had a private beach and an outdoor swimming-pool. The entire building was air-conditioned. We were given two rooms: a twin room for Tatyanchenko and myself, and a single one for Kokkinaki. We were pleased to find ourselves in such nice and comfortable rooms – until we spotted the cost quotes in little frames on our doors. We realised we would not only have to use up our hotel allowances to the last penny, but also add nearly all our respective travel allowances as well. The sad truth as it dawned on us was that, having paid for the rooms, we would hardly have any money left to eat on, let alone to buy souvenirs or whatever (and Soviet citizens were not allowed to possess any hard currency at the time). Our position was as humiliating as during my visit to the air show in England, when two deputy ministers, two world-famous aircraft designers and two generals had to share rooms in a very cheap London hotel because with the beggarly allowance given to us in Moscow we could not afford anything else.

With the attention paid to the Soviet delegation by the organisers and other participants, we simply could not move to a cheaper hotel. We knew a number of people on the conference well, so it would not go unnoticed. Crestfallen and disconcerted, we went to the embassy to ask for advice. To our good fortune it turned out to be the time 'between two ambassadors', as it were: the former one had gone home and the new one had not yet arrived. We were made a generous offer of the spacious ambassador's apartment in the embassy building. A better solution could not have been found. We kept the single room at the Sheraton as our daytime 'base' (our joint hotel allowance was just enough to pay for it) and informed those who knew us among the participants that General Kokkinaki had run into an old friend at the embassy who had insisted that the three of us stay with him as his guests.

The conference was perfectly organised. Our hosts took full advantage of the event, which had brought to Israel representatives of over fifty different states, to show their country off. The meetings took place every other day and hardly ever went on after lunch; the rest of the time was given to sight-seeing and various excursions. There were several coaches provided for us with an Israeli air hostess and a guide assigned to each of them. The three of us always travelled on the coach with the Americans and other English-speaking participants (plus the people who could understand either English or Russian), for our guide was from a family of Russian Jews and had fluent English and passable Russian. We made coach trips to all Israel's main cities: Jerusalem, Haifa, Nazareth, and we were even taken to the Dead Sea. There was a lot of singing on the way, mostly Russian songs; Kokkinaki and Tatyanchenko would start off, and others enthusiastically joined in.

In Nazareth we visited the large church built over the site of Christ's childhood home. In Jerusalem we saw Golgotha, the Temple of David and other holy places. Half of Jerusalem at that time, before the Six-Day War, belonged to the Arabs. The coach took us to see the 'border street', a no-man's corridor between rows of barbed wire on either side. The big yellow signboards warned against coming too close: 'Danger! Frontier ahead!' A journalist girl walking beside me said that there had been occasional shootings here and people had got killed. We entered a large temple and climbed up the steps to an open landing at the top, from where the whole city could be seen. At the door to the staircase we were advised to leave our cameras behind, for a flash of a lens against the sun could be taken for binoculars from the other side and fired at. So my film camera had to be left downstairs too.

Another interesting excursion (by air) was to Eilat, a city-port in the south of the country on the Bay of Aqaba, a long narrow stretch of the Red Sea. West of Eilat was Egypt, to the east of it Jordan, and only about ten kilometres' worth of the coastline between the two belonged to Israel. We were shown a water-desalinating plant, the only local source of fresh water besides an underground spring about a thousand metres deep. As all other tourists on the Red Sea coast we made a trip on a pleasure boat with enormous glass portholes in its bottom, through which we could admire the magnificent underwater view of the bay, with exotic-looking plants covering the seabed and exotic fish floating under our feet. After the voyage we had time to go swimming in the bay. I had already had a dip in the Mediterranean in Tel Aviv, and now I added the Red Sea to my 'collection'. Its water was noticeably saltier than in the Black Sea and swimming was much easier.

An interesting experience of a different kind was a visit to three kibbutzes – the agricultural communes apparently introduced by Russian immigrants in the early twentieth century. They must have shown us their most successful ones, for what we saw in all three of them impressed us by its prosperous (by communal standards, of course) and spick-and-span look: clean and well-tended grounds, neat two-storey cottages with modern conveniences, a canteen, a school and a kindergarten and a civic centre. We were invited to go inside one of the cottages and were shown a typical flat: two rooms and a kitchenette in the hall. A proper kitchen was considered unnecessary for everyone ate in the canteen, and all people would have at home was perhaps a light supper or coffee. All children older than three were actually *living* in the kindergarten (it was more of a boarding-school, perhaps, for there were older children there as well), with only three hours spent at home each afternoon. In the school we saw girls and boys sharing bedrooms for three or four children each. We were told that the mixed upbringing was intended to prevent the children from developing an 'unhealthy interest' in the opposite sex.

All members of a kibbutz would do different jobs on a kind of rota basis. The only salary they would regularly receive for their work was some sort of pocket money, and when they wanted money for larger purchases, for example, a suit or some such thing, it was given to them within the allowance each was entitled to 'by the book'. University education was also paid for by the kibbutz, but it expected one to return and work for it after the graduation. Besides their primary agricultural orientation, one of the kibbutzes we visited was running a roadside restaurant, and another had a jewellery workshop. We were told that out of Israel's three million population about 100,000 people lived in kibbutzes, and that many of the well-to-do and high-ranking citizens sent their children to kibbutzes for a year or two for a taste of 'life and work in a collective'. When we were at a reception at an Israeli minister's house he presented to us his son who was home 'on leave' from a kibbutz.

In those days Israel must have been the only non-Slavic country where a visitor from the USSR could easily get by without any foreign language. Russian seemed to be spoken in Tel Aviv at every corner (even more so today, I believe). The local radio broadcasted Russian songs, and we were shown a forest outside Tel Aviv known as the 'Red Army Forest', a popular picnic ground frequented by Soviet immigrant families. The forest owed its name to their custom of going there every year on 9 May to celebrate the victory over fascism (I later heard that the tradition continued after the breaking-off of diplomatic relations between Israel and the USSR).

In Tel Aviv I had an opportunity to drive around on my own in the car lent to me once or twice by our embassy official. One day I went driving in the company of an Israeli journalist whom I had met at a conference reception. She published a little article in her paper about me entitled 'A vodka for you? – No, orange juice, please'. While in Israel I kept a diary describing all my experiences and impressions, and I wrote a feature story on the basis of it on my return home. A large fragment of it was printed in a Soviet magazine published to be distributed abroad.

On the way back we landed in Athens, where we had a few hours before our connection flight to Sofia, from where we were supposed to catch an Aeroflot plane to Moscow. The head of the Soviet trade mission in Athens was Aram Piruzian, an old friend of my father's and a man who had known me nearly since my birth. He gave us all a warm welcome at his house and invited us to stay in Athens for at least one night as his guests, but Kokkinaki was afraid we would miss our connection from Sofia and insisted that we leave Athens the same evening. Such a pity we did not know we would have to hang around Sofia for two days until the next Aeroflot flight home!

In 1964 the Institute was involved in another aerial demonstration. This time it took place at Kapustin Yar, a missile test range not far from Akhtubinsk where ground-to-air and ground-to-ground ballistic missiles were tested. The event was organised for the higher Air Defence Command, and it involved demonstrations of various anti-aircraft armaments and systems in action. Our part consisted in demonstrating the work of aviation interception complexes, or rather the final phase: shooting down, before the eyes of the audience, a number of remotely controlled air targets. I was sent to Kapustin Yar to give explanations to the guests about the aircraft armaments and to commentate on the actual demonstration. Before each particular type of airborne armament was demonstrated in action, my assistant displayed the corresponding explanatory posters in a large tent, and I gave a short talk about it. When, as I knew, the time came for the air targets and interceptors to approach, I invited the guests to come out onto the viewing ground.

One of the air targets was an unmanned MiG-15 which was to be shot down with a K-13 missile from a MiG-21PF. The interceptors came in a formation of three, with Colonel Kotlov as their leader. The target was hit by the very first missile. The pilotless MiG-15 entered an impeccable loop and dived towards the ground. The officer who acted as our master of ceremonies invited everyone back into the tent for the next talk.

I was the first to enter the tent and was standing by the posters waiting for everyone to come in. Suddenly I heard a noise which could only belong to a low-flying aircraft of the MiG-15 or MiG-17 type. Whatever would a MiG-15 be doing here? I looked into the window in the side of the tent and there it was, a MiG-15 heading right towards our tent at a height of about 100 metres. It was the 'wounded' pilotless target, which must have somehow recovered from a dive and was now travelling in a level flight. A somewhat overdue command to run for cover sounded from the loudspeakers, and some people did make a dash for the trench, though it was obviously too late. The aeroplane went right over our tent and precisely at that moment its tail came off and fell down a few metres behind the tent; the machine itself crashed about 200 metres from us. Luckily no one was hurt. My acquaintance General Timoshkin picked up a piece of exhaust pipe, which fell down more or less under his feet, as a souvenir. If the tail had come off a second earlier the aircraft would have crashed into the tent, where there were about thirty officers and generals of the Air Defence Supreme Command, and me. It must have been everybody's lucky day. When the demonstration was successfully over, all the pilots who had taken part received souvenir gifts from the Air Defence Commander, General Batitsky. I also received a gift from him – a photo camera, which I have since kept as a memento of the event.

At the end of 1964 I received a phone call from Moscow from the Ministry of Radio Industry inviting me to come and see the First Deputy Minister Piotr Stepanovich Pleshakov (later he became minister). We knew each other well, for he was our frequent guest at Akhtubinsk where he came for various technical meetings. When I flew from Akhtubinsk and reported at his Moscow office, he said that Kalmykov, the minister, wanted to offer me a job. He asked me to wait in the reception room and went into Kalmykov's office. After a while the door of the office reopened and none other than Sergo Beria emerged. I knew him well but I had not seen him since the time of Stalin. Unlike me, Sergo was not surprised to see me (he had just heard Pleshakov report my arrival to the minister), and he walked straight towards me to shake hands. We talked a while, and before he left he asked me to thank my father for him. Apparently my father had helped Sergo to be transferred to Kiev from Novosibirsk, where he and his mother had been packed off after Beria's trial. In the old days my wife and I occasionally saw Sergo Beria and his wife Marfa, for both Marfa and my wife were close friends of Svetlana. Once Ella and I visited Sergo and Marfa in their rooms in his father's residence on Kachalov street (we entered Sergo's quarters through a side door round the corner from the main entrance).

I waited alone for another few minutes, then Pleshakov looked out of the minister's office and waved me in. Kalmykov did not beat about the bush and offered me the post of Director of the Flight Research Institute under the auspices of the Radio Industry Ministry. He described his plans for upgrading the Institute's role in the development of various aviation complexes. His idea was that before any new radio, radar, aiming or navigation equipment was installed into a test specimen aircraft it should first be fully developed, tested and finished at this Institute.

I must say that I always treated the 'revolutionary' ideas generated in the offices of 'big bosses' with a great deal of caution and quite a bit of scepticism. No matter how grand an idea might sound, what happened to it in practice was quite a different story. Kalmykov's idea was no exception: I could not help thinking that it was rather unrealistic. I was too familiar with the usual pattern of new aircraft and new equipment development, which consisted in the government taking a decision about the creation of a certain type of new aircraft which provided for its main equipment and accessories – its power plant, its avionics, its aiming system and its armament – to be designed in parallel with the machine itself. However, the designing and building of the airframe almost invariably took less time than the engine and various radio systems. By the time a new machine had been built and prepared for factory and then for military certification tests, most of the onboard systems were usually not quite ready. In such circumstances the Institute of which Kalmykov was talking would not have the opportunity to elaborate and finish all those systems by itself and on its own ground; it would be forced to install them on the waiting aircraft and to go on working on them in co-operation with our Institute. It would have been different, of course, if we had had the same system as in the West, where, as far as I knew, engines, radars and all other sophisticated equipment were created and developed independently on the basis of experience, existing demand and technical feasibility criteria. When an aircraft design company designed a new machine it had certain existing equipment in mind for it, taking it 'from the shelf', as the expression goes.

Another consideration against Kalmykov's offer, and a very important one at that, was that the post he had named was at the time held by Valentina Grizodubova, a well-known former pilot, a holder of several aviation records and the commander of an air force regiment during the war. She enjoyed great respect among all the people who knew her personally, especially those working under her, for she always helped them in every way and always defended their interests. I did not want to have a hand in her dismissal, even though Kalmykov took care to tell me that it was time for her to retire and they were determined to replace her anyway. I thanked him for the offer and refused. I explained my refusal by saying that I did not want to give up my job, particularly flight testing, which formed its most cherished part. It was the heartfelt truth of course, but Kalmykov did not expect me to decline his proposal and his annoyance was evident.

When I returned to Akhtubinsk, the Institute Deputy Commander Molotkov, who had heard from someone of Kalmykov's offer to me, asked if it was true that I refused. When I assured him it was, he asked me to recommend him instead. I rang Pleshakov and named Molotkov to him. He knew him well and agreed that he would be a good choice. Molotkov was in the same category of specialists as I was. He was an experienced test pilot and a good engineer (also a graduate of the Zhukovsky Academy), in the same rank as me, but with greater experience as a commander and organiser.

Some time afterwards I was in Moscow visiting my father at the dacha, and he told me over dinner that Valentina Grizodubova had rung Brezhnev to complain that there was a plot to drive her out. My father was still chairman of the Presidium of the Supreme Council, and Brezhnev had already become General Secretary of the Party, yet there was nothing surprising about Grizodubova calling them both direct; she had quite a reputation for never hesitating before making a phone call to any high-ranking official if she needed to get things done at work or on somebody's behalf. 'They wanted to replace her with your boss, Molotkov,' said father. I told him the whole story then and he said that I had done the right thing in refusing. He must have been pleased our name was not involved in that conflicting situation. It would have been very easy for some people to say that Grizodubova was dismissed to make way for Mikoyan's son. That was something my father would never have allowed to happen.

The outcome of Grizodubova's phone calls to Brezhnev and my father was that she remained in her place, while Molotkov was appointed her deputy. He worked at 'her' Institute for a while, but his position there was rather awkward and soon he asked to return to the air force. The only post available at the time was that of editor-in-chief of the *Aviation and Cosmonautics* magazine. Later he was appointed head of an aviation research institute under the auspices of the Defence Ministry. My misgivings about Kalmykov's plan to increase the role of Grizodubova's Institute proved to be right. The plan was not realised then, nor was it realised later under the two directors who succeeded Grizodubova one after the other. The Institute still continues to develop and test aviation equipment at the early stages of its creation.

When Molotkov left the FTI at the end of 1964, I was appointed its Deputy Commander in his place. In the past, when the Institute had been based at Chkalovskaya, this post had been known as the First Deputy Commander, but after the reorganisation the prefix 'first' was removed (as well as the small addition to the salary that went with it), though the functions and responsibilities remained the same. My position in the Institute involved some new duties, including those of general administrative and organisational character. Quite often I had to take over the Institute Commander's duties as well, when he had business in Moscow, Chkalovskaya or Feodosia, or went away on holiday.

The Institute Commander, General Finoghenov, before he got this appointment, had been an air force bomber corps second-in-command. In Akhtubinsk, besides being at the head of the FTI, he was also the local garrison commander and paid a lot of attention to administrating the latter and looking after its daily needs and the needs of the living compound. As for the Institute itself, his principal concern was to ensure the Moscow bosses' approval and high opinion of himself, particularly since various commanders and commissions from Moscow came to us fairly often. General Finoghenov had had no higher education, his technical knowledge was rather poor and he had never been a test pilot. Therefore he almost never interfered with any technical or other purely professional issues, and they were all left in my charge (as in Molotkov's case before me), which suited me perfectly. Finoghenov signed the final statements of the tests and other technical documents fully relying on the opinion of those who presented them, and in many cases I had to sign them myself.

My new responsibilities brought me into close contact with some types of aircraft and aviation technology with which I had had little or nothing to do before: bombers, missile carriers, anti-submarine aircraft and their armament systems. I found these new experiences and discoveries very interesting, and despite all the differences there was still a lot in common between those new types and the ones I knew well. At that time the Institute was testing the first Soviet supersonic missile carrier and bomber, the Tu-22 (known in the West as 'Blinder'). It was armed with self-guiding K-22 missiles. The tests were superintended by a state commission chaired by the Commander of Long-Range Aviation, Colonel General Agaltsev, while Finoghenov was appointed deputy chairman. From my very first days in my new office, Finoghenov began delegating me to attend the commission meetings in his place.

Just before my new appointment there occurred an episode connected with the Tu-22 tests which created quite a stir when it happened. Before the aircraft and its armaments could be put through the final military certification tests (the stage known as 'stage B' of the joint test programme), the test team, Agaltsev's commission and the Air Force Command in Moscow had to receive the 'stage

A' results, i.e., the results of missile-launching at a target ship in the Caspian Sea (a number of such written-off battleships used for armament tests and for combat training were lying aground in the shallow north-east part of the Caspian). When a missile was fired it seemed to the observer that it hit the deck superstructure, and he reported a direct hit. Knowing how anxious they were in Moscow to know the results, the commander of the Trajectory Measurement Department, Andrei Gladilin, hurried to send them a cipher reporting the success. The next day the state commission made the decision to pass on to 'stage B', i.e. the final stage of military certification tests. The first missile launched in 'stage B' went past the target, and so did the second, and then the third. A scandal erupted. An investigation showed that the original report of a direct hit was inaccurate; the missile had only touched the superstructure of the cruiser on its way and fell into the sea far beyond it. General Gladilin was penalised, and the armament system was returned to 'stage A' to be improved. The missiles had missed their target for a reason: there turned out to be a fault in the guidance system which took a long time and a number of additional launches to be removed before the military certification tests could be resumed.

Another new type of armament I now had to deal with were anti-submarine systems. I made several flights to Feodosia, near which was the base of No. 3 Department of our Institute. Its airfield was about thirty kilometres from the Black Sea coast. At that time the department was finishing the testing of the anti-submarine Il-38 aircraft, the first Soviet Air Force aircraft equipped with a digital computer, even though the computer was rather cumbersome and not very reliable. I took part in the discussion of the results and in writing the final test statement. I must say it did not take me too long to get a working, if relatively superficial, knowledge of this type of armament.

My new duties also made me far better acquainted with the work of the three departments of our Institute that were based at Chkalovskaya. No. 7 Department was testing ejector seats, partial- and full-pressure suits and various safety and survival equipment. The new kinds of such equipment that I now encountered were those intended for cosmonauts. In one of my visits to Chkalovskaya I was present at a training session in which Alexei Leonov was practising leaving the space capsule through an air-lock inside a large space simulation test chamber (soon afterwards he would do it in open space). The domain of No. 4 Department included transport aircraft, helicopters, parachutes and various landing devices for airborne troops. This department had branched off from our old No. 1 Flight Test Department (from which the bulk of my 'own' No. 1 Department had come as well), and so there were many people working there whom I knew well. The same applied to No. 6 Department, which was in charge of testing engines for all types of aircraft, and which often sent its engineers to our base in Akhtubinsk.

In June 1965 I received another opportunity to go to France to represent the Soviet Federation of Air Sports (FAS) at the annual FAI council meeting, timed to coincide with the Bourges Salon. Our delegation was again headed by Vladimir Kokkinaki, who was FAI First Vice-President at the time. The third delegation member was again Tatyanchenko of the DOSAAF. The meetings were held in the building of the French National Aeroclub.

We made three visits to the Bourges airfield to see the air show and to meet up with the Soviet delegation at the Salon. This time the delegation was extremely representative and included three world-famous aircraft designers – Andrei Tupolev, Alexander Yakovlev and Artem Mikoyan – as well as Minister of Aviation Industry Dementiev and Deputy Air Force Commander General Ponomarev. Kokkinaki and I were invited to the dinner party given by the hosts in honour of the USSR delegation, although officially we did not belong to it.

That Salon unfortunately saw two fatal accidents during an aerial demonstration. An American B-58 bomber crashed on landing, performing a flare too low over the ground. It hit an elevation on the field on its way to the landing strip. The pilot of an Italian aerobatic plane, making a low final turn and trying to align with the runway banked too steeply and hit a bus with his wingtip and crashed down onto a group of spectators, killing himself and several other people besides. Unfortunately fatal accidents occur at large air shows nearly every year (in 1973 Bourges saw the fatal flight of our Tu-144 supersonic jet liner).

On one of our visits to the airfield I ran into General Shamir, President of the Israeli Aeroclub, who had been our host in Tel Aviv the year before. We spent some time talking together and I reminded him of the words he had said to me in Tel Aviv about his country's peaceful aspirations. What about the armed skirmishes on the Egyptian border which were now going on? I expected him to find some excuse or justification, but he smiled and said, 'Well, we are, indeed, a peculiar people.'

The official USSR delegation at the Salon was 'reinforced' by an informal group consisting of various aviation specialists who had bought a package tour deliberately timed for the air show. It was a common practice in those days, and such tours were affordable thanks to large reductions made for trade union members (and every person on a job was a trade union member more or less automatically, except for the military, whose trips were paid for by the Air Force Command). Some of my colleagues and friends were in that group, first of all Piotr Kabrelev and Nikolai Dorofeev.

One evening five or six of us went out in Paris together, with me serving as their self-appointed guide on the strength of it being my second visit. One of the sights we saw together that night was the famous wholesale market (which has since been removed from the city centre), the *'ventre de Paris'*. We were told that every night after midnight peasants and farmers from around Paris brought their freshly picked vegetables to that market, where they were sorted out and taken to greengrocers first thing in the morning. The young farmers, their loads off their hands, would fill up the neighbouring taverns or spend some of their takings on girls. The taverns and the onion soup they served became a kind of tourist attraction. We walked into one of them, and I, who had a little more money on that trip than my tourist friends, ordered everyone a bowl of onion soup. Our next experience of *couleur locale* was a visit to a stripshow on Place Pigalle, which was again my idea. We had to pay just three francs each at the door, but inside we were told that we would not get away without ordering, and every item on the menu, even Coca-Cola, was a lot more expensive than in town. The spectacle was quite a bit of a 'novelty' to my friends (I was the only one to have seen it before, on my first visit to Paris, when a friend took me to the *Crazy Horse*), but our morals did not get 'corrupted'.

My friends' hotel was within a short walk from Place Pigalle, while I had to get a taxi to get home. The driver heard our goodbyes and surprised me by addressing me in Russian on the way. He turned out to be from Russia, which he had left with his family in the 1920s. He was working for a private taxi company which operated six cars and twelve drivers who did nothing but drive. All the rest, including the car maintenance, was done by the owner, who 'worked like a horse'. Next time I stopped a taxi and addressed the driver in English, he muttered something in French in reply, and I automatically asked 'What?' in Russian. And again, in Russian, he snapped, 'I'm on my way to the garage.' Another Russian immigrant, and with the worst habits of a Moscow taxi-driver at that.

One day Yuri Gagarin appeared at the Salon, and immediately there materialised people wishing to shake his hand and get his autograph. Once, as we were sitting and talking over brandy and fruit and caviare inside the Tu-104, which served as the Soviet delegation's 'chalet' at the air show, more people gathered outside the aircraft waiting for Gagarin to come out. He did, and when he returned he suddenly said to me, 'You can't imagine how fed up with it I am!'

After the FAI council meeting, its participants, including Kokkinaki and me, were supposed to act as jurors at a festival of films about aviation. The festival was held in Vichy under the auspices of the FAI. We flew to Vichy together with Gagarin and three other cosmonauts who had just performed an orbital flight together: Vladimir Komarov, Konstantin Feoktistov and Boris Yegorov. They flew in from Moscow that day and immediately changed for our flight to Vichy. We spent a few days there watching several films every day and then discussing them and voting as the jury. Our spare time was devoted to sight-seeing and strolling around the town. A couple of times I was invited out by fellow jurors. Once an American I had known from the previous conference asked me to join him and his friends for dinner at an expensive restaurant, with no other Russian participants present. On another occasion I was invited for a drive in the country in the company of FAI Vice-President Hoissbacher, his wife and another jury member who was a friend of the couple. It all sounds perfectly normal, if not trivial, today, but in those days unchaperoned meetings by Soviet people, especially the military, with Westerners were not encouraged, and that is putting it mildly (in my case they might have been one of the reasons why I was never sent by the DOSAAF on such visits again, and in general had no opportunity to go abroad until 1991, i.e. for twenty-six years!).

One day a wealthy Frenchman, an oil tycoon as we were told, invited all four cosmonauts and the Commander of the Cosmonaut Training Centre General Kuznetsov, who had accompanied them from Moscow, to visit his island in the Mediterranean. Gagarin suggested I come along but I refused for I did not fancy being in the 'retinue'. On their return, Gagarin described the splendour they had seen and said it was a shame I had not gone.

The film festival closed with an air sports show by the lake on the outskirts of Vichy. We saw something that we had never seen before: a parachutist towed by a motor boat and going up from the water. And an American pilot, Bob Hoover, to whom I was introduced afterwards, performed low-altitude aerobatic manoeuvres in a Second World War Mustang.

On 25 November 1965 my father turned seventy years old. A formal jubilee dinner was held at Novo-Ogarevo, a state reception residence in the country near Moscow. All my brothers and I were invited to it with our wives. At the dinner both Brezhnev and Kosyghin made toasts to my father and said very warm words about him, with many other Politburo members and government officials following suit. We did not know then that plans for sending him into retirement had already been made.

Some time before Brezhnev came to power, at the beginning of 1964, my father, as he afterwards told me, had had a private conversation with Khrushchev in which they both agreed that the role of elected councils ('soviets') and especially of the Supreme Council had to be elevated. 'There are only two people who could do it: you and I,' Khrushchev said, 'and as I can't be distracted from the Council of Ministers, it will have to be you. You will have to become head of the Supreme Council and take the matter into your hands.' And so in June 1964 Anastas Mikoyan was elected, or rather appointed, chairman of the Presidium of the Supreme Council in Brezhnev's place. Brezhnev kept his post as one of the secretaries in the Central Committee of the Party. The chairman of the Presidium *de jure* was the head of state, *de facto* it was more of an honorary position (it was the chairman's membership in the Politburo which determined his influence in the affairs of state). That was what Khrushchev and my father had planned to change. I do not know whether Khrushchev would have continued to support my father if there had been time to carry out their plan while Nikita Sergeevich was still in power, but neither Brezhnev, who replaced Khrushchev as General Secretary, nor Suslov were happy about his attempts.

An interesting aside to this plan happened, I believe, in 1963, when my father was spending his leave at the government dacha in Pitsunda with Vanya and Zina, his wife. My wife and I joined them there for a week or two. Khrushchev, who was also on holiday at the time, occupied the neighbouring dacha (there were three separate dachas on the large grounds surrounded by a common enclosure). Nikita Sergeevich and my father were spending quite a lot of time together, either in Khrushchev's house or in ours, and often walked together in the park or along the beach.

One day a large party of guests – members of the government – arrived at the dacha. Among them were Kosyghin, Voronov, Dymshyts and several others. Apparently Khrushchev had decided to convene a Cabinet meeting at Pitsunda to discuss the next five-year plan. The visitors were accommodated at the third dacha. They had long working sessions each morning, at which none of us was present of course, but in their leisure hours after lunch, when the whole company led by Khrushchev with his two first deputies – Kosyghin and my father – took long walks through the park or along the sea, I often went along.

In one of these strolls along the seafront path a certain conversation took place which was characteristic of how some important decisions could sometimes be made. Khrushchev, my father and Alexei Nikolayevich were, as usual, taking the lead, with Voronov walking a few steps behind them, and Dymshyts and me bringing in the rear. Suddenly Khrushchev said, 'Our regional party committees are in charge of both the industries and agriculture. What if we break them up into industrial and agricultural party committees?' In terms of the party ideology and the party policy it was a really bizarre suggestion. I noticed that everyone seemed to start at his words. Dymshyts and I looked at each other in bewilderment. At this moment my father made a step or two back, pinched me by the sleeve and whispered, 'Be silent.' He knew my usual penchant for arguing and did not want me to say anything against Khrushchev's words. He needn't have worried however: I was perfectly aware that it was not an occasion for a debate. What my father said aloud was that the proposal was not without interest, but it had to be carefully considered. After a few remarks by the rest of the ministers present, the subject was dropped, but, as it turned out later, not forgotten or given up. However strange it might have seemed at the time, when my friend Sasha Babeshko and Andrei Kertes and I discussed it several years later, we came to the conclusion that it might have been Khrushchev's deliberate attempt to undermine the party bureaucracy (which had a rivalry with the government bureaucracy) by splitting its organs in two ('Divide and rule'!). After Khrushchev's forced resignation everything returned to the old pattern of omnipotent regional party committees.

I am not going to dwell here in detail on my father's position in relation to Khrushchev's dismissal in October 1964; there have been a number of publications where it was described, among them Sergei Khrushchev's account published in the *Ogonyok*.* I shall only record here that father was the only person in the leadership who stood by Khrushchev's side right through and who raised his voice in support. He suggested letting Khrushchev remain as chairman of the Cabinet, but the others were adamant, and Nikita Sergeevich himself decided to give up the struggle and resign. In the last few years of Khrushchev's rule, when he began showing 'voluntaristic' inclinations, my father argued with him a lot and tried to dissuade him from doing certain things, but as a rule he did it in private and said things to his face, never plotting against him behind his back.

Incidentally, Sergei Khrushchev ended his story in the *Ogonyok* by pointing out that his father and mine had never seen each other again after Khrushchev's dismissal. It surprised many people who read it. It certainly does seem strange: they had been close allies, one could even say friends. And yet, what seems odd to us was almost natural to them. It was part of their psychology that had formed back in the 1930s, when all purely social meetings between top officials of the

---

* Sergei Khrushchev, 'A Pensioner of All-Union Importance', *Ogonyok*, No. 40, 1988.

country had ceased. It was too easy to get suspected of a conspiracy against Stalin or the regime as such. The times changed, but that psychology to some extent remained. None of the statesmen continued seeing each other socially after retirement. Molotov and Kaganovich, Bulganin and Malenkov, Voroshilov and any of the above; none of them saw one another as pensioners. My father and Voroshilov had always been on good terms, but after the latter's retirement they only spoke on the telephone two or three times, I believe, and only once met. Besides, as I have already mentioned, both Khrushchev and my father seem to have been informed by their trusted staff members of the insulting comments allegedly made by each about the other. Both were too proud to demand a face-to-face explanation. This could hardly have encouraged their former friendship to continue.

Very shortly after the jubilee and a little over a year after Khrushchev's dismissal, Brezhnev offered my father retirement. My father was already thinking of it himself, in obedience to the resolution earlier passed by the Politburo about its members retiring at the age of seventy (none of his colleagues had honoured that resolution yet). However, his intention was to retire after the coming election to the Supreme Council which was to be held six months later, so that the new Presidium could legitimately elect their new chairman. Yet Brezhnev was not inclined to wait for the election. The reason was simple. The next Party Congress was due in the spring, some time before the Supreme Council election. If Mikoyan remained the Presidium chairman at the time of the Congress, he would certainly be re-elected as a member of the Politburo, and this was exactly what Brezhnev wanted to prevent. After my father's retirement my brother Alexei asked him if he would be allowed to remain a Politburo member. Father replied it was very unlikely, and added, 'I have more experience than any of them and my opinion is respected, but my views are different, and I am in their way.'

In 1995, at an international conference in Moscow, I saw Devi Sturua (the younger son of my father's old friend George Sturua), who came from Tbilisi to attend it. He told me about the book he had written in which he had quoted my father's reminiscences about Stalin and other leaders. Devi had heard them when visiting my father and, being a journalist, he had written them all down (alas, I had never thought of doing it myself). He spoke of both my parents with great respect and said that he had been present at that meeting of the Supreme Council at which my father announced his retirement. When he was given the floor there was a long applause, a real ovation in fact, and when Brezhnev afterwards named Nikolai Podgorny as my father's prospective successor, the audience responded with dead silence.

It seems appropriate here to mention the conflict between my father, then still the chairman of the Presidium, and Konstantin Chernenko, who was in charge of a department in the Presidium administration. Once father gave Chernenko some task and after a while enquired as to how he was getting on with it. Chernenko said the work was done, but later father learnt that he had done nothing whatever. He gave Chernenko a severe dressing-down at a staff meeting, saying that he was no good for the Presidium or, for that matter, for the party either. Chernenko cried it out on Brezhnev's shoulder, and Brezhnev offered him a vacancy in the Central Party Committee administration. The episode must have had something to do with the way things turned out for my father.

He remained a member of the Supreme Council until 1974, when, for the first time in almost forty years, he was not nominated as a candidate in the general election. It was hard to believe that his old constituency in Armenia suddenly decided not to re-elect the only Armenian in the top leadership of the country, especially as, far from being a mere figurehead, he was still active and influential. It was clear that the decision was made in the Kremlin, and either Suslov or Chernenko, or both, might have had a hand in it (characteristically, other members of the 'old guard', for example Voroshilov or Budenny, remained in the Supreme Council until their deaths at the age of almost ninety). Another slight was received by my father in 1976 about three years before his death, when he was not elected a delegate of the Twenty-Fifth Congress of the Party. The pattern was the same: the Central Committee administration forbade his nomination by the party organisation of the large plant in Moscow, whose member he had been for many years. Admittedly he was fairly advanced in years then, but in those days age as such was no object; it was the attitude of Brezhnev and Suslov that decided it all.

There were other minor yet characteristic slights. One evening my niece's husband phoned to say there had been a live episode on the news programme showing the arrival of Harold Wilson at Moscow airport. Wilson made a short speech in which he remembered his first visit to Moscow and mentioned his meeting with my father: '. . . when Anastas Mikoyan and I signed the agreement on credits for the USSR . . .' The episode was certain to be repeated on our main news programme *Vremya* ('Time') in the evening. Needless to say, I turned the television on at nine, waiting to see Harold Wilson and to hear him mention my father. See Harold Wilson I did, but the name of my father did not sound. What Wilson said in the recorded version was, 'when we signed the agreement on credits . . .' Somebody was really averse to hearing my father's name on the national news programme, and it was deftly edited out of the soundtrack.

I believe Harold Wilson referred to the agreement about which I had earlier heard from my father. He told us of his negotiations with the British side about a large credit loan in 1947. As far as I remember, before the negotiations began several Western countries had refused to give us a loan because we had refused to pay for the wartime lend-lease deliveries. Stalin had said to my father, 'You may try to talk them into it, if you like, but it's useless.' My father had a long and sincere conversation with Harold Wilson (who came at the head of the British delegation), frankly describing our severe losses in the war and our grave economic situation following it, and managed to persuade him to agree to that loan. The agreement was signed. Having finished his story my father surprised us by saying, 'It was so vitally important then, that even if it had been the only thing I ever did, I still could have regarded my contribution to the country worthwhile.'

The difficult talks with Harold Wilson were certainly not the only mission involving international contacts that father performed in his career. He made important state visits and headed various high-ranking delegations to dozens of foreign countries. He was often assigned to the most delicate and difficult missions and negotiations with foreign leaders. I have already described his visit to Mao's secret camp before the formation of the Chinese People's Republic, his trip to the USA in 1959 when the Berlin issue threatened a breach in American–Soviet relations, his mission to Cuba during the crisis in 1962. He also visited Japan twice, and there had always been delicate points in our relationship with that country (e.g. the Kuril Islands and disputes over fisheries).

Earlier, in May 1955, father, together with Khrushchev and Bulganin, paid a visit to Belgrade to heal a rift between the USSR and Yugoslavia caused by Stalin's annoyance at Tito's opposition to his will. The rift went back seven years, during which time Yugoslavia was 'officially' considered to be 'pro-capitalist' and therefore almost as good as 'ideologically hostile'. That joint trip was perhaps an unprecedented, or at least a rare case in the history of world diplomacy: three top leaders of a state volunteering a peace-making visit to the country which their official propaganda had been recently and consistently throwing mud at. However, their mission proved successful, and a year later Tito and Kardelj returned the visit. At the end of the official programme in Moscow Khrushchev offered the Yugoslav guests a few days' holiday on the Black Sea, which they accepted. Father accompanied them. One day they all paid a visit to the Soviet Navy cruiser *Frunze*. Several years later, a sailor from the *Frunze* sent me some snapshots he had taken during that visit of Tito, his wife, my father and others on board the cruiser. On leaving Moscow Tito invited father to spend his coming holiday in Yugoslavia. In 1956 my parents (with the Central Committee's official blessing) went there on a two-week holiday. Tito put them up in his residence on the island of Brioni. My mother enjoyed her holiday very much, and she returned full of praise for the fine climate and the beauty of the island. My father, as usual, combined pleasure with business, continuing talks with Tito every time he paid them a visit from Belgrade.

On 25 November (his birthday) 1963, Anastas Mikoyan represented the Soviet Union at President Kennedy's funeral. William Manchester in his book *The Death of a President* wrote of the apprehensions and security problems raised by Jacqueline Kennedy's decision to walk behind the coffin all the way from the White House to the cathedral; they feared that an attempt on General de Gaulle's life could be made by the OAS, and on my father's by Hungarian extremists, and tried to persuade the two of them (and some other dignitaries) to go in the car. Both men flatly refused and walked all the way with the others.

My father's last trip abroad was in 1965 and comprised state visits to India, Burma, Afghanistan and Indonesia. In Indonesia, besides the meetings and talks with President Sukarno and other officials, there was a meeting with the leaders of the Indonesian Communist party which was under the strong influence of Chinese communists. My cousin's husband Feodor Yarikov, who was on the staff of the Soviet embassy in Djakarta, acted as my father's interpreter for that meeting. According to him it was very tense and difficult, and my father tried to persuade the Indonesians – speaking very bluntly, even harshly at times – to renounce extremist policies and find common ground or some compromise with democratic organisations. They responded by criticising Khrushchev's 'thaw' (although it was already on the decline). Here is a fragment from my father's official archives of a shorthand account of father's words at that meeting. He said: 'We are looking for a simple agreement. Supposing you, comrades, dis-approve of our way of building communism, and you choose to describe it as restoration of capitalism. But do not interfere, allow us to do what we are doing [. . .] As for international issues, let us certainly talk them over together, but as true comrades. If you start insulting us, we shall retaliate. We are against quarrelling and we would hate to do so. But I believe we should manage to discuss everything calmly.' Unfortunately they did not yield to persuasion and did not give up their extremist views and tactics. What followed is well known. Just about a year later Indonesia saw a massacre of communists in which about half a million people (mostly their intelligentsia) are said to have been killed.

When my father ceased to be either a Presidium or a Supreme Council member, he continued working in the Presidium administration as a consultant. He was given a small office in the Kremlin with a reception room and was assigned a secretary and a personal assistant. At home he worked a lot as usual, writing his memoirs and articles that were occasionally published in various journals and magazines. Two separate volumes of his memoirs came out, *In the Early Twenties* and *The Path of Struggle**, and he almost finished a third book covering the period from the late 1930s onwards, though it has never been published, just like a number of essays and articles on the war of 1941–5 and other events of our history. But we have not lost the hope of seeing some of it in print one day.

---

* The American edition of the book appeared in 1988; Mikoyan, A.I., 1895–1978, *The Path of Struggle*, Sphinx Press Inc., 1988.

CHAPTER 22

The Su-15 Fighter

From 1959 onwards the FTI test force was involved in testing a new family of aircraft: the Sukhoi interceptors. In 1960 some air defence regiments already began receiving the new Su-9 interceptors. For a time the aircraft continued to give some trouble, and there were a number of engine failure instances as a result of which several pilots had to eject, and some were killed. However, an upgraded version of the Su-9, dubbed the Su-11, was already being tested and developed at that time. It was equipped with a greater-range radar and armed with the more powerful K-8 homing missiles instead of the K-5 type. The Su-9's troublesome engine was replaced with an improved and more reliable modification, but the Air Defence Command insisted on fitting the airframe with two engines instead of one for greater reliability.

This led to the official decision about designing another version of the Su-11, the Su-15. At least it was originally conceived as a version, and a not too different one at that. The only intended alterations concerned the installation of two smaller, lower-thrust engines instead of one. However, the result of these alterations was in fact a new aircraft. The nose engine air intake was replaced with two lateral air intakes behind the cockpit, which allowed for the installation of a larger radar antenna in the nose. Due to the larger antenna the range of the radar increased. There were other changes and innovations, and in the end only the wings and most of the tail remained unaltered.

In 1963 the Su-15 military certification tests began. The two pilots most active in the test project were Stal Lavrentiev of our Institute and Vladimir Ilyushin of the Sukhoi Design Company (the tests were conducted jointly by the two bodies). I was prevented from flying on this project by a silly mishap that had happened to me while I was on leave. In September 1963 I was resting at a health spa near Yalta in the Crimea. One night, after a dinner party with some friends in a restaurant in Yalta, I walked eight kilometres along the road from the town to the spa premises and, rather than wake the attendant to let me through the front door, I decided to get in through the balcony of my room (which I had done every day coming back from the tennis court). I stepped up onto the granite parapet of a service staircase (which led to the basement), stretched my arms up to get hold of the balcony railings and began pulling myself up so as to put a foot on the balcony cornice. Suddenly my right-hand fingers slipped off the railings and I went tumbling down, not onto the ground but onto the bottom stone steps of the staircase on its basement landing. I remember the words 'that's the end' flashing through my mind, and afterwards it occurred to me that I must have experienced the same sense of the inevitable that pilots feel in the last moments before crashing. But at that moment down on the landing my first thought was that I was still alive. My right foot was in great pain, but I somehow managed to crawl up the steps and climb onto that balcony. Limping heavily, I got into bed, hoping that the pain would go. If anything, it was getting worse by the minute, and I scrambled out of the bed and to the door and began banging on it, hoping the night nurse would hear. She did, and called the doctor on duty, who gave me a pain-killing injection.

First thing in the morning I was taken to hospital where an X-ray showed a multiple bone fracture of the heel, which had received the entire impact. A bold young orthopaedic surgeon at the Yalta hospital gave me two options: one was a long cure that would allow a gradual restoration, bone by bone, of the heel structure; the other option was to press the fractured bones back into a semblance of the original shape (under a local anaesthetic, of course) and put a plaster cast on. That was a wild venture, for nobody, least of all the enterprising surgeon himself, could tell me what kind of heel I would end up with as a result. Yet it was what I chose. I flew to Moscow with my foot in a cast and was taken straight to hospital from the airport. It took over three months for the heel to mend, and I had to spend most of that time in hospital (which was where I heard on the portable radio I had with me the announcement about Kennedy's assassination, broadcast within minutes of his death). On my return to work I was suspended from flying for a while and thus I missed the Su-15 certification tests which were going on at the time. However, I had a chance to have a ride in it afterwards, and later tested its various modifications, including the two-seater.

As I have already said, the Su-15 had the same wing as the Su-9, but the weight of the machine had become one and a half times heavier. It meant that the load per square metre of the wing had grown. This load affected many parameters of the aircraft performance, such as its take-off and landing characteristics, its manoeuvrability and range of flight. Although a small wing is generally speaking an advantage at very high speed, the Su-15, like all other advanced fighters of the time, had a potential air speed well above the Mach number limit. Its touchdown speed was too high at 350 to 360 kph, higher than any other contemporary fighter, but the Su-15 was very good in the air, a treat to fly at speeds over 500 kph; it was easy to handle and quite stable, without any lagging or overshooting, and with a very responsive stick. At lower speeds, however, its weight began to tell, and take-off and especially landing were more demanding than in other fighters.

Once, when Pavel Sukhoi himself was visiting the Akhtubinsk air base, I told him in a conversation about the Su-15 that in my opinion its wing was under-sized for its weight. The chief designer did not object. I would not claim to have influenced his decision by that remark, but in any case soon afterwards a new Su-15 with extended wing tips arrived at Akhtubinsk to be tested. The enlarged wing area certainly improved its handling at low speeds, and the other innovation which this aircraft had was a boundary layer control system similar to that of the MiG-21, of which I have written earlier. As a result the touchdown speed went down to 310 kph, and landing grew simpler.

The Su-15 became notorious throughout the world twenty years later. It was with the missiles launched from this aircraft that the South Korean Boeing 747 airliner was shot down near Sakhalin on 1 September 1983.

The 1960s saw the introduction of cockpit automation in Soviet military aircraft, and especially in fighters. It would not be a mistake to say that Pavel Sukhoi's company pioneered this development, though other design companies were close on their heels. Thus, the Su-9 was the first aircraft fitted with an automatically extended air intake cone, and the Su-7B fighter bomber was our first serial fighter equipped with a pitch/roll autopilot. A version of the Su-15 was also being developed to incorporate automated target interception modes.

In automated guidance of an interceptor by the Air-1 guidance system, the commanded values of heading, speed, altitude and target range were automatically transmitted on board from the ground-based computer via a radio data link. By matching the instrument needles to the commanded value marks, the pilot would follow the optimum flight path bringing him within the scanning zone of his radar. As soon as the target mark appeared on the radar display, the pilot closed in, the radar and the missile heads locked on their target, and the pilot fired the missiles. After the missile launch the pilot had to break away immediately to avoid collision with the target or its fragments. In the Su-15 all these modes were automated (which was soon also done in the MiG-25). The commands of the ground-based guidance system and then of the onboard radar signals were now transmitted both to the cockpit instruments and to the autopilot. Thus, the Su-15 developed into a fairly sophisticated state-of-the-art machine with advanced flight and combat capabilities (in addition to missiles, it was also armed with a two-barrel 23 mm gun). But unfortunately its serial production was soon stopped, despite the general satisfaction it caused in air defence units where it was serving. The reason was a trifling episode which involved Soviet government leaders.

Leonid Brezhnev and other dignitaries were visiting the Kubinka air base for a demonstration of new aircraft. As they were shown the aircraft on the ground and the group approached a Su-15TM, Brezhnev walked past it with the words, 'Ah, that's old junk!' Brezhnev's dismissive remark proved a sufficient excuse for the cancellation of the production of the Su-15.

Before it happened I had had an opportunity to take part in some of the Su-15 tests. I was the first military test pilot to test its boundary layer control system and to fire its gun. There was also an interception mission to test the automated control system and the infra-red sight.

Perhaps my most challenging flight in the Su-15 was the one I had not planned on making. As I came to the No. 1 Department building one day to get ready for a scheduled flight, I was approached by the Su-15 stability and controllability test engineer, Vladimir Semeshin, who said, 'Comrade General, could you go up in the Su-15 to determine the landing configuration stall speed, please?' The mission consisted of allowing, with my landing gear and flaps extended, the speed to 'bleed off' to the point of stalling, when the aircraft would begin dropping on a wing. The idea was to do it at the lowest height possible, and that was the main difficulty and danger. The engineers named 2,000 metres, and I agreed. Each of us was perfectly aware that should I linger a second or two with the recovery at the departure point, the machine would go into a spin and ejection would be my only option.

I must say I loved stall speed tests and believed that I had a good feel for the aircraft in the stalling and departure regimes. So I was not particularly nervous about that task, which did not mean that I could allow myself to be anything but extremely alert and careful during the flight; I knew only too well that a second's delay or a tiny mistake could prove fatal. Everything went as it should, and the aeroplane began rapidly falling on the left wing and dropping the nose. I pushed the stick forward and advanced the throttle to gain speed, not losing more than 400 metres of height altogether. The engineers were pleased with the data received.

Many years later, when my colleagues and I were celebrating the successful presentation of my thesis, Vladimir Semeshin (who had helped me in collecting material for my research) remembered that episode in his toast. He confessed that he had not asked any of the other test pilots to make that flight because he was sure their immediate commanders would not allow them to do a departure test at a height insufficient for spin recovery. On the other hand, as I was a commander myself, he knew I could make a decision without asking anyone else. Besides, my particular weakness for aerodynamic performance and stability tests was well known, so he could be sure I would agree. I had not seen through his stratagem then, being pleased to be addressed for a particularly difficult and dangerous flight test. It is in the project engineer's professional (and human) interest that a mission is successfully performed and safely finished. To me the fact that our engineers often asked me to do various complicated tests was a flattering sign of their faith in my professionalism and a boost to my own confidence.

In the meantime the Yakovlev Design Company had followed the recommendations of the Air Defence Command and created a new interceptor, the Yak-28P, on the basis of their Yak-28 light bomber. In 1963 or thereabouts, the Institute received its test specimen for military certification tests. The state commission which superintended the tests was headed by Anatoly Kadomtsev, and I was appointed as his deputy representing the Institute. Lieutenant General Kadomtsev was a deputy of Marshal Savitsky, Commander of the Air Defence Fighter Force. Immediately in charge of the flight testing was Colonel Belodedenko, and Vadim Orlov was project engineer. The pilots involved in the project were Piotr Kabrelev, Boris Adrianov and a number of others. I performed several flights too.

The tests went well, without any mishaps, but the test team conclusion was that the aircraft was obsolete in both its layout and its performance capabilities. Its top speed was only slightly above the speed of sound, and its acceleration was much too slow, especially in high outside air temperatures. Its engines were mounted on the wings rather far from the aircraft's body, and if, on an afterburner take-off, one of them failed, the bank control authority became insufficient for keeping the wings level. It had another serious drawback too: its sweptback large-spanned wings had not enough rigidity in them, and this caused aileron reversal (as in the Tu-128) when the indicated air speed was high.

We at the FTI were against the adoption of the Yak-28P. However, General Kadomtsev was insisting on a favourable decision. His argument was that the Yak-28P was needed for air defence because it was an aircraft with a two-member crew (a pilot and a radar operator), like the Yak-25. The latter had been used in air defence units for a long time and was at the end of its service life. A two-seat aircraft was best suited to the task of intercepting low-altitude targets. There were no look-down radars at the time, and the interceptor had to travel lower than its target so as to avoid so-called 'ground clutter' on the radar display. A low-level flight is a fairly dangerous business, particularly at night or over the sea when it is difficult to determine just how low you are, so it requires the pilot's undivided attention. To give some of it to target-interception tasks would mean to increase the hazard considerably. Hence the obvious advantage of having a radar operator on board. The Yak-28P was rather well suited for low-altitude interception missions, and also for medium-height flights at moderate speed regimes. We had to admit that Kadomtsev was making a good point, and I signed the final statement in its favour.

Incidentally, even though the Yak-28P aircraft were built and rather widely used in combat units, the model itself was never included in the Defence Ministry General Staff official armament inventory, for the same reason we had wanted to reject it: its obsolete design. (The official 'adoption' of every new aircraft always took place after the aircraft had served in an operational force for some time, and after its previously undiscovered faults had been revealed and removed.)

The Yak-28P was not the only aircraft not to have been included in the official armament inventory compiled by the Defence Ministry General Staff. The MiG-19 had had the same fate, although for a different reason. After it had been put on the production lines and had begun its service in combat units, some shortcomings were revealed in it, mainly in the engine and armament installation. Even after the faults had been removed the MiG-19's reputation as a difficult machine to handle persisted among combat pilots, and it continued to serve without being considered for official 'adoption' as a piece of standard AF armament. In the end it must have been forgotten about, for it became obsolete and new aircraft were appearing. I always felt that it was very unfair, for the MiG-19 was an outstanding and remarkably high-performance aircraft for its time. It was built in large numbers, sold abroad and even took part in real combat action (for example in the conflict between India and Pakistan). In China it was produced for many years under a licence purchased from the USSR.

The Yak-28P was armed with self-guiding K-8 missiles, which we had earlier tested in the Yak-27K and the Su-11. Once, when my navigator Nikolai Ivanov and I were up on a launching mission and Ivanov had detected the target, while I, already seeing it through the canopy windscreen, was waiting for the radar and the missile heads to lock on and for the launch-clearance light to come on after it, there was suddenly a loud clap and a telltale whistle: my right engine flamed out. To restart it I would have to descend and bring the speed down, thus frustrating the attack. As the aircraft was still obedient and under control, I opted for going ahead on it with one engine. I pressed the trigger as the lock-on lights appeared, and the moment the launch-clearance lights came on the missiles went off. I waited to make sure that the target was destroyed and then turned away, descended and restarted the engine.

Until the late 1960s all certification tests of all types of aeroplanes, both military and civilian, were the exclusive responsibility of the Research and Flight Test Institute. We tested such passenger aircraft as the Il-12, Il-14, Il-18 and the An-10. Our test pilots, Lieutenant-Colonel Starikov and Major Yakovlev, with Colonel Bagrich as their navigator, tested the first Soviet and the world's second (after the British Comet) jet airliner, the Tu-104. The same crew later performed the Tu-104's first foreign flights and afterwards trained airline pilots to fly it.

The government's decision about the development of a new passenger aircraft at that time presupposed its creation on the basis of an existing transport or cargo military aeroplane; conversely, a military cargo plane could appear as a modification of a passenger aircraft. Thus, the passenger Antonov An-10 was a variant of the An-12 cargo plane, and the cargo aeroplane An-26 was a modification of the An-24 airliner. The Tu-104 was created on the basis of a well-known jet bomber, the Tu-16 'Badger', while the passenger Il-18 gave birth to several military machines: an anti-submarine aircraft, a signal intelligence plane (SIGINT) and an airborne command post.

In the early 1960s a new passenger aircraft appeared: the Tu-124. According to a popular joke of the time its chief designer was Nikita Khrushchev himself. It was he who had suggested to Tupolev that an aircraft 'half the size of the Tu-104' be made, and it proved to be quite a good aeroplane. At that time the French already had their Caravelle, which was the first airliner with tail-mounted engines. The example was soon followed by other passenger aircraft. One of the many advantages of that design was that there was much less engine noise in the cabin. Besides, thanks to the elevated position of the engines, the negative effect of the jetstream on the ground and on people was largely reduced. At the same time there appeared a problem of balancing the aeroplane with different payloads. The weight of the engines on the tail caused its centre of gravity to move backwards, therefore its wings had to be 'pushed' backwards too. Almost the entire passenger cabin ended up with the wings (and the centre of gravity) behind it, with the result that the balance of the aircraft began to depend greatly on the number of passengers on board. (In the Tu-154, for example, they had to make up for the 'missing' passengers by means of special ballast in the nose of the aircraft.)

Nevertheless, the layout with tail-mounted engines remained an attractive idea. Tupolev produced a modification of the Tu-124 with tail-mounted engines, the Tu-134. The No. 4 Department of our Institute at Chkalovskaya received the test specimen of the Tu-134 in the early days of 1966. On 14 February it was to be tested for maximum speed (Mach 0.82) at 10,000 metres. The Mach number of 0.82 corresponded to about 900 kph true air speed. The flight ended in a fatal accident.

According to the cockpit voice recorder tape and the instrumentation data, as the pilots had reached their limit Mach number they detected fuselage oscillations. They seemed very slight, for they were happening far back at the tail. They reduced the speed but then decided to repeat the run to see what kind of vibration it was. This time it was more violent, and then suddenly the aircraft dropped its nose and went into a dive, totally out of control. The co-pilot, Yuri

Rogachev, cried into the intercom, 'Everyone bail out!', and the commander, Major Yevteev, repeated the order, urging everyone to eject but forgetting in the awful strain of the moment that there were no ejector seats in a passenger craft. It is hard to imagine what the crew must have felt, knowing that the aeroplane with people in the cabin was falling and there was nothing they could do. None of the eight people who were on board – the crew, the test engineers and technicians – bailed out, although each of them had a parachute. The reason was that the exit door opened inside the cabin, where the air pressure was more than twice as high as outside. The force acting on the door from inside the cabin meant that to open it was far beyond the means of human strength. The depressurisation of the aircraft by means of the outflow valve would take about ninety seconds, and their fall did not last longer than a minute. The examination of the debris showed that they must have tried to break one of the portholes with a metal object, probably trying to bleed the pressure. But they failed. After that crash all passenger aircraft test specimens were equipped with a fast emergency depressurisation system and with devices making it easier to leave the aircraft in case bailing out was necessary.

The cause of the accident was the hydraulic control booster, or, rather, the insufficient rigidity of the booster attachment assembly. The booster was spontaneously shifting in relation to the pitch control rod and, accordingly, in relation to the slide valve of the actuator, thus forcing the elevator to 'swing' up and down. The swinging became more and more vigorous until the tail disintegrated and the pitch control of the aircraft was completely lost. As so often happened, the design company representatives refused to acknowledge a fault in the aircraft and blamed the accident on the fact that the pilots had exceeded the limit Mach number (which they had, but only by 0.01!). They registered their opinion in our investigation statement, blaming the pilots for the crash, though the aircraft should have been designed with a Mach number safety margin. However, we later found out that they modified the booster assembly unit to remove the fault, thus effectively admitting that we had been right.

Yuri Rogachev had been my very good friend. He had previously worked as a fighter test pilot at Akhtubinsk. He had been an excellent pilot with a talent for testing and the qualities of a good commander. When George Beregovoi left flight testing to become a cosmonaut, Rogachev replaced him as a fighter squadron commander. He was named as a possible successor to 'VG' Ivanov, our universally respected veteran wing commander. Yuri Rogachev was as popular among the Akhtubinsk fighter test pilots as Lyosha Fadeev, and when Lyosha left Akhtubinsk he took his place as the life and soul of all our gatherings and parties, sharing it with another of my close friends, Norik Kazarian. As a test pilot Rogachev had especially distinguished himself in the tests of the Tu-128 and of the Su-7B's various modifications. I have already described how he recovered a Tu-128 from a spin. He had many times demonstrated the aerobatic performance of the Su-7B in operational units and in aerial shows organised for the dignitaries and high commanders visiting the Akhtubinsk air base. I remember once how he impressed everyone with his impeccable low-altitude aerobatic manoeuvres and his simultaneous commentary over the radio for the benefit of all the other pilots, who had gathered around the loudspeaker to listen to him citing his speed, altitude, G-load and the characteristics of each manoeuvre. He ended that flight with a simulated dead-stick landing.

Such demonstration flights, which Yuri had to perform in combat units and in testing many times, subjected him to frequently repeated large G-loads which mainly acted on his spine. This brought a change in his life that in the end proved fatal. I believe it was in 1965 that we had a visit of specialists from the Cosmonaut Training Centre, who came to select their prospective trainees out of the volunteers among our test pilots. The candidates were thoroughly examined by a medical commission, and Yuri Rogachev, who was one of them, did better than most in terms of various physiological, psychological and professional parameters (established through a set of special tests). However, a radiograph of his spine revealed a major vertebrae displacement. As such it was a common fighter pilot occupational disease, but in Yuri's case it was enhanced beyond the tolerated limit by too many high-G-load flights. As a result he was not only prevented from joining the cosmonaut trainees group, but also banned from fighter aircraft and transferred to Chkalovskaya to test transport aeroplanes and helicopters. At the farewell party we gave for him at Akhtubinsk Yuri joked bitterly, 'Well, as things are now, I'll go on flying till I am an old man,' referring to the safety of transport aircraft in comparison with fighter jets. Yet it was just there that death found him. Among those killed in the Tu-134 crash was another man we knew well: the navigator Victor Malyghin, who had taken part in the Tu-128 tests and had often flown as Rogachev's crew member.

In March 1969 I heard about plans for organising a long-range flight to the far north in a Tu-95KM missile carrier. Some time before that my friend and colleague George Bayevsky had flown as the co-pilot on a mission to the North Pole and back. This time the route was different but equally interesting: Akhtubinsk–Bay of Tiksi–Northern Land–Akhtubinsk. I was very keen on taking part (for the first time!) in such a long-distance flight in a heavy aircraft, and I asked to be taken on as the co-pilot.

The crew captain was my good friend General Sergei Dedukh, Commander of the Missile-Carrier and Bomber Flight Test Department. The purpose of the mission was very simple: to test the work of the engines on a new type of oil in a flight that was at least sixteen hours long. The navigators plotted a route that would take about sixteen hours to cover (I wish they had decided to repeat the former route with a turn over the North Pole). We received our food rations for four hours' flight each. They contained chocolate, biscuits and tinned meat (as usual in such cases, we did not touch anything except the biscuits during the flight, leaving the rest to be polished off on our return home). Parachutes and inflatable dinghies were also provided, though everyone knew that in the case of forced landing or bailing out our survival chances in the Far North were practically zero.

We took off after sunset, in the dark. A night take-off with full tanks (and they had been filled to the brim) was a difficult business, so it was performed by Sergei, the aircraft commander and an experienced bomber pilot. As soon as he had climbed up to the initial cruising altitude, we swapped seats and I piloted the machine all the way. When I tried to turn the autopilot on, for some reason it refused to function. It seemed to upset the navigator more than I thought was reasonable. After a while I realised why he was so concerned: he was worried about our chances of finding the Bay of Tiksi and the Northern Land (our check-points) without the autopilot. There were no visual orientation points on our way across Siberia and the Arctic Ocean, so our prescribed route had to be main-tained with precision. With the flight legs being as long as they were, it was an impossible task without the autopilot. However, the autopilot finally 'woke up', and the navigator was relieved, but even with the autopilot on there remained quite a lot for me to do. Besides keeping an eye on the instruments and moni-toring the systems, I had to gradually increase the altitude (via the autopilot) as we were using up our fuel. Another task was to adjust the heading in accordance with the navigator's commands so as to follow the great-circle track (the shortest route over the globe) or to match the change of the wind direction.

I looked down every now and then as we were travelling along the Arctic Ocean coastline and all I could see were great chaotic piles of rocks and cliffs with no vegetation on them or any trace of man's presence: no roads, no houses, nothing. It could have been a different planet for all I knew. When we reached the Bay of Tiksi we came face to face with the rising sun, and later, when we turned back, we overtook it and went back into the night, only to face the sun again after a turn to the south. I performed the approach and the landing at Akhtubinsk myself to the surprise of the rest of the crew; they knew I was a fighter pilot and thus unaccustomed to such long flights, so they did not expect me to pull through after so many hours at the wheel (I had snatched thirty minutes' sleep on the cockpit floor about halfway through the flight).

CHAPTER 23

Early Space Flights and Aviation

W hen, in the early 1950s, the Soviet space programme began, its technology was first developed under the auspices of the Ministry of
Armament until eventually it became the domain of the specially
formed Ministry of General Engineering Industry. The specialised military
research institutes, launch sites and a network of ground-based tracking stations
which had appeared within the Artillery Command were then transferred to the
newly formed Strategic Missile Command, and later also united under a separate
administration. At the same time, the air force was left in charge of testing life-
support and rescue equipment, and, more importantly, of space crew training. A
special centre (now known as the Gagarin Cosmonaut Training Centre) was set
up at Chkalovskaya for the purpose. Although at the beginning the centre was
staffed mainly by specialists from the Flight Test Institute, most of our
personnel – due to the Soviet military command's usual passion for secrecy –
knew nothing of the new organisation beyond the rumours that we were hearing.

Soon the department under my command also became temporarily involved
in these new developments (we were still partially based at Chkalovskaya then).
The fuel supply and lubrication systems in one of our two-seat MiG-15 trainers
were upgraded so that they could function in near zero and zero gravity conditions. In the summer of 1960 or slightly earlier, young pilots whom none of us
knew began to arrive at the airfield one by one (there were seven of them
altogether) to be given rides in the MiG-15 by our test pilots at zero-gravity
regimes. They were brought straight to the aircraft and driven away after each
flight, and whatever we knew about the purpose of their training was pure guess-
work.

Zero gravity conditions can be created in an aircraft only in a push-over
manoeuvre flying along an arch-like trajectory. The curvature of this trajectory
is controlled by the pilot with the help of the onboard G-load indicator, to create
a balance between the vertical centrifugal force and the force of gravity. The
G-load in the zero gravity condition is nil, and the aircraft is flying along
a ballistic trajectory at such an angle of attack that no lift is generated. The
duration of weightlessness achieved in these flights in the MiG-15 was no longer
than thirty seconds or so. Later, similar 'exercises' were performed at a different
department of our Institute and at the Gromov Institute in a Tu-104, where the
future cosmonauts had enough room to 'soar' in the specially fitted section of
the fuselage.

No. 7 and No. 3 Departments were involved in the space projects more than
any other division of our Institute. At the Feodosia base of the No. 3
Department, where the two departments had carried out joint tests of ejector
seats, high-altitude flying suits, parachutes and various items of water search and

rescue equipment, they were now testing return vehicle parachutes, full-pressure suits, orbital airlocks for in-orbit exit and re-entry, and other relevant equipment. Besides, the Feodosia base became an additional training facility for the cosmonauts. In 1966 a launch-escape system was tested at our air base in Akhtubinsk with the help of a Tu-95. I made one such flight in it; we had to drop a mock spaceship on which this system was installed, simulating its operation in an emergency during the launch.

Although the participation of the FTI and other aviation bodies in the development of space programmes was more or less confined to the above tasks, the air force played a key role in the search and recovery of cosmonauts on their return from space (my brother Alexei was for several years in charge of this work as the Commander of the Air Force District in Central Asia, where Soviet space capsules mainly landed).

Those early years saw the appearance of a different direction in the development of space technology which was more closely connected with aviation. It centred around the concept of winged orbital ships which could be launched either vertically (with the help of a rocket booster) or horizontally, from the back of a special aeroplane known as the 'aircraft-type booster'. The latter method of launching helped to save on the fuel required for putting the ship into orbit, and allowed the launch to be performed from various sites and at variable launch inclinations. At the re-entry the winged ships were less subject to heating; they could also perform some essential manoeuvring in the atmosphere and land in an aircraft-like fashion on any suitable airfield.

Somewhere around 1965 the Mikoyan Design Company began designing a vehicle of this type. It emerged as a single-seat aeroplane with small wings and a broad, flat 'lifting' body. As its first stage they conceived an aircraft-type booster that would launch the spacecraft in a steep climbing manoeuvre performed at hypersonic speed. The code name of the project was 'Spiral'. Initially, until the booster aircraft was built, the space vehicle was to be ejected into orbit by a ballistic missile. Many various bodies and enterprises within our aviation and radio industries participated in that breakthrough project. The design tests and experiments that were conducted involved not only the space vehicle itself but also its control and navigation systems, which were aimed at the unprecedented tasks of monitoring an orbital flight and deorbiting and landing the spacecraft after it.

Two types of models were created for the testing purposes: free-flying models of the winged orbital craft to test its potential aerodynamic behaviour in the earth's atmosphere, and a model of a self-guided orbiter, the Bor-4. Besides, a subsonic manned life-size analogue of the orbiter was built to be used for approach and landing tests. It was decided that the analogue, dubbed 'Item 105', would be dropped from a Tu-95 bomber. To accommodate Item 105 in the bomb compartment (halfway in), a hole had to be cut out in the bomb bay doors. Artem Mikoyan asked Andrei Tupolev (the two of them were friends) to instruct his staff to make the necessary adjustments in one Tu-95 for the 'Spiral' project.

Although the project had been initiated by the Aviation Industry Ministry, it got under way without the relevant resolution of the Council of Ministers, which was a must for any new project that needed financing. When eventually the draft of the resolution was signed by all relevant ministers as well as the commanders-in-chief of the air force, air defence and strategic missiles, it was presented for the approval of the Minister of Defence, Marshal Grechko. What Grechko wrote on the draft was: 'Enough of science fiction – Mikoyan should make aeroplanes.' Nevertheless, the project was kept alive by the trickle of money from the Aviation Industry Ministry. The modified Tu-95 was ferried to our airfield, where we were using it as a trainer for our pilots while it was waiting for its 'real' job. It was only in 1977 that the orbiter analogue could at last be tested. I will come to these tests later in my story.

The Cosmonaut Training Centre was then headed by General Kuznetsov, and Yuri Gagarin (with his historic orbital flight already behind him) was his deputy. The centre set out to prepare for the 'Spiral' project. German Titov, Alexander Filipchenko and Anatoly Kuklin were selected as cosmonauts, and it was decided, quite sensibly, that they ought to receive training as test pilots. From the summer of 1967 they began their training at our air base in Akhtubinsk, gradually moving from simple test flight missions to more demanding ones. At the end of their training course their performance was assessed by the Institute qualification commission, and I, as its chairman, signed their certificates as Grade 3 test pilots. They were to continue their practice in Akhtubinsk the following summer, but sadly a tragic event interfered with the plan.

On the morning of 27 March 1968, Air Force Commander-in-Chief Marshal Vershinin had signed an order whereby Titov, Filipchenko and Kuklin were directed to resume their flight test practice at the FTI, and less than an hour later it was reported to him that radio contact with Yuri Gagarin's aircraft had been lost. Vershinin recalled his freshly signed order and struck out his signature. That was the end of the cosmonauts' training as test pilots. Yuri Gagarin had been doing a training course in a special air force regiment based at Chkalovskaya for the chief purpose of providing flying practice to cosmonauts. He had been okayed for a solo flight in the MiG-17, the aircraft he had flown as an air force pilot. I could very easily understand his desire to climb into the cockpit of the dear old fighter and again experience the joy, which I knew so well myself, of taking his machine up into the sky. Unlike those people who knew nothing of a pilot's soul, I was never for a second surprised at Gagarin's craving for flying. Moreover, quite apart from the emotional side of it, I have always been convinced that fighter jet flying should be an essential part of spacecraft captains' preparation for orbital flights. There is nothing like it for getting the psychological, physiological and technical training so important for the involved and demanding task of controlling any flying vehicle. And so on 27 March Gagarin had to perform his last check-ride in a two-seater with the newly appointed Regiment Commander, Vladimir Sereghin. The flight ended in a crash, and both pilots were killed.

A government commission was formed to investigate the reasons and the circumstances of the crash. It monitored the work of two sub-commissions, one of which was concerned with the hardware, the other with the flight and piloting. The latter, of which I was a member, consisted of several generals and flying officers of the air force. (There were two other commissions besides, comprising aviation industry specialists.) Let me first cite what we had known to start with, before the investigation began. Yuri Gagarin was flying the aeroplane from the front seat, while Sereghin occupied the rear cockpit as an instructor. It was meant to be an aerobatic training flight, but it was a cloudy day with two or three layers of clouds one over the other. Being between the layers of clouds, they must have been unable to perform all the intended manoeuvres. In any case, shortly after they had entered their local aerobatic practice area Gagarin reported to the tower in a perfectly normal voice: 'Six twenty-five to tower. Mission completed, request clearance to heading three twenty.' Judging by their previous message, at that moment they must have been at slightly over 4,000 metres. There was no other transmission after that.

As a rule, when an aircraft crashes the instrument needle leaves an imprint at the reading opposite which it was at the moment of the crash; thus the readings can afterwards be determined (the so-called 'black box' was not installed in this type of aircraft then). That was how we established that their speed had been 670 kph and the G-load over eight. These parameters corresponded to pulling up from a dive at the thresholds of human endurance and that of the aircraft (in fact their G-load exceeded its structural limit). By the time frozen on the panel clock and on Gagarin's wristwatch respectively, it was established that they crashed about forty-five seconds (at least, no longer than a minute) after their last radio transmission. According to the calculations made by a team of Zhukovsky Academy specialists, a loss of 4,000 metres in altitude in less than a minute (assuming that something happened right after Gagarin's last message) with a fairly low near-ground speed would have only been possible in a spin, the manoeuvre consuming more energy than any other. A haphazard fall or a dive would have taken more time or been faster. In any case, the assumption that the aircraft had lost height through a spin was accepted by the commission as a fact, and all subsequent analysis proceeded from it. It explained how the crash itself had happened, for it was not hard to imagine what had followed their departure into a spin. There were layers of clouds between them and the ground, and recovering from a spin in the clouds, i.e., without being able to see the ground or the horizon, is a very difficult task. Even though they might have tried to recover earlier, it was obvious they must have made their real attempt at recovery only on coming out of the clouds at just seven or eight hundred metres above ground, a height definitely insufficient for recovering a MiG-15.

One question often asked in connection with this accident is why neither Gagarin nor Sereghin sent any radio message when trouble began. The answer, quite simply, is that when a pilot gets into a really critical life-threatening situation demanding the utmost concentration of all his faculties and psychological powers, it is beyond his physical possibilities to think of or perform any parallel actions on which survival does not directly depend. Virtually the entire tragic record of fatal accidents in aviation testifies that even if a pilot were trying to say something in the last moments between life and death, he hardly ever managed to pass on a coherent message. I will later tell of the crash of my colleague Kadomtsev. He tried to give a radio message, and the taped transmission was studied by audio experts at a specialised forensic laboratory, yet his last message could not be made out. And it was not the only such case. As for Gagarin and Sereghin, they might not even have tried to say anything, too intent on their attempts to recover and hoping to the last they would do it.

Having decided the immediate cause of the crash, we were faced with the question of why their machine had gone into a spin in the first place. Had it happened while they were doing aerobatics in the practice area, we could have supposed a mistake was made in one of the manoeuvres, but the MiG-15 trainer was not the kind of aircraft to go into an unintentional spin easily; it would take a really bad error to 'force' it into it. Even though Gagarin and Sereghin were flying with drop fuel tanks which somewhat affected the performance of the machine, it was very unlikely that the aircraft would stall and spin during aerobatics, and almost totally out of the question in level flight.

There have been recent attempts to explain their fatal spin by their aeroplane accidentally getting into the wake vortex of another aircraft which allegedly happened to fly close by, but the investigation commission after the crash established beyond doubt that all aircraft airborne in the area at the time had been at a perfectly safe distance from Gagarin's MiG-15. And even if there had been an aircraft flying by, getting into its wake vortex could not have led to spinning. It happened to me many times, including in test dog-fight situations when the Su-7B I was attacking was performing high G-load turns (the larger the G-load, the more powerful the vortex from the aircraft), yet I never went into a spin because of it, nor did my aeroplane turn over. The only tangible effect was banking with a jerk and being 'thrown' out of the vortex; control was restored immediately, and my attack went on unhampered. And when I got into another aeroplane's air vortex at an angle, there was almost nothing to feel but a shake. Therefore none of the experienced pilots who gave a thought to Gagarin's crash or discussed it, either after it had happened or when this new explanation was suggested, could even for a minute accept that Gagarin and Sereghin had stalled and spun due to getting into somebody's wake vortex.

This might be an appropriate moment to say a few words about Vladimir Sereghin, with whom I worked for fourteen years. He and I were good friends. Everyone in the fighter testing section, where we had worked together side by side for quite some time, knew Vladimir as a thoroughly good and kind person of remarkable integrity. He was a great friend to have: sensitive, considerate and thoughtful, his only weak point a rather quick temper. An attack pilot during the war, Vladimir had received his title of Hero of the Soviet Union for his distinction in action. He had retrained to become a good fighter test pilot after the war, and he was somebody everyone was fond of and respected.

As a member of the investigation commission, I suggested my own version of what had caused Gagarin and Sereghin's crash. It was the only version that had at least an indirect confirmation, whereas all others were based on nothing but conjecture. It occurred to me when I, along with other commission members, was invited to the Aircraft Maintenance and Repair Institute, where all fragments of the crashed aeroplane were assembled (the enormous task of finding and picking up every single piece had been performed by a battalion of soldiers, and the earth on and around the crash site had been literally sieved). As was usually done in

323

the course of an accident investigation, all the pieces were laid out in a hangar in such a way as to make up the shape of the aircraft. Everything that could be analysed was analysed by experts, who established, among other things, that the engines had been running to the last moment and that the landing gear position lights had been alive until the moment of the crash, therefore there had been no electric power failure. These latest discoveries and other data prompted the commission to conclude that at the time of stalling and departure the aircraft had been in perfect working order and there had been no failures that could have led to the crash. This conclusion was automatically, if indirectly, suggestive of the pilots' own fault, of which there was no indication whatsoever. A number of well-known test pilots, including myself, signed a letter addressed to the government protesting against ungrounded insinuations about the pilots.

General Sigov, who was reporting on the results of the examination of the fragments, pointed out that the cockpit had been airtight on impact with the ground, and the cockpit pressure differential indicator had a mark at minus 0.01. As soon as the report was over and questions were invited, I raised my hand and asked why Sigov regarded that position of the needle as normal. He replied that a difference between outside and cockpit pressures was normally created upon climbing to higher altitudes, while at the ground that difference was nil. Well, minus 0.01 was close enough to zero to be taken as such, I felt. When asked by the chairman if I was satisfied with the reply, I said I was not. What Sigov was saying was true for static conditions, but in a rapid descent there should remain positive pressure differential, for the valve would not have the time to throw off the excessive pressure of the engine-fed air. There was no question of zero, let alone negative pressure difference if the cockpit had remained airtight to the moment of impact. During the break I was asked by the head of the flight and piloting sub-commission whether I had complete confidence in what I had said. I assured him I had. He then asked me to arrange for a relevant flight test at my Institute, which I immediately did, getting on the phone to Andrei Manucharov.

Next morning Manucharov reported to me on the phone that the test pilot Bobrovitsky had performed several steep dives in a two-seat MiG-15 with recovery at ground level, and had registered a minimum pressure difference at the lowest point of the dive of plus 0.2. It was direct proof in favour of what I had said (at high altitudes the pressure differential is about 0.35 to 0.4). Several more flight tests of this kind were performed with special measuring instrumentation on board, and in each steep descent the difference between the outside and cockpit air pressure was above the zero mark. Following our report on the results, similar tests were conducted at the Gromov Institute air base with the same results. The natural conclusion was that the cockpit of Gagarin's MiG-15 had been depressurised *before* the crash. Now, the loss of air pressure at about 4,000 metres (the altitude they had been travelling at) was by no account serious trouble in itself, but my argument was that whatever had caused it must have simultaneously affected the aircraft as such and the pilots.

So what could it have been? Getting into somebody else's air vortex would not lead to the depressurising of the cockpit. It could happen in the case of a collision or a stroke of lightning, but there had been no thunderstorms at the time. A collision with another aircraft had to be ruled out for lack of another damaged aircraft. It might have been a bird that had flown into them, but there was no trace of a bird strike found among the debris. Finally, the loss of pressure might have been due to the breaking of the canopy sealing hose, but it would not have affected either the pilots or the aircraft. I suggested that they might have collided with a meteorological balloon sonde. Such sondes, with instrumentation pods suspended under them, would usually rise up into the air rather fast, and Gagarin might have failed to notice it until it was too late, especially if the balloon had unexpectedly popped out of the clouds. If the instrumentation pod happened to hit the aircraft in the cockpit area it could have led to its being depressurised, and could even have injured the pilots. The aircraft might have gone into a spin because of the impact or else because of the pilots' temporary inability to control it. The sonde might have been launched from the nearby Kirzhach parachute jumping base, as was always done before jumps to determine the direction and force of the wind.

My version was not accepted by the commission leadership, and in a way I understand why not: somebody would have had to be held responsible for randomly launching meteosondes, and many people (not necessarily the ones to blame) would have been penalised 'as an object lesson to others', as was often done with us in cases where publicity was unavoidable (not that the results of the inquiry were or were ever intended to be published). Therefore the official explanation of the depressurisation of the cockpit was that it had resulted from an impact against a tree on the accident site. A special experiment confirmed that with trees about twenty-five metres tall (which was how tall they were in that place), a collision with a tree-top could result in the pressure difference falling down to zero. Even if this version was plausible (which I could not accept it to be), it would have certainly been more correct to accept and to cite both possibilities as to why Gagarin's cockpit might have been damaged and depressurised.

In the end, however, as I heard long afterwards, my version of the meteosonde had been included in the investigation commission's final statement, where it said that Gagarin's aeroplane might have entered a spin as a result of an abrupt evasive manoeuvre performed to avoid collision with a balloon. In any case, the statement was never made public, and so neither the Soviet people nor the world at large received any official explanation of Gagarin's death (which eventually led to the appearance of some wildly improbable and preposterous versions). As I later heard from a man from the Air Force Flight Safety Department, when Brezhnev was told of the investigation results he decided they should not be made public, saying something to the effect that 'the people had calmed down already, there is no need to agitate them again'. Rather a peculiar philosophy, I would say.

Around July 1968 there was another fatal accident near our airfield with which I was indirectly involved. Towards the end of a Su-15 test flight I was heading for the airfield at 10,000 metres, performing a low-speed fuel consumption test run. In this test it was essential to maintain constant air speed, altitude and rpm. It was not an easy task at low speed, so I kept my eyes on the flight indicators, virtually unable to take them off for a look around outside the cockpit. The ADF

325

indication showed I was travelling in the direction of the right side of my airfield, heading towards the northern edge of our test area where it bordered on the firing range of the missile base at Kapustin Yar. I adjusted my path towards home in a gradual turn, taking care to bank left at the shallowest angle possible so as not to spoil the fuel test run. On landing I went straight to the pilots' mess to have lunch. While I was there, Colonel Zagorny came in and said that two Tu-16s had collided and crashed near Kapustin Yar. It was tragic news, but it did not for a second occur to me then that the crash had anything to do with my own flight.

As it turned out, a formation of several Tu-16s was acting as a group target for the air defence systems which were tested at Kapustin Yar. The aircraft were travelling one over another with a height interval of 300 metres between them. It became clear from the cockpit voice recording that the crew of one of the upper aircraft got distracted for a minute or two and lost a bit of their height. One of the pilots said, 'Look, there's a fighter to the left of us – I wonder what his altitude is.' After a couple of casual remarks by the two pilots, a different voice, probably that of the radioman, cried, 'Commander, an aircraft underneath!' These were their last words. The upper aeroplane 'sat down' onto the one below. Of the twelve crew members in the two machines only one survived: a navigator, who must have fallen out accidentally, landed safely with his parachute.

There was no one besides me in the test area at the time, therefore it was my Su-15 that the pilots spotted, although there were over ten kilometres between us. Being intent on instrument flying, I saw no aircraft myself. Even if I had seen them I would not have been worried, for the distance between us was perfectly safe. And it certainly appeared safe to the tower controller who was monitoring my flight on the radar screen and who would have let me know if I had come too close to the test area border or to any other aircraft. The investigation commission, headed by General Agaltsev, examined the radar tracking of my flight and ascertained that I had remained within three kilometres of the test area edge. There was nothing to blame me for, yet my heart was very heavy and the pain has remained to this day.

The year 1968 brought about unexpected and unprecedented changes in Czechoslovakia, and I still remember the amazement caused by some of the news from Prague. Political censorship was cancelled! It was something we could not even imagine happening in the USSR. Czechoslovakia had apparently taken a step on the way towards a society with more freedom. This, of course, was not the way these developments were presented in the Soviet media, controlled by the Central Committee of the party. Their reports and comments grew more and more disapproving and critical.

All my adult life I had sympathised with the ideas of democracy and had hoped for a more humane and liberal system than the one we were living in. Even in Stalin's times, to say nothing of Khrushchev's, I had rejoiced at the slightest sign of our socialism becoming a little more democratic and more 'human'. This is not to say, however, that I doubted the viability and essential justice of socialism as a system to be strived for. As I have already written, the first indications of the country's turn towards some semblance of democracy after Stalin's death caused joy and excitement among most people I knew. So many things ignored or hushed down before – the position of collective farmers, the appalling situation with urban housing (to say nothing of the atrocities of Stalin's regime), and so on – were for the first time openly (or so it seemed) discussed in the press and considered by the government, which began to take measures to improve the state of affairs. We were becoming a more open society, and our people were for the first time allowed to go to the West as tourists, if only in organised groups. (I remember my father, an ardent champion of foreign tourism, saying, with a mixture of joy and surprise, 'Over fifty thousand people have travelled abroad this year, and only five of them defected! It's nothing!')

However, the pro-democratic policy was short-lived. There was no unity in the top leadership, and the clash between the two main factions – the Stalinists and the reformists – resulted in an open conflict and the removal from the position of power of the so-called 'anti-party' group (Molotov, Malenkov, Kaganovich and their immediate supporters). Our passion for stigmatising labels was overpowering, and when such a label was stuck on by those in authority it automatically became a standard term of reference for the person or phenomenon in question. I have always thought that it was then that the retreat from the democratic tendencies really began, despite the ostensible defeat of the anti-reformist forces.

Only today, after all the hurdles and tribulations on the road of *perestroika* begun by Gorbachev, has it become clear how naive our hopes for major changes so soon after Stalin's death were. Most of the old state machine had remained in operation, and neither Khrushchev nor those who supported him could break or dismantle it, particularly since they had no intention of fully dismantling it. And the reformers themselves – Khrushchev, Mikoyan, Kosyghin and others – must have had a kind of 'split personality' complex, the old and the new wrestling in their minds and in their perceptions and decisions. Besides, by the end of his time in power, Khrushchev's initial pro-democratic inclinations had gradually given way to more authoritarian ones. That was probably why those who noticed a change in Khrushchev's policy received the news of his dismissal rather calmly, if not with some relief. Unfortunately, they had misinterpreted the signs: Brezhnev's regime turned out to be a kind of belated reaction against Khrushchev's 'thaw'. Stalinists held up their heads again, and the persecution of ideological and political dissidents resumed (although it was not quite as ruthless as under Stalin). Against this background the democratic developments taking place in Czechoslovakia seemed a very encouraging sign. I am sure I was not alone in hoping that they would eventually be echoed by similar changes in the Soviet Union.

In the early summer of 1968 a group of Czechoslovakian military specialists paid a working visit to our missile testing range on the Volga. They participated in the final evaluation tests of the K-13 missiles, which were beginning to be produced in Czechoslovakia under a Soviet licence. Our obsessive secretiveness was at its daftest: the Czechoslovaks were not even shown our living compound in Akhtubinsk, let alone the air base territory. They were not even supposed to suspect the existence of a flight test centre there (even though it was impossible *not* to be aware of it). A helicopter had brought them from Volgograd straight to a measuring post in the steppe, where all they could see was a barracks for the soldiers, the measuring facilities and a timber cottage, in which they were put up. And Czechoslovakia was our ally and a fellow member of the Warsaw Pact! At the same time, as we all knew, the existence of the Institute and its exact location was no secret to the Americans. Their satellite photography together with 'conventional' intelligence could hardly be suspected of idleness or inefficiency.

Once I visited that measuring post to meet the guests and to see how the work was going. The day ended with an informal dinner with the Czechs, and I remember how one of them, a major in the Czechoslovakian army, was saying with genuine distress that the Soviet party leadership should not have been so opposed to their reforms. They were *not* trying to become alienated from the Soviet Union or to renounce socialist ideals, he said, all they were trying to do was to improve and humanise the system. He spoke of the enthusiasm with which the reforms – the 'Prague spring' – were received by most people at home, especially in Prague itself. Neither he nor I could then understand that the task as they saw it was impossible. Any 'improvement' of that regime (which had no more to do with 'real' socialism than our own) would either have been temporary or else it would have destroyed the regime itself, as our recent *perestroika* has shown.

The news of the Warsaw Pact countries invading Czechoslovakia came as a great shock. It was the end of a faint hope that Czechoslovakia would set an example of a humanised socialist society. It must have been the possibility of such an example that had frightened the party leaders in Moscow into action. One of my friends, Vadim Yudin, an aviation engineer in the air force, was on a short posting in Prague when it all happened. He was an excellent amateur photographer, and on the day he woke up in his hotel to the roar of tanks outside he first took a few pictures from his window and then used up several rolls of films in the streets. Back in Moscow Vadim told me of the tears in the eyes of men who were watching our tanks driving through their city, of the word 'Why?' written in large letters across the roads. The photographs he showed me were more eloquent than any words. It was clear that most people in Prague were shocked and deeply hurt by the invasion; they could not understand why they had to be treated in such a way when all they had done had been aimed at improving the socialist system. Shortly afterwards Vadim hid his pictures away and asked me not to tell anyone about them. He died in 1990, and I have not seen them since the day he showed them to me in 1968.

It was three days after the invasion, when he had just returned from Prague, that I flew in from Akhtubinsk and went to see him at his dacha in Zhukovka near Moscow. Vadim's nearest neighbour in the country was Vyacheslav Molotov, and I ran into him and his wife Polina Semyonovna when I went out for a walk. I have written earlier that they had known me since childhood, for we had been close neighbours in the Kremlin. Polina invited me to have lunch with them. Over lunch she asked me about my brothers, and when she asked about Alexei, I said, half jokingly, 'He's now turned an invader.' Molotov was immediately alerted and asked, 'Invader, you say? So you disapprove of our troops in Prague?' I did not want to enter into an argument, so I said cautiously (and insincerely) that the decision itself might have been right, but the Czechoslovakian people would not forgive us. 'Forget about the people – one day they will understand. It was the only way to act!' he retorted, and his wife asked, 'Does Anastas Ivanovich feel the same as you do?' I said I did not know, and she did not seem to believe me (and if she really did not, she must have suspected that my father's views were different from those of most of his former colleagues in the Politburo). However, I spoke the truth, for I had not seen my father after the events and did not know that he, on hearing the news of the invasion on the radio, exclaimed 'It's a disgrace!' (I heard it from my brother, who had been present in the room.)

Several years later I met Molotov again in the government dental clinic, where we were waiting for our turns and talking. Somebody sitting next to us asked him if he was writing his memoirs. 'I am, I am', he murmured, in a strangely dismissive way, and then suddenly asked, 'Stepan, remember you were upset by our troops in Czechoslovakia? Have you changed your opinion since?' It was amazing he could still remember it. I gave him the most evasive answer I could think of.

The last time I saw Molotov was two years before his death. It was against a medical background again, in a hospital where we happened to be patients together. I visited him in his ward, and was shocked to see that he was even smaller, as if he had shrunk visibly in size. He had hearing problems too, but he recognised me at a glance. He showed me the book he was reading: it was the newly published volume of *The History of the Great Patriotic War*. 'Not that there is anything I do not know, but it's still interesting to read.' Characteristically, in all of my encounters with Molotov after his dismissal from power he never once asked me about my father or asked to pass him his regards. On the other hand, my father also listened to my accounts of my meetings with Molotov without a word of comment or a single question. He never asked me to give his regards if I happened to see Molotov again. It did not surprise me much, for I knew they had never been on friendly terms with each other, and their views were different.

When Molotov died (surviving my father by a few years) I attended the funeral at Kuznetsov cemetery. His daughter, Svetlana, saw me and invited me to their house afterwards. As I was standing there near a small group of guests, I overheard a conversation that was distinctly Stalinist in its character and subject. One of the men, a general from Tbilisi, was boasting that he had organised a memorial museum of Stalin in his dacha near Tbilisi, complete with a statue which he had found among junk and rubbish at some dump. I thought it was rather over the top and said so. Somebody immediately snapped back at me, and I heard someone ask, 'Why did he come here?' I was asking myself the same question. The formal speeches that followed were in the same vein, and after two or three I could take it no more and quietly left.

CHAPTER 24

The Variable-sweep Wing

T he mid-1960s saw the appearance of a new tendency in aircraft design: the use of variable-sweep wings. From the time of the earliest jet engines it had been clear that a jet engine alone was not sufficient for breaking the sonic barrier and that a new type of wing, the sweptback wing, was a must. At the same time, at lower speeds (i.e. at greater angles of attack) sweptback wings create larger air drag than ordinary wings, which means that their lift-to-drag ratio is lower. This affects the range of flight and the manoeuvrability of the aircraft. On landing, other things being equal, the lift of a sweptback wing is lower, therefore its landing speed is higher. Such aircraft require longer runways. In other words, at lower or medium speeds and especially at take-offs and landings, the ordinary wing has an advantage over the sweptback one.

It was this reasoning that generated the idea of designing a variable-sweep wing for supersonic aircraft, so that landings and cruising flights could be performed with a smaller 'sweep' of the wing and therefore with better aero-dynamic characteristics. It was not an easy task to design a wing with a turning mechanism inside it, and the inevitable side effect was that it enlarged the weight of the aircraft (which was to be compensated by a greater fuel economy in the cruising flight). The first aircraft with a variable-sweep wing to become known in the world was the American F-111 fighter, which unwittingly 'gave a push' (as happened in other cases as well) to the Soviet aircraft design.

In spring 1967 our air base at Akhtubinsk received an experimental model from Pavel Sukhoi's company: the S-22I. It was based on an ordinary sweptback Su-7B in which the outer parts of the wings (from the wheel struts to the wing tips) could be moved forward, thus decreasing their sweep. All the pilots who evaluated the S-22I (I was among them) appreciated the advantage of this inno-vation at lower speeds and on landing. The Mikoyan Design Company, which had for some time been developing the concept of a high-performance fighter with moderate landing speed, had preceded the S-22I with two aircraft fitted with additional lift engines (one of them was a preliminary version of the MiG-23). These engines were used only at take-off and landing and their function was to add lift to that of the wings. They certainly shortened the run of the aircraft at take-off and landing, but on the other hand they were nothing but useless extra weight during the flight itself. That was why Artem Mikoyan decided to give up on the idea of additional lift engines and exploited the variable-sweep concept instead. The MiG-23, which appeared soon afterwards, was equipped with a turning mechanism that changed the sweep angle of the entire wing (the wing root was its only immovable part).

In terms of breaking the sonic barrier and high-speed flying (including high-speed flying at low altitudes) a larger sweep angle is an advantage, for the larger the angle the easier it is to break the sound barrier and gain maximum speed, although in manoeuvring, such as dog-fighting or aerobatics, the optimum wing sweep angle is much smaller, from forty to forty-five degrees; in cruising the full-forward sweep is the best. In our first supersonic fighter, the MiG-19, the leading-edge sweep angle was sixty degrees. The possibility of lessening the sweep angle of the wing at take-off and landing allowed for a greater sweep backwards at higher speeds than had been possible before. In the second modification of the MiG-23 the maximum angle at which the wings were swept back was seventy-four degrees, while at the landing it was reduced to eighteen. Its landing speed was 250 to 255 kph as against the 320 kph of the MiG-21, which had the wings permanently swept back at sixty degrees. If the MiG-23 had been designed with an invariable-sweep wing swept back at seventy-four degrees its landing speed would have been 400 kph or thereabouts. In the MiG-23 the wing profile curvature was also increased in the landing mode by the lowering of two sets of flaps: the trailing-edge flaps and the leading-edge flaps.

Apart from higher landing speed, the large wing sweep angle had another side effect: it reduced the control authority of ailerons. Therefore, in the variable-sweep aircraft, ailerons were replaced with a hydro-mechanical tail which allowed the stabilisers to move collectively or differentially to provide either pitch or roll. In addition, the wings were supplied with spoilers, which increased the roll control (they were neutralised at large sweep angles).

The project test pilot in the tests of the specimen MiG-23 was Gennady Butenko, who was the first to fly it in its factory tests at Zhukovsky. A little later the same year (9 July 1968) I had a ride in it too, also at Zhukovsky. It was only next year that the MiG-23 arrived at our air base in Akhtubinsk to be tested there. All in all eight or nine pilots (I was among them) were directly engaged in testing this machine. There were so many pilots involved because it was a very extensive and complex project in which several airframes were tested at various times during the three or so years that the overall programme of the MiG-23 military certification tests took us to accomplish. In the course of this time the aircraft was subjected to considerable modification. Its wings were redesigned twice, as well as its engine and radar, and its control system was seriously modified. The final test statement was issued for a model which was largely different from the original specimen. Altogether about 1,300 test flights were performed in about a dozen airframes of the MiG-23 on that test project.

At about the same time, in July 1969, I flew the MiG-21 testing a new missile designed for the MiG-23. My task consisted of launching two missiles one after the other at limit altitude. I zoomed from 13,000 metres upwards, launched my first missile, and my only engine stalled and flamed out. The aircraft was still climbing from force of momentum, so I decided to go ahead with the mission and launched my second missile at about 2,000 metres altitude. Only after that, as the aircraft went into a descent, did I report the engine failure to the flight controller. He got worried but I had no problem restarting the engine, so everything ended well.

The initial version of the MiG-23 presented to us for military specification tests was the MiG-23S, where the 'S' indicated that it was equipped with the 'Sapphire' radar originally installed in the MiG-21S. The new radar specially designed for the MiG-23 was not ready yet. It was in this preliminary specimen that we first encountered certain features that affected the controllability of the MiG-23. As I have written earlier, control surfaces of all modern aircraft (ailerons, stabilisers, etc.) are operated by means of hydraulic actuators, or boosters, while the pilot only deals with hydraulic valves, which take a minimum physical effort to activate. To simulate the effort on the controls, a special device with springs, known as the artificial feel unit, was installed. In the MiG-23S this device had a double spring with too large a difference in the force gradients. As the pilot pulled the stick with increasing force, the G-load grew accordingly until there came a point (at about 5G, which is characteristic of aerobatic manoeuvres) when the G-load suddenly went up in a leap because of the difference in the force gradients of the two parts of the double spring. Needless to say, maintaining a steady G-load in such conditions was a pretty difficult task. The test pilots' decision was that operational pilots could not be presented with such an aircraft. We all signed the pilots' assessment statement where our opinion was expressed, with the result that the MiG-23 was supplied with a pitch damper with the help of which a steady G-load could be maintained. Despite this improvement, and for the first time in my experience, we wrote down in the MiG-23 pilots' manual that all agile manoeuvres were to be performed with the autopilot stability augmentation mode on.

Another deficiency of the MiG-23 concerned its aerodynamic layout, and it unfortunately revealed itself in a tragic way. In September 1970 we were preparing a demonstration of aircraft and armaments for the members of the high military command. The dress rehearsal was timed to coincide with the fiftieth anniversary of our Institute, which was attended by many distinguished guests, including several air force generals, the Air Force Commander-in-Chief Marshal Kutakhov and a number of aviation industry dignitaries. The guests were watching the demonstration from the stands set up close to the firing range.

One of the items on the programme was a mock low-height air combat between a MiG-23S and a MiG-21, intended to demonstrate the advantages of the new aircraft. Our command post was within a hundred metres of the stands on an artificial mound. The pilots were commanded on the radio by Vadim Petrov and I commentated on the proceedings through the PA system. Three other people at the command post besides us were the Institute Wing Commander Bayevsky, No. 1 Department Commander Manucharov and the navigator N. Ivanov. Sasha Kuznetsov flew his MiG-21 low along the length of the stands and entered a banked turn. Vitaly Zhukov was following closely in the MiG-23. When the fighters had passed over our heads and their roar had gone off with them, I continued my explanations into the microphone. Suddenly I heard Petrov's voice behind me: 'Recover!' I did not get concerned at first, for I thought he meant recovering from the turn. And then he cried, 'Eject!' I looked to the right in instant alarm and saw, at a height of about 200 metres, an aircraft spinning towards the ground at an angle, some two kilometres from where we were. Just above the ground, some twenty metres or so, there was a bright flash over the cockpit and the next moment the machine hit the ground and exploded. After a few seconds of shocked and painful silence I switched the microphone on and said slowly into it, 'We have just lost test pilot Major Vitaly Zhukov.'

There was no doubt of the tragic outcome, although it turned out that the flash we had all seen had come from Vitaly's ejector-seat rocket engine which he had fired, trying to escape. But the aircraft was falling too steeply and the height was too low for the parachute to deploy, and Victor fell down right into the explosion. General Bayevsky and I walked to the helicopter which was standing by near the command post and which already had its rotor running for the flight to the crash site. I will never forget the sight of Vitaly's bare sun-tanned back in the debris, all that was seen of him after the explosion.

Although Vitaly Zhukov was my junior both in age and rank, I always regarded him as a friend. I was on good and easy terms with most pilots, especially fighter pilots, with no consideration for any differences in rank or office, but Vitaly was one in a group of several pilots who were my particular friends, with whom I often met up at our get-togethers, visited in their homes and invited to my own place. Four of them, including Vitaly – the 'four musketeers' as we called them – were particularly close to one another, and all four were killed: first Vitaly, then the other three – Sasha Kuznetsov, Nikolai Rukhlyadko and Nikolai Stogov – following over the next fifteen years. It was as though the four of them had been doomed by fate.

It was first suggested that Zhukov had gone into a spin because he had entered a critical angle of attack, though it seemed strange that he could have made such a mistake in a test specimen; he should have piloted it with a safety margin left. The analysis of the instrumentation data from the training flights showed that in each of them the margin separating the aircraft from the critical angle of attack had been sufficient. (In the crash flight itself the instrumentation was completely destroyed by fire.) I remember the meeting at which we had discussed the programme of that tragic demonstration. I pointed out then that it was still too early in the day to perform low-altitude air combat manoeuvres in the MiG-23; we had only just begun testing the aircraft and did not really know it well enough. I wish I had not been proved right in my apprehensions.

All MiG-23 flights were suspended for a few days. However, the day after the crash George Sedov, Artem Mikoyan's first deputy, came up to me on the airfield and said, 'Stepan Anastasovich, we simply must have one flight in our factory MiG-23 specimen – do you think you could do it for us?' He knew that none of the pilots would be allowed by their commanders to do a test flight before Vitaly's funeral, whereas I was entitled to decide for myself. I agreed. Having performed the mission and already on the way home, I decided to repeat the manoeuvre which had led to Vitaly's death, but at a higher altitude. I found nothing alarming in the behaviour of the machine. However, after a while another pilot went into a spin and crashed in a MiG-23 at the Air Force Advanced Training Centre, and in November 1972 it happened to Boris Orlov of the Mikoyan Design Company, who just managed to recover in time.

In the following year a similar thing happened in a MiG-23B to me. That flight proved to be one of the most critical episodes of my flying career. My mission consisted of testing the manoeuvrability of the aircraft with four under-wing bombs in low-altitude aerobatics. I began a loop at a thousand metres, maintaining about 5.5 G-load to start with. When, with the loss of speed, the angle of attack increased, I took care to keep it at the limit value of twenty-six degrees. Having got over the top, the aircraft nosed down and inverted. I took another look at the instrument – it was still showing twenty-six degrees, so all was well. However, I had barely taken my eyes off the indicator when the aircraft sharply rolled. There had been no warning cues whatsoever; it was as if somebody had forcefully applied the controls without my knowledge. I immediately, almost by instinct, hit the pedal against the spin and pushed the stick fully forward. The rolling stopped at once, luckily with the aircraft the right side up, which made it easier to recover from the dive. It was a narrow escape, and only because of my immediate application of controls for recovery before the spin had time to develop. If the machine had not stopped rolling at once, or if it had emerged from the spin the wrong side up, there would not have been enough altitude left for recovery and I would have had to eject (the safety manual directs ejection if at 3,000 metres the aircraft still continues spinning).

It did seem odd that the aeroplane stalled at a twenty-six degree angle of attack, the critical angle being no less than thirty-two. The onboard instrumentation data showed that just before rolling the aircraft had yawed, and it became clear that this indiscernible yawing had been the cause of all the unexpected spins at non-critical angles of attack. After that flight of mine the angle-of-attack limitation was brought down to twenty-four degrees and operation pilots were temporarily restricted from doing sophisticated aerobatics in the MiG-23. To remove the dangerous fault, the MiG-23 was supplied with a yaw damper and the so-called 'taileron-rudder interconnect' counter-balancing the pilot's roll-control movements with the rudder deflection against the yaw. In addition, the critical alpha (angle of attack) warning lights were complemented with a tactile indicator, a small lever next to the wheel brakes lever on the control stick which began tapping on the pilot's hand as the warning lights came on. Later it was replaced with a more sophisticated device, a stick pusher which automatically pushed the stick forward at the maximum allowance angle of attack (after which it was put up to twenty-eight degrees).

Vitaly Zhukov's crash was the second fatal accident in the still brief history of the MiG-23, and the two of them had happened within one week (the first two fatal accidents involving the Su-24 had happened on one and the same day). A few days before Vitaly, the MiG company test pilot Mikhail Komarov had crashed in a MiG-23 at the Zhukovsky flight testing base. It was established that Komarov had blacked out while speeding up with the afterburner on, exceeding the design dynamic pressure limit (i.e. the maximum speed sustained by the airframe) with full afterburner still on. The aircraft began to disintegrate in the air and fell. In the history of aviation there have been cases of oxygen and nitrogen bottles being mixed up with each other while the aircraft was being prepared for a flight. Nobody could be fully certain of course, but something of this kind might have happened and caused Mikhail Komarov to lose consciousness in his fatal flight. He was buried in Zhukovsky near Moscow, and on the day of his funeral (which was Saturday) a group of us went to what was known in Akhtubinsk as the 'Mikoyan' bungalow to drink to the memory of our civilian colleague together with his fellow pilots from the Mikoyan Design Company. My friends Nikolai Stogov and Vitaly Zhukov were there with us. Nikolai Stogov, a dedicated amateur film-maker, suddenly said, 'What an uncanny co-incidence – I had filmed Rogachev and Komarov only once each, and both of them got killed!' Zhukov's reply came in a flash: 'You've only filmed me once too. Does it mean I'll also get killed?' Two days later he was dead (Nikolai Stogov crashed fifteen years later).

I have already mentioned that the MiG-23's wings had to be redesigned in the course of testing. It was caused by a particular phenomenon, known to most pilots, called 'buffeting'. At high angles of attack, when the steadiness of the flow over the upper wing surface is already upset but the aircraft is still under control, the pilot can usually feel the buffeting of the airframe caused by the unsteady airflow. In the aeroplanes with unswept wings the buffeting starts right before departure into a spin, thus serving as a useful warning cue to the pilot. But as we started flying aircraft with sweptback wings we discovered that in them buffeting began long before the critical angle of attack was reached. Therefore, if buffeting was to be regarded as a cue that warned the pilot against pulling any further G-load, he would then be restricted from exploiting the whole range of possible angles of attack, i.e. from using the entire lift potential of the wing, which would mean considerably limiting the manoeuvrability of the aeroplane.

We first encountered this feature in the MiG-21, in which the buffeting began at the point when the G-load was one or two units lower than it could be at larger but still fairly safe angles of attack. In the MiG-23, with the wing sweep angle at forty-five degrees (which we considered to be the optimum angle for air combat and aerobatics), the buffeting started even earlier than in the MiG-21. We did not regard it a dangerous drawback; nevertheless we mentioned it in our initial assessment statement on the aircraft. The MiG-23 was being tested under the watchful eye of a state commission and the Air Force Commander himself. He demanded the immediate removal of that drawback by the MiG-23 designer team (on which we, the test pilots, were not insisting). So the wing was redesigned and received an extended leading edge with a so-called saw-tooth on it. It delayed the buffeting but brought the spin threshold nearer. Neither the landing nor the take-off was sufficiently safe now, for the angle-of-attack safety margin at touch-down or at the take-off point was just one or two degrees.

The MiG design team was aware of the problem and they were developing a modification of the wing with a deflectable leading edge, which would remove the unpleasant feature. We believed it reasonable to wait until the improved wing modification was ready. However, as Joseph Swejk would say, 'Everything was going well until the General Staff interfered.' The Aviation Industry Minister, under pressure from the Air Force Commander-in-Chief, had already ordered the manufacture of the deficient wings before they were tested. Eighty sets of such wings were made. However, our test statement on the aircraft with these wings said that they could not be allowed to fly in operational units. So, the way things were, to comply with the final test statement the wings had to be discarded and the wingless machines set aside to wait for the improved wings to be made and tested.

This is what ordinary common sense suggested doing, yet the 'big wigs' at the top did not want to lose face.

We received a visit from a number of design company specialists and the Deputy Minister, A. Minayev. A long and heated discussion followed in the office of the Institute Commander, for whom I was officially acting at the time. The industry people tried to talk us into allowing the eighty MiG-23s to go into service with those wings, but we staunchly refused (later one of the Moscow guests confessed to me that they had known we were right all along but had to follow the minister's instructions). It was a stalemate, and to break it I finally agreed to a compromise: the aircraft were to be allowed into temporary service under the condition that their wings would be replaced with the new ones as soon as the latter were tested and approved. As an additional safety precaution we supplemented the pilots' manual with the instruction *always* to take off on after-burner so as to gain the safe speed faster.

I was reminded of this compromise over a dozen years later. The wings of all MiG-23s were indeed replaced, except for one machine which belonged to the Gromov Institute in Zhukovsky. It was flown all that time, and the special entry in the manual was apparently long forgotten. One day the Institute Flight Director Enn Kaarma was taking off to test some autopilot modification and his afterburner was off. As soon as he had unstuck, still at low height and slow speed, he must have removed his left hand from the throttle lever to raise the landing gear and to turn the equipment on. The lever would have then begun to move slowly backwards by itself, the engine thrust would have decreased and so would the speed, while the angle of attack would have reached the critical value (with the afterburner on, the lever would have been fixed with a retainer, and the aircraft would have quickly speeded up). Preoccupied with the equipment to be tested, the pilot must have failed to notice the dangerously falling speed. The aeroplane stalled, went into a spin and crashed.

In September 1971 a dual-control combat trainer for all modifications of the MiG-23, the MiG-23UB, arrived at Akhtubinsk for military certification tests. I made ten test flights in it, with Vladimir Ryaby as my co-pilot. He and I together had rather an unusual experience in this aircraft in March 1972. Our flight mission was to test its performance at supersonic speed with a medium wing sweep angle (normally it is the maximum sweep angle which is used when going supersonic). As the mission required, I sped up to my Mach 2.35 limit (2,500 kph) and moved the sweep control lever from the seventy-four-degree stop to the forty-five-degree position. The sweep indicator needle stirred and moved, but instead of stopping at forty-five degrees it went on moving further down the scale until it reached the bottom limit of eighteen degrees. With such a sweep angle Mach 0.8 was as fast as you were allowed to go, and we were flying at over 2.0! I tried to force the lever but it did not budge. Strange as it was, the behaviour of the aircraft did not change in any way, maybe because we were well above the speed of sound. However, slowing down under the sonic barrier with the wings at such an angle would be dangerous; the aircraft would lose its stability and a pitch-down moment would develop. Our lives hung on what would happen first: whether we would make it to under Mach 1.0 at closed throttle and airbrake extended, or whether the indicated air speed in an unintentional vertical dive would exceed the design limit of the airframe and it would disintegrate in the air. Our luck was with us, it seems, for as the wing reached its full forward position it suddenly became controllable again, and I was able to sweep it back. It turned out later that it was a manufacturing defect in the wing sweep control unit that had caused the problem.

In the 1960s Alexander Yakovlev's designer team had begun their work on the first Soviet vertical take-off and landing aeroplane (VTOL), inspired by the British P.1127. I had first seen a stand model of this aircraft at Farnborough back in 1961, and in 1965 I saw it flying at Bourges. I was really impressed by the way it hovered over the ground and then moved sideways and backwards. It was very odd seeing an aeroplane flying like a helicopter. The Yakovlev team created an experimental VTOL dubbed 'Yak-36' which was demonstrated 'in action' at an air show at Domodedovo airport in 1965. After that they went on developing a combat aircraft of this type.

I believe it was in 1970 that the combat version of the Yak-36, later called the Yak-38, was considered by the mock-up commission. The consideration by this commission was an important stage in the creation of any new aircraft. The commission was presented with a life-size wooden model, or mock-up, of the new machine, along with technical documentation and all the main equipment and instruments (preferably real, but not necessarily) installed in their places. The commission's primary concern was the cockpit layout, followed by the controls, instruments, and instrument panels and consoles, and their main criteria were the ease of the pilot's (or the crew's) work and the pilot's external vision. Other parameters considered were the ease of maintenance (for example, the accessibility of various parts and systems for servicing, etc.). In theory the mock-up commission should sit before a flyable prototype of the aircraft is built, but in practice by the time the commission starts its work on the mock-up the manufacturing of the prototype will have as a rule been started.

The sitting of the mock-up commission to assess a new aircraft was a great event for its designer team. The statement drawn up by the commission at the end of its work had the force of law. Only the commission itself could make amendments to that statement or, for that matter, allow deviations from the air force mission and service requirements, which, after approval by the Air Force Commander-in-Chief, the aircraft designer team had to obey. In the military certification tests that followed later an important function of the Flight Test Institute was to make sure that the aircraft, its equipment and armament corresponded to the air force mission requirements and to the statement of the mock-up commission (the FTI performed this role for aviation commanders in all branches of the armed forces). The mock-up commission was always headed by a high-ranking commander in that particular kind of air force for which the aircraft in question was intended. The bulk of the commission was formed by engineers and test pilots of the FTI, with an addition of maintenance experts, representatives of the AF Combat Training Command and other military specialists. The commission that assessed the mock-up of the Yak-38 was headed by the Naval Air Force Commander Colonel General Borzov (a distinguished naval pilot himself), who had three deputies: a general from the Naval Air Force Command, another from the Naval Air Force Command, and me from the FTI.

The Yak-38 was essentially different from both the British Harrier and the American Av-8, each of which had a single vectored-thrust engine with four pivoting jet nozzles. At take-off the nozzles would be vectored downwards, and the engine thrust would act for the absent lift of the wings. In the air, as the speed was gained and the wing lift appeared, the nozzles would be slowly pivoted backwards and the aircraft would fly as any other. On slowing down before landing the nozzles would be gradually redirected again. In those days we did not possess an engine of sufficient specific power capable of lifting such a machine with all its armament by itself. Therefore the main lift/cruise engine (with two nozzles) had to be supplemented by two additional lift engines, which were installed vertically, nozzles down, and which were meant to be used briefly at take-off and landing. During the rest of the flight they were nothing but useless extra weight. It was impossible to use nozzle vectoring to increase the lift in manoeuvre. The result was an aircraft with lower manoeuvrability and with lower safety margins at take-off and landing. The safety problem was due to the fact that the probability of failure of one out of three engines is higher than of a single engine. Besides, if any of the three failed the aircraft would topple over and the pilot would have to eject at once. Not to waste precious seconds on the canopy removal, he would have to face the through-canopy ejection in which the glass would be broken by the seat headrest. But before it happened the pilot would have to realise the necessity of ejecting, to get hold of the ejector handles and pull them, all of which would take two or three seconds at least; with the aircraft pitching sharply up or down, even two seconds could prove too long. This prompted a new safety measure – an automatic ejection system which fired the seat if the pitch or bank angles got out of limits. Since the system was designed to allow for both the roll and the pitch rates, it could eject the seat even before the critical bank angle was reached. The system switched off automatically as the speed of 320 kph was gained after take-off and turned itself on again on slowing down before landing.

The initial flight tests of the Yak-38 VTOL aircraft were mainly performed by Mikhail Deksbakh and Oleg Kononenko, and also by Vadim Khomiakov of the FTI. Khomiakov was the first to make a night landing on an aircraft-carrying ship. Later both he and Mikhail Deksbakh received the title of Hero of the Soviet Union for these tests. As for me, I did not get an opportunity to fly this machine before I was restricted from fighters by the medical board.

Vadim Khomiakov had one rather bizarre experience with the Yak-38. He had to fly out a production specimen at the airfield of the Saratov aircraft factory and, as he made a vertical take-off and began to speed up, he felt a sudden push, and a few seconds later he was 'hanging' in the air under an open parachute. It turned out later that just as the automatic ejector system was to switch itself off, an accidental electric pulse caused the system to fire and eject the seat. Khomiakov landed safely with his parachute and the aircraft continued flying on its own for another seventeen minutes before it went into the ground. After

Vadim's 'adventure' the circuit design of the system was improved and made more reliable.

The necessity of such a system was later tragically proved by the fatal accident of the military test pilot Nikolai Belokopytov at the air base of our No. 3 Department in the Crimea. He was flying a Yak-38 when his vertical gyroscope, determining the attitude of the aircraft in the air, failed. This meant that the automatic ejection system, which relied on the gyroscope for determining the critical bank angle, had to be switched off to prevent it from firing at random, thus ruling out vertical landing – which was expressly forbidden with the ejection system off. The main airfield of the base was closed for maintenance, and to land horizontally (in the usual way) Belokopytov had to head for another airfield some distance away. But it was a Friday, and he had guests at home who had just come to stay for the weekend; he must have been in a hurry to get home and decided against detouring to the back-up airfield. He said nothing of the failure to the flight controller at the tower and went for a vertical landing. As ill fate would have it, in this first ever landing he attempted without the automatic ejection device, one of his lift engines failed. The machine pitched down sharply and Belokopytov tried to get hold of the ejector handle but his fingers caught a cable instead which had worked itself loose under the negative G-load. He fell with the aircraft, the cable clutched in his hand.

CHAPTER 25

The Fastest and the Highest

In the middle of the 1960s, the Mikoyan Design Company created an aircraft of a new class – a high-altitude, high-speed interceptor with a high-altitude reconnaissance plane as a variant. They were dubbed the MiG-25P and the MiG-25R respectively. Their entire design was ruled by the concepts of height and speed: they were destined to fly at over 20,000 metres and at a speed nearly three times the speed of sound. At such speeds, with the sonic barrier far behind, an aircraft encounters a barrier of a new kind: a thermal one. That was why, for the first time in our aviation industry, the skin of the aircraft had to be made of welded sheets of steel instead of the usual riveted sheets of aluminium alloy. It was our first aeroplane to reach such remarkable altitudes and speeds, and the only aircraft comparable to it in the world was the American SR-71 reconnaissance plane (not counting the X-15 experimental rocket aircraft). In 1967 Piotr Ostapenko reached the average speed of 2,920 kph in a 1,000-kilometre circuit flight (in straight flight it was even higher – over 3,000 kph), and Alexander Fedotov achieved an altitude of 36,240 metres in a zoom climb. The static ceiling of the MiG-25 was about 24,000 metres.

Most test flights in the MiG-25 were performed by Vadim Petrov, Grigory Lesnikov, Norair (Norik) Kazarian, Alexander Kuznetsov and Nikolai Stogov. I made some fifteen flights in it too, the first of them in August 1966, at the beginning of the military certification test programme. The tests of the MiG-25R reconnaissance plane began a little later, and were mainly performed by Ivan Gudkov and Alexander Bezhevets. The MiG-25R was equipped with a navigation complex of great precision, including, in addition to standard onboard equipment, a Doppler radar for measuring ground speed, a LORAN-type long-range navigation system and a digital processor. (Extra-precise navigation is essential for 'matching' aerial photographs with the map of the area.) The tests of this navigation complex demonstrated its remarkable precision and prompted the idea of using this aircraft for high-altitude bombing. The bombs were dropped without aiming on the basis of the target co-ordinates entered into the onboard computer. Despite the great precision of navigation the bombing accuracy from high altitudes was insufficient for ordinary bombs, but suitable for nuclear ones. As a result of those tests the aeroplane received a new name: the MiG-28RB reconnaissance bomber.

The MiG-25 tests bring a tragic episode to my mind: General Kadomtsev's fatal accident in Akhtubinsk. Kadomtsev had become the Air Defence Fighter Aviation Commander in 1966. I liked Anatoly Leonidovich very much, and our regard for each other was mutual. He was a good pilot with an engineering education, and had all the qualities of a decisive and efficient commander. Despite his elevated position, Kadomtsev continued flying combat machines and flying

340

out new air defence aircraft at the completion of military certification tests. I respected him for that, although the Air Force Command was against its high-positioned generals flying and regarded it as a whim which should not be encouraged. Alas, what happened to General Kadomtsev was an argument in favour of their position.

In late April 1969 Kadomtsev arrived at the Akhtubinsk air base. I met him on the airfield and he said that he intended to have a go at the MiG-25P which was then being tested at our base. It would not be his first flight in this machine, for he had flown a MiG-25 at Zhukovsky. Early next morning, 28 April, I met the Institute Commander on the way to my office, and his face immediately told me that something was very wrong. 'Kadomtsev's machine is on fire, he's been ordered to eject,' he said and went out to his car. What happened was as follows. Kadomtsev had taken off in the MiG-25P after an Institute pilot had taken it up first thing that morning. Shortly after take-off the tower controller heard a female voice on the radio – it was the emergency voice warning played by the onboard voice-information unit. Such warnings are usually recorded in female voices so as to stand out against routine radio communication (and also because the female voice is supposed to be more articulate). They are simultaneously played into the pilot's earphones and transmitted over the radio to the tower. The voice warning is accompanied by warning lights on the pilot's cockpit panel. The recording informed of a fire in the right-hand engine and, seconds afterwards, of a hydraulic system failure. After that Kadomtsev's perfectly calm voice said, 'There's a girl talking about a fire – what's it supposed to mean?'

I have said earlier that onboard fire alarm systems could sometimes go off accidentally, and the pilot should judge whether the alarm is real or false by certain additional cues. One such cue in Kadomtsev's case was the information about the hydraulic failure that followed the fire warning. It was clear that the two warnings were related to each other: either the fire was caused by a failure in the hydraulic system or the fire came first and a hydraulic pipe burned out as a result. In any case, the reality of a fire on board was beyond doubt. The tower controller replied, 'It means that your aircraft is on fire!' Still calm and composed, Kadomtsev asked, 'So what am I to do?' The controller's immediate command was, 'Turn right by thirty degrees and eject at once!' He then repeated the word 'eject' several times. I believe that Kadomtsev asked what he was to do because as a high-ranking commander he did not wish his ejection to appear like a panicky decision. What he wanted was the tower controller's command (which is law to all pilots in the air irrespective of their rank) to abandon the aircraft.

Immediately after the fire warning had come through, Kadomtsev turned homewards and flew over the airfield, from which we could see his burning aircraft well. After the ejection command from the tower he turned right towards the steppe as he was ordered and then suddenly began turning left again. We saw a flash right over his machine and thought he had ejected, but then the aeroplane began to descend while flying away from the airfield and fell into the river. Nothing came from Kadomtsev on the radio after the tower's ejection command. It was only shortly before he fell that he had attempted to say something, but his words were unintelligible and no one, not even the audio experts who analysed

341

the tape afterwards, could make out what he was trying to say. It took a long time to find and retrieve the aircraft fragments from under the water. Some remains of General Kadomtsev were found and flown in a sealed coffin to Moscow, where the funeral took place. I went over to Moscow to attend it.

It was established that the accident was caused by a turbine blade that had broken off and cut through a hydraulic pipe. The hydraulic liquid leaked out and caught fire. As to why Kadomtsev failed to eject, it remained a mystery. The accident became widely known and led to another sad event. An inquiry commission was formed and my uncle, Artem Mikoyan, was included in it as the chief designer of the aircraft. He arrived at Akhtubinsk immediately after the crash and then departed a few days later.

Every aircraft designer must have known the bitter pain caused by the death of a pilot in an aeroplane of his design, even of a combat pilot he does not know, to say nothing of his own company test pilot or somebody like General Kadomtsev who was not only a well-known pilot but also a high-posted commander. My uncle was an exceptionally kind and sensitive man and he took every pilot's death very close to heart. His participation in the inquiry – in which he had to examine the aircraft fragments, listen to Kadomtsev's voice on the tape and discuss every detail of the accident again and again – proved too much for him. On his return to Moscow in the early days of May he had a massive heart attack. He had had one before, but this time the attack was very severe and he never recovered from it. Even though he lived a year and a half after it, most of that time was spent in hospital and in bed. Only once was he allowed to come home for a few days and then spent two weeks at a rehabilitation centre in the country, but after that he was taken to hospital again and never left it. The doctors informed Artem, his wife Zoya Ivanovna and his elder brother, my father, that the only chance of recovery was an operation on his heart. Artem gave his consent to the operation, but, alas, the fragile hopes that were pinned on it were not justified.

Two years prior to Kadomtsev's fatal accident another pilot had crashed in a MiG-25. It was the first fatal accident in this type of aircraft, and the pilot killed was Igor Lesnikov, a test pilot on the staff of our Institute. I happened to be indirectly responsible for that accident.

The Soviet Union and the USA were constant rivals in setting up aviation records. Nearly every time there appeared a new aircraft with a greater speed, ceiling or load-carrying capacity, it was used for an attempt to beat a world record. A successful attempt was prestigious for the design company and the country at large. As a rule the aircraft to be used for a record-setting flight was specially prepared, with some of its equipment removed to reduce the weight. Both in America and in Russia it was the task of the company that designed the machine in question. The difference, however, was that in America it was air force pilots who mainly set world records in military aircraft, while in the USSR the task used to be assigned to the civilian test pilots on the staff of the design company.

At the beginning of 1967 a MiG-25 was being prepared at the Mikoyan company for a climb-to-altitude-time record. It was about that time that Artem

Mikoyan paid a short business visit to Akhtubinsk, and I told him that I believed it wrong that all record-setting was entrusted to company pilots, and that it would be fair if military pilots who tested those aircraft could have their share of record flights. I named the MiG-25 project test pilot Igor Lesnikov (having asked his consent first, of course) as a worthy candidate for the coming flight. Lesnikov took off for his record-setting flight from the Ramenskoye airfield near Moscow. He went into a steep climb, with cinetheodolites recording every moment of the flight. We could afterwards see in the film how his aeroplane suddenly rolled to the left at about 1,000 metres. As the roll reached thirty degrees or so, the flames in the nozzles went out, which indicated that the pilot had cut the afterburner. This could only mean that unable to control the roll he had to give up his attempt at a record. A few seconds later the aeroplane turned over and went into a vertical dive. At about 600 metres Lesnikov ejected. An aircraft ejector seat is supplied with a device which provides for a two-second parachute deployment delay at very high speed (thus preventing the parachute from bursting). Lesnikov's machine had been going down at a speed of over 1,000 kph. He ejected, but the two-second delay brought him so near the ground that when his parachute finally opened it was already too late.

The accident was caused by the same controllability problem described earlier in connection with the Yak-28 and the Tu-128: the loss of aileron authority due to wing torsion at high speed. A decrease of aileron authority is a feature shared by all aircraft, but in that first version of the MiG-25 an indicated air speed of slightly over 1,000 kph rendered its ailerons totally ineffective. Lesnikov's mission involved piloting within a safe speed margin, but to reach a maximum rate of climb he might have opted for a speed too close to the dangerous limit. When his machine rolled to one side (due to a slight asymmetry of the airframe), the ailerons proved powerless and he could not level it out. This deficiency of bank control became evident later when the MiG-25 was flown for its armament tests. First Norik Kazarian and then Sasha Kuznetsov had to launch two missiles from one wing at 15,000 metres at high speed. Both of them encountered the same problem: the aircraft started rolling after the launch, and the ailerons proved ineffective. Then the machine rolled over and went into a vertical dive. In both cases the pilots managed to pull out at less than 8,000 metres.

After these two incidents the MiG company undertook to improve the MiG-25 control system, and in 1971 its new version appeared with a differential stabilon installed to assist the ailerons (the way it had been done in the MiG-23). This allowed the indicated air speed limit to be brought up to 1,300 kph. When Norik Kazarian and Vadim Petrov repeated the original missile-launching mission, they encountered no problems whatsoever.

Both these pilots played an important role during the final stage of the MiG-25P tests. Kazarian performed one of the most difficult tasks ever – the interception of a high-altitude, high-speed, winged target in a head-on attack. The target was flying at about 3,000 kph, with the distance between it and the interceptor shortening faster than at 5,000 kph, or one and a half kilometres per second! Both Kazarian and Petrov were excellent test pilots (Kazarian had started his flying career as a marine fighter pilot) and were greatly respected by

343

the entire flying contingent of our Institute. The respect of the pilots' 'brother-hood' was important to each and every one of us, and we all knew that if a newcomer was accepted and 'approved' by it, he would usually live up to the standard set up by it. There were hardly any mistakes or disappointments on either the human or professional score.

Due to its high speed and ceiling, it was decided to use the MiG-25R as a recon-naissance plane in Egypt. A special squadron was formed on the basis of an air force reconnaissance regiment, with Colonel Alexander Bezhevets, a test pilot, as its commander. Among the pilots were Nikolai Stogov (also a test pilot of our Institute), Vladimir Gordienko of the Gorky aircraft factory and four air force pilots. My friends Bezhevets and Stogov told me about the first reconnaissance mission in Egypt. It was preceded by a number of practice flights over Arab terri-tory. The tactical plan of the MiG-25R's reconnaissance flights over Israel was prepared under the guidance of Colonel Kharlamov of the Soviet Air Force, then the chief aviation counsellor to the Egyptian government. The first flight was timed for a Sunday, the day when it would be expected least of all. The aircraft was kept in a hardened shelter where it was serviced and prepared for the flight. The airfield authorities were told that there would be no flying the MiG-25 for some time, for it was in need of some maintenance with the engines running (it was thought that there could be Israeli spies among the airfield personnel and, besides, the Arabs themselves were not famous for their ability to keep a secret). Stogov donned a partial-pressure suit with a pressure helmet, climbed into the cockpit and started the engines.

Then the shelter gates suddenly opened – a total surprise for the Egyptian staff – and Stogov taxied out onto the runway and took off at once without even stopping to request clearance. He climbed up to the limit altitude and cruised from north to south (east of the Suez Canal) over the positions of the Israeli troops at a speed of over 2,800 kph. The Israeli radars spotted him while he was still over Egyptian territory, and over thirty fighters (most of them Phantom 4s) were sent to intercept him. If the Israelis had known of the MiG-25's intended flight in advance, the Phantoms might have met Stogov halfway, as it were, and hit him with missiles launched head-on. Even though the Phantoms would have been flying lower than Stogov's MiG, their missiles would have been able to reach a target flying several kilometres higher (we had this kind of missile too). As it was, all they could do was try to catch up with him from behind, which was out of the question. They were just about seven or eight minutes late for a head-on attack on the MiG. Nikolai returned to the base safely, and the film his onboard automatic reconnaissance camera had taken was immediately processed, and the pictures, almost A4 size, were sent to Moscow the same day and immediately presented to the government there. After that each of the squadron pilots made several flights of this kind.

About that time there began to happen inexplicable but almost identical acci-dents involving the MiG-25. The first one was at an air defence training base at Krasnovodsk when a MiG-25 started rolling over after a missile launch at high speed and crashed. At the Kubinka air base, during a 'dress rehearsal' of an aerial demonstration, the MiG piloted by an air defence pilot flying at high speed in a formation by the spectators' stands suddenly rolled over and, after an incomplete barrel-roll, hit the ground. Finally, Sasha Kuznetsov crashed at our base in Akhtubinsk. He was doing a test flight at 1,000 metres at a speed of about 1,100 kph when his machine suddenly banked sharply and began to roll over. Just how sudden and unmanageable it was became clear from the fact that Sasha ejected barely two seconds after the rolling had begun. Unfortunately, the air speed being very high and the aircraft rolling, he was thrown against some part of the plane, possibly the empennage. His parachute deployed automatically and brought him down, but he was already dead when the rescue party found him. When I arrived at the site in a helicopter he had already been taken away, but there was a trail of blood on the ground where his parachute had dragged him after landing, which meant he had still been alive then.

The inquiry into the cause of the accident revealed a clash of opinions. Our military flight test engineers suggested that the rotation of the aircraft might have been connected to a fault in the hydraulic control boosters, which was flatly denied by the design company representatives. Their idea was that a bird might have hit the cockpit windscreen, but no trace of such a collision could be found in the debris, not even a tiny feather. An empty nest of an eagle was found nearby, and some wise heads decided that its owner had collided with the aircraft! As for the version suggested by our engineers, it was based on a certain phenomenon that was well known to us at the Flight Test Institute. Several years prior to that we had encountered it in the Su-7B and MiG-21. The effort needed for the deflection of the stabiliser could reach several tons. The hydraulic control boosters were designed to cope with the necessary effort and more (i.e. they had a surplus power margin), but it turned out that at very high air speeds at low and medium altitudes the control booster had not enough power, and the control stick seemed to turn on a kind of obstacle and refuse to move any further. In our previous experiences it happened only while the stick was being pushed forward. As the aircraft gained very high speed it would try to go into a climb, and the pilot could not push the stick forward all the way to keep the machine in level flight. It was not really dangerous, for as the aircraft climbed higher and the speed grew slower the control authority was recovered. The MiG-25 had a differential stabilon whose two halves could be deflected differentially in opposite directions. We supposed that one of the stabiliser halves could have been 'stuck' for inadequate booster force, while the other was still turning. That would have led to an asymmetry of control inputs, which would in its turn have caused an uncontrollable rotation of the aircraft.

The aviation industry representatives did not wish to accept our version and decided to do special flight tests at the Gromov Institute in Zhukovsky to disprove it. The first few flights went well, and Oleg Gudkov, the Gromov Institute test pilot who performed them, did not have any problem with the controls (he did not even believe there could be a problem of the kind we described). Come the final flight on that programme, Gudkov had to reach maximum speed at 3,000 metres. However, because of the clouds at the scheduled height it was decided to go for a limit speed at 2,000 metres. The purely fortuitous combination of limit speed with that particular altitude proved to be too much for the booster, and the aircraft went into rotation. All Oleg Gudkov had time to say into his radio mike was, 'She's rolling!', after which he ejected. Unfortunately the height was not sufficient and his parachute did not open. Gudkov was killed as he fell onto the roof of a factory building. (Some aviation psychologists believe that a pilot's sense of real time in a critical situation in the air is distorted – seconds seem to pass more slowly, and he might think he has some time before bailing out whereas in actual fact there is none. This may be the reason why, even when a dangerous situation comes to a head at a high altitude, pilots sometimes delay the ejection until it is too, or almost too, late.)

I was on holiday in Sochi when it happened. One day I decided to go and visit somebody I knew at a neighbouring sanatorium. There were other guests at the time, and one of them said that he had phoned his Moscow office in the morning and had been told that a test pilot, a Hero of the Soviet Union, had crashed in Zhukovsky. Not knowing anything for certain, I immediately thought of Gudkov, partly because there were not so many test pilots with this title. A few minutes later there was a knock on the door and a telegram addressed to our hostess was handed to her. She read it aloud: 'Alla, tell Stepan Gudkov crashed.' It was from Norik Kazarian, who knew I was in Sochi but did not know my address there. An uncanny chain of coincidences! I had known Oleg Gudkov well and we had been on good terms with each other. He had had a well-earned reputation as a first-class test pilot, and had particularly distinguished himself in spin tests (for which he had received the Hero's Golden Star). No other proof of our version was sought for after this tragic episode, and all MiG-25s received stabilisers of an improved design.

When the cause of the accidents had been fully established and, after its removal, the MiG-25 was adopted by the air force, the long-suspended government decree on awards to its designers, manufacturers (except for those who had anything to do with the fatal deficiency) and test pilots was finally acted upon. On 3 April 1975 three test pilots of the Flight Test Institute – Vadim Petrov, Alexander Bezhevets and I – and a pilot of the Gorky aircraft factory, G. Pukito, were invited to the Kremlin to be named Heroes of the Soviet Union and to receive the Golden Stars which go with it (there were other members of our test force receiving their decorations on that day as well).

I must say that until then I had been rather unlucky as far as government orders went (I am not speaking of my wartime decorations or the medals awarded to me as a war veteran on special anniversaries of VE-Day). In the early 1950s there was a series of awards given for long service in the armed forces, and I received a Red Star Order for my fifteen years' service. By the time I had been in the air force twenty years, for which until then everyone had automatically received a Red Banner Order – an order respected by the military people more than any other – the long-service awards were cancelled as such. The same happened with the awards for flights in adverse weather conditions: I had received a Red Star Order, and as I had accumulated a certain number of flying hours in bad weather and, along with other pilots, was nominated for a Red Banner Order, this category of awards was also cancelled before the award list with our names in it was signed. There were two other similar situations when I was nominated for an award and then something interfered (which had nothing to do with me personally) and I never got it. Thus, in my twenty-six-year career as a test pilot I did not receive a single decoration for my flight-testing work, until that day in 1975 when I was awarded the title of Hero of the Soviet Union and presented with its Golden Star. And that, of course, made up for it all.

As I have written earlier, while the Institute was commanded by General Finoghenov most of the technical and professional issues were almost entirely my responsibility. Although test programmes, test statements and recommendations were elaborated and written in the relevant departments under the supervision of their respective commanders, the role of Deputy Institute Commander was quite large: I was responsible for the overall technical policy of the Institute, participated in the work of mock-up boards as their deputy chairman and in various other meetings, organised interaction between the Institute departments and sections and between the Institute and other aviation institutions and the Air Force Command. There were other responsibilities besides these, and all in all I was acting as First Deputy Commander and had to take over the Commander's duties in his absence and to represent the Institute at other organisations.

When, in 1970, Marshal Kutakhov became Commander-in-Chief of the Air Force, he naturally began to change the 'team'. Among other high commanders replaced by him was our Institute Commander, General Mikhail Finoghenov. He was sent into retirement and Ivan Gaidayenko was appointed in his place. General Gaidayenko was not a total stranger to us at the Institute. From the late 1950s to 1962 he had been one of the Institute Deputy Commanders, which was when he had become a general. For a few years prior to his appointment as the FTI Commander Gaidayenko commanded the Central Asian Air Force District with a headquarters in Tashkent. When Gaidayenko was transferred from Tashkent to Akhtubinsk, my brother Alexei was appointed in his place. Alexei was transferred from Lvov where he had been Deputy Commander of an air force army. The army's second-in-command was General Gorelov, and its CO was General Yefimov, the future Commander-in-Chief and Marshal of the Air Force.

I had always thought highly of Gaidayenko and I liked him as a person: he was easy-going, very sociable and friendly, although rather shrewd and somewhat cunning. Unlike General Finoghenov, he took a real interest in technical issues and made a real effort to understand everything about the test programmes, even though he had no engineering background. In many ways he was easier to work with, for he was no formalist and knew what test flying was about (he was an active pilot himself). On the other hand, I was no longer the only one dealing with technical questions, and therefore I could no longer be independent in my decisions.

General Gaidayenko was extremely energetic and full of ideas. He initiated a reorganisation of the Institute, as a result of which the fighter and bomber departments were merged into one large Combat Aircraft Testing Department, with their respective armament and radio-equipment sections transferred to corresponding specialised departments. In other words, instead of having one integrated department which would be fully responsible for comprehensive tests of, for example, fighter jets (together with their avionics and armament), there were now several separate departments, each in charge of a particular aspect of the test programme. In my opinion the elimination of integrated flight test departments was a wrong thing to do, and I put forward my arguments against it at all the meetings when it was discussed – but naturally not after the Commander's final decision was made.

At the same time General Gaidayenko's other initiative – the organisation of a test pilot school under the auspices of our Institute – was certainly for the best. Until then the ranks of our test pilots grew thanks to volunteers who either sent their applications (mostly addressed to me) or arrived at the Institute in person. We would look through the candidate's personal log-book and his service file (if available) and then invite him for an interview and a check-ride. If a candidate suited us, we would formally request the Air Force Command to post him to us (sometimes we failed to overcome the resistance of unit commanders reluctant to let a good pilot go). The new recruits would learn about flight testing as they began to work with us, empirically, as it were, with the help of 'tutors' attached to them from the ranks of our experienced test pilots and engineers who would give them instruction on flight testing methods. All of us had become test pilots this way, and I was no exception. This method had its limitations, but it was not without advantages either (thus, it allowed the newcomers to start learning about the test pilot's job there and then, as it were, through actual experience and through day-to-day contact with fully-fledged test pilots and engineers).

As soon as the test pilot school was formally established, we received the right to select candidates from among military pilots in air force and air defence operational units. The candidates (two or three times more than the official quota of the students-to-be) were invited to report at the Institute for exams and check-rides. The successful candidates would then be listed in a special order to be signed by the Air Force Commander-in-Chief.

One of the good things about the test pilot school was that the students had an opportunity to gain experience of different kinds of aircraft. I, along with most test pilots I know, have always believed that flying different types of aircraft does a lot for a test pilot's proficiency and is an essential part of his professional training. It prepares him for what every test pilot has to do all the time – fly new, unfamiliar aircraft or new modifications of familiar ones. Besides, if each test pilot were assigned to a particular type of aircraft, say the MiGs or the Sukhois, the Institute would need many more pilots and a number of them would remain idle for days and days. In my own experience, on an average day I often had to fly in two or three different types of aircraft. To be able to do this one must naturally have certain technical qualifications, and be psychologically prepared for it. When a pilot has a varied flying experience he is capable of judging each tested aircraft in a more objective and unbiased way. Of course all types and classes of aircraft have their distinctive features and they often differ in their cockpit layout and in the arrangement of the instruments. The pilot's actions in an aeroplane cockpit are not mechanical; even though a certain set of automatic reactions will certainly develop, it is stored in the memory for each separate type of aircraft. When I climbed into, say, a Su-15 or a Su-24 having just landed in a MiG (as often happened), one good look around the cockpit and at the panel before starting the engines would bring it all back, even if it was months since I had flown it last.

Every now and then some inspection commission or another made a move to put a limit on our pilots' flying various types of planes, but all they managed to do in the teeth of stiff resistance was to ban flying more than two different types of aircraft within one and the same day. Even this rule of necessity had to be broken rather often. Operational unit commanders do not usually see any good in their pilots possessing a varied flying experience, and some of them consider it dangerous. A view which seems to be very common among them is that a pilot should fly one type of aircraft only and practise piloting it to the point where he can do it almost automatically. I would never accept this view myself: I have always maintained that the pilot should *think* rather than rely on automatic skills. They are important too, but merely as an 'instrument' and not as a guiding force.

Here is an episode to illustrate my point. During an aerial demonstration organised at Akhtubinsk for the Minister of Defence and his retinue, our pilots were performing the strafing of several ground target aircraft positioned in front of the guest stands. The attack by two pairs of Su-7Bs was successful and the targets were hit, albeit without the visual effects supplied by an explosion. 'VG' Ivanov, who was on the stands, sent a word to the airfield ordering another pair to be taken up. There was only one Su-7B standing by and flight ready, so a MiG-21 had to be used to make it a pair. Norik Kazarian, who had just done the Su-7B attack, hopped into the MiG and performed another successful attack (explosion and all) in tandem with the Su-7B. It was mentioned at the debriefing afterwards. One of the guests who was sitting next to me – a well-known Air Force Commander, Colonel General Kirsanov – asked me in surprise how the pilot could have got from one type of aircraft into another and performed a difficult mission there and then. Norik, who sat on my other side, whispered into my ear, 'What would he say if he knew that I haven't been inside a MiG-21 for almost a year!' I did not dare repeat it to General Kirsanov.

The Test Pilot School of the Flight Test Institute (later renamed the Test Pilot Training Centre) was officially opened in 1973. Its first graduates appeared in 1974. Most of them, as the majority of subsequent graduates, became first-class test pilots of a new generation. The year of the first graduation was the last year when I was still flying fighter jets. I examined three of the graduate students myself, taking check-rides with them in the MiG-21U two-seat trainer. In the next few years I was only allowed to examine the future bomber test pilots in the Tu-134.

General Gaidayenko's interest in technology and innovations of all kinds indirectly brought about another useful development, this time of a purely technical nature. I can say that he contributed to the adoption of the angle-of-attack indicator. The main instrument used for piloting an aircraft has always been the air speed indicator, which in effect measures the dynamic air pressure. The dynamic air pressure characterises the ability of the air to 'support' the aeroplane in flight; the lower the indicated air speed (and the dynamic air pressure), the greater angle of attack is needed to ensure adequate lift. At a very high speed a very small angle of attack is sufficient. Pilots actually used to determine their angle of attack by their indicated air speed (sometimes without even being aware of doing so). Thus, the chief concern of every pilot has always been not to lose speed: that is, not to bring the speed down to the point when the angle of attack would become critical and cause airflow stall and the loss of lift by the wing.

However, the direct interdependence between speed and angle of attack exists only in straight flight. To turn the aeroplane or to pull out (to recover from a dive), one has to increase the angle of attack to obtain the additional lift needed for a curved trajectory. So the angle of attack might become critical, and the aircraft might come to the point of stalling even at fairly high speed. When the flight path is curved towards the ground (for example in a pushover manoeuvre – the transition to a descent from a steep climb), a lower lift is needed than in level flight, therefore the stall speed is also lower. Only the feel of the aircraft and certain warning cues (if there were any), such as buffeting, used to enable pilots to avoid the critical angle of attack (and stalling) in 'energetic' manoeuvres. The idea that both flight safety and manoeuvrability would increase if pilots had an instrument to monitor the angle of attack had been in the air, as it were, for a long time.

One day we happened to get hold of the flight manual for a US fighter-bomber, the F-4 Phantom. I read it through carefully and found many interesting things. One of them was a reference to an angle-of-attack (AOA) indicator, with an illustration showing the cockpit panel with this instrument. I showed it to Andrei Manucharov, who was quick to appreciate the idea and immediately commissioned some particularly ingenious avionics engineer in his department, Lieutenant-Colonel Kondratiuk, to try to produce such an instrument. Kondratiuk installed an ordinary voltmeter in the cockpit and rigged it up with an angle-of-attack vane (a device installed in military aircraft for adjusting the gunsight). Andrei Manucharov and I were the first to test his 'creation' (my first flight in it was on 15 May 1969), and we both enjoyed piloting with the help of this makeshift instrument, particularly when approaching high angles of attack. We put our experience on paper and sent a report to the Air Force Command and the Ministry of Aviation Industry. 'Official' tests at the Gromov Institute confirmed our opinion, but there it all ended and nothing happened after that.

In the summer of 1970 the Air Force Commander-in-Chief arrived at Akhtubinsk to hold a meeting on all the principal aircraft that were tested by our test force. The Aviation Industry Minister and other important people arrived to take part. It was shortly after the war in the Middle East, and the Air Force Command was still studying the air combat experiences of the forces engaged in this war. When they were leaving Gaidayenko, Manucharov and I saw them off at the gangway. Manucharov and I whispered to Gaidayenko to mention the AOA indicator to the guests. He did, and in the conversation that followed we explained its importance for air combat. Not that a pilot would have time to look at it in combat, but while training for it he would be able to get the feel of the aircraft at high, near-critical AOA and then pilot it at such regimes more confidently and safely. The conversation ended in the decision to manufacture a small series of such instruments for trying them out in operational units. The angle-of-attack indicator (with Kondratiuk's original design slightly modified) was approved by one and all and was officially adopted for all fighters and some other aircraft. It was also supplied with warning lights. The AOA indicator could not only prevent stalling but help to maintain pre-set final glide airspeed. All in all it was another example of a useful innovation being adopted on a 'prompt' from abroad. I have earlier written of the G-indicator which was copied from an F-86 Sabre captured in Korea; it was later combined with the new AOA indicator into one integrated instrument, an original design by our own engineers.

Back in the summer of 1967 I had participated in the testing of automatic and semi-automatic modes of the landing-approach system in the MiG-21PF and MiG-21S (with a ground-based instrument-landing system). The ultimate goal of that project was to bring the landing weather minima down and to increase landing safety in bad weather conditions.

In an ADF non-precision approach the pilot can do quite well as regards the runway alignment, but he has no indication of his deviation from the glidepath in height unless he receives a 'tip' from a ground-based radar. His attention focused on his heading, the pilot might inadvertently lose height and come dangerously low. There have been cases of aircraft actually brushing against the ground on the landing glide. This is, of course, most likely to happen at night, even in clear weather. The pilot is looking ahead at the runway, which is traced out in the dark by landing lights, not seeing the ground beneath him and invariably imagining his glidepath to be steeper than it actually is. During the war I had seen this happen to Alexander Suprun, who to his own great surprise landed in his Spitfire on a field before the runway, and once at Akhtubinsk, as I was taxiing back along the runway after a night flight, I saw the navigation lights of an aircraft on final approach. He had descended almost as low as the ground even before he reached the middle marker. I immediately said over the radio, 'Hey there, you on final, stop descending, go up!' The aircraft climbed up a bit and then landed. It happened to be my second-in-command Andrei Manucharov. Whenever he remembered this episode afterwards he always repeated that I had saved his life.

The landing approach system we had tested in the summer of 1967 was known as the 'Flight-1' autoland system (its preliminary stage had been labelled 'Flight-0'; a MiG-21PF with the 'Flight-0' system had arrived in the spring of 1967, and on 25 April I had taken it up for its first test flight). It was an integrated flight control system in which the pilot used the ordinary control stick to assign a particular flying regime to the autopilot. The application of about one kilogram of force to the stick closed the on–off switch of the autopilot, sending it into stand-by mode; after that the pilot could control the aircraft manually. When the pilot eased down on the stick or let go of it altogether the autopilot would immediately take over and maintain the given attitude of the aircraft. Since then this kind of autopilot has been used in all subsequent MiGs.

351

By that time pitch/roll autopilots had been in service for a relatively long time, but the autopilots we tested in 1967 could perform trajectory control; in other words they could guide the aircraft along a certain route on the basis of signals received from the landing, navigation or aiming systems. When used in a landing mode it was tied to the ground instrumental landing system (ILS) called 'Katet'. In the Katet system the right/left signals of the localiser and up/down signals of the glidepath beacons were transmitted to the receivers onboard the aircraft, and as long as the machine was sticking to its pre-set path the beacon signals remained equal. Any deviation from the path was indicated by a changed pattern of signals. The autopilot would then respond by sending a turn- or a pitch-correction command to the relevant controls. The pilot could control the aircraft manually using the same signals with the position needles on the artificial horizon. He would also be helped by special steering command needles on this instrument, showing how much the controls should be applied for maintaining the pre-set route. This is known as semi-automatic flight control, in which the pilot is actually doing the autopilot's job.

Finally, in 1973 the Gromov Institute and the FTI started a joint flight research project (under the code-name of 'Zakhod-73') aimed at reducing the landing minima of fighter aircraft equipped with instrument landing systems. First a two-seater MiG-21U and afterwards the two-seater versions of other fighters were equipped with measuring instruments, and special blinds, or hoods, were installed in their front cockpits. The hood was closed during approach. On finals, the rear-cockpit pilot lifted it up at the height of fifty metres. The trajectory and all other relevant data were taken down, as well as the pilot's pulse and breathing rates. In some flight missions the front-cockpit pilot had to wear special goggles which recorded the direction of his gaze so as to determine at which instruments and for how long he was looking at various points during the landing approach. In each flight at least two landing approaches in each of the three modes were made.

As a pilot I took part in the first stage of that test project, the MiG-21U stage, in July and August of 1974. By the time other types of fighter became involved in the project, I had been restricted from fighter jets by the medical board. All in all the project took three years. It was confirmed in the course of flight testing and research that even in the manual mode of landing approach in which the pilot was guided by position needles showing his deviations from the specified glidepath (the most difficult landing mode to perform, normally used only in emergency), a well-trained pilot was capable of landing with a fair degree of confidence at 500×50 weather minima, i.e. at 500 metres' visibility and fifty metres' cloud base. The two other modes, the semi-automatic and the automatic, ensured even greater reliability. Despite the results of the research project the weather minima determined for the fighters long before instrument landing systems appeared were not changed, not for the next few years at least. For most types of fighters it remained at the $3,000 \times 300$ mark and at $2,500 \times 250$ for some, even though many pilots, including myself, had many times landed in far worse conditions. I am convinced that our weather minima had been set unreasonably high, obviously for the sake of the operational commanders' peace of mind and certainly at the expense of the overall combat efficiency of our air force. To compare, American fighters equipped with the TACAN landing system (a counterpart of our Katet) had a ceiling limit of sixty metres, and for some pilots it was set at thirty. Technically speaking our system also allowed landing with the cloud base at thirty metres, but we suggested setting the official minimum at fifty as a precaution against failure of the automatic modes.

To bring the official weather minima down we had to do more than test the relevant equipment; the most difficult task was to break through the psychological resistance of operational pilots and the Air Force Command. I was convinced that we should allow our best test pilots trained to use the Katet landing system to fly in really bad weather so as to gain experience and then spread it around among combat pilots. I actually wrote a draft of the Air Force Commander's order to that effect and presented it at the Air Force Combat Training Department. After some editing on their part, the order was signed by the Air Force Commander-in-Chief. It directed us to compile a list of FTI test pilots for whom landing at the weather minima of $1,000 \times 100$ could be allowed. They were higher minima than we had suggested, but it was a step forward nevertheless (every test pilot on that list whose opinion I later asked was convinced that operational pilots could be safely allowed to fly at these minima).

A few years later the weather minima reduction suddenly became a concern of the 'high and the mighty'. The Soviet Defence Minister, on a visit to East Germany, arrived at the headquarters of the 16th AF Army deployed in the GDR. The weather was bad and our pilots were all 'sitting it out', yet the ground-based radars showed busy traffic at a US fighter air base across the border. The minister was indignant: 'How come the Americans are flying and we are not?' The reason was that the old weather minima were still in operation in combat units, and they were way over the minima adopted in the US Air Force. The minister made a great noise about it on his return to Moscow, with the result that the retraining of pilots began and the weather minima were brought down.

I was often asked, by people remote from aviation, 'Aren't you afraid to fly?' I always felt somewhat embarrassed answering this question, for to say I was not afraid would seem as if I were boasting, and to say I was would be lying, for genuine fear was something I never really felt when flying. A sense of danger I experienced more than once – a danger that made me mobilise all my faculties and all my moral strength – but there was no fear as such. But it felt awkward to say no. And then in 1970 I had an experience which for the first time caused me to be truly frightened, and since then I have confidently answered, 'Yes, I have known real fear in one flight, and when I felt it I knew I had never felt it before.'

It was a flight to test the manoeuvring performance of the MiG-21 (its last modification) at low altitude. I was flying a loop from 1,000 metres at military power throughout the manoeuvre (normally one would throttle back to idle after the top). When the nose of my machine was already well through the vertical, I felt the aircraft speed up sharply and pitch down, making the dive even steeper. I pulled the stick but nothing happened. There was nothing I could do but eject, yet the speed was too high, over 1,000 kph, and the altitude was already less than

1,500 metres. I hacked the throttle hard and pulled the stick with both hands, and felt that the aeroplane, reluctantly and slowly, was obeying the controls and recovering from the dive. The stress of the situation narrowed my perception down to a minimum: all I could see was the blurred line of the horizon some-where above me, the line to which I somehow had to drag my machine. I could look at or see nothing else; I could not even force myself to steal a glance at the altimeter. I was pulling hard at the stick with just one endlessly repeated thought in my mind: 'Now, a crash, now . . .' I had no idea what my height was, and I was genuinely afraid, no doubt about that. Finally the nose of my machine rose above the horizon. The relief was enormous, and that was when I felt cold sweat running down my face.

Having recovered, I aborted the mission and landed. I went straight to the fighter pilots' briefing room, sat down in an armchair and closed my eyes, trying to get over the frightening experience. One of our project engineers found me there to say that a MiG-23 was ready for my next scheduled flight – cannon firing at a ground target. That meant diving again, and again I would see the ground before my eyes, heading fast towards it. I realised I just couldn't face it so soon. It must have been the only time in my entire flying career that I answered an offer of a flight with, 'Hold it, I think I'll take a break.' The engineer must have been surprised – he did not know what I had just been through.

The instrument readings showed that the large G-load (I had pulled over 6G) had bent the engine control unit rod, which started the afterburner. That was why the speed had suddenly zoomed up to high subsonic. At such a speed the pitch control authority would always deteriorate sharply, and the stabilon deflec-tion which I had had before it happened was no longer enough for pulling out – no wonder the aircraft pitched down the way it did. To pull it out I would have had to deflect the stabilon twice as much, but at a high indicated air speed the arti-ficial feel would have selected the short control arm. In other words the same effort at the stick was producing a smaller deflection of the stabilon, hence such a slow recovery from the loop. It followed from the instrumentation data that my minimum height above the ground had been about 300 metres – not too much of an altitude for a speed of over 1,000 kph!

By association, however indirect, with my own unpleasant diving experience, I would like to say a few words about one of the air disasters of the century – the fatal accident of the Soviet supersonic liner Tu-144 at the Bourges Salon in 1972. There are two or three aspects of that accident which I will mention here. The main cause of the crash was the pull-up manoeuvre which the pilots attempted to do in imitation of their foreign colleagues. This manoeuvre had never been performed in the Tu-144 before. The pilot himself, Mikhail Kozlov, was not experienced in it either; if he had ever done it at all, it would have been only as a student, for he was a bomber pilot and would not do any aerobatics in his normal job. On finding himself in an unusual position with the horizon hid behind the nose of his machine, Kozlov must have pushed the wheel too hastily and too far, overshooting in pitch.

The Tu-144 was a tailless aeroplane and as such would be extremely sensitive to pushing the control column forward. It reacted to Kozlov's aggressive push on the column by rotating sharply from a climb to a vertical dive. And then another factor came into play. As was seen from the video footage, the pilot delayed the pull-out from the dive by a couple of seconds. It has been assumed that the delay was caused by the video camera that was dropped by the cameraman (he was sitting between the two pilots) and landed between the pilot's seat and the control column. It could be so, but I believe there is a more plausible explanation. The negative G-load which accompanied the sharp vertical dive would have tossed the pilot up from his seat – it has been said that Kozlov was not properly strapped in – and at this moment he would unconsciously have pressed on the wheel, thus pushing it further forward instead of pulling it. Even with the other pilot's help he would have lost one or two seconds to settle back in and start pulling the control column.

Finally, one last thing. When you are diving plumb downwards, the ground always seems to be closer than it really is, even if you are a fighter pilot who is used to such manoeuvres. To somebody like Mikhail Kozlov, who would have seen the ground from such an attitude for the first time, it must have seemed even closer. As soon as he had recovered his seat he might have pulled the column back with too much force and exceeded the design G-load limit of his machine. His wing disintegrated as a result, whereas if he had pulled more gently, just balancing on the G-load limit but not exceeding it, he might have had a chance to recover, even though he was indeed very near the ground.

CHAPTER 26

A Farewell to Military Aircraft

On 12 July 1972 I turned fifty. Long before the day came I had begun thinking of how to organise a birthday party so as to invite all those I wanted there. All in all I was envisaging a party for about a hundred and fifty guests.

An unexpected complication interfered with my plans: an epidemic of cholera in the Astrakhan district to which Akhtubinsk officially belonged and the quarantine that was immediately announced. Nevertheless, many people braved the quarantine and flew over, including my wife Ella (my daughter, who had been coming to Akhtubinsk for my birthday for several years before that, had a five-month-old baby at the time and could neither leave him behind nor bring him to a cholera area with her, so she had to stay behind in Moscow). The weather was very hot, and somebody suggested I hold the party outside rather than in the stuffy dining-hall of our only restaurant. I dropped in on my brother Vanya (the technical supervisor of the current MiG tests at the base) and other MiG company representatives, who were living in their company bungalow on the outskirts of the compound, to ask their advice. They offered their 'territory' and their furniture for the party. The tables were set up on the lawn at the back of their bungalow, along the edge of the high bank of the river on which the bungalow (and several others) stood. At an outdoor party space was no object, so there was enough room around the tables for all my guests.

Before that informal party there was a formal celebration meeting at the Officers' Club organised by the Institute administration for me. All our department and section commanders came up onto the stage with their birthday greetings, as well as our colleagues from the missile range at Kapustin Yar and the design companies' representatives. There were more than sixty written greetings from various units within the Institute and many aviation industry enterprises and organisations. I have kept them all, but some of them are particularly dear to me because of their informal expressions of respect and gratitude. Among such special mementoes is the birthday greeting written by my fellow fighter pilots.

A day or two after the party I flew to Moscow, and on my father's suggestion I gave another birthday party for my family and my Moscow friends at his dacha. My father obviously enjoyed socialising with my friends, especially with the four test pilots who were present, and with all their wives. I must say, however, that his gallantry had one somewhat awkward touch. Whenever a previously unfamiliar married couple (or a married woman on her own) appeared in his house as his guests or the guests of any of us, he would sooner or later ask them if they had children and how many. When the answer was one or two, he would reproach them rather bluntly for not having more, and when they said 'None' he would say, 'It won't do! There should be children.' We all felt embarrassed when we heard it. My wife would always reprimand him after the guests had left: 'Anastas Ivanovich, how could you say it – what if they can't have children and suffer from it!' He would look distressed and admit that Ella was right, but next time he would forget and subject other people to the same ordeal. Children to him were the main joy and the meaning of life.

In 1973 a new modification of the MiG-23 arrived at the Institute to be put through military certification tests, the MiG-23B fighter-bomber. On 30 June I performed the first test flight in that machine.

It would be more accurate to describe it as an attack aircraft, but back in the 1950s the Air Force Attack Aircraft Command had been renamed Fighter Bomber Command to assign attack aircraft with some of the fighter aircraft tasks and also because attack aircraft units were mostly equipped with the MiG-15 and MiG-17 fighters (armed with additional bombs and unguided rockets). So when, about the same time, Ilyushin created a good new attack aircraft, the armoured Il-40, it was not adopted by the air force – possibly because officially attack aviation no longer existed. Besides, it revealed a grave fault, first encountered about ten years earlier in the first jet fighter, the MiG-9: its engines would flame out during cannon fire, for the cannon barrels were too close to the air intake and the axial compressor engines were extremely sensitive to the disturbance of the air at the intake. It seemed odd that the MiG-9 experience was not taken into account while designing the Il-40; unfortunately, such things happen.

Later there appeared the Su-7B, which became the principal aircraft to be used by the fighter-bomber force until it was superseded by the Su-17, its modification with a variable-sweep wing. The Su-17 in turn acquired a rival – the MiG-23B. It differed from its 'parent', the MiG-23, in its navigation/attack system and its armament. Its cockpit had armour-plated sides and it had a ranging laser (instead of the radar) which gave it better accuracy in shooting and dive bombing. Thanks to the absence of radar antenna its nose could be slanted further down for better vision, with the lower limit at minus seventeen degrees, better than in any other Russian military aeroplane. The MiG-23B was a preliminary version, followed by its upgraded modification, the MiG-27. It was the first of the lighter machines to possess a navigation/attack system with a digital processor, and the first aircraft to be armed with a six-barrel 30 mm cannon. Since it did not need to travel at very high supersonic speed it was given fixed-geometry air intakes, which made their design simpler. I was the project pilot in the tests of both these machines and so performed a large number of flights in each of them. It was in the MiG-27 that I made my last flight in a military aircraft.

The digital processor 'Orbit-10' had two working modes: the aiming and the navigating ones. One of the flights on that programme I remember particularly well was to test the automated system in a multi-leg-track flight with a combat mission involved. I turned the autopilot on as soon as I got airborne, at fifty metres, and the entire flight was controlled automatically, almost up to the landing. It was only the climb angle and the cruise altitude that I commanded to the autopilot manually. The aircraft went through three turning points, came out on to the range, descended from 12,000 to 5,000 metres, neatly dropped the bombs at pre-set co-ordinates and turned home – all done automatically. When it was time to go on the landing approach I selected the corresponding mode of the autopilot and sat back, watching it perform the base and the final turns and fly down the glidepath. It was only at fifty metres that I took over and landed manually.

On another occasion I was to perform automatic pull-up bombing. As I was approaching the target at 200 metres I matched the gunsight cross-wires with the pre-selected aiming point and pressed the button. The aircraft flew level for a while, then went into a climb, and as it reached the computed height the bombs were automatically released. The recovery from the climb had to be done manually, and when I turned to the right I saw my two bombs explode well within the fifty-metre target circle. I was also the first pilot to test the new six-barrel cannon, first at a ground target and then at an unmanned target aircraft. I still remember the formidable roar of that cannon and its powerful recoil, which noticeably slowed the aeroplane down. My target was spectacularly blown up into pieces.

In 1973 we began testing Pavel Sukhoi's new aircraft, the Su-24 heavy attack aircraft, or medium bomber. The idea had been inspired by the American F-111. Like the F-111, the Su-24 had a variable-sweep wing which at high speed was swept back at sixty-nine degrees. Thanks to that feature the bomber could fly at supersonic speed, including sea-level supersonic speed (i.e. at low altitudes). It could carry both missiles and bombs and had a cannon as well. It was equipped with a two-frequency high-resolution radar which could detect, for example, tanks at night-time and through clouds, and an electro-optic sight which increased the vision range, especially in a haze. Another new feature of the Su-24 was its obstacle-avoidance system for low-altitude flights. The radar installed in the Su-24 could only be used for ground targets, unlike the radar of the F-111. The latter also had an obstacle-avoidance mode effective both in horizontal and pitch planes, while the Su-24 was capable of terrain clearance in pitch plane only with the help of two radar altimeters installed at different angles.

Another distinction of the F-111 unmatched in the Su-24 was its unique escape system. The two pilots sitting beside each other on ordinary seats did not need individual parachutes; in an emergency the entire cockpit was ejected and brought safely down by a large parachute. In 1973 or thereabouts, such a cockpit (in which American pilots had ejected in Vietnam) was handed over to our specialists by the Vietnamese Air Force and brought to the Gromov Institute to be carefully examined by aviation experts. I went there too and spent several hours studying it and was quite impressed by its layout and a number of minor features which showed concern for the pilot's comfort and safety. The Su-24 had individual ejector seats of a new kind, designed by Severin. They proved to be extremely reliable and saved many people in the years to come.

The Su-24 military certification tests at the Flight Test Institute were conducted by our pilot Stal Lavrentiev, who performed most flights. Another test pilot involved in the programme was Vladimir Ilyushin, the chief test pilot of the Sukhoi company (it was rather a rare occasion for the company test pilot to join our team for an FTI test project). On 29 August 1973, towards the end of the test programme, Lavrentiev and his navigator Yurov took off in the Su-24 to perform a bombing mission. After that flight Lavrentiev was to fly to Moscow to receive the badge which went with the title of Honoured Test Pilot (conferred on him shortly before that). Suddenly one of the engines surged and stalled; Lavrentiev cut it off and headed towards the bombing range to get rid of his bombs, but a fire broke out. It was established later that the surging and the fire were caused by a broken compressor blade. The fire burnt through the stabiliser control rod, the hydraulic booster valve went into its limiting position and the two halves of the differential stabiliser deflected fully in the opposite direction (it could be clearly seen on the cinetheodolite film). The aeroplane began rolling at a high rate and seconds later it hit the ground.

It happened a few minutes after I had taken off in a MiG-23 on a cannon-firing mission at our nearest test range. I had already fired my first shots in a dive when the tower controller asked me if I could land promptly. I said I had another seven shooting runs to perform, but even as I said it I realised there was something wrong. 'Is anything the matter?' I asked. 'Yes', he answered curtly, so I quickly approached the target, fired a long burst so as not to land with my cannon loaded, and turned in for landing.

The Institute Commander was away, so it was my duty to fly to the site of the crash. A helicopter with its engines running was waiting for me by the ramp of my MiG-23. I climbed out of the fighter and straight into the helicopter, and we flew to 'the pit', as these sad destinations were referred to by pilots. I will not go into detail, describing the harrowing sight of a huge crater and the debris of aircraft fragments, big and small, littering the place. It was painful to think that two young strong, healthy men, with whom I had talked just an hour or so before, had perished without a trace in this hideous jumble of contorted metal. At first we had a faint hope that they might have ejected, but when two left-foot shoes, one after the other, were found in the debris our last hope was shattered.

I had barely returned to the Commander's office and signed the coded telegram informing the Air Force Commander-in-Chief of the crash (as the regulations required in the case of all major accidents) when the telephone rang. It was a call from the Air Force Advanced Training Centre at Lipetsk, where Lavrentiev had trained several pilots. They said they had just had a fatal accident involving a newly received Su-24, and an instructor pilot, whom Lavrentiev had trained, got killed. They asked me to send Lavrentiev to them to participate in the inquiry. I could not bring myself to tell them of his death and made some excuse, promising to send someone else. The two nearly simultaneous accidents had totally different causes. In Lipetsk the Su-24 was about to land, and as it was going around one of the flaps failed to retract and the aeroplane rolled because of a difference in lift on the two wings. The bank control authority proved unable to cope with the roll.

The misfortunes did not end there. Next day, while I was on the phone to General Gaidayenko reporting on Lavrentiev's accident, there came an internal call from the tower controller, who said, 'Major Ryaby blew up at the downwind turn.' I had to repeat his grim message to Gaidayenko. After I had finished talking to him and hung up, the tower controller called again: 'Ryaby is alive!

He's ejected!' It was a rather remarkable incident. As soon as Vladimir Ryaby had taken off in a MiG-21 he felt that engine thrust was fading. He managed to perform a U-turn to the right, hoping to land on the runway, but realised he would not make it to the airfield. Power was falling and the aeroplane was coming down – he was already just about fifty metres above ground. Ryaby decided to try to land on the ground straight ahead, but spotted a small building on the way. It was only then that he pulled the ejector seat D-rings, but there was not enough height left for the parachute to deploy. As Ryaby told us himself, he was free-falling towards the ground, which was already so close that he could discern separate blades of grass, knowing it was the end; then suddenly there was a blinding blaze and a blast and he felt the jerk of his parachute. His aeroplane, which was ahead of him, exploded as it hit the ground and it miraculously co-incided with the moment when the parachute came out of the pack. The air blast filled his parachute with air and it billowed. When I called Gaidayenko with the news of Ryaby's survival he did not really believe me. 'Let him call me', he said. I met Ryaby on the airfield when the rescue helicopter brought him home and took him to the staff building in my car so that he could call Gaidayenko before being taken to hospital for a compulsory examination.

Another pilot who made many test flights in the Su-24 was one of my good friends, Colonel Nikolai Rukhliadko. In one of his flights, in June 1974, the weapon pylon on one of the wings pivoted across the air stream (its retention rod had broken) and the aircraft rolled down sharply on one side. Nikolai managed to level the wings and decided to test the behaviour of the machine at near-landing speed at 1,000 metres before landing, but ordered his navigator, V. Sidorenko, to be ready to eject. Sidorenko answered calmly, 'I've been ready for ages.' When Nikolai slowed down, the controls lost authority and he could no longer oppose the roll. The aeroplane turned over and went into a steep dive. The navigator ejected at once, while Nikolai, seeing that the machine was diving right into a small village, turned away and ejected at the eleventh hour, as it were, at the minimum height. His parachute did not fully deploy until he was some fifty metres over the ground.

Nikolai Rukhliadko made his last flight on 15 September 1981, testing the one-engine-off performance of the Su-24. He spent thirty minutes flying with his left engine stopped. When he tried to restart it before landing there was an explosion somewhere behind his seat. The right-seat pilot ejected at Nikolai's command, and as he told us later the last thing he saw was Nikolai getting hold of his ejector seat D-ring. However, he did not eject and was killed. As was confirmed later, a prolonged flight with a stopped engine would cause the fuel to accumulate at some point in the system and explode upon an attempt to restart the engine, damaging the ejector unit as it did – a 'discovery' that cost Nikolai his life.

Whenever a fatal accident happened at our air base or when radio communi-cation with a pilot was suddenly lost, all flights were immediately suspended. The routine roar of the flying jets could be well heard from the living compound, and everyone was used to it, but the wives of the pilots or other crew scheduled to fly on this particular day, whatever they might be doing back home or at work, would always listen to the aircraft roar with apprehension. Brief pauses between

360

take-offs were normal, but a pause lasting longer than usual would always fill the women's thoughts with nagging alarm. Maybe the weather has broken? No, the weather hasn't changed. Then, at last, they would hear an engine running, but they would soon recognise it as a helicopter going up. What if it is a rescue helicopter going off in search of a lost aircraft? On the days when their husbands were flying, the most frightening thing for the wives was an unexpected doorbell. Each of them knew that if she opened the door to see her husband's friend and his commander, there would be no hope left. (My daughter, who had spent many summers in Akhtubinsk as a teenager, told me years later that on the days she had known me to be flying she had been terrified of unexpected phone calls. She had not known, and it had not occurred to me or anybody else to tell her, that they would never have phoned if anything had happened to me, they would have come and rung the doorbell.)

The wives of pilots and of other flying crew are a special breed of women. Most of them live in constant fear for their husbands. This creates a unique bond among them. I have, unfortunately, had many occasions to see at pilots' funerals that it is first of all other pilots' wives who cluster around to give comfort and support to the new widow. They have always seemed to me to have something elusive in common, something unknown to people outside their community.

At the beginning of 1974 I decided to take part in the tests of the Su-24 and began to prepare for my first flight. The flight test director on behalf of the Sukhoi company, Mikhail Simonov (the company's present head and designer general), tried to talk me out of it, saying that in my position I would not be able to fly it regularly, while sporadic and rare flights in it were undesirable. He must have for some reason or another been worried for me. Anyway, when he realised he would not prevail he insisted that I make my first Su-24 flight with Nikolai Rukhliadko in the right seat. I grudgingly agreed, and we went up in it together on 5 April 1974. Everything went well, and I had no problem flying it at all.

I was rather piqued at not being allowed to fly as aircraft commander the very first time; I had done it dozens of times before in many different types of unfamiliar or modified military aircraft. Why could I not fly as commander (or solo) in a Su-24? Deep down I knew it was the same old argument between two opposite points of view. Mine had always been that a Grade 1 test pilot should fly machines that were new to him without familiarisation flights, even if a two-seat version of that machine was available. I have kept this view to this day, and I still believe that every experienced test pilot should be always psychologically prepared for a solo flight in a new machine.

Anyway, after my first flight in the Su-24 with Nikolai I made nineteen test flights in it with several different navigators. I did automatic pull-up bombing, semi-automatic radar-aimed low-level bombing, air-to-ground attacks with electro-optic sight aiming, and performed several stability and controllability test flights. I also made a number of flights with four nuclear mock-ups, including four three-minute supersonic runs at the 200-metre altitude (it was a special kinetic heating test). On full afterburner with four big mock-up bombs under the wings the Su-24 would barely reach Mach 1.07 or 1.08, but still it was supersonic and it was certainly more than most other aircraft would be capable of at such a low height.

I liked the Su-24 very much, especially at take-off and landing, when it was very stable and a pleasure to handle. The same was largely true of other flying regimes as well, except for transonic ones and high angle-of-attack flights with the wings unswept, when it would rock. At transonic regimes the Su-24 displayed a feature that distinguished it from all other supersonic jets I had flown (which covers all Soviet military aircraft up to the mid-1970s, with the exception of the Tu-22). At Mach 0.98 and up to 1.04 it would now and then give slight jerks sideways and lengthways, demanding continual, though small, corrective movements of the stick. With the Mach number growing, these jerks would at some point disappear as suddenly as they had come on.

The Su-24 cockpit had quite a clever layout. With the two pilots' seats placed next to each other, the number of instruments and switches could be reduced, for not all of them had to be dual. The pilot and the navigator could now be in direct contact with each other and their co-operation and psychological rapport was much easier; sometimes a gesture pointing at an instrument or even mere eye contact was all that was needed in a critical situation. In an air-to-ground attack the navigator would select the target on the radar or the electro-optic display and then transmit the target mark to the head-up display of the pilot. The pilot would take aim and fire. It was a well-thought-out system and I liked it. I also approved of the new type of instruments used in the Su-24, the so-called 'tape indicators' where the corresponding values were indicated by the height of a column. There were two such indicators installed: the fuel quantity and the rpm gauges. In front of the navigator's seat there was a short control stick, the pedals and the electric switches linked to the engines, which could be used by an instructor pilot. This meant that a special training version with dual controls did not need to be built, and it also gave the navigator a chance to bring the aircraft home if the commander was for some reason unable to pilot it.

There was an unusual incident connected with that short control stick. A combat unit crew was preparing to start the engines before a flight in a Su-24. A distinctive feature of this aircraft was that while there was no pressure in its hydraulic system, the stabiliser would 'hang' with its leading edge down and the control stick would therefore rest in the full aft position. With the engine started, the pressure in the hydraulic system began to build up and the booster would bring both the stabiliser and the stick into the neutral position. In the episode in question, the short control stick had accidentally caught on the ejector drive ring, and none of the crew noticed it. At the start of the engines the stick moved forward and pulled the D-ring with it. The ejector gun fired, and the next thing the navigator knew was that he was hanging over the aircraft under a parachute, before landing safely by its side.

In 1973 my friend Vadim Petrov was on a short-term posting in Syria where he heard from Syrian pilots who used our MiG-21s that they had discovered an effective way of 'shaking off' the Israeli Phantoms: they would go up at a 'crawling' speed at which the enemy aircraft could not keep 'afloat' and had to dive down, at which point the MiG-21s attacked them from above. The Syrians gave an in-flight demonstration of this manoeuvre to Vadim and to the MiG company test pilot Boris Orlov.

On Petrov's return to Akhtubinsk we decided to test it ourselves. The chief pilots were Vadim Petrov and Norik Kazarian. I made one such flight in a MiG-21U two-seater with Norik, and when he performed that manoeuvre I followed suit and made a tight turn at a minimum speed and a zoom with a whip stall and a tail slide. Such manoeuvres had been previously performed only in aerobatic aircraft. Then we made a loop from a very low height and at a very low speed – 500 metres and 500 kph respectively. It seemed incredible but we did it; the aeroplane, having as good as no speed at all, made it to the top and over, completing a near perfect loop. On landing Norik asked me, as his CO, to authorise him to act as an instructor pilot for such manoeuvres, which I did, writing it down in his personal log-book.

These tests broadened our views on the possibilities inherent in low-speed flight. In theory we had known of them before (I had even published an article on the subject in 1973 in an aviation journal),* but it was the first time we actually explored them in the air. It is well known that an aeroplane stalls and goes into a spin when it reaches the critical angle of attack. It happens if the wing is expected to create more lift than it can produce. On the other hand, if you do not expect it to produce excessive lift and don't overpull the stick, the aircraft will not stall. A case in point is a steep zoom and a pushover manoeuvre recovery. In both these cases the centrifugal force is acting upwards and making up for the deficient lift, and this is what makes it possible to slow down to and below the speed at which in horizontal flight the aircraft would normally stall and spin.

The thirtieth of August 1974 was the last day I took a military aircraft up. I had no inkling whatsoever it would be so, and if anyone had predicted anything of the kind to me then, I would have indignantly dismissed it as sheer rubbish, for I felt as healthy and as willing to fly as ever. I first went up in a Su-15TM and then made another flight in a MiG-27.

The next day was a Saturday, and I was playing tennis with my usual partners. There had been a pain in my back somewhere near the shoulder blade since the morning that day (it had happened before), and when, having lost a set, I gave my place to another player and sat down, it seemed to me that the pain had grown. To be honest, I was always somewhat over-anxious about my health, so I thought the pain had something to do with my heart. I asked my recent partner if he had any heart drops or something. One of the spectators offered me a pill of nitro-glycerine, and when I wondered whether it would be a good idea to take it, he said he sometimes took two at a time and was fine (he had a bad heart). I put one tiny pill into my mouth. The next thing I knew I was lying on a bench on the tennis court and a doctor and a nurse were fussing over me. It turned out that I had blacked out, and everybody decided that I had had a severe heart attack.

* S. A. Mikoyan, 'At limit regimes', *Aviation and Cosmonautics*, Nos. 1, 2, 1973, Moscow.

An ambulance was called and I was rushed to the hospital. Apparently at some point my blood pressure was forty by zero! However, as soon as an electrocardiogram was taken the doctors announced that there was nothing to worry about. They said my reaction to nitro-glycerine was almost typical of healthy people taking it for the first time. There was no heart attack and I could go home.

Nevertheless, the head of the Institute medical board declared that since I had lost consciousness he could not allow me to fly until I was cleared at the Central Aviation Hospital in Moscow, which every pilot and crew with any chronic health condition, as well as every pilot over forty, had to check into every year for a thorough medical inspection. It was a real blow. I was afraid I would not get away with a couple of weeks wasted in hospital for the inspection. The previous physical had not gone smoothly, and the cardiogram taken after the centrifuge test had shown intermissions in my heartbeat. There had been some trouble with my blood pressure as well. As a result, I had been restricted to flying under 3G. I was worried that this time the restrictions might be even more severe.

Once in the Central Hospital I seemed to pass all the tests, if not exactly with flying colours, at least with the results only slightly different from last year's – or so I thought. I was apprehensive about the additional restrictions I might get. Finally, with all the tests behind me, I was summoned to hear the decision of the board. I could not believe what I heard: the chairman announced they could not allow me to fly. I was so shocked that I think I shouted, 'You can't mean *not* fly *at all*!' I was shattered. I tried arguing but it was no use. Among the doctors on the board there was somebody I knew well, and I noticed he was keeping silent. I thought that he might have disapproved of the verdict. I declared that I disagreed with their decision and would appeal to the Air Force Chief Medical Commander, General Rudny, but when I phoned him he said he could not over-rule the decision of the medical board. Then I asked him to suspend it, allow me to go on leave, put myself to rights and repeat the physical. To my great joy he agreed, although no doubt it was against the rules.

After the holiday, partially spent in a sanatorium under medical observation, I returned to the Central Aviation Hospital for another inspection. This time they suspected coronary deficiency, and with such a diagnosis every hope of flying would have to be given up there and then. Fortunately a more detailed examination at a civilian cardiological hospital, where they took me for 'an expert opinion', did not confirm that suspicion. As a result I was restricted to transport aircraft with dual controls and to helicopters. It was still a shock – there was nothing I loved more than flying single-seat combat fighters – yet it still allowed me to fly. Of course I had been aware for some time that sooner or later I would have to say goodbye to flying (I was getting on for fifty-three), but it was hard to imagine and seemed impossible to resign myself to. On the other hand, to my mind it would have been even more painful to be grounded all of a sudden once and for all, so in a way being restricted was a blessing in disguise.

I had to part with the cockpit of a combat machine for ever at a time when I was still feeling perfectly fit and in no way affected by ageing. I was as full of energy and confidence as ever, and all I wanted was to go on testing military aircraft. In fact it was at a time when I had been flying more actively than ever since I had become the Institute Deputy Commander: in August 1974 I had made twenty-four test flights – as if I had known it would be the last month of my fighter pilot's career. Twenty-four flight test missions in one month was a fair number for any pilot, and for me it was really a lot, for much of my time had to be given to administrative work. Usually during the best-weather season, from March to October, I would do from ten to fifteen test flights monthly (not counting training flights and flying to other airfields on business).

I would like to give a brief listing of my flight test missions for that last August as written in my flying log-book (I have kept them all): eleven flights in a MiG-27, the missions including level-flight, pull-up and low-height bombing, an assigned route flight in the automatic flight-control mode with target bombing and automatic landing approach, six-barrel cannon firing at unmanned air target, etc; six flights in a MiG-21U under hood (blind flying) down to fifty metres above ground to test automatic and instrument landing approach in reduced weather minima; one flight in a MiG-21PFM to attack a target aircraft, testing an advanced optical sight; three flights in a Su-15TM to perform radar-aided attacks at a target aircraft and to test the performance of the automatic control system in flight and on landing approach; finally, three flights in a Su-24 for bombing and to test the navigation system performance. There was one particularly busy day earlier that year, 26 April, when I did four flights in a row in a Su-24 and then another in a MiG-27. Not every young pilot would find it an easy flying day.

In the next medical inspection the following year a new problem arose: my deteriorated hearing. I could barely make out with my left ear what the doctor was whispering at a metre's distance from me, the required norm being six metres. I remembered that a few years earlier I had gone up in a MiG-25 for a high-altitude flight in a pressure helmet with a bad cold; since then my left ear had got worse and worse. The doctor wanted to ground me on the basis of this alone, but I pointed out that I had never had any hearing problem in flight. It was true; I had never once asked for a radio message to be repeated. I insisted they test my hearing through the earphones, simulating in-flight radio contact. They complied, and I won – with the headphones on I could hear all right. I passed the medical with the same results as the year before.

Flying transport aircraft was something I had done before; when I had to go on business to Moscow or Feodosia (where our Anti-submarine Aircraft Test Department was based) or elsewhere, I would often go into the cockpit and fly the machine from the commander's seat. The aeroplanes I had piloted on such occasions were the Il-14, the An-24, the An-26 and the An-12, as well as the Tu-124, the Tu-134 and the Tu-154. Over the years I had made about thirty flights in the Tu-104 (even before it replaced the Il-14 as our 'shuttle' plane between Akhtubinsk and Chkalovskaya).

There was now not much test flying for me to do, for transport aircraft were mainly tested at Chkalovskaya and there was no question of arriving there for short 'raids' to test their machines. It could only be done systematically, as a fully-fledged member of their team who would know what they were doing. But I had my administrative and commanding work to do at Akhtubinsk, and I could not get away from it for long. However, in 1975 I managed to make a number of flights including two test flights in the aircraft commander's seat of the Il-76, which was ferried to us from Chkalovskaya. One of our test missions involved flying at sea-level (below the slightly elevated coastline) over the Caspian Sea to determine the radar capabilities in such flying conditions. In the same year I asked to be appointed aircraft commander in the tests of a new radar antenna in a Tu-134, and made about a dozen flights, half of which were at night-time.

Not having piloted a helicopter before, I now decided to convert to the Mi-8 helicopter. We had a helicopter squadron at Akhtubinsk (their main mission was to search for the dropped and fired armaments on the firing ranges), but I wanted to be converted by helicopter test pilots at Chkalovskaya. My good old friend Norik Kazarian had been working at the Transport Aircraft Test Department at Chkalovskaya for a couple of years already (he had had family reasons for a return to Chkalovskaya, in addition to the medical restrictions which had ruled out fighter jets for him). He had already converted to all transport aircraft, including the biggest machine in the world, the An-124, as well as to all helicopters. After a short briefing Norik took a few rides with me in a Mi-8 as an instructor, and finally entered a permit to pilot helicopters into my log-book. After that I used to fly the Mi-8 as aircraft commander at Akhtubinsk on a variety of missions and training flights. Once a Mi-8MTV arrived at Akhtubinsk from Chkalovskaya, ferried by its engineering test pilot Vsevolod Ovcharov, who had a mission to test the machine-guns installed in that version of the Mi-8 helicopter. He invited me to have a go in it and perform a fuselage-aiming machine-gun attack at a ground target in a dive, something I had done hundreds of times but never in a helicopter. It was my only test flight in a helicopter.

Some time afterwards we received a high-ranking commission from Moscow which came to inspect the reconstruction of the radar measurements posts on our range. The commission was headed by the Deputy Defence Minister in charge of building and construction. They wished to inspect all building sites, and my duty was to accompany them. I decided to combine business with pleasure, so to speak, by piloting the helicopter in the commander's seat myself. Little did I know of the 'pleasure' I was in for. At first everything went well. We visited three or four sites where I had to land on unprepared ground, every time hovering low to assess the terrain before landing. On our last site I suddenly felt very ill; I was feverish and my head started aching badly. By the time the inspectors were ready to return home I was in a very bad shape indeed and was feeling sick. What was there to do? I had no other pilot on board, for the right-hand seat was occupied by a navigator, and the last thing I wanted to do was to call for a relief pilot. So, without saying anything to anyone, I took off with my passengers on board and headed homewards. It took me all my powers of concentration and a major physical effort to bring down that helicopter. However, nobody seemed to notice that anything was wrong. Everyone went to the mess to have lunch together, and I went too, but after a few minutes I had to admit that I was feeling very ill and left the table. I went to see a doctor, and he immediately packed me off to hospital where they diagnosed severe food poisoning.

Once, after I had already been restricted from combat aircraft, I had a chance to 'play a pilot', as we used to call the situation when a pilot for some reason had to climb in and out of the cockpit without taking the machine up. Our amateur cameramen from Chkalovskaya were making a film about our Institute and its history. They arrived at Akhtubinsk and asked me to simulate a flight in a MiG-23. I donned a flying suit, got into the pilot's seat, strapped in, started the engine and taxied towards the runway, where I made a U-turn and taxied back to the ramp making it look as though I had just returned from a flight. As I was taxiing within a few metres of the runway threshold I was sorely tempted to align the machine and take off. It was only my sense of discipline that kept me from doing it, but I have regretted it ever since.

In the summer of 1975 I was sent with a special mission to Alma-Ata, the capital of Kazakhstan. It was the time when a test range for a new air defence interceptor, the MiG-31, was being constructed. Although its number suggests that it was a more recent aircraft than the MiG-29, in actual fact it was developed before it as a two-seat modification of the MiG-25. It had a powerful and a more advanced armament system and a radar with a longer range than that on the MiG-25. This radar was designed to lock on four targets at a time and to launch and guide four missiles simultaneously. The testing of such a formidable interception complex required a larger testing range than we had at Akhtubinsk. Besides, another measuring post had to be set up in addition to the three we had. It meant that we had to enlarge our grounds by receiving an additional portion of land from the Kazakh authorities. I went to Alma-Ata with a formal and officially approved letter requesting such an addition. My task was to obtain the signature of the Chairman of the Council of Ministers of Kazakhstan. I went as commander in our Tu-134 (which we used as a navigator trainer aircraft). The paper was signed without any problem and so my diplomatic mission was a success. On the way back I took the liberty of making a detour to call on Tashkent, where my brother Alexei was living (he was the Central Asian Air Force District Commander), and stayed there for two days as his guest.

Also in 1975 an American F-5E fighter was brought to our air base. It had been captured in North Korea after a forced landing. The F-5E was not America's most sophisticated fighter; in fact its main distinctive feature was its simplicity. It was also smaller and lighter than other fighters. As far as I knew, the F-5E was not adopted by the US Air Force and was mainly sold abroad. Its top speed and ceiling were both lower than those of its contemporary fighters. It was mainly designed for air combat manoeuvres at low and medium heights and, as our tests showed, was perfectly adequate for that task. Its manoeuvrability was increased by the in-flight use of the trailing and leading edge flaps of the wings, which was unusual at the time (they would normally be used only at take-off and landing). The F-5E had a small, simplified attack radar, and all panel indicators were small yet perfectly readable, with clear graduation. Even the artificial horizon was so small that our pilots at first did not like it. As for the cockpit lighting, it was approved by one and all. Even before our pilots first took the F-5E up, we had a chance to appreciate its cockpit lighting in the hangar at night: we covered up its canopy, turned the lighting on and took turns to spend some time in the cockpit to get the feel of it, imagining a night flight. The lighting of the panel was even and not too bright; all instruments could be seen clearly, without any light reflected in the glass.

Since the F-5E was undamaged and turned out to be perfectly airworthy, it was decided to test it in flight so as to compare its performance and handling with our own aircraft. It was another occasion for me to be sorry that I was no longer allowed to fly fighter jets. The first to take the American fighter up was Alexander Bezhevets, although it was Nikolai Stogov who made most of the flights in it afterwards. By their accounts the F-5E revealed excellent manoeuvring performance, largely due to its low wing load and a high lift-to-drag ratio. It gave it an advantage in simulation dog-fights with our MiG-21 and MiG-23 at low and medium height. However, when the dog-fight was performed at a higher altitude, between 8,000 and 12,000 metres, our fighters proved superior. The F-5E's real advantage over our aircraft was its flight endurance. By the time the MiG-21 had almost run out of fuel and had to pull out of the dog-fight, the F-5E still had nearly half its fuel left. Although the MiG-23 had a greater flight endurance than the MiG-21, it was still inferior to that of the American aeroplane, and their respective tank capacities were not the main reason: the F-5E had a more economical engine and a better lift-to-drag ratio at high G-load manoeuvres. We concluded the F-5E tests programme with a detailed report sent to the Air Force Command, but it seemed they were not particularly pleased with it.

Once I went to Chkalovskaya on some business and ran into Norik Kazarian, who offered to take me on a ride in a L-39 jet trainer with him. Needless to say, I accepted the offer with pleasure. I had twice flown its predecessor, the L-29, and was glad to have a chance to have a go in its more advanced version. I took the front seat and tried out the machine in various flight regimes and aerobatic manoeuvres, including a spin. It was a real treat to fly a manoeuvrable aircraft again after such a long interval, and it felt almost like piloting a fighter. I liked the L-39 very much, although it could have done with a more powerful engine. I arranged with Norik to go up in it again the next day. However, the staff doctor saw my name in the flight schedule and declared that my medical restrictions ruled out aerobatic jets. I tried to reason with him but he would not budge. Then I insisted they phone the Central Aviation Hospital and ask whether with a diagnosis such as mine one could not fly aerobatic jet aircraft. They did, but before answering the chief physician of the hospital wondered which pilot they were talking about. 'General Mikoyan.' The reply that immediately followed was, 'No. With such a diagnosis flying the L-39 is out of the question.' So that was the end of my experiences in that machine.

CHAPTER 27

Back to Moscow: A New Job

My nineteen-year posting to Akhtubinsk came to an end in early 1978 when, following the Defence Minister's order, I was transferred to Moscow. It was to become the last year of my father's life, and it was sadly ironic that the time when I could finally see more of my family and particularly of my father, at least in the few months that remained before his death, could only come with the end of my flying career.

However, my father had never been against my choice of career, although I must say he was particularly pleased when I became a student of the Engineering Academy. When I later decided to become a test pilot he made no attempt to change my mind, even though I felt that he was concerned (especially as Alexei was flying too, but Alexei was an operational commander and there was nothing to be done about it). If not to change my mind but at least to prevent me from going ahead with my decision, he could quite easily have dropped a hint to the Air Force Commander-in-Chief, but of course it would never even occur to him to do such a thing. It was only much later, when he was already retired, that I began to notice he was worried for our lives, especially when Alexei or I told him of our tragically lost friends and colleagues. He would never admit it directly, but he would say something to the effect that it was time I thought of passing my experience and technical knowledge to others, as a lecturer or in some other way. I would pretend that I did not understand his implication and reply that my technical knowledge and my experience were very useful just in the work I was doing, and I was very actively passing them on to young pilots as it was. He would not press the subject, but I knew that he wished I would stop flying.

When, at the end of the 1970s, a new pilots' textbook on aerodynamics and the flight dynamics of manoeuvrable aircraft was being written, I was invited to join the team of authors headed by AF Colonel Lysenko, a scientist and a lecturer at the Air Force Engineering Academy. My father was obviously pleased, both with the offer and my acceptance of it. While still in Akhtubinsk I had begun working on my dissertation. Flight testing by definition provided an enormous amount of material, and its research and scientific analysis gave rich food for various papers. Many of our engineers were perfectly capable of conducting such research of experimental data, but the problem was that the better and the more talented an engineer was, the less time he could devote to theoretical work and to the writing of papers. Therefore we had fewer people with academic degrees than at other MoD institutes and certainly fewer than we could have had with such a wealth of flight test and experimental data.

When I stopped flight testing combat machines I began to have more spare time, and I braced myself for writing a serious academic paper for a degree. The subject I chose concerned various aspects of the flight of aircraft at high angles of attack, i.e. in aerobatic manoeuvres or in manoeuvrable air combat. It involved many complicated issues related both to flight safety and to combat performance (I had earlier published three articles on the subject in the *Aviation and Cosmonautics* magazine). My participation in many flight tests where the angle-of-attack issues were either directly or indirectly involved gave me ample material for research and generalisation. I was working on the thesis in the evenings, staying in my office at the Akhtubinsk air base until eight or nine every evening except Sunday. The final editing of the actual text and the polishing of its final layout I completed in Moscow. My father was happy to hear that I was working on a dissertation and seemed to be proud of me, although he had also been proud that three of his sons had been professional military pilots. Unfortunately the formal presentation of my thesis took place after his death, so he could not congratulate me on the degree I received.

For as long as I remember my father he always led a very healthy life and preached it to us all. As I mentioned earlier, he did not smoke and hardly drank at all, especially after Stalin's death when he no longer had to attend his sumptuous late-night banquets that would go on to the small hours. He was a very light eater, ate very little meat or rich food, but could not live without vegetables and cheese. Living most of the time in the country (from where he was daily driven to work), he liked being outdoors, whatever the weather. In the summer, unless it was raining, all his weekend lunches, especially when the family was present (and the family being large, some of us would always be there at weekends), were eaten at a long wooden table in the garden or on the veranda – even in cool weather.

He loved going for long walks, and was very sensitive to natural scenery. He could not understand how anyone in their spare time could prefer the city to the country. Whenever any of his sons, their wives and, especially, his grandchildren stayed in town for a weekend he would always say, with genuine surprise, something like: 'It's really beyond me! How can you (he/she/they) stick around in town when you have such a wonderful opportunity to spend some time in the country!' I must say we did take that opportunity for granted, and it is only now, when it is no longer there, I often nostalgically remember how easy it was in those days to go to the country and spend a weekend at my father's dacha, where everything was taken care of and where there was nothing to be done except enjoy oneself and the company of one's nearest and dearest. My father would feel offended if any of his sons or daughters-in-law missed two or three weekends in a row. For example, my wife often stayed in town to edit her typescripts which she would bring home for the weekend. My father grumbled that the weekends were for resting, and if Ella could not do without her work she could at least bring her stuff to the dacha and work away to her heart's content, breathing fresh air as she did. But of course she could not really do it; she always used all kinds of reference books in her editing, and it would be unthinkable to 'ferry' them all back and forth every weekend.

Neither he nor my mother had ever kept any pets or been interested in animals, but some time in the 1960s my brother Vanya acquired a small fluffy lapdog, called Tyapa, and the dog accompanied Vanya's daughter Olga and his son Anastas to the dacha, when they went there with all their cousins for the summer.

370

At first father simply ignored the dog, but for some reason the dog got extremely attached to him – in the literal sense as well as in the other. Wherever my father went Tyapa silently followed. When he sat down to read his papers, the dog would lie down at his feet or under his chair. We all watched this curious alliance with interest, and were amused to see that father not only noticed the dog at last but actually grew very fond of him. The children, who were there throughout the summer, told us in wonder how Tyapa always knew when their grandfather's car was on the way to the dacha from town (although he always returned at different times), and a few minutes before he drove in Tyapa would run to the gate and sit there waiting, thus letting the children know that grandfather was about to come home.

Soon after father stopped being a Politburo member he moved (or was moved) to a different dacha. It was much smaller and much more modest than the one where he had lived with his family for forty years, but father never said anything to show that he minded; in fact he liked to stress that the new dacha was beautifully situated (it was built on a high woody bank of the river) and suited him perfectly in every way.

Almost up to the age of eighty my father was justly proud of his good health. He was hardly ever ill, but even when he was unwell and you asked him how he was feeling he would say that it was nothing. I can imagine how bitterly ironic it must have felt to him when, on Brezhnev's 'recommendation', he had to formally ask the Supreme Council to be relieved of his duties as the Supreme Council Chairman 'due to health reasons'! He had just turned seventy and he was perfectly healthy and fit, which is more than could be said of Brezhnev himself at that age. After eighty he aged noticeably and became rather frail. His strong will and spirit were no longer as apparent as before.

In October 1978 he was taken to a government hospital in Moscow with a cold. When he got slightly better, his secretary (in those days she was spending more time with him than any of the family could afford to) talked the doctors into letting him spend a couple of days at the dacha on account of the warm, sunny weather. Once back at the dacha she sat him down in an armchair in the sun on an open veranda. But warm weather in October can be treacherous, and as soon as the sun goes down the autumn chill comes in its place. As a result, my father returned to the hospital with pneumonia. For a man over eighty who had had tuberculosis of the lungs as a young man, it was lethal. When I visited him a few days before his death he was extremely weak but still conscious; he was looking at me and trying to say something, but it was impossible to make out the words. His speech centres must have already been affected (one of my brothers, who had been there just a day before, could still understand some of what he was saying). The last time I came to him, with my eldest son, was a day before he died. He was in the intensive care unit and was breathing through a machine. There was no visible reaction to our presence or voices, though maybe he could still hear us. My daughter, who came on her own later the same day, said he seemed to be looking at her and his lips were moving, but neither she nor the doctor who accompanied her into the ward could be sure he recognised her.

My father died on Saturday 21 October 1978, a little over a month before his eighty-third birthday. We knew we would have to wait until Tuesday to hear the official decision concerning the funeral. Whenever an eminent statesman died, even in retirement, the protocol of the funeral had to be determined by the Politburo (or, to be more exact, by Brezhnev, Suslov and Chernenko), which would not convene until Monday. Even the media could not inform the public of his death without a proper sanction; the editors would not know what 'epithets' they could or should use about him, or on which page of *Pravda*, for example, the formal obituary was to be printed and with whose signatures (and with or without a photograph). Such was the established practice in those days. Suddenly, early on Monday, the press briefly wrote of A. I. Mikoyan's death. As we heard later, they were indirectly forced to do so (before the official obituary was approved by the Politburo) by the Western media, which had already announced it on Sunday.

Until Monday evening the family was in the dark as to whether the funeral was going to be official or private, and where and when the interment would take place. It was very awkward to be unable to say anything definite to the many people who started phoning as soon as they had heard the news. Finally we were informed that on the day of the funeral (two days hence), father's body would be laid out for a few hours in the building of the Scientists' House on Kropotkinskaya Street. About twenty minutes or so before the doors of the Scientists' House were opened to the public, there unexpectedly appeared a group of Politburo members – Brezhnev, Kosyghin, Podgorny, Ustinov and others. They shook our hands and hugged us, the four sons, stood sombrely by the bier for a few minutes and left. I believe they had not really intended to come but then at the last minute one of them must have suggested that it would look better if they did. The papers could now safely say that 'the funeral was attended by the party and government leaders' and print the photographs that showed them standing by the coffin. Kosyghin handed me an envelope with a telegram with condolences from the Prime Minister of Japan, and a typewritten list of the foreign heads of state and other eminent people who had sent their expressions of sympathy. However, the telegrams themselves were not in the envelope, nor did we receive them afterwards. Somebody later told us why not: they had been 'too flattering'.

People were coming into the building and walking past the bier for hours, but several of my friends who left the procession to come up to me with their condolences said that the police on the approaches to the building were keeping people back. I went over to the colonel in charge and asked him what was going on outside. He said that his officers were deliberately 'thinning' the stream of people who were coming through the doors so that the parting ceremony 'would not end too quickly'. He was obviously hinting at the allegedly small number of mourners waiting to be let in. I did not go out to see if there were many people waiting outside or not, but it turned out later that the colonel's hint was a lie. Our various friends independently told us afterwards that the queue of those who came was thick and long, but many of them failed to enter the building for at some point the access was closed by the police (and we were told that the doors were shut because there were no more mourners outside). We later also learned that a number of foreign ambassadors had wished to come and pay their respects, but the Foreign Office informed them that 'the family would prefer to have no foreigners at the ceremony', which of course was sheer rubbish and another lie.

The Politburo decided against having him interred in the Kremlin wall (where most Soviet statesmen were buried) and plumped for the Novodevichy cemetery. It might have been intended as a final slight, and this is how we might have taken it at first, but the feeling that soon prevailed was that it was appropriate that our father was buried next to our mother, his wife, and to his own mother and his parents-in-law, and beside the tablet commemorating his son killed in the war. Many people came to the cemetery, and there were a number of official (though some of them genuinely warm) eulogies over his grave. After the funeral everyone went to the traditional funeral banquet which was prepared in the large dining-hall of the Central Army Club. There were perhaps two hundred people or more, including the entire family and many family friends, celebrities and officials. The latter were sitting with us, the sons, at the top table. There were speeches again, many more than at the cemetery, of course, and most of them far less formal and with greater feeling. However, in the eulogies delivered by the officials we all felt a tendency to emphasise our father's Armenian roots and to mourn his death 'as a great loss for the Armenian people', until Marshal Bagramian, an Armenian himself, when his turn came, protested against what he called 'an Armenian bias' and pointed out that Anastas Mikoyan's death was 'a great loss for the country at large'.

Finally it was time for me to stand up and thank, on behalf of the family, all those who came and said warm words about my father. Even before everyone was seated around the tables Chernenko's deputy had come up to me and whispered that we should by all means express our thanks to Brezhnev. Just before I stood up to speak, some other very important person at my table said I must not forget 'to thank Leonid Ilyich'. Apparently the 'rules of the game' required that he be thanked for his 'fatherly care'. I had no wish to thank him at all, knowing how he had treated my father, but something had to be said. So I thanked everyone who had come to mourn our father with us and all those who were present 'and Leonid Ilyich and Alexei Nikolayevich [Brezhnev and Kosyghin] for having come to pay their last respects'. I deliberately named Kosyghin too to show there was nothing for which I was going to thank Brezhnev separately. I went on to speak about my father and of what kind of man he was, and of his devotion to the interests of his country, which he had always placed before his own or those of his family. I spoke of our pride in him, repeating the words 'we are proud' as a refrain, and detailed what exactly it was we were so proud of: his creation of the country's food industry and trade; his help in our victory in the war by organising the army and rear supplies of all the vital things, from food to ammunition; of how he had been Khrushchev's first ally in the de-Stalinisation period and the initiator of rehabilitation of Stalin's victims, and so on. I had not prepared my speech; it was spontaneous and utterly sincere. It was just that I suddenly felt that I must say it all, maybe because of the humiliating suspense in which we were held after his death while it was decided whether he was worthy of a decent obituary and a ceremonial funeral or not.

The order of the Minister of Defence by which I was transferred from Akhtubinsk to Moscow was his response to the request of the Aviation Industry Minister who had asked for me to be appointed Deputy Director General in charge of flight testing of the newly set up aerospace design company. The company, officially known as Research and Production Company (RPC) 'Molnia', was formed to participate in the development of a Soviet reusable launch space system, our somewhat belated 'answer' to the American Space Shuttle programme, which was well under way by that time.

I have already mentioned the orbital aeroplane 'Spiral', developed by the Mikoyan Design Company back in the 1960s. As no similar project was known to be systematically developed on a large scale elsewhere in the world at that time, the then Defence Minister Marshal Grechko did not show any interest in the Spiral, and it received no official back-up or funding. Serious interest on the part of the decision-making bodies appeared later, when it became known that a reusable launch space system had been developed in the USA. Our aviation industry was accordingly charged with the task to develop our own space shuttle. The RPC 'Energia' (until 1966 headed by Sergei Korolev) was put in charge of the overall system, while the new RPC 'Molnia' was to design the craft itself, a reusable orbital vehicle.

The Molnia united three aviation industry bodies: the Molnia Design Company headed by Matus Bisnovat (specialising in fighter aircraft missiles), the Burevestnik Design Company of Alexander Potopalov (designing air defence surface-to-air missiles) and Vladimir Myasischev's aircraft design company in Zhukovsky. The new syndicate inherited the name of one of its members, and its Director General became Gleb Lozino-Lozinsky, a former deputy of Artem Mikoyan and the chief designer of the Spiral. Many of the specialists earlier involved in the Spiral project now joined the staff of the newly formed RPC.

I had first received an offer of a position at the Molnia at the beginning of 1977, probably in accordance with the long-existing Soviet practice of 'reinforcing' defence-related industries with military specialists. In February 1978 the Molnia Director General, Lozino-Lozinsky, asked the Aviation Industry Minister to apply to the Minister of Defence on his behalf to appoint me his deputy (with my full military rank and status preserved). This application, as I have already said, resulted in a turn in my career.

I will round off the lengthy story told in this book with a description of the orbital vehicle project and my own contribution to its development at the Molnia, where I have been working since 1978. It is only natural that the specialists previously involved in the Spiral project who now assembled at the Molnia should wish to develop an orbital vehicle similar to the one they had been working on before, but Valentin Glushko, whose Energia was in charge of the system as a whole, preferred to stick to the American shuttle design (to avoid the risks an original design might involve). Both the Space and the Aviation Industry Ministers shared his view.

Many of our specialists still believe that the aerodynamic layout of the Spiral had advantages over the American design. The principal distinction of the Spiral from the Space Shuttle is that the former was conceived as a craft with a lifting body, i.e. its lift was to be created mostly by its broad fuselage with a flat lower surface. The main function of the wings was to serve as controls. In comparison with the Space Shuttle, whose design and layout are close to those of the conventional aeroplane type, such layout would yield larger useful space inside the vehicle in relation to the same airframe weight. Such a craft would also be subjected to less heating upon entry into the atmosphere and would be more capable of some sideways manoeuvres.

All published data concerning the American project were carefully studied, and all that could be used in the development of our Buran orbiter was used. Some of the elements were even copied. Nevertheless, our vehicle was not a replica of the American Shuttle, even though it looked very similar to it. The main distinctive feature of our system was that it is based on a large rocket, the Energia, to which the orbiter, the Buran, is attached. The American system is based on the orbiter itself, which is fixed onto a large fuel tank with two solid propellant boosters attached to it. Both the Buran and the Energia have their own flight control systems. After the separation, the rocket re-enters the atmosphere, partially burning up as it does. Thus the only reusable component of our system is the orbiter itself, while the rocket, fitted with the main engines (the most expensive element of the entire system) and with its own flight control system, is 'disposable'. The American Shuttle is itself designed as a winged rocket with all the engines and flight control system fitted directly onto it, and is thus reusable. Even the boosters are not disposable: they separate within minutes of the launch (as soon as they burn up their fuel) and come down on parachutes into the ocean. They are recovered from the water and repaired. Only the fuel tank burns up in the atmosphere, the least costly element of the system (despite its size). So the American system is almost entirely reusable and therefore more economical than ours. The Russian Buran–Energia system can be described as reusable only with serious reservations.

I believe that our choice of a scheme in which the orbiter had no main engines was a consequence of bureaucratic differences between the space and aviation industries. The Energia, as a space industry body, took the opportunity of creating a superpowerful carrier rocket capable of lifting up to a hundred tons' worth of cargo into orbit (the Buran weighs about 105 tons loaded up). Such a rocket could be used for other tasks, independent of the prospects of the orbiter project developed, as it was, under the auspices of aviation industry. The problem was, of course, the immense cost of the rocket, and so the chances of many such rockets appearing in Russia's present economical situation are very small.

The Buran was originally conceived as an automatically controlled vehicle with no crew interference whatsoever, although we later managed to insist on the possibility of such interference, at least during an atmospheric flight, being provided for. The Americans, on the other hand, designed their Space Shuttle (as all other manned space vehicles) with the astronauts' participation in mind. Even its maiden orbital flight was performed with a crew on board, and after more than eighty orbital flights American astronauts have never yet performed a fully automatic landing. At several hundred metres above the ground they turn the automatic control system off, then flare the vehicle out and touch down manually. Both with the visibility sufficient for the flare, and when the instrument landing system is used, the manual landing is safe and not particularly difficult. So in fact there is no need for automatic landing control at the flaring out and touchdown (which are the most difficult tasks for any autoland system). Landing in a thick fog, for example, is a totally different story, and then of course you cannot really do without the autoland system until touchdown, but the Americans never land the Shuttle in bad weather; they 'sit it out' in orbit, or else use a back-up landing facility. Our space industry operates by the rule that no craft should be put into orbit with people on board until after two or more successful unmanned flights. Therefore all orbital systems are designed with a fully automatic function in mind. The Buran was no exception.

The commander of every American spacecrew is always an experienced test pilot, either military or ex-military. With us, especially in the early days of space industry, although future cosmonauts were recruited from the fighter pilots' ranks, the chief criteria were young age and physical and psychological fitness rather than flying experience and professional qualifications. There has been more attention to these qualities since the mid-1970s, and the candidates selected for future orbital flights began to arrive at Akhtubinsk for a training course, at the end of which they received the qualification of Grade 3 test pilots. Still, it is not quite the same professional level as possessed by the US astronauts. Apart from Vasily Lazarev, a test pilot with a limited flight testing experience, the only highly qualified and experienced test pilot among Russian cosmonauts up to the mid-1980s was George Beregovoi. By the time he made up his mind to convert to spacecraft he had been a test pilot at the Flight Test Institute for fifteen years. In the 1980s another two experienced test pilots appeared among Russian cosmonauts. They made several flights on a near-earth orbit, 'practising' for an orbital test flight in the Buran. They were Igor Volk and Anatoly Levchenko. Another two cosmonauts, Alexander Volkov and Victor Afanasiev, also had some experience of flight testing.

In view of the required unmanned flights, our principal task was to develop a fully automatic landing system for the Buran. After de-orbiting, a spaceship glides down and performs a landing approach with the power off. The glidepath can, within certain limits, be updated by means of speed variation or by closing or deploying the airbrakes. To perform research on flight trajectories and flight dynamics of the orbiter, a special dynamic flight simulator on a three-axis base was built at the Molnia, together with a life-size flight hardware simulator for developing and testing actual systems and units (known in Russia under the same name as in the USA – the 'Iron Bird'). Another dynamic flight simulator, on a six-axis base, was purchased in Britain (it was fitted with a French computer system) and installed at the TzAGI in Moscow (Central Institute of Aviation and Hydrodynamics).

The next essential step was to build a variant of the orbiter to be used for the approach and landing tests. The Americans tested their shuttle in the approach and landing modes too: they put their life-size model on top of a Boeing-747, and at a height of 6,000 or 8,000 metres the Shuttle separated and glided down the landing approach. At that time in Russia we did not possess an aircraft that could lift and carry the weight of the Buran, so we decided to have it take off by itself, for which the test version was supplied with four jet engines (of the type used in the Su-27).

Each candidate for future orbital flights performed a great number of dead-stick landings in a MiG-25, and some also in a Tu-22. In such landings the aircraft would glide at a steep angle, and its vertical speed of descent could be up to fifty or sixty metres a second. Then the cosmonauts made many such flights in specially modified Tu-154LL in-flight simulators equipped with the Buran-type control system. Their first landings in them were manual, the autoland being switched on for a little longer in each subsequent flight, until it was ascertained that a fully automatic landing was possible. Then the same pattern was repeated in the Buran. Before each atmospheric flight of the Buran test version, the two test pilots who formed the crew would first practise their flight mission in our dynamic flight simulator, and then perform it in the Tu-154LL. Altogether the test version of the Buran performed twenty-four flights, and in seventeen of them the landing was fully automatic. The craft successfully performed automatically selected approach, gliding, and touchdown, up to the stop at the end of the landing run. These successful landings helped to make a decision concerning an unmanned orbital flight of the Buran.

During the flights of the test version at Zhukovsky, I was in charge of the test control post where we received all downlink telemetry and video data, and where engineers were sitting in front of over a dozen displays monitoring the work of the onboard systems and the trajectory parameters. I had the additional responsibility of approving flight missions and debriefing.

Even before the Buran project was conceived, and while the work on the Spiral orbiter was still going on, its half-scale flying model, named 'Bor-4', was designed for testing its aerodynamics and control systems in orbital flights. Although the Spiral programme had been cancelled for some time, we decided to use such models for tests of heat insulation. Several 'Bors' were built and provided with heat insulation developed for the Buran. The models were then put into orbit with the help of carrier rockets launched from the missile range at Kapustin Yar. Each of the Bors made one orbital circuit and then re-entered the lower atmosphere, where its parachute deployed and brought it gently down into the sea. Four such models were launched altogether. The first two landed in the Indian Ocean west of Australia, and the other two in the Black Sea. Each time a small fleet of several ships went out into the sea to search for and retrieve the models. Another type of model designed was that of the Buran itself, one-eighth of its full size. Five such models, named 'Bor-5', were launched into sub-orbit from Kapustin Yar to assess aerodynamic characteristics of the orbiter. I was in charge of the entire Bor-4 project, and the Test Flight Director in the Bor-5 test programme. Besides, as the Deputy Director General of the Molnia in charge of flight tests, I supervised the technical and flight-simulator preparatory training of the test pilots selected for the future orbital flight of the Buran. As the only professional pilot in the management of the company, I was also involved in the cockpit layout development and in all issues concerning the in-flight work of the would-be crew.

The first orbital flight of the Buran took place on 15 November 1988, twelve and a half years after the RPC Molnia had been formed. The flight was a success, and our unmanned orbiter made a totally unprecedented automatic aeroplane-type landing on the purpose-built concrete runway at Baikonur. Besides the monitor station at Baikonur, the flight was monitored from the Flight Control Centre at Kaliningrad near Moscow. The cosmonaut Vladimir Riumin was Flight Director, with Vadim Krevets as his deputy, and I was his other deputy in charge of the atmospheric flight and landing. The three of us and our large team of operators were closely watching the operation of various onboard systems and the flight as such by the telemetric data appearing on the displays. When, after its re-entry, the Buran received an 'escort' in the shape of a two-seat MiG-25U chase fighter with a cameraman onboard, we were eventually treated to its picture coming live on television screens (in fact we had two pictures – one from the MiG, the other from the ground-based cameras). Unfortunately the weather was cloudy, so for a while after the re-entry we could see nothing, and despite the reassuring data on the displays we could not help being anxious about its progress. So when the Buran finally emerged from the clouds on our TV screens, right before the runway and heading neatly towards its centreline, everyone was delighted. And when it flared out and performed a faultless touch-down we were truly jubilant, and the feeling of triumph was overwhelming.

However, a successful maiden flight did not mean that another Buran flight, which was to consist of several circuits, could take place soon afterwards. The fact was that the first flight realised only a limited flight programme, while the Buran project as a whole had not been fully developed yet. For one thing, the software available at that stage covered only one-circuit flight, and the soft-ware to operate the closing and the opening of the payload bay doors was not ready yet. The opening of the bay doors was essential for a multi-circuit flight, for underneath them were the cooling-system radiators. Some other systems that were dispensable in a short flight but vital for a long one were not finished either. Besides, another Energia career-rocket was not ready yet, and the second Buran, though it had already been fetched to Baikonur, required a number of important finishing touches, including facing with insulation tiles. In short, in 1992 we were not ready for a second launch, and soon financial difficulties began. Two years later, in 1994, the Buran programme was suspended and then cancelled altogether.

It was sad, for the creation of the Buran with its thermal insulation, its highly sophisticated equipment and its unique launching and automatic control systems was a truly remarkable achievement by a large team of first-class engineers and scientists, and it gave a new insight into many scientific and technological prob-lems. At the same time the project turned out to be extremely expensive and took a very long time to develop. Two more unmanned orbital flights were planned after the first one, before a manned launch into orbit. How much more time would it have taken before it took place? And what would we have achieved when it did? We would not come up with anything better than the existing American launching system, and there was no point producing anything worse. So, at the end of the day, sorry as I am that it is all over, I have to admit that the decision to cancel the Buran programme was right. It is evident to us now that the work should continue on a far more promising reusable aerospace launching system, which was conceived at the Molnia several years back. This system presupposes an orbital aircraft, similar to the Spiral, which is launched into orbit from the top of a large transport aeroplane, the An-224 'Mria'. A still more promising idea is a reusable one-stage-to-orbit spacecraft, but this is a matter of the future.

In 1997 an unexpected and extremely rewarding event took place in my life. A US AF test pilot, Colonel Terry Tomeny, whom I had met in 1996 during an exchange visit of the Edwards Air Force Base delegation to Chkalovskaya, wrote to me to say that I had been nominated and elected an Honorary Fellow of the Society of Experimental Test Pilots. I became the second pilot in the Russian, and formerly Soviet, Air Force to have received this honour, after Grigory Sedov of the Mikoyan company, who had been elected an Honorary Fellow in 1992. In September 1997 I made a trip to the United States in the company of my daughter, for the pleasure and privilege of attending the SETP Annual Symposium and the awards banquet, at which I was to receive the diploma of an Honorary Fellow. These were the days I will never forget: the days of my first meeting with America; the days as a guest at the Edwards air base, with so many memories brought back and the roar of fighter jets in my ears again; the days spent among many wonderful people with whom I know I have a bond, for they belong to the same 'breed' as I have always been proud to belong to. They are test pilots. It was truly the crowning moment of my life as a pilot.

Afterword

I have finally come to the end of my rather long narrative. It is indeed long, despite my deliberate though reluctant omission of quite a few events and interesting episodes of my life, as well as of many technical issues in the aviation field.

Looking back on the past years I feel that by and large I have lived a gratifying life – although naturally, as in anybody else's life, there have been disappointments and regrets, and situations with which I would have perhaps dealt differently, had I been given a chance of re-living them. What I have certainly never regretted is the profession and career I chose early in my life and pursued throughout it. Although, again, there are certain things I am sorry not to have accomplished – both as a fighter pilot during WW2 and in my work as a test pilot afterwards.

What has always given me enormous satisfaction is the goodwill and friendship of the many people I have encountered both in my private and professional life. And I can say I have been extremely fortunate in my circle of friends and colleagues.

I hope the reader will get a true notion of my political and social views, which, I believe, are characteristic of most members of the present-day Russian intelligentsia. Having lived the largest part of my life in the Soviet Union as it then was, I was enthusiastic about the changes brought by the *perestroika*, which closed the era of political confrontation between us and the West, put an end to the threat of a nuclear war and proclaimed the priority of human rights and well-being over the 'interests of the State'. I sincerely hope that despite all the hardships, errors and pitfalls on the road of our reforms, Russia will continue to move towards true democracy and will finally become a natural and welcome member of a free world.

I thank all of you who have had the patience to read this book, and I would like to think they have found it interesting and enjoyable.

Stepan Anastasovich Mikoyan

Index

The index is arranged alphabetically on a word-by-word basis, except for entries under Anastas Ivanovich Mikoyan and Stepan Anastasovich Mikoyan, which are in chronological order.